BOSTON

AND THE DAWN *OF* AMERICAN INDEPENDENCE

BOSTON

AND THE DAWN OF AMERICAN INDEPENDENCE

BRIAN DEMING

WESTHOLME
Yardley

To Carol

First Westholme Paperback 2015

Maps by Paul Dangel

Westholme Publishing, LLC
904 Edgewood Road
Yardley, Pennsylvania 19067
Visit our Web site at www.westholmepublishing.com

ISBN: 978-1-59416-240-4
Also available as an eBook.

Printed in the United States of America.

CONTENTS

List of Maps

INTRODUCTION

The world of colonial Boston packed up and sailed away long ago, but it left quite a mark. That town of just eight thousand or so adults put the history of a continent and an empire on a new course; inspired a new nation destined to become an engine of prosperity and a beacon of freedom; and demonstrated that people can and should demand justice and dignity, strike back when precious rights are threatened, and never suffer in silence the whims of arbitrary power.

Behind that powerful legacy is a compelling story. This is the unlikely tale of how Boston, a loyal and contented colonial town in 1760, turned against British rule and by 1775 ignited the American War of Independence.

Back in 1760, no one could imagine the American colonies revolting against Great Britain. The colonists were not hungry peasants groaning under the whip of a brute. They lived well. Land was cheap, wages were good, opportunities abounded. While denying many thousands of imported Africans and American-born blacks of their liberty, the white Americans themselves enjoyed freedom and prosperity far beyond the hope of most people in the world at that time.

Nor were the American colonists chaffing under strange rulers from a foreign culture. They were not Asian Hindus, French Canadians, or Irish Catholics balking at British authority. They were English Christians who loved their king, adored British institutions, and modeled their governments, courts, laws, and lives after what they had known in Britain. While many Americans had been in the New World for generations, they felt themselves British, and England was still "home."

Yet in the space of just fifteen years, the sturdy bonds of affection and loyalty frayed and snapped. The Americans cobbled together a ragtag army to take on not an impotent crumbling kingdom, but a rising, rich, and powerful empire. What a curious turn of events.

Boston did more than any other American town to sever those strings to the old homeland and push the colonies to take up arms. Arguably, if not for Bostonians, and such events as the Boston Massacre and the Boston Tea Party, the Battles of Lexington and Concord would not have happened, the Declaration of Independence would never have been written, and the 1770s would be remembered as just a bumpy patch on the long sloping road to gradual independence and proud membership in the British Commonwealth. Those Bostonians included not just Sam Adams, John Hancock, Paul Revere, and others whose names American children learn in grade school, but also poor shoemakers, feisty printers, brawling seamen, and many others who played fleeting but key roles in this drama.

Many Americans today look back on the turbulence in Boston over those years with great patriotic pride. But those days were anxious, heartbreaking, awful times for many of those who lived them. The crisis divided families, fractured marriages, destroyed dreams, and crushed ambitions. Everybody suffered, but especially the Loyalists, who were ostracized, tormented, hounded, and ultimately chased from the land they loved. And their crime? Obedience to laws, devotion to the king. This is their story, too.

It is also the story of ordinary people just living their lives. Bostonians of that day didn't set out to change the course of history. Most of them, most of the time, were carrying on as they always did: going on fishing outings, picking out ribbons for bonnets, trying not to die of smallpox, and just getting by. To modern readers, there is fascination in their everyday joys and wonder in their struggles, so daunting and even horrifying to us. This was a gritty, pungent world of smoke and fire, where commerce relied on animal brawn and capricious winds, and where innumerable babies sickened and died. From our comfy, well-wired, engine-powered, convenience-laden perch more than two hundred years on, we marvel that they managed to do anything at all, let alone start a revolution. This book honors their fortitude.

AUTHOR'S NOTE: In some places, spelling and capitalization have been modernized when spoken dialogue is being quoted.

ONE

LET LOOSE HIS WRATH

On a March night in 1760, slumbering Boston came to life to the sound of church bells. Windows opened, heads poked out, and hearts quickened as the town's nine fire companies, each with a dozen or so men, sprang into action. The volunteer firefighters jostled, stumbled, and cursed as they positioned their "engines," hardly more than great tubs with handles, hand pumps, and hoses. Other men, as well as boys, dashed about, many with leather buckets, required by law in every household.

Fires were common enough in Boston. Of the town's two thousand or so houses, warehouses, shops, and outbuildings, most were made of wood, and all were heated by fire and illuminated by candles and lamps. This blaze started on Cornhill Street, near the center of town.

It is presumed the fire was fought in the conventional way: two lines forming up at each engine with the strongest and steadiest men in each "wet" line, passing buckets hand to hand from the nearest well to the engine, where the buckets were dumped. Empty buckets returned via the "dry" line of mostly boys. On each engine, two men worked the pump while another directed the hose. Everywhere, men dashed about with shovels, ladders, ropes, and chains. Some, wielding long poles with wet rags on one end, rushed from building to building, slapping out embers on rooftops.

The responding companies were quick, but not as nimble as usual, for they had responded to alarms in two of the previous three days. The evening stillness gave way to breezes, then gusts. Clouds of sparks flew up, scattered, and fell on dry cedar shingles downwind, spawning three, four, ten fires. The fires spread east, skipping to shops on Pudding Lane and leaping to King Street and Quaker Lane. According to one breathless account, people heard "shrieks of mothers and children" as "surrounding flames" roused them from their

Woodblock print of the Angel of Death and the Great Boston Fire, 1760, by Zechariah Fowle and Samuel Draper. (*Library of Congress*)

beds, and saw "the aged, the sick and the bed-rid . . . driven forth to the inclemencies of the weather, not knowing where to shelter."[1] Amid the confusion, some people, with an "amazing pitch of wickedness and impudence," helped themselves to unguarded goods.[2]

Other engines arrived. One came by boat from Charlestown, just across the harbor to the north. The blaze raced to the sea, where sparks found rigging and turned eight or nine vessels into torches. The fire also veered toward a battery where ammunition was stored. A huge explosion tore into the night sky.

The Great Fire of 1760 raged for ten hours, finally ending about noon the following day. Remarkably, the fire took no lives, but ruined 174 houses and 175 shops. One wealthy man alone lost fourteen houses, two wharves, two shops, and a pair of ships. Many others lost far less but still all they had. The catastrophe left over two hundred families homeless. From a Boston pulpit came the words: "It seems that God . . . was determined to let loose his wrath upon us."[3]

In the wake of the worst fire ever to blacken a colonial American town, Boston asked for help. Donations poured in from local and nearby churches, from the province's House of Representatives, but also from private citizens throughout America, from legislatures in five colonies, and from friends across the sea. Pudding Lane became Devonshire Street to honor a benefactor from England. The largest donation by far—about as much as all other donations combined—came from merchants in London.

With the horse gone, Boston shut the barn door. The town ordered certain streets widened and required new structures over seven feet high to be built of brick or stone and roofed with slate or tile. Learning that one firefighter was sixty-two, townsmen drew up rules requiring that the master of each fire company be suitably vigorous. Meanwhile, work began to erase the charred gash in the heart of the town. The town would rebuild, but would it fully recover?

If Boston was not exactly sinking, it was not rising like New York and Philadelphia. Once the largest town on the Atlantic Seaboard, Boston had by 1760 slipped to third place, its population hovering at about sixteen thousand. The town's geographical disadvantages were showing. Boston's Charles River, which meandered and diminished a few miles upriver west of Boston, was no match for New York's broad Hudson, which reached hundreds of miles into the interior, giving New York City a watery thoroughfare to lands far to the north and west. Meanwhile, Philadelphia, with its more central location along the Atlantic coast, had the edge over northerly Boston in domestic trade with southern colonies. Now, with scorched ruins to clear away, Bostonians worried that the town would only lose more ground to the thriving rivals to the south.

Fears were especially acute among the 200 to 250 men who managed Boston's seaborne trade, the lifeblood of the town. Each year Boston docks accommodated, in addition to some twelve hundred or so fishing vessels and small boats that hugged the coast, some five hundred larger trading vessels that carried goods to and from American ports; crossed the Atlantic to the British Isles, the Netherlands, Spain, and Africa; and sailed to the Caribbean.

Boston's prosperity depended on the men who owned these vessels and cargoes. They bought the ships, hired the shipmasters, arranged for the cargoes, fretted about storms, and agonized about prices. These were merchants. They made their money by the ancient formula of finding surpluses in one place and shifting them to where they were scarce.

The cargoes came and went on the tides of supply and demand. Incoming vessels might carry, for example, porcelain from Holland or wine from Portugal. Vessels sailing from Boston might carry furniture or fish. Much of the trade, however, boiled down to two cargoes: molasses coming in and rum going out.

This trade became significant largely because New England farms had so little to spare. Through determined efforts, nearby farmers could coax just enough from the rocky New England soil to survive and to feed Boston and other towns, but little surplus was left over for export. Merchants in Philadelphia could ship grain and other crops harvested from the rich Pennsylvania countryside. Merchants farther south could ship tobacco or rice. Boston merchants, with no tobacco plantations or rich fields of grain nearby, were left with mainly fish and lumber. These weren't enough, either.

The resourceful Boston merchants thus tapped the Caribbean as their prime source of raw products for trade. These islands of the West Indies, divided among Britain, the Netherlands, France, and Spain, had

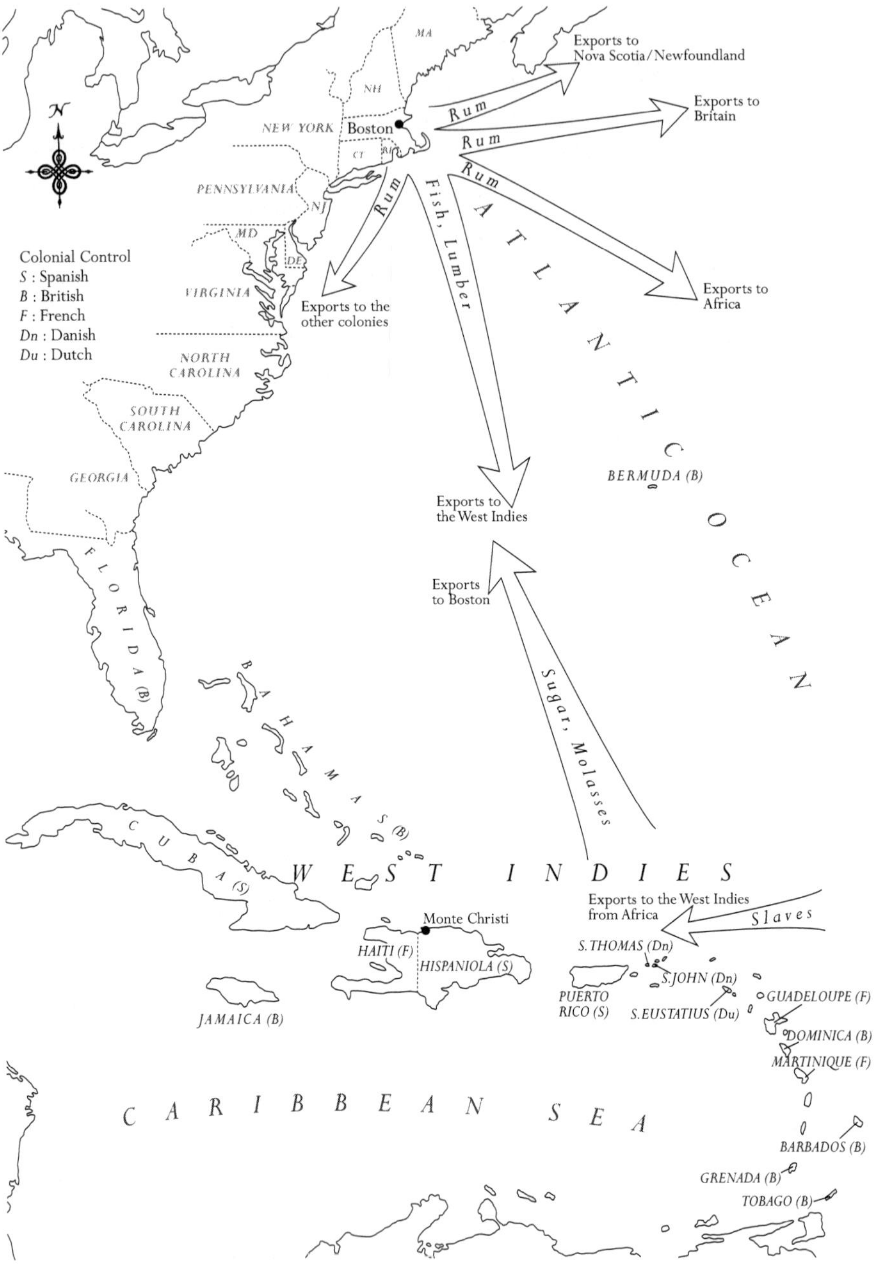

Map 1. Boston trade with the West Indies during the eighteenth century.

been fashioned for one crop and one crop only: sugarcane. Over time, after evicting, slaughtering, and enslaving the natives, the European conquerors brought in African slaves to work the plantations and turn the cane into sugar and molasses.

Boston merchants early on recognized that fortunes could be made from the demand for slaves to work the islands and the huge bounties of sugar and molasses the slaves helped produce. Thus evolved a lucrative trading scheme involving mainly molasses, rum, and slaves.

To enter this trade, a merchant might, for example, arrange for a vessel to sail to Barbados with a cargo of lumber and fish. Lumber was valued in the Caribbean, where land had been stripped of trees to make room for more sugar fields. Cheap fish from New England went to feed slaves. In exchange for the fish and lumber, plantation owners on Barbados stuffed vessels with barrels of molasses, the sweet, dark, sticky byproduct of sugar manufacturing.

From Barbados, the shipmaster then returned to Boston and delivered the molasses to distillers, who transformed the molasses into rum. The holds that brought in barrels of molasses now carried away barrels of rum.

The vessel, laden with rum, then crossed the Atlantic to the west coast of Africa to places where Africans had been captured and corralled in sweltering prison camps. The shipmaster then bargained with the Europeans and Africans who held the captives: so much rum for so many slaves. The deal struck, the slaves were crammed into the vessel's hold. The ship then sailed for the Caribbean, where the shipmaster traded slaves for molasses, and returned to Boston.

This trade evolved over decades, enriching many Bostonians, including Peter Faneuil, who became wealthy enough to give Boston its handsome Faneuil Hall, which served as marketplace and town hall. But it was a costly, risky, messy business. Ships had to be specially equipped with chains and other gear to handle and control the human cargo. Poor timing could ruin a venture. For example, a vessel that arrived at the African coast just as other slave ships left would face a glut of rum and a scarcity of available captives. Then there was the appalling sea voyage from Africa to the Caribbean. On some slave ships, as many as one third of the captives died. The stench of this voyage never reached the merchant's countinghouse in Boston. But the merchant nevertheless took note of lost profits with each corpse tossed overboard. So, by the 1760s, most Boston merchants had abandoned the slave trade to their counterparts in other ports, especially those in Newport, Rhode Island, which by then was the center for slave trade in the northern colonies.

Still, the trade in sugar and molasses from the Caribbean to Boston remained robust. Bostonians acquired a keen taste for such sweeteners.

One visitor to Boston remarked: "Their Woman are pretty enough, but have, almost without exception, bad teeth, w[hi]ch I have observed begin in the youth of both Sexes, to decay, at a very early Age."[4]

Molasses and the Caribbean trade supported not only merchants and distillers, who bought the incoming cargoes, but also seamen–vessels might employ eleven to twenty-five men–and the many dockworkers who wrestled with capstans, pulleys, slings, and hooks to lift and move casks, bales, hogsheads, and cases out of holds and into warehouses. Shipbuilders also tracked the trade to the West Indies. The town, especially its North End, bristled with shipyards, which employed carpenters, painters, carvers, caulkers, and other craftsmen, and also relied on the skills of blacksmiths, tanners, and others. A single vessel might take a year to build and require the handiwork of twenty-three crafts. Meanwhile, vessels needed sails and ropes. Sails were stitched in spacious garrets known as sail lofts. Ropes emerged from ropewalks, long narrow buildings where men, each with a bundle of hemp around his waist, would walk backward while feeding fibers to a lengthening strand as other men–and boys–would twist each strand via a crank with a hook. Thus, the fortunes of Boston rose and fell with merchants and the molasses trade. When a merchant stubbed his toe, all of Boston yelped.

Not all Boston merchants relied on the Caribbean trade. Thomas Hancock, for example, followed another path to fortune. He started off as a bookseller's apprentice at age thirteen, and then, at about twenty, opened his own bookshop at the sign of the Bible and Three Crowns. He expanded his trade from books into cloth, tea, and cutlery. For customers strapped for cash, he accepted goods for payment, leading him away from the bookseller's trade and into the world of a full-time merchant.

In one coup, he dispatched trading vessels to remote whaling settlements, rather than waiting for the whalers to come to Boston. This way Hancock vessels were first in the season to obtain whale oil and whalebone, and thus first in the season to deliver those cargoes to England, where the earliest cargoes always fetched the highest prices. He also learned how the interests of British authorities could dovetail with his own. He won government contracts for bricks and other materials to rebuild and fortify forts in Newfoundland. He profited as a supplier to the British fortress of Louisbourg on Cape Breton Island. Later, when the British military geared up to take Canada from the French, Hancock provided oxen and teamsters. Hancock also stepped up when, in the 1750s, British authorities wrenched the Acadians–the French-speaking settlers–from their homes and farms in Nova Scotia, New

Brunswick, and Prince Edward Island. Hancock provided transports to scatter the refugees up and down the American coast. He had no qualms about cleansing Acadia of "those vermin."[5] But later, when a group of bedraggled Acadians, striving to return north to their old homeland, were captured and confined in Boston, Hancock urged authorities to let them go.

Hancock's rise to riches was so rapid that many assumed he had some secret source.[6] But his secret was just meticulous bookkeeping, a knack for complex trades, innovations, daring, luck, and a capable and helpful wife. Lydia Henchman, the daughter of a fellow merchant, was just sixteen when she married Thomas, who was eleven years older. She was a large, handsome woman and a valuable partner.

The Hancocks showed off their wealth in grand style with a Georgian mansion that stood alone on Beacon Hill overlooking Boston's forty-five-acre Common, which Thomas looked after as if it were his own estate. He saw to it that the Frog Pond was cleaned regularly. He planted a long row of lime trees on the east border. When those trees succumbed to the harsh New England weather, he replaced them with elms.

One day in June in that year of the Great Fire, a collection of Bostonians gathered on the shoreline to see off their outgoing governor, Thomas Pownall, who was leaving for England. He had been popular, a rarity in Massachusetts, where squabbles between the royally appointed governor and the popularly elected House of Representatives were common. Pownall would be remembered fondly: "He was much the gentleman, pleasing manners, short, comely, plump [and] pretty man who had rather gallant and bear the arm of a pretty woman than bear any weight of the government."[7] A new governor had been named but had not arrived.

On board the same vessel with Pownall was John Hancock, age twenty-three, pampered nephew of Thomas and Lydia Hancock, who had raised him.

John shared the name of his dead father and grandfather. The grandfather had been a Congregationalist minister in Lexington, about twelve miles northwest of Boston. His vigor and domineering style earned him the nickname "the Bishop." John's father, also a Congregationalist minister, was a meeker sort, described as having "no great Character for his Abilities Either Natural or Acquired."[8] That John Hancock tended a flock in Braintree, a town about thirteen miles south of Boston, where young John was born, growing up in a modest household with a brother and sister. John's destiny, it seemed then, was the pulpit.

Then, when John was seven, his father died. John's widowed mother was left with little money and no home. She and her brood moved in with the Bishop in Lexington.

Lydia and Thomas Hancock had longed for children but never had any of their own. When they offered to take John in, John's mother agreed. John, like a character out of a Dickens novel, found his life suddenly transformed. He had been an ordinary boy in an ordinary family tumbling with other boys among the trees and fields of Braintree. Now, his father was dead, his mother and siblings were miles away, and he was living in the finest mansion in Boston, with a horse-drawn coach to deliver him to school.

Aunt Lydia and Uncle Thomas showered John with the best money could buy. That included an education at Harvard, the college in nearby Cambridge. There John composed drinking songs and earned a scolding from college authorities for getting a slave dangerously drunk. College authorities fined John at least twice: once for missing chapel and another time for praying when he should have been studying. After college, Thomas introduced John to the business. One of John's first assignments was to apply his distinctive penmanship skills to making neat copies of his uncle's letters: a duplicate for his uncle's files and then as many as six others to be sent on separate ships to ensure at least one reached its destination.

By the year of the Great Fire, John was ready to round out his preparation for the business world with a trip to Britain. Before Governor Pownall and John boarded the *Benjamin and Samuel*, Thomas Hancock gave to John a treasured watch and to Pownall instructions on what to do if the French captured John and demanded a ransom.

While in Britain, John was expected to collect debts for his uncle, introduce himself to his uncle's business agents, and enjoy himself. He did, and also slipped off for a side trip to Hamburg and Amsterdam.

Modern Boston is firmly affixed to the mainland. Trees grow and buildings stand where water used to be, and city boundaries now embrace many old towns that started out as remote settlements. But in 1760, when Francis Bernard arrived to assume the post of governor, Boston was virtually an island, one mile wide and two miles long. Only a flat thread of land known as the Neck tethered the town to the mainland. This Neck, extending from the town to the southwest, was just forty yards wide at its narrowest point and so low that occasionally waves from Boston Harbor washed over it knee deep.

On the peninsula's northern side, where the Charles River mingled with the Atlantic, Bostonians had crafted a cove into a tidal millpond. To the northeast extended the North End, a knob of land jammed with narrow alleys and fringed with shipyards. The South End was roomier, ample enough for grand houses and gardens, one large enough for over forty fruit trees. On the west side, cattle grazed on the Common, which also served as a training ground for men to march and drill. Today's Back Bay section of the city really was a bay then, its waters lapping the Common.

Francis Bernard, after the portrait by John Singleton Copley. (*Library of Congress*)

The peninsula's most distinctive geographic features were its hills, such as Beacon Hill, Fort Hill, Copp's Hill, and Mount Whoredom. Decades later, these prominences would be lopped off to accommodate development and provide fill, and Mount Whoredom would be rechristened Mount Vernon. But in 1760, these barren and steep mounds, looming behind a grove of steeples and masts, defined the town's skyline.

Many dozens of vessels bobbed along Boston's sundry wharves, which stretched out like fingers into the town's handsome harbor on the Atlantic. The types of vessels would have been instantly familiar to the men working along the shore–brigs, brigantines, snows, sloops, schooners, shallops, lighters, pinnaces, barks, and ketches.

By far the grandest wharf was Long Wharf, extending half a mile from the shore. This wharf was also unusually wide, with room enough for warehouses along its north side. Long Wharf made a grand front porch for the town. A distinguished man arriving in Boston would be expected to step ashore there and march directly up King Street to the Town House, the sturdy, three-story brick building that was the province's capitol.

So it was strange that Francis Bernard, the new governor of Massachusetts, would enter Boston by the back door. That is, by land over the narrow Neck.

The son of an English clergyman, Bernard had toiled as an obscure barrister in England until a lucky marriage gave him sufficient connections to win the job of governor of New Jersey in 1758. Bernard's London relatives then won him the more lucrative and prestigious appointment in Massachusetts, a province of about thirty-nine thousand square miles (including what is now Maine), fourteen counties, over two hundred towns, and a population of about three hundred fifty thousand.

Bernard, "a man of little genius, but some learning,"[9] who could recite Shakespeare and dash off elegies in Greek and Latin, looked for-

Map 2. Boston Harbor, c. 1760.

modern shoreline
(approximate)
Charlestown
Peninsula
stown
Noddle's
Island
River
Boston
modern shoreline
(approximate)
modern shoreline
(approximate)
Neck
Castle Island
Dorchester Peninsula

ward to the assignment. Boston was a cultured place for a colonial town. It had music, a good library, and educated men with whom one could have lively and learned conversations. He thought Boston was "perhaps the most polished & scientific Town in America. I shall find there a good public library, many very conversible men, tolerable musick & other amusements."[10] Bernard was confident his time in Boston would be peaceful and pleasant. In advance of his move to Boston, he wrote: "As for the people [of Massachusetts], I am assured that I may depend on a quiet & easy administration. I shall have no points of government to dispute about, no schemes of self interest to pursue. The People are well disposed to live upon good terms with the Governor & with one another."[11]

The prospect of making more money was especially appealing to the new governor because his wife, Amelia, provided her husband with, in addition to political connections, ten children.

To get to Boston, Bernard, with his wife, some of their brood, their baggage, and entourage, had sailed by sloop to Newport, traveled by another boat to nearby Providence, and then set off in coaches. A troop of horse guards and the sheriff of Boston's Suffolk County met Bernard's group as they crossed from Rhode Island into Massachusetts. The next day they continued, with dozens of other coaches and carriages joining the train about twelve miles from Boston. As Bernard followed the road on the windswept mud flats along the Neck, with Roxbury Harbor on his right and the Back Bay to his left, he would have seen the town gallows and, here and there on the bleak landscape nearby, forlorn mounds of stones marking the graves of executed criminals and those who took their own lives. Then he would have come to the brick town gate with its two arches–one for pedestrians and one for coaches, wagons, and livestock–and passed through, entering the intimate world of Boston of 1760, now vanished, but then poised on the watershed of history.

TWO

FAVORABLE SIGNS

The first stop for Bernard and his entourage after they entered Boston was Province House, the venerable, three-story brick mansion that was the governor's residence. We can imagine the new governor looking up at its high roof and cupola, topped with the figure of an Indian drawing a bow.

From Province House, the Independent Company of Cadets, the governor's honorary bodyguard, escorted Bernard to the sound of drums and fifes to nearby King Street and the Town House, where militiamen stood at attention. The Town House served many functions. The ground floor, an open arcade, was an exchange for men to gather and talk business. It was common practice for merchants to shut up their places of business at one in the afternoon, stroll to the Town House, and spend a few hours gathering gossip, negotiating deals, and chatting about promising fishing ponds and such before returning to warehouses, shops, and countinghouses about four in the afternoon. This arcade was often the first stop for ship captains after they stepped ashore from months at sea.

Under the Town House was a cellar rented out for storing wine. The cellar also had room for a copper fire engine. Two staircases led from the arcade to the second floor, where, on the west side, was a courtroom, and in the center was Representatives Hall, the meeting place for the province's House of Representatives. On the east side was the Council Chamber, a large room designated for the Governor's Council.

The entourage of greeters led Bernard to this chamber, where a committee of the provincial legislature presented him with his royal commission. After taking the oath of office, Bernard, a stout man with a round face and blue-green eyes, stepped out onto a balcony, the stage for important public announcements in Boston. As the new governor looked down King Street and beyond to Long Wharf, townspeople jostling below offered three great cheers, while cannons from town batteries and British warships boomed. All signs were favorable for this amiable and scholarly man.

As Bernard mingled that day, he must have strained to understand what people meant when they said "Bast'n" for "Boston," "git" for "get," "hull" for "whole," and "sarve" for "serve." This was a clue that Boston, while similar in many ways to other American towns, and indeed to many towns in England, had its own ways, its own culture, and its own character.

The typical Bostonian was not a man or woman, but a child. White children under sixteen represented 52 percent of Boston's population.[1] Meanwhile, not all the faces in Boston were white. About one in every twenty was black. Of these eight hundred or so blacks, only about eighteen were free. What about Native Americans, or "Civilized Indians,"[2] the term for native peoples attempting to assimilate into white society? Boston had a few. A census from 1765 counted thirty-seven.[3]

Because of Puritan sensibilities, theaters were banned in Boston. But the town had other entertainment venues, such as Concert Hall, at the corner of Court and Hanover streets. Entertainments there included dances with as many as two hundred gentlemen and ladies.

The Hancock house was perhaps the grandest residence in town. It was three stories, made of granite blocks, with brownstone trim at the corners, and had no fewer than fifty-three windows–including the dormers. The Hancocks had five black slaves and two white servants. Meanwhile, the cellar was stocked with the best Madeira. Outside the house was an orchard that included mulberry, peach, and apricot trees.

Few Bostonians lived half as well as the Hancocks. Most townspeople lived more like Edward and Jane Mecom, who had a house on Hanover Street near the Orange-Tree Tavern. In the front room of the Mecom house was Edward's shop. He made and repaired saddles and harnesses, although by the early 1760s, Edward was too sick to do much work. What work was being done in the shop was done by a son, Josiah. From this shop, the family also sold miscellaneous products, including spices, soap, butter, raisins, mustard seed, tobacco, needles, and rum.

The shop couldn't support the growing family, so after the birth of the seventh child (Jane would eventually give birth to twelve, nine of whom survived infancy), the family began to take in boarders. The Mecom boardinghouse was respectable enough for some lawmakers from out of town attending sessions of the provincial assembly at the Town House. The house took in as many as six boarders at a time.

At about this time, the early 1760s, the house may have felt quite empty with just six people living under one roof: Jane, Edward, Josiah, two sickly daughters of Jane and Edward, and a lodger, the stepdaughter of one of Jane's late sisters (Jane had sixteen siblings; all but two were dead by 1760).

It was in this household that Jane played host to another sibling–a brother–along with a niece, for three months in 1762. The brother, up from Philadelphia, was the most famous man in America, Benjamin Franklin.

Jane Mecom and her family struggled–the sheriff threatened Edward at least four times with debtors' prison–but were still better off than many, such as George Robert Twelves Hewes. Born in 1742, Hewes was the sixth of nine children and the son of a tanner rich enough to buy a slave and pay fees for his children's education but not frugal enough to put away savings. When George was about seven, his father died and the family was soon receiving charity. By the time George was fourteen, his mother was dead. Too small to enter a trade where muscle was needed and too poor for a lucrative trade that required an indenture fee, George became apprenticed to a shoemaker, near the bottom rung of the trades in Boston. Unhappy as an apprentice, he tried to enlist in the military but was rejected for being too short.

He eventually completed his apprenticeship and opened a shop, taking time off to go on fishing voyages with his brother to Newfoundland. In 1769, at age twenty-six, he married the seventeen-year-old daughter of a church sexton and washerwoman. He had a hard time making a living and two years later found himself in debtors' prison, apparently because he was unable to pay for the suit he bought when he was courting. He got out of prison but remained poor. In 1773, he and his wife and three children were apparently living with an uncle in Boston.

Others, worse off than Hewes and his family, received charity. Most of the poor who received relief lived at home. An observer noted that the Overseers of the Poor were "very tender of exposing those that had lived in a handsome manner" so gave assistance "in so private a manner, that it is seldom known to any of their neighbors."[4]

Churches also provided poor relief, and some people depended on such charity for years. However, churches tended to be generous only with members in good standing, and even those might not receive help if deemed undeserving. The Boston Episcopal Charitable Society, in its charter, said, "All Vagrants Idle and dissolute Persons of Notorious evil fame are excepted or excluded as unworthy this Charity."[5]

In many small towns in Massachusetts, the penniless stayed in the homes of willing citizens paid by the town to provide such shelter. Boston, by this time, had moved away from such arrangements. The town had its own almshouse, a two-story brick building on Beacon

Street for the poor, aged, and infirm; a two-story workhouse facing the Common for "rogues and vagabonds";[6] and a nearby structure that was both a kind of prison and an insane asylum. A report from that decade told of 230 people in the almshouse and forty in the workhouse.[7] In times of war, the almshouse often received wounded soldiers, housed prisoners of war, and provided shelter for women and children stranded by war.

Boston, like most towns in New England, also employed a practice called warning out to discourage poor people from settling in the town. Each town was responsible only for its own legal inhabitants. Anyone not an inhabitant could be delivered back to the town where he or she was born to receive welfare. Towns defined "inhabitant" in various ways. The definition used in Rhode Island towns was probably typical. There, inhabitants were only those born in the town and those who became legal inhabitants by serving an apprenticeship in the town, by buying land in the town, or, for women, by marrying an inhabitant.

To be warned out was to be told by a constable or some other official that the town would provide no aid–no food, no shelter, no special care–should the person become ill, hurt, or destitute. In some cases, the person being warned out would be immediately taken out of town. In other cases, the warning out was a formality, and the person was left alone.

A noninhabitant might become eligible for welfare benefits if he or she lived in the town for more than twelve months without being warned out. Therefore, towns took great pains to warn people out on a regular basis, even those who appeared well established. A noninhabitant could be quite prosperous, pay taxes, and even hold public office, and still receive warnings year after year and be denied relief during hard times. Also, a person could live in a town for decades and still be considered an outsider. Records tell of an elderly widow who, after living thirty years in Providence, was ordered to leave and return to her "home town."[8]

Almost everywhere, pregnant women with no evident means of support were especially likely to be warned out. Towns acted quickly to hustle such women out of town before the baby was born because the child, once it came into the world, was the responsibility of the town where it was born. No town wanted to be burdened with the care of both mother and child. In some cases, a single pregnant woman arriving at a town to live with a relative would be ordered away just so the town would not have responsibility for the expected child.

The constable escorting the unwanted individual away would deliver the person or family to officials in the next town, who would then relay the person to the town farther down the road. The person would be transferred again and again until reaching his or her native town, which would then have the responsibility for shelter and food. Cases involving families could be especially wrenching because husband, wife, and children could each have been born in different towns, which meant the family would be scattered.

As a port, with many seamen and port workers coming and going, Boston had more than its share of transient noninhabitants. The number of warnings in a given year could be in the hundreds. In 1755, for example, the town issued 222 such warnings.[9]

Concern about outsiders taking advantage of the town's welfare led Boston's leaders to hire a man to check into the activities of every newcomer, especially "Poor, sick, and Lazy" sailors.[10] Inhabitants who failed to report strangers staying with them could be prosecuted.

Boston's character was defined in large part by its churches, taverns, and town meetings. Boston's many churches reminded one and all about the role of faith in establishing Boston in the first place. The first Europeans to come in large numbers to the Boston area were the Puritans. They were English men and women who, irked by the rules of the Church of England, took off for America. Some two hundred to three hundred arrived in five vessels the first year of settlement, 1629. The next year, twelve hundred came. By the time the great wave of Puritan settlement ended in 1643, some twenty thousand had settled in and around Boston.

These Puritans had a charter from the English king that authorized the colony on land that was virtually vacant. Disease brought by earlier Europeans had ravaged the native tribes that once hunted and fished around Massachusetts Bay. The Puritans chose Boston as the colony's capital because of its reliable springs and fine harbor.

The Puritan beliefs were similar to those of the Pilgrims, who had established the Plymouth Colony a few years before, about forty miles southeast of Boston. The Pilgrims and the Puritans both believed that, while no one deserved salvation, God in his mercy selected a few for saving and eternal life. Everyone should be prepared for God's grace by studying the Bible, resisting temptations, and praying.

Also, Pilgrims and Puritans came to America for similar reasons. Both hated the Church of England's popish folderol–the vestments, the candles, the incense, the chanting–so similar to the traditions of the Roman Catholic Church. Services, they insisted, should be in plain English.

The Pilgrims and Puritans also despised the Church of England's structure, with doctrine imposed by the king, bishops, and priests. The Pilgrims and Puritans believed that congregations could read and interpret scripture for themselves, and could choose their own ministers. Pilgrims and the Puritans recognized that prospects in England were bleak for them if they criticized and defied the Anglican Church. In America they could worship as they wished.

But the Pilgrims and Puritans also had their differences. The Pilgrims, known as Separatists, wanted a complete break from the Church of England. When they came to America, they intended to stay. The Puritans had a different aim. They would constitute the "pure" Church of England in America, and they expected eventually to return to England to replace the corrupt church.

The Puritans around Boston were also richer and more numerous than the colonists in Plymouth. The Pilgrims, after stumbling ashore late in 1620 with few provisions, suffered terribly and were nearly wiped out the first winter. The Puritans, by contrast, came well equipped–they even brought forty cows and sixty horses–and most arrived much earlier in the season. They suffered from scurvy and hunger, but, by comparison with the Pilgrims, the Puritans had it easy.

The Puritans quickly outnumbered the Pilgrims in America. Even so, the Puritans adopted many Pilgrim ways. For example, the Puritans took on the Pilgrim practice of calling sanctuaries meetinghouses instead of churches. It seemed a more suitable name for structures used for civic gatherings as well as for worship.

The Puritans, for their part, introduced their own ideas, which were adopted by the Pilgrims and others. One of these ideas was the town meeting, the form of local government that became common throughout New England. They established narrowly democratic institutions. You could vote as long as you were an adult white male, owned property, and were a church member.

The Puritans also stamped Massachusetts with their culture, a culture that included a passion for education. The Puritans were well educated to begin with. The percentage of college-educated men was higher in colonial Massachusetts than in England. The Puritans believed that good members of the faith had to be able to read the Bible themselves. Therefore, reading was important. So towns were required to make teachers available for reading and writing. Also, good pastors were needed. Therefore, a college was important. The college that became Harvard was established early on, within a decade of settlement.

Over time, the religion of the Pilgrims and Puritans came to be called Congregationalism, a term that emphasized the independence of each parish and the power of each congregation to govern itself.

The colony's founders envisioned a model Puritan community. But it could never be. Other immigrants trickled in, and some didn't share the Puritan vision. Meanwhile, Puritan offspring–and Puritans had many children–found their parents' faith too bleak and oppressive. Many congregations loosened rules on membership to maintain their numbers. The early plain, steepleless meetinghouses gave way to steepled buildings that looked more like churches, even though they were still called meetinghouses. Many New Englanders placed comfy Congregationalist cushions on their hard Puritan pews.

Puritanism also never recovered from the witchcraft hysteria that consumed Salem Village (now Danvers), northeast of Boston, in the late 1600s. By the time the colony awoke from that nightmare, twenty people had been convicted of dealing with the devil. Nineteen were hanged, and one was crushed under heavy stones.

The frenzy created new divisions among Congregationalists. Some made no apologies for the witch trials, while others felt deep shame. In Boston, new controversies arose in 1699 when a congregation allowed women, as well as men, to elect the minister, and began to read scriptures verbatim without the usual commentary from the minister.

Some outsiders found Bostonian attitudes toward religion insufferable and hypocritical. An English visitor wrote of Boston: "[I]n Boston there are more Religious Zealots than Honest-men, more Parsons than Churches . . . tho' they wear in their Faces the Innocence of Doves, you will find them in their Dealing, as Subtile as Serpents. Interest is their Faith, Money their God and Large Possessions the only Heaven they covet."[11]

As the years passed, other faiths gained footholds. By 1722, when Boston had at least seven Congregational meetinghouses, Quakers, Baptists, and French Protestants each had a place to worship, and Presbyterians would soon have a church. By that time also, followers of the Church of England had a place to gather: King's Chapel.[12] Dreaded corrupt Anglicanism was thus planted in the heart of the Puritan "city on a hill." Other Anglican churches appeared, including Trinity Church and Christ Church, now known as Old North.

Then came a whirlwind known as the Great Awakening, a religious upheaval that raged through America in the 1730s and 1740s. This religious revival touched all of the colonies, renewing interest in religion and roiling established practices.

The man most identified with the Great Awakening was George Whitefield, from Gloucester, England. He crossed the ocean seven times to spread his message in America. Speaking quietly and with solemn pauses, he moved his audiences in ways unheard of before. Benjamin Franklin, upon hearing Whitefield, wept. No one knew for sure what would happen at a Whitefield sermon. His listeners might scream or even fall on the floor and start writhing. This certainly never happened at any other Protestant service, especially Congregational services, where worshipers were properly restrained and silent, and nothing was spontaneous.

When Whitefield came to Boston for the first time in 1740, enthusiastic followers crammed the Summer Street Church where he was to preach. But the building was too small for the crowd, and a panic resulted in five deaths. Whitefield eventually spoke out on the Common to a throng of five thousand.

So into the 1760s, in Boston, as echoes of the Great Awakening still reverberated, Congregationalism's grip was slipping, its doctrine drifting, its tone softening. On gravestones, macabre skulls were giving way to sweet cherubs.

Meanwhile, Anglicanism was gaining ground, and even becoming fashionable. Some Presbyterians and Congregationalists came back to the Church of England, drawn in part by its association with power–it was, after all, the king's faith–and social prestige.

The growth of Anglicanism did not go unnoticed. Some warned that the Church of England planned to establish a bishop in America. With the Anglican Church tightly bound to British authority–the monarch was the head of the church–the imposition of a bishop would be the first step, some feared, toward government supervision of religion, plainly a threat to all non-Anglicans.

Meanwhile, and more horrifying to many devout Congregationalists, some Roman Catholics were settling in Boston. Barriers were high for anyone attempting to practice the Catholic faith. At least as late as 1755, laws barred priests from even entering the province. Into the 1760s, Boston had no Catholic church. But the town had Catholics nonetheless, as well as a surprising number of people who seemed to follow no faith at all. A Boston clergyman estimated around this time that, of two thousand families in Boston, 420 belonged to no denomination.

John Adams dismissed taverns as dens of "idlers, thieves, sots, and consumptive patients,"[13] which they were. But many others spent time in taverns as well. Indeed, Boston townsmen likely spent more time on tavern benches than church pews. People went to taverns not just to eat or drink, but to borrow books, read newspapers, pick up mail, play cards, or obtain loans. In winter, a poor man with little money for firewood would go to a tavern to get warm.

One source counted thirty-two taverns in 1769 and twenty-three in 1774.[14] But there were many other drinking establishments. In 1765, one in every thirteen houses in the town was licensed to sell alcohol. Some must have been cramped dram shops with a stool or two and little else. Permits to sell liquor were often awarded to poor widows, especially war widows, as a way to help them eke out a living. For that reason, women may have outnumbered men as vendors of alcohol in Boston.

Most taverns were known by their distinctive signs. The Salutation's sign showed two gentlemen bowing to one another. A visitor to the Bunch of Grapes would see three gilded clusters of grapes over the entrance. Royalists, it was said, crossed the street rather than pass by Cromwell's Head just to avoid bowing under an image of Oliver Cromwell hanging low over the footway.

Taverns often acquired reputations. People said the Orange-Tree Tavern on Hanover Street had the best well water in town. Tanners often met at The Three Horse Shoes. A merchant in the market for a vessel likely went to the Royal Exchange on King Street, probably the finest tavern in town.

Some taverns could be quite large, and many offered rooms to paying guests. One Boston tavern, the Golden Ball, had four chambers and a garret in addition to large and small front rooms, a bar, and kitchen. Taverns without separate chambers might put a bed in the public rooms to accommodate overnight guests.

Taverns had other uses. In a pinch, they were places of worship. The Green Dragon served temporarily in 1764 for religious services while a church was being built.

Usually, though, taverns specialized in spiritual needs of another sort: drink, especially rum. Each tavern had its own rum punch recipe and a variety of rum-based concoctions. Other drinks might include cider, beer, applejack, and peach brandy.

Many taverns also served food. In front of the Bunch of Grapes, a bell sounded each day at 2:00 p.m. to signal mealtime. Guests might be served salmon, veal, beef, mutton, fowl, or ham, along with vegetables, pudding, and a pint of Madeira.

Many taverns had books that patrons could read in the tavern or borrow. Politics and history were favored subjects. Books at the Bunch of Grapes included an eleven-volume history of England, essays by Jonathan Swift, and John Milton's *Paradise Lost.* An inventory from a colonial tavern earlier in the century tallied eighty-eight books and thirty-one pamphlets. One or more local newspapers were generally available for anyone to read.

Many patrons, even those with good employment, had difficulty coming up with ready cash to pay for food and drink because coins were always in short supply. Tavern owners addressed this problem by keeping a ledger with records of what patrons owed. Debts might be paid back in cash, goods, or services. A surviving ledger from a Massachusetts tavern showed credit given to a man for shoeing the tavern keeper's horse.[15]

Travelers or post carriers often entrusted letters with tavern keepers, who would hold them until the recipient stopped in. To attract patrons, tavern keepers might permit scholars to lecture, musicians to play, or unusual animals to be exhibited. In taverns one could attend a "Philosophical Lecture of the Eye"[16] or see a moose on display. Boston had no official slave marketplace, so taverns often served that role.

As sacred as religious services and as lively as the taverns were the town meetings, which were held at least once each year, mainly to choose the town's selectmen–the men who managed the town during the year–and to elect representatives to the provincial House of Representatives. Much other business was also conducted. Over the course of one meeting in March 1762, for example, townsmen cast votes to choose seven selectmen, twelve overseers of the poor, the town treasurer, the county treasurer, twelve town wardens, twelve constables, four tax collectors, seven assessors, twelve firewards, twelve clerks of the market, six fence viewers, twelve surveyors of boards, twelve scavengers, ten cullers of staves, one surveyor of hemp, two informers of deer, one hayward, two assay masters, four sealers of leather, four hog reeves, and three purchasers of grain.[17]

In other business, townsmen authorized ringing of church bells at 5:00 a.m. (!); accepted a report on the keeper of the granary; directed selectmen to look into the "Law relating Hogs"; named a committee to draw up a petition regarding "the pernicious practice of forestalling the Market"; set fees for tax collectors; advanced money to the town almshouse; prohibited any "Tanner, Shoemaker or Currier" from serving as a sealer of leather; and on and on. Altogether, at least forty votes were taken at Faneuil Hall that day.[18]

Another town meeting took place that year in May. There townsmen elected Boston's four representatives to the province's House of Representatives and then attended to other business, such as setting aside money for poor relief, approving salaries for schoolmasters, authorizing the selectmen to fix or enlarge the town gates, and ordering that all wood and bark brought into the town be properly measured and certified. The town also addressed the issue of hogs: they would no longer be allowed to roam at large, except those being driven to market. Anyone catching a runaway hog would get half the fine from the owner, the other half designated to "the Poor of this Town."[19]

How many people were at these meetings and voting on all of these issues? Town records only counted votes cast for representatives to the House when 629 people voted.

For most issues, voting was done by a show of hands or voice vote. Special town meetings, called by selectmen or by a petition from ten citizens, also took place from time to time.

For its day, Boston's town meeting form of government was about as democratic as any form of government in the world, but still a far cry from full democracy. Fewer than half of the adults could participate. Women, blacks, and Indians could not. White men without property could not vote either, in theory. In practice, however, many did. All white men, even those without property, could attend town meetings to discuss and debate issues, and once a poor man was inside the hall, who was going to stop him from raising his hand or saying "aye"?

It might be assumed that the Town House at the head of King Street was the setting for Boston's town meetings. Indeed, that was the case when the Town House was built. However, by the 1760s, nearby Faneuil Hall was where most town meetings took place. Faneuil Hall had an open-air marketplace at ground level and an ample public hall on the second floor with a capacity of about twenty-five hundred. Similar in appearance to the Town House, Faneuil Hall was brick and topped with a handsome cupola with a distinctive weather vane in the form of a grasshopper. It easily accommodated most town meetings. Sometimes, however, especially large meetings were moved to the Old South Meetinghouse, near the Province House. Old South, the largest building in town, could accommodate five thousand people.

Not everyone admired the town meeting form of government. Some argued that the town meeting was a sham–a democratic façade for a shabby political structure of cronies and insiders.[20] Boston, they said, would be better off with something akin to English city government, with a powerful mayor and with aldermen and councilmen who elected their own replacements. Such a government would put the towns firmly in the hands of a wealthy elite few.

That faction lost this battle, but it had a point. The town meetings were choreographed, with most actions of consequence planned beforehand in caucuses, semisecret meetings where key townsmen determined just who would be selectmen for the next year, who would hold the various town offices, what issues would be addressed, and what issues ignored.

Maybe Boston's experience with town meetings and self-government had something to do with the people's obsession with contracts, solemn resolutions, and legal matters. This was a town where seven boys in 1750 organized themselves as a society of bell ringers with a covenant promising, among other things, to go to Christ Church "once a week on Evenings to Ring the Bells for two hours Each time from the date hereof to one year."[21] Meanwhile, filing lawsuits was virtually a pastime. As a Loyalist historian later wrote: "[T]he People of the Province seem to be born with litigious Constitutions."[22]

That prickly nature went way back and may explain the province's unhappy history with its governors. The first settlers of the Massachusetts Bay Colony made their own laws and elected their own governor and lawmakers, as allowed in the charter granted to the colony by the English king. Authorities in London paid no attention until the 1670s, when they discovered that colonists were ignoring

British navigation laws and thus cheating the king of customs duties. Massachusetts lawmakers, alarmed at the possibility that their virtual independence would be taken away, argued that they didn't have to enforce such laws. They dispatched a message to London with an argument that would echo a century later: "[T]he laws of England were bounded within the four seas and did not reach America."[23]

British authorities scoffed and, in 1684, threw out the colony's charter and imposed a new one. The colonies of Massachusetts Bay, Plymouth, Maine, and New Hampshire were roped together as the Dominion of New England. (This dominion would later be expanded to include Rhode Island, New York, Connecticut, and what is now New Jersey.) Furthermore, a "president" appointed by the king would govern the dominion.[24] The days of virtual self-government in Massachusetts were over.

Massachusetts sulked but didn't protest when Sir Edmund Andros arrived on the scene in Boston in 1686 as first–and last–president of this new dominion. Andros made enemies quickly. He demanded to use the Congregational Old South Meetinghouse for Anglican service, and then he pushed measures that appeared to invalidate nearly all land transactions made over several generations.

New England soon longed to be rid of the wretched Andros. Then, over the winter of 1688–89, word trickled into Boston that King James II had fled to France and that William of Orange from the Netherlands had invaded England. While Massachusetts citizens had recognized Catholic James as their king, many were pleased to learn that he was on his way out and Protestant William was on his way in.

However, the outcome of this crisis–the Glorious Revolution, as it would be known–was not yet certain. Some speculated that President Andros was plotting to somehow join New England with French Canada as part of a plan to restore James to the British throne. The scheme was plausible enough, and it gave colonists more motivation to send Andros packing.

That opportunity presented itself on April 18, 1689. Authorities sought to arrest some militiamen who had deserted their posts in the north and showed up in Boston. Friends of the militiamen intervened. Meanwhile, mutineers from a navy frigate in the harbor seized their captain while he was ashore. All this sparked rioting, which spread through the town. Militiamen and armed citizens seized various officials of the dominion and hauled them to jail. Andros found refuge with the military garrison.

As word of the clash spread and hundreds of militiamen streamed into Boston, civic leaders made the best of a chaotic and dangerous situation and called on Andros to surrender. He finally did, and with other ousted allies, was shipped to England.

How did new King William III react to these curious events in Boston? He neither restored the dominion nor the old charter, but imposed a wholly new charter that refashioned boundaries and jurisdictions. All of the Plymouth Colony would be incorporated into Massachusetts. Massachusetts would also oversee Maine and the islands off Cape Cod, including Martha's Vineyard and Nantucket. The new charter also trimmed the political influence of the Puritan church: the right to vote would no longer hinge on church membership. Furthermore, the new charter directed that the Crown choose the governor, who would have veto power over proposed laws from local legislators. Thus, there would be no return to the days of virtual independence, when the people of Massachusetts elected their own governor.

By the time Francis Bernard arrived on the scene, this charter, the Charter of 1691, had been in place for almost seventy years, and it still rankled. The very presence of the royal governor under the imposed charter was a reminder of what Massachusetts once had and lost.

The person best suited to teach Bernard about this history was Lieutenant Governor Thomas Hutchinson, a forty-nine-year-old widower, a "tall slender, fair-complexioned, fair-spoken, 'very good gentleman.'"[25] He knew Massachusetts history better than anyone, and was also widely admired, even revered, and certainly more suited to be governor than Bernard. If the people of Massachusetts could have voted for governor, they would have elected Thomas Hutchinson.

Hutchinson descended from a family of merchants going back many generations in America. His great-great-grandmother was Anne Hutchinson, the defiant and outspoken religious leader banished from Massachusetts in 1637. Thomas Hutchinson had none of her religious fervor but inherited another family passion–that for careful business deals and the steady acquisition of wealth. Business mastery made the Hutchinsons prosperous and established the family in the upper ranks of Boston society.

At Harvard, then more like a preparatory school for boys than a modern college, young Thomas scrupulously recorded how he spent every coin. After graduation at sixteen, he spent several years in the family's merchant business before gradually engaging in public affairs. An inheritance and shrewd business skills made him wealthy. But he was never ostentatious. When persuaded that he needed a more stylish carriage, he ordered one from England, saying a used one would be suitable and "it can't be too plain if neat and light."[26]

Along the way, he acquired a suitable wife–Margaret Sanford, daughter of the governor of Rhode Island–and even fell in love with her. Peggy, as he called her, bore him a dozen children, of which five–

three sons and two daughters–survived childhood. As it turned out, Peggy's older sister married another man who would become important in Massachusetts government, Andrew Oliver. Thus, the Sanford sisters established the first link between the Oliver and Hutchinson families, whose members occupied many government posts in the late 1760s and early 1770s. Over the years, that link would evolve into a braided chain. Each of Thomas Hutchinson's three children who married would marry an Oliver.

Peggy died in 1754 after childbirth. Her last words to Thomas were "best of husbands."[27] No event of his life, not even the many humiliations and defeats, was more painful than her death. With it, he said, he lost more than half his soul.

Hutchinson found comfort in the affection of his children, and by 1760, in his spare time, had immersed himself in the study of local history. He collected documents and stocked his library with nearly every book available on New England's past. He had achieved all his ambitions but one: he was not yet governor. That would be the pinnacle of his public life. He had the experience and skills. He was certainly popular enough to be elected. But his chances of becoming governor were remote; for such posts, the king favored men born in England.

Over the years, Hutchinson's fellow townsmen had elected him not once, not twice, but many times–every year but one between 1737 and 1749–to represent Boston in the province's House of Representatives, where his colleagues chose him speaker. After serving in the House, Hutchinson was named by the governor, with the blessing of the House, to the Governor's Council, on which Hutchinson served for more than a decade.

He had also been entrusted with many other important posts and key assignments. He had represented the province in boundary disputes. He had managed the province's lottery. Back in 1754, he represented Massachusetts at the Albany Congress, where he worked with Benjamin Franklin, among others, to produce a scheme–never implemented–for greater cooperation among the thirteen American colonies. Over the years, he had also served as a judge and was a member of the Board of Overseers for Harvard College. Furthermore, he was, without question, courageous and willing to do more than his bit for his town and province. He risked his life during the Great Fire of 1760, putting himself in the path of the flames to toss gunpowder into the sea.

The great majority of people, the powerful and the powerless, held him in high esteem. Pownall, the departing governor, wrote of him, "He has . . . universally the best character of any man in this continent, both as to his head and heart."[28] John Adams, musing about Hutchinson in his diary in 1766, wrote:

> Have not his Countrymen loved, admired, revered, rewarded, nay almost adored him? Have not 99 in an 100 of them really thought him, the greatest and best Man in America? Has not the Perpetual Language of many Members of both Houses, and of a Majority of his Brother Councillors [been], that Mr. Hutchinson is a great Man, a pious, a wise, a learnd, a good Man, an eminent Saint, a Phylosopher &c, the greatest Man in the Province, the greatest on the Continent?[29]

It must have galled Hutchinson to see Bernard arrive to take the job he so coveted. But the lieutenant governor did his duty. That was his nature. He was pragmatic and realistic. He once advised an ally that, in this imperfect world, it is better to be a willow than an oak: "[W]hen we can't have perfection, we ought to comply with the measure that is least remote from it."[30] He was also cool, prudent, deliberate. Hutchinson wrote about himself: "My temper does not incline to enthusiasm."[31] Cautious by nature, he could never just dash off a letter and rush it out by next post. Every letter had a draft or two, and then a revision or two. Some letters, with multiple drafts and revisions, he never sent, but simply filed.

A careful, hard-working, brave, smart, respected, capable man who loved Massachusetts and, it seemed, understood the workings of the colony better than anyone–that was Hutchinson. Yet in a few years, he would be the most despised man in America: "dark, intriguing, insinuating, haughty and ambitious,"[32] "arch fiend,"[33] "vile hypocrite and slanderer,"[34] "a parricide who has attempted to ruin his country to save his own narrow selfish purposes,"[35] and a "damn'd arch traitor."[36] By the time of the American Revolution, Hutchinson was more hated than King George III.

Bernard quickly came to depend on Hutchinson, for the new governor understood well–but not well enough–the importance of cultivating cordial relations with local politicians. By appearances, Bernard was answerable only to the king; he had no apparent need to seek the support of the people or their representatives. Furthermore, Bernard could veto any law brought before him, and lawmakers could not override that veto.

However, there was the problem of money. For money to run the government and for his own salary, Bernard had to get along with the General Court, which was not a court of justice but the province's legislative branch.

The General Court was made up of two houses–the House of Representatives and the Governor's Council. Members of the House were elected by the people–that is, white men with property–at town meetings in each of the towns. Boston had four representatives in a body made up of more than one hundred members. Meanwhile, members of the Governor's Council were chosen by the House together with the members of the outgoing Council. Those choices required the governor's approval. The House and Council drew up proposed laws for the province. Once the General Court passed a measure, it went to the governor to sign or veto.

The House also had two other important roles: it authorized taxes and decided how those taxes were to be used. Meanwhile, the twenty-eight members of the Council, in addition to passing judgment on measures from the House, served as advisers to the governor. The governor was free to ignore the Council, but he did so only with great reluctance.

To some, this structure represented a fine balance of power not unlike that of Britain: the House of Representatives equated with the House of Commons, the Governor's Council with the House of Lords, the governor with the king. But to the man who happened to be governor, the structure might seem tipped to his disadvantage and could be a source of frustration.

The same month Bernard arrived in Massachusetts, the province's chief justice died. This meant that one of Bernard's first official actions as governor was to appoint a new man to head the province's highest court. The position was not lucrative but was highly prestigious.

Many inquired about the appointment. One who asked was James Otis Jr., not for himself, but for his father, known as the Colonel. The position of chief justice, the Colonel thought, would be a grand way to cap off his rise in the world. Colonel Otis of Barnstable started as a clerk in the family store, prospered in business, stumbled into law, entered politics, and rose to become speaker of the province's House of Representatives.

The Colonel also raised a family, which included the junior Otis, by this time a respected lawyer in his midthirties. Young James, with muscular shoulders and a thick neck below a round, boyish face, was the eldest of thirteen children. After Harvard, he studied law, started a practice in Plymouth, and eventually relocated to Boston, quickly establishing himself as one of the best lawyers in town.

He also married. His bride, Ruth Cunningham, a merchant's daughter, was quite unlike her groom: she placid, he impetuous. The marriage may have started well–it produced three children–but later soured when their views about the evolving political crisis diverged.

Later, Otis Jr. would exhibit strange, alarming behavior: shooting off guns in his house; entering the courthouse through a window; proposing at a town meeting that he personally grapple with Britain's prime minister on the floor of the House of Commons. But at this time, there

Thomas Hutchinson, left, painted by Edward Truman. (*Massachusetts Historical Society*) James Otis, right, painted by Robert Chase. (*Bostonian Society*)

was little to suggest a brittle state of mind. Otis decided the best way to get Bernard's attention–and get the judicial appointment for the Colonel–was through Hutchinson, who seemed to have a good opinion of the younger Otis.

So, on behalf of the Colonel, Otis paid a friendly visit to Hutchinson. He reminded Hutchinson that promises had been made: two previous governors had pledged the prestigious judicial post to the Colonel. Hutchinson needed no reminder that the Otises were considered, in the parlance of the times, "friends to government."[37] That is, part of Hutchinson's own political faction bound up with the governor.

Checking out a rumor that Hutchinson himself might ask for the post, Otis asked the lieutenant governor directly if he would ask Bernard for the job. Hutchinson's answer: he was not seeking the office. The younger Otis left the meeting satisfied that all had gone well, that the appointment of the Colonel to the court was virtually a done deal.

THREE

SMALL SPARK

This year of the Great Fire and Bernard's arrival was also a year of war. Britain and its American colonies were fighting France in a conflict that became known as the Seven Years' War. North America, where the duel of European giants was known as the French and Indian War, was a vast battleground and a prize. The winner would likely control Canada and most of America east of the Mississippi River.

The war kept Boston on edge. In 1757, it feared that a French fleet would sweep down the coast and bombard the town. The sails never appeared on the horizon, however, and the tide of war turned with a climactic battle in 1759, when British forces routed the French before the walls of Quebec City.

Now, in September 1760, word reached Boston of the fall of Montreal. Boston rejoiced in a frenzy of British patriotism. The governor, the Governor's Council, and the House of Representatives each celebrated the long connection between the colonies and Britain. Governor Francis Bernard underscored the blessings the people of Massachusetts derived "from subjection to Great Britain, without which they could not now have been a free people."[1] The Council responded: "[T]o their relation with Great Britain they owe their present freedom."[2] In its turn, the House of Representatives declared that the connection with Great Britain "is founded on the principles of filial obedience, protection and justice."[3] Then, in December, news reached Boston that King George II was dead, succumbing to a stroke while at his toilet. The new king, George III, was the late king's grandson. Boston looked forward to the rule of a vigorous young king. Starting his reign at age twenty-two, George could be expected to rule for decades. Sadly, George was dull, immature, and insecure. Although astute enough to recognize his shortcomings, he was not wise enough to choose the right people to guide him.

For most of its colonial history, America was an untended garden. Britain paid scant attention, yet the provinces bloomed. Into the 1760s, oversight from London was confused, lax, and illogical. The main responsibility of the secretary handling American matters was Europe, not America. The government's Board of Trade was interested in America, but only in matters involving trade. Sometimes the Privy Council, the monarch's core advisory body, dealt with American issues. But the Privy Council's interests were wide and varied, with America rarely at the top of the agenda.

As for Parliament, its 558 members barely noticed what was happening in Britain, let alone America. Many came into Parliament with an eye only on narrow and local issues and took notice of nothing else. Rare was the member with fresh, sound ideas about broad policies. More rare still was the member with knowledge and interest in America.

Over the years, the colonists had taken on most of the responsibility for arming and defending themselves. When native tribes threatened, the colonists organized, marched, and risked their lives. Most of the time, the awesome power of the British army and navy was too far away to be of much help. An American could live a lifetime and never encounter a single British government official dispatched from London. Out of mind and out of sight of British rulers, the colonies had handled their own affairs, collected and spent their own taxes, struggled, and prospered.

Meanwhile, each of the American colonies evolved separately in near isolation from the others. Communications were spotty. A 1699 report on extending postal services from the northern colonies into Maryland and Virginia concluded that such an extension was not worth the trouble because only about one hundred letters a year passed between those two colonies and the colonies to the north.[4]

Americans in their isolated colonies were happy to have nothing to do with their neighbors. Even in times of grave crisis, they couldn't work together. Around the middle of the eighteenth century, a Swedish traveler in America wrote:

> [I]t is to be observed that each English colony in North America is independent of the other, and that each has its proper laws and coin, and may be looked upon in several lights, as a state by itself. From hence it happens, that in time of war things go on very slowly and irregularly here; for not only the sense of one province is sometimes directly opposite to that of another; but frequently the views of the governor, and those of the assembly of the same province, are quite different; so that it is easy to see

> that, while the people are quarrelling about the best and cheapest manner of carrying on the war, an enemy has it in his power to take one place after another. It has commonly happened that whilst some provinces have been suffering from their enemies, the neighbouring ones were quiet and inactive, and as if it did not in the least concern them. They have frequently taken up two or three years in considering whether they should give assistance to an oppressed sister colony, and sometimes they have expressly declared themselves against it.[5]

Thus, in the French and Indian War, a determined France might well have swallowed up these thirteen colonies one by one. But British might prevailed, and victory over France would extend George III's realm in North America far beyond the ports and plantations clustered near the coast. British authority would now embrace lands, forests, rivers, and mountains far to the west and north, and would include many French-speaking farmers, fishermen, trappers, and traders, as well as tribes of native peoples.

Here was an opportunity that a stronger, wiser, more imaginative king and Parliament might have seized. But the rich promise of America was not so apparent, and for now the main topic on the minds of king and Parliament was the war debt.

In the view of the British government, the war in North America was fought for British America, thus British Americans should pay at least some of the cost. That was only fair, according to the government's reasoning, especially considering that Americans were paying far less in taxes than their fellow subjects in the homeland.

So young King George III, his advisers, and Parliament, desperate to shore up Britain's tottering finances, contemplated how best to gather more taxes from America.

A few steps down King Street from Boston's Town House stood the brick Custom House. In this building, one of thirty such offices in America, customs men carried out British laws regulating shipping to and from American ports. The Custom House, more than any other building in the province, embodied British authority.

The bureaucratic, complex customs process employed many. In charge of the Custom House were the customs collector and the customs comptroller, the two men who regulated the port. As a vessel came into Boston Harbor, its captain was required to provide the collector with sealed certificates, known as cockets, which described the vessel's cargo, including quantities and weight, and named the consignees for these goods.

In the meantime, a tidesman or tidewaiter, another customs officer, was dispatched to the vessel. His job was to list all the goods on the vessel and to poke around for possible illegal goods. Following this work, the cargo could be "landed"–unloaded. Now another official, a landwaiter, watched as the goods came out of the holds and onto the shore or dock. If unloading could not be completed in a single day, or if illegal activity was suspected, yet another official was called in. This was the watcher, who guarded the goods overnight to prevent anyone from moving cargoes.

As the goods were landed, other officials came along to inspect, weigh, and measure them so that an accurate calculation of the duty could be made. Suspicious goods and goods not properly accounted for might be locked up for later investigation. Once all information was checked, and the duties calculated and paid, the consignees could take away their goods.

While the collector and comptroller checked the work of these lower officials and of each other, yet another official, the surveyor, in turn checked them.

According to the rules, goods originating in Europe, such as wine from Portugal and porcelain from Holland, could not come directly to America. They had to be shipped first to England or Scotland. There they had to be unloaded and duties had to be paid. Then they could be reloaded and shipped on to America. Goods from the West Indies, chiefly sugar and molasses, could come directly to Boston and enter duty-free only if they came from such British-controlled islands as Barbados. Goods directly from Dutch or Spanish islands carried stiff duties. And anything from France or French possessions at this time was forbidden.

Many Boston merchants, perhaps nearly all, were smugglers, one way or another. Smuggling had gone on for so long, and was so common, that it was halfway respectable. John Rowe, diarist and a leading merchant, was one of the most active smugglers. Some smuggling had to do with goods from Europe, but most was connected to trade with the West Indies, and much of that had to do with molasses. Molasses would prove, as John Adams later pointed out, an "essential ingredient in American independence."[6]

Merchants had many tricks. One involved passing off cheap molasses from French islands as the more expensive molasses from British islands. Shipmasters would sail to Monte Christi, a Spanish-controlled port close to French-owned plantations in Haiti, and arrange for French molasses to be put in British barrels. In Boston, the shipmaster would present the tidewaiter with plausible documents indicating that the molasses was British, and import the French molasses duty-free.

Other smugglers didn't bother with such deception. It was a simple matter to avoid the busy ports, where customs men lurked, and unload in a quiet, out-of-the-way bay.

Colonial merchants were so adept at smuggling, and British authorities so lackadaisical about enforcing the laws, that nearly 90 percent of the molasses imported into the American colonies came from French islands. Trading with the enemy was a matter of course.

So, in Boston, customs men pretended to enforce the law, merchants pretended to obey it, and all was cozy and pleasant until one day in 1760 when the customs men did the unthinkable: they seized a vessel. Such seizures were so rare they were practically unheard of. Sixteen years had passed since the last such confiscation. Boston merchants took notice. The customs office was getting serious about applying the law.

Other seizures followed. Then evidence came to light that much of the money from seizures that was supposed to go to the king was instead going to informers against the merchants. The king was being cheated. Oh my, harrumphed the merchants, who had been cheating the king for as long as anyone could remember. The inflamed merchants were now poised to take to the barricades in defense of their rights as good honest smugglers.

The smuggling merchants had friends and allies. Among these were the publishers of the *Boston Gazette*, the most spirited of the town's few newspapers and not the first to rattle the people at the top.

At the *Gazette*, Benjamin Edes, with partner John Gill, early on set a bold editorial policy, which earned a scolding from the town's selectmen for printing articles that "reflect grossly upon the received religious principles of this People which is very Offensive." Edes solemnly vowed to "publish nothing that shall give any uneasiness to any Persons whatever" and then continued to publish as he pleased, earning for the paper the sobriquet "Weekly Dung Barge" from printers on the other side of the political divide.[7]

Boston merchants, as they grumbled about increasingly tight enforcement of customs regulations, zeroed in on one especially powerful tool of customs enforcers, writs of assistance. These were like search warrants. A writ, obtained from a judge, authorized the holder to enter or break into warehouses, cargo holds, and other places where goods were stored. Significantly, however, unlike a modern search warrant, a writ was general, not specific. That is, the document did not name a particular location of a suspected illegal cargo, or identify the owner of the cargo in question, or tell why illegal activity was thought likely. The writs simply gave the tidewaiter broad authority to search where he pleased.

As Boston merchants stewed about the hated writs of assistance, they learned about a certain article first printed in an obscure British journal about imports of fabric into Britain. The article, eventually reprinted in Boston, seemed to suggest that in Britain, writs were obtained and applied case by case for specific cargoes in specific places.

Merchants in Boston pored over the article. With Britain an ocean away, no one could confirm the facts of the article. But if true, the implications for Boston were huge: possibly, the writs as applied in Boston were illegal, and customs men had no authority to conduct searches as they did. If writs of assistance had to be specific, an official would have to obtain a new writ for every cargo and would have to demonstrate to a judge why the cargo was under suspicion. Efforts to stop smuggling would be crippled. The article galvanized Boston merchants into action. They would challenge the writs in court. Thus emerged a lawsuit, recalled today as the Writs of Assistance case, but known then as the Paxton case.

Charles Paxton, surveyor and searcher of customs, must have had a thick skin. That's the only way he could have survived amid so many enemies. The *Gazette* called him "perfidious and treacherous to the last degree, as oppressive as a tyrant, and an intire stranger to truth."[8] Others described him as an extremely polite man who was everyone's humble servant but no one's friend, a sort of colonial Uriah Heep. Paxton may indeed have been an oily character, but his only real "crime" was no crime at all, just rigid enforcement of customs regulations. The writ of assistance was Paxton's favorite tool. With the death of King George II, Paxton had to reapply for a writ, as was customary. The suit challenged the renewal of the writ.

At about the time merchants were contemplating legal action, the new governor named the province's next chief justice. Bernard, ignoring the promises of previous governors, did not appoint Colonel Otis. Instead he chose a man arguably far more qualified; a man who had served the province with distinction for many years; a man with proven courage, good judgment, and judicial experience; a man widely admired. In short, Bernard chose his own lieutenant governor, Thomas Hutchinson.

The appointment seemed sound. Hutchinson was respected and had judicial experience. Even so, many found the selection irksome because it further concentrated power and influence in the hands of Hutchinson, his family, and allies. With the appointment, Hutchinson would have four government positions at the same time. He was already, in addition to lieutenant governor, a member of the governor's Council and a judge of probate. Now he would be joining a five-member court that already included three relatives and a close friend.

Meanwhile, the appointment bothered many in the legal community because Hutchinson had no legal background or training.

Finally, the appointment infuriated the Otises, father and son. Had Hutchinson lied when he said he did not seek the job? No, according to Hutchinson. He wrote that he never asked for the job and accepted it only after Bernard confided that he had no intention of offering it to the Colonel.[9]

Whatever the reasons, the Otises felt betrayed and deceived. Such slights and misunderstandings are part of political job jockeying everywhere. The historical consequences usually are nil. In this case, however, the repercussions would be profound indeed, as Hutchinson later acknowledged. From this time, the Otises, two former friends of the government, became its implacable enemies. As Hutchinson later wrote, "From so small a spark, a great fire seems to have been kindled."[10]

FOUR

TWO YOUNG EAGLES

As the Writs of Assistance case was coming together, the younger Otis was the province's advocate general, which meant he would be expected to argue for the government in support of Paxton and the writs of assistance, and against the sixty-three merchants who brought the case.

But rather than take up the government's case, Otis quit his job and promptly offered to represent the merchants. So passionate was he about the principles in this suit–and bitter at how Bernard snubbed his father–that he agreed to take on the case for nothing.

The Council Chamber in Boston's Town House served from time to time as a courtroom, as it did in February 1761, when, for three frigid days, with the town deep in snow, the fine room was packed with bewigged merchants and lawyers to hear arguments in the Paxton case before the province's highest court. The case was compelling in and of itself, for a decision favorable to merchants would hamstring the customs office and give merchants a virtual license to smuggle. But the case was also interesting for the expected dramatic sparks between Otis, as attorney for the merchants, and Hutchinson, one of five justices hearing the case.

The case aroused interest beyond Boston. One young attorney traveled up from Braintree just to watch and learn: twenty-six-year-old John Adams. Adams was just beginning to become a familiar face in Boston. He came up to town from time to time to sit in on court cases, to learn from such legal virtuosos as Otis, to chum with his old Harvard pals, and to glance at Boston's assortment of pretty young women.

Adams had grown up on a farm in Braintree, where he and young John Hancock were briefly schoolmates. Showing scholarly promise, Adams was admitted as a fifteen-year-old to Harvard. His father sold a precious ten acres to pay part of the cost of the boy's education. A partial scholarship paid for the rest. Following graduation, Adams landed a job as teacher at a one-room school in Worcester, forty-five miles west of Boston.

In his spare time in Worcester, Adams read and looked in on activities in the local court. Finding teaching unsatisfying, and intrigued by the goings on in court, he soon chose a future in law. He signed a two-year contract to study under the guidance of a local lawyer, the usual path for aspiring attorneys. There were no law schools. Following that training, Adams moved back into his parents' house in Braintree to work on the farm while preparing for admittance to the bar, which he attained in 1759. After setting up his office in his parents' home, he soon experienced the humiliation of losing his first case. A stew of self-doubts and fierce ambition, Adams, by 1761, was starting to look beyond Braintree. Boston, he was starting to think, was where an up-and-coming lawyer should be, although years would pass before he would move there.

On this winter day in February 1761, he was not a participant, but a spectator, sitting at a table, scribbling notes on folded sheets of paper. More than half a century later, he conjured the scene when he was an awestruck young man "looking like a short, thick, fat Archbishop of Canterbury . . . lost in admiration." He remembered gawking about the great square room with its nine tall windows, a fireplace, a central chandelier, and full-length royal portraits of Charles II and James II. Governor Bernard had ordered those portraits taken out of storage, dusted off, and displayed in "splendid golden frames." Many Bostonians would have preferred that the images remain "stowed away, in a garret, among rubbish"–or burned. To Puritan Boston, the two royals were despots. But the great paintings dazzled young Adams: "If my young eyes or old memory have not deceived me, these were the finest pictures I have seen. The colours of their long flowing robes, and their royal ermines were the most glowing, the figures the most noble and graceful, the features most distinct and characteristic." Seated at a long table were "all the Barristers of Boston" and some from out of town, Adams recalled, "in their gowns, bands, and tye-wigs," and in dress "more solemn and more pompous than that of the Roman Senate."[1] Also seated in this chamber, closest to the fire, sat the five judges in their scarlet robes and great wigs. Among them was Thomas Hutchinson, now chief justice, as well as lieutenant governor.

So the stage was set: Otis teaming with fellow attorney Oxenbridge Thacher, age forty-one, representing the merchants. Thacher, from a highly respected family that produced "a whole race" of ministers, had once studied for the ministry but abandoned that ambition on account of his unsuitable voice, "slender frame," and fragile health.[2] Then he tried business–and failed–before discovering law, where he excelled.

John Adams, after the portrait by John Singleton Copley. (*Library of Congress*)

Both Otis and Thacher studied under veteran lawyer Jeremiah Gridley, who once remarked that "he had reared two young eagles who would one day peck out his eyes."[3]

Would this be the day? For opposite the two eagles in this case was fifty-nine-year-old Gridley himself, on the side of the government, the customs office, and the tidewaiters.

Gridley, in defending the legality of the writs of assistance, acknowledged that the writ was indeed a powerful tool. But, he said, the writ was applied in much the same way as the legal tools for collecting taxes in Massachusetts. Also, he said, while ordinary subjects may not enter another's house, the king can in a criminal matter. The tidewaiter, possessing a writ of assistance, represents the king. Thus, the writ is perfectly legal.

Thacher, in questioning the writ of assistance, zeroed in on a technicality. With "softness of manners" and "cool reasoning,"[4] he called the writ of assistance in Massachusetts illegal because a Massachusetts court issued it. Only a specific court in London, the Exchequer Court, had authority to issue such a document.

Then Otis rose and charged the pallid case with energy and blood. "I will to my dying day oppose, with all the power and faculties God has given me, all such instruments of slavery on the one hand and villainy on the other as this writ of assistance is." It is "the worst instrument of arbitrary power, the most destructive of English liberty, and the fundamental principles of the constitution that was ever found in an English law book."[5] Otis battered the writs of assistance in arguments stretching over five hours.

Otis pointed out that writs, easily obtained and transferred from person to person, invited abuse: "Every man prompted by revenge, ill humour, or wantonness to inspect the inside of his neighbour's house, may get a writ of assistance. Others will ask it from self-defence; one arbitrary exertion will provoke another, until society be involved in tumult and in blood."[6]

Voicing sentiments echoed later in the Declaration of Independence, Otis roared that every person at birth has a right to life and liberty. The right to property was equally indisputable. Only an idiot would voluntarily surrender those rights, which–by way of old Saxon laws, the Magna Carta, many acts of Parliament, and much strife–had become embedded into the English constitution, the collection of laws and traditions that underpin British justice. People living in Massachusetts, as much as people in Britain, were entitled to those rights.

Decades later, old John Adams remembered how Otis left young John Adams breathless: "Otis was a flame of fire! With a promptitude of classical allusions, a depth of research, a rapid summary of historical events and dates, a profusion of legal authorities, prophetic glare of his eyes into futurity, and a rapid torrent of impetuous eloquence, he hurried away all before him."[7] This time, this place, this moment was, to Adams, pivotal in American history: "American independence was then and there born."[8]

That's how Adams remembered it. At the time, though, the judges were not so dazzled. While admiring Otis's soaring oratory, Hutchinson doubted the attorney genuinely cared a whit about the rights of ordinary folk. Hutchinson later wrote, "Mr. Otis' zeal in carrying on these causes was deemed as meritorious as if it had sprung from a sincere concern for the liberties of the people."[9] In any case, these stirring words were, to Hutchinson, beside the point.

At the conclusion of arguments, Hutchinson and his fellow judges left the chamber to talk things over. When they returned, Hutchinson, speaking for the court, announced that there would be no verdict that day or for many months. Hutchinson was instinctively pragmatic. The case arose out of a suspicion, based only on a journal article, that the writs of assistance were being applied differently in Massachusetts than in Britain. Yet no one in Massachusetts knew for certain one way or the other. Clearly, from Hutchinson's view, the writs of assistance should be applied in Massachusetts the same way they were in Britain. Therefore, questions should be dispatched to Britain to determine precisely how the writs were handled there. If in Britain writs of assistance were specific–requiring, for example, that a specific structure be identified before a search–then perhaps the merchants had a valid argument. If in Britain the writs were general, as in Massachusetts, then the merchants' case could be tossed out.

So the case was adjourned and the Council Chamber emptied. Inquiries were dispatched to London and, after many months, word came back that the Boston merchants were misinformed. In Britain, writs were being applied more or less as they were in Massachusetts. In November, in light of this information, the case was reargued. The court eventually decided that tidewaiters could continue to use the writs in the customary way. The case was over, and the merchants had lost.

So nothing changed as far as tidewaiters were concerned. Yet something did change. Otis had lit a fire. He was now the merchants' champion and emerged as the head of a vigorous alliance. In May 1761, in the interval between the adjournment in February and rearguments in November, Boston elected Otis to the Massachusetts House of Representatives. In that role, and as an attorney representing merchants, Otis continued to battle the governor and his allies. He usually lost these skirmishes, but along the way he gained allies and chipped away at the reputations of both Hutchinson and Bernard. With dazzling arguments and ceaseless energy, Otis emerged as the feisty voice of the opposition. His message, spread in influential, widely read pamphlets, was not radical, not revolutionary, but absolutely loyal–in his view–and essentially conservative in calling for a return to the past, to the way things should be, a message reasonable and appealing not just to merchants but to rural folk.

On the surface of Boston society, the ripples from the Writs of Assistance case vanished. The House, the Council, and the governor seemed to be in harmony. In May 1761, the House and the Council gave Bernard a pat on the back, agreeing that "the civil rights of the people are not in danger; nor are we in the least degree suspicious, that they ever will be under your excellency's administration."[10] In June 1761, Bernard wrote: "The new Assembly has proved a very good one and business goes on very well. The commotions that were heretofore raised are subsided in general."[11]

Meanwhile, young John Hancock was back from England, where he watched the installation of George III at Whitehall. As 1763 began, John's uncle Thomas announced that John was officially his business partner. With Thomas Hancock's health in decline, John, ready or not, took on a larger role.

Hancock found himself courted by several of the many clubs in Boston. Thin, nervous, chatty, slightly stooped, and prone to headaches, he was not robust or impressive. But he was young, handsome–with almond eyes, aquiline nose, dimpled chin, and brown hair beneath a small white wig–and possessed qualities that clubs valued: he was likable, rich, and generous. Hancock joined the Masonic Lodge of St. Andrew, one of two Masonic lodges in Boston. He also joined a large club of merchants.

This particular club had existed for more than a decade, meeting regularly, often at the British Coffee House on the north side of King Street. Loosely organized and unfocused, the group had done little up to this time to address common problems. In April 1763, that changed as its 146 members gave the organization a hefty name–The Society for Encouraging Trade and Commerce within the Province of Massachusetts Bay–and charged it with purpose. This was no revolutionary group, but more akin to a chamber of commerce. And its members would certainly not be taking up arms. They would lobby, putting forward their concerns to lawmakers in Massachusetts and Parliament. Having lost the Writs of Assistance case and sensing further threats from the government in London, they were pushing back. The idea caught on. In the Massachusetts ports of Salem, Marblehead, and Plymouth, other merchants got together and formed similar lobbying groups. To the south, merchants in Newport, New York, and Philadelphia followed suit. An infrastructure for sharing ideas and coordinating action was emerging.

Boston society was fracturing, with Otis and his allies on one side, and Hutchinson and his allies on the other. Otis represented many who chafed at customs regulations and fumed at the influence and power of Hutchinson and his circle. Hutchinson, meanwhile, represented many wealthy families in town, but also others who sincerely felt that Hutchinson and those around him were the steadiest, most competent, proven, and capable people available.

So Boston was divided, but not on the issue of patriotism or loyalty to Britain. Bostonians considered themselves loyal British subjects. They professed love for their town, their province, and their king. This was amply demonstrated in May 1763, when word reached Boston of the treaty ending the French and Indian War. No one was more ardent than Otis in praising the firm bonds between Britain and its American colonies:

"No other constitution of civil government has yet appeared in the world, so admirably adapted to these great purposes, as that of Great Britain. . . . The true interests of Great Britain and her plantations are mutual, and what God in his providence has united, let no man dare attempt to pull asunder."[12]

Peace with France brought relief, but also hardship as war-related business stopped. Boston had to deal with more idle men, more people with their hands out.

About this time, the faction surrounding Otis started calling themselves Whigs and applying the term Tory to those friendly to the government. These were old terms that made little sense in the context of colonial Boston in the 1760s. The terms had emerged in Britain in the previous century. Generally, Whigs supported the supremacy of Parliament while Tories were those who favored the absolute power of the monarch. Over the decades, Toryism in England disintegrated. By the 1760s, almost no one in Britain subscribed to absolute royal authority. Virtually everyone acknowledged Parliamentary authority. Thus, almost everyone was a Whig under the accepted definition. Rare was the person claiming to be a Tory.

Similarly, in America, true Toryism was extinct. Bernard, Hutchinson, and their allies did not believe in absolute royal authority any more than Otis did. In the English sense, they were Whigs–supporters of Parliamentary authority. Indeed, they were arguably more "Whiggish" than those in the Otis faction, who were starting to raise questions about Parliament's authority.

But the terms stuck, an important propaganda victory for the Otis faction because most people associated the term Tories with people on the wrong side of history.

Popular opinion of Bernard plummeted. Some of this decline had to do with frictions with prickly lawmakers who insisted on interpreting the governor's well-meaning actions as power-mad antics of a dictator. A case in point: During one legislative recess, word reached Boston that the French had taken St. John's, Newfoundland. The towns of Salem and Marblehead, alarmed at the potential threat, pleaded with Bernard to order two vessels fitted out to protect fishing fleets. With the advice of his Council, Bernard authorized the expenditure. The matter seemed urgent, the spending prudent. When the House returned to work, representatives threw a fit, roaring that the governor and the Council, spending money without the House's approval, were "annihilating one branch of the legislature."[13]

This and other tiffs with lawmakers battered the goodwill Bernard tried so earnestly to cultivate. That goodwill was further shredded by the governor's actions connected to smuggling. As governor he was entitled to one-third of goods seized. He thus supported strong enforcement. To merchants, this looked like profiteering at their expense. It didn't help that Bernard was especially chummy with the hated customs enforcer, Charles Paxton.

Bernard's reputation might have withstood this appearance of greed. After all, the governor's job was to see that the law was enforced. If he made a profit, well, that was the way things were done. But then it was discovered that Francis Bernard wasn't so diligent about enforcing the law as it applied to Francis Bernard. The governor was a smuggler.

We know this mainly thanks to John Temple, a remarkable creature. He was a diligent customs man who strictly enforced the customs regulations yet remained in the good graces of Boston merchants. Born in Boston, Temple had powerful relatives across the Atlantic, which explains how he sidled into the job of surveyor general in Boston in 1760 at age twenty-eight. Temple earned the respect of Boston merchants by cracking down on enforcement in other ports, thus correcting what Boston merchants thought was a competitive disadvantage.

He also opposed the use of informers for evidence in smuggling cases, a practice that deeply aggravated merchants.

Furthermore, Temple had the novel idea that the customs men under him should act within the law and not extort money from merchants. While investigating just such an attempt to squeeze ship owners, Temple uncovered evidence that Bernard was mixed up in shady schemes to cheat the treasury of its due in exchange for personal deliveries of wine, fruit, and other goods.

The upshot of this revelation and other hints of shady dealing: customs man Temple and Governor Bernard became enemies; Temple was further confirmed as, if not exactly a friend to merchants, someone they could work with; and Bernard's hope of ever regaining popular trust was forever dashed.

Meanwhile, a war of words burst forth on the religious front. A key soldier on this battle of quills was Jonathan Mayhew, pastor of Boston's Congregationalist West Church and a man identified with the emerging Whig faction.

By this time, into the 1760s, Mayhew's credentials as an agitator were well established. Back in 1750, Mayhew caused a sensation when he proclaimed from the pulpit that the Apostle Paul not only authorized but required citizens to resist a tyrannical king "whenever this shall be necessary to the public safety and happiness."[14] When, said Mayhew, a king "turns tyrant, and makes his subjects his prey to devour and destroy, instead of his charge to defend and cherish, we are bound to throw off our allegiance to him, and to resist."[15]

When Mayhew's sermon was published, it was "read by everybody; celebrated by friends, and abused by enemies," according to John Adams,[16] who read and reread the sermon, starting at age fourteen, until "the Substance of it was incorporated into my Nature and indelibly engraved on my Memory."[17]

On matters of faith, Mayhew was an "amiable heretic" who dismissed such bedrock Calvinist principles as predestination and was the first minister in Boston to reject the notion of the Trinity.[18] He did not belong to the Boston Association of Congregational Ministers, but that didn't bother his loyal congregation, to whom he preached for nineteen years, "loving his people, and by them beloved."[19]

Mayhew also stood tall on the barricades against the Church of England. He and others suspected that the church was plotting to place an Anglican bishop in America and eventually make Anglicanism the official faith in America. Since early in the century, Americans, especially in Puritan New England, worried about the church's moves to worm its way into American life. Back in 1701, the

Church of England created the Society for the Propagation of the Gospel in Foreign Parts, with the stated purpose of bringing the gospel to pagan Indians and blacks. But then missions began appearing in Massachusetts in such places as Cambridge, where no Indians lived. By 1760, some thirty Anglican ministers were scattered among New England towns to spread that faith.

Following the death of an Anglican missionary in Braintree, a pamphlet war erupted. A Boston newspaper, in commenting on the death, took the opportunity to attack the church's practice of placing missionaries in settled communities. This produced a response in pamphlet form from the Anglican missionary in Cambridge. Then Mayhew entered the fray with his own pamphlet. Counterattacks followed, and Mayhew blasted back with two more pamphlets. This was answered by a final pamphlet, in 1764.

In this dispute, Mayhew charged that the Cambridge mission and others like it have "all the appearance of entering wedges . . . carrying on the crusade, or spiritual siege of our churches, with the hope that they will one day submit to an episcopal sovereign."[20] Mayhew reminded readers that New England settlers had fled the Church of England: "Is it not enough that they persecuted us out of the old world? Will they pursue us into the new, to convert us here, compassing sea and land to make us proselytes, while they neglect the heathen and heathenish plantations?"[21]

This controversy is now forgotten, but some contemporaries, such as John Adams, looked back on the quarrel as critical in spreading fear of authority from across the Atlantic: "It excited a general and just apprehension, that bishops, and dioceses, and churches, and priests, and tithes, were to be imposed on us by Parliament."[22]

For the time being, there would be no incursion of bishops, but there would be another kind of invasion–that of a peacetime army. To King George III, placing British soldiers in America seemed reasonable, even clever. During the Seven Years' War, the size of the British army ballooned. Many officers in this army had provided political support to the king and his ministers. To suddenly shrink the army would put these supporters out of jobs. Why not keep the soldiers employed in America?

The king's advisers agreed that putting a standing army in America was a good idea, and they had even better reasons: Indians. In Canada, in frontier regions to the west, and elsewhere, native tribes posed a threat. Soldiers were necessary to keep the peace, as well as to block Americans from settling in areas west of the Appalachian Mountains designated for Indians. Parliament gave its blessing with barely a murmur.

But how to pay for this army? From the government's point of view, it was not only fair but also imperative that Americans pay at least some of the cost. England was desperate for money. The government, with an income of only about £8 million, groaned under a £137 million debt.

Thus was born the American Revenue Act of 1764, also known as the Sugar Act. It would raise some of the money for the army in America. It would also crack down on smuggling in America and push sales in America of British-made goods.

On its face, the act seemed a blessing for the merchants of Boston. It would cut the duty on foreign molasses in half. If a merchant wanted to legally import molasses into Boston from Dutch islands, for example, he would pay half the duty he paid before–assuming he had all along actually imported the molasses legally and had paid the required duty. The British authorities hoped that because they had cut the duties so drastically, merchants wouldn't trouble with smuggling. Authorities anticipated that much more molasses would enter colonial ports legally, resulting in the collection of much more revenue.

But merchants in Boston and in ports up and down the Atlantic Seaboard were not fooled. The duty, though cut in half, was still staggering, representing 25 percent or more of the wholesale price. Furthermore, other provisions of the act seemed designed to drive colonial merchants into bankruptcy.

For example, the act added more products to a list of goods that could no longer be exported from the colonies directly to non-British destinations. Such products as beaver skins for hats and logwood for dye could no longer go straight to Holland or Germany, but had to be shipped to Britain first, adding to shipping costs. Also, the act gave customs officials the upper hand in any legal action related to smuggling. Before this act, legal cases related to smuggling were usually brought before an American court, where American judges and juries tended to side with the merchant. The act created a new court in distant Halifax, Nova Scotia. The court would have no jury. Its judge, far away from Boston, New York, and Philadelphia, would feel no local pressure to rule in merchants' favor. Meanwhile, for merchants, the cost of challenging the customs seizure was now especially burdensome, requiring travel to Halifax.

What was more outrageous from the merchant's point of view was the presumption of guilt before this court. Furthermore, even if he proved his innocence, a merchant could not sue to recover the cost of defending himself.

Boston merchants seethed and raised questions about Parliament's right to even enact such a law. In protesting the act, Massachusetts merchants and their counterparts along the Atlantic coast seized upon the stated purpose of the Sugar Act–to raise revenue. From the colonial point of view, that aim made it different from other forms of taxes on the colonies, which were crafted to promote trade with Britain and British islands or to discourage trade with other countries. Americans argued that Parliament stepped beyond its authority when it imposed taxes on Americans to support the government. By tradition, the Americans had taxed themselves to support their own government. Never before had they been required to pay taxes to support the government in Britain or the soldiers sent by Britain to defend them.

In Massachusetts, Lieutenant Governor Thomas Hutchinson was one of the first to recognize the principle here. While others quibbled about the size of the tax, Hutchinson pointed out the alarming precedent. He asked, wouldn't this tax violate the "much esteemed privilege of English subjects–the being taxed by their own representatives?"[23]

All these changes coming from Parliament were accompanied by other reforms intended to make tax collection more efficient. It had been common practice for the collectors and comptrollers to remain in England and appoint deputies to carry out their tasks in America. These deputies, as often as not, turned out to be corrupt, incompetent, or lazy. They quickly learned that to rigorously enforce the king's laws was to invite hatred up and down the waterfront. Now authorities in Britain demanded that customs collectors move to America or quit. Many did quit, replaced by men determined to be more diligent.

As these collectors got to work, the British navy beefed up its role in preventing smuggling. The navy followed the letter of the law, going well beyond its spirit. Many hundreds of vessels–barges and such, not meant for the open sea–hugged the craggy American coast and rarely went more than a few miles. The navy, interpreting the rules rigidly, stopped even these vessels, asked for papers, and from time to time seized them. Americans were infuriated.

FIVE

MOST ESSENTIAL RIGHTS

While Boston puzzled and complained, another crisis suddenly arose to make the Sugar Act seem but a trifle. An outbreak of smallpox early in 1764 brought business to a standstill.

Smallpox is a silent and vicious terror. After exposure to the virus and an incubation period of about twelve days, the victim experiences pounding headaches, stabbing pains in the back, chills, fever, and overall weakness. A child with the disease might go into convulsions. On the second day, the fever spikes, and the victim might become delirious or even fall into a coma. Those who remain conscious wish only to die. On the third day, the symptoms diminish and the fever comes down. The victim looks better and may feel almost normal, with only a sore throat and a rash.

But this is merely a prelude to a new nightmare. Painful sores appear in the mouth and throat, and then on the face and forearms, spreading to the chest, stomach, back, and finally the legs. Each red sore, about one-third of an inch in diameter, eventually swells, bursts, and then scabs over. Meanwhile, the fever returns.

Physicians knew how to gauge the severity of the disease. If the sores did not touch each other, the victim would probably live. If the sores touched, chances of survival were even. If the victim bled beneath the skin and from the nose and mouth, death was certain.

After two weeks, the disease disappears. The last scabs fall away after a month. The victim, if he or she survives, might be blind and would certainly be scarred. Smallpox scars were a common disfigurement of the age.

Smallpox was a familiar visitor. An epidemic less than a century before took the lives of about one in five townspeople. When an epidemic broke out in 1752, the provincial government packed up and temporarily relocated twenty miles northwest to Concord just to be safe.

This time, in 1764, lawmakers fled to Cambridge, setting up shop in buildings of Harvard College, where, on a snowy, blustery January night, a fire to warm legislators somehow set Harvard Hall in flames, destroying the building, a fine library, and valuable scientific equipment. The governor, lawmakers, and Cambridge citizens pitched in to save other college buildings.

In Boston, measures were enforced to control the disease. A guard brandishing a red flag stood outside the home of Paul Revere. The flag was a signal that someone inside had the disease. The guard, enforcing a quarantine, prevented anyone from entering or leaving. Later, Revere's role in the Revolution would become the stuff of poetry and legend. But at this moment, he was just a husband and father trying to save his family.

Revere turned thirty in 1764. He was a husky man of average height, with a thick neck, a round face, brown eyes, and meaty arms. He spoke his mind, and sometimes he spoke with his fists. Just three years before, a court found him guilty of "assaulting & beating"[1] one Thomas Fosdick, hatter. Evidently Fosdick was not badly hurt–or maybe got what was coming–for the fine was a trifle.

Revere was half French. His French Huguenot father, Apollos Rivoire, had been shipped off alone to America at age twelve to make his way in the world. Apollos became a goldsmith and did well. Paul never learned his father's mother tongue, but he did learn his trade. When Apollos died in 1754, Paul, at nineteen, took over the business and gradually learned to work not only gold but also silver, copper, and brass, while crafting, among other things, silver chains for pet squirrels, spatulas for surgeons, and baptismal basins for churches, as well as coffeepots, teapots, chocolate pots, pepper pots, punch bowls, creamers, salvers, and cups. He also acquired skills in copperplate engraving and found time as well to dabble in dental work. He advertised that "persons so unfortunate as to lose their Fore-Teeth by Accident, and otherways, to their great detriment not only in looks but speaking may have them replaced by artificial ones . . . by PAUL REVERE, Goldsmith."[2]

In August 1757, he married. Eight months later, he was a father. Other children would soon come along. By the time of the epidemic he had three "lambs," as he called his little ones. One had come down with smallpox, and the family would be shut up until the illness abated. Revere had battled with the town's selectmen for the quarantine as an alternative to sending the child to a pesthouse on the edge of town. Revere guessed that the child's chances of survival were better at home. But by keeping one sick child at home, Revere risked losing all his children. He guessed right. Everyone in the family survived, and during the quarantine period, Paul's wife, Sarah (whom he called Sary), gave birth to a fourth child.

Everyone knew that anyone who survived smallpox never got it again. Everyone also knew about variolation, which might provide the same immunity but was almost as dangerous as the disease itself because it was the disease itself, in a weakened form. Variolation first required the collection of dried smallpox scabs from victims. Then, a physician, after scratching the arm of a healthy person, applied a bit of scab to the scratch and bandaged the arm.

In Britain, people learned of variolation by way of Turkey, where English visitors had observed the practice. Bostonians became aware of the technique from a slave who had been inoculated in this fashion in Africa, where the practice had also been common.

Many were terrified of variolation for good reason: those treated came down with some symptoms of smallpox, and some died. A brother of Thomas Hutchinson's was one such victim of the treatment. A safer method did not come along until after 1796, when English physician Edward Jenner discovered that germs from cowpox, a much milder disease, could provide immunity from smallpox.

Because variolation was risky, the town banned the procedure when the smallpox outbreak first appeared and seemed confined to the North End. But then the disease flared up again, and all those who couldn't leave town "resolved to be inoculated at all events."[3] The town selectmen gave in to public demand and permitted anyone to "inoculate at their pleasure."[4]

As the epidemic worked its way through the population, many other Bostonians rushed to make arrangements to be inoculated. To accommodate demand but still limit the risk of epidemic that the inoculations themselves might cause, the town designated inoculation sites. One was Castle William, the military post on eight-acre Castle Island, about two and one-half miles out in the harbor.

The epidemic transformed sleepy Castle William–a small square fort with four bastions, two ravelins, and thirty-eight guns–into a bustling medical station with forty-eight rooms converted for this health emergency, each room accommodating ten people.

Some people, such as John Adams, came from out of town to take advantage of the opportunity to get inoculated. One of the physicians treating Adams was twenty-two-year-old Joseph Warren. He was from nearby Roxbury and, like Adams, a Harvard graduate, a former schoolteacher, and a farmer's son. Adams described Warren as a "pretty, tall, Genteel, fair faced young Gentleman."[5] A rare anecdote about young Warren at Harvard is telling. Finding himself locked out of an upper story chamber, he got on the roof and climbed down via a "spout," hurling himself into the chamber through a window just as the spout gave way.[6] He was brave, to be sure, but also reckless.

In this year of 1764, handsome Warren would marry "an accomplished young lady with a handsome fortune."[7] Over time, Warren

A view of Castle William in 1770. (*Library of Congress*)

would become famous as a speaker and as a key figure in the emerging political crisis, especially in the critical months just before and after the Battles of Lexington and Concord, more than a decade away.

Adams sent out a stream of letters from Castle William to Miss Abigail Smith, soon to be Mrs. Abigail Adams, describing his experience cooped up with nine other men in a room with a "card table, Chequer Bord, Flute, Violin, and singing" for distractions as they waited for the sickness to come and go. Worried that Abigail might pick up an infection from the letters, Adams advised her to "Smoke all the letters from me, very faithfully, before you or any of the Family reads them."[8] Adams said his sickness was but a trifle: "A short shivering Fit, and a succeeding hot glowing Fit, a Want of Appetite, and a general Languor."[9] He counted on his body no more than ten pocks.

In a few months, the epidemic was a memory. The massive inoculation effort was imperfect, as everyone knew it would be. Overall, however, the numbers showed inoculation saved lives. Of about five thousand people inoculated, forty-six died, about one in one hundred. Of about seven hundred people who contracted smallpox in the natural way, 124 died–about seventeen of every one hundred.

The survivors, some with ghastly scars, buried the dead and restarted their lives. The town came back to life and resumed its old quarrels.

About this time, a certain failed businessman who made a poor living as a tax collector took on a more prominent role at town meetings. This was Sam Adams, a cousin of John Adams's (their great-grandfather was Joseph Adams of Braintree). Sam Adams was thirteen years older than his cousin and, unlike John Adams, was a true Bostonian, born and raised in the town. Sam Adams had accomplished little and failed at much. He lived in a ramshackle house, and his clothes were shabby.

Young Sam Adams had shown promise. He had a Harvard education. But following college, Adams fumbled his chances. His father, known as Deacon Adams, gave Sam money to embark on his own venture. Sam promptly lent half the money to a friend–who never paid it back–and frittered away the rest. Eventually his father took him in as a partner in his malting business, a service for brewers. Sam, who made the rounds delivering malt, became known as Sam the Maltster. After Deacon Adams died, Sam couldn't keep the business going. Meanwhile, the deaths of three of his five children in infancy cast a shadow over Sam's personal life, and by the time of the Great Fire he was a widower.

His fascination was politics. He had toiled on various town committees, one related to schools, another concerning chimneys. He was also a fire warden and worked to put in place measures against smallpox. His first elected office, at age thirty-one, was that of town scavenger. Later he won election as a tax collector, making his rounds in his tattered red coat and disheveled wig, which he left at home on warm days. In the part of the job that involved meeting people and listening to them, Adams was very good. But in the part that involved collecting tax money and turning it over to the town, he was inept. Unwilling to press townspeople to pay their taxes, Adams established a spotty record for collecting. His lack of diligence robbed the town of money and also kept Adams and his children in frayed clothes, because his income was based on the money he collected.

In 1764, Sam Adams turned forty-two, but he seemed much older because his hands often trembled. He suffered from essential tremor,[10] a progressive condition that made it difficult for him to write–late in life he would have to dictate his letters–and was always worse when he was under stress. Sam Adams, the failed businessman and careless tax collector with unsteady hands, could barely support his family. He certainly didn't seem to be much of a threat to the British Empire.

Adams had a deep and longstanding distrust of people in authority. This view likely stemmed from his father's financial downfall while Sam was at Harvard. Deacon Adams and his allies proposed a bank that would issue bills based on the value of land. It was a popular idea, with support from many up-and-coming entrepreneurs. Opponents included the governor and such wealthy men as Thomas Hutchinson, who favored an alternative bank that would issue bills backed by silver instead of land.

In the end, Parliament shut down both banks, leaving Deacon Adams, among others, ruined. Young Sam, perhaps with his father's experience on his mind, chose as his thesis at Harvard "Whether it be lawful to resist the Supreme Magistrate, if the Commonwealth cannot be otherwise preserved." His answer was yes.

Sam Adams spent years sorting out his father's financial wreckage and far longer blaming Hutchinson. Thus, Adams and Otis had something in common–grudges against the lieutenant governor. Following the Writs of Assistance case, Adams allied himself with Otis. Adams became the man behind the scenes, organizing, listening, planning, advising. He was, sneered an observer, Otis's "pimp."[11] John Adams later likened his cousin and Otis to the two great Reformation leaders. Otis was like Martin Luther, "rough, hasty, and loved good cheer." Sam Adams was like John Calvin, "cool, abstemious, polished, and refined, though more inflexible, uniform and consistent."[12]

Samuel Adams, from a portrait by John Singleton Copley. (*Library of Congress*)

Sam Adams might have agreed. He once considered becoming a clergyman. He chose another path, but he took on politics like a religious vocation, and in spirit and attitude he was a true Puritan. For him, shabby clothes were emblems of virtue. "I glory in being what the world calls a poor man," he said.[13] To him, riches were inherently suspect: "[L]uxury and extravagance are . . . destructive of . . . virtues which are necessary for the preservation of liberty and the happiness of the people."[14] He drank little and valued temperance as well as "Sobriety of Manners."[15]

A devout Congregationalist, Adams regularly attended services at Old South. He loved to sing, had a good voice, and led a men's singing club. He was sociable and had many allies, but no intimate friends, and he was emotionally cool to the point of seeming to be uncaring. John Adams noted in his diary a conversation with Sam: "He says he never looked forward in his life, never planned, laid a scheme, or formed a design of laying up anything for himself or others after him."[16]

While Sam Adams worked behind the scenes, Otis was center stage, the man merchants and others counted on to be their voice. Otis raged at the Sugar Act like he roared at the Writs of Assistance. This was not just a matter of how many pennies might be collected on a barrel of molasses. This went to the issue of rights. The Massachusetts House of Representatives took up the cause. It drew up a message to Parliament: the measure "deprives People of their most essential Rights."[17]

But Britain never heard this cry. Lieutenant Governor Hutchinson advised lawmakers to take a cooler approach. It's not that Hutchinson disagreed. He just thought it more prudent–and Hutchinson was meticulously prudent–to soften the message. A strident tone would only offend Parliament and get the colonists nowhere, he thought. Opposition to Hutchinson was building, but still his advice was widely respected. So the message was watered down to be more submissive.

Meanwhile, outside the circles of merchants and their lawmaker allies in port towns, the Sugar Act did not rouse much interest. What did farmers care about imports of molasses? So from Massachusetts, the British government heard only a distant squeak.

But that squeak along with squawks from other colonies did perk up some sleepyheads in London. In the distance, they heard a cry of "No taxation without representation"–that is, because Americans had no representation in Parliament, Parliament had no right to tax Americans. This warranted a response. Americans were indeed represented, so went the argument from Britain. While the Americans did not actually elect any members of Parliament, neither did most Britons. Only a small minority of British citizens residing in Britain could vote. Yet, so went the government's argument, members of Parliament virtually represented all Britons, as well as all Americans and all others within the empire. Parliament represented all and therefore could tax all.

So protests against the Sugar Act went nowhere. Meanwhile, Parliament prepared to dig deeper into American pockets. Mixed in with resolutions related to the Sugar Act was another hinting of a later measure calculated to further increase revenue from the Americans. That would become known as the Stamp Act.

One might ask today what many asked then: Were Americans, in protesting the Sugar Act, simply trying to dodge taxes? In the case of Massachusetts, facts demonstrate a willingness to pay the taxes. In summer 1764, the Massachusetts House of Representatives asked Governor Bernard to allow a special session of the assembly for the express purpose of passing a tax. The lawmakers were ready to support a measure to collect and hand over to Britain the revenue meant to be gathered via the Sugar Act and the anticipated Stamp Act. This way Parliament would win–it would get the revenue it wanted–and Massachusetts would win–preserving its principle that only Massachusetts could tax Massachusetts.

The idea was not new; it had come from the prime minister himself. George Grenville had hinted back in March that such a solution might be possible. But Grenville was never serious about the offer. Likely he did not want to be seen as giving in on the principle of Parliament's right to impose taxes. Grenville never gave Bernard clear guidance about permitting such a tax, and without specific instructions from London, Bernard refused the Massachusetts lawmakers' request.

So the Sugar Act stayed in place, and the months passed. On August 1, 1764, Thomas Hancock, after climbing the circular stairs of the Town House, collapsed on the floor of the Council Chamber. Two hours later, he was dead. In his will, he promised freedom for his slave Cato upon Cato's thirtieth birthday, provided the slave behaved. He also bequeathed to nephew John two-thirds of the estate. John's aunt Lydia soon signed over to him the grand Hancock house, where she continued to live. John, twenty-seven, was now one of the richest men in America.

November 5, 1764, was like every November 5 had been in Boston for years: noisy, violent, chaotic, and dangerous. Also this November 5, like some others, was deadly. The day, known as Pope Day, was given over to the North End and South End mobs. Made up of apprentices, laborers, porters, ropewalkers, and other rough-and-tumble men and boys on the lower rungs of society, each mob was led in a loose military fashion. In the case of the South End mob, the leader was "Captain" Ebenezer Mackintosh, a twenty-six-year-old unmarried shoemaker who for one day a year ruled Boston's streets–or at least the streets of the South End.

The tradition varied little from year to year. In the weeks before, each mob would separately and secretly fashion grotesque effigies and put them on carts, about forty feet long and six feet wide, which served as rolling stages. The effigies represented real and imagined figures, both famous and infamous. They might include, for example, Nancy Dawson, a dancing scarecrow; Admiral Byng hanging from a gibbet; Joyce Jr. riding an ass; and the devil, with pitchfork and tail. Nancy Dawson was a famous London actress and dancer. Byng, a British admiral, had been court-martialed and executed in 1756. Joyce Jr.–actually George Joyce–had captured King Charles I in 1646 during the English Civil War. Always, seated in the center of the cart would be an immensely fat pope made to look as preposterous as possible.

Sometimes a lantern made of oiled paper and measuring perhaps five feet wide by nine feet tall would be displayed at the front of the rolling stage. On this would be painted "The devil take the pope" and either "North end forever" or "South end forever," depending on whose cart it was. Sometimes the heads of the pope and the devil would be mounted on poles. A boy hidden below would manipulate the poles so the heads would sway back and forth.

On November 5, the carts–one in the North End and one in the South End–would appear, usually about dusk. The noisy mobs would push the carts from place to place, each following a boy with a bell who would shout:

Don't you remember,
The fifth of November,
The Gunpowder treason and plot?
I see no reason,
Why Gunpowder treason
Should ever be forgot.
From Rome to Rome
The Pope is come,
Amid ten thousand fears,
With fiery serpents to be seen
At eyes, nose, mouth, and ears.
Don't you hear my little bell
Go chink, chink, chink?
Please to give me a little money,
To buy my Pope some drink.[18]

The monstrous popes drank little, but the mobs found plenty of rum, wine, and beer to fuel their antics. The carts would turn down this street and that, accompanied by racket from conch shells, drums, whistles, and horns. From time to time boys, their clothes covered with tar and feathers, would leap onto the carts to dance with the pope and kiss the devil. Periodically, particularly in front of grand houses, the carts would creak to a stop and the effigy of the devil would be hoisted high in the air on a pole to peer with great red eyes into second-story bedrooms. Boys and sometimes girls, too, would go from door to door and ask for money. Residents were expected to play along, greet paraders at the door, and pass out coins or dole out rum punch.

Invariably, the mobs would meet, taunts would fly, then stones and bricks, then shoving, leading to punching, biting, and gouging, each side defending its own pope while attempting to capture the other's.

If the South Side "won," all would gather at the Common for a bonfire. If the North Side was victorious, the bonfire would take place on Copp's Hill. Some years it was agreed to pull the carts to the gallows on the Neck for a bonfire there. Save for the cartwheels and the heads of the effigies, all would be tossed onto the pyre, along with some pilfered barrels, tubs, and bits of fencing.

The strange event was not unique to Boston. Others like it, but usually smaller and less violent, took place in towns up and down the colonies, as well as in Britain. It was a celebration of British patriotism and anti-Catholic prejudice as well as an excuse for the have-nots–workmen and boys with little money or power–to blow off steam.

Everyone understood, at least vaguely, the historical significance of the date. In 1605, Guy Fawkes and other conspirators in London

A woodcut depicting a Pope Day procession in 1769. (*Library of Congress*)

planned to blow up Parliament along with King James I. The conspirators had hoped to spark a rebellion that would lead to the crowning of a Catholic king and a return to Roman Catholicism in England. The Gunpowder Plot, planned for November 5, was thwarted. Fawkes and others were executed.

Boston authorities tolerated the havoc while trying to dampen its excesses. Laws intended to discourage the rioting required that the celebrations take place only during daylight. But that law, by encouraging mobs to bring out their carts earlier, simply produced more hours of mayhem. The town seemed helpless to stop or even contain these annual riots. Boston had no police. The day-to-day duties of law enforcement fell on the shoulders of Sheriff Stephen Greenleaf, who could handle isolated pickpockets and wayward drunks but had no chance against these mobs. In a pinch, he could call upon perhaps a dozen constables with law-enforcement authority. If the mobs got out of hand, town authorities might turn to the militia, civilian men with some military training. But even with the militia's help, the sheriff would have his hands full.

Pope Day 1764 began more or less the way all Pope Days began. Early on, however, a five-year-old boy, one of many boys skipping, jumping, and running about or near the North End cart, slipped and fell. The cart could not be stopped in time, and a wheel crushed the boy's head. The child died, the mob sobered up, and the sheriff appeared. He ordered both popes destroyed. This Pope Day would be cut short. Or would it?

Mackintosh ignored the sheriff's orders. What did the dead boy have to do with him and his South End mob? That night, Mackintosh and his gang brought out their cart once again. Word spread to the North End, and soon the North End mob patched together its pope and resumed its parade. As usual, the mobs met up and a massive brawl ensued, ending with a parade through the town gate at the Neck and the burning of the popes near the town gallows.

In the days that followed, authorities got around to charging some rioters with disturbing the peace and destroying property. Some were tried and acquitted. Some paid small fines. So far as we know, no one answered for the death of the boy.

As the year closed, the widower Sam Adams married for the second time, seven years after the death of Elizabeth, his first wife. His new twenty-four-year-old bride, also named Elizabeth, was eighteen years younger than her groom. He called her Betsy.

Less than two years hence, Sam and Betsy would call upon John and Abigail Adams in Braintree. The visit left an impression on Abigail. A "charming pair," she called them: "In them is to be seen the tenderest affection toward each other, without any fulsome fondness, and the greatest Complasance, delicacy and good breeding that you can imagine, yet separate from any affectation."[19]

SIX

A FARTHING

In the 1760s, as Americans started pushing against the authority of the king and Parliament, they looked across the ocean for heroes and allies. One champion was William Pitt. The Great Commoner, as he was known, even thought of himself as a voice in Parliament for colonists overseas. But while Americans admired Pitt, they adored John Wilkes, a rogue who left a trail of scandal everywhere he went. With crossed eyes and an outsized jaw, Wilkes had a startling appearance. Pregnant women, one man warned, should not be allowed to look at this man. Furthermore, the dimensions of Wilkes's jaw meant that his lower teeth were exposed when he spoke, giving him a lisp. Yet he oozed self-confidence and wit, winning the admiration of many men–and the amorous attention of many women–despite his physical peculiarities. When the Earl of Sandwich remarked that Wilkes would either die of syphilis or on the gallows, he famously replied, "That depends on whether I embrace your principles or your mistress."[1] Wilkes amused himself with indecent diversions: He belonged to a club that mocked Catholic rituals and reveled in sexual pleasures; he collaborated on a bawdy parody of Alexander Pope's *Essay on Man.*

In 1762 Wilkes established a political newspaper, the *North Briton,* to trumpet his opinions and attack Lord Bute, the king's adviser. In addition, since Bute was a Scotsman, Wilkes used his columns to stir up English hatred of Scots. Wilkes's notoriety spread. After one piece, an enraged reader challenged Wilkes to a duel. Wilkes accepted. When the fateful moment came, the men fired simultaneously, missed, and then went off to an inn to share a bottle of claret.

The patience of the king and his ministers with Wilkes wore thin and finally shredded with the publication in April 1763 of the forty-fifth edition of the *North Briton,* which seemed to stain the king's honor and question his honesty. Wilkes was arrested for seditious libel and tossed into the Tower of London. He stayed there only a week. A court ordered his release because, as a member of Parliament, he was shielded from arrest.

Wilkes and his allies subsequently brought lawsuits challenging the tool authorities had used to arrest him, the general warrant. The document spelled out the crime that was alleged to have been committed but did not name the suspected perpetrators. The person holding the warrant could arrest anyone. Wilkes won his legal battle against such warrants and continued with his writing, assuming that his position as a member of Parliament gave him protection. For defying authority, Wilkes became hugely popular in Britain, especially among the working and middle classes. Wilkes's distinctive image appeared on tobacco papers, porcelain dishes, teapots, and punch bowls.

To Benjamin Franklin, who was living in London at this time, Wilkes was "not worth a farthing."[2] But many other Americans venerated him. The phrase "Wilkes and liberty," which crowds shouted as Wilkes emerged from the courtroom in May 1763, became a toast throughout the colonies. "Wilkes and liberty" was as much a byword in Boston as in London. The number forty-five–for the particularly controversial edition of the *North Briton*–became a hallowed symbol for discontented Americans.

Americans were drawn to the figure of Wilkes because they shared his hatred of Bute, who was seen as responsible for the king and Parliament's missteps, and because Wilkes spoke boldly against government ministers. He came to represent freedom to criticize authority. It also helped that Wilkes battled to do away with the general warrant. His efforts echoed those of Otis and the merchants in Boston's Writ of Assistance case. Both cases challenged the tendency of authority to poke into people's lives and business.

As radical Americans learned more about Wilkes, they also came to feel that they shared with him a common view of British history. This view, the so-called Whig view, pointed to the Glorious Revolution as enormously important. Bostonians of the 1760s looked back on that event with nearly the same reverence as Americans today look back on the American Revolution.

The Glorious Revolution of 1688 brought William and Mary to the British throne under conditions set by Parliament, bringing Britain into line with the ideas of John Locke that government was a social contract between the ruler and the people, as represented in Parliament. To Wilkes and many of his followers, and to many Americans, the Glorious Revolution established a perfect balance–the House of Commons, the House of Lords, and the monarch–each with a role and each positioned to check the power of the others.

Now, in the 1760s, Wilkes, along with his followers and many Americans, detected a dangerous imbalance. To them, too much power was in the hands of the king and his ministers, and they were corrupting or intimidating a supine Parliament. Other leading men in England, such as William Pitt and Charles Fox, recognized this same problem. But none challenged the king as boldly as Wilkes did. Without trying to woo Americans, Wilkes had stolen their hearts.

John Wilkes by William Hogarth. (*Library of Congress*)

While Wilkes gloried in his court victory, his enemies in Parliament and among the king's ministers maneuvered to have him kicked out of the House of Commons. Wilkes was in Paris when he was tried in absentia and found guilty of seditious libel for no. 45, and also of impious and obscene libel for the naughty parody of Pope's *Essay on Man.* As 1765 began, Wilkes was an outlaw living in exile in France, but still very much a hero to many in Britain and America.

Meanwhile, the British government, unable to get at Wilkes, took out its fury on his allies in Britain. In February, authorities set the publisher of no. 45 in a pillory for an hour for his role in the alleged libel. The ten thousand or so people who gathered in New Palace Yard, instead of tormenting the man, shouted "truth in the pillory" and "Wilkes and liberty" while passing a hat. They left a pile of donations at the publisher's feet and then hanged a jackboot and a Scottish bonnet–symbols of Bute–and a petticoat–symbol of the king's mother, who was Bute's ally and suspected lover.

This event was merely background noise for Parliament, which shrugged at whimpers from America about the Sugar Act and promptly brought forth the Stamp Act. The vote, in March 1765, wasn't close, 294 to 49, without vigorous debate.

In Boston, the year 1765 began ominously when a prominent merchant, Nathaniel Wheelwright, went bankrupt, starting a financial crisis that rippled through the community. Wheelwright, forty-three, owner of a large wharf, had borrowed from many people. His personal IOUs with a promise to pay at 6 percent interest had circulated almost like paper money. People believed he would easily repay eventually in "lawful money." But his wealth was based largely on war profits. After the wartime money spigot ran dry, Wheelwright stopped honoring his staggering debts.

People holding Wheelwright's notes, now unable to pay their own debts, scrambled for cover. Wheelwright's bankruptcy would be followed by dozens of others. Governor Bernard wrote: "This was like an earthquake to the town; numbers of people were creditors, some for their all. Every one dreaded the consequences; lesser merchants began to fail; a stop to all credit was expected and a general bankruptcy was apprehended for a time."[3] John Hancock, writing to his business agents in London, offered an ominous forecast: "[T]imes are very bad & precarious here & take my word my good Friends, the times will be worse here, in short such is the situation of things here that we do not know who is and who is not safe."[4]

In May, just as Boston was reeling from the Wheelwright debacle, news about the Stamp Act arrived. While Americans had known since early 1764 that such an act was planned, only now did Americans learn its details. Unlike the Sugar Act, which directly affected a narrow group of colonists–merchants–the Stamp Act would touch the lives of almost everyone. Under the Stamp Act, which would go into effect November 1, six months away, special stamped paper would be prepared and bundled in England. The Stamp Act did not involve stamps in the modern sense, that is, devices like postage stamps stuck to paper. With the Stamp Act, the paper itself would be embossed, or stamped, so a portion of the surface was raised in a distinct pattern that could be seen and felt. This stamped paper would be shipped to the colonies and distributed to designated agents, who would sell the paper to colonists at a price set by the government. The agents would turn over this money, minus their fees, to the government. Thus, the government would take in revenue from the sale of this paper.

The act required the use of stamped paper for nearly all printed and legal documents. That included all diplomas, deeds, mortgages, indentures, leases, contracts, bills of sale, articles of apprenticeship, and liquor licenses. Beyond its requirement for legal and formal documents, the paper was also required for such items as almanacs, advertisements, pamphlets, and even playing cards. Thus the tax would touch anyone who bought and sold land, needed a handbill printed, or stepped into a tavern for a hand of whist. The tax varied–three pence on a deed, one shilling on a pack of cards, two pounds for a diploma–but was applied so broadly that it couldn't help but get people's attention. Furthermore, and crucially, the act required that newspapers be printed on the stamped paper. Just about every newspaper in the colonies beat the drum against the tax.

If Britain had deliberately set out to rile colonists, it could hardly have devised a more effective method. The tax annoyed everyone, and it particularly irritated merchants, who had money and influence; lawyers, who were well educated and articulate; and newspaper publishers, who had the horns to trumpet their anger.

Penny stamp proof set. (*British Library*)

In London, some fretted that Americans would howl, but most of those in authority felt the tax was only fair. Charles Townshend, the government's architect of the act, said: "[N]ow will these Americans, children planted by our care, nourished up by our indulgence until they are grown to a degree of strength and opulence, and protected by our arms, will they grudge to contribute their mite to relieve us from the heavy weight of that burden which we lie under?"[5]

Member of Parliament Isaac Barré, scarred veteran of the French and Indian War, ripped into the government's justification for the tax: "They planted by your care? No! your oppression planted them in America. They fled your tyranny to a then uncultivated and inhospitable country, where they exposed themselves to almost all the hardships to which human nature is liable, and, among others, to the cruelty of a savage foe. . . . [Y]et, actuated by the principles of English liberty, they met all those hardships with pleasure."[6]

Barré continued, along the way calling Americans "sons of liberty" who are "as truly loyal as any subjects the king has; but a people jealous of their liberties, and who will vindicate them if ever they should be violated."[7] Barré would join Wilkes and Pitt in America's pantheon of heroes and for many years would be America's best friend in Parliament.

In spring and summer 1765, Americans contemplated the coming act, which was making much more of a stir than the Sugar Act. In Boston, the coming of the Stamp Act galvanized townspeople, no one more so than John Hancock. In a letter venting to his agents in London, his quill all but burst into flames:

> I would sooner subject myself to the hardest Labour for a maintenance, than carry on the Business I now do under so great a Burthen, & I am Determin'd as soon as I know they are Resolv'd to insist on this act to Sell my Stock in Trade & Shut up my Warehouse Doors. Thus much I told our Govr the other day, &

> is what I am absolutely Determin'd to abide by, without some very extraordy intervention, indeed, wch is not likely–I am very sorry for this occasion of writing so boldly, & of being obliged to such Resolutions, but the Safety of myself & the Country I have the honor to be a Native of require some Resolutions, I am free & Determin'd to be so I will not willingly & quietly Subject myself to Slavery.[8]

After his closing, "Your Sincere Friend but an enemy to the Stamps" Hancock added a postscript with an eye to history: "This Letter I propose to remain in my Letter Book as a Standing monument to posterity & my children in particular, that I by no means consented to a Submission to this Cruel Act, & that my best Representations were not wantg. in the matter."[9]

Protests against the Sugar Act had failed. Now the Stamp Act was coming. Its consequences were worse. What to do? Some joined a nascent movement to spend less on mourning. For years in Boston, it had been the custom for bereaved families to buy imported rings and gloves and pass them out as tokens at funerals. Also, mourners bought expensive imported mourning clothes. Even before the Stamp Act, some merchants vowed to quit this practice just to save money and stem the flow of hard currency from the province.

Now, with the implementation of the Stamp Act approaching, that movement to cut back on mourning took on the character of a protest, a genteel slap at Britain. Many people signed on to refrain from buying mourning goods or even wearing black cloth during mourning.

Tory Peter Oliver later poked fun at the movement: "A Funeral now seemed more like a Procession to a May Fair." It was better before, Oliver wrote, when "a Widow, who had been well rid of a bad Companion, could conceal her Joy under a long black Vail."[10]

But the movement caught on. Hutchinson wrote in 1766, "The scheme for laying aside mourning succeeded to my surprise and scarce any body would now dare to wear black for the nearest relation."[11] The movement inspired other measures to both discourage imports and promote self-sufficiency. For example, many people in Boston signed a pledge to eat no lamb for the year. The aim was to ensure more sheep for the local production of wool.

Thus Bostonians began pushing against a powerful consumer trend that had been building for decades. By this time, Bostonians and other Americans were eager consumers of imports and relied on England and other foreign sources for certain basic products, especially woolen, linen, and cotton cloth and garments; sugar; wine; and tea; but also iron, paper, and glass. Spinning wheels were no longer all that common. In Boston's Suffolk County, only about one in four households had one, and many of those were gathering dust. It no longer made much sense to spin thread and make cloth at home when it could be bought so cheaply from England, where advanced machinery, low wages, and economies of scale kept costs low. Few consumer products were mass-produced in America. Americans created almost no porcelain tableware or anything made of brass, such as candlesticks. Britain discouraged American manufacturing by throwing up barriers. For example, one law prohibited the transportation of wool products in America by water; another made it illegal for Americans to export hats; yet another made it illegal to establish a furnace in America for making steel. But even without these barriers, American manufacturers would not likely have prospered: labor costs were too high. Also, with so much cheap land, America was better positioned for agriculture.

Thus, sailing against a stiff headwind of consumer demand and economic realities, efforts to curb imports and encourage local manufacturing didn't go far. But they had the effect of building a sense of unity and reviving Boston's Puritan spirit equating modesty and simplicity with virtue.

So, one response to the Stamp Act was to shun imports and promote local industry. Another was to threaten people, throw rocks, and make a lot of noise. That was the approach of a group called the Loyal Nine. Benjamin Edes of the *Gazette* was its most prominent member. Another member was John Avery, a distiller and Harvard graduate, giving the group a patina of respectability. Another member, Henry Bass, was a cousin of Sam Adams's. Five of the remaining six were a distiller, a painter, a jeweler, and two braziers. Sources disagree on the identity of the remaining member.[12]

Neither Sam nor John Adams was a member, but they each met with the group in gatherings that sounded anything but revolutionary. Sam was a guest at a "very Genteel Supper" on an evening spent "in a very agreeable manner Drinkg Healths etc."[13] John Adams met with them in a small room at a distillery: "We had punch, wine, pipes and tobacco, biscuit & cheese, &c. I heard nothing but such conversation that passes at all clubs, among gentlemen, about the times. No plots, no machinations."[14]

The Loyal Nine looked for a vulnerable cog in the tax-collection machinery and found it: the distributor. Distributors would receive the stamped paper shipped from Britain and then sell it to printers and others. Under normal circumstances, the job of distributor would be easy and lucrative: he would have a monopoly on a product that just about everyone would be compelled to buy. After selling the paper, the distributor would turn over the proceeds, minus a handsome fee, to the British government. But the Loyal Nine were determined to intimidate, threaten, and terrorize the distributor and prevent him from selling stamped paper. They assigned this dirty work to Ebenezer Mackintosh and his mob, and were "not a little pleas'd" to let Mackintosh get the credit.[15]

The Loyal Nine's strategy was hardly an innovation. Englishmen and Americans were well acquainted with the idea of breaking windows, throwing bricks, and raising a ruckus on the streets to make a point. Rowdy crowds were common enough in the 1700s. For many thousands of voteless and poor people in England and America, rioting or something like it was their way of being heard. Sometimes mobs were festive, with no focused political motivation, as with the mobs that roamed the Boston streets on Pope Day. But sometimes mobs rose up in response to grievances and had specific aims.

In the previous seven decades or so, several dozen riots of one sort or another had taken place in Boston, many more than in New York and Philadelphia. At least three had to do with a shortage of bread. In two riots, the targets were brothels. On at least one occasion, a mob acted in the interest of the town against a private citizen. The town had proposed a new street, conducted a survey, and found that a man's barn stood in the way. Rather than waiting for the tedious process of acquiring the property and compensating the obstinate owner, townspeople gathered one night, blackened their faces, and tore the barn down.

The largest riot occurred during the so-called Knowles Affair in 1747. British warships under Commodore Charles Knowles had gathered outside Boston Harbor in preparation to sail to the West Indies. During that time, several dozen sailors deserted, leaving ships without full crews. Knowles ordered gangs of sailors to sweep through Boston and seize able-bodied men to fill his ranks. Impressment crews snared forty-six men, including apprentices, carpenters, and other land laborers.

Enraged townspeople, many armed with sticks and clubs, roamed the streets looking for revenge. In frustration, the mob took hold of a deputy sheriff and set him in the public stocks. Later, a throng of several thousands massed on King Street. Some hurled stones at windows of the Town House, shattering every pane on the ground floor. Others battered in the door. The governor fled to Castle William and pleaded with Knowles to release the impressed men or make some compromise. After some days of crisis, Knowles released most if not all of the impressed men, and his squadron sailed off.

The memory of this triumph of the mob lingered, which is perhaps what inspired the Loyal Nine. Rioters served the town well back in 1747. Perhaps they would be useful now.

Also about this time, a hardware dealer in Boston by the singular name of Harbottle Dorr began saving Boston newspapers. Week after week he would set aside the *Boston Gazette* (also titled *Boston-Gazette and Country Journal*), the *Boston Evening-Post*, or the *Boston Post-Boy*. Some weeks he would save two papers. In addition to carefully preserving these newspapers, he would jot comments in the margins or between columns. These remarks would identify otherwise anonymous authors of letters or articles, or would explain obscure references, or would offer sharp commentary on matters in the articles. Thus we see Dorr's notations preserved at the bottom of the front page of the Monday, March 25, 1765, edition of the *Boston-Gazette and Country Journal.* The page is entirely given over to the actions of the Virginia House of Burgesses. As Dorr and other Bostonians were learning, Virginia had been especially assertive with a series of powerful resolutions, including one denying Parliament's right to levy taxes on Americans. While records are murky, historians believe that some of the most radical resolutions reported in the newspapers were never actually adopted in Virginia.[16] But Bostonians didn't know that and were amazed at the apparent boldness of the Virginians. Thus wrote Dorr, at the bottom of this page, "Noble spirited Petitions! how much unlike ours!"[17] The news from Virginia "proved an Alarm bell to the disaffected," as Governor Bernard later wrote, and set a fire under the *Gazette,* "an infamous weekly Paper," which from then on "swarmed with libells of the most atrocious kind."[18]

The reports from Virginia also stiffened the spines of the assemblymen in Massachusetts, now determined to retake the initiative. The Massachusetts lawmakers figured that a joint protest from many colonies, perhaps all thirteen, would be hard for Parliament to ignore. The Massachusetts House drew up a plan to have a meeting–a congress–of representatives from each of the colonies. The idea was not altogether fresh. A similar proposal had been floated the year before. But no meeting took place.

This time, with reports from Virginia and elsewhere of boiling discontent, the Massachusetts representatives were more confident that an invitation to a congress would get an eager response. In June, a circular letter was sent to each colony inviting representatives to gather in New York in October. The wording of the invitation was guarded. The assembly would consider a "general and united, dutiful, loyal and humble representation of the condition to his majesty and the parliament; and to implore relief."[19] This was no rebellion.

As it turned out, even though Massachusetts called for the congress, it would provide no strong leadership. Two of the three Massachusetts representatives at the so-called Stamp Act Congress were allies of the governor's. The third was Otis, who seemed now inexplicably to be wavering.

Meanwhile, in July, death took a key Whig, Oxenbridge Thacher, who was also one of Boston's representatives in the Massachusetts House. In September the town elected Thacher's successor. On the second ballot, the town settled on Sam Adams, who quickly made his presence known and worked in tandem with Otis as leaders of the faction opposing the government. Tory Peter Oliver later described the two men: "He [Sam Adams] was all serpentine Cunning, Mr. Otis was rash, unguarded, foulmouthed, & openly spitefull."[20] According to Oliver, Adams soon overtook Otis in popularity and won the hearts of ordinary men through a common interest in, of all things, music:

> [H]e could transform his self into an Angel of Light with the weak Religionist; & with the abandoned he would disrobe his self & appear with his cloven Foot & in his native Blackness of Darkness–he had a good Voice, & was a Master in vocal Musick. This Genius he improved, by instituting singing Societys of Mechanicks, where he presided; & embraced such Opportunities to [inculcate] Sedition, 'till it had ripened into Rebellion. His Power over weak Minds was truly surprising.[21]

SEVEN

RAGE OF DEVILS

At the corner of Essex and Newbury streets (present day Essex and Washington) stood a handsome elm more than a century old. On the morning of Wednesday, August 15, 1765, Bostonians passing by this tree, already known as the Liberty Tree, saw two objects swaying from its massive limbs. The first was an oversized boot, its sole painted green, with a devilish head and horns "peeping out of the top."[1] The second was an effigy of a man labeled "A.O."[2] and an attached verse: "A godlier sight who'er did see; A stamp man hanging on a tree!"[3]

The boot was a visual pun representing the Earl of Bute (pronounced "boot"), the hated royal adviser. The green paint on the boot was the "Greenville sole," another pun referring to George Grenville, prime minister and another object of scorn in Boston. "A.O." was Andrew Oliver, wealthy merchant, brother-in-law of Thomas Hutchinson, and the man rumored to be tapped for the job of distributor of the stamped paper.

Already at 5:00 a.m., an imposing crowd had gathered. The tree's owner came out to cut down the ornaments, but he quickly retreated so as not to "occasion the Demolition of his Windows."[4] Many of those around the Liberty Tree were the same South Enders who made up Mackintosh's Pope Day crowd. Leading them was Mackintosh himself, strutting and giving orders as if commanding a regiment, which in a way he was. This was not an aimless mass. These men and boys were, in a haphazard way, disciplined. Mackintosh had his followers well in hand. As the human sea around the elm extended farther and farther down adjacent streets, word reached the Town House a half mile away about the effigy, the boot, and a possible riot. Hutchinson, wishing to nip the tumult in the bud and fearing for Oliver's safety, ordered Sheriff Greenleaf to go with some men to cut the objects down. Greenleaf left but soon returned. The crowd was too big and threatening, he said. He would not risk his life and the lives of his men.

Meanwhile, Governor Bernard asked the Council how the government should respond. Most councillors opposed taking any action. It was a mere "trifling Business," and "would subside of itself," said some. Others said interference would only "inflame the People" and create worse havoc.[5] Talk went on throughout the day, and as darkness fell and the governor and Council continued to hem and haw, the mob itself, now in the thousands, came calling, escorting Oliver, in effigy form, to the Town House. The rough crowd delivered three shouts directed at the windows of the Council Chamber. Then, led by "forty or fifty tradesmen, decently dressed,"[6] the crowd paraded into the Town House, up the steps, and into and out of the chamber where the governor and Council were meeting.

From the Town House, the mob moved down King Street toward Long Wharf and then to Kilby Street, where Oliver owned a building he planned to rent. Mackintosh and his men, guessing that Oliver intended the new brick building as an office for selling stamped paper, encircled the structure, broke the windows, beat down the doors, and finally battered the edifice to rubble. One person was hurt: a spectator standing too close to a brick wall when it collapsed.

The mob then moved on to Oliver Street to Andrew Oliver's family residence, where, in front of the house, with Mackintosh in full control, the mob paused for a bit of theater. Men brought forth the effigy and, in a mock ceremony, cut off its head amid roars and laughter. Soon stones were flying at the house and shards of glass were dropping from the window frames. Oliver and his family, cowering inside, were relieved when the mob moved off with the newly executed effigy and bits and pieces of the building from Kilby Street. The rioters took these prizes to the summit of a nearby hill, built a bonfire, and threw the effigy into the flames.

The night was not over. Mackintosh later led the mob back to Oliver's house. By this time, Oliver and his family had left the house in the hands of trusted friends while they found protection with neighbors. The friends barricaded the doors.

The mob, louder and drunker than ever, crashed through the garden fence, beat on the doors and broke windows. Someone shouted a threat to kill Oliver. Oliver's friends now abandoned the building, and soon men entered the home and began a frenzy of furniture smashing. Before the night was over, a huge mirror, said to be the largest in North America, was in fragments.

Bernard wrote out an order to call out the militia. The colonel in charge of the militia advised against it. Any drummer sent out to beat the alarm would have his drum quickly smashed, said the colonel. Besides, "probably all the drummers of the Regiment were in the Mob."[7]

Map 3. Boston, c. 1765.

Soon Bernard fled to Castle William. Lieutenant Governor Hutchinson showed more courage and initiative. He and Sheriff Greenleaf set out to face the mob alone. At the Oliver house, they shouted over catcalls for the crowd to disperse. The response was a blizzard of stones. Hutchinson and the sheriff scurried away, "not without some bruises."[8]

At midnight, the triumphant rioters shambled to their homes. Property–targeted property–was wrecked, but no one killed. Sam Adams pronounced the mob's actions entirely justified. The crowd, he said, had "deliberately" and "rationally" destroyed that property as the "only means of securing the property of all."[9]

The next morning, several townsmen called on Oliver and formally asked him to resign as stamp distributor. Oliver replied that he could not quit the job because, technically, he did not have it. He had not yet received his commission. He promised, however, that if the commission came, he would quit. He gave his word that he would take no steps in the meantime to carry out any requirements of the Stamp Act. It was a complete surrender to Mackintosh and the Loyal Nine. That evening the mob formed up again, "not to insult the distributor, but to give him thanks."[10] They built a bonfire on a hill near the Oliver house.[11]

The next evening, the Mackintosh mob gathered again, this time around the fine North End home of Thomas Hutchinson, who had the nerve to confront the mob the previous night. Also, according to rumors, the lieutenant governor secretly favored the Stamp Act. Hutchinson actually opposed the Stamp Act and worked to undo it. Arguments he drafted matched many of those used by members of Parliament fighting to do away with the Stamp Act.[12] But no matter what Hutchinson said or did, many in Boston remained convinced he backed the act.

Hutchinson's brick home on Garden Court Street was one of the finest in town. It featured a tasteful cupola on the roof and gardens extending to nearby Hanover and Fleet streets. The house announced elegance and British pride: dark mahogany lined the parlor walls; the crown of Britain surmounted each window. The library displayed portraits of Queen Anne and several royal Georges, a tapestry of the coronation of George II, and busts of Stuart monarchs.

As Hutchinson waited and listened inside, some rioters tried to enter the house, but the doors and windows were barred. Then voices called for Hutchinson to appear on a balcony and declare that he had never written in support of the stamp tax. Fulfill this demand and the crowd would disperse, came a shout from outside. Hutchinson heard the demand but remained hidden. It was, he later wrote, "an indignity" to which he "would not submit."[13]

The men outside weighed their options. Then a brave neighbor called out from a nearby window. The lieutenant governor, he said, had left earlier that day for his country house. The rioters accepted the story. The men and boys broke some windows but soon drifted away.

Eleven days later, the Mackintosh mob gathered once again. After assembling around a great bonfire on King Street, it moved under Mackintosh's direction to the residence of Charles Paxton, the reviled customs man connected with the Writs of Assistance case. The mob would have ripped apart the house but for the quick thinking of Paxton's landlord. He brought out punch for the crowd and told rioters that Paxton was away. The mob paused for refreshments, spared the house, and then moved on, splitting up to attack other properties and then eventually joining up once again and streaming north toward the Hutchinson home.

Hutchinson House. (*American Almanac and Repository of Useful Knowledge*)

The mob seemed to have no more reason for attacking Hutchinson's house this day than it did days before. This time, however, the rioters "ripened in Ebriety and Madness"[14] were more inflamed and determined. As the mob was making its way to the house at about twilight, Hutchinson was changing from a warm suit to a thin dressing gown and preparing to sit down for supper with his children: two older boys, Thomas and Elisha, who had finished Harvard; younger Billy; Sallie, soon to marry; and Peggy, the youngest and favorite. Likely the children's unmarried aunt was also there, as well as five servants. When word reached the house that the mob was coming, Hutchinson ordered everyone except his sons to leave. As the others found refuge at a neighbor's house, Hutchinson and his sons prepared to barricade themselves in the mansion. Just as the mob was about to arrive, daughter Sallie reappeared, determined to either drag her father away or join him and her brothers in defending the home. Afraid for her, and unable to shoo her away, Thomas Hutchinson slipped away with her, and soon her brothers followed.

Then, as Hutchinson later described it, a "hellish crew" attacked the house "with the rage of divels." In a moment, "axes split down the door." They went upstairs and down searching for the lieutenant governor and then tore the place apart, battering walls, pulling down drapery, laboring two hours on the roof wrenching off the cupola and then tearing off the slate. Outside, the mob trampled the garden fence and demolished fruit trees.[15]

A witness wrote to a friend that the drunken rioters broke Hutchinson's windows, "threw all his Furniture out of his House, stamp'd upon the Chairs, Mahogany Tables, very handsome large gilt-framed Pictures, the Peices of which lay in Piles in the Street, open'd his Beds and let all the Feathers out, took ten thousand Pounds in Cash, took all his Cloathes, Linnen, Plate, and every Thing he had."[16]

Meanwhile, a few of the rowdy crowd trailed Hutchinson to where he found refuge, at the home of his sister. When the rioters shouted for Hutchinson, his brother-in-law, the Reverend Samuel Mather, son of the illustrious Cotton Mather, appeared at the door and defiantly pledged not to hand over the lieutenant governor. The mob left, but Mather feared they might come back, so he arranged for Hutchinson to be spirited away. Hutchinson's niece, thirteen-year-old Hannah Mather, guided him out of the house some back way, through an alley, to a more distant house of safety. There, uncle and niece spent the night awake, listening to the shouting and crashing as the Hutchinson house came down. He returned to the Mather house in the morning and joined the family for breakfast. Wrote Hannah, many years later, "He conducted like a calm philosopher through the whole scene."[17]

The destruction continued until the approach of dawn. No militia drove the mob away. No leaders tried to halt the lawlessness. No friends came to defend Hutchinson's property. No one intervened. Hutchinson, appearing at the Town House in the morning as scheduled, wore the same clothes he had on when he fled his house before the mob. After apologizing for his appearance, he affirmed his opposition to the Stamp Act. Hutchinson later wrote:

> I call my Maker to witness that I never, in New England or Old, in Great Britain or America, neither directly nor indirectly, was aiding, assisting, or supporting, or in the least prompting or encouraging what is commonly called the Stamp Act, but on the contrary, did all in my power, and strove as much as in me lay, to prevent it. . . . I hope all will see how easily the people may be deluded, enflamed, and carried away with madness against an innocent man. I pray GOD give us better hearts.[18]

The destruction of the Hutchinson house shocked townspeople. A special town meeting was called, and despite the short notice–not more than two hours–it drew the largest crowd in memory to Faneuil Hall. Townsmen, including Mackintosh, declared "detestation of the extraordinary & violent proceedings of a number of Persons unknown against some of the inhabitants" the previous night. Townsmen passed a motion urging that future disorders of this kind be suppressed. No mention was made of trying to identify and punish the "Persons unknown."[19]

The public was alarmed. Wrote one man: "Its perilous times wt us here, a man dars't speak a word in favour of ye act without running the risque of having his house pulld down, his goods destroyd & pillaged, or his life lost."[20] Fearing further riots and looting, some wealthy people quietly asked poorer neighbors to store valuables. Ordinary people were also horrified. Jane Mecom, writing to her brother, Benjamin Franklin, said Hutchinson's suffering "was never equaled in any nation, our Saviour's only excepted."[21]

Preacher Jonathan Mayhew was distraught. He thought a fiery sermon the day before the riot had unleashed the mayhem. He sent off a letter of apology to Hutchinson: "In truth I had rather lose my hand, than be an encourager of such outrages as were committed last Night." He also begged Hutchinson not to divulge what he wrote "[f]or it could do no good in the present circumstances . . . and might bring their heavy vengeance upon myself."[22]

Even the *Gazette*, generally the most strident voice of the patriot cause, was shocked, dismayed, and mystified. The newspaper drew a distinction between the violence earlier in the month and the violence that destroyed the Hutchinson house:

> Most people seem dispos'd to discriminate between the Assembly on the 14th of the Month, and *their* Transactions, and the unbridled Licentiousness of *this* Mob; judging them to proceed from very *different* Motives, as their Conduct was most evidently *different*–the Countenances of People almost universally on the former Account, apparently discover'd an Approbation; on the latter, as might reasonably be expected, every Face was gloomy and we believe every Heart affected–at some Times and in some extraordinary Cases, the Cause of Liberty requires an extraordinary Spirit to support it; but surely the pulling down Houses and robbing Persons of their Substance . . . is utterly inconsistent with the first principles of Government, and subversive of the glorious Cause.[23]

Bernard felt helpless. He wrote a plaintive letter to General Thomas Gage, commander of British forces in America: "The Town of Boston is in the possession of an incenced & implacable Mob; I have no force to oppose them. . . . Under these difficulties, I have nothing to do, but to apply to you, as his Majesty's Military Commander in chief; and I can only recommend to you to use such means as you shall think proper to preserve his Majestys Dominion over this Town."[24]

But the governor need not have been so fearful. The people were now firmly on the side of law and order. When the governor called out the militia, the militia responded. When the town asked the fire companies to pitch in to keep the peace, they helped out as well. So for weeks, militiamen and volunteer firemen patrolled the streets.

No rioters would ever be prosecuted for the destruction. Sheriff Greenleaf, ordered to arrest Mackintosh, easily found the shoemaker right on King Street. But before the sheriff could jail him, officers from the Custom House approached. They wanted Mackintosh released! They had heard rumors that the Custom House was next on the list of targets for mob attacks. They had also heard that unless Mackintosh was free, no one would respond to defend the building. Greenleaf let Mackintosh go, earning a scolding from Hutchinson: "[Y]ou have not done your duty."[25]

Later, some six or eight others were rounded up and jailed. But after a few days or weeks, a group of men showed up at night at the jail keeper's house and demanded the rioters be released. Soon free, those men slipped away for several months. Then, realizing no one was after them, they returned and went about their business. No authority laid a hand on them.[26]

The motives behind the attack on the Hutchinson house, so much more ferocious than any other assaults on property in Boston during this period, remain a mystery. While Hutchinson had lost a good measure of his popularity, he retained enormous respect, as demonstrated just the year before when the House of Representatives, with only eight dissents, selected Hutchinson to go to London to argue the province's case regarding the Sugar Act, boundaries, and other issues. Hutchinson never made the trip. Still, that vote demonstrated the high regard people still had for the man.

At the time, and today, some have speculated that motives were at play other than–or in addition to–the desire to intimidate or punish the lieutenant governor. One theory is that someone wanted certain papers to vanish and paid or encouraged Mackintosh to turn the mob loose on the house to ensure that those documents were lost or destroyed. Hutchinson, as lieutenant governor, as a historian, and as a merchant, possessed many rare and valuable papers, and reports confirmed that among the lost and damaged property were "large Files and Records . . . relating to the Claims and Title of this Province."[27] Hutchinson himself wrote that the mob "scattered or destroyed all the manuscripts and other papers I have been collecting for 30 years together besides a great number of Publick Papers in my custody."[28]

The destruction of the Hutchinson house and the other violence did nothing to change the Stamp Act. The law was still scheduled to go into effect November 1, and Parliament still expected the tax to be collected. In early September, a ship arrived in Boston carrying the dreaded and despised stamped paper that the distributor was supposed to sell. On board the same ship was a man assigned to distribute stamps in New Hampshire. On learning of the "proceedings of the mob" in Boston, he promptly resigned, whereupon he "was received with acclamations & carress of ye people, who conducted him to ye Exchange Tavern, where they applauded him & treated him in a grand manner."[29] Meanwhile, the paper was unloaded at Castle Island and put under guard.

Hutchinson, writing in despair, envisioned a province in paralysis: "You cannot conceive the wretched state we are in. Such is the resentment of the people against the stamp duty that there can be no dependence upon the general court to take any steps to enforce or rather advise the payment of it. On the other hand, such will be the effects of not submitting to it that all trade must cease all courts fail and all authority be at an end."[30]

Colonial representatives gathered in New York as planned in October, with twenty-seven delegates attending. Nine colonies were represented at this meeting, known to history as the Stamp Act Congress. New Hampshire declined the invitation. Virginia, North Carolina, and Georgia were absent because, in each of those colonies, the alarmed governor would not let representatives assemble, and thus blocked the election of delegates. Those governors need not have worried. The congress generated little excitement among the people. Newspapers barely gave it notice.

Still, the congress proved surprisingly assertive. Instead of merely arguing that the Stamp Act was too harsh and would create too much hardship, the delegates focused on how the act threatened two essential rights: the right of the colonists, and no one else, to impose taxes on them, and the right of trial by jury. The delegates agreed that Parliament was violating both of these rights by imposing taxes through the sales of stamped paper and by giving juryless courts jurisdiction in Stamp Act cases. The delegates called for Parliament to repeal the act.

The congress also addressed the issue of representation in Parliament. Some, such as James Otis, had suggested that if the problem was taxation without representation, the solution would be representation in Parliament. Why not have the colonies each elect members of Parliament to travel to London and vote in the House of Commons on an equal footing with other members?

The notion was not novel. Indeed, Otis's nemesis, Governor Bernard, had the same idea. He had already sent off an essay to Britain on the subject of government reform in America. Representation in Parliament would, at the very least, force Americans to stop hollering "no taxation without representation." Bernard would raise the idea again, begging for someone in Britain to take the idea seriously: "If they will not be obedient to Parliament without Representatives, in Gods Name let them have them."[31]

But the idea never gained traction on either side of the ocean. In Britain, one writer was appalled to even imagine "Pumkin" lawmakers from New England and other Americans in the House of Commons: "Shall we live to see the Spawn of our Transports occupy the highest seats in our Common Wealth? Degenerate Britons! how can ye entertain the humiliating Thought!"[32]

Meanwhile, on the American side, views were mixed, but on the whole, people felt there was more to lose than to gain from representation. One writer cataloged the disadvantages: too expensive to maintain representatives in London; Parliament would limit American representation so severely as to make American influence negligible; America, with no nobility, would not be represented in the House of Lords; and American members of Parliament, so far from home, would be easily corrupted. Furthermore, representation in Parliament would gut the power of colonial legislatures. To accept representation in Parliament would be to "virtually . . . surrender our liberty and property to be held by the meer will and pleasure of a body of men in Britain; it will be to put it in their power to enslave us whenever they please."[33]

So the Stamp Act Congress dismissed the idea, stating that "the people of these Colonies are not, and from their local circumstances cannot be, represented in the house of commons in Great Britain."[34] The only real point of debate at the congress was trying to define precisely where Parliament's authority over the colonists ended. The delegates sidestepped the question: colonists owed "due Subordination" to Parliament. But just what, exactly, was "due"?

The astonishing actions of the congress bewildered Otis. Arriving with a reputation for bluster and bombast, he proved quite subdued and reluctant to rock the boat. He wanted from the congress an unambiguous message that the colonies were, after all, fully subordinate to Parliament, and he wanted to include conventional statements of loyalty to the king. When the congress failed to incorporate these points in its final declaration, Otis initially refused to sign the document. Only after a plea from one of his fellow delegates did Otis, on the final day, add his signature.

EIGHT

JOYFUL DAY

By that fall, everyone in Boston understood that on November 1, when the Stamp Act was to go into effect, the stamped paper would remain bundled and untouched. But then what? Should all activities requiring the paper cease? That would mean the courts would stop functioning, newspapers would stop publishing, and all kinds of business would come to a halt. Or should the people go about their lives as if the Stamp Act had never been passed? That was the simplest course, but it raised concerns. For example, would legal documents filed without stamps later be deemed invalid?

Attention focused on three areas where the stamped paper was required: the courts, the ports, and the newspaper offices. Would judges insist on stamped paper, or recognize legal documents without the stamps? Would merchants allow ships to sit idle rather than obtain the required stamped paper for various shipping documents? Would newspapers publish with stamped paper, with unstamped paper, or stop publishing altogether?

By this time, the Loyal Nine had melded into a large, loosely organized group that embraced the label Barré roared in Parliament: Sons of Liberty. Up and down the Atlantic Coast, other groups with the same name and the same aim–to defeat the Stamp Act–also sprang up. The Sons of Liberty, which included many shopkeepers and artisans, such as Paul Revere, considered themselves loyal British subjects devoted to the king. They didn't blame George III or even Parliament for the Stamp Act, but tended to focus anger on the king's advisers.

As November 1 approached, the Massachusetts House and Council weighed their options. Debate centered on a resolution calling for business to carry on as usual without the stamps–to act as if the Stamp Act didn't exist. After all, the distributor had resigned, and the people could not obtain the controversial stamped paper. But the House rejected the resolution. This was a sticky point. Representatives felt that by passing the measure, the House was actually acknowledging Parliament's right to tax Americans. It was better to leave the issue alone.

With the House thus taking no position, attention focused on the Sons of Liberty. Bernard nervously considered how to prepare. Would there be riots November 1? And what about Pope Day, November 5? He received word that he could, if he wished, have one hundred British regulars dispatched to Boston to keep the peace that crucial week. Bernard turned down the offer. They would be worse than useless: more than enough to annoy townspeople but too few to provide security. So he waited and wrung his hands: "[T]he real authority of the Government is at an end: some of the principle ringleaders in the late riots walk the streets with impunity; no Officers dare attack them; no Attorney General prosecute them; no Witness appear against them; and no Judges sit upon them."[1]

At the end of October, he finally took action. He ordered the militia to be called to keep the peace. A drummer sent out to beat the alarm had his drum smashed. Militia officers duly informed Bernard that the militia would not be available. Thus impotent and uneasy, the governor slunk away yet again to Castle William to be out of sight on the red-letter day.

November 1 began like a day of mourning, with the tolling of church bells and the "melancholy blast"[2] of conch shells. Printer John Boyle recorded in his journal, "Every one joining in the general Solemnity; little or no business was done; main Shops and Stores were wholly shut up, and the Ships in the Harbour had their Colours hoisted half-mast in token of . . . Lamentation and Mourning."[3]

Grenville's effigy was strung up from the Liberty Tree alongside the effigy of a New Hampshire man blamed for the idea of the Stamp Act. At 2:00 p.m., the effigies were cut down, placed on a cart, and, with an escort of thousands in perfect order, marched past the Town House. The parade wound its way back eventually to the gallows at the Neck, where the effigies were properly hanged and then cut down, torn to bits, and scattered into the wind. All was carried out peacefully and precisely, as if to prove to the governor and anyone else that Boston mobs were orderly folk. The day passed with no broken windows. Meanwhile, every sheet of stamped paper remained on Castle Island.

Pope Day, just four days later, was similarly tepid, "remarkable for the peaceable orderly behaviour" of participants.[4] About noon, the North End and South End mobs as usual rolled out their carts with the requisite popes, devils, and assorted effigies. But instead of noisily parading around the town, the two mobs came together on King Street where a "Union was established in a very ceremonial manner," led by Samuel Swift, of the North, and Mackintosh, of the South, in "Military Habits" with "small canes" on their left arms.[5] The ceremony was a model of civility, according to the *Gazette*: "[N]ot a Club was seen among the whole, nor was any Negro allowed to approach near the Stages"[6] The united mobs then marched peacefully to the Liberty Tree, and then to Copp's Hill for a bonfire. "[E]verything was conducted in a most regular manner."[7]

The press in Boston defied the Stamp Act from day one and kept publishing on unstamped paper. The *Gazette* helpfully advised Grenville to kill himself:

> To make us all Slaves, now you've lost Sir! The Hope,
> You've but to go hang yourself.–We'll find the Rope.[8]

Most other newspapers in America also ignored the Stamp Act. No paper in the thirteen colonies printed on stamped paper. A few printers outside Boston interrupted publishing after November 1 to avoid using stamped paper. But that was risky. One New York printer who opposed the Stamp Act got a message that he would be in danger if he did not publish his newspaper as usual. Most newspapers simply kept publishing without interruption.

In the ports, everyone knew a crisis would come after November 1, when vessels loaded with cargo prepared to sail. They would require clearance papers from the Custom Houses, and, according to the new law, these documents had to be on stamped paper. Complicating the problem for everyone in Boston was another circumstance: amazingly, no one in town had an official copy of the Stamp Act. Governor Bernard, like everyone else, was relying on unofficial copies and what he read in newspapers.

In Boston, the two customs men caught in this predicament scrambled for a way out before the November 1 deadline. One was William Sheaffe, collector of customs. The other was Benjamin Hallowell, comptroller of customs, whose house was wrecked by rioters in August. Before November 1, these two men turned for guidance to various superiors, including John Temple, the surveyor general of the customs, and his nemesis, Governor Bernard, each of whom passed the buck or dodged the issue. No one dared give the okay to clear vessels without stamped paper.

As November 1 approached, Sheaffe and Hallowell had no instructions on how to handle clearances, but that didn't really matter when the day arrived, for the port was nearly empty. Anticipating the controversy, many ship owners arranged to load up their vessels as best they could and sent them out to sea before the deadline. So, initially, Sheaffe and Hallowell had no clearance requests to handle. But as the November days passed one by one, pressure began to build. Vessels arrived, were unloaded, reloaded, and prepared for sea. As more merchants demanded clearances, customs men were hearing that the Sons of Liberty might attack the Custom House if the port was not opened soon.

Then on the last day of November, a ship arrived carrying Andrew Oliver's commission, the document authorizing him to sell stamped paper. Sheaffe and Hallowell, groping for a way out of the crisis, had gone to Oliver once before for stamped paper. Now they asked again. Oliver said no. Having already faced the mob and having "resigned," Oliver had no intention of inviting more trouble from the Sons of Liberty. When Sheaffe and Hallowell asked a third time, Oliver was as explicit as he could be: "In answer to your Letter of this date demanding my determinate and absolute answer to this question, whether I will or will not deliver you any stamp'd papers after having answered it twice already: I say No."[9]

As the customs men squirmed, the Sons of Liberty also learned that Oliver's commission had arrived. There was consternation that Oliver, under pressure from Sheaffe and Hallowell, would renege on his earlier promise not to sell stamps. The Gazette published a letter from Oliver acknowledging that he received the commission, but protesting that he had no intention of distributing the stamped paper.

This did not satisfy the Sons of Liberty. Late on December 16, Oliver received a demand that he appear at the Liberty Tree at noon the next day. "Provided you comply with the above, you shall be treated with the greatest Politeness and Humanity."[10]

Oliver arranged for John Avery, a friend and also a member of the Loyal Nine, to meet him in the morning. Avery might at least help him save a shred of dignity. At noon the next day, in a rainstorm, Oliver marched to the Liberty Tree, with mob leader Mackintosh on hand as an escort. About two thousand people heard Oliver deliver his new resignation from an upper window of a house near the tree. The dripping crowd rewarded Oliver with three cheers. Oliver responded with gritted teeth and surprising grace: "I shall always think myself very happy when it shall be in my power to serve this people."[11]

Hallowell and Sheaffe were well aware of Oliver's ordeal. How long would it be before the Sons of Liberty demanded that they appear at the Liberty Tree? Finally, they received clear guidance from someone in authority: Robert Auchmuty, the advocate general of the Admiralty Court, said clearances could be issued without stamps. On the afternoon of December 17, about the time Oliver's torment was over, the Custom House started processing clearances. The port was open.

Merchants and customs men in other American ports faced the same dilemma as those in Boston. Responses varied, but one by one, ports opened, some before Boston, some after. By the end of February 1766, all the ports were open. Only in Savannah, Georgia, did merchants go along briefly with the use of stamped paper. About sixty vessels were cleared with stamped documents. This produced fury in Georgia and outside the colony. An armed mob of about six hundred persuaded the Georgia governor to lock away the stamped paper. The port stayed open.

Americans were appalled that anger about the Stamp Act did not spread to other British-controlled North American ports–in Quebec, Nova Scotia, Florida, Barbados, Grenada, and Jamaica–where the stamp tax was paid and the stamps were used. Curiously, however, when cargoes from the American colonies arrived in those ports, no one seemed to mind that shipping documents carried none of the required stamps. Stranger still, cargoes sent to England from America were unloaded there with no questions asked about improper, unstamped documents.

The Stamp Act did not apply to court documents concerning criminal cases. So in Massachusetts and other colonies, trials concerning those accused of murder, robbery, and other crimes carried on as usual. But the Stamp Act did apply to all kinds of documents related to civil matters. Judges and lawyers were in a quandary. No one dared use stamped paper, which was unavailable anyway. But at the same time, no one could be sure that documents on unstamped paper would be recognized as legal. Because documents were involved in so much legal work, the courts in Massachusetts were paralyzed.

Then the Sons of Liberty, fresh from their triumph in prying open the port, applied pressure on authorities to get the courts back to work. At a special meeting in Faneuil Hall, townsmen influenced by the Sons ratified a request to open the courts. Bernard as usual tried to pass off the decision. He left it up to the Council, which met on December 19. The Council didn't want to make the decision either but agreed to meet the next day.

Now lawyers got involved. They showed up at the December 20 meeting also urging that courts be opened. John Adams asserted Americans are not obliged to obey the Stamp Act because they had no say in creating the act: "A Parliament of Great Britain can have no more Right to tax the Colonies than a Parliament of Paris."[12] Otis followed with melodrama. "It is with a great Grief that I appear before your Excellency and Honours upon this Occasion," he said. "A wicked and unfeeling Minister has caused a People, the most loyal and affectionate that ever a King was blessed with, to groan under the most insupportable Oppression." He also pointed out that the government, by allowing courts to remain closed, is failing in its duty. "The shutting up of the Courts is an Abdication, a Dissolution of Government."[13] Attorney Jeremiah Gridley provided a pragmatic view. What if the stamped paper had been lost at sea? Would the courts then have ground to a halt? "There is now as much an Impossibility to use those Papers, as though they were all in the Bottom of the Ocean."[14]

Governor Bernard and the Council discovered in these learned arguments an excuse to foist the tough decision onto someone else. These lawyerly thoughts sounded like matters for a judge. Why not let the courts decide whether it was okay to handle legal matters without stamped paper? The judges proved bolder than the Council and governor. By the end of January, some courts had resumed their work without stamped paper. The House of Representatives applied pressure on the remaining courts with a resolution urging they be opened. On March 20, 1766, a newspaper claimed that "all the courts of Justice in this province are now to all Intents and Purposes open."[15]

In Rhode Island, the courts never closed. But in the other colonies, as in Massachusetts, the doors to the courts slammed shut and proved sticky when pressure was applied for them to open. Debtors were more than happy to keep court doors bolted shut to creditors trying to sue. This was especially the case in Connecticut, where many local people owed money to lenders outside the colony.

Meanwhile, pressure to open the courts diminished as the weeks passed in 1766, when rumors reached the colonies that the Stamp Act would be repealed. Many judges and lawyers were content to wait for the law to end rather than violate it, however misguided the act was. In most colonies, at least some courts refused to defy the Stamp Act and remained closed until word was received of its repeal.

Across the Atlantic, American opposition and hostility against the Stamp Act got under the skin of many Britons. New Englanders were, as one writer vented, "a crabbed Race, not very unlike their Half Brothers, the Indians, for unsocial Principles." He speculated about New England leading a war of independence:

"They are the Joke of America. I cannot reasonably imagine that such a Hated and sour tempered Province can find any Allies. . . . He must have little Sense, who would become liable to be treated as a Rebel for the Sake of a shunning Payment of a Shilling or Eighteen Pence for a sheet of stamped Paper."[16]

But there were also writers who sympathized with the Americans, and Parliament was now having second thoughts about the Stamp Act. Parliament noted the violence of the Sons of Liberty and was well aware of the Stamp Act Congress. But what really caught lawmakers' attention was the howling from their own British manufacturers.

British manufacturers told members of Parliament that the act was stifling trade. These complaints, coupled with bad economic times in England, plus political shifts favoring opponents of the law, meant the Stamp Act was doomed.

However, as it turned out, the Americans, in railing against the Stamp Act, complicated what should have been a simple matter of undoing it. Americans had repeatedly brought up the issue of whether Parliament had the right to impose taxes like those of the Stamp Act.

How could Parliament repeal the Stamp Act without appearing to give in, without appearing to acknowledge limits in its authority over the colonies?

So weeks went by. In Boston, Mackintosh and his followers kept the issue alive with theatrics in late February 1766, following the arrival of another ship with stamped paper. Mackintosh obtained some of the paper, fixed a sheet to a pole, and put the pole in the public stocks. A designated "executioner" set the stamped paper on fire.

Parliament's solution to the dilemma was to couple repeal of the Stamp Act with passage of the Declaratory Act, which asserted that Parliament retained its authority over the colonies "in all cases whatsoever."[17] For now the Americans would have their way in getting rid of the Stamp Act, but Parliament still claimed supremacy. The dispute about rights remained unresolved.

In Britain, repeal of the Stamp Act set off rejoicing and the tolling of church bells. The British public as a whole despised the act and blamed it for the hard times. On May 16, the brig *Harrison*, owned by John Hancock, sailed into Boston Harbor with an official document proclaiming news of the Stamp Act's repeal. Within hours, all of Boston was abuzz. A day of celebration was quickly planned for May 19, a day no one would sleep. Those celebrations began at one in the morning with church bells across the town waking everyone. At two in the morning, men with bugles, fifes, and drums marched in the streets playing as raucously as possible. Cannons from the shore battery boomed. At the first light, men and boys climbed all over the Liberty Tree, leaving it festooned with banners. Flags appeared on housetops all over town. At noon, ships in the harbor joined in the festivities with a chorus of cannonades.

Merchant John Rowe recorded in his diary, "This day is the Joyfull Day indeed for all America." He joined dozens of men at a celebratory dinner. "[W]e drank fifteen Toasts & very Loyal they were & suited to the Occasion."[18] A newspaper reported, "[J]oy smiled in every countenance, benevolence, gratitude and content seemed the companions of all."[19] Money was gathered up to free everyone in the debtors' prison.

On the Common, the Sons of Liberty erected a great pyramid adorned with no fewer than 280 lanterns along with sketches of the king, queen, and fourteen "worthy patriots."[20] John Hancock, now a town selectman, saw to it that his house was brightly illuminated and ordered a pipe of Madeira set out for everyone to come and enjoy. He and the Sons of Liberty treated townspeople to fireworks displays. A newspaper account said "the air was filled with rockets–the ground with beehives and serpents–and the two stages with wheels of fireworks of various sorts."[21] Days later, Jonathan Mayhew intoned from his pulpit, "[N]ever did the tide of joy swell so high or roll so rapidly

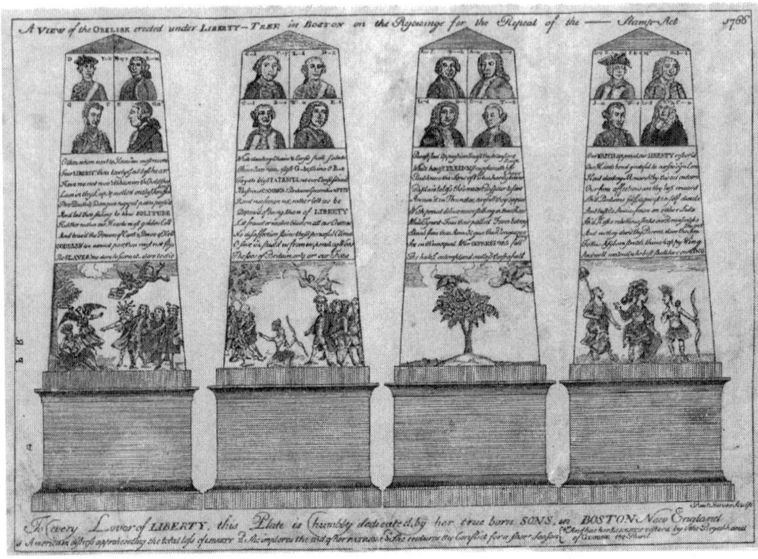

"A view of the obelisk erected under the Liberty-tree in Boston on the rejoicings for the repeal of the–Stamp Act 1766," engraved by Paul Revere. (*Library of Congress*)

through the bosoms and veins of the people in general, on any public occasion, as on the news of the REPEAL."[22]

Mayhew's sermon on the repeal of the Stamp Act was one of his last. He died July 9, 1766, of an "obstinate nervous disorder in his head."[23] Taking his place on the barricades against the Church of England, and on the side of the Whigs, was Charles Chauncy, of the Congregationalist First Church. Another clergyman who identified with the Whigs was Samuel Cooper, pastor of the Congregationalist and affluent Brattle Street Church, where his flock included John Hancock, Joseph Warren, and occasionally John Adams, but also Tories. Cooper worked with Whigs behind the scenes without offending Tories from the pulpit, where he preached "with a voice melodious in the tones of a delicate flute."[24] Clergymen on the Tory side were rare, but there were some. One was Mather Byles, an eccentric Congregationalist preacher at the Hollis Street Church. He was notorious for his mischievous wit. A sample: when a man with a toothache asked Byles where he could have his tooth "drawn," the clergyman directed him to the house of a portraitist.[25] Through thick and thin, he never budged from his Tory mindset, but he kept politics out of his sermons. Some Tories, longing for a champion, asked why Byles didn't speak out? His response:

> In the first place, I do not understand politics; in the second place, you all do, every man and mother's son of you; in the third place, you have politics all the week,–pray let one day out of seven be devoted to religion; and in the fourth place, I am engaged in a work of infinitely greater importance. Give me any subject to preach upon of more consequence than the truths I bring to you, and I will preach upon it the next Sabbath.[26]

But Byles, among Congregationalist preachers in Boston, was almost alone in toeing the Tory line. Most of the others sided with the Whigs and spoke out either from the pulpit or behind the scenes, making up a "black regiment"[27] in the movement leading to the revolution. After the bloody battles to come, a British officer scowled at an American prisoner: "It is your God damned religion that has ruined your country. Damn your religion."[28]

Surprisingly, however, considering the importance of churchmen in Boston's history, merchants, lawyers, and even physicians overshadowed the clergy as the chief voices and actors of the movement. Of those physicians, Thomas Young and Benjamin Church would join Joseph Warren in key roles. Young, the son of Irish immigrants to Ulster County, New York, was already in his mid-30s and a figure of controversy by the time he appeared in Boston in 1766. In 1756, Young was indicted in Dutchess County, New York, for calling Jesus "a knave and a fool." Young renounced "that opinion," and begged the "pardon of God Almighty the world of Mankind and the present Court of Sessions."[29] But the blasphemy charge, and his outspoken Deism, haunted him in Puritan Boston.

As a physician, Young found it difficult to be accepted in Boston's medical community. He was an outsider, had no formal education, and raised eyebrows with some outlandish medical theories. Church had a far better reputation. First of all, his pedigree was thoroughly American: he was a Mayflower descendant, and his grandfather, Captain Benjamin Church, was a famous participant in King Philip's War, a bloody and terrifying Indian uprising in New England the previous century. Church's educational credentials were also impressive. He graduated from Harvard, in the same class with Hancock, and went to London for training in surgery. Furthermore, he had an established record for public service. He had treated the ill at the public almshouse and, during epidemics, freely administered smallpox inoculations to the poor.

Jane Mecom knew better than anyone about all the head butting in the Massachusetts House of Representatives. Her boardinghouse was often full of representatives from outside Boston, and she heard the talk. She wrote to her brother, "I have six good Honist old Souls who come groneing Home Day by Day at the Stupiditey of there Brethren."[30] Still, from time to time, representatives found a way to work together. At this time, the House was more than usually of one mind, with Otis and his allies in control. Emboldened in the wake of the repeal of the Stamp Act, they took aim at the Governor's Council.

In the game of Massachusetts politics, with the House on one side and the governor on the other, the Council generally tilted in the governor's favor because the House generally offered candidates to the Council the governor could accept, including many of his friends and allies.

Now the House was determined to tilt the Council the other way. When it came time for the House to nominate candidates for the Council, it bypassed Hutchinson and others most favored by Bernard. Bernard howled in protest: the House was depriving the government "of its best and most able servants, whose only crime is their fidelity to the crown."[31] Bernard vetoed six of the House's nominees. The House answered back by refusing to nominate other men.

That same year of 1766, the governor and the House also collided about compensating Thomas Hutchinson and Andrew Oliver for the ransacking of their properties during the Stamp Act crisis the year before. When Bernard asked the House to pay Hutchinson, Oliver, and two others for their losses, lawmakers at first shrugged. Eventually, the House and the Council authorized compensation, but with a condition:

> [T]hat all riots, routs, and unlawful assemblies, councelled, commanded, acted, done, or made within this province, between the 1st day of September, 1765, and the 1st day of May, 1766, and all burglaries, felonies, rescues, and breaches of the peace whatsoever, committed in, by, or during such riots, routs, or unlawful assemblies, be, and hereby are pardoned, released, indemnified, discharged, and put into utter oblivion, and that all and every person or persons, acting, advising, assisting, abetting, and counseling the same, be, and are hereby pardoned and discharged from the same, and from all pains of death, and other pains, judgments, indictments, convictions, penalties, and forfeitures, are hereby declared null and void.[32]

In short, Massachusetts lawmakers wanted no one, not Mackintosh nor any of the other rioters, to ever face justice for the wreckage. When this bill found its way to the king, he rejected it and demanded that a new compensation bill be passed "unmixed with any other matter whatsoever."[33] But by the time word of the king's command reached Massachusetts, the money had already been paid out.

So Mackintosh dodged prosecution, and after this time he slipped from prominence. Did he voluntarily step back, or was he pushed aside? We don't know. William Molineux, a hardware merchant, would emerge in place of Mackintosh as mob organizer and "first Leader of Dirty matters."[34]

Meanwhile, mobs continued to spring up from time to time. One notorious case in fall 1766 involved merchant Daniel Malcom. The hated Charles Paxton and other customs men, suspecting smuggling, came to Malcom's house armed with a writ of assistance. When customs men insisted on access to a certain locked cellar, Malcom pulled out two pistols and threatened to "blow the brains out of the first person to break a lock or door."[35] The customs men retreated, returning some five hours later with a writ of assistance and a more specific search warrant. By that time, Malcom had turned his house into a fortress, and a mob of about three thousand had gathered in his defense. The customs men backed off, and Malcom treated his defenders to "buckets of wine."[36]

Despite the rancor, Bostonians felt themselves firmly loyal as 1766 drew to a close. In early December, Rowe noted in his diary a dinner. Guests included Otis, Hancock, and Molineux. Rowe listed twenty-seven toasts, starting with the king, then the queen and royal family, then the Parliament, and then "His majesty's Ministry." Number twenty-two was "The United & inseparable Interest of Great Britain and her Colonies."[37]

Bernard, meanwhile, was ready to give up on Boston. Discouraged, fed up, and frustrated, he wrote:

> [I]t is high time for evry Crown Officer in America, who has distinguished himself by his fidelity to the King, to get away before his retreat is cut off. If the Administration of Great Britain is not able to take necessary Measures to support its Authority over the Colonies, it cannot be expected that they should be able to protect the King's Officers against the popular power of the Colonists.[38]

He wanted a new job far from cantankerous Massachusetts. Barbados, perhaps, or even Nova Scotia, which "at another time, I should consider as a banishment" but would now prefer rather than "to be left here to fight the King's Battles. Without protection, support, or maintenance."[39]

NINE

TAIL OF A RATTLE SNAKE

As a businessman, John Hancock was not remarkable. He didn't need to be. He inherited a fortune. His talent wasn't in making money, but in spending it. He spent plenty on himself but also gave generously to his community. The effects of this charity pleasingly dovetailed with his political ambitions, making him popular and quickly pushing him up the political ladder, as was demonstrated in 1767, when he turned a disaster into an opportunity. A February fire that started in a building Hancock owned spread overnight and consumed twenty structures, leaving fifty families homeless. The House of Representatives responded with £400 for relief. Hancock matched that amount and also made a donation of firewood for the poor for the remainder of the winter. Boston thanked Hancock by electing him to the House.

Tory Peter Oliver characterized Hancock as a fool with deep pockets under the spell of Sam Adams, "so thorough a Machiavellian" who would whisper in Hancock's ear "in the same Manner that the Devil is represented seducing Eve." Hancock, according to Oliver, "was as closely attached to the hindermost Part of Mr. Adams as the Rattles are affixed to the Tail of a Rattle Snake."[1]

For Sam Adams, these were uneasy times. His prominence in the triumphant wake of the Stamp Act's repeal made him a target for those whose property was wrecked and reputations soiled during the crisis. Some raised questions about Adams's work as a tax collector. He had fallen far behind in turning over to the town taxes from his assigned ward. Was he crooked? Was he an embezzler?

Maybe, but if so, he wasn't spending his ill-gotten gains on himself. The man wore frayed clothes and lived in a dilapidated house. Possibly, though, he was using his position for political advantage. By overlooking tax debts, he could win votes and favors. Whether Adams embezzled, bargained for a political edge, or simply failed to do his job, his enemies had a point. Because of Adams's ineptitude, corruption, or dishonesty, the town was being cheated, and some people were not paying their fair share of taxes.

Adams had his excuses. Times were tough. The fire in 1760, the more recent smallpox epidemic, and economic blight had put many people in a bind. They couldn't pay their taxes, so he couldn't turn over sums the town expected. Indeed, other tax collectors were behind as well, although not to the extent Adams was.

But the town took legal action. His own ally, Otis, as attorney for the town, prosecuted Adams, who was eventually ordered to pay £1,463. Much of it was eventually paid back, but not all. An inspection of town records in 1772 showed that Adams still owed £50.[2]

Adams's days as a tax collector were over, and his predicament spattered his reputation. Tories would bludgeon him with the scandal for years. However, the affair did little damage to Adams's standing among Whigs. In 1767, townsmen again sent him to the House of Representatives. A writer submitting a letter to the Boston *Gazette* described qualifications for a representative. Wealth is not a requirement, said the writer: "on the contrary tho' he is intimately acquainted with poverty, yet if he is in all respects otherwise qualified his poverty should be no obstacle to his choice, especially if he has been proved and found faithful: because his virtues will surely keep him out of the reach of temptation than the riches of others."

Shopkeeper Harbottle Dorr wrote in the margin of his copy, "A true Character of Samuel Adams . . . who has always Proved himself a Steady wise Patriot in the Worst of Times."[3]

The Stamp Act was dead, but for merchants in Boston, times were still tough. They may have triumphed for the time being in their quarrel with king and Parliament, but they still needed to make money, and that seemed to be getting very difficult, with too many shopkeepers chasing too few customers. In seven years, the number of merchants had increased by nearly 50 percent, and the number of shopkeepers had tripled.

Then, at this moment of intense competition and thin profits, word came in summer 1767 that Parliament had devised another plan to squeeze Americans for taxes. This plan was embodied in the Townshend Acts, which would take effect November 20. Would this be the Stamp Act all over again? Would the Sons of Liberty rise up in anger again? At first, it didn't seem so. One day in August, about sixty Sons of Liberty gathered around the Liberty Tree not to hang effigies, but to drink the king's health.

In a way, the colonists had themselves to blame for Parliament's actions. Or perhaps the blame could be placed squarely at the feet of Benjamin Franklin. If any one man spoke for all the colonies, it was Franklin. He was living in London and serving as an agent–a lobbyist–for both Pennsylvania and New York. His job was to advocate on behalf of the two colonies to members of Parliament, British authorities, and anyone who would listen. Other colonies had agents. But because of Franklin's stature, his opinions were received as the views of all Americans.

In urging Parliament to kill the Stamp Act, Franklin had said that Americans readily acknowledged Parliament's right to levy "external" taxes on Americans, but not "internal" taxes. Taxes on newspapers and legal documents, as proposed with the Stamp Act, were "internal." "External" taxes, according to Franklin's reasoning, were duties on imports, such as tea and glass.

Many in Parliament found the distinction absurd. A tax is a tax. If Parliament has the authority to impose one tax, it has the authority to impose the other. One man who found the internal-external tax distinction silly was Charles Townshend, who became chancellor of the exchequer in 1766. Townshend laughed at the American argument and let it be known that there must yet be a painless way to extract taxes from the Americans.

Parliament, taking Townshend at his word, reduced a land tax in England and then challenged Townshend to replace those lost taxes with new taxes from America. So the Townshend Acts represented Townshend's answer to Parliament's challenge and to Franklin's assertion that Parliament had every right to impose "external" duties. The Townshend Acts added new products to the list of goods for which an import duty must be paid. Duties would now be collected on five varieties of glass, on red and white lead, on painters' colors, on sixty-seven grades of paper, and on tea.

These taxes were irritating enough to Americans, but there was more. The acts included other measures to prevent colonists from obstructing tax collectors. For example, the acts specifically allowed the general use of writs of assistance, thus obliterating any lingering doubts about the authority of customs officials to break into holds and warehouses.

The acts also stipulated that the duties collected from Americans would be used to pay judges and civil officers in America. This sounded reasonable enough: American taxes going to pay officials serving in America. Colonial legislatures would not have to set aside other tax money for those salaries. However, this meant that the colonists, through their elected lawmakers, would have no leverage against those officials. Colonial legislatures would not be able to cut off salaries to key officials whom lawmakers didn't like.

Furthermore, the acts provided for the establishment of the juryless Vice Admiralty Courts in Boston, Philadelphia, and Charleston, thus ensuring that any cases related to the duties were heard by a judge beholden to the king and not to American juries sympathetic to merchants.

The Townshend Acts also set up a new customs office in Boston that would be in charge of customs throughout all of British North America, as well as Bermuda and the Bahamas. Boston would be the center of customs enforcement in North America. Five commissioners would run the office.

By late October, Townshend was dead, but the acts he contrived lived on. They would go into effect in November as planned. As with the Stamp Act, merchants and the Sons of Liberty had months to prepare. Bernard was nervous. He grumbled that a small faction was again stirring up trouble:

> The minds of the common people are poisoned to a great degree; so that (to use an expression of one of their own partisans) their bloods are set on boiling. It is a melancholic consideration that this rich and populous town should be thus distracted and disgraced by a set of desperadoes (perhaps not a dozen), whose own ruined or insignificant fortunes make the distraction of their country a matter of indifference to them.[4]

One of the most strident voices was that of twenty-three-year-old Josiah Quincy Jr. Surviving a sickly infancy and overcoming the disadvantage of crossed eyes, Quincy proved a strong student, graduating from Harvard in 1763 and acquiring along the way a fascination for Shakespeare. Later, upon taking a master of arts degree, he "pronounced the English oration" on the subject of patriotism.[5] He studied law under Oxenbridge Thacher and by 1767 was showing promise as an up-and-coming attorney. Josiah's brother Samuel affectionately called him "Wilkes" because, like John Wilkes, Josiah had crossed eyes and a fiercely radical point of view.

Fired by the implications by the Townshend Acts, Josiah Quincy submitted in the fall of 1767 two articles to the *Gazette* under the name Hyperion. He all but invited the bloodshed to begin:

> In defence of our civil and religious rights, we dare to oppose the world; with the God of armies on our side, even the God, who fought our fathers' battles, we fear not the hour of trial, though the host of our enemies should cover the field like locusts. . . . For, under God we are determined that, wheresoever, whensoever, or howsoever we shall be called to make our exit, we will die freemen. Well do we know that all the regalia of this world cannot dignify the death of a villain, nor diminish the ignominy

> with which a slave shall quit his existence. Neither can it taint the unblemished honour of a son of freedom, though he should make his departure on the already prepared gibbet, or be dragged to the newly erected scaffold for execution.[6]

His was a lonely voice. No one else was quite ready for such talk of armies and battles, let alone gibbets and scaffolds. The violence of the Stamp Act riots appalled and frightened many Bostonians, including many of those most opposed to the stamps. The destruction of the Hutchinson house made clear how easily violence could get out of hand. Many people were also afraid the violence would only harden attitudes in London and mark Boston as an unruly outpost overrun with frenzied mobs. Articles appeared under the names of town selectmen asking people to refrain from "all outrage" or lawlessness. Otis, presiding over a town meeting, denounced rioting: "[N]o possible circumstances, though ever so oppressive could be supposed sufficient to justify private tumults and disorders." Relief, he said, should be sought "in a legal and constitutional way."[7] An article in the *Boston Gazette* called for peace and thrift: "Let the persons and properties of our most inveterate enemies be safe. Let not a hair of their scalps be touched. Let this be the language of all,–no mobs, no confusions, no tumults. Save your money and save your country."[8]

Sam Adams and most other radicals recognized that armed resistance was rash. They also understood that the rioting, for all the noise and attention it got, was less effective than other tools. Experience from the Stamp Act crisis had demonstrated that the best way to get Parliament's attention was to strike at British pocketbooks. That meant nonimportation, or, to use a word not yet coined, boycotts. Such a boycott of British imports required vigorous, unified support throughout the colonies, and that required time and organization.

Meanwhile, Boston acted on its own to revive and strengthen the earlier movement to curb imports and to foster local production. At a town meeting in October, townsmen passed a resolution to discourage "excessive use of Foreign Superfluities." The town asked people to "lessen the use" of a such imported items as hats, gloves, shoes, nails, gold and silver thread, lace, gold and silver buttons, snuff, mustard, "all sort of Millinary" ware, clocks and watches, "Muffs, Furrs, and Tipetts," stays, linseed oil, glue, silk and cotton velvets, and cheese. Townsmen also voted to encourage the use of American-made glass and paper.[9]

Cutting back on imports was a hardship for consumers and well-to-do merchants but a catastrophe for some marginal businesses struggling to exist. Take, for example, the enterprise of Jane Mecom. By this time Mecom, now fifty-five, was a widow using all her wits and energy to make ends meet. In late 1766, she had made arrangements for brother Benjamin's London landlady to send her fabrics and paper patterns of London fashions. Mecom hoped to sell these in Boston. The goods arrived in May. By November, advertisements were appearing in Boston newspapers: "to be sold by Jane Mecom at her house . . . a few articles of Millinary . . . all new from London" and "made from the newest Fashion Patterns with Care and Expedition." By December, the venture was faltering. She wrote her brother, "It proves a Litle unlucky for me that our People have taken it in their heads to be so Excesive Frugal at this Time."[10]

Amid all this, Mecom wrestled with crushing depression over the recent deaths of loved ones, especially that of her nineteen-year-old daughter, Polly. Writing to thank Franklin for the money to support her business, Mecom's letter overflowed with grief and despair: "I am not unsenceable of the obligation you contineualy Lay me under but Realy my Spirits are so much Broken with this Last Hevy Stroke of Provedenc that I am not capable of Expressing my self as I ought. Oh My Brother she was Every thing to me."[11]

In December, Bostonians pored over the first edition of the *Chronicle*, a new weekly newspaper in Boston. Filling much of the front page of the first edition was an excerpt from a letter by "a Farmer in Pennsylvania." The "Farmer" was actually Philadelphia lawyer John Dickinson. His letters, which appeared in newspapers throughout the colonies, would be an early rallying cry for Americans to unite against efforts of Britain's Parliament to tax colonists.

So at first glance the paper seemed, like the *Boston Gazette*, on the side of Boston Whigs. However, the same issue had a scalding criticism of British politician William Pitt, a hero to the Whigs. So this was not a Whig trumpet. But what was it?

The publishers of the new paper were two Scotsmen. One was John Mein, who after arriving in Boston three years before, took over a shop, the London Book Store, which sold, besides books, linen and "excellent bottled Bristol beer."[12] Mein also established a lending library. A fee of one pound, eight shillings per year would give a reader access to twelve hundred books from his store on the north side of King Street. He touted it as the first such library in New England: "Something of this kind has been long wanted, to amuse the Man of leisure; to afford an elegant and agreeable relaxation to the minds of Men of business, and to insinuate knowledge and instruction, under the veil of entertainment to the FAIR SEX."[13] Mein eventually teamed with Scotsman John Fleeming to establish a print shop with two presses and seven frames of type. From their presses came such titles as *The Vicar of Wakefield* and *Four Dissertations on the Reciprocal Advantages of a Perpetual Union between Great Britain and the American Colonies*.[14]

Now, with the *Chronicle*, Mein and Fleeming were newspaper publishers. From the first edition, the editors aimed for the *Chronicle* to be independent and evenhanded, to be a forum for Whig and Tory opinion. That noble intention would soon fall by the wayside after the *Gazette* printed a letter from "Americus" that heaped abuse on the *Chronicle* and implied that Mein was a Jacobite. In the context of that time and place, such an accusation was the worst insult imaginable. Jacobites were supporters of the deposed Stuart royal family. The last Stuart king had been ousted in 1688, but there were still Jacobites who denied the legitimacy of George III as king and sought restoration of a Catholic Stuart king. Thus, with the mere word "Jacobite," Americus announced to Boston that Mein might well be a traitor and, almost as shocking in Puritan Boston, a Catholic. Americus produced no supporting facts. But everyone knew Mein was a Scot, and many assumed Scotland was awash with Jacobites. Americus knew well how best to smear Mein.

In choosing to enter the prickly business of newspaper publishing, Mein should have had a thicker skin and let the insult pass. But that was not his nature. Early in the new year, 1768, Mein stormed into the offices of the *Gazette* demanding to know the identity of Americus. The letter was likely the handiwork of Otis. That's what Mein thought. But editor Edes refused to say. Mein stalked out but returned the next day. Again Edes remained silent. That evening, on the streets of Boston, Mein came upon Gill, Edes's partner and a man much smaller than Mein. When Gill failed to give Mein the answers he wanted, Mein cracked his walking stick against Gill's head. Gill survived. Mein paid a fine and dealt with civil damages. Meanwhile, the *Chronicle* veered to the Tory side, and Mein's name soared to the top of the Whigs' list of enemies.

The Townshend Acts generated smoke but not the fire that rose up with the Stamp Act. Three times at Boston's town meetings, radical Whigs called for a boycott of British-made goods. Three times that failed. A similar proposal came before the House of Representatives and was crushed.

Why didn't the Townshend Acts generate a more explosive reaction? The Townshend duties, except for the tax on tea, touched few. Lawmakers in rural western Massachusetts would never bluster over a tax on paints for portrait painters or for the lead in windows of Boston mansions. The Townshend duties, unlike the stamp tax, were no big deal to most people in Massachusetts.

Even so, Sam Adams and his cohorts still hoped to drum up a united outcry from all colonies similar to that put forward earlier by the

Stamp Act Congress. To that end, the Otis-Adams faction drew up a series of resolutions protesting the Townshend Acts. Otis, Adams, and their allies' plan was to get these resolutions through the Massachusetts House, and then send them on as a letter to the assemblies of each of the other colonies for their consideration and, it was hoped, endorsement. The Massachusetts Whigs hoped by this method to deliver to authorities in Britain a powerful message that the Townshend Acts were unacceptable. These resolutions, contained in what became known as the Massachusetts Circular Letter, were intended to be as striking and vigorous as Virginia's reported response to the Stamp Act.

But first, the Massachusetts House had to actually approve the letter, and many Representatives refused to go along. With representatives from western Massachusetts standing firmly against, the House rejected the letter by a two-to-one ratio.

But Sam Adams was not content to let matters stand. He was now clerk of the House, where he was in the best position to choreograph activities in the 109-member chamber. Adams showed his skills as dance master during the cold weeks of February 1768. Boston was an expensive place to live, and, as usual, many of the representatives from western Massachusetts had quietly left town for home to save money. The House was not officially adjourned, but it seemed not to matter. No important business was planned.

Then amid the empty seats, Adams and his allies brought out the letter again and managed to jam it through. Then for good measure, the House ordered that the earlier vote, the one in which the letter was defeated, be erased from the House Journal. The maneuver was sneaky but within the rules. Soon the Massachusetts Circular Letter would go out to each of the other twelve colonies.

The letter restated many familiar arguments: Americans, as British subjects, have an "equitable claim to the full enjoyment of the fundamental rules of the British constitution"; one of those "sacred and irrevocable" rules asserts that "what a man has honestly acquired is absolutely his own, which he may freely give, but cannot be taken away from him without his consent"; and because Americans are not represented in Parliament, the Parliament's imposition of duties on Americans amounted to the taking of property without consent.[15]

The letter also pointed out the problem of salaries for judges and other civil officials. Appointed by the Crown and paid by the Crown, such officials were left "independent of the people," a situation that might endanger "happiness and security."[16]

Furthermore, the letter raised the specter of the colonies being overrun with troops and officious customs men. Commissioners of the newly established customs office in Boston could "make as many appointments as they think fit, and to pay the appointees what sum they please, for whose malconduct they are not accountable; from whence it may happen that officers of the Crown may be multiplied to such a degree as to become dangerous to the liberty of the people."[17]

The letter anticipated the possibility that Parliament, and maybe even other colonies, might consider the most obvious answer to the complaint of taxation without representation: American representation in Parliament. Massachusetts wanted no part of it. Without even gathering opinions from other colonies, its representatives stuck a dagger in that idea. It would be worse than the status quo:

"[C]onsidering the utter impractability of ever their ever being fully and equally represented in Parliament, and the great expense that must unavoidably attend even a partial representation there, this House think that a taxation of their constituents, even without their consent, grievous as it is, would be preferable to any representation that could be admitted for them there."[18]

Meanwhile, the letter went on, "enemies of the colonies" have led government ministers and Parliament to believe that the Massachusetts House was "factious, disloyal, and having a disposition to make themselves independent of the mother county." Not so, harrumphed the House. "[T]he charge is unjust."[19]

So, the Massachusetts House blew the trumpets, and within weeks, Boston merchants beat the drums. In March, 102 agreed to refrain from importing from Britain for one year starting June 1. This was far from unanimous: At least forty-one importers refused to sign. Also, those who did sign hedged their bets: the boycott would go ahead only if merchants in both Philadelphia and New York agreed to a similar boycott. Boston merchants were not about to go it alone and risk losing business to their counterparts to the south. Word of this agreement went out.

The same month, merchant Rowe jotted in his diary about a dinner marking the second anniversary of the repeal of the Stamp Act. As usual, the king, queen, and royal family topped the requisite list of toasts. This time, though, unlike the previous two anniversaries, there was no toast for Parliament. Rowe also noted that "a considerable Mob of young fellows & negroes got together this Evening & made great Noise & Hallooing." Rowe wrote that about eight hundred appeared on King Street and at the Liberty Tree and then made their way into the North End to the home of a customs inspector, "but did him no damage." Rowe noted that two effigies were seen hanging from the Liberty Tree.[20]

TEN

RIPE FOR RIOT

Amid the rising tensions, John Hancock did his bit to heighten the drama. He made it known that he would not allow any customs men on his vessels. To the customs office, that sounded like an invitation.

On April 8, Hancock's brigantine *Lydia* tied up at Hancock's Wharf with goods from London. Two tidewaiters were sent to board the ship. Hancock, despite his threat, followed the law and let them come on board. However, while the law allowed tidewaiters on deck, it banned them from belowdecks without permission. Hence the commotion when the next evening, one of them, Owen Richards, was found below pawing through the cargo looking for goods that required a duty. He poked around for about three hours before Hancock and eight or ten others, unarmed, came aboard demanding Richards come on deck. Richards refused. Hancock asked to see his orders. Richards handed them up. Hancock inspected them and found no date. Hancock asked if Richards had a writ of assistance. Richards said no. At Hancock's orders, two seamen grabbed Richards and hauled him out of the hold and onto the deck. Now Hancock asked Richards if he wanted to search the vessel. Richards said no.[1] He was let go and scuttled away.

The incident put the customs office in an uproar. How dare Hancock treat an agent so roughly. The customs office demanded that Hancock be prosecuted. The attorney general looked at the facts: the men who confronted Richards were unarmed; Richards had gone belowdecks illegally; Richards had explicitly said that he did not want to search the vessel. Plainly, prosecution was not warranted. Hancock was off the hook.

This was but the latest in a long trail of defeats and setbacks for the customs office. In a confidential report to London months earlier, the customs commissioners summarized their pathetic situation.

Smuggling was rampant, yet over thirty months they had netted only six seizures, and of those, only one was successfully prosecuted. Meanwhile, newspapers spread reports of tumults in Boston and, thus, "the spirit which first shewed itself in this town, was diffused thro' the neighboring Provinces, where the people seem to be as ripe for riot, and mischief, as they are here."[2]

The commissioners let it be known that, if duties were to be collected, some muscular show of power was essential: "[N]ow, that the right of Parliament to lay any taxes whatever in the Colonies, is denied, we have every reason to believe that we shall find it totally impracticable to inforce the execution of the Revenue Laws, untill the hand of Government is properly strengthened."[3]

We can imagine the pleasure of the customs men when in May they saw in the harbor the brooding outlines of the *Romney*, a fifty-gun warship arrived from Halifax. Brought in at the request of the enlarged and emboldened customs office, the warship was positioned to remind colonists of just who was in charge.

The *Romney*'s captain wasted no time in giving the town a poke in the eye. He dispatched from the ship a small boat, well-manned and armed, to prowl among incoming merchant vessels, to stop and board ships, and to seize mariners to fill in gaps in the *Romney*'s crew. Impressment–nothing short of bombarding the town could have produced more fury, especially among the common workmen and mariners, the usual quarry of impressment gangs. Even Hutchinson was dismayed. Just the fear of impressment was disruptive because masters of coastal vessels, so important for shifting goods among coastline communities, no longer felt free to come and go from the harbor. In addition, impressment just added to the enormous tension in the town: "[I]t adds more fewel to the great stock among us before."[4]

Among the men snatched by the *Romney*'s impressment gang was Thomas Furlong, a mariner grabbed off the *Boston Packet*. The impressment happened so quickly that Furlong didn't have a chance to collect his belongings or his pay. His mates on the *Packet* seethed, but what could be done? By and by, that vessel tied up at a wharf to prepare for its next voyage. Then, one day in June, a small boat launched from the *Romney* glided toward the *Packet*. Aboard were an officer and two midshipmen from the *Romney* and none other than Furlong. They were bringing the mariner to the *Packet* to collect what he left behind.

The crew of the *Packet* saw what was happening, as did other workers near the wharf. They streamed toward the *Packet*, and soon a crowd was shouting insults. Outnumbered and unnerved, the *Romney* men rowed away, leaving Furlong behind. It was a bloodless rescue. Mariners and wharf workers had defied the British navy and won.

That incident was a prelude to another, more violent dockside confrontation that month involving the *Liberty*, a sloop owned by

Hancock. Upon arrival at Hancock's Wharf late one day in May, two tidewaiters were dispatched as usual to stay on the vessel overnight. The next day crews unloaded the cargo. All seemed to go strictly by the book: cargo inspected, documents signed, duties on goods all paid in full by Hancock.

But to the customs office, something seemed askew. First of all, the cargo of twenty-five pipes of Madeira was surprisingly small for so large a vessel. Second, about that same time, John Marshall, the master of another vessel Hancock owned, was found dead. He had overly exerted himself while unloading his own vessel, so the story went. This was odd because shipmasters normally did not do the work of unloading or loading their own ships.

The customs men were puzzled but did nothing until Thomas Kirk, a tidewaiter who had been stationed overnight on the *Liberty*, came up with a new story about what happened that night. He now said Marshall had confronted him with "proposals" for landing the wine illegally. Kirk didn't give the response Marshall was looking for, so Marshall and five or six muscular helpers forced Kirk into a cabin and nailed the hatch shut. For three hours, Kirk heard the thumping of cargoes being moved. Then the noise stopped, the hatch was opened, and Kirk was let go with a warning. Marshall's death from "overheating" was likely a heart attack while illegally unloading cargo that night. What about Kirk's partner, the other tidewaiter who was also supposed to be on board? He could not confirm the story, saying he had been asleep. Kirk said he wasn't even there, that he was drunk and had gone home.

Even though Kirk's tale had no corroboration, the customs officials were thrilled. They had enough evidence, they thought, to prove cargo had been landed illegally. Now they were going to take their prize: Hancock's *Liberty*. They would seize the ship, as the law demanded. That would be tricky. It would have to be pulled off jointly by the navy and the customs office working together. But with so much anger along the shore against the navy and the customs men, a clash of some kind was almost certain.

The assignment to reel in the big fish went to Joseph Harrison, the customs collector. Though "so ill as to be just able to stirr abroad,"[5] Harrison roused himself and, with Benjamin Hallowell, the customs comptroller, set out for Hancock's Wharf at about dusk on a Friday in June. On the way to the wharf they met up with Harrison's eighteen-year-old son, Richard, who joined them. About the same time, a small boat packed with well-armed military men rowed toward the *Liberty* from the *Romney*, anchored in the harbor.

On the *Liberty*, on the wharf, and on shore, seamen, laborers, and shore workers could see something was up. Many bombarded the men in the small boat with stones as it approached the wharf. Preoccupied with the *Romney* men, the crowd around the *Liberty* let the Harrisons and Hallowell pass. The elder Harrison boarded the *Liberty* and "put the Kings Mark on the Main Mast"[6] as a signal that the vessel was now officially in possession of the customs office.

Once men from the *Romney* came onto the wharf, Joseph Harrison turned over the *Liberty* to them. While the *Romney* men had "special directions" not to fire on civilians "but in the very last extremity," the mob didn't know that and gave way after some scuffling. The *Romney* men boarded the *Liberty*, cut her lines, and "carried her off in triumph." She was soon snugly anchored "under the Guns of the Romney." Wrote a navy man, "[W]e happily accomplished our purpose, at the expense of some blows and bruizes of no great consequence."[7]

Meanwhile, the Harrisons and Hallowell, after handing off the *Liberty*, walked off the wharf unmolested. But by this time the goings-on had attracted many others to the shore. A crowd of four hundred to five hundred took note of the three men. As the elder Harrison wrote later:

> [W]e had scarce got into the street before we were pursued by the Mob which by this time was increased to a great Multitude. The onset was begun by throwing Dirt at me, which was presently succeeded by Volleys of Stones, Brickbatts, Sticks or anything that came to hand: In this manner I run the Gauntlet near 200 Yards, my poor Son following behind endeavoring to shelter his Father by receiving the strokes of many of the Stones thrown at him till at length he became equally an object of their Resentment, was knocked down and then laid hold of by the Legs, Arms and Hair of his head, and in that manner dragged along the Kennel [canal? ditch?] in a most barbarous and cruel manner.[8]

While all this was happening, someone staggered the elder Harrison with a whack in the chest: "I verily believe if I had fallen, I should never have got up again, the People to all appearance being determined on Blood and Murder."[9] But then, as the crowd was focused on Harrison's son, a courageous man grabbed the elder Harrison and rushed him away to safety. Still, he was so badly hurt that he spent the next two days in bed.

The younger Harrison, too, was plucked from out of the mayhem, "tho' pulling and hauling between Friends and Enemies had like to have been fatal to him."[10] Meanwhile, Hallowell was likewise set upon, and likewise rescued. He received cuts to the back of his head and to his cheek.

The Harrisons and Hallowell were safe, but the mob was not done. By 9:00 p.m., the mass–estimates range from five hundred to three thousand–of "chiefly sturdy boys and negroes"[11] gathered at

Hallowell's house. Told he was not there, they broke windows and moved on to the Harrison house. Before they arrived, someone warned Joseph Harrison's wife, who, with her remaining brood, slipped off to the safety of a house nearby. As at the Hallowell house, the mob was told no one was home. Again, the mob was satisfied with a few broken windows and went on, now to the home of yet another customs man, where it broke more windows. Around this time, someone reminded the boisterous throng that the elder Harrison had a fine little boat that he sailed around the harbor for pleasure. Off they went, pulled the boat out of the water, dragged it to the Liberty Tree "where she was formally condemned," and then to the Common, where it was set ablaze.[12]

The elder Harrison later wrote about the incident. After nearly losing his son and his life, after the damage to his house and the torching of his dear sailboat, all because of a matter involving John Hancock, Harrison's opinion of Hancock was surprisingly sympathetic. Harrison wrote as if the rich merchant himself was a kind of captive of malevolent forces. Hancock, wrote Harrison:

> happens to be the Idol of the Mob, just as Mr. Wilkes is in England. Hancock and Liberty being the Cry here, as Wilkes and Liberty is in London! tho' in other respects Mr. Hancock is a generous and benevolent Gentleman but unluckily subject to the influence of Otis and other Incendiaries. . . . On this Occasion I can not help observing the unhappiness of Mr. Hancocks Situation: He is a Young Gentleman of the Largest Fortune in this Town of a generous benevolent Disposition and very charitable to the Poor. These Qualities must necessarily render him extremely Popular and being unluckily connected with Otis and the other Ringleaders of the Faction they have artfully drawn him by little and little into all their Measures and have now placed him at the Head of their Party; tho' I verily believe in his own Mind he disapproves of their Proceedings, but being naturally of a timid pliable Temper is frequently bullied into a Compliance with them the contrary to his own Inclination.[13]

The *Liberty* riot was over, but the uproar was just beginning. On one side were the customs office, the governor, and their allies, alarmed and furious at the attack on customs men. On the other side were merchants and wharf workers angry at what appeared to be an arbitrary and unjust seizure.

Four of five customs commissioners were so fearful they slipped out of Boston with their families to the *Romney*. Sixty-seven people in all joined the navy men on the warship. For Ann Hulton, sister of Commissioner Henry Hulton, the experience was terrifying, but also a bit thrilling. She wrote to a friend in Liverpool, England, how "Marines with bayonets fixed" took her and more than sixty others by barge to the warship, where they were "well accommodated, & very genteelly entertain[d]" for nine days.[14] They were eventually sheltered at Castle William.

The one customs commissioner who did not at first flee the town was John Temple, the former surveyor general of customs, and Bernard's old enemy. Temple, who agreed with Bostonians who opposed the very existence of this commission, was seen as a friend of the Whigs and therefore left in peace by the mobs. He could have remained in Boston. But for appearances' sake, he eventually moved out to the island as well to join the other commissioners.

Life for the commissioners on the island was not only bearable, it was pleasant. To Ann Hulton, it was like "one of the Publick water drinking places in England"–a spa. They had regular visitors from Boston, who would secretly slip out to the island and back by boat. Rare was the dinner with fewer than twenty people. The governor came out and, over tea, confessed to the exiles that if the next two years are anything like the past two years, the British Empire "is at an End."[15]

For Hancock, the seizure of the *Liberty* forced him to make a crucial personal decision. As a businessman, it was in his interest to get the *Liberty* back so it could resume moving cargo. Initially, he arranged to do that, working out a deal with the Custom House to provide a personal bond in return for the ship. Under this deal, he promised to hand over the vessel if a court ultimately ruled against him. But then, in his parlor, he met with Sam Adams, Otis, Warren, and other key Whigs. Over glasses of Madeira, they urged him to abandon the arrangement. Such an agreement, he was told, would be seen as a political surrender. To Adams, there was also an important symbolic importance of letting the vessel in full view of all Boston remain under the control of the warship, a reminder to all of what was at issue. The name of the vessel gave the symbolism clarity: *Liberty* shackled. Hancock finally agreed. Hallowell received a midnight visit from Warren informing him that Hancock had called off the deal.

On a rainy morning later that same eventful month, June 1768, throngs met at "Liberty Hall"–that is, around the Liberty Tree–in response to notices posted by the Sons of Liberty. After the mass grew into the hundreds, the boisterous procession began toward Faneuil Hall, passing under the windows of the Town House, which Bostonians were now starting to call the State House.

The mob crowded into Faneuil Hall, and in a kind of parliamentary alchemy, the so-called "meeting" of the Sons of Liberty was adjourned and a formal town meeting was brought to order. The hall was too small, so the assembly poured out into the street, marched noisily past the State House again, and filed into the bright sanctuary of Old South, nearly square with balconies along three sides, the great pulpit rising high in front of a tall arched window with clear glass. The town meeting came to order again, and in a few minutes a petition was read out asking Bernard to order the provocative *Romney* removed from the harbor.

With a roar, the mob gave the petition its approval. Quickly a committee of twenty-one was named to take the document to the governor, who was at his country home at Jamaica Plain about five miles away. No fewer than eleven carriages set off with Otis, Sam Adams, Warren, Hancock, and others. Bernard received the twenty-one, patiently heard Otis present the petition, served wine all around, and said he would respond in the morning.

Back at Old South, the town meeting considered a related matter, a set of instructions for the town's four representatives in the House: Otis, Sam Adams, Hancock, and Thomas Cushing. Like the petition, these instructions had been drawn up ahead of time. Their author was a newcomer to Boston and a new member of the circle of opposition to the government. He was John Adams, the same man who traveled up from Braintree to take notes at the Writ of Assistance case in 1761. In the intervening years, Adams had established a law practice in Braintree, married, started a family, and dabbled in local politics. When the Stamp Act crisis arose, he submitted long legalistic articles to the *Gazette* arguing against the tax. These articles won admirers in Boston and drew him into the circle of men who opposed Bernard, Hutchinson, and their allies.

For the young man from Braintree, Boston represented excitement, a wealth of potential clients, and a possible future in politics. John Adams moved his family from a farmhouse in Braintree to within steps of Faneuil Hall, the very center of the political whirl. His instructions to the representatives were stunning:

> [W]e are continually alarmed with rumours and reports of new revenue Acts to be passed, new importations of Officers and Pensioners to suck the life-blood of the body politick, while it is streaming from the veins: fresh arrival of ships of war to be a still severer restraint upon our trade; and the arrival of a military force to dragoon us into passive obedience. . . . [It] is our desire that you inquire and use your endeavors to promote a parliamentary enquiry for the authors and propagators of such alarming rumours and . . . that you forward, if you think it expedient, in the House of Representatives, resolutions, that every such person who shall solicit or promote the importation of troops at this time, is an enemy to this town and province, and a disturber of the peace and good order of both.[16]

This would get the governor's attention: if Bernard dared to call in more military, he would be an enemy of Boston and Massachusetts. Furthermore, the Adams instructions asserted "loyalty and duty to our most gracious sovereign" and "a reverence and due subordination to the British parliament" as the supreme lawmakers–"in all cases of necessity."[17] In all cases of necessity? How subtle. There might be exceptions to Parliament's supremacy. Parliament's authority was not absolute.

As for the petition to Bernard, the governor did respond as promised. He would do what he could to stem impressments. He also said he didn't have power over the *Romney*, but by this time the warship had been repositioned to seem less threatening to the town.

Controversy about the *Liberty* continued. The Sons of Liberty complained that there was no need in the first place for the customs men to seize it. The vessel and its cargo would have been perfectly safe docked at the wharf. The customs office answered with a trap. It secretly arranged for another seized vessel, a schooner loaded with molasses, to be tied at a wharf guarded by two customs men. Thirty men appeared, shut the customs men in a cabin, and unloaded the molasses. Officials at the Custom House gloated. That just proved that the Sons of Liberty were wrong. The town was effectively lawless.

The Sons of Liberty answered back. A threat went out to the schooner's captain. Before long, the molasses magically reappeared in the schooner's hold. But the Sons of Liberty did not win all the confrontations. Sometimes all it took was one brave and clever customs man to defeat the mob. On the night of July 15, a mob showed up at the residence of customs official John Williams, whom the mob visited in March. Williams, fully armed, met the crowd in the courtyard. Shouts and taunts gave way to demands: mob leaders ordered Williams to appear at the Liberty Tree the next day to announce his resignation. Williams refused. He said, however, that he would be glad to meet with the mob at noon the next day on King Street near the State House. The mob wavered. Some assented, and the mob drifted away.

More than a thousand curious people appeared the next day on King Street to witness the drama's next act. Williams appeared, as promised, but not on the street. He stepped out on the balcony of the State House looking down King Street. He announced that he would answer any questions. If anyone had objections to his role as customs inspector general, speak out. He would be happy to respond.

Silence.

He stood waiting. Murmurs could be heard, but no one spoke up. Fifteen minutes passed. Where were the voices of the Sons of Liberty? More waiting. A meaningless shout from someone in the crowd broke the tension. Laughter rippled through the crowd. Soon the disappointed audience left King Street. Williams went home, victorious.

ELEVEN

GLOOM AND UNEASINESS

As Bostonians awaited the next bit of mayhem on the streets and wharves, Boston merchants heard from New York and Philadelphia about the proposed boycott of British goods. New York merchants agreed to the plan. Philadelphia merchants did not. The boycott thus collapsed before it began. As for the Massachusetts Circular Letter–the powerful statement of protest against the Townshend duties–the answers from other colonies were tepid. Only some assemblies endorsed the tough resolutions contained in the letter. In most colonies, the heart wasn't there to turn bluster into action.

Then the new British secretary of state for American affairs, Wills Hill, known as Lord Hillsborough, went out of his way to kick the hornet's nest. Years later, King George III would say that he had never met a man "with less judgment" than Hillsborough.[1] Certainly Hillsborough demonstrated his penchant for lack of good sense with his response to the Massachusetts Circular Letter. Hillsborough ordered that Governor Bernard demand the Massachusetts House rescind the letter. If the House refused, Bernard was to prorogue, or suspend, the House. Thus the elected House of Representatives had to follow Hillsborough's command or be forbidden from meeting. Furthermore, Hillsborough sent letters to the governors of each of the other twelve colonies ordering that any assembly that endorsed the Massachusetts Circular Letter should likewise be forbidden to meet.

Thus Hillsborough made the most radical, extreme, paranoid American arguments seem reasonable: the British authorities were stifling American democratic institutions just for disagreeing with the British government.

Hillsborough's demand set Massachusetts on fire. "We are asked to rescind," roared Otis in the Massachusetts House. "Let Britain rescind her measures, or the colonies are lost to her forever."[2] Rural lawmakers, who were earlier horrified by the Massachusetts Circular Letter, now joined Sam Adams and his allies in defending it. The Massachusetts House voted 92 to 17 not to rescind. The number 92 joined 45 as a symbol of liberty and defiance. Paul Revere crafted a silver bowl honoring the 92. In other colonies, lawmakers inflamed by Hillsborough's threats refused to kowtow. No colony voted to withdraw support for the Massachusetts letter.

Following the vote, Bernard did exactly as ordered: he prorogued the House of Representatives. Lawmakers could not legally meet again until the next spring. Meanwhile, the Custom House was paralyzed, its men terrified of working on the wharves or walking the streets, and Bernard was under pressure to give them the protection they needed to do their jobs. The sheriff and his assistants had neither the power nor the will to protect them, and it was laughable to think about calling out the local militia.

The customs office wanted Bernard to call in more military support. The *Romney* wasn't enough. Soldiers were needed to occupy the town. How could tidewaiters do their work–their legal work of enforcing the king's laws–in this atmosphere of intimidation? Bernard dearly wanted the military to come and restore his authority, and Major General Thomas Gage, the military commander in New York, wanted to send them. But Gage did not want to send any without a direct request from Bernard, and the governor, with his popularity plummeting, was reluctant to openly make such a request and make himself a target of mob reprisals.

The issue of shipping troops to Boston to control civilians would have touched a nerve under any circumstance. But at this time, the question was especially delicate because of shocking events earlier that year in London. Playing a starring role in this drama was none other than John Wilkes, the darling of mobs in Britain and idol to many Americans. Sorely in debt, Wilkes had returned to Britain from the Continent in early 1768 and promptly got himself re-elected to Parliament, which would have shielded him from arrest for his earlier run-ins with the law. But then Wilkes waived his privilege. He volunteered to pay the price for the "crimes" that had made him an outlaw since 1764. So off he went to prison. But it wasn't as simple as that. On the way to King's Bench Prison, a friendly mob intercepted the coach carrying Wilkes. The guards fled and the mob paraded with Wilkes through London streets. He had to finally disguise himself to flee his adorers and turn himself in.

In those days, prisoners with money could avoid bleak, dank cells for more tolerable prison apartments. Wilkes was broke, but someone else made sure the cross-eyed hero landed in a comfortable ground-floor suite. From this prison window, Wilkes could see open land used for gatherings, military drills, and picnics. From the first day Wilkes was in prison, crowds would gather on this ground, called St. George's Fields, to catch a glimpse of their champion. In early May, the crowds grew to an alarming size. They included many admirers of Wilkes's, but also many hungry souls suffering after a bitter winter of rising bread prices. Along with shouts of "Wilkes and liberty," someone was heard to mutter, "It's as well to be hanged as to starve."[3]

On May 6, authorities dispatched soldiers to St. George's Fields to tighten security. Initially, the presence of the troops did not ruffle the crowd. Indeed, the scene was almost festive. But on May 10, the crowd was so large and boisterous that prison guards feared a swarm of people would try to break into the prison to set Wilkes free. The guards urged the soldiers to force the mob back from the prison entrance. When the soldiers pushed, the crowd responded with insults, and a detachment of soldiers went off in pursuit of one especially offensive man. That detachment soon cornered a fellow in a barn and shot him dead. It turned out to be the wrong man.

Word spread of the death of the innocent William Allen. Now the crowd started throwing rocks. Efforts to disperse the people failed. In the confusion, soldiers began firing on the crowd. Down fell five or six people.

The sullen crowd drifted away at last. However, as it spread through the city, so did word of events at St. George's Fields. Riots broke out among coal heavers, weavers, sawyers, and others. The anarchy lasted for days and was so great that the king considered abdicating.

The people of Boston received news of the St. George's Fields shooting in July. To many, the lesson was obvious: the danger of using soldiers for police duties. Word later reached Boston that no one would be held accountable for the deaths at St. George's Fields. The official message to the troops on duty at the shootings–termed a massacre by some–was that "his majesty highly approves of the conduct of both the officers and men."[4]

With this news on everyone's mind, no wonder Bernard fretted about calling in soldiers to Boston. He also knew that his Council should approve such a request, and he was certain that councillors would reject the idea, further demonstrating the governor's impotence and unpopularity. He just dithered, and by dithering antagonized the customs office, virtually his only allies. Bernard had lost respect from all sides. He longed to escape. Finally, he did go to his Council with a proposal to ask for troops. Sure enough, the Council rejected it. If Bernard were to request troops, he would have to do it alone, without the Council's support.

Eventually, Hillsborough saved Bernard by making the tough decision for him: Hillsborough ordered Gage to send soldiers to Boston. The orders called for Gage to station at least one regiment in Boston "to give every legal Assistance to the Civil Magistrate in the

Preservation of the Public Peace and to the officers of the Revenue in the Execution of the Laws of Trade & Revenue."[5]

Bernard also received instructions. These orders, dispatched after Hillsborough received word of the *Liberty* riots, called for Bernard to corral the perpetrators of the riots and consider shipping them to England for trial, investigate the disturbances, and have lawmakers meet outside of Boston, away from the mobs. Also, should the question of impressment come up, Bernard should note that impressment in America is perfectly legal.

Amid the hubbub over the Massachusetts Circular Letter and the *Liberty*, Boston merchants revived the idea of a boycott. In August, sixty merchants signed an agreement not to import from Great Britain. With the exception of a few products, such as gear for fisheries, nothing would be shipped in from Great Britain for one year beginning January 1, 1769, so the men promised. This time the agreement was unilateral; these Boston merchants would march on alone no matter what merchants in New York and Philadelphia did. Other Boston merchants came forward one by one to sign. Almost two hundred signed by the middle of the month, but more than a dozen refused.

Just as the Boston merchants hoped, merchants in other ports felt compelled to follow suit. Merchants elsewhere in the province–in Salem, Plymouth, Cape Ann, and Nantucket–drew up similar agreements. When word reached New York and Philadelphia, merchants in those two towns also agreed to a boycott.

Also in August, legal action involving the *Liberty* moved forward. A judge determined that Hancock had forfeited the vessel. The *Liberty* was thus offered for sale. No one in Boston dared to make a bid on it. Harrison, the very man attacked the day the *Liberty* was seized, finally bought the vessel and transformed it for service catching smugglers. It served that role until, less than a year later, a mob in Newport stormed it and burned it to the water line.

Meanwhile, authorities charged Hancock and five others with customs violations. Hancock cast about for a lawyer to represent him. As the richest man in Boston, he could have his pick. He chose John Adams.

Hancock was not the only man to recognize Adams. Governor Bernard also took note of the rising lawyer. More moderate than his cousin Sam and uneasy about the activities of the Sons of Liberty, John Adams still wavered about his political alliances. Bernard sought to entice Adams to his side with the offer of a lucrative and prestigious government position. If Adams accepted, he would have to quit as Hancock's lawyer. He would also have to hold his tongue–no more instructions implying that the governor was an enemy. Adams declined.

Bernard gave no official word that troops were on their way, but many Bostonians assumed so. One September morning, townspeople glancing in the direction of Beacon Hill saw at the summit a pole holding up a barrel. This was reminiscent of the days when Britain and France were at war and townspeople hoisted a tar barrel filled with turpentine above the hilltop. At the first sight of French masts, a watchman on the hilltop was to set the barrel alight as a signal to the countryside to come to Boston's aid.

But of course, in September 1768, the French and British were at peace. So why was the alarm erected? Clearly it was the handiwork of the Sons of Liberty. The "enemy" was the British military. Bernard wouldn't stand for this provocation. Soon Sheriff Greenleaf and several volunteers were dispatched to bring down the barrel. Greenleaf returned and reported that barrel was not a tar barrel at all, but a nail barrel, old and empty.

On the Monday night after the barrel incident, residents who crowded into Faneuil Hall for a town meeting found the hall buzzing with apprehension, heightened by the presence–right there in the middle of the hall–of four hundred muskets, cleaned and racked. The town's selectmen had, months before, removed the muskets from the hall's attic. They needed to be cleaned, so the selectmen said. However, once cleaned, the muskets were not put back in the attic but left ready for use on the floor of the hall, as if a threat were imminent. With the gleaming muskets in view, men sputtered about the expected arrival of the military to Boston. Some spoke openly about resistance, armed resistance; about seizing Castle William; and even about confronting the British troops as they attempted to come ashore on the island and into the town.

Otis took the floor, silencing the hubbub and then launching into a tirade, while also tamping down notions of armed resistance. By the time of this meeting, another warship had made its appearance near Boston. With that ship positioned as it was, any attempt to take the island military post was doomed. The town meeting would not propose any such action. The meeting instead brought forth resolutions carefully drafted beforehand. One asked Bernard to clarify his own hints about troops coming to Boston. Another created a committee to recommend further steps. The meeting ended with nothing settled.

The next evening, another town meeting. The same anger and apprehension charged the hall. First, a report was made about Bernard's cagey response: the governor said he received no "publick Letters"[6] notifying him that troops were being sent. Faneuil Hall rumbled with skeptical muttering.

Armed resistance, discouraged the night before, was now again being contemplated. More than one speaker underscored the need to fight an "enemy," always identified as France, as if the French army were massed in Dorchester. Everyone understood the charade. To baldly call for armed resistance against British soldiers was sedition.

Otis pointed to the muskets beckoning in the center of the hall as he roared out a call to arms against the "enemy." Someone put forth a motion to immediately distribute the muskets. More shouts and murmurs. Sam Adams, of all people, intervened. The time was not right, he said. He urged that the motion be defeated, which it was. The message from the leaders seemed to be mixed. Was it a call to arms or not? Someone asked for clarification. Otis pointed again to the muskets: "There are the Arms; when an attempt is made against your Liberties, they will be delivered."[7] The meeting then wound down. Before it was over, townsmen vowed "at the utmost peril of their Lives & Fortunes" to defend King George and British liberties.[8] But they also asserted their rights "to be consulted; and to give their free Consent in person, or by Representatives of their own free Election to the raising & keeping of a standing army among them."[9] They also called for a "convention" on September 22 that would be made up in a way identical or similar to the House of Representatives. This was provocative. Just the term "convention" was alarming. Today the word is benign. But then, in that context, it suggested upheaval. The term "convention" had been used in England for meetings at times of great crisis and in Boston when governor Andros was sent packing the previous century. Was this convention legal? The governor had dismissed the House. The town meeting was, in effect, usurping the governor's authority and calling the assembly back together.

In a further provocative act, the meeting voted to urge each householder in town–because of "a prevailing apprehension, in the Minds of many, of an approaching war with France"–to have at hand "a well fixed Fire Lock Musket Accoutrement and Ammunition."[10] Armed opposition to the British landing of troops seemed possible. That's what investors in London thought. When news reached England of these alarming activities, stock prices plummeted.

Boston's call went out, but the response was mixed. Hatfield, far to the west, spurned the invitation, calling Boston's ideas "unconstitutional, illegal and wholly unjustifiable, and what will give the enemies of our constitution the greatest joy; subversive of government, destructive of that peace and good order which is the cement of Society, and have a direct tendency to rivet our chains, and deprive us of our charter rights and privileges."[11]

View of Faneuil Hall in Boston, c. 1789. (*Library of Congress*)

Hatfield also poked a hole in Boston's phony claim of a possible French attack: if Boston was truly worried about the French, it would welcome the British soldiers. Ninety-two other towns did send delegates to the convention, but most of them were sent off with strict orders to be moderate. The country towns were not going to feed Boston's fire.

The convention came together at Faneuil Hall as planned, despite messages from Bernard that the meeting was illegal and should disperse. For six days delegates met, with Cushing, former speaker of the House, as chairman, and Sam Adams, clerk of the House, as secretary. In the end, the meeting produced nothing of consequence in Massachusetts, but it did further harden attitudes in London. Bernard's powerful relative and patron, Lord Barrington, learned about the convention and later wrote to Bernard that members of the assembly committed "high crimes and misdemeanors, if not treason."[12]

The convention also gave authorities in London good reason to believe that Boston was alone in this quarrel, and that the Massachusetts countryside was solidly loyal. This was true enough. By 1775, however, attitudes in the countryside would be vastly different.

While failing to generate any meaningful action, the now-forgotten convention demonstrated the willingness of most towns–even those in the conservative countryside–to meet in defiance of royal authority. As Thomas Hutchinson later wrote, "this represented a greater tendency towards a revolution in government, than any preceding measures in any of the colonies. The inhabitants of one town alone took upon them to convene an assembly from all the towns, that, in every thing but in name, would be a house of representatives; which, by the charter, the governor had the sole authority of convening."[13]

One by one, vessels packed with British soldiers arrived in Boston, and by the morning of October 1, 1768, twelve warships were anchored in the harbor, their broadside guns trained on the town. At noon that day, small boats crowded with armed men in red and scarlet pushed off from the warships and rowed toward Long Wharf. Thousands on shore watched in silence.

By the dozens and then hundreds, the soldiers hoisted themselves, their packs, pikes, muskets, belts, drums, and other gear out of the boats. Columns formed. Then, to the sound of fifes and drums, they marched up Long Wharf onto King Street. The marching soldiers–officers with swords drawn wearing cocked hats with silver lace; drummers in yellow jackets; infantrymen wearing black, three-cornered hats with white lace; imposing grenadiers transformed to giants in their tall, bearskin hats–passed the State House, entered Queen Street, and soon turned at Tremont in the direction of the Common.

Thomas Hutchinson, slowly recovering from an illness–likely a stroke[14]–wrote, "the red-coats make a formidable appearance and there is a profound silence among the Sons of Liberty."[15] Elsewhere in the colonies, news of redcoats ruling Boston streets after so much "Puff and Bombast"[16] from radicals prompted ridicule. It also led some Americans to wonder what other colonial towns would be forced to swallow the same medicine. A patriot in New York wrote, "Our metal may be tried next in the same hostile manner as is that of our neighbors in Boston."[17]

Spats between soldiers and civilians began almost from day one. On the day after the troops came ashore, Rowe reported in his diary about a confrontation at a coffeehouse. A British captain told Rowe, "You are an Incendiary & I hope to see you hanged yet in your shoes." Rowe walked away. "I thought it Prudent not to take any Notice of it just then but came home to dinner."[18]

Josiah Quincy, as Hyperion in the *Gazette*, attempted, as he had in an earlier crisis, to shame Bostonians into a muscular show of resistance:

> Oh, my countrymen! What will our children say, when they read the history of these times, should they find we tamely gave away, without one noble struggle, the most invaluable of earthly blessings? As they drag the galling chain, will they not execrate us? If we have any respect for things sacred; any regard to the dearest treasure on earth;–if we have one tender sentiment for posterity; if we would not be despised by the whole world;–let us, in the most open, solemn manner, and with determined fortitude swear,–we will die,–if we cannot live freemen![19]

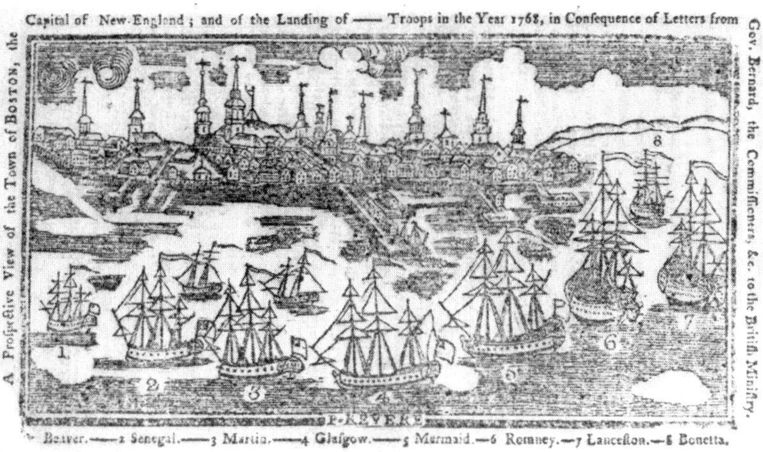

"A prospective view of the town of Boston, the capital of New-England and the landing of troops in the year 1768, in consequence of letters from Gov. Bernard, the commissioners, &c. to the British ministry." (*Library of Congress*)

But, again, the people of Boston weren't ready for bloody confrontation. The leaders of the Sons of Liberty reluctantly agreed that there would be no violence, not even harassment of the soldiers: "There is no more talk of resistance. The present disposition is to treat them, the troops, with civility but to provide nothing. All is at present quiet; but there is a general gloom and uneasiness."[20]

For the time being, soldiers camped on the Common. But that would not do for the duration of the occupation, which could take months or years, no one could say. Places indoors for these men had to be found and soon, for winter was approaching. This was no small problem. Space was needed for four thousand men in a crowded town of sixteen thousand.

Bernard had wrestled with the problem of how to house the soldiers, but nothing had been resolved by the time of the landing. He had designated for use as a barracks a former manufacturing building owned by the colony. However, tenants–poor but rent paying–were living in the dilapidated building, and they refused to leave.

Now the military took a more aggressive approach. Lieutenant Colonel William Dalrymple went to the town selectmen. Give me quarters for my men, he demanded. The selectmen replied: Not our problem. Then he marched his men to Faneuil Hall and, as his men waited in formation outside, had a long harangue with town officials. After several hours, the hall doors opened.

The next day, Bernard cleared the way for the entire State House, except for the Council Chamber, to be occupied by the soldiers. Soon soldiers were bedding down in the chamber of the House of

Representatives hall where Sam Adams had engineered so much trouble for the governor.

But Faneuil Hall and the State House could only accommodate some of the men. Many were still camped on the Common, and still more were on their way to Boston. The barracks at Castle William, three miles out in the harbor, could accommodate some. But even that was not enough.

The search for housing continued, leading to the first inevitable mob confrontation. The governor dispatched Sheriff Greenleaf and two deputies to try once again to clear the decrepit manufacturing building. The people still refused to leave. Bernard then sent Hutchinson. As lieutenant governor and chief justice, Hutchinson, it was thought, could speak with more authority than Greenleaf in telling the poor tenants they must leave. But the tenants had consulted lawyers. With all due respect, the tenants said, the law is on our side. We're staying.

So Hutchinson and Greenleaf left. A few days later, Greenleaf returned secretly. With soldiers positioned nearby, the sheriff found an unguarded basement window and entered the building. Perhaps he planned to make his way to a door and let the soldiers in the building. But the plan, whatever it was, was cut short when he was discovered and taken prisoner by the tenants he was trying to evict. The soldiers came to Greenleaf's rescue. They managed to free the sheriff, but by that time they were surrounded by a mob. For two days, the soldiers laid siege to the building while townspeople bombarded them with curses. After a few days, the troops around the building went away. The effort to clear the building was abandoned.

As it happened, the first to die at the hands of the soldiers was a soldier. The troops were no fools. They recognized civilian life in America was bliss compared to military life as a redcoat. In America, wages were good and land was cheap. If a man could desert, he could easily travel to a colonial town a safe distance away, find good work, and quickly make enough to buy land. It was all so enticing. So desertion rates were alarming. Within the first three weeks of the occupation, more than three dozen soldiers slipped away. Drastic measures were required. Thus, unlucky Private Richard Ames (or Arnes), caught attempting to desert, was court-martialed and sentenced to die. Local women submitted a petition pleading that the pitiful man be pardoned, but it was brushed aside. At 7:00 a.m. on October 31, to the sound of a slow drum cadence, every soldier in Boston was marched into formation on the Common to witness the killing of the private, dressed in white, who marched in with his casket carried beside him. The squad assigned to carry out the execution took aim and fired. The soldiers were marched past the bloody heap.

TWELVE

IMPUDENT, VIRULENT, AND SEDITIOUS LIES

Eventually, the military leased enough warehouses and stores to solve the housing problem. Officers and some enlisted men found space in private homes. Some who had sung in the chorus against the occupation couldn't resist the prospect of steady rental income. Royall Tyler, an important ally of Sam Adams's, leased space to a grenadier's wife and three children. Mob leader Molineux rented several warehouses and another building to the military.

Meanwhile, the military took steps to address frictions. Assertive sentries became passive. Exercises were modified so the rat-tatting of drums and squealing of fifes did not disturb Sunday church services.

While most soldiers behaved decently and Boston was quieter than anyone might have expected, that was not the impression the rest of America got. The British troops had taken the bite out of the radicals, but they still could bark.

Even before the arrival of British troops in October 1768, radical leaders set to work to transform the occupation into a propaganda triumph. They composed daily articles geared not so much for readers in Boston but for those elsewhere in America and even London. These articles, ranging in length from a few dozen words to many hundreds, focused mainly on news in Boston–incidents, crimes, and trials, for example–connected with the military occupation. Many included helpful commentary lambasting the governor, customs commissioners, British ministers, British policies, and British soldiers.

These reports, now known collectively as *The Journal of the Times* or *The Journal of Occurrences*, first appeared in the *New York Journal* on October 3, 1768, and soon after in the *Pennsylvania Chronicle.* Many were later widely reprinted in many other American newspapers and in a pamphlet distributed in England. Eventually, the reports found their way into pages of the *Boston Evening Post.*

Who, exactly, wrote these articles? Governor Bernard pointed at Sam Adams and his pals. Historians suspect collaborators included William Cooper, the town clerk; publisher Benjamin Edes; John Adams; and Josiah Quincy.

Among the authors' favorite targets were the customs commissioners, whose grave transgressions included an attempt to "invert the order of nature" by dining at the "courtly hour" of 4:00 p.m., even though "one or two o'clock has been the hours for dining in this town, time out of mind."[1] The balance of reports, however, formed a catalog of outrages committed by soldiers, conflicts between soldiers and civilians, and irritations or problems stemming from the military occupation of Boston. Individual soldiers were sometimes named. A certain Captain John Willson, for example, got frequent mention for "wickedly soliciting the Negroes of this town, to abuse their masters and cut their throats, &c."[2]

By and large, soldiers were never identified, nor were their alleged victims: "A married woman living in Long Lane, returning home in the night, was seized by the neck and almost strangled."[3] "Gentlemen and ladies coming into town in their carriages, threatened by the guard to have their brains blown out unless they stopped."[4] "A householder in this town was met by three soldiers" who knocked down, "stamped upon him," and "robbed him of all the money in his pocket, which happened to be but three pistareens."[5] A soldier–an "abandoned wretch"–visiting an "aged woman in the north part of Boston . . . seized her, by the shoulders, threw her upon the floor, and notwithstanding her years, attempted a rape upon her."[6] "A girl at New-Boston, was lately knock'd down and abused by soldiers for not consenting to their beastly proposal."[7] "A worthy old gentleman, the other morning discovered a soldier in bed with a favourite grand-daughter."[8]

A skeptic might suspect some incidents were exaggerated or made up. Thomas Hutchinson said only a tenth of what was reported was true. Bernard called the reports a "collection of impudent virulent & Seditious Lies, Perversions of Truth & Misrepresentations."[9]

Before the *Journal* went silent–its last item was dated August 1, 1769–it also reported on the continuing legal fiasco concerning Hancock's *Liberty*. The smuggling trial of Hancock and his codefendants went on and on. Attorney General Jonathan Sewall brought forth witness after witness, but nobody said anything helpful for proving Hancock and the others guilty of illegal shifting of cargo. John Adams, representing Hancock, found the trial unbearably tedious. The *Journal* crowed that the whole exercise amounted to harassment. Finally Sewall found a witness to say something useful. But the man's credibility was dubious, and his evidence was eventually declared inadmissible. Later, a different court indicted the man for perjury. Sewall finally gave up. On March 25, charges against Hancock and the others were dropped. Hancock, instead of being humbled, emerged from the affair a martyr and a hero.

The *Journal* also covered the fallout of a bloody confrontation just fifteen miles offshore in late April. For weeks, two navy vessels, the schooner *Hope* and the frigate *Rose,* had patrolled Massachusetts Bay, stopping merchant vessels and boarding them. Their ostensible purpose was to look for evidence of smuggling, but their real aim was to seize seamen to fill out crews depleted by desertions.

The captains were under orders to be polite and reasonable, to a point. The kidnapping was to be done courteously. They were not to use "unbecoming"[10] language. They were to first ask for volunteers. If no volunteer stepped forward, they were supposed to ask the captain of the merchant vessel to offer a man he was "most willing to part with . . . provided he is not distempered."[11]

Under such orders, the *Hope* and the *Rose* snatched crewmen one by one without incident until April 21, when the *Rose* stopped the *Pitt Packet,* a brig loaded with salt, wine, gin, and lemons, and manned by six men besides the ship's master, mate, and cook. When Lieutenant Henry Panton with two midshipmen and seven seamen from the *Rose* boarded the *Pitt Packet,* four crewmen on the brig hid. One of Panton's men found them in a scuttle, a storage area. The seamen refused to come out, and they had weapons: a musket, hatchet, harpoon, and double-pronged spear. With a crowbar and adze, men from the *Rose* began prying a new hole into the scuttle so they could yank the seamen out. When the barrel of a musket poked out of the cramped room, a sailor grabbed it and then fired a pistol blindly into the scuttle. The pistol had only powder, no ball. Still, the force of the shot left Michael Corbet, one of the cornered seamen, with a bloody lip.

Corbet now waved his harpoon through the new hole, which was growing ever wider. As the men with the tools continued their work, and as Panton sat and watched, the tip of the harpoon caught his neck, bringing forth an "Effusion of Blood."[12] A *Rose* man responded by firing into the scuttle. The bullet struck and broke the arm of another cornered seaman. The bleeding Panton was carried to a cabin, but within two hours was dead. Meanwhile, the seaman with the broken arm came out of the scuttle and was carried to the *Rose.* The standoff with the remaining three seamen continued for hours, but eventually they all surrendered. Now Corbet, the man with the harpoon, faced a problem worse than serving on a navy ship: he faced a possible death sentence. The navy men attempting the impressment faced no charges.

When details of this incident circulated, Bostonians instinctively sided with Corbet, according to the *Journal of the Times*: "The inhabitants were not a little alarmed to learn that those who were the aggressors . . . are left at liberty, while the men who stood only upon their defence against an illegal attempt upon their liberty are confined in irons."[13]

Competing with the navy for the town's hatred and disgust was Governor Bernard. Suspicions had lingered for months that he had been feeding his superiors exaggerated and misleading accounts of the situation in Boston. In May, the *Boston Gazette* reported that "persons of credit" consider Bernard "a Snake in the Grass" who "writes double Letters pro and con, to be used as Occasion serves; and that he is a Ministerial Canker Worm."[14]

These suspicions were confirmed when Boston radicals received copies of Bernard's letters obtained by friendly agents in London. The letters complained of how the town and the Governor's Council were uncooperative in helping to find housing for soldiers the previous fall and winter. That was exactly the truth. But Bernard, not knowing the letters would one day resurface in Boston, had expressed himself a little too bluntly. In his letters, he also suggested that the Massachusetts charter be recrafted to bring the Council more tightly under the control of the king–and therefore under the governor's thumb.

The Council, angry and now thoroughly alienated from the governor, had the letters published with their comments. Councillor James Bowdoin, whose daughter was married to John Temple, Bernard's enemy, sputtered, "Never was there a Council that have borne so much from a Governor, as the present Council have borne from Governor Bernard."[15] The Council then officially requested that Bernard be shipped out.

Bernard's relationship with the House of Representatives was even worse. At the end of May, it assembled at Boston's State House as usual, according to the charter. Almost immediately, the House protested that the presence of the soldiers everywhere was intolerable: "That an armament by sea and land investing this metropolis (*Boston*) and a military guard with cannon pointed to the door of the state house where the assembly is held, are inconsistent with that dignity and freedom with which they have a right to deliberate, consult and determine."[16]

The House demanded the governor remove the troops. Bernard said he lacked the authority. The House was incredulous. If Bernard's claim were true, then the military in Boston had no civilian supervision in Massachusetts: "This military force is uncontroulable by any authority in the province: it is then a power without any check here, and therefore it is absolute."[17] The House refused to do any business. Bernard responded not by kicking the soldiers out, but by kicking the House out. He ordered lawmakers to meet in Cambridge.

The House did as told, and by late June was meeting in a chapel at Harvard College. Then the House gave Bernard a sharp poke. Saying that "a standing army in this colony, in time of peace, is an invasion of natural rights,"[18] the House denied the governor money in connection with quartering troops in Boston and on Castle Island. The House also refused to authorize any money for the administration or for Bernard's salary. The snit between the House and the governor culminated in a petition from the House, approved 109 to 0, asking the king to "remove Sir Francis Bernard forever from this government."[19]

All Boston awaited the June trial of the *Pitt Packet* seamen, the most sensational courtroom event in memory. Representing Corbet and three other seamen were none other than James Otis and John Adams. Otis, uncommitted to the case and increasingly unreliable, left the bulk of the defense work to Adams.

First, certain legal questions had to be settled. Should the trial be held in England or America? Was a jury required, or could the case be tried before a panel of judges? The applicable laws seemed to conflict. Otis and Adams plainly favored a trial in America before a jury. A jury of sympathetic Boston men–who universally despised impressment–was Corbet's best hope.

Thomas Hutchinson, as chief judge, dashed that. He interpreted the laws to mean the case could be tried in America but without a jury. Instead, a special panel of judges would hear the case. That panel included Governor Bernard, Lieutenant Governor Hutchinson, and Commodore Samuel Hood, the very man who ordered the impressments. Corbet seemed doomed.

Wharf workers and seamen united in their hatred of impressment crowded the courtroom in the new courthouse on Queen Street, near the State House. In this case, the facts were not in dispute. Corbet's fate hinged on the question of self-defense. How threatening were Panton and the other men from the *Rose*? In preparing his closing arguments, Adams underscored Corbet's right to resist:

> He saw a desperate Gang of armed Sailors, before him, other Pistals, cocked and presented at him, and his Companions, their Heads and Breasts, drawn swords in the Hands of some, continual Threats to blow their Brains out, could he expect any Thing but Death? In these Circumstances what could he do? but defend himself, as he did? In these Circumstances what was his Duty? He had an undoubted Right, not merely to make a push at Lt. Panton, but to have darted an Harpoon, a dagger thro the Heart of every Man in the whole Gang.[20]

Adams also planned to assert the illegality of impressment itself. He was prepared to cite a statute from 1707, a statute ignored, forgotten, or assumed to be a wartime measure no longer in force. But it was not a wartime measure, as indicated by its purpose, "for the encouragement of trade in America," and should not be ignored. Adams wrote in his notes: "If . . . this Statute is now in Force, all that Lt. Panton did on board the Vessell was tortious and illegal, he was a Trespasser from the Beginning, a Trespasser, in coming on board, and in every Act that he did, untill he received the mortal, fatal Wound."[21] Thus, if impressment is illegal, then certainly Corbet and the other three seamen had a right to resist, and Panton's "Blood must lye at his own Door."[22]

Thus prepared, Adams began his arguments. But, as Adams recalled many years later, he barely had a chance to utter "justifiable homicide" before Hutchinson, "in a very indecorious manner," interrupted and adjourned the court. Everyone, recalled Adams, was "thunderstruck." In a separate chamber, the justices gathered "like a conclave of cardinels, in secret intrigues for the rest of the day."[23] The courtroom emptied, and Adams spent an anxious night wondering if Hutchinson was plotting with the other judges to ship Corbet to England.

In court the next afternoon, Bernard stood with a "countenance so solemn and gloomy as made the audience shudder, as if a sentence of death was coming." Then he announced that the court was "unanimously of the opinion" that the charge "amounts only to justifiable homicide; you are accordingly acquitted and discharged from your imprisonment."[24]

In the wake of this stunning decision, many, including Adams, puzzled not only about the verdict but also why Hutchinson cut short Adams's closing arguments. Adams suspected that Hutchinson knew the legitimacy of impressments would be attacked, and he didn't want that issue raised. Possibly, but more likely, Hutchinson, practical and prudent, saw no reason to waste everyone's time. Hutchinson later explained that, to him, the case was clear-cut: "It appeared that neither the lieutenant nor any of his superior officers were authorized to impress," and the judges, including Hood, all believed "the prisoners had a good right to defend themselves."[25]

Over the weeks before, during, and after the trial, the town seemed to acquiesce to a kind of truce. The customs men did their work in peace. Life returned to a kind of normal. On June 5, Rowe recorded in his diary: "Spent the evening at the Concert Hall with a very Brilliant company of Gentlemen & Ladies–a fine Ball, excellent Musick & a good large Plumb Cake."[26] In July he noted that some twelve hundred people crowded into Faneuil Hall on an afternoon to hear "Mrs. Rachel

Willson, the famous Quaker preacher." Rowe wrote, "She seems to be a Woman of Good Understanding."[27]

Ann Hulton, in a letter that year, mentioned concerts every other week and, just as often, "assemblies"–dances–with about sixty couples. There was also the alternative "Liberty Assembly" for gentlemen and ladies who abhorred sharing a dance floor with Tories.[28]

With the apparent calm, Hillsborough in London gave Gage in New York the authority to remove, if he wished, some or all of the soldiers from Boston. Gage sent orders for about half of the troops to pack up. In July, hundreds began to leave.

With half the soldiers gone, one might have expected a further easing of tension. But just the opposite occurred. Many Bostonians behaved like long-suffering prisoners just discovering one morning that half their jailers had vanished. Taunting and confrontations increased. Minor conflicts between soldiers and civilians threatened to explode into full-blown riots. One morning, for example, a constable appeared at the guardhouse on the Neck with a warrant against Ensign John Ness for stealing wood and assaulting civilian Robert Pierpont. Ness, in charge of the sentries at the Neck that morning, promised that as soon as he was off duty, he would call upon the appropriate judge. The constable left.

Minutes later, Robert Pierpont himself appeared with a mob and surrounded Ness and his fellow sentries. Curses flew and the crowd pressed close. Ness ordered the mob to disperse. The mob responded by pushing closer. Amid the jostling, Ness commanded the sentries to fix bayonets and form up in front of the guardhouse. Now stones flew at the soldiers, who remained silent and in formation. After about a quarter hour, relief sentries arrived.

Ness and the other soldiers started marching in formation back into town. The mob trailed, growing larger as the hubbub attracted rowdy boys and passersby. The soldiers kept marching as stones flew. Several raucous men charged into the formation, and the neat columns snarled. As officers struggled to restore order, a blast exploded from a soldier's musket. A bullet crashed into a nearby blacksmith's shop. Ness, aghast that the musket was loaded contrary to orders, now commanded his men to make certain their weapons were not loaded.

The mob was more cautious for the moment, staying some distance from the soldiers but still keeping up a rain of stones, one of which left a bloody gash on a soldier's head. Then a man appeared out of the crowd and smacked his fist square into the face of one of the soldiers. Another soldier stopped a second attack with the butt of a halbert, while four other soldiers directed their bayoneted muskets at the mob. Again the throng fell back.

Three officers now appeared to help Ness and his men. One took charge, shouting, "If any man strikes you, put your bayonet through him."[29] This kept the crowd at bay. The soldiers marched without further incident to their barracks.

Ness was eventually acquitted of the charges of stealing and assault, the allegations that evidently prompted the near-riot. However, the soldier who fired the weapon was now in trouble, as was the one who used his halbert to block an attack, and the officer who gave the command to "put your bayonet" through anyone who struck. None of the soldiers received harsh punishment. In court, though, the judge, Richard Dana, berated the soldiers and praised the mob:

"There is no walking the streets at day or night, for the hourly abuses committed by the soldiers. The inhabitants of the town acted properly. They had a right not only to strike a man of the guard for firing his gun, but to have dragged him from among the rest of the guard and brought him before a justice."[30]

Through all this, the Townshend duties remained in place. The official attitude in London was summed up in the words of Frederick North, Lord North, chancellor of the exchequer: "Whatever prudence or policy might hereafter induce us to repeal the paper and glass act, I hope that we shall never think of it till we see America prostrate at our feet."[31]

The Boston merchants who had signed the nonimportation agreement were getting edgy. More than six months had passed since the pact went into effect, and there was no sign that Britain was caving in to the economic pressure. This was different from the Stamp Act crisis, when Parliament quickly responded to nonimportation and abolished the stamp tax. This time, with the British economy in a stronger position, Parliament was holding firm. British woolens were in high demand in Germany, and good harvests in Britain were keeping bread prices low for British workers. The pinch from the American boycott was bearable.

Also, the boycott was leaky. While many merchants signed the nonimportation agreement, some did not and continued to openly import British goods and distribute them to retailers, who had little trouble attracting customers. While homespun clothes were fashionable in these times–to save money and as a show of solidarity and patriotism–many people still quietly continued to buy British goods.

Week after week, merchants who stopped importing lost sales to the minority of merchants who, despite pressure, continued to bring in British-made goods. Among those who openly imported was Mein of the *Chronicle*. Mein opposed the Townshend duties, but nonimportation would destroy him, he said. He sold stationery and ran a newspaper. He thus needed paper, and American paper mills could not supply him with the quality and quantity he required. If he ceased to import, he would be out of business and twenty-one people would be out of work, he said. Mein expressed what many believed, that the nonimportation movement was mainly a scheme for large, well-established merchants to drive small newcomers out of business. The *Chronicle* asked, "Do the Public begin to suspect that a certain scheme is principally calculated to crush all the young Merchants and Importers, that the trade may still remain in the hands of a few grave 'well-disposed' Dons who are believed to be exceedingly well-stocked with Goods?"[32]

Those arguments made no headway with the nonimporting merchants. Angry resolutions were passed. Handbills were printed and distributed urging the public to boycott those businesses violating nonimportation. Mein's name was on those handbills.

Amid these events, Bernard's nightmare came to an end. London called him home. On August 1, he boarded a vessel bound for Britain. His wife and children would follow later. As calm winds delayed the departure, Bernard heard cannons booming and bells ringing from the town. At night, a great bonfire blazed atop Fort Hill. These were not to honor Bernard but to celebrate his exit. The *Gazette*, in its note on the departure, gave Bernard a poke in the eye, saying that "for nine Years past, [he] has been a Scourge to this Province, a Curse to North-America, and a Plague to the whole Empire."[33]

Hutchinson was now acting governor, and eventually he would achieve his life's wish of becoming governor, but at the worst possible time.

In mid-August, the Sons of Liberty sponsored a triumphant dinner in Dorchester, just outside Boston. On a field adjacent to the Sign of the Liberty Tree tavern, over 350 joined Sam Adams, John Hancock, James Otis, and their radical friends. The event drew long-time allies of the Sons, but also newly won friends, people still straddling the fence, and even some linked to the Tories. With Bernard gone, half the soldiers shipped off, and sentiments in Boston cresting in favor of the radicals, many men took the opportunity to rub elbows with the Sons of Liberty just to be safe. Such was the case with John Adams, who wrote, "I felt as if I ought not loose this feast, as if it were my Duty to be there. . . . [M]any might suspect I was not hearty in the cause if I had been absent."[34]

The Sons of Liberty made the trip to Dorchester worthwhile. Guests feasted on three pigs roasted over charcoal pits and helped themselves to boiled codfish with egg sauce and blueberry pie washed down with Madeira. Under a great sailcloth awning, they raised glasses for precisely forty-five toasts, first to the king, then to the queen, and on and on to the last: "Strong halters, firm blocks and sharp axes to all such as deserve either."[35] Still, somehow, no one got drunk, so John Adams claimed.

They joined as one to sing to a new song by Benjamin Church and then *The Liberty Song*, an old British tune with new American verses. The tune was the same as *Hearts of Oak We Are Still*, written with the British navy in mind. Americans had invented new verses and made it their own anthem. Sam Adams, standing on a chair, performed the verses solo and then directed the three-hundred-plus voices in the chorus:

In Freedom we're born and in Freedom we'll live,
Our purses are ready,
Steady, Friends, Steady,
Not as Slaves, but as Freemen our Money will give.[36]

When all was over, a line of 139 carriages–Hancock at the front, Otis in the rear–returned to Boston.

THIRTEEN

WEAKNESS OF GOVERNMENT

Just three days after that massive fest in Dorchester, Mein's *Chronicle* dropped a bomb on John Hancock and the nonimportation movement. At first glance, the mid-August issue of the *Chronicle* did not appear sensational. The front page was taken up mainly by lists of goods:

271 Casks of Nails
96 Casks Cheese
70 Baskets Cheese
26 Casks Wrought Iron
14 Bales Woolens
24 Bundles Pans
12 Packages Linen

The lists went on and on. There were also names of prominent men, including John Hancock, listed four times, twice in all-capital letters.[1]

At closer inspection, readers could see that what Mein had published were the manifests of four vessels, three owned by Hancock. The manifests showed that Hancock and many others who had loudly vowed not to import were quietly importing, and not just a few trivial items, but whole cargoes of supposedly banned products. Mein had disclosed wholesale deceit in the ranks of Boston's "Well Disposed"[2] merchants–Mein's sneering reference to the signers of the nonimportation agreement.

Mein had published a similar manifest earlier in the month, an embarrassment to the nonimportation movement. This new revelation, with Hancock's name attached, was more stunning. Subsequent issues of the *Chronicle* revealed more names and listed other cargoes, demonstrating that the nonimportation agreement was a sieve. Over several editions, Mein listed fifty-five cargoes detailing wholesale flouting of the pact. The *Chronicle* reported that no fewer than 190 people imported items from Great Britain from January to the end of May–during the period of the supposed boycott.

These revelations circulated around Boston and Massachusetts in the *Chronicle*'s usual press run of fourteen hundred copies. But Mein went further. He compiled various lists, printed up four thousand copies, and sent them down the coast as far as Florida and up as far as Nova Scotia. Mein was playing Sam Adams's game of spreading news–and propaganda–about Boston.

Seeing that Boston merchants were trampling their own agreement for business advantage, merchants in New York, Philadelphia, and elsewhere would be tempted, even compelled, to resume importation to keep up.

Mein's exposé shattered the credibility of the nonimportation movement. Whigs tried to control the damage. The *Gazette* painted over the hypocrisy: the imports were inconsequential, mainly single items for personal use, not for resale. At a town meeting, Sam Adams raged that importers should be "stigmatized & declar'd Enemy's of the Country."[3] But despite his bluster, he could not afford to turn his back on Hancock or reject other secret importers. The nonimporting merchants gathered in Faneuil Hall and renewed their vows not to import. The movement hung together.

Advocates of nonimportation turned their attention toward Mein: he needed to be silenced. Advertisements appeared calling him an enemy of America. Letters went out to selectmen in other towns urging them not to patronize Mein's businesses. Mein began to receive letters so threatening and alarming that he took to packing a pistol. Duly frightened, but still determined, Mein would not back down. The *Chronicle* remained defiant.

Meanwhile, James Otis, once the leading light of the Whig faction, was behaving more and more like a crazed fool. Gripped by a hatred and fear of Customs Commissioner John Robinson, Otis attacked him in the press. Then in the British Coffee House, the King Street lair for customs and military men, Tory merchants, and anyone sympathetic with the Tory authorities, Otis confronted Robinson and demanded "A gentleman's satisfaction."[4]

Otis intended, apparently, to have a fistfight out in the street. Robinson had another idea. He reached for Otis's nose to give it a vigorous twist. Soon the two parried with walking sticks like absurd swordsmen. Then Robinson dropped his stick, and a bystander snatched Otis's away. Others joined in the fight on the side of Robinson, one man holding Otis and other delivering a gash to his forehead. The bleeding Otis, now without his hat and wig, was certain to get further pummeling but for Customs Comptroller Benjamin Hallowell, of all people, and another man, who extracted Otis from the melee.

Otis recovered physically. Mentally, he was more unstable than ever and clearly an embarrassment for the Whigs. Later that year, Otis took on town assignments and moderated several meetings. But increasingly, radicals turned elsewhere for leadership–to wealthy John Hancock, to legal star John Adams, to ardent Joseph Warren, and especially to wily Sam Adams.

That fall, a town committee that included both Adamses, Otis, and Warren touched on news that some of the Townshend duties–those on paper, glass, and painters' colors–might be lifted. That, the committee reported, was not enough:

> [T]he Grievances which lie heavily upon us we shall never think redressed, till every Act passed by the British Parliament for the express purpose of raising a Revenue upon us without our consent is repealed; till the American Board of Commissioners of the Customs is dissolved; the Troops recalled, and things restored to the state they were in before the late extraordinary measures of Administration took place.[5]

Townsmen also turned up the heat on Mein and other men who openly imported in defiance of the nonimportation agreement. A town meeting ratified a resolution expressing "Astonishment and Indignation, that any of its Citizens should be so lost to the feelings of Patriotism and common Interest, and so thoroughly & infamously selfish" as to continue importing from Great Britain. The resolution then named several importers, including Mein and Thomas Hutchinson's sons Thomas and Elisha, so "that Posterity may know, who those Persons were that preferred their little private advantage to the common Interest of all the Colonies, in a point of the greatest Importance."[6]

A few weeks later, a gang prowling the streets fell upon a man and began beating him before moving on to another man and beating him as well. In the darkness, each of the men vaguely looked like Mein, who apparently was the intended victim. Word soon reached Mein about the attacks. Terrified, he went with his partner, Fleeming, to Hutchinson and pleaded for some kind of help. Hutchinson asked the men if they could put a name to anyone who might attack them. They could not. Then, Hutchinson said, there was nothing he could do. In this town crowded with soldiers manning checkpoints and patrolling, Mein and Fleeming were left to fend for themselves.

On October 28, about 4:00 in the afternoon, Mein and Fleeming, both armed with pistols, were walking along King Street on their way to their print shop. The two men, nervous and wary, noticed that the shops along the street appeared busier than normal for a late fall day.

Then, in what seemed an instant, Mein and Fleeming found themselves surrounded by about twenty men, including Molineux, the apparent leader. After some menacing talk, a man lifted his cane and jabbed Mein in the stomach. It was not a gentle poke. Eight days later, the bruise would still be visible.

Mein pulled out his pistol, cocked it, and took aim. The crowd fell back but did not scatter. Mein and Fleeming backed their way down King Street, the crowd following at a distance. Someone shouted, "Knock him down. Kill him."[7] Fortunately for Mein and Fleeming, they were backing toward one of the few places in town where they might find safety–the Main Guard, the largest military barracks in town. This was on the south side of King Street, near the State House.

The officer on duty saw what was happening and ordered the sentries to step aside and allow Mein and Fleeming to step between the sentry boxes. Now sentries were between the mob and the two printers. They were safe, or so it seemed for a moment. Then, just as Mein was climbing the steps of the guardhouse, down came the blade of a shovel on his shoulder. A tailor named Thomas Marshal had grabbed a shovel out of a nearby store, slipped around the sentries, and prepared to split Mein's head. Marshal missed Mein's skull but struck his shoulder, leaving the printer with a two-inch gash.

Just behind Mein was Fleeming with a stick in his left hand and a pistol in his right. Fleeming swung his stick at Marshal as the tailor was fleeing. Fleeming missed and stumbled. A moment later, Mein and Fleeming at last slipped into the guardroom and safety.

At some time in these chaotic moments, at least one shot was fired. Mein later explained that Fleeming, as he tripped, inadvertently yanked on the trigger of his pistol. Others, including a witness who was no enemy of Mein's, said it was Mein who fired the pistol. One newspaper reported that Mein fired from inside the guardhouse and that either the bullet or the wadding used to hold it in place in the barrel caught a soldier's sleeve.[8]

In the guardhouse, Mein and Fleeming could breathe easy for a second or two, but their ordeal was not over. More people joined the mob outside. As rumors spread that the shot came from Mein's pistol and that he had deliberately fired into the crowd, the mob became more agitated and pressed so close to the sentry posts that the sentries could not be relieved in the usual way, but had to be ordered off one by one.

Meanwhile, Molineux and Sam Adams sought an arrest warrant for Mein. They got one, and soon they, a deputy sheriff, and a constable, warrant in hand, entered the guardhouse in search of Mein. They scoured the building for more than an hour but failed to find him hiding in the garret.

The search was abandoned. Soon after, Mein borrowed a soldier's uniform and, thus disguised, left the guardhouse to find refuge in the house of a friendly military man. What happened to Fleeming? That's unclear. The mob seemed to have lost interest in him.

Poor George Gailer would not be so lucky. Gailer had been a crewman on the sloop *Success*, which had recently been seized for improperly bringing ashore a cargo of wine. Someone evidently tattled to the customs officials, and the Sons of Liberty pointed at Gailer. At about the same time one mob chased Mein and Fleeming up King Street, another collection of Sons of Liberty tracked down Gailer and soon treated him to a special kind of torment and humiliation.

Back in June of the previous year, news of an incident in Salem caught the attention of colonists up and down the coast. An enraged crowd had taken hold of a man suspected of informing officials about smuggling. The crowd "stripped him, then wrapped him in a Tarred Sheet, and rolled him in Feathers; having done this, they carried him about the Streets in a Cart, and then banished him from the town for 6 weeks."[9]

This was not the first tar-and-feathering. Such torment dates back at least to the Middle Ages. Nor was it the first tar-and-feathering in America. But until this time, the practice was rare. Now patriotic groups seized on this ordeal as dandy for intimidating, humiliating, and hurting enemies without–usually–killing them. Within two years after the incident in Salem, at least a dozen similar episodes took place in America. The tar might be heated, but usually it was daubed on as is, sometimes on bare skin, sometimes on clothes, sometimes on a garment given to the victim to protect his clothes. Meanwhile, goose feathers from two pillows were enough to complete the job. Records tell of at least one episode where tormentors flung a live goose at the victim.[10]

In the case of Gailer, the torment was especially humiliating. First, the crowd brought him to the State House, where he was stripped, covered in tar and then feathers, and placed on a cart. Then, forced to hold a lantern, he was pulled through the town accompanied by up to two thousand people. The procession led toward the Liberty Tree, where Gailer was made to swear never to inform again. Then the procession was off to the North End, then to the west side of town, back to the State House, and then down King Street to the Custom House, where people broke a few windows and gave the sentry three cheers. The crowd then forced Gailer to once again promise never to inform. He also had to beg pardon for whatever he did wrong, and express his gratitude for not being put to death. Then the mob returned his clothes and let him go.

Days went by. Mein, in hiding, slipped a message to the lieutenant governor asking about protection. Mein said he would willingly surrender "provided I have a proper force to prevent any injury to my Person from a Licentious Mob."[11] Hutchinson gave a messenger his response: Mein was free to come out of hiding, as long as he was mindful of "the Weakness of Government."[12]

It all seemed incredible to Mein, who responded that the weakness of government could be addressed at a stroke. All Hutchinson had to do was call upon the soldiers. Mein also relayed a warning. While in hiding he had managed to gather affidavits from friendly witnesses about the night in question. If he was forced to flee Boston and return to England, he would take those with him and report all of this: "If I go I shall carry with me proper Authenticated Representations of the Power and Support being withheld while the most evident necessity demanded its being exerted."[13]

Hutchinson, ever prudent, would not call out the soldiers for the sake of this lone printer so widely despised. He, too, was frustrated, however, and shared Mein's sense of helplessness. Civil authority was at its lowest point since the stationing of British soldiers in Boston. Soldiers were still everywhere, but authorities would not use them. Hutchinson agonized, but what could he do? The sheriff and his deputies were too feeble to face a mob of one thousand. If he tried to call up the militia, he would be laughed at. As for calling upon the military, he would be damned if he did and damned if he didn't. If he did ask the military to protect Mein and control the streets, the people would likely rally to the side of the radicals, who had been huffing all along that the troops had been sent to intimidate the populace. But if Hutchinson did nothing, his bosses in England could say he failed to use power at hand to maintain order.

In the end Hutchinson did just enough to say he did something, but not enough to do Mein any good. Hutchinson directed the justices of the peace to find the men who assaulted Mein and bring them to justice. The justices, however, were not inclined to act. As Hutchinson later wrote, they disapproved of the way Mein was treated, and they would normally "exert themselves in carrying the law into execution against all offenders in like cases," but made no promises to lift a finger on Mein's behalf.[14] In any case, even if the justices were willing, they had no chance of carrying out their duties without some force behind them. They were powerless.

Mein eventually concluded that his future in Boston was hopeless. On Pope Day, when his own effigy made an appearance, he slipped out to a naval ship, where he was given shelter. In the middle of the month, he was on his way back to England aboard the schooner *Hope.*

Mein, as promised, wrote his own report about events. The report, as expected, cast Hutchinson as weak and ineffectual. Hutchinson, for his part, was kinder toward Mein. Hutchinson's full report to

Hillsborough, which Mein carried across the ocean, concluded, "I am fully convinced that Mr. Mein is a very great sufferer and that his suffering took their rise from his opposition to the doings of the Merchants and I could not deny him a just representation of his case to your Lordship."[15]

The events involving Mein and Gailer demonstrated that the Sons of Liberty had reasserted control of the streets. Remarkably, some merchants still scoffed at threats and continued to openly import. These included sisters Anne and Betsy Cuming, whose modest shop offered imported linens. They had watched the mob chase Mein and saw in front of their very door a Sons of Liberty victim, probably Gailer, "in a gore of blood."[16] Yet they quietly continued to trade in imports. Shortly after receiving goods from England, the sisters found a "Comitey" at their door charging them with violating the nonimportation pact. The women admitted they never promised not to import "for it was verry trifling owr Business." Then they went on the attack: How dare the committee try "to inger two industrious Girls who were Striving in an honest way to Git there Bread"?[17]

We can imagine the chastened committeemen slinking away, but they still duly included the Cuming sisters in a list of importers to be shunned. That backfired. At the end of the year, the Cumings reported higher sales than the year before. The publicity, they said, "Spirits up our Friends to Purchess from us."[18] A correspondent tittered to a distant friend, "Would you not be diverted to see . . . the two little Miss Cumingses Posted together in a News Paper as Enimys to their Country?"[19]

As Britain watched events in Boston, so Boston tracked events in Britain. The fascination with Wilkes, the eccentric crusader for English liberties, continued. A modern scholar reviewing several newspapers in Virginia noted that Wilkes, from 1768 to 1771, was discussed and quoted more than any other man.[20] In Boston, interest in Wilkes took on the traits of a cult. About this time, the following political creed was reprinted in Boston:

> I believe in Wilkes, the firm patriot, maker of number 45. Who was born for our good. Suffered under arbitrary power. Was banished and imprisoned. He ascended into purgatory, and returned some time after. He ascended here with honour and sitteth amidst the great assembly of the people, where he shall judge both the favorite and his creatures. I believe in the spirit of his abilities, and they will prove to the good of our country. In the resurrection of liberty, and the life of universal freedom forever. Amen.[21]

This continued devotion to Wilkes demonstrated that Bostonians, like most Americans, still craved a solution to their problems as British citizens. They were not yet looking for independence, but reform, and they believed that Wilkes could be the instrument of that reform. A committee that included John Adams, Joseph Warren, Thomas Young, and Benjamin Church wrote to Wilkes:

"[Y]ou are one of the most incorruptibly honest men reserved by heaven to bless, and perhaps save a tottering Empire. . . . Permit us, therefore, much respected Sir, to express our confidence in your approved abilities and steady Patriotism. Your Country, the British Empire, and unborn millions plead an exertion, at this alarming Crisis."[22]

In addition to other fawning letters brimming with tributes, the Sons of Liberty shipped across the ocean a pair of turtles, each over forty pounds, "as a small testimony of the great esteem and respect for [Wilkes's] . . . magnanimity and perseverance in the cause of constitutional freedom."[23]

What of Wilkes's obscene parodies? Did that bother the puritanical Bostonians? One older member of the Sons of Liberty wrote that if he ever read what Wilkes "wrote on Women," he had the strength to bear up, "fortified" as he was from enduring "sixty cold North American winters."[24]

However, the news about Wilkes was dispiriting. After voters in Middlesex elected the imprisoned Wilkes to represent them in the House of Commons, that House promptly expelled him. When Middlesex voters elected Wilkes again, the House declared him "incapable" of election to Parliament. When Middlesex elected Wilkes yet again, Parliament declared the election void. When Middlesex chose Wilkes a fourth time, Parliament declared that the man receiving the second-most votes would represent the county. Here was yet another abuse of English liberties for Bostonians to chew on. Parliament, at the king's urging, had denied–not once, but four times–the choice of the people of Middlesex County for representation in Parliament.

These events riveted Bostonians, who started to despair that reform in Britain was possible. Wrote Thomas Young to Wilkes, "Nothing less than an entire change of men and measures will ever regain the confidence of Americans."[25]

FOURTEEN

BLOOD OF THE RIGHTEOUS ABEL

The first day of 1770 brought a new crisis in Boston. January 1 was the day the flimsy, year-long nonimportation agreement was supposed to end. But radical supporters of nonimportation wanted the boycott to continue. After all, the hated Townshend duties were still in place. Divisions among Boston merchants now came to a head. In one camp were those committed to nonimportation and firmly allied with the Sons of Liberty, Sam Adams, and James Otis. Most of these merchants wanted the boycott to continue. John Hancock was among these men. Trying to scrub his blackened reputation, Hancock put a notice in the *New York Journal*: "This is ONCE AND FOR ALL to certify to whom it may concern, That I have not in one single instance directly or indirectly deviated from said Agreement; and I now publicly defy all Mankind to prove the CONTRARY."[1] Hancock remained at the forefront of the movement, apparently forgiven for his hypocrisy.

Another faction was made up of the few, very few, merchants who openly continued to import. They had never signed any nonimportation agreement and were pariahs in their own town. For some of these merchants, the decision to openly import had brought not profits, but ruin. Their business had dried up. Customers who opposed importation avoided them. Others shunned them out of fear that trade with a tainted merchant would invite an evening visit from the Sons. Merchants who openly imported were nearly extinct.

Then there was a third group, those in the middle. These were the merchants who never wholeheartedly supported nonimportation. They only went along with it because of threats and intimidation by other merchants and by the Sons of Liberty. Many of these merchants had initially continued to import in defiance of the nonimportation agreement, but then caved in. These merchants had warehouses stuffed with imported goods under lock and key. They had been looking forward to January 1 as the day they could unlock the warehouses and resume trade as usual.

Sure enough, in the first days of January, more than a half dozen of these merchants unlocked their warehouses and removed their goods. Among this group were two sons of Thomas Hutchinson, Elisha and young Thomas.

Meanwhile, the open importers remained defiant. In January, newspaper readers in Boston perused the remarks of Theophilus Lillie, who operated a North End shop:

> [I]t always seemed strange to me that people who contend so much for civil and religious Liberty should be so ready to deprive others of their natural liberty–that Men who are guarding against being subject to Laws [to] which they never gave their consent in person or by their representatives, should at the same time make Laws, and in the most effectual manner execute them upon me and others, to which Laws I am sure I never gave my consent either in person or by my representative. . . . I own I had rather be a slave under one master; for if I know who he is, I may, perhaps, be able to please him, than a slave to an hundred or more, who I don't know where to find, nor what they will expect from me.[2]

Anti-import merchants, scrambling to hold the fraying movement together, called for a mass meeting at Faneuil Hall in mid-January. This was not a regular meeting of merchants, nor was it a regular town meeting. For merchants, this gathering represented a new stage in the evolution of their lobbying group. With this meeting, what began in 1760 as a the Boston Society for Encouraging Trade and Commerce, a lobbying organization just for merchants, became a kind of grand, unofficial group that included anyone who happened to walk in the door. Termed "the Body" by Sam Adams, it was open to all–even women, servants, and apprentices[3] (but apparently not slaves or free blacks). Attendance at this and later meetings of the Body ranged from one thousand to fourteen hundred, larger than most town meetings.

From this meeting, a committee went out to urge defiant merchants to make an appearance before the throng. Some of those merchants could not be found. Others flatly spurned the invitation.

Stronger action was called for. Soon a throng from the hall marched to the shop of William Jackson, a notorious importer. We can imagine Jackson's chest tightening as he looked down upon the crowd of about a thousand and wondered how it would feel to be stripped naked, tied to a cart, and tarred and feathered. He opened a window to hear mob leader Molineux demand that he put in the mob's custody all his imported goods from Great Britain. Jackson bravely refused.

Molineux was silent, as if not quite prepared for Jackson to do anything but give in. What now? Molineux muttered something about it being "beneath the dignity of this committee to be parlied with in the street"[4] and then ordered a retreat. Molineux and his "committee" returned to Faneuil Hall, where news of the humiliating setback further deflated the discouraged townspeople.

But there were other, more hopeful, reports. It was rumored that the lieutenant governor's sons Thomas and Elisha Hutchinson were prepared to put their imported goods back into storage. The next morning, radical merchants sent wagons to the lieutenant governor's rebuilt mansion in the North End, where the two adult sons lived with their father. The wagons had arrived to pick up tea and other imported cargo and return it to locked and guarded warehouses for safekeeping and to prevent its distribution and sale. One of the Hutchinson sons appeared. No, he said, he and his brother would not hand over their cargoes. The wagons left empty.

The reports from the day before had been authentic. The Hutchinsons had been planning to give in and give over their cargoes. But overnight the brothers changed their minds. Jackson's example, combined with the arguments of other holdouts, restored their will to defy the radicals.

There followed yet another meeting at Faneuil Hall. Molineux proposed a massive march to Hutchinson's doorstep. The packed hall roared approval. But then attorney Josiah Quincy warned that such an action might be a fatal mistake. Indeed, it might be a trap and the very action that the lieutenant governor had been waiting for. The restless audience fell silent as Quincy explained that the appearance of a threatening mob before the acting governor's house might be viewed as a threat to the king and thus high treason.

Quincy's words sobered everyone. High treason? A mob had ransacked that very house only a few years before. No one had been charged with high treason or punished in any way. But then Hutchinson was not the acting governor.

Quincy's warning was enough to frighten some leaders. A committee was needed to lead the massive visit to the Hutchinson house. John Hancock was asked to join. He refused. James Otis also declined. Molineux, frustrated and angry, threatened to leave the hall and quit the movement altogether. He was persuaded to stay, and a committee was formed that included Sam Adams. Otis changed his mind and agreed to be on the committee as well. Then the committee, escorted by about one thousand others, trooped into the North End and in the late afternoon stood before the great Hutchinson house.

The lieutenant governor himself opened an upper story window and asked what the gathering wanted. Molineux responded, "It is not you, but your sons we desire to see." Hutchinson replied, "I am the representative of the king of Great Britain, the greatest monarch on earth, and in his name require you to disperse."[5]

The crowd held its ground. Molineux then produced a document and read the committee's demand that the young Hutchinsons surrender the tea. The lieutenant governor asked for documents showing the vote for this demand. Molineux was in a spot. Quincy's words probably echoed in his mind. What sort of jeopardy would men named in the document possibly face? Molineux refused the request. His excuse: he had only the original and had no authority to give that or a copy.

Now Hutchinson took command from his window. He saw Otis in the crowd and scolded him, saying the lawyer had to know the gathering was illegal. Hutchinson continued, referring to the looting of the very same house some years before. "Gentlemen, when I was attacked before, I was a private person; I am now the representative of the greatest monarch upon earth, whose majesty you affront in thus treating my person."[6]

Hutchinson disappeared from the window. Molineux conferred briefly with his committee. They decided to slink away. The Hutchinsons had won.

The committee, with the crowd in tow, tried its hand with other recalcitrant merchants. They trooped to Jackson's shop once again, and once again Jackson flatly refused to give in. They moved on to Theophilus Lillie's shop. He told the crowd that "they had already ruined him and his Business, and if they now wanted his life, they might take it when they pleased."[7] They visited two other defiant merchants. None gave in.

The next morning, many of the same people trudged in the bitter cold to Faneuil Hall for yet another meeting. The failures and humiliations of the day before pointed in one direction: the utter collapse of nonimportation and the sullen acceptance of the Townshend duties.

However, just as the meeting started, two men arrived with news from Thomas Hutchinson. He had given in to all the demands of the day before. His sons would hand over their cargoes to the merchant committee assigned to guard them and prevent their sale. Furthermore, the sons would hand over the money they had received for goods already sold.

As the news was announced, Faneuil Hall erupted in cheers. It seemed a kind of miracle. That evening, several of the other holdouts, apparently influenced by the Hutchinsons' example, sent word that they, too, were prepared to agree to demands. Suddenly, nonimportation was back in place.

The about-face of the Hutchinsons, father and sons, was astonishing. The lieutenant governor had determined that as acting governor he had to find a way to work with the radicals. For that he needed to regain some public trust, and for that he could not allow his family to be seen as gaining a trade advantage during this crisis. He hoped that by giving in he might gain some popular support. But Hutchinson's retreat won him little affection from the radical faction, making him appear both weak and irresolute. At the same time, by giving in, Hutchinson lost the confidence of the merchant holdouts, who now despised and distrusted him.

The episode shattered much of the respect and trust Hutchinson and his sons had among merchants and among the Hutchinsons' own friends and allies. A Whig observer wrote:

> Afterwards He [Hutchinson] was greatly embarras'd, sensible that He and his sons were considered as the chief Bulwark of those who wish'd to see the Merchants agreement annihilated. He was blam'd for appearing below His Dignity as a negotiator in this business, His sons were blam'd even by his own Friends for their inconsistency and Dishonorable conduct with the Merch[ants]: The [customs] commissioners were offended with what they call'd his weakness in this Instance, declaring that he had now given the reins of Government into the Hands of the People, and that he c'd never recover them: – His Unpopularity is increased by this step.[8]

Hutchinson himself admitted later that the decision to cave in to radical demands was a disaster. He confessed that he "felt more trouble and distress of mind from this error in his publick trust" than "from the loss and damage to his private fortune" when his house was demolished during the Stamp Act crisis.[9]

By giving in, Hutchinson heartened and emboldened the radicals. The mood in Faneuil Hall was buoyant when hundreds crammed the building later that month for yet another meeting of the Body. The speakers first took on the military commanders. Had they exceeded their authority in quartering troops in the town? Was it proper for the military to post a guard outside the home of one of the holdout merchants?

The news of this meeting further exasperated Hutchinson. The leaders of this unauthorized gathering were acting as if it had some legitimate authority. Who were they to debate military matters? He sent off Sheriff Greenleaf to Faneuil Hall with a declaration. Greenleaf duly stood in front of the crowd and pronounced that the gathering should immediately break up. After a round of catcalls and hisses, Sam Adams responded, "[I]t is the unanimous opinion of this body after serious consideration and debate that this meeting is warranted by law."[10] No one asked, what law?

Thus ignoring the acting governor's demand to break up, the assembly took on Jackson, Lillie, and two other holdout merchants. They were, the Body voted, "obstinate and inveterate Enemies to their Country, and Subverters of the Rights and Liberties of the Continent."[11] Furthermore, the group resolved to withhold from them "not only commercial Dealings, but every Act and Office of common Civility."[12]

Yet another resolution condemned six others, including Mein–who was already gone–"to be driven to that Obscurity, from which they originated, and to the Hole of the Pit from whence they were digged."[13]

Then shortly before adjourning, the assembled took a solemn pledge: they would drink no tea. This was another tactic to punish tea importers and ultimately to get Parliament to kill the Townshend duties. The idea caught on. In February, about three hundred women of Boston promised to deny "ourselves the drinking of foreign tea, in hopes to frustrate a plan that tends to deprive the whole community of all that is valuable in life."[14] Tory Peter Oliver later wrote that these women had a loophole: tea when ill was permitted. He said some patriotic women "were forced to take Turns to be sick, & invite their Acquaintance[s] to visit them; & so the Sickness went on by Rotation."[15]

February 8 was a Thursday, market day in Boston. As usual, schools were closed. That morning, attached to the town pump, a board appeared reading "IMPORTER" next to the figure of a hand pointing at Jackson's shop. A cluster of boys, loitering near the entrance to the shop, flung dirt and hissed at customers coming and going from the store. From time to time, when Jackson emerged to tear down the sign, boys with sticks would send him scurrying back into the building. Other merchants gathered. Molineux appeared. No one tried to stop the boys. At about 1:00 p.m., the sign disappeared, and soon so did the boys, but only after giving Jackson's windows a coat of mud.

A week later, the sign of the hand again turned up in front of Jackson's store. Attached to the sign were effigies of some importers, and a second sign promised that the next week the Liberty Tree would feature an assortment of effigies, including those of some of the customs commissioners, five of their "understrappers," and several targets of hate from England.[16] When four soldiers came to take down the signs, a crowd drove them off.

After another week, on February 22, the sign of the hand again went up by Jackson's shop. Another appeared at the shop of Theophilus Lillie. A crowd of men and "hundreds" of boys stood around Lillie's shop and prevented customers from going in.[17]

Just after 10:00 a.m., one Ebenezer Richardson appeared in the street and began talking to a man with a horse and wagon. Richardson was a pariah. Scandal and disgrace had forced him to slink from his hometown of Woburn. But he couldn't shake his reputation, which included, as John Adams recalled, adultery, incest, and perjury.[18] Most Bostonians despised Richardson all the more as an assumed informer for the customs office. That may have suggested at least he had friends there. But even among some customs people, he was detested. Paxton, the customs man who also had few friends in Boston, called Richardson a "villain."[19] Richardson did little to cultivate warm feelings. Indeed, he seemed to be itching for a scrap. Days before he had been heard to remark, "Let 'em come on me I'm ready, for I've guns loaded."[20]

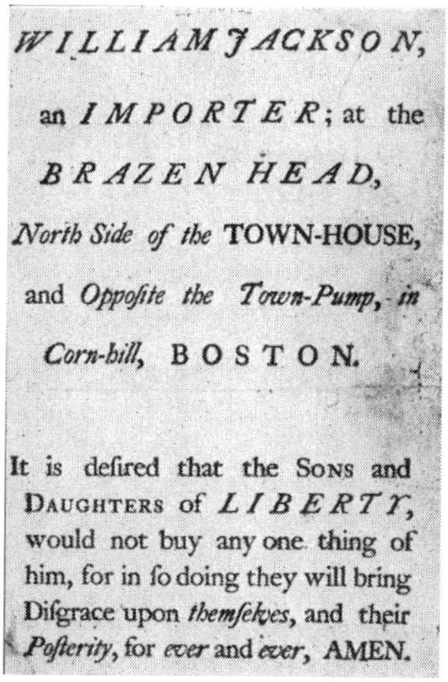
WILLIAM JACKSON,

an *IMPORTER*; at the

BRAZEN HEAD,

North Side of the TOWN-HOUSE,

and *Oppoſite the Town-Pump*, *in*

Corn-hill, BOSTON.

It is deſired that the SONS and DAUGHTERS of *LIBERTY*, would not buy any one thing of him, for in ſo doing they will bring Diſgrace upon *themſelves*, and their *Poſterity*, for *ever* and *ever*, AMEN.

Broadside urging a boycott of the merchant William Jackson. (*Library of Congress*)

On this morning, after talking to several men, he seized the reins of a horse pulling a wagon. Soon the wagon, with Richardson aboard, lurched toward the infamous hand. Richardson was determined to smash the notorious sign. But the rowdy boys showered him with mud and stones. He abandoned the horse and cart and retreated to his house. On his way he recognized a member of the Sons of Liberty. "By the Eternal God," Richardson said, "I'll make it too hot for you before night."[21]

Richardson entered his house, and three Sons of Liberty were soon at his door. "Come out you damn son of a bitch," roared one. "I'll have your heart out, your liver out."[22]

Richardson soon emerged, shaking his fists and uttering more threats at the boys now gathered in front of his house. He shouted at them to go away. The boys, properly schooled in their rights, gave no ground. They were free to stand in the king's highway, they said. Small stones and bits of garbage began to patter off the walls of the structure. Richardson stepped out of sight and then reappeared with a stick. If they did not go away, he promised to "make a Lane thro them."[23]

About this time someone tossed a rock or a brick fragment through a window, and in an instant boys on all sides of the house began a bombardment of eggs, sticks, and stones. Windows cracked and shattered.

One missile hit Richardson's wife and a daughter. Richardson and his family faced the mob alone until George Wilmot, an out-of-work seaman, appeared, got Richardson's attention, and was allowed into the home. The gallant Wilmot volunteered to help Richardson defend his home and family.

Where were the authorities during all of this? When word reached Hutchinson about the scene outside the Richardson house, he ordered Sheriff Greenleaf to take action and "suppress" the "unlawful assembly." Greenleaf refused, fearing for his safety.[24]

No authority–no militia, no justices of the peace, no officials of any kind–came to intervene. As the mob became more aggressive, Richardson appeared in an upper story window, musket in hand. He snapped the lock. Was the weapon loaded? Only Richardson knew for sure. By now Wilmot could also be seen with a musket. Richardson, resting the barrel on a windowsill, pointed the gun down at the boisterous boys below. They continued throwing stones, believing the gun was not loaded. If it were, even Richardson, as outraged as he was, would not dare fire, so everyone assumed.

Then came a blast. Pellets sprayed the crowd. One tore through a sailor's trousers, a few bloodied the hand of a young man, and eleven pierced the stomach and chest of an eleven-year-old boy who was holding a stone in his hand.

Even after the blast, in the stunned confusion, another boy picked up a stone and hurled it at Richardson. "Damn ye," Richardson thundered, pointing his musket at the boy. "I'm ready for you."[25] Wilmot, with a musket at another window, shouted, "Stand off or I'll fire."[26]

A crowd huddled around the wounded boy, Christopher Seider, lying on the frozen street, bleeding horribly. Doctors appeared. Men carried the boy to a nearby house.

The gunfire, instead of scaring the mob way, fed its rage. The sound of nearby church bells brought forth more men, doubling and tripling the size of the mob outside the Richardson house. The boys and men were afraid to enter the front door, so many moved around to the rear to find a back way in. Men flooded into the back yard and began battering a wall, quickly tearing off boards, creating an opening. Men by the dozens poured in through the back and then clambored up the stairs. Wilmot quickly gave up his weapon. Richardson held out. He stood, his back to a wall, cutlass in hand, facing a room full of men ready to tear him apart.

Someone told him he had killed a boy. That was not true, not yet. The boy would linger for hours. Richardson snarled, "I don't care what I've done."[27] He was soon overwhelmed. The fierce mob dragged him and Wilmot out of the house and into the street. Someone produced a noose. A sturdy signpost was close by. A hanging was almost certain.

Then Molineux, of all people, came forward and calmed the crowd. Sobered by the shooting, stunned by how events had spun out of hand, Molineux was not prepared for a lynching, and the mob accepted his decision. Molineux knew about rock throwing, smashing windows, threats, and roughing people up, and those were his limits. A killing? He would not go that far.

Later, in Faneuil Hall, four judges charged Richardson and Wilmot with discharging a gun and wounding a boy, and then sent the men to jail. At about 9:00 p.m., the Seider boy died. The charge against Richardson would be murder. Wilmot would be charged as an accessory.

Sam Adams and the Sons of Liberty now went to work to make the most out of the bloody death of Christopher Seider. Three days after the killing, a letter in the *Gazette* notified all the "friends of Liberty" that they would have the opportunity to pay their "last Respects" to the boy, "this little Hero, and first martyr to the noble Cause." The letter writer, "A Mourner," deduced from the boy's behavior as he was dying and from the "heroic Pieces" of poetry in his pocket that he had "martial Genius, and would have made a clever man."[28]

A few days later, late in the afternoon, dozens, then hundreds, then thousands of Bostonians trudged along snow-clogged streets to gather around the Liberty Tree as part of the largest funeral procession anyone could remember. Placards with suitable biblical quotations were displayed. Read one: "Thou shalt take no satisfaction for the life of a MURDERER–he shall surely be put to death."[29]

Leading the procession in the waning light were more than four hundred boys, solemn and well scrubbed under their winter coats, walking slowly two by two from the Liberty Tree toward the State House. Then followed the bier, with Latin inscriptions. Six young men carried the coffin, behind which walked the boy's family, his friends, and then some two thousand mourners, followed by no fewer than thirty carriages.

In the *Gazette*, an article assured readers that someone would pay for the death of the boy (referred to as Snider), in contrast to what happened in London after the killing of the man mistaken for a rioter at St. George's Fields: "The Blood of young Allen may be cover'd in Britain: But a thorough Inquisition will be made in America for that of young Snider, which crieth for Vengeance, like the Blood of the righteous Abel."[30]

The actions against importers continued. Hutchinson seemed helpless. He urged his Council to take some action to end the tumults. But the Council, solidly on the side of the radicals, would authorize nothing.

Patrick Walker, like many other poorly paid soldiers in Boston, sought part-time work. Thus, on March 2, 1770, a few days after Seider's funeral, Walker appeared at the rope factory of John Gray. Many casual laborers were employed in the vast building, which was almost 750 feet long and stood south of Milk Street. A rope maker, observing Walker, asked, "Soldier, do you want work?"

Walker was eager. "Yes, I do, faith."

The rope maker answered, "Then go and clean my shithouse."[31]

The banter went downhill from there. Other rope makers gathered, and Walker swung his fist at somebody. Someone responded in kind. A cutlass clattered to the street from beneath Walker's coat. Walker soon scuttled away without his weapon but with a huge grudge. He returned minutes later with eight or nine fellow soldiers. The rope makers sent out word, and soon they had more than enough reinforcements, most wielding clubs.

The soldiers, outnumbered, retreated to their barracks, but returned within the hour, this time with about forty men. Soon, around the rope makers' tar kettle, a free-for-all ensued. As more civilians joined the fray, the soldiers took a beating and eventually retreated once again to their barracks.

In the following days, soldiers and civilians scuffled here and there, with the soldiers usually getting the worst of it. One private suffered a fractured skull and broken arm. When a sergeant missed a roll call, many suspected he had been killed. He eventually reappeared unharmed.

Hutchinson, well aware of the soaring tensions, sought advice from his Council. The only solution, councillors said, was to get the soldiers out of town.

FIFTEEN

FIRE AND BE DAMNED

About a foot of crunchy snow and chunks of ice covered King Street on the cool, still evening of March 5, 1770. A bright quarter moon from a clear sky offered faint light. Boston had no streetlamps. At the corner of King Street and Royal Exchange Lane, only a short block from the State House, stood a sentry box where Private Hugh White was on duty this particular evening. Behind White, up three steps and to his left, was the door to the brick Custom House. White was bored, nervous, and eager to be relieved. He was well aware of all the trouble in town. Somewhere, sometime this evening, a brawl or bloody mayhem could be expected. If some sort of organized attack on property were planned, the Custom House was a likely target. It was not hard to imagine a mob gathering, hurling stones and ice, and storming the building.

White could hardly defend the Custom House alone, but he took comfort in knowing that reinforcements were nearby. The Main Guard, the chief quarters for his regiment, was in view across and up King Street, near the State House. This was the same place that Mein fled into to escape the mob. White knew that if trouble arose, soldiers would be dispatched quickly to assist him.

The street was quiet, but never deserted. From time to time people came and went from the Custom House. Business hours were over. But a portion of the Custom House was also a dwelling for a family, the Greens, and visitors periodically dropped by and left.

White, fighting the tedium, called out to a civilian he knew walking by. How were things at home? The man responded and went on his way. Then came an officer. White recognized him, too: Captain Lieutenant John Goldfinch. Then a boy appeared. That was Edward Garrick, a wigmaker's apprentice. The boy gave a shout, not at White, but at Goldfinch: "There goes the fellow that won't pay my master for dressing his hair."[1] Goldfinch, a receipt for the wigmaker's service in his pocket, didn't bother to respond.

Somehow, though, the boy's snide accusation got under White's skin. Soon another apprentice appeared on the scene with two girls. They joined Garrick. One of the girls lived in the part of the Custom House that served as a dwelling. On the Custom House steps, the foursome dawdled, with White just steps away.

By and by an older brother of one of the girls emerged from the Custom House and ordered both girls in. The two apprentices wandered away, but not far. Before long, Garrick and his companion returned to King Street, where Garrick returned to the topic of Goldfinch. As people wandered past, Garrick blabbed to them that Goldfinch had no money.

This was too much for White. From his sentry post he shouted that Goldfinch would pay whatever debt he owed. Goldfinch, White assured Garrick, was a gentleman.

Garrick shouted back that that regiment had no gentlemen.

Now White stepped away from his post and out into the street. The cheeky Garrick approached.

"Let me see your face," said White.

"I am not ashamed to show my face," said Garrick.[2]

The words were hardly out of the boy's mouth when White slammed the musket against the side of the boy's head. The boy staggered and began to wail. White and the other apprentice traded insults.

About this time, a church bell somewhere in town starting tolling. Here and there shouts of "fire" could be heard.

The apprentice boys did not flee, but now started taunting White as more people began to gather on King Street to inquire about the supposed fire. Fresh taunts and curses rained down on the sentry. "Lousy rascal." "Damn you, you lobster son of a bitch!"[3] "Damned rascally scoundrel lobster son of a bitch!"[4]

The crowd grew to fifty or so, some with fire buckets. On edge, White retreated to the steps of the Custom House, where he would have the advantage of a slight elevation and where no one could get behind him. He also loaded his musket. More people gathered, more shouts, and now snowballs flew in White's direction. White fixed his bayonet and lowered the barrel in a threatening way.

A stout young bookseller, Henry Knox, worked his way through the crowd and spoke to White. Knox recognized the mortal danger. He told the soldier that if he fired his musket, he would die.

"Damn them," said White. "If they molest me, I will fire."[5]

At least one man stepped forward to urge the crowd to leave the sentry alone. Some people stepped away. Most people stayed, many edging closer to White. Now jagged chunks of ice were crashing near the soldier. This hail of missiles–ice, snow, oyster shells, chunks of wood, and perhaps stones and bits of brick–may have seemed more terrifying than it really was. A witness later remarked that after all this, not one pane of glass in the hated Custom House was broken.[6] But White was becoming unnerved. He pounded the butt of his musket on the steps hoping that would get the crowd to move back. He rapped on the Custom House door. Someone opened it about halfway. Then it was shut. White missed the opportunity to safely slink inside.

The screaming intensified. "Kill him, kill him, knock him down." "Fire, damn you, fire, you dare not fire."[7]

Another voice of calm reached White. This man, a town watchman, reminded White that, after all, his tormenters were mainly just boys. They would not really hurt him. But White remained jittery, verging on panic. He let out a shout: "Turn out. Main Guard!"[8] One eyewitness reported that no more than twenty people were on King Street near the Custom House when White shouted for help. Other estimates suggest more. Whatever the number, it quickly multiplied.

Almost simultaneous to the events on King Street, altercations between soldiers and civilians were erupting only a few streets away. One took place in Brattle Street in front of a barracks, where four or five officers faced a crowd of twenty townspeople.

"Why don't you keep your soldiers in their barracks?" a man shouted. "Are the inhabitants to be knocked down in the street? Are they to be murdered in this manner? . . . We did not send for you. We won't have you here. We'll get rid of you or drive you away."[9]

An officer tried to soothe the man and "begged" him to help disperse the crowd. Amid the mayhem, a seven-year-old boy appeared at the barracks gate, crying, screaming, holding his head. An officer grabbed the boy and "damned him for a rascal and asked him what business he had out of doors."[10]

As the officers looked for some peaceful way to calm and disperse the crowd, soldiers in the barracks seethed. One soldier dashed out of the barracks with his musket and, as the officers were distracted, began to take aim down the crowded alley. "Damn your blood. I'll make a lane through you all,"[11] he shouted. Before he could fire, officers grabbed him, took his musket away, and hustled him back into the barracks. Moments later, another soldier slipped out and likewise aimed his gun at the mob. Again, officers averted a massacre, disarmed the man, and got him back into the barracks.

Meanwhile, down the crowded alley a group of soldiers were fending off a snowball attack with a shovel. Officer Goldfinch, the same man pestered on King Street, came by. Civilians advised Goldfinch to get the soldiers back to a barracks before they got hurt or killed. Goldfinch pushed through the crowd and then led the soldiers through the volleys of curses and snowballs to the nearby barracks.

At the barracks the crowds pressed close to the gates. One angry man growled at an officer that soldiers had no business being out in the streets after 8:00 p.m. The officer tried to calm the situation. A civilian tried to help: "You hear what the officers say, you had better go home."[12] Many people sullenly obeyed and wandered away toward their homes. But many followed the shouts of "let's go to the Main Guard" and headed toward King Street.[13]

So King Street continued to draw more people–first from the confrontation between Private White and the apprentices, then from the tolling of church bells, and then from the mob on Brattle Street looking for a fight.

Meanwhile, in Dock Square, outside Faneuil Hall, several hundred men and boys from the North End had gathered, many with sticks and cudgels. Shouts of "fire" could be heard, but there was no fire anywhere, as many knew, for they were tearing apart nearby market stalls for hefty table legs, not much use for putting out a blaze. On the signal of a tall man in a white wig and red cloak, the mob quieted and then listened to his spirited tirade. The speech over, shouts of "Main Guard," echoed around the square, and this mob pushed toward nearby King Street, joining the swelling crowd.

Bells continued to ring out, now from two churches, and more and more men appeared on the street prepared to fight a fire, buckets in hand, as well as bags for stuffing the belongings from threatened dwellings. Here and there around town men hauled out fire engines and lugged them around in search of the phantom fire. Eventually word passed from man to man, crew to crew, that there was no fire, but there was some sort of disturbance on King Street. By twos and threes and then by the dozens these men found their way to King Street to see what was going on.

King Street, especially the short stretch between the Custom House and the State House, was now packed with people, mostly men, but many boys and some women. Most were just curious. Some people were looking for trouble. Many had sticks. At least one had a Highland broad sword.

One person drawn to King Street was Samuel Maverick, a seventeen-year-old apprentice to an ivory turner. He had been a guest for dinner at a friend's house. He heard the bells, gulped down his meal, and dashed out to see where the fire was. Another was Michael Johnson, a mariner in his late forties, about six-feet two-inches tall. Some said he was black. Others said he was Indian. He was likely a little of both. He was also a runaway slave. About twenty years before, when he was known as Crispus Attucks, he had fled his master in Framingham. Now, after eating dinner at a victualing house, a cheap eating place popular among off-duty soldiers, Johnson went out among the club-wielding clusters of whistling, shouting sailors who prowled the streets that night.

By now, of course, the soldiers of the Main Guard were alert to the crisis. No one at the Main Guard fully understood all the commotion–the bells, the armed men streaming into King Street, the shouting in front of the Custom House. But a crisis was at hand, and everyone in the building awaited orders. What would Captain Thomas Preston do? Preston, an Irishman, forty years old, happened to be captain of the day and had responsibility over White. Preston was highly regarded on all sides, with a "character of a benevolent, humane man," according to a civilian entirely opposed to the military presence in town.[14] Preston had been at his nearby lodgings when the bells first tolled and had gone up to the roof to see where the fire was. While he was on the roof, several soldiers came with word of a mob at the Main Guard on King Street. Preston soon appeared at the Main Guard, where townspeople told him that the sentry at the Custom House was at risk of being "murdered."[15] Preston had just seconds to consider his options, all highly risky. He could send out a large number of soldiers to reinforce White and make a stand in front of the Custom House. But the crowd they would face was huge, well armed, and angry. Just getting those soldiers to the Custom House without provoking a riot would be a miracle. But then what? Dozens or even hundreds of soldiers would probably not overawe this crowd.

Preston could also do nothing. The fury of the huge mob might burn itself out. Could White hold out? Would he survive? Preston looked out over the sea of waving sticks and fists at the figure of White. He might fire his weapon at any moment. Then he'd be torn apart.

Preston latched onto a third option–to relieve White. That is, rescue him. This meant dispatching a small group of six or seven soldiers to push across King Street, through the mob, gather in White, and march back with him through the mob to the Main Guard. This was perhaps the best of the three choices. But as Preston knew, if he extracted White without putting another sentry in his place, the Custom House would be left unguarded. It was entirely likely that the mob would smash into the building and loot it.

Preston went forward with this third option. A relief party formed up. Preston would lead a corporal and six privates, all large men made to loom taller with lofty, bearskin caps. The men marched two by two, muskets at their shoulders. The weapons were not loaded, but bayonets gleamed from the end of each barrel.

The eight marched slowly down King Street and then across, toward the Custom House. The mob gave way by inches, crowding so close that the soldiers brushed them as they passed. On orders, the men repositioned the muskets in a diagonal fashion. The bayonets now poked threateningly at anyone who failed to keep a safe distance. One bayonet grazed a man's hat. Another jabbed a man's back. "Damn you. Stand out of our way," shouted a private to a man in the way. The man refused: "I will not move for no man under the heavens."[16] The column split, veering left and right around the obstinate man.

Knox, the bookseller who pleaded with White earlier not to fire, had all this time tried to dampen the charged atmosphere. He had shouted at the boys to stop harassing White. Now, as the soldiers pushed through the crowd, he elbowed his way to Preston and pleaded with the officer to "take his men back again, for if they fired his [Preston's] life must answer for the consequence."[17]

Preston said he was aware of the danger.

By now the soldiers had reached the sentry box, which was empty, for White was on the Custom House steps. The soldiers paused, rested the butts of their weapons on the ground, and began to load them. All the while, the shouting, jostling, and snowballs continued. Men and boys pressed closer, screaming into the soldiers' ears, shoving, bumping, doing all they could short of assault to annoy, disrupt, and provoke the soldiers.

With loading completed, Preston ordered White to fall in. White quickly, awkwardly squeezed in among his fellow soldiers. Now the tiny force of nine turned and attempted to push its way back to the Main Guard. But they came chest to chest, chin to chin against men determined to block their way. Preston anticipated a brawl if they tried to push further. Amid the scuffling and cursing, Preston ordered the men to form up in a semicircle in front of the Custom House.

The men obeyed as best they could. Their line extended from a hitching post at the corner of the Custom House to the sentry box. A space of about the length of an arm separated each of the men. They thought their flanks and rear were protected, but amid the hubbub, people filtered in behind the soldiers, slipping through between them and the Custom House wall.

A woman somehow found herself near the very front of the mob and close to the soldiers' bayonets. White knew her and recognized her. "Go home," he shouted. "Or you'll be killed."[18]

Preston, standing in front of his men, shouted for calm, but his voice was drowned out by the crowd, screaming for the men to fire: "Fire, fire damn you fire, fire you lobsters, fire, you dare not fire."[19] All the soldiers saw were a sea of angry faces, hundreds of flailing fists, and flying bits of ice, shells, bricks, and bottles. Some people in the back of the mob had climbed on men's shoulders for a better view. "Why do you not fire?" came a shout. "Fire and be damned."[20]

Those who yelled such taunts were confident the soldiers would not dare fire. The boys who screamed and the men who boldly taunted had heard over and over again that the soldiers could not fire without permission of Hutchinson or some other civil authority in Boston. Hutchinson would never give such an order. So many men and boys felt untouchable: They could do anything to these soldiers without fear.

Those boys and men were wrong. The soldiers were not supposed to fire without civilian orders. But soldiers, just like civilians, might legally fire weapons when sufficiently threatened.

Still the soldiers held their fire. The men of this regiment were an unruly bunch, but Preston held them in check. More taunts. A well-dressed man at the back–unusual in this throng of mostly sailors and workmen–now could be heard: "Fire," he bellowed. "By God, I'll stand by you whilst I have a drop of blood. Fire!"[21]

A man moved in close to Preston. "Are your soldiers' guns loaded?" he asked.

"With powder and ball," said Preston.[22]

"I hope you don't intend the soldiers shall fire on the inhabitants."

"By no means," said Preston, noting that he stood in front of the guns and thus would be shot if the soldiers fired.[23]

Now there was laughter, and then three derisive cheers from the mob. Confidence that the soldiers would not fire rose with the din. Amid this cacophony and tumult, a man at the very front of the mob raised a club and brought it down on the shoulder of a soldier, Private Hugh Montgomery, who instantly lost his grip on his musket and fell on his back. Montgomery, in pain, in anger, in fear, quickly pulled himself up, snatched up his weapon, let out a fateful curse–"Damn you, fire!"[24]–and pulled the trigger.

The sound of the shot reverberated up and down King Street, silencing for a moment the shocked mob that had gotten what so many had been screaming for. Some began to flee. Samuel Maverick, some distance from the soldiers, sensed danger and started running in the direction of the State House. Space opened up directly in front of the soldiers as many backed away, although some took the gunfire as a signal to charge into the soldiers.

Then the roaring quickly resumed. If anyone was hit, no one seemed aware of it. Many in the mob assumed the guns were loaded only with powder–all sound, but no deadly force.

Richard Palmes, a merchant at the front of the mob, swung a stick at Montgomery, hitting his left arm, and then swung the stick at Preston, striking his arm. Perhaps this blow stunned Preston. Otherwise there is no explanation for why he failed to give any order at this crucial moment. He did not order his men to fire. Nor did he shout "Recover," the order to stop firing.

Now standing behind his men, Preston hesitated. Then another musket fired. Then another, and another, and another, not in a volley, but in quick succession.

In that instant, Michael Johnson, club in hand, fell backward to the street, blood gushing from his chest. Near the State House, many yards away, Maverick collapsed, struck in the chest by a deflected bullet. Elsewhere, rope maker Samuel Gray sank to the icy street with a hole in his head as big as a hand. Another man caught a bullet in his hip. Another man standing in his own doorway was struck in the arm.

The soldiers frantically started to reload. Preston, incredulous, shouted at his men, asking why they fired. Some said they heard orders. Now the mob, which had fallen back in panic, clustered around the fallen. The nervous soldiers, fearing an assault, raised their weapons. Preston dashed forward and pushed the barrels aside. "Stop firing. Do not fire."[25]

Most of the mob scattered. Some remained spellbound, still thinking the guns fired no bullets and assuming the dark mounds on the street were winter coats left behind in the panic. Others heard the screams, saw the blood, and were now coming back to attend the fallen, who were moaning, crying, writhing on the street.

Preston quickly brought the men into proper formation to march back to the Main Guard. With the mob scattered, the way was now clear, and the soldiers returned to the Main Guard without further incident.

The groaning wounded and the silent dead were handled haphazardly. There were no hospitals or morgues. Johnson's body was delivered to a tavern near the Custom House. Another body was carried to a doctor's house and simply plunked down by the locked door. Maverick was taken to his mother's house in the North End, where he died a few hours later.

Preston had good reason to expect, after the shooting, a full-scale mob assault on the Main Guard. He positioned a force by the Main Guard in anticipation of such an attack, while also ordering a drummer to beat a call to arms for the entire Boston garrison. As if in response, church bells from all over Boston joined the bells that already had been ringing. A full-scale battle between civilians and soldiers seemed certain. Many officers here and there about the town, now making their way on snowy streets back to their regiments, found themselves bombarded with stones and snowballs or attacked with sticks. Civilians talked about distributing the muskets stored in Faneuil Hall.

When word of the catastrophe on King Street reached the Hutchinson mansion in the North End, the acting governor set off immediately, joined by a cluster of men, including radicals who knew that Hutchinson might be the only man in town who could restore calm. On the way to King Street, Hutchinson's group encountered a crowd of men, some armed with clubs, others with cutlasses. Hutchinson explained who he was. Someone answered with the swing

Henry Pelham, half brother of John Singleton Copley, made a sketch of the shooting and gave it to Paul Revere (see page 160). Revere, without giving Pelham credit, made an engraving, printed it, and sold it, establishing the picture as the defining image of what became known as the Boston Massacre. (*Library of Congress*)

of his club. Hutchinson and the others fled that mob and found a roundabout route to King Street.

Hutchinson soon was pressed by the crowd "almost upon the bayonets" of the soldiers and stood face-to-face with Preston. Hutchinson asked, "How came you to fire without orders from a civil magistrate?"[26]

Preston bristled: "Sir, we were insulted. I was obliged to save my sentry."[27]

Preston invited Hutchinson to the Guard House. Hutchinson declined. He understood that just by stepping into it at this critical moment would suggest to some that he somehow endorsed the military action. But Hutchinson had to do something. He found himself swept into the nearby State House, where in the Council Chamber on the second floor he faced, among others, radical mob leader Molineux. Hutchinson was asked to tell military commanders to order all soldiers to their barracks. Under the circumstances, it seemed a prudent action to take.

But Hutchinson was wary. He had all along argued that he didn't have the authority to direct the actions of the soldiers. Thus if Hutchinson gave the order now and the soldiers obeyed, it would prove that Hutchinson had the authority, and had it all along. On the other hand, if Hutchinson gave the order and the military refused, that would prove that the military in Boston was not under civilian control. That would amplify the message Boston had been shouting to the world, that the town was being held in chains by an unwanted military force unresponsive to the will of the king's own civilian authority in Massachusetts.

Hutchinson thus refused to make any request of the military. Instead he stepped out onto the balcony overlooking King Street. He promised a full investigation. Go to your homes, he said. "The law should take its course. I will live and die by the law."[28]

The words had some effect. Some people drifted away. But many stayed, refusing to leave the street until the soldiers, in position around the Main Guard, left the street first.

Molineux again approached Hutchinson with the demand to use his authority with the military. Hutchinson talked to the lieutenant colonel in charge but made no demands. He simply made an observation: if the soldiers went into the barracks, the people would probably go home. The officer got the point. He issued orders. Soon the soldiers were back indoors. Not long after, the civilians abandoned bloody King Street.

Meanwhile, back in the Council Chamber, work began on sorting out what happened. Witnesses were found. Preston was brought in at 2:00 a.m., and by 3:00 a.m. he was ordered to jail. Later, eight soldiers turned themselves in.

By morning, soldiers and civilians realized how close the town had come to a much larger and bloodier clash. The town was alive with tales of how riders had gone out from Boston to alert the countryside, and how clusters of armed men had been seen in the night marching toward Boston. Others reported that a barrel of tar had been carried to the summit of Beacon Hill to be lit as a general alarm.

The tar barrel was never ignited, and the men from surrounding towns turned back, but nerves continued to be on edge. Hutchinson, in the Council Chamber again, huddled with the Council and two military men, Lieutenant Colonel William Dalrymple and Lieutenant Colonel Maurice Carr.

The Council was divided, but some councillors urged Hutchinson to order the military to get the troops out. When the town's selectmen arrived, they made the same demand. Following the selectmen, another contingent appeared: the town's justices of the peace and some justices from nearby towns. They urged the same thing–get the soldiers out–or there would surely be more bloodshed.

Hutchinson said what he had said before: he did not have such authority.

The selectmen left, called to a town meeting at Faneuil Hall. This was unorthodox to say the least. The selectmen had not scheduled the meeting. They were being summoned by townsmen. According to town records, "freeholders and other inhabitants" had appeared at the hall at about 11:00 a.m., Town Clerk William Cooper acting as chairman. He recorded: "The selectmen not being present and the inhabitants being informed they were in the council chamber, it was voted that Mr. William Greenleaf be desired to proceed there, and acquaint the selectmen that the inhabitants desire and expect their attendance at the hall."[29]

At this meeting at Faneuil Hall, townsmen voted to solicit from anyone information about the shooting the previous day. So many people wanted to speak that a committee was created to gather further statements.

At the same gathering in the packed hall, townsmen, at the urging of Sam Adams, demanded what others had cried for over and over: get the soldiers out of town. A committee of fifteen, including Adams, Hancock, and Molineux, was soon on its way to the Council Chamber at the State House to deliver the demand. At the chamber, Adams spoke for the group: "Nothing can rationally be expected to restore the peace of the town and prevent blood and carnage, but the immediate removal of the troops."[30]

Hutchinson received the message impassively. After Adams and his town committee retreated to a nearby room, Hutchinson and his Council deliberated with Lieutenant Colonel Dalrymple present. Hutchinson again told the Council he did not have the power to remove the troops and would "upon no consideration whatever, give orders for their removal."[31]

Hutchinson's only concession was to agree to another meeting with the Council that afternoon, about the time yet another meeting of townspeople would be taking place at Faneuil Hall. During this interval, consultations continued in the Council Chamber. Dalrymple, trying to be helpful, made a crucial remark: he said that without formal orders from Gage, he could order one regiment, the one that seemed most troublesome, out of town if Hutchinson and the Council simply indicated that such a move was desirable. In other words, Hutchinson and the Council could express a vague wish for such a move–not an order–and Dalrymple could make it happen. This pulled the carpet out from under Hutchinson's feet. The lieutenant governor, contrary to his repeated denials, had the power to remove the soldiers from the town.

Also during this interval, a councillor, Royall Tyler, said that ten thousand men from surrounding towns were prepared to come to Boston if need be to force the soldiers out. Other councillors from out of town confirmed to Hutchinson the threat from the countryside.

At 3:00 p.m., townspeople jammed Faneuil Hall. The meeting was immediately adjourned, to be reconvened at more spacious Old South. So the people filed out of Faneuil Hall, trooped past the Town House, and into Old South, which also proved too small to hold the throng. They bided their time in the church, outside the church, and near the State House while Sam Adams's fifteen-man town committee went off to the State House to call upon Hutchinson. Writing later, Hutchinson acknowledged that this was no mob, but earnest citizens seeking a peaceful way through the morass. They were "warmed with a persuasion that what they were doing was right, and that they were struggling for the liberties of America."[32]

When the town committee arrived at the State House, Hutchinson had a written response: "I have in council consulted with the commanding officers of the two regiments which are in town: They have their orders from the general at New York; it is not in my power to countermand his orders."[33]

In his response, Hutchinson also admitted that the Council now favored the removal of the soldiers to Castle William. The response also included Dalrymple's offer to evacuate one regiment from the town and make other changes in the soldiers' stationing to prevent more trouble.

The committee then departed, led by Adams, making its way past onlookers to Old South amid shouts of, "Make way for the committee."[34]

Adams entered Old South and delivered his report. A vote was soon taken on the question of whether Boston would accept the removal of one of the two regiments. One brave soul said yes. Everyone else roared no. It was the answer Adams wanted: all or nothing. The town demanded the removal of all soldiers.

A new committee was named. Joining Adams on this one were Hancock, Warren, Molineux, and three others. Out of Old South they went and up the street to the State House. They appeared before Hutchinson, the Council, and the military men–an assembly of great wigs, scarlet cloaks, and gold braid–seated at a long table in the Council Chamber, the same room where the Writs of Assistance case had been hashed out years before.

The committee told Hutchinson that the town meeting found his reply "by no means satisfactory."[35] Sam Adams then confronted Dalrymple and Hutchinson. John Adams told the story best:

> With a self-recollection, a self-possession, a self-command, a presence of mind that was admired by every man present, Samuel Adams arose with an air of dignity and majesty . . . stretched forth his arm, though even then quivering with palsy, and with an harmonious voice and decisive tone said, 'If the Lieutenant-Governor or Colonel Dalrymple, or both together, have authority to remove one regiment, they have authority to remove two, and nothing short of the total evacuation of the town by all the regular troops, will satisfy the public mind or preserve the peace of the province.'[36]

But John Adams wasn't there and wrote this almost half a century after the event.

Andrew Oliver, kinsman of Hutchinson, was there and reported a confrontation only between Sam Adams and Dalrymple, with Adams warning Dalrymple that if he did not remove all the soldiers, "it was in his peril."[37]

Adams later boasted that he saw Hutchinson's legs tremble during this dramatic scene. Possibly, but likely out of anger and frustration, not fear. Even today, no one fully understands what happened on March 5 on King Street, and certainly no one understood the day after the events. But Hutchinson then was convinced that the whole crisis leading up to and including the shootings had been planned and managed. In his view, it was a violent confrontation concocted to make the soldiers appear to be in the wrong in order to force their evacuation and eventually also the removal of the customs officials. It galled Hutchinson to give in to Adams and his ilk, who conceivably provoked the killings on King Street for political ends.

Dalrymple now said the threat from the countryside that Tyler mentioned was reason to keep soldiers in town, not remove them. But he was not going to make a decision. He dumped the responsibility on Hutchinson, saying, "I await your orders."[38] The acting governor must have wanted to hurl Dalrymple over the State House balcony. At the beginning of the day, Hutchinson had asserted that he was powerless and that the soldiers could not be moved without orders from Gage in New York. Then Dalrymple had battered that claim by offering to remove troops without orders from Gage and with only a nudge from Hutchinson. Now Dalrymple was literally asking Hutchinson for orders, completing the demolition of Hutchinson's contention and conceding Sam Adams's point that Hutchinson had the power to get the troops out.

The town committee left, and Hutchinson put the matter to the Council, which now seemed unanimous in calling for complete evacuation of the soldiers. Hutchinson asked: If all the soldiers are at Castle William three miles out in the harbor, who is going to protect the customs officers? One councillor argued dubiously that customs officers would be safe and always had been. Another said they'd be as safe as they were with troops in town. Tyler suggested that the safety of the customs men was no longer relevant; the people were determined to be rid of the soldiers, "failing of other means, they were determined to effect their removal by force, let the act be deemed rebellion or otherwise."[39]

Hutchinson felt abandoned. Would no one consider the consequences? With the soldiers gone, the protection of the customs commissioners and customs men could not be ensured. Enforcement of the Townshend Acts would lapse. This would be a capitulation and an acknowledgment that the king's laws could not be upheld. But no one seemed to care. The bloody events on King Street had left him no choice. He made the request. Dalrymple, to protect himself from later inquiries, insisted it be in writing, and Hutchinson complied.

Dalrymple understood Hutchinson's dilemma. "What else could you do?"

Hutchinson responded: "Retire to the Castle and remain there until the people come to their senses."[40]

In the dark, Sam Adams's town committee strode in triumph back to Old South with its trophy: a promise to evacuate all the soldiers.

SIXTEEN

HANG THE DOG!

As preparations began for the soldiers to leave Boston, plans were also being made to bury victims of the bloody events of March 5. Sam Adams and the other radicals would do for these victims what they did for the Seider boy only a few weeks earlier: the King Street martyrs would receive a grand funeral procession.

More than ten thousand people accompanied the four coffins containing mariner Johnson (whose given name, people now learned, was Attucks); apprentice Maverick; James Caldwell, a young mariner; and Sam Gray, rope maker. The solemn parade wound through the town, passed by the Liberty Tree, and eventually reached the cemetery known as the Granary Ground.

Tories watched and stewed. Was this a funeral, or political theater? One Tory recalled Attucks–"that half Indian, half negro, and altogether rowdy," who should have been "strangled long before he was born."[1] Tory pastor Byles muttered, "[W]hich is better, to be ruled by one tyrant three thousand miles away, or by three thousand tyrants not a mile away?"[2]

A fifth victim, Patrick Carr, a maker of leather breeches, died later that month, prompting still another somber procession.

On March 10, five days after the bloody confrontation on King Street, one regiment marched to the wharf and boarded boats for Castle William. The other regiment followed the next day. During embarkation, Molineux marched alongside a redcoat commander to ensure that townspeople did not harass the troops on the way to the wharf. Finally the soldiers were gone from the town, though still on a nearby island. When news of these events reached Great Britain, Lord North, the prime minister, wryly acknowledged that Boston radicals had trumped his military men. He gave a name to the troops exiled to Castle William. They were no longer under the king's command, but were "Sam Adams' regiments."[3]

Two days after the shootings, Preston and the others were arraigned. The indictment is striking to modern eyes for its archaic language: the men, acting "without the fear of God before their eyes," were "moved and seduced by the Instigation of the devil and their own wicked Hearts."[4] The indictment named only one victim: Attucks. Nothing in the document suggested that any of the men were soldiers; most were identified as laborers.

Within days of the shooting, Henry Pelham, half brother of painter John Singleton Copley, made a sketch of the shooting. Copley by this time was internationally famous, thanks mainly to his *Boy with a Flying Squirrel*, a painting exhibited in London. Pelham, eleven years younger than Copley, was the boy in that painting. Now twenty-one or twenty-two, Pelham had his own artistic aspirations and expected to make some money on his massacre drawing.

Pelham gave silversmith Paul Revere the drawing, and Revere, without giving Pelham credit or even getting his permission, made an engraving, printed it, and sold it, establishing the picture as the defining image of what became known as the Boston Massacre. This engraving, inaccurate and provocative, showed a neat row of soldiers firing in a volley on command into a cluster of well-heeled townsmen.

Pelham put his own print on the market about two weeks after Revere's went on sale. Pelham also wrote an indignant note to Revere for his "dishonorable Actions." Pelham complained that Revere had deprived him "not only of any proposed advantage but even of the expense I have been at, as truly as if You had plundered me on the Highway."[5] We don't know if the letter was sent. We do know that Pelham settled his differences with Revere: four years later they formed a business arrangement.

Meanwhile, opposing committees–one representing the radicals, the other speaking for Tories and the military–set to work cobbling together reports, bolstered by depositions, to send off to London.

The radical publication, *A Short Narrative of the Horrid Massacre in Boston*, was a pamphlet of nearly 150 pages made up chiefly of a report, mostly the work of James Bowdoin, spiced with italic type for emphasis. Supporting Bowdoin's report were depositions from ninety-six people, including seven women and one slave but no soldiers or officers. Bowdoin's report bristled with anger not so much at the soldiers occupying Boston, but at the customs commissioners and Bernard, the former governor. As Bernard and the commissioners "were the procuring cause of troops being sent hither, they must therefore be the remote and blameable cause of all the disturbances and bloodshed that have taken place in consequence of that Measure."[6]

In discussing the troops, the *Short Narrative* explained that the military had set up two field pieces aimed at the State House, with the

John Singleton Copley painted his half brother Henry Pelham in 1765. The portrait, *A Boy with a Flying Squirrel,* was exhibited in London and brought Bostonian Copley to the attention of established European painters.
(Reproduction © 2013, Museum of Fine Arts, Boston)

Main Guard posted just yards away: "This situation of the main guard and field pieces seemed to indicate an attack upon the constitution, and a defiance of law; and to be intended to affront the legislative and executive authority of the province."[7]

The report itemized some past outrages of military men. At the top of the list were the actions by a certain "Capt. Wilson" to incite local slaves to kill their masters, steal their masters' property, and "repair to the army for protection." Soldiers were also guilty of shooting off a musket "in a public street," an "attack" on "some of the magistrates of this town," and "the frequent wounding of persons by their bayonets and cutlasses."[8]

As for the confrontation at the ropewalk, Bowdoin recast the outhouse insult as a genteel "difference" leading "to a boxing match."[9]

The *Short Narrative* insists that in the days and hours before the Massacre, the town was in a state of terror as soldiers, and even the wives of soldiers, itched for an excuse to slaughter townspeople. Indeed, that is the scene painted in many depositions. Ten days before the Massacre, John Wilme heard a soldier's wife say that in the event of a shooting, if any townspeople were wounded, she would take the opportunity to "take a stone in her handkercshief & beat their brains out."[10] On the morning of the Massacre, Jane Usher heard someone, apparently a soldier, say "he hoped he would see blood enough spilt before morning."[11] Minutes before the Massacre, John Brown was staggered by a blow from soldiers "cursing and damning, toward the townhouse with naked bayonets in their hands."[12]

To the modern reader familiar only with the accepted story of the Massacre, the most surprising parts of the report are the allegations–supported by more than a half dozen depositions–that at least some of the bullets whizzing around King Street that evening came not from soldiers on the street but from an upper window of the Custom House. Four men, including Cato, "a Negro man, servant to Tuthill Hubbard, Esq.," thought they saw the flashes of gunfire from a Custom House balcony or window.[13] George Coster thought he heard gunfire from a Custom House window. Samuel Drowne "clearly discerned" a gun pointing through balusters on the balcony and witnessed "the person who held the gun, in a stooping posture withdraw himself into the house, having a handkershief or some kind of cloth over his face."[14]

Bowdoin may have been skeptical of these allegations. In his *Short Narrative*, he did not even mention a deposition from a boy claiming to be one of the second-story shooters! This was the deposition of Charlotte Bourgatte, a teenage servant of customs officer Edward Manwaring. Bourgatte claimed he was "carried" into an upper story chamber, given a gun by a "tall man," and told to fire it. When the boy refused, the tall man drew a sword "out of his cane" and threatened to "run me thro' the guts" if "I did not fire" the gun.[15] The boy said he shot it out the window twice, after which the "tall man came and clapp'd me on the shoulders . . . and said that's my good boy." The boy, in his deposition, said he saw other men in the room, including his master, Manwaring, whom the boy said was pointing a gun out the window.[16]

As for what provoked the sentry and soldiers on King Street, Bowdoin found in the depositions evidence of only spouting foul words and lobbing snowballs.

While Bowdoin and the radicals worked fast, their version of events arrived in London only after the military version, with its own supporting depositions, was in the hands of ministers. This document, *A Fair Account of the Late Unhappy Disturbance at Boston in New England*, contained a twenty-eight-page unsigned report followed by twenty-nine depositions.

The men collecting the depositions for the *Fair Account*, fully aware of depositions in the *Short Narrative*, took pains to include a deposition shattering Bourgatte's wild tale incriminating Manwaring. According to this deposition, the boy and Manwaring were not in the Custom House, but at Manwaring's lodgings at the time of the incident.

Another deposition revealed just how far patriotic attitudes had evolved. Henry Dougan, a regimental surgeon, told how just a few days after the Massacre he faced a "number of people, inhabitants armed with fire arms and clubs." According to Dougan, "I heard them repeatedly say, 'they had but one life to lose, and that they were willing to lose it for their country.'"[17] These sentiments, so similar to Nathan

Laſt Thurſday, agreeable to a general Requeſt of the Inhabitants, and by the Conſent of Parents and Friends, were carried to their *Grave* in Succeſſion, the Bodies of *Samuel Gray*, *Samuel Maverick*, *James Caldwell*, and *Criſpus Attucks*, the unhappy Victims who fell in the bloody Maſſacre of the Monday Evening preceeding!

On this Occaſion moſt of the Shops in Town were ſhut, all the Bells were ordered to toll a ſolemn Peal, as were alſo thoſe in the neighboring Towns of Charleſtown Roxbury, &c. The Proceſſion began to move between the Hours of 4 and 5 in the Afternoon; two of the unfortunate Sufferers, viz. Meſſ. *James Caldwell* and *Criſpus Attucks*, who were Strangers, borne from Faneuil-Hall,

March 12, 1770, newspaper illustration showing coffins bearing the initials of four civilians killed in the Boston Massacre: Samuel Gray, Samuel Maverick, James Caldwell, and Crispus Attucks. (*Library of Congress*)

Hale's famous last words six years later, show that these Bostonians no longer thought of Britain as their "country." But what was their country? Boston? Massachusetts? America?

Though the radicals were beaten in getting their story across the Atlantic, articles in British newspapers, just like those in American newspapers, tended to side with the townspeople. In Boston, the *Gazette* lumped the shooting on King Street with the death of Seider and the brawl involving Otis as "Villainy acted by dirty Banditti."[18] The *Gazette* also carried a notice placed by Captain Preston, who from jail was trying every strategy to save his neck. The notice gave "my Thanks in the most Publick Manner to the Inhabitants in general of this Town–who throwing aside all Party and Prejudice, have with the utmost Humanity and Freedom stept forth Advocates for Truth in Defense of my injured Innocence." Furthermore, "I shall ever have the highest sense of the Justice they have done me."[19]

At about the time Boston readers pored over that message, Preston was composing another, more honest, message for the eyes of readers in England. This report said the people of Boston "have ever used all Means in their Power to weaken the Regiments, and to bring them into contempt, by promoting and aiding Desertions, and with Impunity, even where there has been clearest Evidence of the Fact, and by grossly and falsely propagating Untruths concerning them."[20]

In this statement, Preston confessed doubts about the justice he would get in Boston, where "Malcontents . . . are industriously using every Method to fish out Evidence to prove [the Massacre] was a concerted Scheme to murder the inhabitants." Unless the king intervened, he wrote, he would have "nothing in Reason to expect but the Loss of Life in a very ignominious Manner."[21]

Meanwhile, Preston, hedging his bets, wrote General Gage in New York to beg the commander to do what he could to obtain a pardon from the king.

Townspeople also thought about the prospects of a pardon or some other trick that would enable Preston to escape the noose. As it turned out, they were correct. Before the trial, Gage wrote that should the verdicts come out against Preston and the soldiers, they would be "respited by the King."[22]

Rumors circulated that the Sons of Liberty planned to "Porteous" Preston. The meaning was well understood. In 1736, John Porteous was a commander of a force in Edinburgh assigned to execute a man regarded locally as a hero. When the spectators sympathetic to the condemned man started rioting, Porteous ordered his men to fire into the crowd. Some people died. For giving those orders and for firing himself, Porteous was later condemned to death. After the queen postponed the execution, a group of men snatched Porteous out of prison and hanged him. Thus, in colonial Boston, to Porteous meant to lynch.

Hutchinson was by now thoroughly fed up with his hometown: "I cannot help an attachment to the place of my birth, and I have some personal interest, 140 or 150 pounds sterling annual rents, besides the house I live in, but I would now give up all, if the town could be separated from the rest of the province. I do not see how that can be done, but something may and must be done to humble the leaders of the people of this town."[23]

With the soldiers gone, conversations in Boston day in and day out now dwelt on the upcoming trials of Preston and the soldiers for the shootings on King Street, and of Richardson and Wilmot in connection with the death of the Seider boy.

The trial of Richardson and Wilmot was set for March 23. By the time that date came around, the hated Richardson still had no lawyer. He tried to interview witnesses himself, but, he told the judges, constables refused to summon them. His jailer, he said, wouldn't even let him talk with friends. Meanwhile the newspapers were full of "the most infamous and false libels" against him, he said.[24] The judges took pity, postponed the trial, and saddled Samuel Fitch, a Loyalist-leaning attorney, with the task of representing Wilmot and Richardson. Fitch was half-hearted but managed to delay the trial into April.

Preston and the soldiers had better luck finding representation. A friend of Preston's approached Josiah Quincy, a radical, and Robert

Auchmuty, a Loyalist. They both agreed, but only if John Adams would be on the defense team. The friend then went to Adams "[w]ith tears streaming from his eyes."[25] Adams said yes. This was a coup: a Tory attorney and two of the best Whig lawyers in town. A juror might reasonably think that if fiery Mr. Quincy and brilliant Mr. Adams believed Preston was innocent, then maybe he was. If it was brave for Auchmuty to take on the case, it seemed even more so for Adams and Quincy. Why would they risk alienating their radical friends and jeopardizing their professional futures?

Adams, recalling the event years later, underscored his sense of duty. He remembered saying, "Counsel ought to be the very last thing that an accused Person should [lack] in a free country."[26] Quincy had a similar response. When his "shocked and bewildered" father asked him if it were true that he would "become an advocate for those criminals," he pointed out that "these criminals, charged with murder, are not yet legally proved guilty, and therefore, however criminal, are entitled, by the laws of God and man, to all legal counsel and aid; that my duty as a man obliged me to undertake; that my duty as a lawyer strengthened the obligation."[27]

As it turned out, neither Adams nor Quincy was taking much of a risk politically or professionally. Quincy pointed out to his father that he took up the case only after receiving the advice and urging of Sam Adams, Hancock, Molineux, and various other prominent radicals. John Adams did not record any meetings with his cousin or the other radicals before taking up the case, but it is reasonable to assume that he did consult them and heard no objection.

As historian Hiller Zobel suggests, the radicals were likely so confident of a conviction that they were quite willing to stand back and let the star lawyers do their best. That way no one could argue later that the convictions were the result of inadequate representation.[28] As Zobel also notes, radicals understood that fiercely Loyalist attorneys might use the trial to cast the town as a lawless, violent place, and underscore the fear that soldiers and customs officials felt. Radicals may have thought that Quincy and John Adams, their allies, would not play that card on behalf of their clients.[29]

So the defendants had a stroke of luck in having John Adams and Josiah Quincy on their side. Another bit of good luck landed in the defendants' laps with the illnesses of several judges. Hutchinson, looking for any reason for delay to allow passions to cool, seized on this excuse to push the trial at least to June. Meanwhile, Sam Adams pushed in the other direction. He knew that the sooner the trial–while outrage was raw–the greater the chance of a conviction. He rammed through a resolution at a town meeting calling for the appointment of special judges. He said a prompt trial was essential lest the prisoners escape.

Also, he pointed out, many witnesses were mariners and would soon be off to sea.

To make his point, Sam Adams, along with other leaders, such as Joseph Warren, led a "vast concourse of people" right into the courtroom, where they "harangued the judges."[30] The judges caved, scheduling the case for April. But the date still proved slippery. Even with the delays, a hanging–of Richardson, of Preston, of somebody–seemed a foregone conclusion. Workers began rebuilding the gallows.

At the trial of Richardson and Wilmot, beginning April 6, attorney Fitch told the court that he needed more time to track down a lead in an "anonymous" letter indicating that "somebody could swear something" that might be helpful to Richardson.[31] The court granted more time. Eleven days later, as the trial was set to resume, Fitch was ill. Giving up on Fitch, the judges tossed the case into the lap of Josiah Quincy. With the legal assistance of one Sampson Salter Blowers, Quincy had all of three days to prepare.

So the trial finally began April 20 before a jury that included no Bostonians. The courtroom was packed with "a vast Concourse of Rabble." Many stood, a few pockets were picked, and a noose was "ready at the Door of the Court Room." The jurors were not much better. To Judge Peter Oliver, they were "Tygers, whose tender Mercies were Cruelty."[32] Oliver later alleged that the process of obtaining juries had by this time been corrupted by the patriot faction, who managed to cull Tories from the lists of potential jurors, thus ensuring verdicts in line with the patriot point of view. In this case, jurors seemed to lean in that direction.

Opposite Josiah Quincy was his own brother Samuel, who did not share Josiah's radical tendencies but favored the Tory view. Worried that Samuel Quincy might not be suitably aggressive in prosecutions, the radicals had arranged for Robert Treat Paine, whose politics tilted toward the Whigs, to be part of the prosecution team. Important events were coming fast and furious for Paine, who practiced in southern Massachusetts and Rhode Island. He was newly married, having tied the knot at age thirty-nine just ten days after the Massacre. His bride gave birth to their first child two months after the wedding.

Samuel Quincy, in arguing the prosecution's case, stressed that Richardson fired on harmless schoolboys who posed no real threat. Richardson was reckless. He was guilty of murder. In response, Josiah Quincy argued self-defense. His witnesses, including Richardson's children, underscored the danger Richardson and Wilmot were in.

During closing arguments, Josiah Quincy hammered on the theme of "A Man's house is his Castle."[33] Paine, closing for the prosecution, noted that the shooting occurred before anyone actually broke into Richardson's house.

The judges had their turn at giving jurors their observations. Defying the testy audience, the judges clearly favored acquittal or a verdict short of murder. Judge Oliver asserted that the shooting was justified, inviting a chorus of hisses. Oliver was not intimidated. The people who are guilty, he said, are those who encouraged the mobs, and the civil magistrates who failed to take action against the mobs.

The courtroom seethed. "Damn that judge," shouted one man. "If I was nigh him I would give it to him."[34] Jurors, as they filed out at around 11:00 p.m., got plenty of advice from the rough crowd: "Hang the dog! Hang him!"[35]

For jurors, there was no break for sleep, or even food or drink. Deliberations began immediately. Most of the crowd, meanwhile, stayed in the courtroom. Only after some of them left was it possible for the judges to leave–to more hisses–and for Richardson to be safely escorted to the nearby jail.

Deliberations continued through the night. At dawn the court reassembled and the jury returned with its verdict. The foreman, one Jonathan Deming, announced that Wilmot was not guilty. Richardson, however, was guilty of murder. The courtroom exploded with cheers and applause.

The judges were plainly displeased. They received the verdict and ordered it recorded. Normally, they would immediately pass sentence. But they did not. They seemed to be playing for time to come up with some sound reason to spare Richardson's life. This was no small act of courage. The judges risked harassment, maybe assassination, to spare this pariah.

Though frustrated and on the defensive, Hutchinson and his Loyalist allies managed to further delay the trial of Preston and the other soldiers. Some radicals whined, but others agreed that in the interest of justice, time should pass for the town to calm down.

The soldiers gone, the town took steps to get rid of military families. The sheriff was dispatched to visit several wives of soldiers now housed at Castle William. He informed two women, one with three children, that they were officially "warned out" of town. They would have to leave within fourteen days.

Out at Castle William, crammed with soldiers, conditions were intolerable. Orders came from General Gage to dispatch a regiment south. Ferries carried that regiment ashore on May 17 for the march to Providence. From there, vessels carried the troops to New Jersey.

Work at the Custom House went on without soldiers nearby for protection. One afternoon in May, two customs men, John Woart and Owen Richards, noticed unusual activity aboard the *Martin*, a schooner from Connecticut. They investigated and found the vessel stuffed with hogsheads, barrels, and other containers of brown sugar, all undeclared to the customs authorities. The ship's master was obviously trying to smuggle the sugar into Boston.

The ship's master pleaded with Richards for leniency, and then offered a bribe. Richards scoffed. With chalk, he marked the containers and then marked the mainmast. The cargo and the ship were being seized. Soon more customs men boarded the vessel and moved it to a more secure place for safekeeping.

At about eight that evening, Owen Richards left the vessel to fetch his coat at home. On his way back to the *Martin* an hour later, he suddenly found himself surrounded by men and boys armed with sticks and clubs. The mob attacked as the streets rang out with shouts of "Informer!"[36] Richards tried to defend himself with a walking stick but soon fell under dozens of blows. The mob seized the bloodied man, groggy from the beating, and hoisted him onto a cart. The boys and men then pulled the cart to the Custom House, the site of the Massacre. Richards was soon stripped above the waist. A bucket of tar was produced, and the hot black goo was smeared over the man's upper body. Then came the blizzard of feathers. As a last gesture of cruelty, the feathers were set alight. Then, on the chest of the smoldering, semiconscious man, a sign was placed: "The True Informer."[37] Richards meekly protested that he was no informer but merely carrying out his job.

The hubbub attracted dozens and then hundreds of people once again to King Street. In his diary, Rowe reported "upwards a thousand people."[38] No one stepped forward to stop the torment.

Now the mob put the cart in motion, and Richards, amid shouting and roars, was pushed through the town, up one street and down the next.

While Richards was undergoing his humiliation, two groups of men and boys broke off from the rest. One group made its way to the *Martin*, pushed aside the tidesmen on duty, and unloaded most of the containers of brown sugar. The other group sought Woart, the tidesman who had been with Richards during the seizure. They found him aboard another vessel, dragged him to shore, through the streets of town, and all the way to Beacon Hill, where that group met up with the main mob, which still had Richards. Finally, some voices of moderation were heard. Enough was enough, and the two men were allowed to slip away.

Despite the constant threat of such humiliation and agony, defiance of the radicals went on. Theophilus Lillie and another stubborn and determined trader, bent on profiting from huge demand in the countryside for imports, attempted a breakout of sorts. They loaded two wagons, each pulled by four horses, with imported goods. Then they charged down the one road out of town, over the Neck. But like a scene from the Wild West, members of a nonimportation committee saddled up and gave chase. They caught the wagons, retrieved the goods, and locked them up.

Another merchant, Patrick McMaster, got far worse treatment for suspected importing. He and his brother James specialized in acquiring linen, silk, and tobacco from London and Glasgow and selling it out of their shop and to other retailers. Because they obstinately kept importing, they found their windows broken, their shop smeared with dirt, and their reputations trashed at town meetings and in newspapers. Still they persisted and participated in meetings supporting an end to nonimportation. On the evening of June 1, a mob of men and boys led by Thomas Young delivered to the McMasters's shop a "warning out." The McMasters had until June 4 to close up shop and leave Massachusetts or "expect the consequence."[39] The McMasters went to Hutchinson for help and somehow got reassurance nothing would come of the threat.

Then on June 19, a crowd showed up at the McMasters' shop. Men tore down the signboard, forced their way in, grabbed Patrick, who was alone, and dragged him out. Many decades later, shoemaker George Robert Twelves Hewes–one of the mob, or at least an observer–recalled that the mob treated McMaster gently because they saw he was so frightened: "They gave him some cordials, revived him, seated him comfortably on a chair in the cart, dragged him very good-naturedly" to Roxbury, over two miles away, and "there, on his promise of good behavior, dismissed him with cheers." The Boston mob never actually applied tar and feathers but carted McMaster through town "with a bag of feathers and a barrel of tar by his side."[40]

Accounts of the time confirm that McMaster was not literally tarred and feathered. However, the accounts also say he was given not cordials but smelling salts, and that while in the cart he was beaten, spat on, and cursed. Then, outside Boston, a Roxbury mob resumed some sort of torment. Around dusk, McMaster escaped, hid until dark, and then made his way to Castle William, probably by going down the Dorchester Peninsula and getting someone to ferry him to the island.

On the same night of McMaster's ordeal, the household of Customs Commissioner Henry Hulton was also the target of terror. Possibly the two attacks were linked. Hulton's sister Ann thought so.[41] She, her brother, and his family were living in Brookline, about five miles west of Boston. Brookline was then a country village of about six hundred residents. Situated amid thirty acres of orchards, the family believed that by being outside tumultuous Boston they would not be harassed. But this night, someone went out of their way to find them and scare them out of their wits. The Hultons heard a knock at the door between midnight and 1:00 a.m. A voice from outside announced an "Express from New York." Henry Hulton was wary. With sword in hand he opened a parlor window and asked for the letter. An arm from the outside tried to push the window open. Hulton "clap'd it down."[42] In the ensuing struggle, window glass, sash, and frame were all shattered. Hulton kept the man out, but then that man and his fellows circled the house, battering the walls and smashing the ground-floor windows. "Most hideous Shouting, dreadful imprecations, & threats ensued."[43] A stone nearly struck Hulton's wife. Just as in the aftermath of the *Liberty* riots, the family soon took refuge at Castle William, where they encountered Patrick McMaster, an "honest industrious Tradesman," and his brother, "ruind men & forlorn."[44] By midsummer, all the customs commissioners had packed up their families and moved to the safety of the island outpost.

SEVENTEEN

STUBBORN THINGS

Finally news arrived in Boston that Parliament had done away with all the Townshend duties–all, that is, except the duty on tea. It was a shrewd tactic. Parliament was trying to calm the tumult without surrendering its principle: the tax on tea demonstrated its authority to tax without the consent of the Americans. But by removing the duties on everything else, Parliament made most Americans feel they had won the game.

Indeed, the storm clouds passed. Many Americans thought they were gone forever. Predictably, nonimportation quickly collapsed. While radicals in Boston wanted to maintain the boycott there while the duty on tea remained, shopkeepers in Albany, Providence, and Newport abandoned the boycott when word of the repeal reached America. New York and Philadelphia could be expected to follow.

Bostonians found other news from England discouraging. Frustrated Britons had initiated a petition movement. Many people, angry with the king's ministers, had petitioned George III directly. But his response was icy. In Boston, the *Gazette* observed: "Is this the virtuous the religious k[ing], who was to bring back the Golden Age, and banish vice and impiety from the realm. How long is England to be the sport of Libertines and Tyrants."[1] Attitudes toward the king were shifting. Until now, he had been sacrosanct. It was assumed his ministers had pulled the wool over his eyes. Now Bostonians in increasing numbers, and people elsewhere in America, were rethinking their opinion of George. Maybe the king was not a dupe but a villain.

As attitudes shifted, a Tory voice fell silent and a new radical Whig newspaper shouted for attention. The *Chronicle* had limped along without Mein but could not survive. In June, the paper died. A month later, another newspaper was born. This was the *Massachusetts Spy*. Its publisher was Isaiah Thomas, age twenty-one. In starting out, the paper's aim was not unlike that of the *Chronicle* when it began: Thomas initially wanted to make the *Spy* an independent paper open to Tories and Whigs. But Thomas couldn't hide his affinity for the Whigs. Where Mein and the *Chronicle* made enemies of the Whigs, Thomas and the *Spy* alienated Tories. The *Spy* gradually became even more strident and more unscrupulous than the *Gazette* in attacking Tories and supporting the Whig cause.

Weeks passed after the Boston Massacre with news and rumors swirling through the town like fall leaves. Word spread that the king would not permit any sentence to be carried out against Preston without his express command. Thus, more than likely, no matter the verdict, Preston would not face the noose–or at least not a legally sanctioned noose.

A lynching was still possible, though. Worried military authorities proposed moving the prisoners to Castle William or to a navy ship. But the prisoners stayed put, and the threat of lynching and other street violence subsided. In July, Samuel Cooper wrote that townspeople "universally wish him [Preston] a fair Trial."[2]

In August, Bostonians were distracted by the return visit of revivalist George Whitefield. This was Whitefield's seventh, and last, tour of America. In late September, after arriving in Newburyport east of Boston, the preacher had an asthma attack and died. No fewer than fourteen notices from Boston presses commented on his passing. No other death in the whole century received such attention.

Boston streets, calm during Whitefield's visit, remained quiet as the nonimportation movement fizzled out. New York threw in its cards on the boycott in midsummer. Philadelphia followed. Boston merchants could not go it alone very long. By October 12, nonimportation in Boston was dead. Merchants could import as they pleased with no more threats from the Sons of Liberty.

At the start of the process for prosecuting Preston and the soldiers, the plan was for a single trial of all the men. By October, a decision had been made to split the case in two. Preston would be tried first, with a single trial for all the other men to follow. John Adams, Josiah Quincy, and Auchmuty would represent all the defendants at both trials. Today, legal ethics would bar the same lawyers from representing all the defendants in two trials of this nature. The reason is obvious. In defending Preston, the attorneys, if they could, would try to prove that Preston gave no orders to fire. In defending the soldiers, the lawyers would try to prove the opposite: that Preston gave orders and the soldiers were just following them.

The problem did not seem to trouble Adams, Quincy, and Auchmuty. The soldiers, however, had qualms–not with their lawyers, but with the idea of separate trials. They feared that if Preston were tried first, his word would be believed over theirs. They thus favored a single trial. In petitioning the court, they wrote: "[W]e only desire to Open the truth before our Captains face for it is very hard he being a Gentelman should have more chance for to save his life than we poor men that is Oblidged to Obay his command."[3]

The soldiers' concerns were brushed aside, and the trial of Preston, alone, began October 24 on the second floor of the new courthouse on Queen Street. The courtroom likely would have had a long table, big enough for a panel of five judges, set before a fireplace. Also in the courtroom would have been a jury box, a clerk's table, a witness stand, chairs and tables for the lawyers, a box for the prisoner, a bar running across the room, and space for about sixty onlookers. At this trial, unlike the Richardson trial, "the greatest order and decorum"[4] prevailed, with an audience made up largely of military and customs men.

Preston had amazing luck in getting several rock-ribbed Loyalists on the jury. With this, he virtually won his case before any evidence was presented. As in modern cases, attorneys on both sides were permitted to block a certain number of jurors considered biased. In this case, both the prosecution and the defense rejected so many veniremen–potential jurors provided by the town–that when the last venireman had been called, only seven jurors had been empanelled, with five vacancies remaining. So judges simply directed the sheriff to go out and gather up potential jurors, called talesmen, from among the men nearby. Lo and behold, among the men the sheriff rounded up was Gilbert Deblois, a wealthy merchant and well-known Loyalist who had actually aided in Preston's defense by giving him all the information he knew about potential jurors. He was joined by several other Loyalists, including one who had been heard to say Preston was "as innocent as the Child unborn."[5]

Of the three other talesmen, one sold bread to the military, another was Deblois's brother-in-law, and the other had long made himself known as a Loyalist. Years later, five of the twelve jurors would be among the Loyalists who left Boston. Considering that the jury had to be unanimous to convict, Preston could breathe easy.

Why didn't the prosecution make a fuss? Why weren't the Sons of Liberty furious? It was as if the radicals had lost interest in the case. Sam Adams wasn't even in the courtroom.

Samuel Quincy for the prosecution called Garrick, the wigmaker's apprentice, as his first witness. He described the initial encounter with Private White. The second witness noted an ample interval between the initial shot and the later shots, plenty of time for Preston to have given the command "Recover," which would have stopped the shooting.

The most powerful evidence for the prosecution came toward the end of the first day. One witness reported Preston saying, "Damn your bloods, fire, be the consequences what it will." Another heard Preston say, "Damn your bloods, fire again, let the consequences be what it will."[6]

Criminal trials in those days usually took no more than a day, so courts rarely had to worry about sequestering and accommodating jurors overnight. This case would take longer than one day, and maybe far more than two, so accommodations for the jurors were prepared in the nearby house of the jail keeper. The defense and the prosecution would each send a "keeper" to watch the jurors overnight.

When the trial resumed, a prosecution witness said he heard Preston give orders twice to fire. "I looked the officer in the face when he gave the word and I saw his mouth," said Daniel Calef.[7] The next witness pointed out Preston. "That's the person who gave the word to fire. . . . I was so near the officer when he gave the word fire that I could touch him," said Robert Goddard.[8]

More witnesses followed. Then, before the day was done, John Adams opened the defense's case. Three witnesses were called before the court adjourned for the day.

On the third day, jurors heard from twenty-two witnesses, including Jane Whitehouse, a friend of White's. Witnesses were not required to swear on a Bible, but Whitehouse insisted. She said she was certain the order to fire came from a man dressed in dark clothes–not like the clothes Preston was wearing–standing behind the soldiers. Another witness said the man giving the command to fire was "dressed in blue or black velvet or plush trimmed with gold"[9] Again, this description did not match descriptions of what Preston was wearing that night. What was Preston doing? Said a witness, "I am very certain he did not give the word fire."[10]

Perhaps the strongest testimony for the defense came from Richard Palmes, who had from time to time identified with the Sons of Liberty. He was as close to Preston as anyone at the time of the shooting: Palmes had his hand on Preston's shoulder moments before the shooting, and moments after the shooting he whacked Preston on the arm with a stick. The flash from the first shot scorched Palmes's coat. Palmes said he did not see or hear Preston give the order to fire.

Another key witness was Andrew, a slave owned by Oliver Wendell, a merchant and a member of the Sons of Liberty. (Oliver Wendell would become grandfather of Oliver Wendell Holmes, poet and author, and great-grandfather of Oliver Wendell Holmes, associate justice of the US Supreme Court.) The prosecution never questioned Andrew's reliability as a witness. Even so, the defense put Wendell on the stand to vouch for his slave. Wendell testified that Andrew's "character for truth, integrity and understanding is good."[11]

Andrew had been in the middle of the action and, according to a summary taken by an anonymous recorder, recalled the mob "making a great noise or screeching huzzaing and bid the Soldiers fire damn you, you dare not fire." Amid the chaos, Andrew "heard a voice cry fire and immediately the first gun fired. It seemed to come from the left wing from the second or third man on the left. The officer [Preston] was standing before me with his face towards the people. I am certain the voice came from beyond him."[12]

Eventually, the defense attorneys got around to introducing evidence about the violent atmosphere in the town on the night of the Massacre. This was tricky for Adams and Quincy. As Preston's lawyers, they needed jurors to hear testimony about threatening townspeople run amok. But as radical politicians, Adams and Quincy would have preferred to keep such testimony off the public stage. Statements that underscored the violence would put the Sons of Liberty on trial.

A man on the stand told of a gang of civilians brandishing clubs, sticks, and swords at least two hours before the deadly events on King Street. This testimony was apparently too much for Adams. Quincy wanted to bring in more such evidence, Auchmuty deferred to Adams, and Adams vetoed the idea, threatening to quit the case if Quincy persisted. So the testimony concluded with almost nothing said about events away from King Street that fatal night. Also, Preston didn't testify on his own behalf. Such testimony was actually forbidden. It was assumed that the defendant would lie.

Also, none of the soldiers testified. The prosecution could have called them, and their testimony might have helped convict Preston, especially if they said they fired after hearing Preston's orders. But such testimony at the Preston trial would make it harder to convict the soldiers at their own trial.

In closing, Adams underscored the right of self-defense. A man may kill, even if he has an avenue of retreat, if he is "assaulted in such a manner, and such a place, that he cannot go back without manifestly endangering his life."[13] Also, such a man could not be blamed under the law if, in killing his attacker, he also killed an innocent onlooker.

Adams went on to emphasize the testimony of Palmes, the man who heard no order to fire. As for the fateful pause between the first shot and the subsequent shots, when Preston did not give the order to recover, Adams dismissed Preston's failure as a simple matter of surprise. Preston was so taken aback that he was unable to react promptly. This was a stretch. Preston was an officer in command of a group of men with loaded guns in a highly volatile situation. He of all people should have been anticipating the possibility that a shot would be fired. That was his job.

Adams finished and then Auchmuty said a few words, winding up at about 4:30 p.m. The court adjourned and resumed the following Monday.

Paine then launched the prosecution's closing arguments. Palmes was "certainly mistaken." Andrew's account amounted to "flights of Fancy." The soldiers could not have truly felt themselves in mortal danger: "This violent attack turns out to be nothing more than a few snowballs thrown by a parcel of boys . . . and one stick that struck a Grenadier but was not thrown with sufficient force to wound or even sally him." Paine used Palmes, the key witness for the defense, to shore up his argument: "Would he place himself before a party of soldiers and risk his life at the muzzles of their guns when he thought them under a necessity of firing to defend their life?"[14]

Starting about noon, the four judges, each in turn, spoke to the jurors, as was the normal practice. The first to speak, Edmund Trowbridge, said he did not think Preston gave orders to fire. If the jurors thought otherwise, then, according to the evidence, the crime could not be murder. The only possible crime was "excusable homicide."[15] The other three judges concurred. The last to speak, Benjamin Lynde, said evidence proved that townspeople, not Preston, behaved disgracefully that fatal evening:

"Happy I am to find, that, after such strict examination, the conduct of the prisoner appears in so fair a light; yet I feel myself, at the same time, deeply affected, that this affair turns out so much to the disgrace of every person concerned against him, and so much to the shame of the town in general."[16]

The jurors retired at the end of the day and sent word within three hours that they had reached a verdict. The next morning that verdict was announced: not guilty.

Preston quickly made use of his new freedom to slip away to Castle William. From there he wrote a letter of thanks to Auchmuty, but not to Adams or Quincy. He later wrote, "My Counsel . . . were men of parts, and exerted themselves with great spirit and cleverness, particularly Judge Auchmuty."[17]

Next came the trial of the eight soldiers. Again, Paine and Samuel Quincy handled the prosecution. Adams and Josiah Quincy, without Auchmuty, teamed up again for the defense. In late November, the selection of jurors began. By the time the list of veniremen ran out, nine jurors had been selected, none from Boston. As in the Preston case, talesmen were rounded up. Various Bostonians were brought in and then rejected for possible prejudices. Finally, three men from out of town were found and determined to be acceptable. Sam Adams, who attended this trial, grumbled that no townsmen were on the jury. But no one else seemed troubled.

The verdict in the Preston case likely aided the prosecution, if only because of natural sympathy for the Massacre victims. With Preston off the hook, many people likely shared the view of one prospective juror who was heard to say, "Innocent blood had been shed, and therefore somebody ought to hang for it."[18] But also, the first trial seemed to take away the soldiers' best defense: that they were just following orders.

Six prosecution witnesses were called the first day, November 27, setting the scene of the shooting. The next day, a witness exposed the prosecution's sloppy preparation, saying, "I don't know any of the prisoners, nor anything."[19]

The testimony of another witness also caught the prosecution off guard. Sailor James Bailey remarked that Attucks, one of the victims on King Street, had been seen earlier brandishing a hunk of cordwood at the head of a noisy gang of sailors, some armed with sticks. Bailey also said that one of the soldiers, Montgomery, had been struck on the arm and knocked down before firing the first shot. These statements worked in favor of the soldiers by showing that they faced threatening civilians and were attacked.

Palmes testified, telling much the same story that he told at the Preston trial. He helped the prosecution by contradicting Bailey and saying Montgomery had not fallen until after firing. But the damage was done. Doubts, contradictions, and confusion were muddying the prosecution's case.

Another witness chimed in with recollections of several dozen men "dressed in sailor's clothes,"[20] half armed with cordwood, heading toward the State House that night. The image jurors were getting was not that of soldiers threatening civilians, but of civilians on a rampage.

At last a witness came forward with solid evidence that, indeed, the soldiers may have harbored plans, or at least notions, of shooting civilians. That witness heard one of the soldiers, Private Mathew Kilroy, say no more than two weeks before March 5 that "he would never miss an opportunity, when he had one, to fire on the inhabitants and that he wanted to have an opportunity ever since he landed."[21]

Then other witnesses told of being treated roughly by soldiers in the days before the Massacre. One man showed a scar from a bayonet wound. The prosecution's message was clear: the soldiers had been itching for a fight and, indeed, had been stirring up trouble before the events on King Street.

In his closing remarks, Samuel Quincy downplayed the idea that people had gathered in the street to threaten the soldiers. The bells, indicating a fire, had drawn people to King Street because that was a natural gathering place when the location of the fire is unknown.

Now Samuel Quincy, the Loyalist trying to hang the British soldiers, gave way to his brother Josiah, the radical trying to free the soldiers. Josiah reminded jurors that many eyes were upon them to see how Boston administers justice: "It is of high importance to your country, that nothing should appear on this trial to impeach our justice or stain our humanity."[22]

No thought, he said, should be given to the town's "character, conduct, and reputation":

> Boston and its inhabitants have no more to do with this cause, than you or any other members of the community. You are, therefore, by no means to blend two things, so essentially different, as the guilt or innocence of this town and the prisoners, together. The inhabitants of Boston, by no rules of law, justice, or common sense, can be supposed answerable for the unjustifiable conduct of a few individuals hastily assembled in the streets.[23]

Of the first fifteen witnesses for the defense, only two actually saw the shooting. The rest saw the violence and mayhem that took place elsewhere that night. The defense wanted to give jurors the impression that soldiers had reason to feel themselves in danger.

Several witnesses described a man in a white wig and a red cloak who spoke to the people in Dock Square. No one then or since had been able to identify the man. This bit of testimony was significant because it suggested that well-positioned men of the town directed the actions of civilians; that these were not just spontaneous aimless brawls of workers and sailors but calculated violence guided from the upper ranks of Boston society.

The direction of the trial was upsetting to both Adamses. Sam Adams wrote a note to Paine giving the prosecutor a litany of unsolicited advice. Paine didn't need it because, on the other side, John Adams was threatening to quit the case, just as he threatened to quit the Preston case, and for the same reason: he wanted Josiah Quincy to stop piling on evidence showing townspeople in a bad light.[24]

Quincy once again gave in. Most of the witnesses for the remainder of the trial were people who had been on King Street. Andrew once again testified, and once again his master, Oliver Wendell, reassured jurors about Andrew's character. Two witnesses told jurors how Patrick Carr, one of the victims, tried to go out that night with a hidden sword. The most touching and powerful testimony came from the doctor who had spoken with the dying Carr:

> I asked him whether he thought the soldiers would fire? He told me he thought the soldiers would have fired long before. I then asked him whether he thought the soldiers were abused a great deal after they went down there? He said he thought they were. I asked him whether he thought the soldiers would have been hurt if they had not fired? He said he really thought they would, for he heard many voices cry out, kill them. I asked him then, meaning to close all, whether he thought they fired in self-defence, or on purpose to destroy the people? He said, he really thought they did fire to defend themselves; that he did not blame the man whoever he was, that shot him.[25]

Immigrant Carr, as his life was ebbing away, told the doctor that he had seen soldiers fire on civilians in his native Ireland. There, he said, they weren't provoked half as much before they fired on the people. On the doctor's last visit to the dying Carr, "He particularly said, he forgave the man whoever he was that shot him, he was satisfied he had no malice, but fired to defend himself."[26]

After an adjournment, the trial resumed with the summation from the defense. Josiah Quincy reminded jurors of the taunts, how the soldiers were called cowards, bloody-backs–in reference to the frequent whippings–and lobsters. "To be compared to the most despicable animal that crawls upon the earth was touching indeed a tender point."[27] No man could ignore these insults:

> Gentlemen of the jury, for heaven's sake, let us put ourselves in the same situation! . . . Consider the temper prevalent among all parties at this time. Consider the then situation of the soldiery; and come to the heat and pressure of the action. The materials are laid, the spark is raised, the fire in kindles, the flame rages, the understanding is in wild disorder, all prudence and true wisdom are utterly consumed. Does common sense, does the law expect impossibilities? Here to expect equanimity of temper, would be as irrational, as to expect discretion in a mad man.[28]

Quincy also briefly noted that townspeople were "guilty of indiscrete conduct."[29] But, probably in deference to John Adams, he said little else about civilian responsibility for what happened.

After Quincy sat down, John Adams started in. He reminded jurors of the law and how even a slight aggravation could be enough to reduce murder to manslaughter:

> The law considers man as frail and passionate, when his passions are touched, he will be thrown off his guard, and therefore the law makes allowances for this frailty, considers him as in a fit of passion, not having the possession of his intellectual faculties, and therefore does not oblige him to measure out his blows with a yard stick, or weigh them in a scale; let him kill with a sword, gun or hedge stake, it is not murder, but only manslaughter.[30]

Like Quincy, Adams tried to put the jurors in the soldiers' shoes:

> Consider yourselves, as knowing that the prejudices of the world about you, were against you; that the people about you thought you came to dragoon them into obedience to statutes, instructions, mandates, and edicts, which they thoroughly detested; that many of these people were thoughtless and inconsiderate, old and young, sailors and land men, negroes and mulattos; that they, the soldiers had no friends about them, the rest were in opposition to them; with all the bells ringing . . . the people cry-

> ing "Kill them! Kill them! Knock them over!"; heaving snowballs, oyster shells, clubs, white birch sticks three inches and an half diameter. Consider yourselves in this situation and then judge whether a reasonable man in the soldiers' situation would not have concluded they were going to kill him.[31]

He touched on the guilt of the mob, saying that in a case of an unlawful assembly, all and every one of the assembly is guilty of all and every unlawful act, committed by any one of that assembly. Adams shrewdly likened the soldiers' predicament to that of townspeople facing a press gang snatching men off the street: "How far do you suppose the inhabitants would think themselves warranted by law to interpose themselves against that lawless press gang?"[32]

The next morning, Adams resumed his summation, attacking simultaneously the King Street mob and the authorities who ordered the soldiers to Boston:

> We have been entertained with a great variety of phrases to avoid calling this sort of people a mob. Some call them shavers, some call them geniuses. The plain English is, gentlemen, most probably a motley rabble of saucy boys, negroes and mulattoes, Irish Teagues and outlandish jack-tars. And why we should scruple to call such a set of people a mob, I can't conceive, unless the name is too respectable for them. The sun is not about to stand still or go out, nor the rivers to dry up because there was a mob in Boston on the fifth of March that attacked a party of soldiers. Such things are not new in the world, nor in the British dominions. . . . Soldiers quartered in a populous town, will always occasion two mobs, where they prevent one. They are wretched conservators of the peace![33]

Adams splashed some of the blame on the victims themselves, while also hinting to his white American-born Protestant jurors that victims included outsiders who were not white, not Protestant, and not born in America. Specifically, "Carr from Ireland" and Attucks, the "stout mulatto fellow, whose very looks was enough to terrify any person [and] to whose mad behavior, in all probability, the dreadful carnage of that night is chiefly to be ascribed."[34]

Adams was nearly finished:

> Facts are stubborn things; and whatever may be our wishes, our inclinations, or the dictates of our passions, they cannot alter the state of facts and evidence: nor is the law less stable than the fact; if an assault was made to endanger their lives, the law is clear, they had a right to kill in their own defense; if it was not so severe as to endanger their lives, yet if they were assaulted at all, struck and abused by blows of any sort, by snowballs, oyster

> shells, cinders, clubs, or sticks of any kind; this was a provocation, for which the law reduces the offence of killing, down to manslaughter, in consideration of those passions in our nature, which cannot be eradicated.[35]

The prosecution's response was feeble. Paine jabbed at the words of the dying Carr. Why should they be given weight? Carr's "character and disposition we know not."[36] He did not take an oath to tell the truth. He had just arrived on the scene when the shooting occurred, and thus knew less than other witnesses. Paine's best argument was to assert that the soldiers had assembled illegally and thus are collectively guilty even if it can't be shown who fired the fatal shots:

"The moment they turned their arms on the people without just cause they became an unlawful assembly. . . .The King's troops have undoubtedly a right to march through the streets and as such are a lawful assembly. But if in such marching without just cause they fire on the inhabitants and but one man is killed they surely are all answerable though it can't be proved who did the execution."[37]

The defense had argued that every individual in the mob was responsible for the actions of the others. Paine said the same could be said for the soldiers, if the soldiers assembled unlawfully.

The prosecution closed at 10:00 a.m. The judges then took three and a half hours to explain the charges. At 1:30 p.m., jurors finally began considering verdicts. They returned to the courtroom at 4:00 p.m. One by one, the verdicts were announced.

Corporal William Wemms, Private James Hartigan, Private William McCauley, Private Hugh White, Private William Warren, Private John Carroll: not guilty.

Private Mathew Kilroy and Private Hugh Montgomery: not guilty of murder, but guilty of manslaughter.

Kilroy and Montgomery thus remained in custody. As for the six others, "They went their way thro' the streets, with little, if any, notice."[38]

Kilroy and Montgomery went into court for their sentence on December 14. The punishment for manslaughter was death, as everyone knew. However, as everyone also knew, no one in this case would be executed. When asked why they should not be sentenced to death, both Kilroy and Montgomery "prayed clergy," a kind of legal life raft for almost anyone convicted of manslaughter.

This quirk in English law traced back to the twelfth century when King Henry II and the royal courts said that any member of the clergy below a priest, if accused of a capital offense, such as manslaughter, would be immune from punishment in secular courts. That special immunity was gradually extended to anyone remotely connected with the church. By the time of the Boston Massacre, this exemption no longer could be applied in some capital cases, but it continued to be available to those convicted of manslaughter, and it extended to virtually any literate layperson. To take advantage of this loophole, all the convicted person had to do was demonstrate an ability to read–often by reciting the 51st Psalm.

Thus, Kilroy and Montgomery, though convicted of manslaughter, escaped serious punishment. They had only to submit to branding on the thumb, the custom in such cases to prevent anyone from claiming benefit of clergy more than once.

The two soldiers soon rejoined their regiment. But before they did, Montgomery made a quiet confession regarding the events of March 5: The command to fire that some heard that night came from him. He admitted that after being knocked down, he shouted the order.

What remained was the trial of tidewaiter Edward Manwaring and three other civilians. The Sons of Liberty had pressed for the prosecution of these four suspected of shooting on townspeople from a window overlooking King Street that bloody night. This flimsy case finally came up in December. Samuel Quincy, attempting to prosecute, likened himself to Don Quixote in a "Windmill adventure."[39] If a lawyer was there to represent the defendants, the man's name is lost to history. They may have represented themselves.

The prosecution had virtually no evidence against three of the civilians. The case focused mainly on Manwaring, and evidence against him was slight: only unbuttressed testimony of a single witness, Bourgatte, Manwaring's fourteen-year-old servant. Though Bourgatte was born in France, his English was thought to be good enough for him to answer questions without an interpreter. Bourgatte said his master fired from an upper window of the Custom House while another tall man forced the boy to fire two guns out the same window. Bourgatte said the tall man, after the shooting, offered him money for his silence.

Four defense witnesses quickly shredded this testimony. These four had been standing across from the Custom House during the shooting. One had been wounded. Each said he saw no shooting from any upper window of the building. Then two women who were in the building during the shooting further demolished Bourgatte's story. They told jurors that neither Bourgatte nor Manwaring were in the building at the time. Finally, Manwaring's landlady testified that Manwaring and Bourgatte were at her boardinghouse from the time the bells started ringing until 10:00 p.m.

The judges then gave the boy a chance to reconsider his testimony. He remained steadfast. The landlady's story was false, he said. The judges gave the boy even more slack. Figuring that he did not fully understand English, no fewer than four interpreters were brought in. Questions were asked again in French. The answers were much the same. The boy would not give an inch.

His testimony did not stand up. But why would the boy lie? Subsequent testimony provided plausible reasons. James Penny had spent some time in jail with Bourgatte in late March, after the shooting. Penny, in jail for unpaid debts, said the boy told him and another debtor that William Molineux asked the boy to tell the tale. Molineux warned that if the boy refused, a Boston mob would murder him. According to Penny, Bourgatte also said that a woman from the North End, who have him gingerbread and cheese, asked him to testify against his master.

The jurors, without leaving the room, or even their seats, found all four defendants not guilty. No investigation was ever conducted, so far as we know, into Molineux's possible threat against the boy.

The next time the superior court sat, the grand jury indicted Bourgatte for perjury. The boy was quickly convicted and sentenced to stand in the pillory for an hour and to receive twenty-five lashes. The sentence made some radicals uneasy. At the first attempt to carry out the flogging, a crowd stepped in to stop it. The lashes were administered anyway two days later.

With the trials over, some felt a miscarriage had been done. The day after the acquittal of the civilians, someone tacked to the door of the State House a paper that attacked the judges and called on people to "rise up at the great call of nature and free the world from such domestic tyrants."[40]

But most townspeople seemed to accept the verdicts, at least at first. Some people in sympathy with the radicals regarded the judicial outcome as admirable. Reverend Samuel Cooper, normally in agreement with Sam Adams, was proud of the outcome and hopeful it would moderate attitudes among authorities in London about Boston. In a letter to a correspondent in London, he wrote, "These Trials must one w'd think wipe off the Imputation of our being so violent and Blood Thirsty a People."[41]

Ann Hulton, who detested the radicals, thought the verdicts "opened the Eyes of the People in general, convinced them that they have been deceived by false opinions & false representation of Facts."[42]

Before the year was over, Boston was so quiet that the commissioners of customs could return to the mainland from Castle William and work without "Insults or Molestations."[43] Wrote Ann Hulton, "Peace and Order takes place, & the past Scenes of confusion & disorder, appears as a dream."[44] She, along with Commissioner Hulton and family, resumed their placid life in Brookline, where they "met with every civility & respect possible."[45] Still, the earlier attack was not forgotten. The Hultons got a dog and put a bell on top of the house as an alarm. Neighbors volunteered to guard the house.

As for Sam Adams, he grudgingly accepted the verdicts and then blamed the Massacre once again on policymakers in Britain: "How fatal are the effects . . . of posting a standing army among a free people."[46]

Adams made sure he had the last word. He worked to establish March 5 as an annual day of mourning to include, in addition to the tolling of bells and the exhibition of illuminated displays, spirited oratory that would, year after year, extol the "martyrs," hammer the British authorities, and trample the truth. People coined a new term for the Custom House: Butcher's Hall.

This continuous drumbeat would fix the impression that the trials were a sham. In 1815, some forty-five years after the trials, John Adams wrote, "To this hour my conduct in it is remembered, and is alleged against me to prove I am an enemy to my country, and always have been."[47]

And what of Ebenezer Richardson, found guilty of killing the Seider boy? He lingered in jail for months. In early 1772, Richardson's attorney, Josiah Quincy, wrote an anonymous letter to the Gazette:

"This Richardson is either guilty or innocent.–If guilty, why not punished; if innocent, why not released. Twenty Two months imprisonment for a capital crime–in tormenting suspence between life and death–is what no man undeserving of death ought to bear. . . . The pretense that Richardson has been a profligate and abandoned wretch, is no good argument for his treatment."[48]

The judges in the case remained in a dilemma, convinced the jury was wrong but without a sound legal excuse to retry the case or let Richardson go. There was another way out: royal pardon. The judges seized on this option, telling Hutchinson that Richardson "was a proper subject for his majesty's pardon."[49] Hutchinson thus wrote to England, and in early March had a pardon in hand waiting for the right moment to issue it without stirring a riot. Finally, on March 10, while many Boston men were at a town meeting, Richardson was hastily shuttled into court, granted his pardon, and allowed to get away.

EIGHTEEN

EVERY STEP BUT ONE

The reputations of John Adams and Josiah Quincy among radicals seemed not to have suffered at all for defending Preston and the soldiers. In June, the town meeting, controlled by radicals, chose Adams as one of Boston's representatives in the House. Meanwhile, Quincy pitched in on formulating the town's instructions for those representatives. Many of the instructions had to do with an issue that, with all the other controversies at the time, seems hardly an issue at all: the meeting place for the lawmakers, or more specifically, whether the governor or acting governor acted properly in commanding lawmakers to meet a few miles up the Charles River from Boston.

Just days after the shooting on King Street in 1770, Hutchinson had called for the House of Representatives and Council to meet not in Boston, but in Cambridge. This was not an innovation. Over the years, for one reason or another–such as during smallpox epidemics in Boston–lawmakers had met several times in Salem and elsewhere outside Boston. Bernard, in his snit with lawmakers, had exiled them to the college town the previous summer. Hutchinson's decision to keep lawmakers out of Boston for the time being seemed reasonable, considering the bloody mayhem that had occurred just outside the State House.

So on March 15, ten days after the Massacre, the Council met miles away from the State House in the quiet library at Harvard, while the House assembled in the college's chapel. "The further from Boston, the better," wrote Hutchinson in a letter to London. "The house will be sour and troublesome enough; but all they can do will be a perfect trifle compared with the trouble the town of Boston gives me."[1]

But the decision to keep the lawmakers in Cambridge touched off a new spat that went on for months. The Boston town meeting, in instructing its representatives, sniped at Hutchinson. The town griped that forcing lawmakers to meet in Cambridge was "unwarrantable unconstitutional illegal and oppressive."[2] Sam Adams saw the eviction of the House from Boston as a small-minded way to irritate lawmakers. What was the justification, he asked.

Hutchinson's response: "his majesty's pleasure."[3]

Adams fumed, doubting that King George had anything to do with it. Adams asked Hutchinson to produce some evidence that indeed the king or someone from Britain had demanded the move. Hutchinson refused.

Adams responded with articles in the *Gazette* ridiculing Hutchinson's claim that King George, three thousand miles away, sent such orders. The articles found their way to ministers in London. Included with them were Hutchinson's remarks about Adams: "I doubt whether there is a greater incendiary than he in the king's dominions."[4]

It was all silly nonsense. Gathering in the serene college town could hardly be called oppressive, so Adams's complaints could hardly be taken seriously. At the same time, Hutchinson was being cagey. He had received instructions before the Massacre and after that gave him plenty of discretion "if you think it best" to shift Adams and his band of malcontents back to Boston.[5]

By spring 1770, Hutchinson felt he couldn't retreat, and Adams and his allies dug in for a long siege. The quarrel was needless, but at its heart brought up some fundamental questions: What were the limits on the power of the king and his appointed governor? Should the king or the governor have the right to dictate with a mere wave of the hand where the people's elected representatives should meet?

In May 1770, insisting that they should meet in Boston, representatives in Cambridge refused to do any business. Hutchinson dismissed the assembly. In July, the House met again in Cambridge and again refused to do business. Hutchinson again prorogued them.

In September, representatives were called together once again in Cambridge. The House now was confronted with a new issue: a move was afoot to withdraw the provincial garrison at Castle William and replace those men with regular troops–redcoats. Of course, British troops had long been stationed at Castle William. But the post was nominally in the province's control, and some local militia had always been stationed there. This change would seem to take control over the key military outpost completely out of the hands of the province. The representatives wanted to at least register a protest, but that would mean violating their vow to conduct sessions only in Boston. The House dedicated a day of prayer "to seek the Lord for his direction and blessing."[6] The Lord apparently advised the representatives to get back to work, for soon–in Cambridge–they were busy issuing an objection to the change of control at Castle William. Then the House conducted a flurry of other business at lightning speed. Hutchinson observed that

View of Harvard College buildings at Cambridge, Massachusetts, engraved by Samuel Hill. (*Library of Congress*)

he could not remember a legislative body accomplishing so much in so little time–despite the "inconvenience" of working in Cambridge.[7]

As 1771 began, merchants up and down the Atlantic Seaboard scrambled to replenish stocks. American consumers snapped up everything. Imports to America from England soared 47 percent beyond levels of the period just before the now-dead nonimportation movement.

In Boston, with the last of the Massacre trials over, a weary calm prevailed. The soldiers were gone. Most of the Townshend duties had been repealed. Samuel Cooper of Boston noted the moment of quiet and hoped for further concessions: "[T]here seems now to be a Pause in Politics. . . . Should [the British] Government be so Temperate and Just as to place us on the old ground on which we stood before the Stamp Act, there is no danger of our rising in our demands."[8]

John Rowe, in his diary, chirped: "The Queens Birth Day, fine weather, Guns firing Jovial Day–Spent the Evening at Concert hall with a very Grand Assembly, Governor, Lieut. Govr Commodore, Colonel, Captains of the Navy & Army, Commissioners, all the Best people in town–A General Coalition so that Harmony Peace & Friendship will once more be Established in Boston–Very Good Dancing & Good Musick but very Bad Wine & Punch."[9]

Looking back years later, Thomas Hutchinson recalled this brief interval of tranquility: "Four or five months passed away in Massachusetts Bay, more quietly than any other like space of time for seven years preceding. This seems to have been a favorable period for a general amnesty, and a return to the former orderly state of government, if both sides had been inclined to it."[10]

The Boston radicals weren't inclined to it. On the first anniversary of the March shootings, church bells tolled from noon to 1:00 p.m., and then for another hour in the evening. Paul Revere drew solemn crowds outside his North End house to view images displayed in three windows: in one, the ghost of Christopher Seider, amid weeping friends, trying to stem his bleeding with a finger; in another, soldiers firing into a group of people, blood streaming everywhere; in the third, a figure of a woman–representing America–sitting on a stump, one foot on the head of a Grenadier lying before her, serpent in his hand.[11]

Citizens crowded Faneuil Hall in early April to hear an oration on the "barbarous murder."[12] The speaker at this first Massacre speech was a schoolteacher, James Lovell. Lovell had the same profession as his father, John. But father and son were on opposite sides of the political divide: John leaned Tory; James sided with the Whigs. James hammered, predictably, on "the ill effects of placing standing forces in the midst of populous communities." But the tone of his speech was moderate. He urged that customs officials be left in peace: "The right which imposes duties upon us, is in dispute; but whether they are managed by a Surveyor-General, a Board of Commissioners, Turkish Janissaries, or Russian Cossacks, let them enjoy during our time of fair trial, the common personal protection of the laws of our constitution. Let us shut our eyes, for the present, to their being executors of claims subversive of our rights."[13]

Lovell seemed to express the mood of weary Boston, which generated not a squeak of protest later that year when all British navy vessels in North America were ordered to Boston Harbor. By August, Boston Harbor held a dozen warships, guns totaling 260, and Boston was silent.

At the same time, most Bostonians and other Americans sighed and accepted the remaining legacy of the Townshend duties: a tax on tea. They were tired of conflict and grateful that Parliament had retreated. After all the fury going back nearly a decade, most Americans submitted to taxation without representation with hardly a murmur.

Amid this interval of political calm, Boston found distraction in a literary controversy of sorts. Was it possible that a girl, brought into Boston from Africa as a slave, could by herself craft decent English poetry? For many, it seemed unlikely. Thus a panel was formed to examine the slave Phillis Wheatley, age about eighteen, who had been attracting attention for poems attributed to her. The panel's task was to give its expert opinion as to whether this young woman was indeed capable of writing what she said she wrote.

Phillis's native language was likely Wolof, and she probably came from the area of modern-day Senegal or Gambia. She arrived in Boston in July 1761 aboard the schooner *Phillis,* just returned from Africa. About that time, Susanna Wheatley, the wife of a prosperous tailor and merchant, needed a house servant. Responding to advertisements in Boston newspapers, she paid a visit to the slave ship. The captain, figuring the frail girl of about seven would soon die, eagerly sold her to Susanna at a bargain price.

Phillis Wheatley. (*Library of Congress*)

Phillis survived, and a teenage Wheatley daughter, Mary, soon began teaching her to read. In the grand Wheatley house on the corner of King Street and Mackerel Lane, Mary instructed Phillis in English, Latin, and the Bible. Four years after arriving in Boston, Phillis wrote her first poem.

Phillis soon astonished Boston and beyond with poetry on such subjects as the Boston Massacre ("Long as in Freedom's Cause the wise contend, / Dear to your unity shall Fame extend; / While to the World, the letter's Stone shall tell, / How Caldwell, Attucks, Gray, and Mav'rick fell").[14] Her poem on the death of Reverend Whitefield won particular acclaim and was published not only in Boston but also in Newport, New York, Philadelphia, and London.

Phillis's skills impressed Susanna Wheatley so much that in 1772, she sought out subscribers for a book of twenty-eight of Phillis's poems. Sales were hampered, however, by widespread doubts that the girl actually composed the poems attributed to her. This was the reason for the panel.

Eighteen men made up this illustrious tribunal. They included Thomas Hutchinson, John Hancock, seven ordained ministers, and three poets. Most of the men were slave owners. At least one traded in slaves. We don't know how Phillis was tested, but in the end everyone on the panel agreed to sign a document that stated:

> We whose Names are under-written, do assure the World, that the Poems specified in the following Page, were (as we verily believe) written by Phillis, a young Negro Girl, who was but a few Years since, brought an uncultivated Barbarian from Africa, and has ever since been, and now is, under the Disadvantage of serving as a Slave in a Family in this Town. She has been exam-

ined by some of the best Judges, and is thought qualified to write them.[15]

The judgment of the panelists did not help Susanna get Phillis's poems published in America. No publisher in the colonies was interested. But one in London was willing, and produced *Poems on Various Subjects, Religious and Moral.* The book was widely talked about, and Phillis briefly was possibly the world's most famous African.

Another matter concerning artistic creativity also came up about this time in the House of Representatives. This had to do with William Billings, a composer. No one was questioning Billings's authorship. The problem in this case was copyright. Billings was trying to prevent others from copying and profiting from his collection of songs.

Billings embodied the American spirit of enterprise and exuberance itching to push the boundaries of tradition and accepted forms. After his father, a Boston shopkeeper, died, Billings, at age fourteen, was apprenticed to a tanner. While learning the tanner's trade, he found time to obtain some rudimentary musical instruction. He became so obsessed by music and the idea of composing that he would, it is said, use his spare moments in the tanner's shop to chalk tunes on pieces of leather and on the workplace walls.

By 1770, he had opened a music shop and was organizing singing classes. He continued to work as a tanner, a prudent measure considering he had little musical training, no formal credentials, and a raspy voice. Furthermore, he was blind in one eye, had a withered arm, and one of his legs was shorter than the other. To add to his peculiarities, he dressed carelessly and consumed huge quantities of snuff. For all these handicaps, he found plenty of students attracted by his boundless enthusiasm for music. His classes for teenagers and adults were as much social as educational activities and were so popular that at times his rehearsal rooms couldn't accommodate all of his student singers.

Meantime, he was always composing. Unhappy with the grave hymns so prevalent, he aimed to create music that was more playful. Some of his songs were fuging tunes similar in some ways to songs in England from the time of Elizabeth I. Sung in a manner similar to a round, these tunes have been described as a "sort of musical horse-race."[16] At age twenty-four, the busy tanner-teacher-composer put together a songbook. Publication was delayed because Billings insisted Edes and Gill print it on American-made paper–hard to find in those days. But in 1770, the year of the Massacre, Billings's *The New England Psalm Singer* appeared, with a frontispiece by Paul Revere. The songbook contained 120 hymns and a few anthems, all composed by Billings. This was the first tune book of entirely American music.[17]

Billings went to lawmakers for copyright protection. They rejected his request the first time, but the second time, possibly with the help of

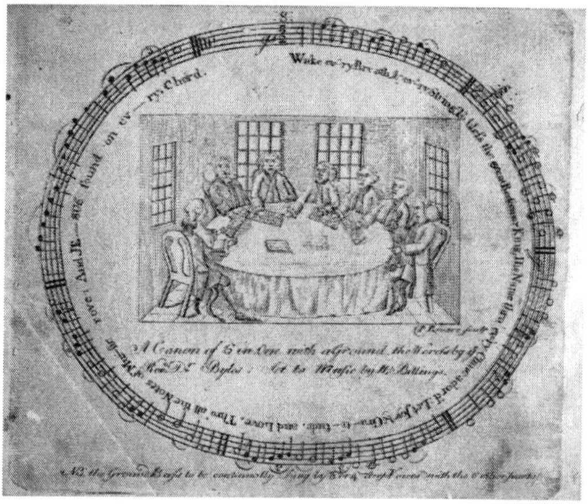

Frontispiece drawn and printed by Paul Revere for William Billings's *The New England Psalm Singer* (1770), the first book of entirely American music. (*Library of Congress*)

friend Sam Adams, who also loved vocal music, the William Billings Copyright Act was passed to give Billings the "Sole privilege of printing and vending" his tunes.[18] The measure never became law, however. Hutchinson refused to sign it, possibly because he was in no mood to do any favors for Sam Adams's friends.

Hutchinson by this time was at the end of his rope. In frustration and despair after the Massacre, he asked in a letter to London that someone "of superior powers of body and mind"[19] take his place. But before that letter arrived in London, George III approved the commission elevating Hutchinson from acting governor to governor. When word of this reached Hutchinson, he wavered. Friends and allies rallied to his side and pleaded with him to take the job he had so long coveted. He couldn't refuse. In March 1771, Hutchinson took the oath of office. Andrew Oliver, his brother-in-law, was the new lieutenant governor. As governor, Hutchinson faced a powerful radical majority in the House of Representatives determined to fight him on almost every question.

The radicals, meanwhile, had to deal again with their unstable figurehead. James Otis, having returned to Boston in apparent command of his senses, seemed in a conciliatory mood. A court case stemming from his coffeehouse fracas–the dustup at the Tory haunt on King Street in 1769–was settled, with Customs Commissioner John Robinson admitting he was "greatly in Fault" and "very sorry" for attempting to take Otis "by the Nose." Robinson agreed to pay Otis's medical, legal, and other costs related to the incident. Otis graciously forgave Robinson, considering him "infinitely less to Blame" than others who incited Robinson "to so unworthy an action."[20]

Otis also returned to the House of Representatives, still meeting in Cambridge. Sam Adams, perpetually riled about the inconvenience, brought forth a motion demanding that the House do its business in Boston only. Otis had no patience for this tiff. He argued that the governor certainly could, if he wanted, order the House to meet in Housatonic, about the most remote place in the province.[21] Otis and Sam Adams, for the moment, were at loggerheads.

About this time, Adams also had a falling out with Hancock, who was dissatisfied with the direction politics was taking and distracted by a family crisis. His brother, Ebenezer, whose wife was pregnant, had fled to Rhode Island to escape creditors. John bailed him out, scolded him, and installed him as a manager of a retail store. This incident may have convinced John that he should step back from the political fray to devote more energy to his business, which had suffered from his neglect. Hancock, as it turned out, did not abandon politics, but his friendship with Adams for the moment was dissolved. Hutchinson gleefully wrote to London, "Hancock and Adams are at great variance."[22]

Meanwhile, John Adams, too, had grown so disenchanted with public life that he swore nevermore to become involved in such messy business. He confided to his diary: "I shall be no more perplexed, in this manner. I shall have no journeys to make to Cambridge–no general court to attend–But shall divide my time between Boston and Braintree, between Law and Husbandry. Farewell Politicks."[23]

Hutchinson, in a letter, summed it up: "Hancock and most of the party are quiet; and all of them, except [Sam] Adams, abate of their virulence."[24]

As for Sam Adams, he still loved public life, but did the public still love him? He ran for registrar of deeds in Boston's Suffolk County. A Braintree man and a Tory, no less, thrashed him, receiving twice the number of Adams's votes. According to John Adams, who had campaigned for his cousin, the victorious Tories crowed "like dunghill Cocks."[25]

As most of Boston savored the return to normal, Sam Adams stewed. He hated the idea that now, in the wake of all the boycott efforts and the troubles leading to the Boston Massacre, a tax on tea was still in place. Merchants had given up the boycott. Consumers, however, could still register a protest by refusing to buy and consume tea. That's what he did. But he went further, taking pains to use, as much as possible, only goods made in America. He would not wear English cloth, for example. He also encouraged others to follow his example. "It behooves every American," he wrote, "to encourage home manufactures, that their oppressors may feel through their pockets the effects of their blind folly."[26]

Adams also groped for a mechanism by which he and his allies in Boston could share ideas–and perhaps coordinate action–with like-minded Americans in the hinterlands of Massachusetts and in the other colonies. Experience had taught him that in times of controversy, when lawmakers in assemblies most needed to communicate and coordinate with other assemblies, the governors in the respective colonies simply shut down the legislatures. Thus the governors each had the power to squelch efforts by elected representatives to reach out to other colonies.

Adams found a possible solution to this problem from England. There, the Society of the Supporters of the Bill of Rights, alarmed about threats to liberty in England, was working to influence lawmakers. This organization came together in February 1769 to raise money to pay off the debts of John Wilkes, still a hero to many in England and America. Over time the organization, based in scattered committees on both sides of the ocean, moved on to other issues. It put pressure on candidates to Parliament to promise "to restore to America the essential right of Taxation by Representatives of their own free election."[27]

Sam Adams envisioned political organizations in America along the lines of this society. Such organizations would work with the society in Britain and other groups of discontented people in Britain to put America and Britain back on the right track. In a breathless letter to Arthur Lee, an American ally in London, Adams proposed not independence but closer ties with Britons who had the same gripes as Americans with the British government:

> The grievances of Britain as well as ours, as you observe, spring from the same root of bitterness and are of the same pernicious growth. The Union of Britain & the Colonies is therefore by all means to be cultivated. In every colony societies should be formed out of the most respectable inhabitants, similar to that of the [Society of the Supporters of the Bill of Rights], who should once in the year meet by their deputies, and correspond with such a society in London. . . . This is a sudden thought and drops undigested from my pen. It would be an arduous task to awaken a sufficient number of colonies to so grand an undertaking. Nothing however, should be despaired of.[28]

Adams by this time was also contemplating independence. In another letter to Lee, Adams summarized his view of the situation in America, especially in Boston:

"The body of the people are uneasy at the large strides that are made and making towards an absolute tyranny. Many are alarmed, but are of different sentiments with regard to the next step to be taken. Some, indeed, think that every step has already been taken but one. The ultima ratio would require prudence, unanimity, fortitude. . . . I have long been of the opinion that America herself, under God, must finally work out her own salvation."[29]

Inspired by the Society of the Supporters of the Bill of Rights in England, Adams began thinking about creating committees of correspondence, clusters of men in every community up and down America who would receive and send out letters about common problems. These independent groups would form a network that once established could not be easily disrupted by a royal governor.

In America, efforts to form associations of correspondents had been tried before. Such committees faltered mainly because so much work was needed to get them off the ground. Success depended on extraordinarily passionate and determined participants united around an especially vital issue.

In refining his plan, Adams worked with other prominent Whigs, such as Thomas Young and Plymouth merchant James Warren (no relation to Joseph Warren). They decided that, to begin with, a correspondence network extending across the Atlantic or even outside Massachusetts was overly ambitious. They narrowed the focus to just Massachusetts. They also figured out how to reduce the work of establishing such committees. Instead of individuals around the province coming together privately to set up such committees, the towns would each set one up. They could be quickly established by town meetings. That would save time. It would also ensure that members of each committee would be respected citizens and that the committees themselves would be sanctioned by their respective towns.

Also, as Adams and other leaders thought out the scheme, they elaborated on the role these committees might play. Committee members could do more than write letters. They could also be political watchdogs, keeping close tabs on their own communities and rooting out those who didn't toe the Whig line. According to Mercy Otis Warren, who was in a position to know–she was the wife of James Warren and sister of James Otis–the committees would "take cognizance of the state of commerce, of the intrigues of toryism, of litigious ruptures that might create disturbances, and every thing else that might be thought to militate with the rights of the people, and to promote every thing that tended to general utility."[30]

Adams had a hard time selling this vision even to his most passionate allies. The plan, first of all, seemed ill-timed. Hadn't the time of crisis passed? Weren't most people content with the way things were?

But even assuming a sense of crisis, the plan seemed dubious. Would people in towns and hamlets far away from Boston share the anxiety? Would men in the hinterlands want to bother spending their spare time poring over diatribes from remote towns and scribbling responses? Would people in frontier villages feel they had anything in common with port towns? Would Americans scattered along the Atlantic Seaboard find any purpose in exchanging views?

Recognizing that groundwork was needed, Adams allowed the idea to mature as he wrote a series of articles for the *Gazette*. He well knew these would be reprinted in newspapers in each of the colonies. He understood that Americans experienced the various crises since the Stamp Act as separate events. He sought to put those events into a context in which Americans could see their common threads, recognize the trends, and detect, as Adams did, the threat.

Mrs. James Warren (Mercy Otis) by John Singleton Copley. (*Reproduction © 2013, Museum of Fine Arts, Boston*)

Starting in September 1771, Adams submitted these articles under the name Candidus. In these articles, he reviewed events since the Stamp Act and noted the hubbub over the famous circular letter. He reminded readers that British authorities shut down legislatures that approved the letter. Adams went beyond recent history and into political theory: self-government, natural rights, separation of power. He drew from the Magna Carta, William Blackstone's *Commentaries on the Laws of England*, Locke, Montesquieu, and David Hume. He expected from his readers an astonishing level of sophistication. He warned against complacency in the face of the steady erosion of long-held freedoms and rights:

> The liberties of our country, the freedom of our civil Constitution are worth defending at all hazards; and it is our duty to defend them against all attacks. We have received them as a fair inheritance from our worthy ancestors. They purchased them for us with toil, and danger, and expense of treasure and blood, and transmitted them to us with care and diligence. It will bring an everlasting mark of infamy on the present generation, enlightened as it is, if we should suffer them to be wrested from us by violence without a single struggle, or be cheated out of them by the artifices of false and designing men.[31]

Bostonians who perused Adams's essays in the *Gazette* may have also picked up the *Spy* to read the thoughts of Centinel, Leonidas, and Mucius Scævola, three feisty contributors in 1771 and 1772. They rivaled Adams in needling the Tories and raging against oppression, real and imagined. Centinel picked on Hutchinson, blaming him for almost everything wrong in the province, and even gave the king a scolding: "[T]he King has no right to send troops, or any thing else here that may be disagreeable to the people."[32] Leonidas and Mucius

Scævola produced spirited essays pummeling William Tryon, the governor of North Carolina. For these attacks, the *Spy* earned the distinction of being condemned in North Carolina to be "publicly burned under the gallows by a common hangman."[33]

No one knows for sure who these three writers were. Historians have guessed that attorney Josiah Quincy was Centinel and that Dr. Thomas Young was Leonidas. Joseph Greenleaf, a printer and justice of the peace in Plymouth County, was suspected at the time and still today of being Mucius Scævola, though Greenleaf denied it in public at least three times.

Whoever Mucius Scævola was, he, more than the others, got the attention of Hutchinson and the Governor's Council. In an issue of the *Spy* of late November 1771, Mucius Scævola asserted that the governor had no legitimate authority: "I . . . absolutely deny his jurisdiction over this people, and am of opinion that any act of assembly consented to by him in his capacity as governor is ipso facto null and void and consequently not binding upon us."[34]

Two days after the article appeared, a messenger showed up at the *Spy*'s office asking publisher Isaiah Thomas to appear immediately at the Council Chamber in the State House. Thomas said he was too busy. The messenger reappeared an hour later with the same request. Thomas had the same answer. The messenger came a third time, stating that Thomas was now ordered to the chamber. Thomas, now armed with legal advice, asked if the order was in writing. The messenger said no. Thomas replied, "Then, sir, with all due respect to the Governor and Council, I am engaged in my own concerns and shall not attend."[35]

Unable to muzzle the *Spy* and the *Boston Gazette*, Hutchinson and his allies at least found some printers and writers to snarl back. Of the three other newspapers in Boston at this time, one, the *Boston Evening-Post*, was, or at least tried hardest to be, neutral. The other two, the *Post-Boy* and especially the *Massachusetts Gazette*, leaned in favor of the administration.

Shielded behind such pseudonyms as Americanus, Benevolus, Lelius, Verus, Impavidus, and Causidicus, a dozen or so pro-Tory writers marched into the arena like inky Roman gladiators. Another pro-Tory publication was the *Censor*, whose contributors included Hutchinson. In one article, Hutchinson took on the irresponsible press. If, under the influence of "a party," he wrote, the press "becomes a vehicle in the hands of the licentious to calumniate the amiable and virtuous, and by insidious arts to create fears, jealousies, and distractions, to the great interruption of publick peace and happiness; such prostitution of the Press I am persuaded every judicious man must condemn, and wish that measures might be taken to prevent."[36]

But Hutchinson and his allies were too weak to make that wish come true. The attacks kept coming and were ever more vicious. Boston readers were treated to more attacks on Hutchinson, including a play from a woman's pen. The woman was Mercy Otis Warren. Her play was *The Adulateur, a Tragedy*. Hutchinson is represented by Rapatio, a tyrant who finds joy in the sight of his suffering land. In one scene Rapatio says:

O'er field of death, with hasting step I'll speed
And smile at length to see my country bleed;
From my tame heart the pang of virtue fling,
And 'mid the general flame, like Nero sing.[37]

It seemed that anything Hutchinson tried to do, no matter how benign, innocuous, or well meaning, exploded into controversy. For example, late in 1771, he issued a customary Thanksgiving proclamation offering "thanks to Heav'n for the Continuance of our Privileges." Bostonians huffed in indignation. According to minister and patriot friend Samuel Cooper, "This was deem'd by the People an open Insult upon them, and a prophane Mockery of Heav'n. The general cry was, we have lost our Most essential Rights, and shall be commanded to give Thanks for what does not exist."[38] Congregations throughout Boston told their ministers to ignore the proclamation, and so it was except in the church that Hutchinson attended, and there "Numbers turned their Backs" on the minister and walked out "in great indignation."[39]

NINETEEN

BLACKHEARTED FELLOWS

As 1771 wound down, momentum shifted further in the Massachusetts House of Representatives in favor of Sam Adams and his radical point of view while madness took hold of Otis once again. In the fall, his unsteadiness was again apparent: "At some time he is raving at all times he is so bewildered as to have no dependence on him,"[1] wrote Henry Pelham, who had engaged Otis to handle a legal case. In December 1771, Otis was so out of his mind that he had to be carted out of town with his hands and feet bound. He was put under the care of a guardian and shuttled off to Nantasket (now Hull).[2] Otis was thus out of the way, removing one possible check on Sam Adams's impulse to turn every issue into a confrontation with the governor.

A few months later, in March 1772, the radicals stoked the embers of patriotism with the second annual Massacre oration. The speaker, Dr. Joseph Warren, was now thirty years old and had a household on Hanover Street that included his wife, four children, and a slave. He was prominent in the Masons, a member of the Brattle Street Congregation, and had a busy medical practice, where he helped train several medical students, including his brother. Warren was now emerging among the leading figures and orators of the movement, standing alongside Sam Adams as one of the boldest radicals in challenging British authority. At Old South, Warren addressed a "very respectable assembly" of men and women, including people from nearby towns.[3] His oratory soared beyond just describing actual events the night when "our streets were stained with the blood of our brethren; when our ears were wounded by the groans of the dying." Said Warren:

"[O]ur alarmed imagination presented to our view our houses wrapt in flames; our children subjected to the barbarous caprice of the raging soldiery; our beauteous virgins exposed to all the insolence of unbridled passion; our virtuous wives, endeared to us by every tender tie, falling a sacrifice to worse than brutal violence, and perhaps, like the famed Lucretia, distracted with anguish and despair, ending their wretched lives with their own fair hands."[4]

Following the mayhem on King Street, only "inbred affection to Great Britain"[5] stopped Bostonians from slaughtering the British soldiers in vengeance, said Warren.

In April 1772, Hutchinson flattered Hancock by naming him colonel of the Cadets, the governor's honor guard. Hancock seized the appointment with glee. He encouraged people to call him "Colonel" and set about equipping the eighty-man unit with splendid uniforms: scarlet coats, white gaiters (leg coverings below the knee), and cocked beaver hats, each with ornament attached to a gilt button by a golden tie. An advertisement was placed for "Two fifers that understand Playing."[6] Hancock even asked the British military to lend a sergeant to drill the men at dawn every Wednesday on the Common in good weather. A man who missed a drill risked a fine usually paid by buying a round of ale at the Bunch of Grapes.

In stroking Hancock's vanity, Hutchinson hoped to pry the merchant loose from the radicals. To an extent, the ploy worked. Hancock, as head of the Cadets, seemed to push back against the violent and lawless elements of the Sons of Liberty, to which about half the Cadets were connected. Under Hancock, two Cadets were canned from the unit for throwing mud at commissioners of the customs. According to Hutchinson, Hancock said he "would never again connect himself with the Adamses."[7]

But the breach was soon repaired, and Hancock was firmly back in Sam Adams's camp, even while proudly retaining his role as colonel of the Cadets. Adams and Hancock patched up their differences with the help of mutual friends. To reaffirm their bonds, Hancock commissioned Copley to create portraits of the two in summer 1772. Hancock displayed them side by side in his front parlor.

The squabble over where lawmakers would meet came to an end after Hutchinson, in June 1772, said he would consider a straightforward petition from the House asking to move back to the State House in Boston, provided the petition did not contain any nonsense questioning the king's authority to instruct the governor.

When the petition was drawn up, Sam Adams, true to form, could not resist including a charge that the shifting of lawmakers to Cambridge in the first place had been unnecessary. Hutchinson at first balked at the snide insertion, but eventually accepted the petition and ended the lawmakers' exile. In retrospect, the matter seems trivial, but it later found its way into the Declaration of Independence in the section accusing the king of calling "together legislative bodies at places unusual, uncomfortable, and distant from the repository of their public records for the sole purpose of fatiguing them into compliance with his measures."[8]

Soon, the House and Hutchinson were embroiled in another squabble. The House learned that from now on the king would pay the salary of the governor. This would seem to be a boon for the people of Massachusetts. No longer would their taxes have to go for such purposes. But many people recognized the threat. The *Spy*'s Centinel asked whether a governor "independent of people, not paid by them" and "absolutely subservient to ministerial instructions, rather than the standing good and wholesome laws" could truly represent the people. Centinel's answer: no.[9]

Hutchinson's *Censor*, in defending Hutchinson's royal salary, said that taking control of the governor's salary away from the people had the effect not of upsetting the balance of power but of preserving it. The British constitution was designed so that each branch–Crown, Lords, and Commons–could act and deliberate independently before coming together to agree on enacting laws. In Massachusetts, the House of Representatives, the equivalent of the Commons, was dangerously close to upsetting the balance by its interference in the other two branches, the Council (equivalent of the Lords) and the governor (equivalent of the Crown). Such a trend led Rome to anarchy and eventually despotism under the Caesars, according to the *Censor*. In Massachusetts, a kind of anarchy was possible if the balance was not restored.

The House of Representatives wailed. Plainly, the change was meant to strip the province of its leverage over the governor. No longer could the House twist the governor's arm by threatening to cut off his salary. The governor could veto bills without fear of financial retribution. But what could the House do? It sputtered and sent off a petition to London.

Before long rumors reached Massachusetts that the king would likewise pay the salaries of the key judges in Massachusetts. Until this time, the situation of judges was much the same as that of the governor: the king appointed them, and the province paid them. The House had jealously guarded its role in setting and paying these salaries as a way to balance the king's influence over judges.

Under the new plan, the House, and thus the people, would have no influence over judges. This was arguably more alarming than having the king pay the governor. There was some logic in having the governor's salary come from the king. The governor was, after all, the king's direct representative. But judges were supposed to be impartial. Now, in cases with the interest of the king–or the governor, Parliament, and British authority–at stake, how could defendants count on judges to be fair?

For this controversy, the scene shifted from the State House, where the House of Representatives met, to nearby Faneuil Hall, where the Boston town meeting assembled. Sam Adams was convinced that the issue of judicial salaries was the hook on which to hang his plan for committees of correspondence. With judicial salaries as the focus, he was determined to set in motion his network of such committees in Massachusetts.

People around Adams were doubtful. John Hancock, Speaker of the House Thomas Cushing, and others thought it better to wait. The change in the way judges were paid was still unconfirmed. Also, the issue of who pays the salaries of judges was not likely to set people's blood boiling. Was this issue important enough to trigger such an arduous effort?

Adams went ahead. As a first step, he started a petition drive, collecting 198 signatures, and arranged for a town meeting, where he expected to announce the plan. Predictably, the issue of salaries did not set Boston aflame. Attendance at the meeting was disappointing. Adams put off the announcement.

Instead, a committee that included Adams, Warren, and Benjamin Church prepared an address for Hutchinson inquiring about the issue. In that address, the committee politely informed the governor that the plan of the king to pay judicial salaries appears "big with fatal evils, so obvious that it is needless to trespass on your Excellencys time in mentioning them."[10]

Hutchinson replied–in a long-winded way–that it was none of the town's business: "It is by no means proper for me to lay before the Inhabitants of any Town whatsoever in consequence of their Votes and Proceedings in a Town Meeting any part of my Correspondence as Governor of this Province or to acquaint them whether I have or have not received any advice relating to the public Affairs of the Government."[11]

After receiving the governor's reply, the town shot back another request: call provincial lawmakers back in session so "Joint Wisdom of the Province may be employed, in deliberating and determining on a matter so important and alarming."[12]

The governor's answer was no. The town's reasons were not sufficient. Besides, by agreeing to the request, he would be surrendering to the town his power to call the assembly "and should be unable to Justify my conduct to the King." Furthermore, such a precedent would only encourage towns to submit similar requests or "to debate & transact other matters which the Law that authorizes Towns to Assemble, does not make the business of a Town Meeting."[13] In other words, a town meeting shouldn't meddle in anything outside its narrow responsibilities.

Hutchinson's response was read several times at the November 2 town meeting. Townsmen then voted on whether the reply was satisfactory. No, they said, and then resolved, "As the Opinion of the Inhabitants of this Town that they have ever had, and ought to have a right to Petition the King or his Representatives for the Redress of such Grievances as they feel or for preventing of such as they have reason to apprehend, and to communicate their Sentiment to other Towns."[14]

The governor's answer was a gift to Sam Adams for two reasons. First, it gave him a sound excuse for pushing his plan of establishing a committee of correspondence. If Hutchinson had bowed to the town's request and called lawmakers together, Adams would have been hard-pressed to explain why his committee of correspondence was needed. But by rejecting the town's plea, Hutchinson blocked the established avenue for discussing provincial grievances. Now Adams had a compelling reason for introducing his innovation. Second, the governor's answer was dismissive. He said the subject of the town's earnest petition was not important enough, and, besides, the town meeting should not concern itself with such matters. Of course, this brush-off got under the skin of townsmen, generating the passion needed to give Adams's plan momentum.

Next came a resolution to establish the Boston Committee of Correspondence. Adams made a motion to form a committee of twenty-one to state the rights of the colonists and the province "as men, as Christians, and as Subjects"; to communicate this to other towns in the province "and to the World"; and to request responses from each town.[15] The motion passed unanimously.

So Adams got his committee of correspondence. Still, some of Adams's allies saw little value in the exercise. Hancock and Cushing, among others, said they were too busy to participate. But Adams managed to round up twenty-one townsmen. James Otis, back in Boston and, for the moment, rational, was named chairman. The other men, described by Hutchinson "as blackhearted fellows as any upon the Globe,"[16] were all professional men or men of property. One-third had degrees from Harvard. Committeemen included Joseph Warren, Benjamin Church, and Thomas Young, all physicians; Oliver Wendell, a town selectman; William Cooper, town clerk and brother of Brattle Street pastor Samuel Cooper; William Greenleaf, an overseer of the poor; attorney Josiah Quincy; and William Molineux, merchant and mob leader. Also on the committee were Joseph Greenleaf, widely suspected of being the face of Mucius Scævola in the *Spy*, and Nathaniel Appleton, a merchant who had published a pamphlet in 1767 attacking slavery.

The committee first met in the House of Representatives Hall in the State House. The group's first act: approving a declaration of secrecy. It later met at such places as Molineux's house, working from 6:00 p.m.

to 9:30 p.m., but never from Saturday until an hour after sundown on Sunday, as was the New England custom.

Early on, the committee's secrecy caused some to think something fishy was going on with town money. To lay these suspicions to rest, the committee voted to charge the town only for the "Candles & Firing" for their meetings. Members taxed themselves for the cost of "Rhode Island Beer."[17]

This committee embarked on a three-part statement–actually, a pamphlet of more than seven thousand words–to be dispatched to towns in Massachusetts. Each part was assigned to a subcommittee, one led by Adams, one by Warren, and the third by Church. In the pamphlet, the question of salaries, the issue that kicked off momentum to establish the committee, was barely mentioned, characterized mainly as the latest in a list of grievances.

Hutchinson regarded the correspondence plan as a "foolish scheme" certain to make its organizers "ridiculous."[18] But Adams was so enthused about the project that he couldn't wait for the work to be completed. On his own, he sent letters to leaders in other towns pushing for the establishment of similar committees. Such towns as Marblehead and Plymouth moved forward on establishing their own committees even before the Boston committee finished its work.

Tories, meanwhile, took shots at Boston's committee. Attendance was meager at the town meeting establishing the committee, they said, so it was a stretch to claim it truly represented the town's wishes. Also, the committee did not include the most prominent men but was merely "a set of Atheists or Deists, men of profligate manners and profane tongues."[19]

The initial work of the Boston committee was soon completed, and Faneuil Hall was packed November 20 to hear the full statement. Otis was there, and Adams thanked him for helping to draft the document–though Otis probably did little–and explained to the throng that Otis wished them to approve the statement. They did. With that, Otis left the public stage for good. The meeting was his last as a public figure.

The first section of the statement, by Adams's subcommittee, contained ideas familiar to colonists. Echoing arguments made long before by Locke, this section summarized the rights of the Americans. First, men have a natural right to life, liberty, and property; society was formed to defend those rights; and any person can enter or leave society as he pleases. All religions should be tolerated except for those "subversive to society." Thus, Roman Catholics should not be free to worship because, among other reasons, "their recognizing the Pope in so absolute a Manner, is Subversion of Government."[20]

Government exists as a referee to sort out differences among individuals in society, and by entering society, each person agrees to this role of government. The governor, meanwhile, is merely a servant of the people and hired by the people to perform essentially a judicial function. "Governors have no right to seek what they please; by this, instead of being content with the station assigned them, that of honourable servants of society, they would soon become Absolute masters, Despots, and Tyrants."[21]

Colonists had certain rights that could not be touched by lawmakers. Lawmaking bodies had no God-given authority and certainly no "absolute arbitrary Power over the Lives and fortunes of the People." While Parliament was the highest authority in England, its power was not absolute. The statement ridiculed the very idea of parliamentary authority over Americans:

> The inhabitants of this country in all probability in a few years will be more numerous, than those of Great Britain and Ireland together; yet it is absurdly expected by the promoters of the present measures, that these, with their posterity, shall be disposed of by a house of commons at three thousand miles distant from them; who cannot be supposed to have the least care or concern for their real interest, but must be in effect bribed against it; as every burden they lay on the colonists is so much saved or gained to themselves.[22]

In the section on grievances, Warren's subcommittee itemized and explained a dozen. First on the list was the problem of legislative power: Parliament had assumed it without consent of the people of Massachusetts. Second was the problem of taxation: Parliament had used its assumed legislative power to raise taxes in the colonies without the colonists' consent. Later items on the list depict swarms of "petty officers," supported by "Fleets and Armies," inflicted on the colonies and given unconstitutional powers to make searches and seize property. "Thus our houses and even our bed chambers, are exposed to be ransacked, our boxes, chests & trunks broke open, ravaged and plundered by wretches, whom no prudent man would venture to employ even as menial servants."[23]

Warren's subcommittee noted that a balance of power between the governor and the lawmakers had been upset when the Crown took over responsibility for paying the governor. This made the governor "independent of the Assembly, whereby the ancient connection between him and this people is weakened, the confidence in the Governor lessened and the equilibrium destroyed."[24]

This section also attacked the juryless admiralty courts: "We may be harassed and dragged from one part of the Continent to the other . . . and finally be deprived of our whole property, by the arbitrary determination of one biased, capricious Judge of the Admiralty."[25]

Also targeted were laws that inhibited manufacturing in the colonies. This section pointed out, for example, restrictions forbidding transport of wool by water: "[T]hey restrain us from carrying our Wool, the produce of our own farms, even over a ferry; whereby the Inhabitants have often been put to the expence of carrying a Bag of Wool near a hundred miles by land, when passing over a River or Water of one quarter of a mile, of which the Province are the absolute Proprietors, would have prevented all that trouble."[26]

The list of complaints also noted fears that the Church of England was thinking about sending over a bishop. "We think . . . that every design for establishing the Jurisdiction of a Bishop in this Province, is a design both against our Civil and Religious rights."[27]

The last section, the "Letter of Correspondence," by Church's subcommittee, zeroed in on the issue of salaries: "[W]e cannot but be extremely alarmed at the mischievous tendency of this innovation; which in our opinion is directly contrary to the spirit of the British Constitution, pregnant with innumerable evils, and hath a direct tendency to deprive us of every thing valuable as Men, as Christians and as Subjects."[28]

Edes and Gill printed six hundred copies of the statement under the unwieldy title *Votes and Proceedings of the Freeholders and Other Inhabitants of the Town of Boston, in Town Meeting Assembled, According to Law.* The forty-seven-page pamphlet included four pages explaining the establishment of the committee as well as an appendix with the governor's response. The pamphlets went out to Massachusetts towns and to important sympathizers in other colonies. The name displayed most prominently on the pamphlet was that of John Hancock–in all capital letters. He was merely moderator of the town meeting that approved the pamphlet. But his fame and stature–as town selectman, member of the House of Representatives, Whig leader, and wealthy merchant–gave the pamphlet added credibility.

Still, some sympathizers expected the pamphlet to be tossed aside. James Warren, writing to Sam Adams from Plymouth, said: "I shall not fail to exert myself to have as many towns as possible meet, but fear the bigger part of them will not. They are dead, and the dead can't be raised without a miracle."[29]

Adams replied, "All are not dead; and where there is a spark of patriotic fire, we will rekindle it."[30]

Tory observers were right in saying that much in the pamphlet had been said before. What the committee was doing differently was targeting a new audience. Most earlier statements in a similar vein were meant for audiences in England, especially the decision makers in London. This pamphlet was aimed mainly at people in Massachusetts.

Responses to the Boston statement came back by the dozens in January 1773. Over seventy of the 260 towns and districts in Massachusetts had responded by month's end. Forty more answers arrived soon thereafter. Some towns, especially those in remote areas, amazed at receiving the pamphlet, confessed ignorance, and deferred to Boston's judgment. Townsmen of Lenox, way to the west "in a remote wilderness Corner of the Earth; and almost the remotest and youngest Town of the Province" admitted that they knew "but little of the Circumstances of the Affairs you write us upon. . . . Therefore as we are Children about five Years old we depend on you, our Fathers, to dispose of Things we know nothing about."[31]

Even though most towns ignored the pamphlet, or were still considering it, members of the Boston committee were pleased with the response. Predictably, those towns with the closest ties to members of the Boston committee, generally those in the east, responded most enthusiastically. Western towns and those whose leaders were friends of the governor's, such as Springfield and Hatfield, were more inclined to disregard the pamphlet. As months went by, sixty more would respond, bringing the total to 170, more than half of the towns in the province.

Nowhere in the pamphlet does the Boston Committee of Correspondence specifically ask that other towns form similar committees. But that is what some towns did. Cambridge instantly formed a committee of correspondence, which answered Boston's with its "concern to maintain and secure their own invaluable rights, which were not the gift of kings, but purchased with the precious blood and treasure of their ancestors."[32]

The committee in Roxbury declared, "Our pious forefathers died with the pleasing hope that we their children should live free; let none, as they will answer it another day, disturb their ashes by selling their birthright."[33]

Even before these answers came in, Governor Hutchinson felt the statement of the Boston Committee of Correspondence required a Loyalist response. In a speech to lawmakers in January 1773, he jabbed at the committee's arguments. The colony's charter did not exempt the people of Massachusetts from Parliament's authority. People in the colony were subject to Parliament, just as someone at sea would be. Furthermore, he said, people who came to America had voluntarily given up their voting rights when they left Britain's shores. If they returned to Britain, they would have those voting rights again and would again be represented. Hutchinson hoped to sober up his fellow Americans by distilling their options to two–one prudent, one unthinkable: "I know of no line that can be drawn between the supreme authority of Parliament and the total independence of the colonies." To Hutchinson the idea of total independence was shocking–America could not survive independent of Britain–and he expected that most Americans shared his view: "Is there any thing that we have more reason to dread than independence?"[34] Hutchinson didn't understand how far American thinking had evolved. By this time, the idea of independence was quite thinkable and by no means dreadful.

Certain that his arguments were watertight, Hutchinson challenged opponents to respond. Sam Adams seized the gauntlet. Adams argued that because it was so difficult to determine the extent of Parliament's authority over the colony, the colony's charter allowed the colony to govern itself. The king said colonists could pass any laws they wanted, so long as they were "not repugnant to the laws of England."[35] He dredged up a quote from King James I: "America was not annexed to the realm, and it was not fitting that Parliament should make laws for those countries."[36] Adams also rejected Hutchinson's notion that by voluntarily leaving England, colonists had forfeited their right to govern themselves.

As Hutchinson's standing plummeted, Sam Adams's stature among patriotic factions soared. Leaders in Rhode Island wrote to him for advice. A crisis there was coming to a head. It stemmed from an incident in June 1772, when the *Gaspee*, a British navy schooner, ran aground off the coast in pursuit of smugglers. A mob rescued the crew but set fire to the vessel. British authorities gasped. The head of the British admiralty promised to strip residents of Rhode Island of all political rights. Now, a leader in Rhode Island asked Adams what should be done. Adams's response: form committees of correspondence and knit closer ties with other colonies.

Rhode Island's predicament suggested to Adams that the time had come for Massachusetts and the other colonies to establish networks of communication, such as committees of correspondence, and seek out support across borders. Adams knew that such an initiative would have the best chance of success if it originated–or appeared to originate–in Virginia, the largest colony. Adams wrote to Richard Henry Lee, a key political figure in Virginia, and brought him up to date on activities in Massachusetts. Virginians already had been contemplating the formation of such committees. Whether influenced by Adams or not, Lee pushed a plan for a committee of correspondence through Virginia's House of Burgesses in March 1773. Virginia's newly formed committee of correspondence quickly dispatched invitations to the other colonies to participate in developing a common list of complaints.

TWENTY

REPROACHED AND REVILED

By happy coincidence, this was about the time firebrand Josiah Quincy set off for the South. A lung ailment, likely tuberculosis, was sapping the life of this young attorney. His physician suggested a journey to a warmer climate. Thus, when Quincy in February 1773 set off on the *Bristol Packet* for South Carolina, he was traveling mainly for his health. But he was also on a mission to get to know fellow patriots in the South. His efforts would help stimulate the formation of committees of correspondence beyond Massachusetts. The first days on board nearly killed him: "I became pale, wan, and spiritless; . . . every person on shipboard gave me over and concluded I should never reach land."[1]

Quincy barely recovered when the vessel brushed up against a hurricane: "I believe every soul on board expected to perish."

The terror seemed to invigorate him, for once on shore in Charleston, he quickly dove into the social whirl. Women North and South, he observed, were "pretty much on a par" when it came to "noise and flirtation." Many southern gentlemen, he wrote, "dressed with richness and elegance, uncommon with us; many with swords on."

He quickly learned about attitudes toward Boston. At a dinner, he heard from a "flaming tory": "You may depend upon it . . . that if Great Britain should renounce the sovereignty of this continent, or if the colonies take themselves clear of her authority, that you all [the Carolinas and other provinces] will have governors sent to you from Boston. Boston aims at nothing less than the sovereignty of the whole continent,–I know it."

Another guest at the dinner echoed the same view: "Take away the power and superintendence of Britain, and the colonies must submit to the next power. Boston would soon have that. Power rules all things; they might allow the others a paltry representation, but that would be all."

Recognizing the deep suspicions that divided the colonies, Quincy quietly planted the idea of "a general, permanent, continental literary correspondence"–committees of correspondence to share grievances and coordinate action among provinces.

From South Carolina, Quincy went into North Carolina, where he found enthusiasm for "Continental correspondence." He traveled from there up through Virginia, to Maryland, and then to Pennsylvania. In Philadelphia he dined with the famous "Farmer" John Dickinson, among others.[2] He hurried through New Jersey to New York, where he attended a concert and found "the music indifferent; the ladies sprightly and beautiful."[3] Then, by water, Quincy went on to Rhode Island, bypassing Connecticut, reaching Newport on May 17.

At the conclusion of his journey Quincy wrote, "Were I to lament any one thing, it would be the prevalent and extended ignorance of one colony of the concerns of another." The trip helped address this ignorance. By establishing personal connections with important men in various colonies, Quincy fostered links between those colonies and Massachusetts.

Other patriot leaders continued to stoke the fires. Benjamin Church's 1773 oration to commemorate the "horred Massacre" to "a large and crowded Audience" at Old South was "elegant and spirited."[4]

Church was not the first choice for the speech. Leaders had asked John Adams to deliver the address. But Adams was still on the political sidelines. In his diary he wrote, "I was desirous to avoid even thinking upon public Affairs."[5] But ignoring public affairs was impossible for John Adams, and by this time he was already itching to get back in the game. In his period out of politics, he had moved his family to Braintree but still commuted to his office in Boston and kept in contact with Sam Adams and others. After sixteen months, he moved the family back to Boston but still steered clear of direct political involvement. One day he found himself troubled after a strange encounter at the shop of Edes and Gill with James Otis, "Eyes, fishy and fiery, looking as wildly as he ever did." The conversation had to do with military issues. Adams recorded it in his diary:

> Says Otis to me, Youl never learn military exercises. –Ay why not?–That You have a Head for it need no Commentary, but not an Heart.–Ay how do you know–you never searched my heart. Yes I have–tired of one Years Service, dancing from Boston to Braintree and from Braintree to Boston, moaping about the Streets of this Town . . . and seemingly regardless of every Thing, but to get Money enough to carry you smoothly through this World.[6]

Adams privately fumed at this "Rant." He told his diary, "I have been in the public Cause as long as he. . . . I have sacrificed as much to it as he."[7] Still, the remarks, coming from a man Adams had admired, cut deep. Had he become wholly self-involved, interested only in making money?

Otis's words rankled. The excitement of politics beckoned. Finally, at the urging of friends, Adams agreed to run again for office, and in May 1773, he won election to the House of Representatives. He was back in the maelstrom for good.

That month, Joseph Warren was left a widower when his wife died, at twenty-six. With four motherless children to look after, Warren might have taken leave of the political battlefield, but he did not. His radical activities intensified.

Still in that same eventful month of May 1773, another political bombshell shattered what was left of Hutchinson's popularity and credibility. The source of this incendiary was none other than Hutchinson himself, by way of Benjamin Franklin.

The eminent Franklin was now the agent in London for the Massachusetts House of Representatives. His job was to prod ministers and members of Parliament on behalf of the Massachusetts House, and report back to Massachusetts on matters pertaining to the province. The Boston radicals viewed Franklin as a tepid patriot. Sam Adams was so doubtful of Franklin's politics that he didn't want him as the colony's agent. But Franklin now proved to be an enormous help to Adams in his war with Hutchinson. One of Franklin's early assignments from Massachusetts was to present to the king and Parliament the Massachusetts House's petition opposing the Crown's new practice of paying the governor's salary.

Franklin first brought the petition to Lord Dartmouth, the new secretary of state handling American affairs. Dartmouth had replaced the hated Hillsborough and seemed likely to be much friendlier to American interests. Americans knew Dartmouth had favored repeal of the Stamp Act. He was thus initially quite popular in America.

Dartmouth convinced Franklin that the timing of the petition was bad. It would be certain to offend the king and invite censure from Parliament. Better to let time pass. Besides, changes had taken place in London since the House drew up the petition. Dartmouth suggested that Franklin simply send a letter to Boston and ask the House, in consideration of the new situation in London, to revise or reconsider the petition.

Franklin agreed. He reasoned that Dartmouth was new to his post and, by taking his advice in this case, Franklin would help their relationship get off on the right foot. Franklin probably also agreed with Dartmouth that the petition in this form would only put more strain on relations between America and Britain. Thoughtful reconsideration was unlikely to hurt, and might result in a more effective petition.

But Franklin was also uncomfortable with the decision to delay. Would the Massachusetts House view this as disobedience? Franklin reasoned that if he could offer the House some other service, or a scrap of valuable information, the House might overlook his failure to do as directed. He wrote to his correspondent at the Boston House of Representatives, Thomas Cushing, and explained the matter of the petition. "If after deliberation they should send me fresh orders, I shall immediately obey them," Franklin wrote.[8]

Then, in the same letter, Franklin told Cushing, "[T]here has lately fallen into my Hands Part of a Correspondence that i have reason to believe laid the foundations of most if not all of our present Grievances."[9]

That correspondence was a bundle of thirteen letters dispatched from America between 1767 and 1769, the period after the repeal of the Stamp Act and before the Boston Massacre. The letters came from various authors, all Americans. All but one was written to Thomas Whately, a member of Parliament who had played an important role in Britain in drafting the Stamp Act. Whately had, before he died in 1772, established correspondence with several Americans.

How did Franklin acquire these letters to Whately? Franklin would only explain later that he received them from a "Gentleman of Character and Distinction."[10]

The most important of these letters were written by Hutchinson, then lieutenant governor and now governor, and Andrew Oliver, Hutchinson's brother-in-law and now lieutenant governor.

Oliver and Hutchinson, in writing to Whately years before, had been trying to influence Parliament in that troubled period. They wrote that Americans were generally content with British rule and that the strife was the product of a vigorous and determined minority. Both Hutchinson and Oliver in these letters suggested what should be done. Oliver, for his part, proposed the creation of a colonial aristocracy. These aristocrats would sit on the Council and ensure a Loyalist counterweight to the democratic House. Hutchinson's ideas were more startling: "I never think of the measures necessary for the peace and good order of the colonies without pain. There must be an abridgement of what are called English liberties. . . . I wish the good of the colony when I wish to see some further restraint of liberty rather than the connexion with the parent state should be broken; for I am sure such a breach must prove the ruin of the colony."[11]

Franklin knew these letters would set off sparks in Boston, where no one would consider the context of the letters and everyone would gasp in horror at the notion of "abridgement" of "liberties." Franklin hoped that through these letters, the House would redirect its anger. London was not the villain here. The villains, in Franklin's view, were Hutchinson and his allies in Massachusetts. Franklin, wanting America and Britain to reconcile, believed that if British authorities could get the true picture of what was happening in America, they would respond appropriately and smooth over the troubles. He also believed that if the Massachusetts House understood how London was being misled, its members would cool down and show more restraint.

Franklin sent off this bundle of letters to Cushing in December 1772. Cushing passed them on to Sam Adams. The problem for Adams and other radical leaders was that Franklin asked that the contents of the letters not be revealed or copied.

To Sam Adams, Hancock, Cushing, and the other radicals privy to the letters, this issue was too important to be kept under wraps. They chose to ignore Franklin's request and made the letters public despite the scandal that would engulf Franklin. In late May, Hancock told the House of Representatives about the letters. Days later, Adams read the letters to a closed session of the House, which then condemned them by a vote of 101 to 5.

Adams, with the support of the House, later had the letters printed. He explained that because copies of the letters were being circulated abroad and in Boston, they were no longer secret. Adams also pushed through the House a request to authorities in London for the removal of both Governor Hutchinson and Lieutenant Governor Oliver. This vote was 80 to 11.

Tories came to Hutchinson's defense. One, writing under the name Philanthrop, stoutly called for people to read Hutchinson's letters in context. Hutchinson's statement about "abridgement of English liberties" was not meant as a wish or recommendation, Philanthrop argued; rather it was a prediction. As Hutchinson himself explained: "It gave me great pain to think the colonies could not enjoy every liberty which the Kingdom could, but I did not see how it could be helped."[12]

Nobody listened. Radicals fumed. Josiah Quincy now blamed Hutchinson for every injustice under the sun. He is, Quincy wrote: "the first, the most malignant and insatiable enemy of my country; . . . he is the author and chief supporter of the severest calamities under which the people labor; . . . he has done more general mischiefs and committed greater public crimes than his life can repair or his death satisfy; and . . . he is the man against whom the blood of my slaughtered brethren cries from the ground."[13]

Today, this scandal receives scant attention as a cause of the American Revolution. But to Hutchinson, this was the pivotal event. In exile he later wrote, "[I]f it had not been for the plot laid by Franklin and others here in England, and the sending over my private letters, and the false representation made of them, I doubt whether there would have been a Rebellion to this day."[14]

Hutchinson had enough. Exhausted, frustrated, heartbroken that he had failed to smash the claims of the extremists, supported only by a shrinking groups of Loyalists, most of whom were too timid to speak out, Hutchinson longed only to be somewhere far from this "most perverse set of men upon earth."[15] He dispatched a letter asking for official leave to go to England. His aim was to trade his governorship for a less stressful position, one that might permit travel and that would give him the money at least equal to what he received for the offices he held before he was governor. Loathed in his home town, burned in effigy in Philadelphia and Princeton, compared to Nero, Catiline, and Caligula, Hutchinson in a private letter recalled ruefully words of his father: "Depend upon it, if you serve your country faithfully you will be reproached and reviled for doing it."[16]

During this time, the Boston Committee of Correspondence began working closely with the House of Representatives. This was easy enough: Sam Adams was clerk of the House. With Cushing, the speaker of the House, attending correspondence committee meetings, the committee and the House worked hand in glove. For example, a petition about judges' salaries originating with the correspondence committee emerged as a resolution from the House.

The committee also printed up and sent out to towns the Virginia Resolves, which promoted a network of correspondence committees among the thirteen colonies. Some Massachusetts towns responded to the Virginians with amazement and delight. Cambridge wrote, "[O]ur hearts even leap for joy upon Reading the Resolves of the Patriotick House of Burgesses in Virginia."[17]

The Massachusetts House responded by setting up its own committee of correspondence. Its fifteen members included, predictably, Sam Adams. By July 1773, provinces with committees of correspondence included not just Massachusetts and Virginia but also Rhode Island, Connecticut, New Hampshire, and South Carolina.

All this seething political drama gives the impression of a society on edge. But political drama was nothing new to Massachusetts, and it was not readily apparent that this political storm was any more threatening than all those that came before. Life went on, and people went about their business mostly as usual.

Out in Brookline, between trips to Boston to do his work as customs commissioner, Henry Hulton busied himself on the farm growing apples, making cider, harvesting hay, and raising sons. "When at home

I am fully employed with my family and farm, my little pratlers are becoming very agreeable companions, & my domestick comforts make up for any chagrine I may have suffered from outward circumstances." He also noted that his "pratlers"–sons about four and two–"both have the true Boston disposition for rioting."[18]

Henry's sister Ann, in her correspondence during this interlude, described some of the "pleasures" of a winter in New England: "[T]here are few days but what we might make excursions in Sleighs (carriages without wheels that travel extreamly quick 10 or 12 Miles and hour)."[19] She also reported that, despite being miles from Boston, they were not lonely. Her sister-in-law "had near 50 Ladies from Boston &c to vissit her in her Lying in."[20]

Boston in 1772 took up the issue of installing street lamps for the first time. John Rowe led a committee that determined that three hundred were needed. The committee called for a tax on "every Wheel Carriage" and on liquor licenses to pay for the lamps, oil, "Wick Yarn attendance and repairs."[21]

Merchant Rowe didn't let his associations with Whigs stop him from cultivating friendships with military men. He went along on a pleasant fishing outing at Menotomy Pond in August 1773 with an admiral, the admiral's wife and daughter, various other naval officers, ladies, and others. "We were very jolly," wrote Rowe, but the fish were small.[22]

In October of the same year, Hugh Finley, an inspector for the British government, passed through and reviewed the work of the royal postal service in Boston. Finley discovered that the post rider who carried the mail between Boston and Newport was not as "expeditious" as he claimed, requiring twenty-six hours to cover the eighty miles to Newport. Finley also remarked, "Complaints are made of the stupidity of the man who attends the office at Boston."[23]

For Paul Revere, the year 1773 brought grief and joy, with hardly an interval between. In April, his wife, Sary, died. In September, his infant daughter, Isanna, followed her mother to the grave. In October, Revere remarried. Rachel Walker Revere would care for Sary's six surviving children and have eight of her own.

A glimpse of a girl's life in this period comes from Anna Green Winslow, who as a ten-year-old had been sent from her home in Nova Scotia to stay with her aunt and uncle, Sarah and John Deming in Boston, and to be educated in proper schools for reading, writing, and sewing. From November 1771 to May 1773, Anna kept a journal–a series of letters to her family–to keep "Mamma" informed of her activities and demonstrate her writing skills.

She recorded, for example, a snippet of an Old South sermon with an uplifting message for young people: "[W]hile you are without holiness, your beauty is deformity–you are all over black & defil'd, ugly and loathsome to all holy beings, the wrath of th' great God lie's upon you, & if you die in this condition, you will be turn'd into hell, with ugly devils, to eternity."[24]

She also wrote about dancing. She described a "constitation,"–a "very genteel well regulated assembly"–attended by seventeen girls, no boys, in a "handsome, large, upper room in the new end" of a house from 5:00 to 10:00 p.m. As two fiddlers played, the girls danced the minuet and, "for variety . . . woo'd a widow, hunted the whistle, threaded the needle, & while the company was collecting, we diverted ourselves with playing of pawns, no rudeness Mamma I assure you." Watching over the event were eleven adults. Snacks and refreshments included "nuts, rasins, Cakes, Wine, punch, hot & cold, all in great plenty."

In her letters, Anna agonized over her appearance: "Dear mamma, you dont know the fation here–I beg to look like other folk. You dont know what a stir would be made in sudbury street, were I to make my appearance there in my red Dominie & black Hatt. But the old cloak & bonnett together will make me a decent bonnett for common ocation (I like that) aunt says, its a pitty some of the ribbins you sent wont do for the Bonnet."

Anna wrote of her "roll"–an elaborate, high, decorated hairpiece in the latest fashion–when she tried it on for the first and, perhaps, last time:

> I had my HEDDUS roll on, aunt Storer said it ought to be made less, Aunt Deming said it ought not to be made at all. It makes my head itch, & ach, & burn like anything Mamma. This famous roll is not made wholly of a red Cow Tail, but is a mixture of that, & horsehair (very course) & a little human hair of yellow hue, that I suppose was taken out of the back part of an old wig. . . . When it first came home, aunt put it on, & my new cap on it, she then took up her apron & mesur'd me, & from the roots of my hair on my forehead to the top of my notions, I mesur'd above an inch longer than I did downwards from the roots of my hair to the end of my chin. Nothing renders a young person more amiable than virtue & modesty without the help of fals hair, red Cow tail, or D–– (the barber). Now all this mamma, I have just been reading over to my aunt. She is pleas'd with my whimsical description & grave (half grave) improvement, & hopes a little fals English will not spoil the whole with Mamma. Rome was not built in a day.

References to civic discontent in Boston are scant. The picture Anna paints in her seventy-two-page journal is of a town getting on as usual.

What about John Boyle, a printer attuned to community affairs and a man sympathetic to the patriot cause? Boyle's record of events through the first ten months of 1773 says little to suggest a coming storm. He noted local fires (five). He entered the names of more than fifty people who died and remarked on September 27 about a wave of children's deaths: "The Disorder that generally attends young Children at this Season of the year, has lately proved very mortal. Upwards of 20 have died the Week past."[25] He mentioned seventeen marriages. He noted Phillis Wheatley's departure to London on May 8 and her return September 15. He remarked about the opening of two new meeting-houses, the appointment of John Hancock as treasurer of Harvard College, a duel on Noddle's Island (not mortal), and the mustering of militia in Cambridge ("they made a most ridiculous appearance"). Boyle noted the last months in the life of one Levi Ames, jailed for burglary. On September 9, Ames was tried, found guilty, and sentenced to death. Before his hanging, "he gave convincing Proof of his dying a True Penitent." His age: twenty-one.

Only three of the seventy or so items in Boyle's journal over this ten-month span give a hint of political discontent. None of these suggest British authorities had anything to worry about. One was the expulsion of a cadet in the town's honor guard for throwing mud at customs men. Another was a reference to Church's Massacre oration. The third was an item about a feast of the Sons of Liberty, an event that went comically awry. This gathering on August 14, marking the eighth anniversary of the Stamp Act protest that destroyed the Oliver property, took place on Roxbury Common and drew about four hundred "True born Sons of Liberty." Two rows of tables were set, each extending about 150 feet. Just after the blessing, as the men sat down, the tables and benches in one of the rows collapsed. "By this misfortune about 200 Persons, genteely dressed, were mingled with Gravies, Sauces, Salt, Pepper, Sugar, Marrow, Flesh and Bones, Rum, Cyder, Punch and Wine, Plates, Dishes, Knives and Forks."

Then, on November 4, Boyle, in his journal–after noting the marriage of John Foxcroft and Sally Whitworth, and the death of John Proctor, master of the writing school on Queen Street–told of a notice "found stuck up in all Parts of the Town" that morning:

> To the Freemen of this and the Neighboring Towns,
> Gentlemen,
> You are desired to meet at Liberty-Tree, this day at twelve o'Clock at Noon–Then and there to hear the Persons to whom the Tea, shipped by the East India Company is consigned, make a public Resignation of their Office as Consignees upon Oath–And also swear that they will Re-Ship any Teas that may be consign'd to them by sd. Company, by the first Vessel sailing for London.
> V.C. Secretary

TWENTY-ONE

FIRM, INTREPID, AND INFLEXIBLE

The calming pleasure of tea was all but unknown in Europe before 1610, when the Dutch began to import it into Europe from Asia. Then, for at least fifty years, the Dutch East India Company had the tea trade in Europe all to itself. In 1667, the English East India Company began dabbling in the business and soon battled head to head with the Dutch. Other competitors, including merchants from France, Sweden, and Denmark, also entered the trade. In a little over a century, an obscure and negligible trade became huge and fiercely competitive. During the eighteenth century, the volume of the tea trade grew from not even one hundred thousand pounds per year at the start of the century to over four million pounds per year in the 1760s. A habit for only the rich became so common and affordable that even chambermaids could frequently imbibe.

The primary sort of tea imported into Europe was Bohea, a black tea from China's Fukien Province. Tea leaves harvested and processed in summer would be shipped to Canton for sales in the fall. The English would trade for the tea with shipments of bullion, woolens, tin, and lead. At the end of the year, vessels packed with tea would sail for Europe, arriving in the middle of the spring.

The British thirst for tea was astonishing–almost three hundred cups per year for every man, woman, and child. Americans, too, acquired a taste for tea. Regular imports began in the 1720s, and by the 1760s, American demand surpassed one million pounds per year–ample, though a fraction of the thirteen million pounds per year consumed in England.

Like their counterparts in Britain, Americans had no qualms about drinking smuggled tea, usually from Holland. Probably less than one quarter of the tea consumed in America was brought in legally from England. Efforts to stop the flow of smuggled tea were futile. A letter from Boston in 1773 reported that "not one chest in five hundred has been seized in this Province for two to three years past, and the custom house officers seem unwilling to run any risk to make a siezure."[1] Even so, despite all the smuggling, the trade in legal tea to America remained robust. It was the fourth-largest category of imports, trailing only cotton and woolens, linens, and ironware.

Typically, tea came to America tightly packed in chests, often lined with lead, weighing 450 pounds. Bohea tea represented 90 percent of the tea trade to America, and by the late 1760s, the ports of Boston, New York, and Philadelphia handled about 90 percent of all legally imported tea.

In America, the idea of reducing consumption of tea emerged at first not as a protest against taxes, but as a way to save money during the drive for more frugal living in the late 1760s. As early as 1767, newspaper articles, resolutions in town meetings, and petitions complained about the use and cost of this import. Then, as the protest against the Townshend duties developed, tea became an especially obvious target of the drive against imports because, of all the articles taxed under the law, tea was the most commonly used. As an alternative, patriots proposed Labrador (or Labradore) tea, also known as Hyperion tea, made from a bush that grew widely in swampy areas in New England. For a while, Americans tamed their tea habit. In the two-year period of 1769–1770, imports of tea from England to America dropped to less than one-third of imports in the previous two years.

When the nonimportation movement collapsed in late 1770 following the repeal of most Townshend duties, so did the fad for Labrador tea. Pledges to stop consuming tea were quickly forgotten, as trade in English tea rebounded despite the duty on it that Americans had so loudly opposed. Legal tea imports to Boston soared from 48,000 pounds in 1770 to 265,000 pounds in 1771. Tea imports in 1772 and 1773 were almost as high.[2]

The Boston men who imported the English tea were not only the hard-line Tories who had always sneered at nonimportation. They were also men who considered themselves ardent patriots. Some forty-five thousand pounds of dutied tea were carried into Boston in 1771 and 1772 on vessels owned by John Hancock.[3] As it turned out, demand for English tea was far stronger in Boston than in New York and Philadelphia because smuggled Dutch tea was so widely available in those towns, where from 1771 to 1773, it sold for less than English tea in Boston.

So in the months preceding the Boston Tea Party, plenty of English tea was coming into Boston and merchants were paying the duties, just as the law required. The craving for tea trumped outrage over taxation without representation. There was every reason to think that Americans would continue to quietly pay those duties despite having no representation in Parliament. If only Parliament had let well enough alone.

Then came a crisis unrelated to America. This one had to do with the United Company of Merchants Trading to the East Indies, more popularly known as the East India Company. The company came into being in 1709, bringing together two former competitors, one founded in 1603, the other in 1690.

Thanks to a charter that gave it a monopoly on virtually all English trade in Asia, the East India Company grew rich and mighty, and even came to establish its own military force to support and extend its commercial operations. The company dealt in many goods, including spices, silks, cotton, and precious metals. But by the mid-1700s, tea was the company's main stock in trade, accounting for about half its income and 90 percent of its profits.

Meanwhile, the British government increasingly came to count on the custom duties connected to the tea and other imports brought in by the company. By the 1760s, those duties represented about one-third of all custom revenues in Britain and about 6 percent of the government's budget. It was all a tidy arrangement that couldn't lose. The British people were hooked on tea. The company had a monopoly on delivering it. The government, feeding on tea duties, pampered this golden goose. Meanwhile, investors scooped up shares of company stock, sending prices soaring. The company doled out wildly generous dividends to investors, who included many members of Parliament.

But in paying out those dividends, the company had little money to plow back into its business and couldn't afford to lower prices. The edifice trembled when Britons received news in 1769 that the French might attack company outposts in India. Stockholders panicked. The price of the stock plunged.

Back in England, a more insidious crisis was looming. The British people didn't like to pay duties any more than Americans did. If they could get cheap, duty-free tea smuggled in from the continent, that's what they would buy. So enterprising lawbreakers responded to the market for cheaper tea, sneaking it in by the boatload, and thus undermining East India Company profits as well as government revenues. By the end of the 1760s, perhaps more than half of the tea consumed in Britain was smuggled in. The widespread smuggling also left the company with mountains of tea it couldn't sell.

Parliament looked for a way to help the company straighten out its financial mess. Members of Parliament and company directors seized on an obvious plan: dump the huge surplus of East India Tea, some eighteen million pounds, onto the European market. This would generate revenue and reduce the cost of storing the tea. America was not mentioned.

Upon investigating the plan, however, company directors became discouraged. By taking tea out of British warehouses and selling it on the European market, prices of tea would rise in England and fall in Europe. This would lead to more smuggling of cheap tea from Europe into Britain, once again cutting into East India Company sales.

So company directors looked at a map and calculated that an excellent way to get rid of the surplus and gain some revenue would be to sell the tea, duty free, in America. That would require Parliament to remove the controversial remaining Townshend tax–the duty on tea. The company submitted a complex petition to Parliament on March 2. The problems went beyond the issue of tea, so more than a month passed before Parliament finally delved into the question of tea exports.

The measure introduced by Lord North in Parliament on April 26 included the proposal to export the surplus tea to America. It did not include any plan, however, to remove the duty on tea. That would still be in place.

A member of Parliament, William Dowdeswell, pointed out the significance of the duty to Americans. Without that duty, Americans would certainly buy more tea, he said, adding, "I tell the Noble Lord now, if he don't take off the duty, they won't take the tea."[4]

North responded that the duty raised revenue needed by the government. Dowdeswell countered that the amount the duty brought in was hardly worth it, only £400 per year after deducting the costs of collecting the taxes. North would not budge. As the debate carried on, no one raised the issue of whether Parliament had the right to tax.

The Tea Act of 1773 passed on May 10 with the Townshend duty untouched. In the press and outside the halls of Parliament, the issue of tea exports was hardly noticed. Newspaper articles about the bill did not mention that surplus tea would be sent to America.

The tea would be shipped to four ports: Boston, New York, Philadelphia, and Charleston. In each of those towns, merchants selected as consignees would receive the tea. The merchants for Boston were the firms of Thomas & Elisha Hutchinson, Richard Clarke & Sons, and Faneuil & Winslow. Those merchants would then arrange for the public sale of the tea. From the proceeds they would deduct costs, including a 6 percent commission.

At first the company planned to ship seventeen hundred chests of tea. That was increased to two thousand. Finding available ships was a slight problem. Anticipating trouble, several New York captains and the captain of one of Hancock's vessels refused to carry the tea. But other captains were willing, and by September, shipments were ready. Soon the *London* was off for Charleston, the *Polly* bound for Philadelphia, the *Nancy* on its way to New York, and the *Dartmouth*, *Eleanor*, *Beaver*, and *William* heading to Boston.

The full text of the Tea Act was first printed in America in New York, where handbills opposing the shipments began appearing on the streets in October. An article in the *New York Journal* warned consignees of the awful fate awaiting them if they attempted to sell the tea: "A thousand avenues to death would be perpetually open to receive and swallow you, and ten thousand uplifted shafts, ready to strike the fatal stroke whenever a favourable opportunity offered for the purpose."[5] The consignees stood firm for a few weeks, but by late November they caved in and agreed not to handle the dutied tea.

The story was similar in Philadelphia. There an October 17 mass meeting of about seven hundred asked consignees to resign so as to keep "the peace and good order of the province." The consignees capitulated on December 1.[6]

In Boston, consignees were more stubborn thanks mainly to Thomas Hutchinson. In New York and Philadelphia, the provincial governors gave no special support to the consignees. In Boston, by contrast, Governor Hutchinson stood behind them. After all, two of them were his sons, and another consignee, Richard Clarke, was the father of young Thomas Hutchinson's wife. The governor also was emboldened by the presence of the British military at his doorstep. Naval vessels were in the harbor, and plenty of soldiers occupied Castle William. And Hutchinson had had enough with the patriots. He was not giving ground. And who could blame him? Back during the Stamp Act crisis, those followers of Sam Adams and his ilk had looted Hutchinson's house. For that, no one had ever been brought to justice. Since then, as lieutenant governor, acting governor, and governor, Hutchinson had endured an almost constant barrage of criticism and insults. Then came humiliation–the publication of his private letters–and shame–the vote by the House for his removal.

So now with the tea crisis, what could he lose by pushing back against his enemies? He could hardly be less popular. He knew that once the tea was landed and distribution began, consumers in Massachusetts would be eager to buy it. Why wouldn't they? Since the collapse of the nonimportation movement, they had been buying, brewing, and gulping dutied tea with hardly a murmur. The certain success of the tea plan would embarrass the patriots and prove that the majority of people in and around Boston did not fear British oppression–at least not enough to forgo their steaming pots of Bohea.

Curiously, Sam Adams and his Boston Committee of Correspondence were so focused on the issue of judges and salaries that they and their allies in Boston were slow to see the significance of the Tea Act. Through the middle of September, all was calm. The September 27

Boston Gazette published a letter saying the abilities of Lord Dartmouth were a promising sign for better relations between America and England.

That same issue of the *Gazette* contained a proposal from Sam Adams calling for what became the First Continental Congress. Readers pored over Adams's proposal that "a CONGRESS OF AMERICAN STATES be assembled as soon as possible." This call apparently stemmed from the general concern about erosion of rights and from particular concern about events in Rhode Island following the *Gaspee* incident. Now was the time for the colonies to link arms, he said. Adams proposed that this congress draw up and publish a "Bill of Rights." It would also choose an ambassador to Britain, determine where the congress would annually meet, agree on how it might be brought together in special circumstances, and take "farther steps" as necessary.[7]

His article on October 11 was more explicit in stating the goal of creating a new nation: "[T]he question will be asked. 'How shall the colonies force their oppressors to proper terms?' This question has been often answered already by our politicians, viz: 'Form an independent state,' 'AN AMERICAN COMMONWEALTH.'"[8]

This was about the time public opposition to the tea plan finally heated up in Boston. But even then it seemed to be just a move to catch up with opposition activities in New York and Philadelphia.

Among Boston merchants, the issue didn't seem important at first. Merchant John Rowe, in his diary for October 1773, mentions some of the same events that printer Boyle described in his journal: a duel on Noddle's Island and the hanging of Levi Ames "with many Thousand Spectators."[9] Tea is not mentioned. John Adams said years later that Boston would likely have accepted the tea peacefully and silently had the town not been stirred to action by reports of opposition in other towns.

Also, initially, opponents of the tea in Boston did not even raise the issue of the tax. When protests began, the chief argument against the Tea Act was that it might lead to a monopoly for the East India Company. One merchant, in writing about the issue, made no reference to taxes, but only to the loss of business and hard currency: "The East India Company has liberty to export teas to America, which makes us uneasy, as it will not only hurt our sales, but drain the continent of silver."[10]

But soon critics of the Tea Act zeroed in on the tax. The *Gazette* argued that the aim of the plan involving the tea was to raise money to pay the salaries of the governor and judges, and thus make them untouchable by the people.

Finally the Boston Committee of Correspondence got into the act, but still treated the business of tea as a side issue. A letter of October 21, addressed to committees throughout colonial America, spoke of the tea shipments almost as an afterthought following a long discussion of other questions:

> We cannot close without mentioning a fresh Instance of the temper & Design of the British Ministry; and that is in allowing the East India Company, with a View of pacifying them, to ship their Teas to America. It is easy to see how aptly this scheme will serve both to destroy the trade of the colonies & increase the revenue. How necessary then it is that each colony should take effectual methods to prevent this measure from having its designed effects.[11]

Soon, the most radical elements of the opposition decided that intimidation was called for, as in the days of the Stamp Act crisis. On November 2, at 1:00 a.m., Richard Clarke and his family, tucked in bed in their School Street home, were awakened by a ferocious pounding on the door. Looking out the window, the Clarkes could clearly see the figures of two men in the moonlight. They were delivering a letter from the country, they said, and soon handed a paper over to a servant. This was no letter, however. It was a "summons." The note demanded that Clarke appear at the Liberty Tree at noon on November 3 "to make a public resignation of your commission."[12]

Copies of the note were delivered to the other consignees and, in the morning, Bostonians read handbills tacked up all over town asking them to come and watch Clarke and the other consignees quit and agree to send the tea–still on its way to Boston–back to England.

These handbills did not go unanswered. Other handbills, signed by "The True Sons of Liberty," raged against the "illegal and underhanded" demands of the anti-tea faction: "You are hereby advised and warned by no means to be taken in by the deceitful Bait of those who falsely stile themselves Friends of Liberty." Defiantly, the authors of this handbill resolved "to walk uprightly, and to eat, drink, and wear whatever we can honestly procure by our Labour; and to Buy and Sell when and where we please."[13]

Just before the appointed time, a town crier circulated through Boston streets calling citizens to the Liberty Tree. Church bells started ringing and kept on ringing until noon. Sure enough, five hundred people appeared and so did Sam Adams, Joseph Warren, the town's selectmen, including Hancock, and other patriot leaders. The Liberty Tree was festooned with flags. But the consignees did not answer the call. They were among the twenty or so men meeting at Clarke's warehouse on King Street.

William Molineux then led a delegation, including Joseph Warren and Benjamin Church, followed by just about everyone who showed up at the tree, to call on the absent invitees. At the warehouse, Molineux told Clarke that he and the other consignees had, by failing to appear at the Liberty Tree as demanded, "committed an high insult on the people."[14] Molineux produced a paper for Clarke to sign. It was a promise to ship the tea back to England.

Clarke refused. Molineux warned that Clarke and his allies could expect "the utmost weight of the people's resentment." Molineux stalked away, and so did most of the crowd. But a few people lingered around a tavern nearby. Soon enough they built up the gumption to attack Clarke's warehouse. With the fierce mob approaching, a servant moved to slam the door. Soon, a brave justice of the peace stepped up to order the crowd away. Someone in the crowd answered by slugging the peace officer, who retreated into the building, joining Clarke and the others. Soon thereafter, the mob yanked the door from its hinges. Men charged into the building and rushed to get at the men gathered on the second floor. But the stairway was narrow, too narrow for more than one or two men at a time. Clarke and his friends kept the attackers at bay for about ninety minutes. Finally, the attackers had enough and sauntered away. Clarke and his allies eventually left their refuge, walked up King Street, and dispersed to their homes "without molestation, saving some insulting behavior from a few despicable persons."[15]

On Friday, November 5–Pope Day–townsmen stuffed Faneuil Hall for a special town meeting. Those at the meeting, with Hancock as moderator, railed at the tax on tea and called for a stand against the importation plan. It was an echo of resolutions ratified in Philadelphia in mid-October. Committees formed to take on the task of again asking the consignees to resign.

When the consignees later received the request, they dodged. They could not answer because they did not yet know the exact terms of the consignment arrangement: "When we are acquainted with these circumstances, we shall be better qualified to give a definitive answer to the request of the Town." The town meeting rejected this "daringly affrontive" response.[16]

Meanwhile, letters in the newspapers kept the issue on boil. Figures appeared showing that three thousand chests of dutied tea had been imported into Boston since 1768. Everyone knew this tidbit would circulate to other towns in America. What an embarrassment for the patriots in Boston. How could they claim to be at the vanguard in the movement against these duties? This heightened the sense among patriots that they had something to prove with this confrontation. They had been late in seizing the issue. Their record of inhibiting the flow of tea into Boston was abysmal. To give in to the consignees would be another failure.

Meanwhile, Hutchinson, his allies, and the consignees continued to feel threatened and vulnerable. The governor ordered the colonel of the

Cadets, Hancock, to prepare for possible action. Hancock did nothing. Each night the uneasy consignees slipped out of Boston to the homes of friends in neighboring communities.

On November 17, a ship's captain just arrived in Boston reported that he left England at the same time as the tea ships. Boston thus knew that the controversial cargoes of East India Company tea would likely turn up within days. That same night, a mob appeared outside the Clarke home on School Street as the family was enjoying a reunion. Amid the raucous noise of the crowd, women of the family fled upstairs. Meanwhile, one young male family member poked a pistol out a chamber window and hollered, "You Rascals, be gone or I'll blow your brains out!"[17] The rascals didn't leave, at least not fast enough for young Clarke. He fired.

No one was hit, but the shot touched off a frenzy. The mob set upon the house, shattering windows and splintering window frames. A blizzard of stones and bits of brick sailed through the openings, scarring furniture and striking people inside. The Clarkes held their own, refusing even to bargain with the mob. The crowd, after an hour or more, went away.

The next morning, another town meeting sent off yet another committee to ask the consignees to give up. Again the consignees stood firm. But weary of the threats and demands, they looked for a temporary measure that might provide some breathing space. On November 19, they submitted a petition begging the governor and Council to take control of the tea until the consignees can "be at liberty, openly and safely, to dispose" of it, or until they received further directions.[18] The governor was sympathetic. The Council, however, needed time to think about it. After more than a week of meetings and debate, the consignees still awaited a decision.

Frustrated, the consignees sought some compromise from the Boston town selectmen. Now eager to get the tea controversy off his back, Clarke said he would do whatever the selectmen wanted. They said the only solution was to ship the tea back to England. Clarke said he couldn't do that. The law, he said, prevented the reimportation of the tea back into England. If that were tried, authorities might seize not only the tea but the vessel as well. After lengthy debate, a compromise was reached: Clarke promised that when the tea ships came in, they would not be secretly unloaded.

Meanwhile, the Boston Committee of Correspondence worked to stir up opposition throughout Massachusetts. On November 22, it played host at Faneuil Hall to a meeting of committees from nearby Roxbury, Dorchester, Brookline, Cambridge, and Charlestown. This meeting produced a joint letter addressed to other towns. Accepting the tax, the letter warned, was the first step down a slippery slope:

> [I]n a very short time, taxes of the like or a more grievous nature, will be laid on every article exported from Great Britain, which our necessity may require, or our shameful luxury may betray us into the use of, and when once they have found the way to rob us, their avarice will never be satisfied until our own manufactures, and even our land, purchased and cultivated by our own hard labouring ancestors are taxed to support the extravagance and vices of wretches, whose vileness ought to banish them from the society of men.[19]

On November 28, a Sunday, word spread that the first of the tea ships, the *Dartmouth*, had come through the outer islands near Boston and dropped anchor in the harbor. On board were 114 chests of East India Company tea.

The crisis was at hand. There seemed to be no solution. The consignees couldn't bear the potential financial loss of sending the tea back, a request Hutchinson called "monstrous."[20] Yet, the patriots had no intention of allowing the tea to be landed and distributed. Meanwhile, leaving the tea in the *Dartmouth* indefinitely was not an option either. According to customs rules, dutiable goods had to be landed and their duties paid within twenty days of the vessel's arrival. If the tea remained in the ship past December 17, customs officers could seize it.

Other options for the tea were not acceptable to the patriots. One was to permit it to be unloaded and placed in a government warehouse, where it would be under the care of Governor Hutchinson. Patriots felt they could not trust him to keep the tea out of the hands of the consignees, especially since two were his sons. Another option was to let the tea come into Boston and call on fellow citizens to boycott it, to refrain from buying dutied tea. But that was sure to fail. New Englanders, by paying the tea duty for years, had already demonstrated an eagerness to cast aside the cause of liberty for a cup of tea.

With no time to waste, patriots arranged a town meeting for the next day, November 29, at Faneuil Hall. Posters shouted: "Friends! Brethren! Countrymen! The Hour of Destruction or Manly Opposition to the Machinations of Tyranny stares you in the Face."[21] This was not a legally sanctioned town meeting, which would normally be officially called by the selectmen. This was simply an open meeting. The chairman of the meeting was not Sam Adams or John Hancock or another of the usual cast of radicals, but Jonathan Williams, a moderate merchant. Everyone was welcome, and, to the sound of church bells, many came, some even from surrounding towns. The meeting began at Faneuil Hall and then shifted to Old South to accommodate the vast throng. A motion was proposed that the *Dartmouth* be ordered back to England with its tea.

As the motion was thrashed out, the throng heard the lonely plea of Francis Rotch, the twenty-three-year-old part owner of the *Dartmouth*. This young Quaker, whose family was big in the Nantucket whaling business, wanted to get the tea ashore, load up with a cargo of whale oil, and be off. We can imagine his anxiety. The name Rotch was not favored in Boston. The Rotch firm had a history of business rivalry with Thomas and John Hancock. Also, in 1769, Rotch joined the names Hutchinson, Clarke, and others on a published list of families who ignored the call to boycott British imports.

To the restless crowd at Old South, Rotch summed up his dilemma: To leave Boston, the *Dartmouth* needed permission from the governor; the governor had no intention of giving permission without proper clearance from the Custom House. If the *Dartmouth* tried to slip out without permission, the navy would snare the vessel. Should the *Dartmouth* miraculously get past the navy, it might be seized in London for having no clearance out of Boston. On top of it all, the return voyage would be costly, an unfair financial blow. Taking the tea back to England was thus out of the question.

Sam Adams took the floor and brushed off Rotch's claim. Taking the tea back was entirely possible, he said. Vessel owners, when cargoes were lost at sea, often went to the Custom House for special consideration. Similarly, Rotch could convincingly tell the Custom House that, because of a "Political Storm" and "a Mob of several Thousands," he was compelled to take the tea back across the ocean without the duty paid.[22]

Soon, the massive meeting passed the resolution: the tea must go back. Nothing suggested a scheme to burn the tea or dump it into the harbor. A man from out of town who stopped in on the meeting later reported that from "observing the countenance, and attending to the discourse of this body of people, he was then fully persuaded, that the tea would not be destroyed."[23]

The meeting assigned twenty-five men to stand guard over the vessel. These guards were assigned to discourage violence. But clearly, they were also there to prevent anyone from unloading the vessel.

About this time, the governor finally got his answer from the Council. Would the Council take control of the tea? No. That, the Council decided, was beyond its authority. The Council's helpful advice for Hutchinson: remind peace officers "to exert themselves to the utmost" to keep the peace.[24]

Meanwhile, handbills appeared, signed "THE PEOPLE," stating that anyone who tried to unload the tea ships would be treated as "Wretches unworthy to live, and will be made first victims of our just Resentment."[25]

Fearing more and more for their safety, the consignees made arrangements to be out of Boston as much as possible, either at Castle William or in homes in nearby communities. The governor, too, usually stayed away at this time, residing at his country home in Milton. Once, before leaving town, the consignees left a letter that was read at the beginning of the next mass meeting, just after 9:00 a.m. on Tuesday, November 30. In the letter, the consignees said that returning the tea to England was "utterly out of our power to do."[26] However, they said they would be willing to have the cargo stored until they received further instructions from the company. At the same meeting, Sheriff Greenleaf suddenly ambled in with a message from the governor: their meeting the day before was illegal. Those who participated were guilty of "openly violating, defying, and setting at naught the good and wholesome laws of the Province." The present meeting was also illegal. "As his Majesty's representative within the Province . . . I warn and exhort you and require you and each of you unlawfully assembled forthwith, to disperse and to surcease all further unlawful proceedings at your utmost peril."[27]

The "unlawfully assembled" answered with "a loud and very general hiss."[28] Sam Adams delivered a fifteen-to–twenty-minute rant shredding the governor: "He? He? is he that shadow of a man, scarce able to support his withered Carcase or his hoary Head! is he a Representation of Majesty?"[29] A motion was duly put forward to "disperse and surcease." It failed unanimously.[30]

Portrait painter John Singleton Copley came forward. His sympathies were with the consignees, for the Clarkes were his in-laws. Even so, patriots respected him as honorable and evenhanded. He volunteered to fetch the consignees if the crowd promised to be courteous and listen to their statements. The great assembly agreed, allowing Copley two hours to retrieve the consignees from Castle William.

After an adjournment, the meeting came back to order at two in the afternoon. *Dartmouth* owner Rotch, along with its captain, watched while the assembly passed a resolution ordering the *Dartmouth* back to England with the tea. Rotch then complained that "he should protest the whole proceedings" but said he would comply.[31] About this time, two other owners of tea ships were sent for. One was John Rowe, merchant, diarist, and political chameleon. Many townspeople saw him as a Tory, but on this day, he prudently took on a patriotic hue. He was sorry, he said, that his vessel, the *Eleanor*, still on its way to Boston, "should be concerned in bringing any of that detestable and obnoxious Commodity." Seeing how much his audience appreciated his apology, he asked, "Whether a little Salt Water would not do it good, or whether Salt Water would not make as good Tea as fresh."[32] Was the idea of the Tea Party thus conjured at that moment? Rowe won applause. Some in the crowd crowed that "now they had brought a good Tory over to their Side–that Mr. Rowe had now become a good Man and they should soon make all the Rest of the Tories turn to their Side as Mr. Rowe had done."[33]

By and by, Copley returned, but without the consignees, who, Copley reported, felt their appearance at the meeting would accomplish nothing. However, they said once again that they would agree to have the tea stored and now were willing to have it warehoused under the oversight of a patriotic committee.

Sam Adams was not impressed. He asked for a vote on the question of "whether the Consignees had offered any thing in the least Degree satisfactory." The people answered: no.[34]

Riding this wave of indignation, Adams put forward a forceful resolution that, besides restating the call to ship the tea back to England, jabbed the many local merchants who quietly kept importing tea:

> Whereas sundry Merchants in the Province basely preferring their own private Interest to the General Good and contrary to the Opinion of N. York, Philadelphia and the other Colonies have imported Tea from G. Britain while subject to a Duty, and whereas they have justly incurred the Displeasure of the other Colonies by so doing, Resolved, that whoever shall import Tea from G. Britain into the Province while that accursed and unrighteous Act laying a Duty upon it is in Force, shall be deemed an Enemy to his Country by this Body, and we will effect a Return of the same to the Place from whence it came.[35]

For many in the hall, this resolution was over the top. They had no problem with returning the tea. But was it necessary to take a swipe at so many local merchants? William Cooper, the town clerk, protested that some importers of tea were "otherwise worthy citizens" and there was "no Necessity of exposing the Conduct of a Number of Merchants and of the Town to the reproach of other Colonies."[36]

Adams gave a Puritan answer: "[T]o the Shame and Scandal of this Province and to the just and great Grief of Philadelphia and N. York, many in this Province had continued to import dutied Tea while the other Colonies had not."[37] Massachusetts should confess, not conceal, this disgrace, he said.

A sharp discussion followed, with debaters coming "well nigh to Loggerheads." Finally the resolution was watered down. According to the amended resolution, some merchants had "inadvertently imported dutied Tea,"[38] as if the tea accidentally fell into a cargo hold in England and came ashore in Boston without the merchant knowing it. Still, the modified resolution was powerful enough: from now on, anyone who imported tea from Great Britain shall be "deemed by this body an enemy to his country." Furthermore, "we will prevent the landing and sale" of tea from Britain and "effect" its return.[39] The resolution was ordered printed and dispatched to England and all the seaports in Massachusetts.

As the meeting finally wound down, John Hancock stepped forward with a benediction: "My Fellow Countrymen, we have now put our Hands to the Plough and Wo be to him that shrinks or looks back."[40]

Now all eyes were on the calendar. The days fluttered past toward December 17, the day customs officials would seize the tea if it were still on board the *Dartmouth.* On December 1, the *Dartmouth* was docked at Griffin's Wharf, and in the days that followed, men emptied the vessel of all its cargo, except for the tea. Meanwhile, Rowe's *Eleanor* arrived. The Boston Committee of Correspondence asked the ship's captain to position it near the *Dartmouth* so the same patriot guards could watch it. He complied. A third tea ship, the *Beaver,* approached Boston Harbor but was found to have smallpox on board. After cleansing, it was brought up to Griffin's Wharf as well. The fourth Boston-bound tea ship, the *William,* ran aground off Cape Cod and never made it to Boston.

In late November and early December, messages of encouragement to resist the landing of the tea reached Boston from Dorchester, Brookline, Roxbury, Marblehead, Medford, Plymouth, and Lexington. By December 13, Boston learned that consignees in New York and Philadelphia had either resigned or given up responsibility for the tea.

Meanwhile, Hutchinson took pains to see to it that none of the tea ships slipped out of the harbor without permission. At the governor's request, the navy positioned warships to block channels not already under the guns of the battery at Castle William.

On December 14, a great crowd of people came together at Old South for yet another session concerning the tea. The moderator this time was a Weston man, selected presumably to emphasize that the issue was not just Boston's concern, but also a concern in other communities. The captains of the *Eleanor* and *Dartmouth* attended and were asked to request permission from customs officials to leave Boston Harbor and return to England without unloading the tea or paying the tea duties. The captains both reluctantly agreed.

With time running out on the *Dartmouth* deadline, a committee of ten from the mass meeting, including Sam Adams, escorted Rotch, the *Dartmouth* owner, to the lodgings of customs man Richard Harrison. Harrison listened to the request for clearance but refused to make an immediate decision. He said he would make up his mind by the next day, the fifteenth. When word of this result reached the meeting at the Old South, that group adjourned to meet again on the sixteenth.

So for the moment, the fate of the tea was in the hands of Harrison, who consulted with Robert Hallowell, the comptroller of customs. The *Dartmouth*'s cargo, by this time, had formally been entered at the

Custom House. This meant that, technically, the tea had already been imported, even though it was still sitting in the vessel's holds. Letting the ship leave without paying the duty would thus seem to be illegal, according to a strict interpretation of the rules. Still, in this special case, perhaps Harrison could employ some discretion. But Harrison was not especially keen on helping the patriots. After all, this was the same Richard Harrison who, during the *Liberty* incident, was dragged through the streets by a mob. Thus, when Rotch reappeared for his answer, Harrison told him that the requested clearance was refused.

So at Old South on Thursday, December 16, the great mass of five thousand or so, including about two thousand from outside Boston, considered this news and pondered what to do next. Someone suggested to Sam Adams that customs officials should be allowed to unload the tea on the seventeenth. The tea still had to be auctioned. Patriots could identify those who dared buy it at auction and deal with them accordingly. This option was not considered. The patriots had repeatedly demanded that the tea be shipped back to England. To now allow it to land would be seen as backpedaling.

The meeting began with Rotch once again explaining why he couldn't just set sail. The gathering then voted to have Rotch ask the governor for permission to clear. This seemed to be the last possible way to resolve the issue peacefully. The meeting adjourned to give Rotch time to complete the fourteen-mile round-trip journey to the governor's estate in Milton.

Out in Milton, Hutchinson was prepared for this eventuality. In a letter written two days before, he said the law stipulated that the only vessels he could allow out of the harbor were those cleared by the Custom House. As far as he was concerned, his hands were tied. In any case, just like Harrison, he had no intention of helping the patriots wiggle out of this fix. Hutchinson later explained that to allow the tea to go back would have been a breach of his duty. As governor, he "was bound, as all the king's governors were, by oath, faithfully to observe the acts of trade." Allowing a vessel out without clearing customs "would have been a direct violation of his oath."[41]

When Rotch arrived, Hutchinson inquired about activities at the meeting and the mood of the people. Rotch said that the people continued to demand that the tea be returned to England. He also said, however, that the people were open to a gesture short of that goal that might open the door to an honorable way out of the impasse. Perhaps the *Dartmouth* could move out into the harbor as far as Castle William. Then the battery could fire a shot across the bow. The tea ship would then surrender to the military. This would satisfy at least some people, who could claim that Boston tried to send back the tea and only submitted to overwhelming force.

Hutchinson did not dismiss the idea out of hand. However, the governor insisted that to carry out the plan, the vessel first had to be towed out near the navy fleet to be under the protection of naval guns. Rotch rejected this, fearing that somehow the move would be misinterpreted and make him the target of a mob. Hutchinson then said he could not cooperate in carrying out the plan, nor could he issue a pass for the *Dartmouth* without proper clearance from the customs office. Rotch started back for Boston.

The meeting at Old South resumed at 3:00 p.m., before Rotch's return. The group occupied itself with speeches and resolutions on the same theme: opposition to the tea. Among the speakers was Josiah Quincy. He was characteristically provocative, so much so that he invited a scolding from another speaker for the intemperance of his language. Quincy shrugged it off with an allusion to the illness that was slowly killing him: "Personally, perhaps, I have less concern than any one present in the crisis which is approaching. The seeds of dissolution are thickly planted in my constitution. They must soon ripen. I feel how short is the day that is allotted to me."[42]

By 5:00 p.m., Rotch had still not returned, and patience was wearing thin. A vote to break up the meeting was followed by a plea for more time, another hour, to hear what Rotch had to report. At 5:45 p.m., with daylight fading, a cold rain falling, and the broad hall of Old South glowing with candlelight, Rotch finally arrived. The meeting quickly came to order, and Rotch spoke. His news set off an uproar. When the crowd quieted, Thomas Young spoke up to plead that Rotch and his property be left alone. The ship owner, after all, had done what was asked of him. Two more questions were put to him: Would he send the *Dartmouth* back to England with the tea? Answer: no, because that would ruin him. Would he land the tea? Answer: only if authorities asked him.

Newcomers appeared at the doorway, men dressed vaguely as Indians. From the gallery came a war whoop, echoed by the newcomers near the doorway. Now other shouts rang out, and then came the momentous statement from Sam Adams, likely a prearranged signal: "This meeting can do nothing more to save the country."[43]

Now came a great push to the exits. People later remembered men hollering "Boston Harbor a tea pot tonight!", "Hurrah for Griffin's Wharf!", "The Mohawks are come!," and "Every man to his tent!" The noise was loud enough and startling enough to get the attention of John Andrews, a merchant living three blocks away who happened at that very moment to be having his own cup of tea. He hustled to Old South to see what the hullabaloo was all about, but he couldn't get in because of the crowd rushing out. He later remembered the astonishing noise: "You'd have thought that the inhabitants of the infernal regions had

An early nineteenth century illustration of the Boston Tea Party. (*Library of Congress*)

broke loose." But the excitement wasn't enough to distract him for long. As others by the dozens were coming to the scene, "I went contentedly home and finish'd my tea."[44] Meanwhile, the people pouring out of Old South pushed their way down Milk Street, to Hutchinson Street, and on to Griffin's Wharf.

They were all following a group of thirty to sixty men, perhaps fifteen or twenty dressed as Indians but in a way that fooled no one–maybe a bit of paint on the cheek and a blanket over the shoulder. Shoemaker George Robert Twelves Hewes, a participant, recalled years later that he dashed into a blacksmith shop, found something black to rub on his face, and then borrowed a blanket to wrap around himself. That was the extent of his disguise. Most did not bother to alter their appearance at all. Many of the men carried hatchets.

The operation was well planned and carefully organized. At the wharf, three groups formed, each with a leader. Many men had assigned roles. Hewes, for example, known for his peculiar whistling skills, was stationed to give signals. To help keep identities secret, the men were told only the name of their particular commander. By this time the rain had stopped and the moon was out.

The groups quickly went to work on the *Dartmouth*, *Eleanor*, and *Beaver*. A customs officer was on board each of the vessels. So the first item of business was to firmly escort these men to shore. Then, with light from the moon and a handful of lanterns penetrating the darkness, the "Savages"[45] entered the holds of each vessel. Sets of block and tackle were put to work, and soon chests were lifted up and brought on the decks. As men worked below attaching block and tackle, and as other men hoisted the tea, still others took hatchets to the chests, scooped the tea out, and flung it overboard. The chests, as they were emptied, were also cast onto the water.

In the low tide, with the water just a few feet deep, mounds of tea began to form alongside the ships. As the work went on, the heaps grew, threatening to collapse back onto the decks of the vessels. Men leveled off the tea piles so more could be piled on. They were forbidden from taking away any of the valuable commodity. According to a letter, an "interloper" who "found the means to fill his pockets with tea, upon being discovered, was stripped of his booty and his clothes altogether, and sent home naked."[46]

Watching all this from shore was a crowd, large but so quiet that the sound of the hatchets working away could be distinctly heard at a distance.

By 9:00 p.m., less than three hours after they started, patriots completed the "destruction of the tea"–it would be many years before anyone would refer to the event as the Tea Party. As if to underscore their own underlying respect for law and order, the men carefully replaced a small padlock they had broken.

John Adams didn't take part but soon learned of the event. He gushed in his diary the next day: "There is a Dignity, a Majesty, a Sublimity, in this last Effort of the Patriots, that I greatly admire. The People should never rise, without doing something to be remembered–something notable and striking. This Destruction of the Tea is so bold, so daring, so firm, intrepid, & inflexible, that I cannot but consider it as an Epocha in History."[47]

TWENTY-TWO

DOCTRINE OF DEVILS

Two days after the Tea Party, John Andrews, the merchant who returned home to finish his tea as the destruction began, wrote a letter: "However precarious our situation may be, yet such is the present calm composure of the people that a stranger would hardly think that thousand pounds sterling of the East India Company's tea was destroy'd the night, or rather the evening before last, yet it's a serious truth."[1]

Questions about the event still beg answers: When did patriots seize upon the idea of destroying the tea? When and where was the destruction planned? Who took part?

The idea of destroying the tea came up as early as November 29, when Thomas Young proposed it at a meeting. The idea was not accepted then but won converts as the days passed and frustrations grew. Plans for the destruction were probably made at the meeting of the committees of correspondence from Boston and other towns at Faneuil Hall on Monday, December 13. The identities of those who participated were kept secret at the time, an amazing feat considering how many were involved and bore witness. And the secret was kept a long time, although it's difficult to believe John Adams's claim, writing fifty years after the event, that he could not name a single man who took part.[2]

From evidence based largely on recollections of old men who had watched or helped out in the event decades earlier, historians have concluded that some of those who tossed tea overboard were members of Hancock's Cadets, others belonged to the Masons, and many were members of the Sons of Liberty. Some apprentices also pitched in, along with such artisans as Paul Revere. Organizers deliberately wanted men who were not well known so they would not be easily recognized. Joshua Wyeth, a blacksmith, later said he was selected to take part just hours before the event. He was picked, he said, in part because he was not prominent.

It seemed every level of society was represented. If family stories told years later are to be believed, at least two merchants took part, including Thomas Melvill, a Princeton graduate with a master's degree from Harvard. William Molineux and Thomas Young seem to have been the only well-known radical leaders to step aboard the tea ships that night. Apparently, Sam Adams, John Hancock, and Joseph Warren did not directly participate in the destruction that December evening. We know John Adams was away.

The day after the Tea Party, Hutchinson tried to gather his Council in Boston but couldn't get a quorum. He tried the next day at his home in Milton. Again he couldn't get enough to attend, apparently because the councillors feared for their safety. Finally, on December 21, he managed to gather with his Council in Cambridge, at the house of William Brattle.

Hutchinson wanted strong action: an offer of reward for information useful for convicting those who destroyed the tea. The Council wanted no part of that. It would only go along with an investigation. Whatever was found would be presented to a grand jury, which, as everyone knew, would likely see the destruction as no crime at all, no matter the evidence.

In Boston, no one felt the Council's tepid response had let the town off the hook. Amid rumors that the patriot leaders would be rounded up and shipped off for trial in England, members of the Boston Committee of Correspondence, with the exception for some reason of Joseph Warren, promised to "support and vindicate each other, and any Person or Persons who may be likely to suffer for any noble Effort they have made to serve their Country."[3]

Meanwhile, the committee sent off Revere on the first of many urgent rides on behalf of the patriotic cause. Thomas Young summed up the man: "Steady, vigorous, sensible and persevering."[4] Patriot leaders knew he was someone they could rely on. While other messengers were assigned to towns in Massachusetts to spread the word about the Tea Party and the committee's justification for it, Revere went off with the same errand to New York and Philadelphia.

No committee member was rounded up, and except for one man, no one was ever arrested for the Tea Party. The one unlucky man was a barber named Eckley, who, for lack of evidence, was never convicted.

As for the people of Boston and surrounding areas, those who spoke out were gleeful about the destruction of the tea. The *Gazette* reported that "the people are almost universally congratulating each other on this happy event."[5] Hutchinson, in letters to London, admitted that the people seemed to have endorsed the action. In a letter to a friend in

New York, a Bostonian wrote, "We are in a perfect jubilee."[6] But some people, afraid to speak out, were appalled. John Rowe confided to his diary, "Tis a Disastrous Affair & some People are much Alarmed."[7]

News of the Tea Party spread and emboldened patriots in other ports where the tea ships went. When word of the Tea Party reached Philadelphia on Christmas Eve, church bells rang in celebration. The tea ship *Polly* finally arrived on the twenty-sixth, and just forty-six hours later it was on its way back out to sea, its cargo untouched. The customs officials and governor in Pennsylvania, unlike their counterparts in Massachusetts, were not sticklers about enforcing rules preventing the tea from being shipped out. In Charleston, patriots failed to stop the tea from coming ashore. However, no duty was paid on the tea, which ended up moldering in warehouses. In New York, the arrival of the tea ship was delayed. Storms nearly wrecked the *Nancy*, forcing it to seek repairs and provisions in Antigua. It finally approached New York the following year, in April 1774. Passions were still high then, and the captain was not keen on a confrontation. So, after taking on more provisions, the *Nancy* headed back to England with the tea still on board. All across the American colonies, the Tea Party riveted attention on the Townshend tax on tea, which Americans had sullenly been paying for many months. In many places, including Boston, the consumption of tea–any tea, smuggled or taxed–was called into question. Seventy-nine out of about one hundred tea merchants in Boston agreed to suspend sales of English and Dutch tea. Many agreed with the writer who wanted all tea banned because, "If you suffer Dutch Tea, you will soon be over-run with dutied tea under that Name."[8] In Boston that winter, sales of coffee soared.

The news of the Tea Party arrived in England with John Hancock's *Hayley* on January 20, 1774, a little over a month after the event. Directors of the East India Company reacted calmly. They wanted compensation but sought no punishment for those who destroyed the tea. The government, however, wanted sterner measures. Lord Dartmouth suggested that the provincial seat of government and the Custom House be shifted out of Boston. The cabinet approved, acknowledging the need to punish the town. Soon afterward, an official report found that the Tea Party amounted to "the levying of war against His Majesty."[9] The report suggested a dual policy of punishing both the town and the people responsible. However, authorities never seriously tried to snare and prosecute guilty individuals. British leaders concentrated almost entirely on collective punishment. To many, the town was due a comeuppance. Boston had been a bawling troublemaker almost constantly from the time of the Stamp Act riots in 1765. King George's view was that Britain, in repealing the Stamp Act, had foolishly granted concessions to the Americans. This pushed Americans toward "independency . . . quite subversive of the obedience which a colony owes to its Mother Country."[10] Now, he believed, coercion was needed to make America submit, and his subjects in England tended to agree. One man, writing to Dartmouth, said Bostonians, in addition to being "morose and sour" religious hypocrites, were also deadbeats. Furthermore, "They are not only the worst Subjects, but the most truly immoral Men of any he [the writer] has had to deal with." Finally, as if that weren't enough, the writer called Boston as wicked "as Sodom itself was for a Vice which ought not be named."[11]

By unhappy coincidence, news of the Tea Party arrived in London when British lawmakers and ministers were already steaming over another issue concerning Massachusetts: the brash request from the House of Representatives that Governor Hutchinson and Lieutenant Governor Oliver be yanked from office. This was connected to the damning correspondence from Hutchinson, Oliver, and others to Thomas Whately.

Reaction in London to the letters was far different to that in Boston. What was interesting in London was not the content of the letters but the question of who sent them to Boston. Fingers pointed at John Temple, the customs official who was suspiciously popular with the Boston patriots. The swirling rumors and accusations led to a duel between Temple and Whately's brother, William, on December 11, 1773, which left Whately wounded. To avert a possible second duel, Benjamin Franklin confessed that he alone had "obtained and transmitted" the letters. Now Franklin was tainted with dishonor: he was linked to a possible theft and certainly was guilty of revealing other men's private correspondence.[12]

No one has solved the mystery of who gave Franklin the letters. Possibly it was Thomas Pownall, member of Parliament and former governor of Massachusetts. Pownall sympathized with the Americans, corresponded with radicals in Boston, and seemed to share many of Franklin's views. He once thought highly of Hutchinson, but now believed as Franklin did that relations between Britain and Massachusetts could only be repaired if Americans recognized that Hutchinson had been leading ministers in London astray.

Whatever the source of the letters, Franklin stood alone in Whitehall's "Cockpit," a large hall with a gallery, before the Privy Council on January 29, just after news of the Tea Party reached London. The public watched and cheered as Alexander Wedderburn, the solicitor general, tore into Franklin in words so harsh that newspapers would not print the speech verbatim.

Wedderburn tossed aside the question of Hutchinson's competence. The governor, Wedderburn said, was honorable, conscientious, and had done nothing wrong in his four years on the job. Now, thieves who stole his letters had set in motion a conspiracy to bring him down, but not for what he said in the letters. Hutchinson was being tormented for daring to challenge the Massachusetts House of Representatives as it threatened to "blow up the province into a flame, which from thence was to have spread over the other provinces."[13] Wedderburn made it clear that Franklin's actions, not Hutchinson's, were the issue here. Franklin, as if on trial, stood silent as Wedderburn accused him of giving seditious advice, having harmful aims, and using unscrupulous means.

Among the spectators at Franklin's humiliation was General Thomas Gage, who happened to be visiting England at this time. In a letter to Hutchinson, he wrote, "I suppose no man's conduct and character was before so mangled and torn as Dr Franklin's was at this time: people wondering he had the confidence to stand it, with the contemptuous looks of the audience upon him."[14] Gage also informed Hutchinson that the relationship between Britain and its American colonies had reached a crossroads: "People talk more seriously than ever about America: that the cricis is come, when the Provinces must bee either British Colonies, or independent and separate States."[15]

The Privy Council's later report cleared Hutchinson and expressed "astonishment" that lawmakers in Massachusetts concocted such unfair accusations against the governor. Hutchinson's days as governor were dwindling, but he would leave the post of his own accord.

Back in Boston, no one yet knew London's reaction to the Tea Party, and a determined tea drinker could still buy the beverage. In an advertisement in the *Gazette* weeks after the Tea Party, a merchant offered "Choice Bohea and Souchong Teas" at his shop "near the Town House."[16] But by late January, pressure was on all retailers to stop sales of all tea. To mark the end of all tea sales, two barrels of Bohea were torched in front of the customs house to the "acclamation of a vast concourse of People."[17]

Meanwhile, reports came in that some people had salvaged soggy remnants of the East India tea that had drifted ashore. The radicals could not ignore this. A group of men, described coyly in the *Gazette* as "Cape or Naragansett-Indians,"[18] entered a home between Boston and Milton, seized this tea, brought it back to Boston, and burned it on the Common.

The mere drinking of tea became an issue of debate. What if a person had tea that was purchased, with duty paid, before the destruction of the tea? Was it right to drink this tea? "A Friend to the Cause" wrote in the *Gazette* that it was "certainly" a moral good to "abolish and destroy" such an article "so every way pernicious to the constitution."

He hoped that his fellow "Countrymen, and the fair Sex in particular, will convince the world of our uprightness, by destroying all Tea for which they have imprudently paid the duty."[19]

Meanwhile, consignees and customs men remained under threat. In late January, emboldened Bostonians let loose on Boston-born customs man John Malcom. Bostonians revered the memory of Malcom's brother Daniel, by this time deceased but remembered as a hero of a confrontation with customs men years before. Opinions about John Malcom were quite the opposite. Patriots loathed him for three reasons. First, he was a customs man. Second, he had fought on the side of the hated governor of North Carolina four years before to suppress the Regulators, a group fighting high taxes and government corruption. Third, he was a prickly cuss. On January 25, Hewes, the shoemaker, came upon Malcom squabbling with a boy. The boy told Hewes that the day before, Malcom had tipped over the boy's sled loaded with kindling. As the dispute escalated, Malcom lifted his cane to clobber the boy. Hewes stepped between them and took the blow. With bystanders gathering, Malcom fled to his home near North Square.

Meanwhile, Hewes staggered away, blood streaming down his face. Dr. Joseph Warren patched up Hewes and told him he should have Malcom arrested. Hewes got a warrant from a judge, fetched a constable, and brought him to Malcom's house, where a threatening mob had gathered. The constable talked to Malcom through a back window. According to the story Hewes told many years later, Malcom begged the constable not to take him away for fear the mob would tear him apart. The constable and Hewes then left.

For a man terrified of the mob, Malcom behaved strangely: From a second-story window, he taunted the crowd. Armed with a sword, pistols, and broadax, he announced that he would "split down the Yankees by the dozen and receive twenty shilling sterling a head."[20] In the meantime, an acquaintance tricked Malcom's wife into letting him through the back door. That man reached Malcom and talked him into putting down his weapons. Soon Malcom was delivered to a waiting cart, where he was tied and stripped from the waist up. The mob then spread hot tar on him, showered him with feathers, and led him about the town, stopping now and then to administer a flogging. Eventually Malcom was brought to the Liberty Tree, placed on a platform, and commanded to quit his customs job. With astonishing bravery, he refused. For this insolence, he was beaten again and threatened with death. Still he refused to resign. A ladder was placed against the tree and a noose was put around his neck. Still he held out. A cat-o-nine tails was brought out and he was flogged. Someone threatened to cut off his ears.

Finally he gave in, a little. He uttered a curse against the governor as an enemy to America. But the ordeal still wasn't over. He and the cart went around the town for the next four hours and then, half frozen, he was taken home and "rolled out of the cart like a log."[21]

On March 26, a letter appeared in the *Boston Evening-Post* from an author identified only as A. Z., but who was probably Malcom. It recounted Malcom's military service where "bullets flew thickest"–he served at the Siege of Louisbourg and in the French and Indian War–and his efforts to prevent smuggling "which is a damage to all fair traders." The writer sought to shame his fellow townsmen: "Oh! Ungreatful inhabitants of the town of Boston to stand still and see and permit such an inhuman thing to be done in your streets."[22]

"The Bostonians paying the excise-man, or tarring & feathering." This print published in England in 1774 shows five men forcing a tarred and feathered customs officer–possibly John Malcom–to drink from a teapot beneath the Liberty Tree where a noose hangs from a limb. In the background, figures on a ship dump tea overboard. (*Library of Congress*)

Hutchinson, in reporting the event to superiors in London, noted the unwillingness of anyone in the town to stand on the side of government: "There is no Spirit left in those who used to be Friends to Government to support them, or any others, who oppose the prevailing Power."[23]

In England, the story of Malcom's ordeal was embellished. Published reports said he was forced to drink tea until he vomited. This was unlikely. Malcom's own detailed statement of the event does not mention such torture. Still, the story formed the basis for widely circulated cartoons with a figure in tar and feathers puking.

Like the Boston mob, the Massachusetts House of Representatives felt the urge to flex its muscle. On February 11, the House demanded that Hutchinson remove from office the province's chief justice, Peter Oliver, a relative of Hutchinson's and the younger brother of Lieutenant Governor Andrew Oliver. Impeachment, John Adams's idea, had never been tried in Massachusetts. But there were cases in England where the House of Commons had impeached justices.

Adams reasoned that if the British House of Commons could impeach, so could the Massachusetts House of Representatives.

Peter Oliver's "crime" was accepting a salary from the Crown. When challenged by the House, the other four justices gave in and promised not to take Crown money. Oliver, however, would not be cowed. Thus, from the House's point of view, Oliver violated the province's charter, which stated that the House of Representatives paid the judges.

By this time Hutchinson was packing his bags. He was making arrangements for himself, his daughter Peggy, and two servants to board one of the larger and more comfortable vessels expected to leave for England in the coming months. But the matter concerning the chief justice brought him back into the fray. Hutchinson refused to remove Oliver, and when the House responded with a formal impeachment on February 24, Hutchinson stood his ground. He thought he could block the impeachment by ignoring it. When a Council meeting was called to present the articles of impeachment, Hutchinson simply failed to appear. Sam Adams, chairman of the committee handling the impeachment, got around this by concocting rules out of thin air. He announced that the governor was "presumed" present. The impeachment then went forward with the absent governor "presumptively" occupying his empty seat in the Council Chamber. Thus, the House's *Journal* would record the lie that Oliver was impeached before the Council and the governor. Hutchinson denied the validity of the proceedings and did not remove Oliver from his post.

John Rowe's diary entry for March 3, 1774, noted a milestone in Boston's history: the first streetlights: "Last evening the Lamps were Lighted for the first time–they Burnt Tolerable Well." He also noted the death of Andrew Oliver, the lieutenant governor and brother of beleaguered Chief Justice Peter Oliver.

Andrew Oliver had been Hutchinson's brother-in-law, political ally, and closest friend. The exposure of the Whately letters had been harder on Andrew Oliver than on Hutchinson. For Oliver, the demoralizing effects of that scandal, combined with recurrence of an old "bilious disorder" and a stroke, were too much.[24]

For Hutchinson, the death of his friend also meant a further delay in his departure. He could not leave now because there was no lieutenant governor to take his place even temporarily. Hutchinson ached to be gone, but he felt duty bound to stay on. He canceled his travel arrangements: "[M]y private views must terminate whenever the King's service comes in the way."[25] He would hold on in Boston and endure more weeks of humiliation until his replacement arrived from England.

He was by now thoroughly despised just about everywhere in Massachusetts. The town of Gorham, in a letter to the Boston

Committee of Correspondence, called Hutchinson "the most restless, secret, plotting enemy to our free and happy constitution."[26] Feeling unsafe and unwelcome in Boston, Hutchinson spent most of his time at his estate in Milton.

On March 5, two days after Andrew Oliver's death, citizens packed Old South to hear the annual Massacre oration. In the wake of the Tea Party, this event was especially momentous and, according to Rowe, attracted more people than any previous Massacre speech: "I tried to get in but could not."[27]

The speaker: John Hancock. A severe case of gout had confined Hancock to his house for most of the weeks following the Tea Party. He couldn't even meet with other town selectmen. Some wondered if the sickness was a ruse–that Hancock was making himself scarce to distance himself from the Tea Party controversy.

But the speech, likely a collaboration of Hancock, Sam Adams, Warren, and Samuel Cooper's, demonstrated that there was no ideological gap between Hancock and those who masterminded the destruction of the tea. From the high pulpit at Old South, Hancock, as the occasion called for, focused on the Massacre, with the requisite descriptions of gore, condemnation of Preston and his men, and ire at British authorities. According to the published version of the speech, the people in Old South heard about "sluices of New England blood," land "polluted with the dead bodies of her guiltless sons," "unprovoked murders," and "bloody butchers." Hancock pointed out in the audience Christopher Monk, who at seventeen was shot in the back that fateful March night four years before, and still suffered from the wounds: "Unhappy Monk! Cut off in the gay morn of manhood from all the joys which sweeten life, doom'd to drag on a pitiful existence without even a hope to taste the pleasures of returning health!"[28]

Then Hancock touched on Sam Adams's favorite issue–salaries of the governor and the judges–before finally coming to the issue of tea. Here, instead of focusing on the problem of taxation without representation, he framed the tea issue mainly as an attempt to strip the tea trade from American merchants: "We soon shou'd have found our trade in the hands of foreigners, and taxes imposed on every thing which we consumed; nor would it have been strange, if in a few years a company in London should have purchased an exclusive right of trading in America."[29]

He moved on to applaud the work of the committees of correspondence and to urge a union of the colonies:

> But permit me here to suggest a general Congress of Deputies from the several Houses of Assembly on the Continent, as the most effectual method of establishing such a Union as the present posture of our affairs requires. At such a Congress, a firm

> foundation may be laid for the security of our Rights and Liberties; a system may be formed for our common safety, by a strict adherence to which we shall be able to frustrate attempts to overthrow our constitution; restore peace and harmony to America, and secure honor and wealth to Great-Britain, even against the inclinations of her ministers, whose duty it is to study her welfare; and we shall also free ourselves from those unmannerly pillagers who impudently tell us, that they are licensed by an act of the British parliament to thrust their dirty hands into the pockets of every American.[30]

Afterward, Edes and Gill printed copies of the speech. Four editions came off their presses.

Two days after Hancock spoke, another group of "Indians" tossed more tea into the harbor. The brig *Fortune* had recently arrived carrying hemp, gunpowder, other articles, and sixteen chests of tea. The ship owners quickly made it clear that they would be happy to send the tea back to Britain. However, Richard Harrison, the customs man in authority, stood his ground. He believed it his duty not to allow the ship to turn around with its cargo. He threatened to seize the *Fortune* and fine its captain.

Before that happened, a band of about sixty patriots who were, as in the first Tea Party, vaguely disguised as Indians appeared on the evening of March 7 at Hubbard's Wharf, where the *Fortune* was tied. After shutting the tidesman into a cabin, the men hoisted the tea out of the hold and flung it into the water. The event proved the obstinacy of Harrison, who by then was well aware of events in Philadelphia, where tea was allowed to be sent back. It also demonstrated that patriots in Boston had no regrets about the first Tea Party.

About this time, Sam Adams and the Boston Committee of Correspondence welcomed a visit from Philadelphia printer William Goddard. Goddard's idea was to establish a post office in America that would be independent of the royal postal system authorized by Parliament.

Adams blessed the idea. An independent American postal system would be out of the control of British authorities. Adams, always attuned to the importance of communication, recognized that if shoves came to blows, patriots could not rely on any system that British authorities could easily use to intercept or disrupt communications among Americans. By the end of that summer, the northern colonies of America had their own postal system.

Back in London, the hammer came down on Boston: the cabinet pushed a bill to close the port of Boston altogether. Under the Boston Port Bill, no vessel moving goods or passengers along the coast or from foreign countries would be allowed to enter Boston Harbor after June 1, or leave Boston Harbor after June 15. Only boats carrying fuel and provisions specifically for the people of Boston would be allowed to come and go. These vessels, however, would be required to first stop at Marblehead, about twenty miles to the northeast, to be inspected. Furthermore, the Custom House in Boston would be shifted down the coast to Plymouth, while the offices of the customs commissioners would be moved up the coast to Salem, which would also for the time being be the seat of government. All these measures would remain in place until Bostonians came to their senses and paid full restitution to the East India Company and anyone else harmed in connection with the destruction of the tea.

In defending the bill before Parliament, Lord North said he recognized that the measure would punish both the innocent and the guilty. But this was not unprecedented. On separate occasions, the cities of London, Glasgow, and Edinburgh had each been punished for "neglect" in stopping crimes or apprehending criminals. By comparison with those cases, Boston, "upwards of seven years in riot and confusion," was more deserving of a firm slap. In the weeks leading up to the destruction of the tea, "Boston had been a ringleader in all riots," and "the act of the mob in destroying the tea . . . belong to the act of the public meeting." The issue now was not legislation or taxation but authority: "It is very clear we have none, if we suffer the property of our subjects to be destroyed."[31]

Lord North's speech was met with neither cheers nor hisses, but silence for several minutes. The noise started when opponents of the Boston Port Bill, few and far between, tried to speak. One couldn't be heard above the uproar and had to sit down until "the gentlemen had done coughing." When this brave voice finally could be heard, he suggested that Parliament simply ask the town to pay for the damage. He was sure the town would "make satisfaction." Other opponents spoke up. One recommended that nothing be done, and that Parliament should stop taxing Americans merely to demonstrate its authority. "Leave America alone, and it would return of itself to obedience." Another member questioned why Boston was being punished. After all, other ports had also prevented tea from being landed. Furthermore, he said, Boston was being convicted without even an opportunity to explain its case. Edmund Burke, the political writer and prominent Whig member of Parliament, stood with those who opposed the bill.

He could not abide by a "doctrine of devils" that punished people for failing to stop a riot: "This Bill involves those who have never in the least been guilty."

But most members thought the bill was the appropriate "restorative and palliative." Some, indeed, thought it rather mild. Americans are "a strange set of people," said a member, and it is "vain to expect any degree of reasoning from them." Instead of making arguments, they "decide the matter by tarring and feathering." Another sounded off like a Roman senator, actually calling for Boston to share the fate of Carthage: "[T]he town of Boston ought to be knocked about their ears, and destroyed: Delenda est Carthago. . . . I am of the opinion you will never meet with that proper obedience to the laws of this country, until you have destroyed that nest of locusts."

Even Colonel Barré, usually America's best friend in the House of Commons, could not bring himself to defend Boston. He promised to give the bill his "hearty affirmative." Furthermore, he said, "I think Boston ought to be punished. She is your eldest son." Then, after the laughter died down, "I mean daughter."

The House of Commons could not be bothered to even hear Boston's case; it rejected a plea from William Bollan, agent in London for the Massachusetts Council, to speak on Boston's behalf.

When one opponent warned that an army would be needed to enforce the bill, Lord North answered that a mere "four or five frigates" could do the job. But if troops were needed, troops would be sent.

Not surprisingly, when Thomas Pownall, the former governor of Massachusetts, told the House that Americans "have a real love for government; they love order and peace," the House responded with laughter. Eventually, opponents offered an amendment to at least give Boston a chance to pay for the damage before closing the port. But the proposal went nowhere.

Few opinions were turned. On March 25, Parliament passed the Boston Port Bill. According to an estimate of the voice vote, at least five members approved for every one in opposition. The bill soon sailed through the House of Lords, and George III gave his assent on March 31. The prevailing assumption among lawmakers and most Britons was that Boston would quickly pay for the destruction and that colonists outside the town would have no sympathy for Boston's predicament.

Though the Boston Port Act set off a furor in New England and elsewhere in America, it alone might not have triggered armed rebellion in Massachusetts. After all, some 95 percent of the province's population lived outside Boston, and for many on distant farms, the closing of its port was not reason enough to take up arms. But then Parliament made another blunder, this one fatal to prospects for peace in Massachusetts. That was the Massachusetts Government Bill, introduced in late March. Including ideas that had been tossed around at least since 1770, this legislation, unlike the Boston Port Act, was not meant to punish but to reform colonial government in the province and, in particular, to strengthen the governor's hand. "The authority of that government is in so forlorn a situation that no Governor can act," said Lord North, in introducing the bill.[32] Whatever its intention, the bill drove a dagger into long-treasured democratic institutions of Massachusetts and achieved what Sam Adams and his committee of correspondence could not: it set the countryside in flames. Erstwhile moderates in rural areas instantly became more radical than the wildest Boston hotheads.

The bill had four main elements, each of which shifted power out of the hands of the people and into the hands of the king and his appointed governor. First, the Governor's Council would be cut out of any role in approving the appointments and dismissals of such officials as judges, justices of the peace, sheriffs, and marshals. From now on, the governor alone would make such appointments. Until this time, the people had at least an indirect influence on such appointments because the House of Representatives, elected by the people, had a hand in appointing the Council. Now the people would not even have that modest influence over key government posts. Second, the House would no longer have a hand in appointing the Council. According to prevailing practice, each year the House met with the outgoing Council to determine who would be in the new Council. The governor always had the power to veto any nominee. Now, according to the bill, the House and the outgoing Council would have no say in who would be on the next Council. Councillors would be appointed by the governor, the king's representative. Third, town meetings would be emasculated. Every town in the province would have to submit its town meeting agenda to the governor beforehand for approval. Furthermore, each town could normally have meetings only twice, once in March to elect town officials and on another day to elect their representatives to the House. Any other meeting could be held only with the governor's consent. Fourth, the jury selection process would be altered to ensure that no verdicts would be contrary to the wishes of the governor. Under the system that had been in place, towns provided lists of potential jurors. Jurors were selected from those lists. Under the system proposed in the bill, the sheriff would select all jurors. Because the governor appointed the sheriff, that change ensured that the views of jurors would align with those of the governor. This change was especially significant for people in the countryside. It meant, for example, that a farmer deeply in debt might no longer face a jury of fellow farmers who knew what it felt like to owe lots of money. Instead, jurors for such a trial would more likely be members of the governor's own class: wealthy, established men who were lenders and generally unsympathetic to any man who could not live up to his financial obligations.

In April, two other measures were proposed to give the royal government in Massachusetts a stronger hand. The first was the Administration of Justice Bill, which stated that if government officers were accused of crimes in connection with the performance of their jobs, the governor could send them to England for trial. This plainly meant that if an event like the Boston Massacre occurred again, any officer involved would not have to stand trial in Massachusetts. The last measure, the Quartering Bill, said that the head of the British military in America could take over barns and unoccupied buildings to house his troops in places where barracks were not nearby. Collectively, these measures–the Massachusetts Government Bill, the Administration of Justice Bill, and the Quartering Bill–were known by opponents as the Coercive Bills or Intolerable Bills and prompted louder outcries from government critics in London than were heard during the debates over the Boston Port Bill.

Some members of the House of Commons warned of dire consequences from this tampering without even giving the province a hearing: "Chartered rights have, at all times, when attempted to be altered or taken away, occasioned much bloodshed and strife." Another member protested that the British government had made itself the aggressor in this crisis: "These Acts, respecting America, will involve this country and its Ministers in misfortunes, and I wish I may not add, in ruin." Another: "It is war, severe revenge, and hatred, against our own subjects." And Barré, who had favored the port bill, thought this measure went too far: "You are, by this Bill, at war with your colonies."[33] Barré was especially incensed at the measure allowing trials of military men to be shifted out of Massachusetts. No evidence had ever been presented that soldiers could not get a fair trial in New England: "Captain Preston and the soldiers, who shed the blood of the people, were fairly tried and fully acquitted. It was an American jury, a New England jury, a Boston jury, which tried and acquitted them. . . . You have stimulated discontent into disaffection, and you are now goading that disaffection into rebellion."[34]

But the majority of the House agreed with the measures. Said a supporter, "America, at this instant, is in a state of downright anarchy; let us give it a Government."[35]

As these measures were being debated, news reached London of the second dumping of tea in Boston Harbor. This added to the momentum behind the Coercive Bills and dashed the flickering hope in London that Bostonians would feel sorry for their deeds. British public opinion sided with government ministers. One writer, calling himself Sagittarius, recommended that Hancock and the other Boston "ringleaders ought to be taken up, and hanged round their own Town Hall."[36]

Sagittarius turned out to be none other than John Mein, the printer chased out of Boston about five years before. Financially ruined and nearly killed in Boston, he had good reason to hate the town and its "vain and blustering"[37] people. That loathing had ripened from months–perhaps years–in debtors' prison. After arriving in England from Boston, Mein had paid a visit to Thomas Longman, to whom Mein was deeply in debt. Mein pleaded for more time to sell off his business in Boston and gather up funds. Longman had Mein arrested.

Now out of prison, and probably in the pay of the North government, Mein ripped into Boston and Massachusetts with relish in sixty-two essays in the form of angry letters published in London's *Public Ledger.* Some were reprinted in Boston. Backed with documentation and steeped with historical references, the essays oozed sarcasm about the "virtuous and universally loyal Saints of Massachusetts" while shedding light on their "encroachments, their knaveries, their hypocrisies, their persecutions, their independent notions, their detestable injustice to the Indians, and their horrid blasphemies."[38]

According to Mein, Boston's selectmen were "the most ignorant, assuming, and despicable fellows in the Creation"; Boston's young people: "bred up hypocrites in religion, and pettifoggers in law"; Boston town meetings: "the herd of Fools and Knaves collected together in Faneuil Hall"; the Puritans of New England: "factious and turbulent, and ever in opposition to legal government"; Boston merchants: they will "say any thing rather than part with their money and their clandestine trade"; members of the Council: "despicable and willing tools of the factious independents and smugglers."[39]

Mein took special delight in cutting apart Hancock, his old nemesis. Mein dredged up Hancock's infatuation more than a decade before with a servant girl in London. As Mein told it, Hancock was a would-be seducer "sneaking and lurking about" with the lust but not sufficient manly attributes to complete his conquest: "[T]hough nature had bestowed upon him a human figure, she had denied him the powers of manhood." [40]

Like many in England at the time, Mein took pot shots at Benjamin Franklin, "an old factious agent, who vomits out his venom in the newspapers." In France, he said, Franklin would be executed. "In England, however, we act with greater moderation; instead of taking the worthless life of a traitor, we give him our contempt."[41]

As for the province's charter, that must go, said Mein: "[T]he Charter of the Massachusets must be annihilated. It is constructed on principles much too democratic, and subversive of all peace, good order, and government; it is held forth to us by the Bostonian rioters not only as their warrant for the commission of all sorts of criminal violence, but also as their shelter and defence against just chastisement."[42]

Other writers were no less vehement. One suggested that "about one hundred of these Puritanical Rebels" be hanged. A common view was that the relationship of Britain and America was akin to that of a parent and child. As one writer said, "Is it not rather a Duty incumbent on the Parent when every . . . Expedient has been tried in vain, to bring [their children] back to their Allegience by a gentle Correction?"[43]

In Parliament, one voice meekly suggested that Americans be offered a carrot as well as a stick. Member of Parliament Rose Fuller moved that the controversial tea duty be repealed to help the other measures succeed. This touched off more debate. Burke urged repeal. The duty, he said, only provoked Americans. Besides, getting rid of it would not reduce revenues. He won some support, but opponents said such a move would be a sign of weakness. Commons soundly rejected the proposal, 182 to 49.

So the tea duty stayed in place, and all the Coercive Bills passed. While most lawmakers and members of the public felt the measures justified, a few predicted disaster. Said Fuller, "If ever there was a nation running headlong to its ruin, it is this."[44]

Just for good measure, Parliament about this time added another blunder to its list of errors. This was the Quebec Act. As its name suggests, this measure was mainly concerned with Canada. But it had several elements guaranteed to alarm and irritate Americans. First, the act assured Roman Catholics in Canada that they would be free to practice their religion. With about four hundred Catholics to every Protestant in Quebec, what else could the British do? But this would unsettle many Americans, especially New Englanders, so wary of papist inroads into their Puritan enclave. Second, the act established a government in Canada that had no elected assembly. Tolerating Catholics was one thing; allowing them to vote was something else. Lord North found it "not prudent in a protestant Government to establish an assembly consisting entirely of Roman Catholics."[45] But this, too, was frightening to Americans. If Parliament could simply impose such a government in Canada, might it one day do the same in America? Third, the act shifted boundaries, extending Canada's borders at the expense of territorial claims by Connecticut, New York, and Massachusetts. Here was more aggravation to dismay and unite Americans.

In the first few months after the Tea Party, Bostonians seemed unconcerned about the possible backlash from authorities across the Atlantic. Early reports from Britain were not alarming. The mood was lighthearted enough that, in April, the *Gazette* reprinted an item from

London that said Bostonians now found that their fish tasted like tea. Even when the first details of the port bill found their way to Boston, residents reacted calmly, assuming that Parliament would not pass such a measure.

The full text of the act arrived in Boston on May 10. Then the implications quickly sank in. On May 18, Boston merchant John Andrews sent off a letter to his brother-in-law in Philadelphia: "Imagine to yourself the horror painted in the faces of a string of slaves condemn'd by the Inquisition to perpetual drudgery at the oar! Such is the dejection imprinted on every countenance we meet in this once happy, but now totally ruin'd town." Andrews thought about leaving: "I sincerely believe they intend to put their threats in execution; which is, to make the town a desolate wilderness, and the grass to grow in our streets."[46] Merchant John Rowe called the act "a Great Evill" and "the Severest Act ever was Penned against the Town of Boston."[47]

It might seem that the shutting down of Boston's port would be a great boon to other Massachusetts seaports. Not so, wrote Boston Selectman John Scollay. Other seaports needed to move cargoes to Boston to be sold. If the blockade lasted, he argued, ports like Newburyport, Salem, and Marblehead would have to "haul up their vessels, for no place but Boston can take off their cargoes."[48] Boston, he wrote, was already contemplating putting the poor to work building a bridge across the Charles River to Charlestown to accommodate all the new overland cargo traffic between Boston and the ports to the north.

Boston reached out. The Boston Committee of Correspondence gathered at Faneuil Hall on May 12 with committees from eight nearby towns. They approved a circular letter for all the other colonies proposing that, in protest of the Boston Port Act, all trade with Britain be suspended: "This Attack, though made immediately upon us is doubtless design'd for every other Colony, who will not surrender their sacred Rights and Liberties into the Hands of an Infamous Ministry. Now therefore is the Time, when ALL should be united in opposition to this violation of the Liberties of ALL."[49]

The response was swift and firm. In Farmington, Connecticut, nearly one thousand people gathered to witness the burning of the port act. Elsewhere, attacks on cargoes of tea became something of a trend. In April, New Yorkers boarded the *London* and tossed eighteen quarter chests of tea into the salty drink. In June, citizens in Portsmouth, New Hampshire, redirected a cargo of tea to Halifax. After another cargo of tea arrived a few months later, a mob attacked the house of the merchant who planned to sell the tea. Other violent demonstrations of one kind or another occurred at Greenwich, New Jersey, and at York River, Virginia. In Annapolis, Maryland, a confrontation led to the burning of the tea and the vessel that brought it.

George Washington, a member of Virginia's House of Burgesses, had an opinion that was perhaps typical: he was disturbed by the destruction of the tea but appalled by Parliament's reaction. He wrote, "The cause of Boston, the despotick measures in respect to it I mean, now is and ever will be considered as the cause of America (not that we approve their conduct in destroy[in]g the Tea)."[50]

But what specific sacrifices were people willing to make? In Newburyport, merchants got together on May 12 and agreed that in sympathy with Boston, they would stop foreign commerce after June 14, provided other ports in the province did the same. On May 13, Boston's town meeting formally adopted a similar resolution, asking all the other colonies to stop trade with Britain and the West Indies. In New England, Providence, Newport, and Westerly seemed willing. But the idea of closing ports in sympathy was not popular everywhere. Boston got no commitment from New London, New Haven, or Portsmouth.

Within Boston, amid the bluster, some suggested that the town should swallow its pride and pay for the tea. That idea might have gotten traction had Sam Adams allowed a certain letter from Benjamin Franklin to be circulated. In that letter, Franklin said Boston's best course of action would be immediate repayment. That, he said, would put America in a better position to gain sympathy in Europe should Britain apply military force against the colonies down the road. Adams disagreed and kept the letter out of sight. Maybe it would have made no difference because once the news about the Boston Port Act arrived, opinion swung solidly against payment. Most Bostonians now saw such payment for the tea as a ransom.

Some Loyalists still pushed for payment. One man, George Erving, offered to pay one quarter of the damages, provided others contributed as well. But even this generous offer could not spark widespread interest. More astonishing: few voices from outside Boston called upon the town to pay for the destruction.

Others, frustrated and angry, directed their ire at patriot leaders. Josiah Quincy received a long anonymous warning from "Your Well-Wisher" of "the imminent hazard which I consider you to be in, of the loss of life, and confiscation of your estate." The author predicted that Britain would punish Quincy as a traitor or rebel, or that Boston people ruined in this crisis would attack him. "You have gone to such lengths that I fear nothing can save you."[51] The author suggested that Quincy make a public apology.

Quincy brushed off the threat and published a lengthy pamphlet, packed with historical references ranging from the Mamertines of Messina to Louis XI of France, ripping into the Boston Port Act, condemning the stationing of troops in Boston, and fanning the fires:

What regular government can America enjoy with a legislative a thousand leagues distant, unacquainted with her exigencies, militant in interest, and unfeeling of her calamities? What protection of property, when ministers under this authority shall overrun the land with mercenary legions? What personal safety, when a British administration (such as it now is, and corrupt as it may be) pour armies into the capital and senate-house, point their artillery against the tribunal of justices, and plant weapons of death at the posts of our doors?[52]

TWENTY-THREE

WHEN THE WICKED BEARETH RULE

The debate about whether to pay for the destroyed tea was still ongoing when Hutchinson's replacement finally appeared. On May 13, 1774, just three days after Boston received official word about the Boston Port Act, General Thomas Gage, age fifty-four, arrived at Castle William. He was taller than most men and had large eyes and a long aristocratic nose. He bore a striking resemblance to, of all people, Sam Adams.[1] Gage was now the top military officer in America and the governor of Massachusetts. On May 17, he entered Boston with all due ceremony. Members of the House and the Council joined prominent citizens and the town Cadets, under Hancock's command, in escorting Gage from Long Wharf up King Street to the State House, passing along the way assorted militia and regular military units. About noon, a proclamation was read, a crowd gave out three cheers, and small arms and cannon were shot off to mark the event. Then, after receiving friends and reviewing the militia, the new governor was off to Faneuil Hall for dinner, where his toast to Hutchinson prompted hisses. Rowe, in his diary, noted, "There were but very few Gentlemen of the Town asked to dine there."[2] Hancock, for example, was absent. The welcome was perhaps not as exuberant as it might have been, but considering the circumstances, all went pleasingly. "They are making a good deal of ceremony with me," Gage wrote.[3]

The choice of Gage as governor was ominous. He was, after all, a military man. His battlefield resume included Fontenoy in 1745, and Culloden Moor in 1746, two bloodbaths. In America, during the French and Indian War, Gage had barely survived the disastrous Braddock expedition in 1755 in the wilderness of western Pennsylvania. Gage was leading an advance guard when the combined British and American force stumbled into an ambush. In the aftermath, some blamed Gage for the fiasco, but nothing dishonorable was proven. Indeed, evidence suggested that Gage had performed gallantly. Later, in campaigning along the shores of Lake Ontario, his caution had enraged a commander but was probably prudent. Neither incident derailed Gage's rise to become commander in chief of military forces in America in 1763.

In naming a military man as governor, British authorities were telling the Americans they meant business. But from the American point of view, prospects for the colony under Gage were not entirely bleak. Indeed, looking further into Gage's resume, a colonist could even be hopeful. Gage had been military commander of Montreal for three years after the French departed. In the town of sullen, defeated French Canadians, Gage had dealt nimbly with such urban problems as dumping of chamber pots over town walls, hogs running amok in the streets, and sleighs blocking entrances to churches. He also instituted practices that must have been widely resented. For example, he put in place a system for collecting duties and compelled the civilians to provide quarters for troops. After all this, Gage somehow made himself at least moderately popular. If Gage could earn the grudging respect of twenty-five thousand habitants with good reason to despise the English, he might find a way to succeed in Boston.

By most accounts, Gage had an exceptional character. Unlike too many military men, he was not infatuated with either drinking or gambling. In his early years in the military, his straightforward manner earned him the nickname "Honest Tom."[4] He was known to be modest, tactful, and generally decent. Also, he was thoroughly familiar with America, having served on the western side of the Atlantic about twenty years. American friends had included, at least for a time, George Washington, who had also served in the Braddock disaster. Washington and Gage maintained a correspondence for at least three years. In a 1757 letter, Gage wrote to the Virginian, "I shall always be glad to hear of your health, happiness & success."[5] Furthermore, Gage had married an American, Margaret Kemble of Brunswick, New Jersey, where she was known as "Duchess."[6] By 1774, the marriage had produced six children.

To be sure, Gage maintained some strong prejudices against Americans. He was convinced, for example, that New England soldiers were, by and large, both boastful and cowardly. He had opposed any role for colonists in directing the French and Indian War. He was also tainted in Boston for his share of the responsibility for the Massacre.

Still, here was a man who might, given a little luck, succeed where Hutchinson had failed in winning back respect for Parliament and Crown authority. Rowe, in despair over the Boston Port Act, was hopeful about Gage: "God Grant his Instruction be not severe as I think him to be a Very Good Man."[7]

How did Gage feel about the Coercive Acts? He had no objection to them. Indeed, he virtually drew them up. Gage had been in England, visiting his boyhood home, when news of the Tea Party reached England. The king summoned the general. Impressed with Gage's analysis of what needed to be done, the king encouraged his ministers to work with Gage. As a result, Gage's fingerprints are all over the Coercive Acts, which included many measures he had been calling for as early as 1770, when he wrote: "I hope that Boston will be called to strict account, and I think it must be plain to every man that no peace will ever be established in that province, till the King nominates his council, and appoints the magistrates, and that all town-meetings are absolutely abolished; whilst those meeting exist the people will be kept in a perpetual heat."[8]

With Gage on the scene, Hutchinson could finally say his goodbyes. In Hutchinson's final days in Massachusetts, many moderates and friends bravely signed testimonials to the departing governor thanking him and wishing him well. One, signed by over 120 "merchants and traders," testified to Hutchinson's "wise, zealous, and faithful administration." The testimonial gently chided Parliament for the Boston Port Act but acknowledged the justice in requiring restitution to the East India Company for the destruction of the tea. The testimonial was also self-serving: The merchants had one more favor to ask of Hutchinson. They hoped that upon arriving in England, he could speak "in our behalf, and make such favorable representations of our case, as that we may hope to obtain speedy and effectual relief." The signers applauded Hutchinson for discharging "your trust with honor and fidelity" despite "all the mortifications."[9] In signing the testimonial, the merchants were taking a risk. Those signatures made them targets of patriot wrath. The signers included the McMaster brothers and Theophilus Lillie, who had already suffered at the hands of the Sons of Liberty. Another signer was John Singleton Copley, the painter who just a few years earlier had attended the great Sons of Liberty banquet in Dorchester.

Twenty-four attorneys and barristers also presented Hutchinson with a testimonial "of our sincere respect and esteem." Like the merchants, the lawyers inserted their own plea for Hutchinson to advocate for Boston in London: "Permit us, sir, most earnestly to solicit the exertion of all your distinguished abilities in favor of your native town and country, upon this truly unhappy and distressing occasion."[10]

Other testimonials were drawn up. Thirty-three men in Marblehead expressed their "entire approbation of your public conduct." They likewise hoped that Hutchinson would put in a good word for the province in London: "[W]e beg leave to entreat you, that when you arrive at the court of Great Britain, you would there embrace every opportunity of moderating the resentment of the government against us."[11]

Six Milton men also signed a letter offering "sincere wishes for your health and happiness" and noting "faithful and prudent Discharge of your Duty exposed to Calumnies, Trials and Sufferings, as unjust and severe" and "bearing them all with becoming Meekness and Fortitude." This testimonial was too much for other Milton townsmen. The signers were "taken to task" at the town meeting and forced to sign and read out an apology: "Now since the Temper of the Times is such, that what we meant to please has eventually displeased our Neighbours. We, who desire to live in peace and good will with them are sorry for it."[12]

General Thomas Gage painted by John Singleton Copley. (*Reproduction © 2013, Museum of Fine Arts, Boston*)

By now others besides Hutchinson were looking to escape tumultuous Boston. One was Copley. Back in April, a mob appeared at his home and asked for George Watson, a Tory from Plymouth. Copley said the man had left town. A mob leader warned the painter that his "blood would be on [his] own head" if he deceived them. Copley wrote, "[W]hat if Mr. Watson had stayed (as I pressed him to) to spend the night, I must either have given up a friend to the insult of a Mob or had my house pulled down and perhaps my family murthered."[13]

Now, as a signer of a testimonial to Hutchinson, Copley was fully identified with Tories. He conveniently arranged to leave Boston for a European jaunt. In some respects it was ideal timing. For nearly two years he had thought about making such a trip. He longed to see first-hand the great art of Europe, especially Italy. He wanted to explore the possibility of settling in London or somewhere in Europe, to broaden his repertoire beyond portraits and into paintings of great historic events, and to aim for glory in the European art world. He was in his midthirties. He couldn't put it off much longer.

Furthermore, he wanted to escape Boston before he was drawn deeper into the conflict. Now might just be a good time to slip away and come back after the storm had blown itself out. Also, his business was suffering. Amid the tumult, few people asked to have their portraits done.

On the other hand, it was a terrible time to go. He had a pregnant wife and three small children. How could he leave them behind at a time like this?

But he did, putting them in the care of his half-brother Henry Pelham and other relatives. He probably expected to return to Boston, but he never did. By July he was writing to his wife–"My Ever Dearest Sukey"–from England and dining on "Choice Salt Fish" with other Bostonians in London. By September he was writing from Paris. We can only imagine Sukey's thoughts when, dealing with pregnancy and small children amid soaring tensions in Boston, she read, "I beleive there is somthing in the Air of France that accelerates or quickens the Circulation of the fluids of the Human Body."[14]

Gage joined provincial lawmakers and others in the usual round of ceremonies marking the start of a legislative session in Boston. Early on May 25, Sam Adams took his oath as clerk, and Thomas Cushing took his as speaker. Then members of the House, along with the Council and Gage gathered at the Old Brick Meetinghouse. There Gad Hitchcock of Pembroke delivered the traditional election sermon. He chose a message from Proverbs: "When the righteous are in authority, the people rejoice; but when the wicked beareth rule, the people mourn."[15]

From Old Brick, lawmakers and Gage moved on to Faneuil Hall for "elegant entertainment"[16] and many toasts.

In June, the lawmakers resumed their work in Salem. They handled considerable routine business, passing dozens of measures despite the looming crisis. They grumbled about the shift from Boston, but the legislative work went on. One item was the incorporation of a new town in Worcester County. The townspeople wanted the name Barre. But when the bill found its way to Gage's desk, he filled in the name Hutchinson.

The closing of Boston's port was a huge calamity but only a side issue to one segment of Boston's society: the slaves. They had a more pressing concern: finding freedom. They had been hearing the chatter about liberty and rights for years, and they had reason to hope that attitudes were changing. In 1765, townsmen of Worcester had instructed their representatives to the House to work toward ending "that unchristian and impolitic practice of making slaves of the human species."[17] In May 1770, Samuel Cooke, preaching to lawmakers then meeting in Cambridge, boldly scolded them for allowing slavery to continue: "We the patrons of liberty have dishonored the Christian name, and degraded human nature, nearly to a level with the beasts that perish."[18] In 1771, the House and Council approved a law to forbid the importation of slaves into the province, but Governor Hutchinson blocked it. The issue of abolition was important enough to be the topic of Harvard's commencement debate in 1773.

For all those years, slaves had remained peaceful, but not passive. Some had sought justice in the courts. John Adams witnessed such a case in Salem in 1766: "This is called suing for liberty; the first action I ever knew of this sort; though I heard there have been many."[19]

In going to court to seek freedom, some slaves pointed at the province's charter, which said that all persons born or living in the province are as free as subjects in Britain. Many slaves won such cases, but victory depended a good deal on how vigorously the master fought the case. Sometimes the master put up a meager defense, especially if the slave was old and hard to handle. By losing the case, the master got out of his obligation to care for the slave in sickness and old age. So slavery in Massachusetts continued, but the success of some slaves in winning freedom chipped away at the institution.

Outside courtrooms, slaves applied what pressure they could on lawmakers and the governor. In 1773, a "humble PETITION of many Slaves," signed only by "Felix"–actually Felix Holbrook, a free black–was presented to Governor Hutchinson, the Governor's Council, and the House of Representatives, asking the governor and lawmakers to relieve the province's slaves from their "unhappy State." The language was passionate but submissive: "We have no Property! We have no Wives! No Children! We have no City! No Country! But we have a Father in Heaven, and we are determined, as far as his Grace shall enable us, and as far as our degraded contemptuous Life will admit, to keep all his Commandments: Especially will we be obedient to our Masters, so long as God in his sovereign Providence shall suffer us to be holden in Bondage."[20]

Later the same year, another petition appeared, this one in the form of instructions to the "Representative of the Town of Thompson" on Thompson Island in Boston Harbor. This had four signatures: Peter Bestes, Sambo Freeman, Felix Holbrook, and Chester Joie. This time, the words were more assertive: "We expect great things from men who have made such a noble stand against the designs of their fellow-men to enslave them. We cannot but wish and hope Sir, that you will have the same grand object, we mean civil and religious liberty, in view in your next session."[21] The instructions told of the slaves' intentions to gather money and transport themselves to Africa for resettlement.

Now, in May 1774, a similar petition came to Gage, the governor's Council, and the House of Representatives. This "Petition of a Grate Number of Blackes," which had no signature, was yet more forceful: "[Y]our Petitioners apprehend we have in common with all other men a naturel right to our freedoms without Being depriv'd of them by our fellow men as we are a freeborn Pepel and have never forfeited this Blessing by aney compact or agreement whatever."[22]

The petitioners underscored the injustice for the children of slaves: "[I]f there had bin aney Law to hold us in Bondage we are Humbely of the opinon ther never was aney to inslave our children for life when Born in a free Countrey."[23]

Nothing came of these petitions. Patriot leaders, their hands full, didn't want to touch that issue. However sympathetic they might be to the idea of abolition, they knew that pushing to end slavery would kill any chance of union with southern colonies, and such a union was essential for any successful resistance against British authority.

On June 1, Hutchinson, with daughter Peggy and son Elisha (but not Elisha's pregnant wife), stepped aboard the *Minerva* and was soon off to England and exile.

The same day, the Boston Port Act went into effect. Naval vessels were positioned to stop inbound traffic, and that was that. The port was slammed shut. There was no violence, no noisy mobs on the streets. Just the tolling of bells and calls for fasting and prayer, as if in mourning. Printer Boyle predicted in his journal that soon "this devoted Capitol will be reduced to the utmost distress. God send us speedy Relief."[24] Rowe noted in his diary: "Poor Unhappy Boston. God knows only thy wretched Fate. I see nothing but misery will attend thy Inhabitants."[25]

The next day, Rowe learned for the first time about Parliament's act to change the Massachusetts government. He predicted it would "sour the minds" of the people: "I am afraid of the Consequences that this Act will Produce. I wish for Harmony & Peace between Great Britain Our Mother Country & the Colonies–but the Time is far off. The People have done amiss & no sober man can vindicate their Conduct but the Revenge of the Ministry is too severe."[26]

Soon soldiers came ashore. One regiment on June 14 and another the next day stepped onto Long Wharf and marched to the Common, where they set up camp. The Common, wrote Henry Pelham, "glows with warlike Red. The fireing of Cannon, the Rattling of Drums, the music of the fife, now interrupt the pleasant silence which once rendered it so peculiarly deligh[t]ful."[27] Another Bostonian, Thomas Newell, recorded in his diary: "Most of the stores on the Long Wharf are now shut up. Thus we are surrounded with fleet and army; the harbor shut, all navigation cease, and not one topsail to be seen but those of our enemies. Oh, let not posterity forget our sufferings."[28]

On July 4 and 5, two more regiments came ashore. In Salem on August 6, yet another regiment arrived, and orders were sent for still more. Gage was confident that this massive force would give Loyalists, so long intimidated and cowed into silence, some backbone to demonstrate support for British authority. Gage wrote to Lord Dartmouth:

"Your Lordship will observe, that there is now an open opposition to the faction, carried on with warmth and spirit unknown before, which it is highly proper and necessary to cherish and support by every means; and I hope it will not be very long before it produces very salutary effects."[29]

John Rowe. (*Tea Leaves, 1884*)

In enforcing the Boston Port Act, Gage followed the letter of the law, no matter its wasteful consequences. For example, it had been common practice for farmers on the mainland to grow hay on the many islands that dotted the harbor, to harvest that hay from time to time, and ferry it to the mainland. Now such transport of hay was forbidden. Also in the crowded town with many wharves, it was often more convenient to haul goods from wharf to wharf by boat, rather than by wagon. This, too, was prohibited.

The transport of food and fuel to Boston by water was allowed, as permitted by the act. But each vessel still had to first travel to Salem, unload the cargo, reload the cargo, and obtain proper paperwork.

The act was even applied to newly launched ships. Any vessel produced by a Boston shipyard would be seized as soon as it touched water. The economic consequences were predictable. The shipyards shut down. That meant no jobs for the carpenters, caulkers, ropewalkers, sail makers, and others dependent on the industry. Obviously, with the port shut down, many other men whose livelihoods depended on the sea were also out of work. These included sailors, longshoremen, and fishermen.

In the grip of this economic chokehold, Boston might have coughed up the money for the lost tea. But that didn't happen. Instead, Boston and patriotic leaders organized and set in motion an aggressive charitable relief and public works effort to relieve suffering and put men to work. The closing of the port resulted in the doubling, perhaps tripling, of the town's needy. Recognizing that the crisis would overwhelm the Overseers of the Poor, the town created a special twenty-six-member group to handle donations. Members included many of the best-known patriot leaders, including Sam Adams, Joseph Warren, John Adams, Josiah Quincy, Thomas Cushing, and William Molineux. Merchant John Rowe was also on the committee. The committee spent ten days interviewing people to identify those most in need.

The committee's work depended on donations from outside Boston. To get the word out, the Massachusetts House of Representatives asked the people of the province to give what they could "till the sense and advice of our sister colonies shall be known."[30] The response was astonishing not just from people within Massachusetts but, as word spread, from other colonies and beyond. Printer Boyle was amazed: "Every part of this extensive Continent, appears to be deeply interested in the Fate of this unhappy Town. Many and great are the Donations we have already received, and many more we have reason to expect. Even our poorest people have not yet suffered for want of Bread."[31]

With the donations came letters of support. The "sense and advice" from everywhere was similar to that from the town of Beverly, Massachusetts: "Stand firm, and let your intrepid courage show the world you are men and Christians, who contend earnestly for the liberties once granted to this Province by charter."[32]

The humanitarian crisis, created by the British Parliament, generated wholesale sympathy for Boston, widespread condemnation of British authorities, and pledges of patriotic fidelity. Falmouth sent, along with firewood, a note of solidarity: "We are but few in number, and of small ability; and as we earn our bread by the sweat of our brow, shall ever hold in utter detestation, both men and measures that would rob us of the fruit of our toils, and are ready with our labor, with our lives, and with our estates, to stand or fall in the common cause of liberty."[33]

While most donations came from towns, some individuals sent along contributions. Aaron Cleaveland of Canterbury, Connecticut, sent in his donation with a note of explanation:

> Being affected with a sense of the righteousness of the cause that the people of Boston are suffering under, as it concerns all the people of America to be roused to support them, that they may not faint under their distress, it took hold on my covetous heart, and made me willing to contribute my little mite, which I have sent by Mr. Green, of Mendam, a beef cow for the distressed, and ordered him to deliver it to the Committee for that purpose; and may the Lord deliver the people of America out of the hands of a wicked and despotic power, who are exerting all the subtilty and malice of hell to enslave us.[34]

The donations committee welcomed cash. But in this bankless society with cash in short supply, most donations came in the form of goods, such as grain, especially corn, or livestock, especially sheep. Other goods included butter, bar iron, cheese, brandy, and even cocoa. Much was sent with the understanding it might be sold or traded for preferred goods. Men assigned to drive a herd of swine to Boston sold several along the way and gave the donations committee cash and the remaining herd.

From Brooklyn, Connecticut, came 130 sheep driven by Israel Putnam, something of a legend in New England. He had acquired a reputation for reckless courage through such feats as having himself lowered by rope into a wolf's den. Putnam had also served in the French and Indian War, where he demonstrated bravery and leadership. He was thus well known in Boston by people on both sides of the political divide. "The old hero," wrote Thomas Young, "cannot get away, he is so much caressed both by officers and citizens." Putnam stayed long enough to hobnob with General Gage and other British officers. Conversations, naturally, turned to the crisis and possible war. Someone asked if five thousand well-equipped British veterans would have any trouble marching "through the whole continent of America." Putnam replied no, if they behaved and paid for everything. But if they were hostile, "the women, with their ladles and broomsticks, would knock them all on the head before they got half way through."[35]

Other donations came from as far away as England and the West Indies. Quebec sent wheat. Montreal sent money. Most of the charity came from American towns and counties: corn, rye flour, pork, and bread from Baltimore; sheep from Kingston, New Hampshire; corn, flour, and pork from Perquimans County, North Carolina; rye and corn from Hartford; corn and beef from Talbot County, Maryland; money and sheep from Providence; flour, pork, and butter from New York City; wheat corn and peas from Chesterfield County, Virginia. These are but a few examples.

The donations committee responded with lengthy thank-you notes. Many of the notes underscored the transparency of the donations work, assuring the donors, as in the following excerpt, that all charity collection and distribution was aboveboard: "We should be extremely well pleased, if any of the worthy inhabitants of Medfield are coming to Boston, that they would examine our books, and satisfy themselves with respect to our application of the several donations received from our kind brethren on this continent, which are open to the inspection of the whole world, and hope will meet with their approbation."[36]

The donations committee, in addition to doling out charity, also put idle men to work, chiefly on fixing streets. The committee also planned a brick works and proposed the construction of a model house that would be built by unemployed men and then sold. The committee bought wool, flax, and cotton for spinning and knitting and set up looms for weaving. Other projects included the manufacture of hoes and axes, which were eventually shipped off to Virginia for sale on consignment. The donations committee apparently pushed its crews to make certain they earned their pay. According to merchant John Andrews, some men grumbled for being made to work so hard for "that which they esteem as their right without work."[37]

Over the subsequent weeks and months, more letters and donations came in. As tensions escalated, distant correspondents offered more than just goods and good wishes. A letter from Virginia in December reported that one thousand volunteers had been collected. They were "as fine fellows and good woodsmen as any on our continent, who have put themselves under the command of Col. George Washington, a brave and experienced officer, whom it is said, has undertaken command of them, and that they are soon to march for your place."[38] They didn't march to Boston, as it turned out, but the offer was appreciated and remembered. Later, the following April, a few weeks before Lexington and Concord, a committee from Monson, Massachusetts, sent, along with a "small present" for the poor of Boston, a note declaring "ready cheerfulness to shed our blood to oppose tyranny and oppression." Furthermore, it said, "We have eighty stout fellows in this district, a great part of which are not only disciplined, but excellent marksmen. I dare be bold to say that at about thirty rod distance, they would pick up tories as fast as so many hawks would kick frogs from a frog pond."[39]

As Boston's donations committee continued their work, more words flowed out from the Boston Committee of Correspondence. The committee, under Sam Adams's direction, called for a province-wide boycott of British goods until the British reopened the port. Working secretly and without even consulting Boston merchants, the committee sent out a call for a "Solemn League and Covenant" to towns around the province. Unlike previous actions, where merchants directed nonimportation agreements, this would be a boycott led by consumers, the people in the towns and on the farms of the province. Adams had learned a lesson from the earlier wobbly nonimportation agreements. As long as demand for goods was strong, nonimportation agreements tended to reward violators and to quickly fall apart. But if the people agreed to stop buying, a nonimportation agreement would not be needed. Signers agreed to buy no goods that had been imported after the effective date of August 31, 1774. Furthermore, they promised to shun anyone who did not sign. The names of those who refused would be published. The covenant with a covering letter was dispatched June 8.

But the ploy nearly backfired. The messages to the countryside from the committee of correspondence gave the impression that Boston had approved this boycott. That was not the case. Many Boston citizens, not just Tories but Whigs as well, were livid when they learned that this Solemn Covenant was being pushed upon the province in the town's name without Bostonians even being aware of it.

The men most opposed to the Solemn League were the merchants. They, through their nonimportation agreements years before, had been the first to promote boycotts as weapons of resistance. But now they had no heart for another trade stoppage and expected a boycott would bring only disaster to Boston.

Beyond Massachusetts, the Coercive Acts broadened the debate about the conflict between America and Britain. Before, talk focused on the right to tax. Now, Americans were asking themselves about the entire scope of Parliament's power. If Parliament today could, in a fit of pique, simply brush aside established democratic practices in Massachusetts and shred that province's charter, the same Parliament tomorrow could flick aside democracy in every other colony. William H. Drayton of South Carolina, who had opposed nonimportation in 1769, was now thoroughly alarmed: "The question now is not whether Great Britain has a right to tax Americans against her consent, but whether she has a constitutional right to exercise Despotism over America."[40]

However, when Sam Adams sent off his Solemn League and Covenant–the call for an immediate consumer boycott–to other colonies, they were no more enthused about it than Boston merchants had been. From New Hampshire, Jeremy Belknap thought it was madness. Members of the Boston committee, he said, were "acting like persons out of their senses & blindly rushing upon their own Ruin."[41]

The New York Committee of Correspondence didn't like it either, but at least it responded with a constructive alternative. That committee proposed a meeting–a congress–of representatives from each colony to talk about how best to respond to the crisis. Sam Adams was not pleased. He had long favored a continental congress because he recognized that a united response was essential. But in this case, he believed more urgency was required. A congress would take many months to form and act. Boston was suffering. The town could not wait. Furthermore, a congress was certain to have just enough Tories or moderate Whigs to declaw any meaningful proposal to strike back against Britain. Indeed, it was quite possible the congress would abandon the Massachusetts radicals completely, give Boston a good scolding, and call for the town to pay for the tea. Adams wrote: "A Congress is of absolute Necessity in my Opinion, but from the length of time it will take to bring it to pass, I fear it cannot answer for the present Emergency."[42]

The Boston Committee of Correspondence asked its counterparts in New York and Philadelphia to at least put in place some sort of nonimportation agreement before calling together a congress. Adams lost his argument. The Solemn League was rejected as wheels were set in motion for a meeting of colonial representatives in Philadelphia. The First Continental Congress thus came together not as a radical act but as a prudent alternative to an extreme proposal coming out of Boston. Moderates figured it might be a way to derail or at least put off such severe measures as nonimportation. Meanwhile, radicals figured a congress might at least demonstrate some kind of unity among the colonies. Independence was not expected to be on the agenda.

Now the dilemma for Adams and his allies in Massachusetts was how to officially appoint delegates to such a congress. The proper body to name such a delegation was the Massachusetts House of Representatives, now meeting in Salem in the lower story of Salem's two-story wooden Town House. However, openly debating about participating in the congress was too provocative. With the mere mention of such a plan, Loyalist members of the House, and there were some, would immediately go to Gage, who would instantly dissolve the assembly to cut off any formal vote on sending a delegation.

So Sam Adams pulled some tricks from his bag of parliamentary magic. From June 10 to 17, a committee met in the daylight hours talking about tea, as if it seriously considered paying for the damage from the Tea Party. This was all a game to fool Loyalist Representative Daniel Leonard, a member of the committee. In the evenings, the committee, without Leonard, met again to patch together a plan to send a delegation to the Continental Congress.

On June 17, after representatives had gathered for what was supposed to be a routine day of legislative work, Adams ordered the galleries cleared and doors shut and locked. He kept the key. Those few Loyalist representatives smelled a rat. One of them, pleading "the necessities of nature,"[43] was allowed out. He went straight to Gage.

Gage immediately dispatched his secretary, Thomas Flucker, to order the House to stop whatever it was doing and dissolve. The secretary pounded on the door. But no one let him in, and the House kept at its business. Flucker shouted Gage's proclamation at the locked door. Still the representatives kept at their work. Defying Gage and over the opposition of twelve dissenters, the House voted to participate in the Congress. Gage's proclamation eventually brought all legislative work to an end. But the critical work had been done. The delegates chosen for Massachusetts were Sam and John Adams, Thomas Cushing, James Bowdoin, and Robert Treat Paine. Bowdoin later declined the appointment to attend to his ill wife.

Meanwhile, back in Boston, Tories and others opposed to the committee of correspondence and appalled by the Solemn League and Covenant were plotting to deliver to Sam Adams a mortifying embarrassment. They crowded the June 27 town meeting hoping by their votes and arguments to denounce the covenant and disband the committee of correspondence. Merchant Samuel Eliot, with goods on the way arriving after August 31, maintained that the covenant would devastate him and would do no good anyway because British products would continue flowing into other colonies. Others raised valid questions about whether the committee had exceeded its authority. At dark, the meeting broke up, resuming the next day with more debates. Finally votes were taken. By ratios of about four to one, townsmen first voted to retain the committee of correspondence and then endorsed the committee's "upright Intentions" and "honest Zeal."[44] No serious offer to pay for the tea was proposed. The Tories failed. Still, curiously, the town never specifically voted its support for the covenant itself.

Outside Boston, the Solemn League won some firm and passionate backing. On June 29, Gage issued a proclamation: all magistrates were to arrest anyone who signed the Solemn League and Covenant and anyone who asked others to sign it. The town of Marlborough had an answer for Gage: his effigy went up in flames along with the proclamation. Of other towns writing in about the Solemn League and Covenant, two-thirds indicated support, and none opposed the action. Worcester boldly agreed to a covenant even stricter than the one proposed by the Boston Committee of Correspondence. However, most towns were far less enthusiastic, and few formally adopted the covenant as proposed. Some complained that the deadline of August 31 was too soon. Others balked when they learned that Boston had not actually endorsed the idea. Some towns crafted watered-down covenants. Still others said they would do nothing until they heard from the Continental Congress. Thus, leaders in the Massachusetts countryside, which until now had looked to Boston for guidance, already had their eyes on Philadelphia and the Continental Congress for direction. Boston, the center of the crisis, was no longer the center of political power.

TWENTY-FOUR

SHARPEST THORN

Hutchinson, upon arriving in England and without even having a chance to change his clothes, was immediately brought before the king. He talked to George for two hours and then quickly recorded from memory the conversation. His record reveals that the king was keenly interested in events in Massachusetts but still, in July 1774, did not have a clear idea of the key personalities affecting events. Like many in England, the king believed that Thomas Cushing, speaker of the Massachusetts House, was behind most of the trouble.

> King.–Then there's Mr. Cushing. I remember his name a long time. Is he not a great man of the party?
> Hutchinson.–He has been many years a speaker; but a speaker, sir, is not always the person of greatest influence. A Mr. Adams is rather considered as the opposer of Government, and a sort of Wilkes in New England.
> King.–What gave him importance?
> Hutchinson.–A great pretended zeal for liberty and a most inflexible natural temper. He was the first that publicly asserted the independency of the colonies upon the kingdom, or the supreme authority of it.[1]

Following his long chat with Hutchinson, the king was more convinced than ever that his policies were correct. He wrote to Lord North: "I have seen Mr. Hutchinson, late governor of Massachusetts, and am now well convinced they will soon submit. He owns the Boston Port Bill has been the only wise and effectual method."[2]

Before the year was over, Hutchinson lived for a while under the same roof with Francis Bernard. The two former governors of Massachusetts got along grandly. Hutchinson wrote that Bernard "has been with me as a lodger for 10 or 11 days in a house which I have taken three doors above Park Place, very pleasant and well furnished. We live in great friendship."[3]

For everyone in Boston and surrounding communities, this was a momentous and painful time. People had to choose sides. For many that meant a parting of ways from old friends on the other side of the political divide.

So it was for John Adams and Jonathan Sewall. The two men had been dear friends going back more than a decade. Their lives were nearly parallel–Sewall, too, had gone to Harvard, taught school briefly, and turned to law. Their private lives had intersected: John had once courted Hannah Quincy, a sister of Sewall's wife, Esther. Adams and Sewall had quite different personalities. Adams was chronically earnest; Sewall was something of a prankster who had to grovel his way back into Harvard after his high jinks led to expulsion. As lawyers, the two had followed different paths. Adams remained in private practice, while Sewall rose to become attorney general for the province. He was the prosecutor opposite Adams in the *Liberty* case. Just as Adams frequently wrote and spoke passionately in support of the Whig view and against the governor, so too did Sewall write with vigor in defending the Tory position and the governor. Sewall was Philanthrop, the Tory who defended Hutchinson in the Whately letters fiasco. Adams later described their politics "as opposite as east and west," although in most ways they thought as one: Sewall, like Adams, wanted Britain to repeal the laws that bothered Boston so much; Adams, like Sewall, was uncomfortable with the violent methods of the Sons of Liberty. Sewall and Adams differed mainly in how best to deal with the crisis. Sewall believed resistance to Britain could only lead to devastation and had to be avoided. Adams ultimately concluded that resistance was essential. Through all this, Adams and Sewall remained fast friends–like brothers–bound together by a common passion for the law. Meanwhile, Sewall, despite his prominent position in the government, maintained the esteem of many Whigs and mingled socially with radicals, even Josiah Quincy, just about the hottest firebrand on the Whig side. But now, old friendships and ties had to give way.

As attorneys, Adams and Sewall were obliged to travel to courts in Massachusetts and Maine, and so they often saw each other on the road. Thus they were together in Falmouth on the Maine coast soon after Adams was named a delegate to the Continental Congress. Early one morning, Sewall invited Adams for a walk. As they sauntered on a hill above Casco Bay, Sewall pleaded with Adams not to go to Philadelphia. Sewall was convinced that participation in the Continental Congress was a huge mistake for his friend. Britain, said Sewall, was just too powerful. In attending the Congress, Adams not only risked his law career, but his very life. He might well be tried for treason. Adams said it was too late: "[T]he die was now cast; I had passed the *Rubicon*; swim or sink, live or die, survive or perish with my country, was my unalterable determination." The conversation continued, but Adams's mind was made up. He recalled his parting words: "I see we must part, and with a bleeding heart I say, I fear forever; but you may depend upon it, this adieu is the sharpest thorn on which I ever set my foot."[4]

Among the military men who went to Boston that year, one of the most fascinating was Lord Hugh Percy, an aristocrat and colonel of his own regiment. By appearance, he was unimpressive: he was gaunt and had a large nose. He was also sickly. At thirty-two, he already suffered from gout. But otherwise there was much to admire in this man. Indeed, he seemed to embody all the qualities of an ideal aristocrat: generosity, courage, good manners, decency. In an era when floggings were common, he was unusually good to his men and inclined to march beside them, despite the gout, rather than ride. It helped that he was hugely rich, rich enough to charter a ship to bring to Boston the wives and children of his men. He also could afford to buy the finest riding horse in New England and to import a pair of carriage horses.

Before going to America, he had some sympathy with the American point of view. Percy had, as a member of Parliament, voted against the Stamp Act. After arriving in Boston, however, his attitude toward Americans changed. In late July, he wrote to his father: "The people in this part of the country are in general made up of rashness & timidity. Quick & violent in their determinations, they are fearful in the execution of them (unless, indeed, they are quite certain of meeting little or no opposition, & then, like all other cowards, they are cruel and tyrannical). To hear them talk, you would imagine that they would attack & demolish us every night; & yet, whenever we appear, they are frightened out of their wits."[5]

Percy said submission to Britain will never happen until Britain rounded up the members of the various committees of correspondence and delegates to the Continental Congress, shipped them to England, and tried them for treason. Percy also told his father about how bold Boston's ministers were in stirring up trouble:

"They preach up sedition openly from their pulpits. (Nay, some of them have gone so far as to absolutely refuse the sacrament to the communicants till they have signed a paper of the most seditious kind, which they have denominated the Solemn League and Covenant)."[6]

As Percy and other British officers were forming opinions about Bostonians, the Bostonians formed opinions about the military men, whose behavior was not always admirable. On August 1, merchant

John Andrews wrote about fifteen officers dining at the Erskine house one evening. They "committed all manner of enormous indecencies, by exposing their anteriors, as well as their posteriors, at the open windows and doors, to the full view of people, either men or women, that happened to pass by, with a great deal of opprobrious language."[7]

The officers then waved pistols at some boys who had gathered near the house. Later the men went off, two or three at a time. Some insulted and threatened people they passed. Others upset the merchandise at an old woman's "apple shop." Five, "with their cutlasses drawn," came upon Abra Hunt, a wine cooper, walking with his wife. The officers, according to Andrews, insulted Mrs. Hunt, whereupon her husband "aim'd a blow" with his hickory walking stick at the head of an officer, and "laid it open." Like high noon in the Old West, the streets cleared for a confrontation between Abra Hunt and the officers. Four civilians, including "a negro fellow," appeared on the side of Hunt to even the odds. In the ensuing brawl, one civilian blocked the stroke of a cutlass with his hand: "[H]e is likely to lose use of two or three fingers."[8]

A committee of the town reported the matter to Percy, who apologized and assured that if prosecution was called for, "he would see that ev'ry one of the culprits was delivered up."[9]

On August 1, 1774, the Massachusetts Government Act went into effect. This law would be far more difficult to enforce than the Port Act, especially outside Boston, where the Government Act virtually set the outraged countryside on fire. One of Gage's first duties under the act was to choose his own Council, which would be done, unlike before, without input from either the House or the outgoing Council. In his choice of men to serve on the new thirty-six-member Council, Gage demonstrated that he would make no concessions to public opinion. Only three of the men selected for the new Council had served on the previous one. Meanwhile, fourteen of the others had once served as councillors but had lost their posts because they were, in the House's view, too friendly to the royal government.

Gage was in a hurry to have his Council in place before his opponents could respond or perhaps intimidate the appointees. He quickly sent out messages calling for appointees to come to Salem to be sworn in. Initially, only eleven of the thirty-six men appeared, while two declined, four required more time to think about it, three accepted but for some reason were not sworn, and sixteen lived too far away to receive notification and travel to Salem in time. In any case, Gage had his Council. The first part of the act was implemented. The men appointed to Gage's Council became known as "mandamus" councillors, from the "royal writ of mandamus" used by Gage to make the appointments. "Mandamus" is Latin for "we command."

Meanwhile, outside Boston, committees of correspondence were not idle. Parliament had banned unauthorized town meetings, but nothing was said about other meetings. So on August 9, no fewer than fifty-two men representing committees of correspondence from twenty-two towns gathered in a Worcester tavern. They drank, debated, and cobbled together resolutions throughout the day. Reconvening the next day, the Worcester County Convention unanimously passed a series of resolutions, the first of which neatly expressed the limits of their loyalty to Britain: "Resolved, That we bear all true allegiance to his majesty king George the third, and that we shall, to the utmost of our power, defend his person, crown, dignity, but at the same time, we disclaim any jurisdiction in the commons of Great Britain over his majesty's subjects in America."[10]

Having grudgingly acknowledged allegiance to the king, these fifty-two patriots, in the next resolution, let loose a thunderbolt. It argued that the Massachusetts Government Act did away with the 1691 charter, the contract between the people of Massachusetts and the king. With the contract broken, the people of Massachusetts no longer had any obligations to the king. In effect, the king had made the province independent: "Resolved, that an attempt to vacate said charter, by either party, without the consent of the other, has the tendency to dissolve the union between Great Britain and this province, to destroy the allegiance we owe to the king, and to set aside the sacred obligations he is under to his subjects here."[11]

The third resolution called upon the people of Massachusetts and the other British colonies to come together. It had the ring of a call to arms: "Resolved, that it is the indisputable duty of every American, and more especially in this province, to unite in every virtuous opposition that can be devised, in order to save ourselves and posterity from inevitable ruin."[12]

Bold words. But the proposed actions of the convention were tepid: they would eschew British-made goods and offer up censures of judges who dared say something favorable about General Gage. That was it. They were not quite ready, after all, to bring out the muskets.

The time for the Continental Congress in Philadelphia was approaching. Nearly ten years had passed since the Stamp Act Congress, the last gathering of representatives of the various colonies. Now the stakes were higher, and Americans were still in many ways foreigners to each other. John Adams had never been out of New England. Sam had never been out of Massachusetts. This was like a mission to a foreign country. Joseph Hawley of Northampton gave John Adams some advice: everything "to cement the body ought to be practiced; and everything in the least tending to create disgust or strangeness, coldness, or so much as indifference, carefully avoided." The Massachusetts delegates must overcome the widespread opinion that the patriots of the province, and especially those from Boston, "do affect to dictate and take the lead in continental measures; that we are apt, from an inward vanity and self-conceit, to assume big and haughty airs."[13]

Others also worried about first impressions in Philadelphia. Before the departure, friends of Sam Adams's bought him a new wardrobe–wig, hat, six pairs of silk hose, six pairs of fine thread hose, six pairs of shoes, silver buckles, and a gold-headed cane–to make sure the penurious republican would fit in with the wealthy gentlemen from the other colonies. Another friend slipped Adams some cash.

On August 10, the four delegates–the Adamses, Cushing, and Paine–departed from Cushing's house in Boston not secretly, but in an opulent procession. With two white servants mounted and armed in front, and four black servants behind, two on foot, two on horseback, the delegates' coach-and-four glided past Gage's five regiments camped on the Common.

Gage might have stopped them. But that would have only stoked the flames and wouldn't have stopped the Congress. Anyway, he seemed to doubt the Congress would amount to much. In his correspondence, he reported the view among some that the gathering "has been consented to in other Provinces, only to amuse those amongst themselves who have been strangely violent in Support of Boston." It seemed the very worst that could come out of the Congress was some sort of nonimportation agreement, which in the past tended to be porous, brittle, and short-lived. Ultimately, Gage believed that, if push came to shove, colonies to the south would leave the New Englanders to deal with their quarrels alone: "I conceive we shou'd have to oppose this Province and Connecticut; I do not apprehend any assistance would be given by the other Colonies."[14]

All along the route to Philadelphia, the delegates were greeted and entertained in grand style, starting with a fine dinner at the Coolidge Tavern in Watertown. Throughout Connecticut, the delegates heard bells and cannons as they rode through. The reception was especially warm at New Haven. Seven miles outside the town, the travelers met a delegation that included the town constable, the county sheriff, and the justices of the peace, in carriages and on horseback. As the procession approached the town, amid the tolling of bells, people crowded windows and doorways of adjacent houses along the way. At an appointed time, a dozen cannons boomed.

The party was on the road ten days before finally arriving in New York City. There, in addition to visiting sights and meeting their patriot counterparts, they dined in splendor. Still, for all the gracious entertainment, John Adams couldn't resist a snide observation. In his diary, he confided: "With all the opulence and splendor of this city, there is very little good breeding to be found. We have been treated with an assiduous respect. But I have not seen one real gentleman, one well-bred man, since I came to town. At their entertainments there is no conversation that is agreeable. There is no modesty, no attention to one another. They talk very loud, very fast, and all together."[15]

After a week, they moved on to New Jersey. In Princeton, they stayed at the Hudabras Tavern and visited the college. After attending a church service there, John Adams remarked that the scholars sang "as badly as the Presbyterians at New York."[16]

At last the travelers approached Philadelphia. An escort of carriages and gentlemen on horseback met them five miles out and guided them to Front and Market streets, where stood the London Coffee House, which, to John Adams, was "the most genteel tavern in America." There the men dined and joined a stream of delegates and other visitors eager to meet the Massachusetts representatives.[17]

The historic first meeting between delegates from Virginia and Massachusetts, the two largest colonies, took place September 2 in a tavern. On Monday, September 5, the Continental Congress sat down to business at Carpenters' Hall.

In the few weeks following the delegates' grand sendoff to Philadelphia, much had transpired in Massachusetts. Far from Boston, Tories faced threats and harassment, sometimes administered in makeshift democratic fashion. In Berkshire County, in the distant west, David Ingersoll, who had once represented the area in the General Court, woke up one morning to face a club-wielding mob outside his door in Great Barrington. The "ruffians," as he called the members of the mob, carried him fourteen miles, just into Canaan, Connecticut, and there accused him of such "crimes" as supporting the Massachusetts Government Act. The mob demanded Ingersoll sign an oath. He refused but offered to formulate his own pledge. The mob agreed. Ingersoll, in later describing what happened, said the mob periodically took votes over one matter or another. By and by, after Ingersoll had made his revised oath, the mob let him go.[18]

In Pittsfield, also in Berkshire County, townspeople proposed a more radical yet straightforward way to defy the Massachusetts Government Act: shut down the courts. On August 16, some fifteen hundred unarmed men surrounded the plain, wooden, unpainted

Berkshire County courthouse to block the arrival of judges and magistrates. Move aside, the sheriff commanded. They didn't budge. The court remained closed. In the Berkshires, the revolution had begun.

Back east, more of Gage's mandamus councillors took their oaths. Some paid a high price for joining the Council. Daniel Leonard of Taunton found life in his hometown so intolerable that he fled to Boston. Similarly, Timothy Ruggles of Hardwick faced angry crowds as he tried to return to his hometown after being sworn in. He stopped in Dartmouth overnight and awoke to find his horse painted and its mane and tail cut off.

The experience of mandamus councillor Joshua Loring was more terrifying. He recorded that, at midnight on August 29 at his home in Roxbury, "I was awakened by a very hard knocking at my door; immediately I jumped out of bed and threw up the window, when I saw five men disguised, their faces black'd, hatts flapp'd, and with cutlasses in their hands."[19]

Those men, supported by fifty to sixty others, were demanding Loring's resignation. They returned the next night and threatened to level his house. Loring did not resign, but fled to Boston. Thus Boston, once the bastion of radicals, was becoming a Tory refuge.

Another mandamus councillor, Abijah Willard, on his way home to Lancaster, took a side trip into Union, Connecticut. There Connecticut patriots spotted him, jailed him, and handed him over the next day to four hundred patriots in Brimfield, just over the Massachusetts border. The Brimfield patriots organized themselves in a roughly democratic fashion and duly ordered Willard to be locked up in a town six miles away. Willard escaped the sentence by declaring "that I am sorry that I have taken the said oath, and do hereby solemnly and in good faith promise and engage that I will not sit or act in said Council, . . . and do hereby ask foregiveness of all honest, worthy gentlemen that I have offended."[20]

Another of Gage's councillors, Timothy Paine, was forced by a crowd of some two thousand men in Worcester to stand on Main Street and read his resignation not once, not twice, but numerous times to be sure everyone heard it. Despite the humiliation and the threatening circumstances, Paine noted the mob's restraint: "I met with no insult excepting they obliged me to walk with my Hat off when I passed through them." Furthermore, Paine understood the crowd's passion. In a letter to Gage, he wrote: "Thus Sir you see an open opposition has taken place to the Acts of the British Parliament. I dread the consequences of enforcing them by a military Power; people's spirits are so raised they seem determined to risque their lives and every thing dear to them in the opposition, and prevent any person from executing any commission he may receive under the present administration."[21]

The Worcester patriots went after another mandamus councillor, John Murray, to force his resignation. After Murray managed to evade them, members of the mob sent a letter to a Boston newspaper calling on him to resign, saying "a large Number of Men from several Towns are assembled, who are fully determined to prevent your holding said Office as Councillor."[22] Murray found refuge in Boston, and he, along with fourteen other councillors, stood their ground and did not resign. However, Murray never saw his home in Rutland again.

Another mandamus councillor, George Watson, got a frigid reception in his hometown of Plymouth. The *Boston Evening-Post* reported that a "great number" of the congregation immediately walked out of the meetinghouse after Watson entered. They preferred not to "'worship in fellowship with one, who was sworn to support that change of our constitution, which professedly established despotism among us.'"[23]

Watson promptly resigned. As he explained to Gage, "I am reduced to the alternative of resigning my Seat at the Council Board, or quitting this, the place of my Nativity, which will be attended with the most fatal Consequences to myself, and family."[24] One by one, others resigned as well, including Andrew Oliver and Thomas Hutchinson Jr.

In the end, eleven of the thirty-six men named as mandamus councillors never took the oath. One was dead. One was out of the province and prudently stayed out. Some others pleaded "Age and Infirmities" as a cover, according to Gage, to "avoid present Disputes." One said he feared losing some position. Others just said no.[25]

Meanwhile, the brave men who took the oath and stayed on as councillors proved to be less pliable than Gage would have liked. They refused to be rubber stamps. When, for example, he asked the Council to concur on the removal of a sheriff, the councillors balked. That was Gage's responsibility alone. They would have no part of it.

As time went on, Gage wouldn't even bother looking to the mandamus councillors for advice or support on issues that mattered. More and more, he was on his own.

Boston was safer than the countryside for Tories, but even in town they faced harassment. In response, Loyalists organized in New England fashion by drawing up a covenant. Using language not so different from that of patriots on the other side, the Loyalist Association, with about 180 members, pledged to support each other's rights in freely "eating, drinking, buying, selling, and communing and acting," and to resist "at the risk of our lives if need be" the "pretended Authority of any Congresses, Committees of correspondence, or other unconstitutional

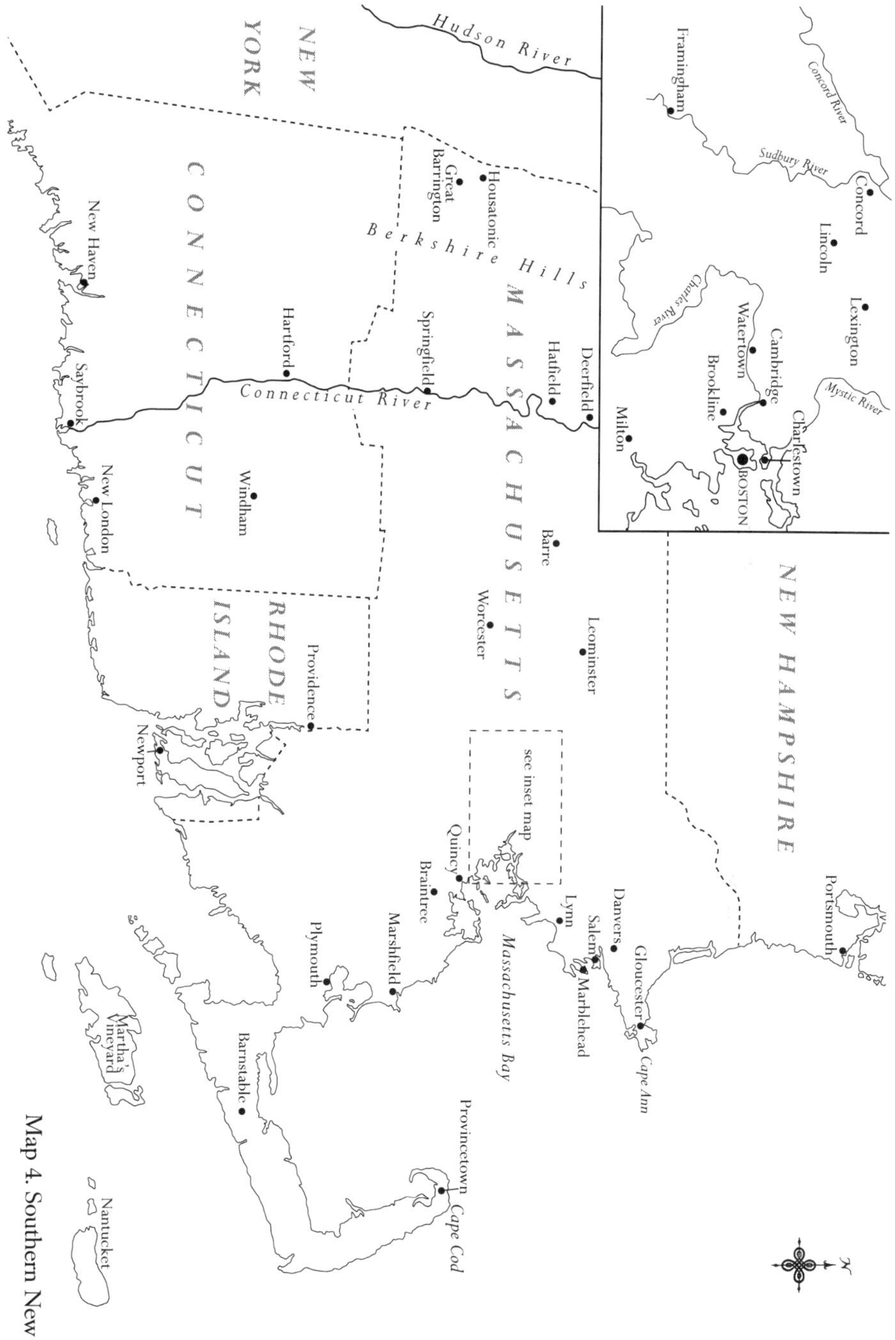

Map 4. Southern New England.

Assemblys of Men."[26] Another group of thirty-six promised to take up arms if called upon to defend Gage's government.

The Tory refugees rubbed elbows with hard-core patriots on Boston streets, and those patriots made up juries in Boston and were balking at playing a part in royal justice. On Tuesday, August 30, the first day of the next court session, Peter Oliver, with other justices, various attorneys, and "High and Deputy Sheriffs," formed up at the State House and walked in procession to the Court House on Queen Street. In the Court House, the justices took their seats and, after the usual proclamations were read, received the list of names of the men there to serve as grand jurors. The foreman was then called up to be sworn. But he refused. The next man was called. He, too, declined to be sworn. Then the next and the next. All twenty-two, including Paul Revere and Ebenezer Hancock, refused. Asked why, the men referred to a paper they had prepared.

The justices turned to the men selected to be petit jurors. Those thirty-three men likewise refused to be sworn and also referred to a list of reasons they had prepared. Both sets of jurors wanted their reasons to be read out in court. The judges, in no mood to let the court be a stage for Sam Adams's propaganda, refused to have the papers read aloud, but they took a glance at them.

When the court adjourned, the jurors gathered at a tavern and there voted unanimously to have the reasons for their refusals published. For both sets of jurors, the main reason for refusing was the presence of Oliver, "who has been declared" by the House of Representatives "unqualified to act as Judge of that Court." The prospective grand jurors had other reasons, including the recent acts of Parliament making appointment of judges dependent "solely on the King's pleasure." The men asserted that by serving as jurors, they would be validating that act. The grand jurors also noted that three of the five justices were mandamus councillors sworn to execute the recent acts of Parliament, which are "utterly repugnant to every idea of justice and humanity."[27] The statement from the petit jurors was shorter but similar. The court stayed open but conducted only business that didn't require juries.

This same month, Gage fired Hancock as head of the Cadets. On August 16, the Cadets fired back: they quit. According to Andrews, the Cadets "pass'd a vote to return their Colors to his Excellency, and acquaint him that they should not in future esteem themselves as his body guard; as also to deliver their Equipage, Musical instruments, &ca. into Colonel Hancock's keeping till some future time."[28]

On August 26, at Faneuil Hall, delegates from towns in Boston's county, Suffolk, met with counterparts from Essex, Middlesex, and Worcester counties, and together recommended that a provincial congress be created to develop "an effectual plan for counteracting the systems of despotism."[29] This was a provocation if ever there was one. This gathering, much like the Massachusetts House of Representatives but without the sanction of the governor, had the ring of an independent provincial government in defiance of British authority.

As tormented Tories flocked to Boston, miserable soldiers continued to slip out. With ranks thinning, Gage needed to make a point. An unlucky and inept would-be deserter was condemned. Led by "curiosity natural to most men," John Andrews went out early one morning in September to witness the killing. The doomed soldier, while his grave was being dug, and after "the Parson had pray'd with him," spoke for thirty minutes "very fluently and compos'd" to the soldiers around him. Then, when brought to the place "from which he was not to remove but into an awfull eternity," he began to lose his composure. After fifteen more minutes of his "exortation and prayer," six soldiers standing about eight yards away raised their muskets and fired. The wretched soul still breathed, so an executioner stepped up, aimed close, and blasted a bullet into the man's head.[30]

After the corpse was laid on the lid of his coffin, the assembled soldiers were ordered to slowly file past. All this was meant to terrify the soldiers and discourage desertions. But, Andrews wrote, it would have the opposite effect and would "create in them an utter detestation to remain subordinate to a set of men, who were instrumental in committing such an unjust act of cruelty."[31]

While Gage was applying the swift and brutal discipline he felt essential to maintaining an army, he also was trying to make life more comfortable for his men. Winter would be coming soon. The town, crowded with Tories, could not accommodate all the soldiers, and the tents on the Common were inadequate for the dark freezing months. Barracks needed to be built. But even this project was a headache. Town selectmen and the committee of correspondence proclaimed that anyone working on such barracks would "probably incur the displeasure of their brethren . . . who may . . . deem them as enemies of the rights and liberties of America."[32] That was enough to prompt town workers to walk off the job. Carpenters from the navy were brought ashore to do the work, but their skills were not suited to the task. Gage eventually recruited carpenters from out of town. Then, lumber and bricks were hard to come by because of threats to suppliers. In Portsmouth, New Hampshire, a skipper of a vessel was seized and dragged through the streets when the people discovered he was loading lumber for barracks in Boston.

Civilians did what they could to make the miserable lives of the soldiers more miserable by, for example, igniting loads of the straw intended for the military. The soldiers, in return, sometimes took their frustrations out on civilians by roughing them up or insulting them. John Andrews recognized that the atmosphere was not too much different from 1770 on the eve of the Massacre: "I am in continual apprehension we shall soon experience another fifth of March."[33]

A massacre was one possibility. Another was wholesale arrest of patriot leaders for trial in England. Thomas Young, a likely target, would soon find it judicious to slip away. In September, he would remove to Providence. But the most prominent leaders–Warren, Hancock, and Sam Adams–coolly retained their residences in Boston and openly came and went from the town. Gage gave no hint of rounding up anyone and gave townspeople plenty of leeway. A town meeting in late September went off as planned, even though it was held without the governor's permission.

With Sam Adams away in Philadelphia for much of this period, Warren was left with the lead role in Boston, keeping the pressure on Gage, organizing meetings, plotting strategies. He seemed to be everywhere and corresponding with everyone. He found time to send off advice to his brethren in Philadelphia about such matters as flaxseed. Believing that Ireland was heavily dependent on flaxseed from America, he suggested an export ban would "throw a million people in Ireland out of bread" and put economic pressure on Britain. In the same letter, he also asked Sam Adams to put in a good word for a Mr. William Turner, "persecuted for his political sentiments," who was now seeking a position as a dancing and fencing instructor in Charleston, South Carolina.[34]

Warren also dispatched letters full of thanks, encouragement, and inspiration to towns that had sent relief supplies. To Stonington, Connecticut: "We esteem no sacrifice too great, no conflict too severe, to redeem our inestimable rights and privileges. 'Tis for you, brethren, for ourselves, for our united posterity, we hazard all." To the town of Preston: "It gives us pleasure amidst our sufferings to find our brethren determined to assist and support us while we are struggling for American freedom."[35]

TWENTY-FIVE

EAGERNESS AND SPIRIT

As Gage pondered chances that patriots would follow Berkshire County's lead and shut down courts everywhere, he also learned of many meetings planned or taking place in defiance of the law. Gage felt he had to do something. He zeroed in on an illegal meeting right under his nose called by the Salem Committee of Correspondence. Gage issued a proclamation forbidding anyone from attending. The day after the proclamation, on August 24, the meeting assembled anyway. Gage dispatched troops to disperse it but, before the troops arrived, the meeting had adjourned, its business accomplished.

About this time, Gage packed up and returned to Boston to run the government from the Province House. The customs commissioners joined him in Boston, now the safest place in the province for customs men. Gage didn't seem to mind that this move to Boston violated Parliament's order to operate the customs office from Salem. Gage was trying to avoid a "bloody Crisis," but was expecting it any day: "Reasoning is over, Nothing can be done but by forceable Means. Tho' the People are not held in high Estimation by the Troops, yet they are numerous, worked up to a Fury, and not a Boston Rabble but the Freeholders and Farmers of the Country. A Check anywhere would be fatal, and the first Stroke will decide a great deal."[1]

Gage continued to take steps to ensure that on the day of that "first Stroke," he would have the edge. On a hill six miles northwest of Boston was a windowless stone silo, built as a windmill, that now held gunpowder and other munitions placed there by the province and several towns. After learning that the towns had removed their powder, Gage thought it sensible to take what was left–the province's share–and put it in a more secure place: Castle William, the island in the harbor. So a secret operation was drawn up. Before dawn on September 1,

1774, a force of 260 troops in thirteen boats departed from Long Wharf, rowed around Boston's North End, and slipped up the Mystic River. After landing northwest of Charlestown, the soldiers marched to the powder house nearby. There they waited for dawn, not daring to light lanterns near the gunpowder. Once the sun was up, the men extracted the province's 250 barrels of powder. While some soldiers loaded those barrels into the boats, a detachment went on up to Cambridge to take away two brass field pieces positioned there. No confrontation occurred in Cambridge or at the powder house. The men completed their assignment, delivered the guns and powder to Castle William, and were back in their barracks by noon. The mission was flawless.

But then the trouble started. Word spread in and around Cambridge about what happened. People gathered around the stone tower, now empty. Gage, as governor and general, had a perfect right to take the powder. Still, to the Americans there, the act seemed at best sneaky, at worst belligerent. The Americans were determined "by some means to give a check to a power which so openly threatened their destruction; and in such a clandestine manner robb'd them of the means of their defence."[2] The soldiers were gone, though, so what could be done? As the day passed, some drifted home, but many remained. With the approaching evening, those who stayed walked en masse to Cambridge's "Tory Row," today's Brattle Street, to the home of William Brattle, a notorious local Tory. By this time everyone knew that Brattle had informed Gage that towns had taken their powder from the powder house. The mob did not find Brattle at home; he had slipped away to the safety of Castle William.

So the crowd of about fifty, "mostly boys and negroes,"[3] moved on to the home of Attorney General Jonathan Sewall, who had recently accepted another royal post. He was away, but his wife, Esther, was there with their three children. At least one family friend was also in the house. Esther talked to the crowd and might have peacefully ended the confrontation. But then a pistol went off from somewhere inside the residence. This set off a frenzy of window smashing. Eventually those inside convinced those outside that the discharge was accidental. According to a later report from an unnamed person who was in the house, the rioters, after receiving apologies, "appeared to be satisfied about the gun, told us we had fought like brave fellows & if we would give them something to drink they would not" riot at another man's house. Wine was dispersed to the rioters, who "cordially bid each other Good-Night."[4]

By eight the next morning, a crowd of about three thousand (some said eight thousand),[5] had gathered on Cambridge Common. They were farmers from Cambridge and surrounding communities fired up by news of the gunpowder raid. They intended to make some sort of demonstration but certainly had no wish for a full-fledged battle with redcoats. They had left their guns in Watertown and were armed only with sticks.

By this time rumors were rife. Some people heard that British troops were preparing to march on Cambridge. Some heard that masses of armed farmers were plotting an attack on Boston. Patriot leaders in Cambridge frantically took steps to defuse the explosive situation. They went to Thomas Oliver, the new lieutenant governor, who lived in Cambridge. Oliver was a Tory. But he was also "a gentleman of great mildness of temper, and politeness of manners,"[6] and no relative of the hated Peter or Andrew Oliver. He was considered someone Whigs could work with. The patriot leaders wanted him to go to Boston to urge Gage not to send troops to Cambridge. Impressed that the group was "orderly," Oliver was glad to help and was soon off to Boston.

The former Massachusetts provincial powder house in Somerville which was the focus of the military operation that triggered the Powder Alarm. (*Library of Congress*)

At the same time, the Cambridge leaders sent off separately a message to their counterparts in Boston. Joseph Warren, in Boston, thus received a message "requesting me to take some step in order to prevent the people from coming to immediate acts of violence."[7]

So about the time Tory Oliver was arriving in Boston on his mission to reassure Gage, patriot Warren in Boston was rounding up colleagues to come out to Cambridge to likewise calm down the unsettled farmers.

Meanwhile, the farmers on Cambridge Common did not simply hang around. They confronted two local mandamus councillors and demanded they resign. But they also respectfully let the men have their say. When one of the men spoke in the open air on the Common to perhaps four thousand, "such was the order of that great assembly that not a whisper interrupted the low voice of that feeble old man from being heard by the whole body."[8] The two men said they already had resigned and showed a paper to prove it. The crowd voted to accept the men's statement.

The crowd also went after David Phips, the sheriff and a Tory. He had obediently given over the keys to the powder house to the British officers when they appeared the morning before. The crowd demanded an oath from Phips. He promised in writing never to enforce the Coercive Acts.

All this time, the crowd remained solemn. In a letter, one witness said "every man appeared just as composed as if they were at a funeral." Some, he wrote, appeared to be over sixty or seventy years old.[9]

It was still before noon when the committee of patriot leaders, including Warren, Molineux, and William Cooper, arrived from Boston. Having worked over months to bring passions to a boil, they now had the task of cooling them down. Molineux and Cooper found themselves defending Gage. The general, they told the assembled farmers, could take the powder because it belonged to the king. Another patriot from Boston, John Bradford, disagreed. Gage had no right to take it because he had not obtained the Council's advice, as required under the old charter.

At Warren's urging, the assembled men unanimously approved a statement asserting "that they abhorred and detested all petty Mobs, Riots, breaking Windows and destroying Private Property."[10] They did not want to be confused with the louts who broke Sewall's windows the night before, although likely some who did the deed were among the throng that morning. Around this time, Oliver was in Boston talking to Gage and getting his assurance that no troops would be sent out. It appeared further violence would be averted.

As the farmers on Cambridge Common awaited word from Oliver about Gage, another incident occurred to ratchet tensions back up. Customs Commissioner Benjamin Hallowell, on his way from Salem to Boston by chaise and ignorant of the powder house hubbub, happened to be passing through Cambridge. Another man was with Hallowell in the open carriage. A black servant rode separately on another horse. A group of men, some on horseback, recognized Hallowell, cursed the "Tory Son of a Bitch,"[11] and spread the word to other riders.

Soon Hallowell decided to get out of town fast. Off toward Boston went his carriage at high speed, followed by 150 or so riders giving chase. The patriot committeemen from Boston, speaking on Cambridge Common, were alerted to what was happening. Having defended Gage, they now tried to save Hallowell, sending a rider to get the others to call off the chase and let Hallowell go.

That worked, almost. Most riders turned back. But six or eight galloped on, and the chase continued. One rider got close enough to shout at Hallowell and to strike his horse. Hallowell pulled out a pistol. The rider tore on ahead of the chaise, yelling along the way, according to Hallowell, "Stop the Murderer the Tory Murderer he has killed a man."[12]

Hallowell drove the carriage on, but about a mile from Boston the poor horse began to falter. Hallowell brought the vehicle to a stop, mounted the servant's horse, and rode on. Leaving servant, passenger, and chaise behind, a pistol in each hand, Hallowell galloped on headlong toward Boston Neck. John Andrews later told what he heard. One rider overtook Hallowell on the Neck, "at whom he snap'd his pistol, which luckily missed fire, when he put on with full speed, and flung himself into the protection of the guard posted there."[13]

Hallowell was safe. But his escape did not end the story. Just past the guards, Hallowell's horse gave out. Hallowell then hurried away on foot to tell military authorities "he was pursued by some thousands who would soon be in town."[14]

Back in Cambridge, Oliver was back from Boston to soothe the assembled farmers. A committee of farmers listened, thanked him, and then one said, as Oliver later reported, that, by the way, as "I was present it might be proper to mention a matter they had to propose to me." The proposal: that Oliver quit the Gage government.[15]

Oliver was offended but said that if other members of Gage's Council quit, and that seemed to be the will of the province, he would resign too. A "very great majority" of the committee voted its approval of Oliver's answer. But that wasn't the end of it. Later that hot afternoon, as more and more people poured into Cambridge, Oliver looked out of his house to find it surrounded by three thousand to four thousand people. A committee of five approached him. Now the polite request for his resignation was a hardened demand. "I was shocked by their ingratitude and false dealings," Oliver later wrote. "I found I had been ensnared, and endeavored to reason them out of such ungrateful behavior."[16]

He also refused to quit. He told the committee that "my first considerations were for my honor, the next for my life; that they might put me to death or destroy my property, but I would not submit."[17]

One observer, a traveler from Connecticut who happened to be passing through, saw an orderly, quiet crowd. "[T]here was no Tumult, but an awful stillness, Silence thro' the Lines, and among the surrounding Body of People."[18] But that's not the way Oliver remembered it. The throng outside the house appeared to him more hostile than the farmers on the Common. Also, about one in four had a weapon. As the minutes ticked by, he sensed growing impatience. Oliver said he could hear people "swearing they would have my blood if I refused." He agonized, weighing his honor against his life, property, and the welfare of his family. He suggested that the committee "call in the people to take me out by force." The committeemen, genuinely worried for Oliver's safety, were not confident they could hold the edgy crowd in check. They thought the idea mad. "[T]he people were enraged." The committee "would not answer for the consequences." Oliver insisted. The committee refused. Finally, he signed the prepared document, but he did more than that: he made it clear he was being coerced. He wrote, "My house at Cambridge being surrounded by four thousand people, in compliance with their commands, I sign my name, THOMAS OLIVER."[19]

The Connecticut traveler reported that the document containing Oliver's resignation "was immediately handed along the Lines & read publickly at proper Distances till the whole Body of the people were made to hear it. Upon which Satisfaction was diffused thro' the whole Body, which thereupon dissolved; the solemn Silence broken & succeeded by a chearful Murmur or general universal Voice of Joy."[20]

Meanwhile, back in Boston, Gage's officers scoffed at Hallowell's tale of terror. They did not believe an army of militiamen was thundering toward Boston. Even so, Hallowell's arrival triggered a noticeable bustle around the barracks. Patriotic observers took note and sent out warnings that maybe, after all, the British were contemplating some sort of attack. When key patriot leaders heard these reports, they dismissed them, but not before some riders had already galloped into the hinterlands with the warning, spiced with wild rumors. By the time the message reached Connecticut, it incorporated a tale that British soldiers had marched on Framingham to seize powder and had gunned down six Americans in their way. People in New London, Connecticut, heard that British ships were bombarding Boston and that troops were slaughtering residents. Saybrook, Connecticut, learned that Boston was a charred waste.

The reports were shocking, but accepted as plausible, and not especially unexpected. At Windham, Connecticut, the "alarming news" was considered "undoubtedly authentic."[21] The reaction in these towns far from Boston was astonishing, immediate, and overwhelming. Men by the hundreds, then thousands, picked up arms and began marching toward Boston. The farmers were ready to fight. A letter in the *Boston Gazette* told about the response in Windham:

> "To Arms! To Arms!" was the universal cry.–Instantly nothing was seen on all sides, but men, of all ages and characters, cleansing and burnishing their arms, furnishing themselves with provisions and warlike stores . . . gentlemen of rank and fortune, exhorting and encouraging others, by their advice and example, and the very women lending their helping hands, with the utmost readiness and assiduity, to expedite the march, which began in a few hours from the receipt of the intelligence.[22]

In one Connecticut community, the militiamen forming up in haste found their footwear inadequate for the long march. The captain strode into the meetinghouse and asked for help. On the spot, people in the hall gave over shoes, stockings, and other clothes.

Israel Putnam was at the center of this mobilization in Connecticut. The old war hero was naturally looked to for leadership when reports from Boston first arrived, and the information he received sounded reliable. The man who delivered it had taken the trouble of dispatching his son to confirm it. That young man rode to within thirty-five miles of Boston. People assured him that the story about an attack on Boston was true. The young man returned to Connecticut with what seemed to be verification.

Thus Putnam was convinced, and when he lent his credibility to the call to arms, militiamen from all over flooded onto roads heading east. One observer figured some twenty thousand men went on the march toward Boston just from the Connecticut Valley.[23] Another man reported in his diary of a traveler on his way to Boston who had seen armed men, some on foot, some on horseback, along the road, and had noted that women and children in "every house" were making cartridges and bullets, packing pouches of food, and baking biscuits, all the while "crying and bemoaning and at the same time animating their husbands and sons to fight for their liberties, though not knowing whether they should ever see them again." The traveler thought, "if anything the Women surpassed the Men for Eagerness & Spirit in the Defence of Liberty by Arms."[24]

Few people dared to speak against the mobilization. But some did. Reverend John Smalley, preaching a sermon in New Britain, Connecticut, bristled at the disruption of his services, with comings, goings, and chatter about something happening in Boston. He found the news impossible to believe and "verily thought there was not a call for us to muster on the Sabbath, and rush down from this distance."[25] In Saybrook, one Hezekiah Whittlesey opposed mobilization activities, saying "many disagreeable and opprobrious expressions concerning the people of Boston."[26] For their honesty, Smalley was widely denounced, and Whittlesey was forced to make public apology.

So the Connecticut men, as well as Massachusetts men and others, marched toward Boston until learning along the way that after all the alarm was false. In the wake of the alarm, as New Englanders returned home, Patriot leaders were amazed and jubilant. The countryside, by tormenting counselors, obstructing courts, and now taking up arms at the rumor of trouble, had clearly caught the fever of Boston radicals. Paul Revere wrote to a leading Whig in New York:

> [T]he Spirit of Liberty never was higher than at present; the Troops have the horrors amazingly, by reason of some late movements of our friends in the Country the week past, our new fangled Councellors are resigning their places every Day; our Justices of the Courts, who now hold their commissions during the pleasure of his Majesty, or the Governor, cannot git a Jury that will act with them, in short the Tories are giving way everywhere in our Province.[27]

Warren likewise sent out an exultant missive to Sam Adams in Philadelphia underscoring the massive military response from the countryside: "I never saw a more glorious prospect than the present. . . . The accounts from the western counties are such as must give the most exalted idea of the resolution and intrepidity of the inhabitants. . . . Had the troops marched only five miles out of Boston, I doubt whether a man would have been saved out of their whole number."[28]

The Powder Alarm, as the event came to be known, demonstrated that by this time, autumn 1774, communities across the province were on edge and willing to take up arms and march wherever needed. Gage took note and was astonished. He weighed the risks of a second mission, this time to send troops to Worcester forty miles away to protect judges there. Gage postponed the mission, which was eventually canceled.

Had Gage ordered the mission, the war might have started in Worcester, for there thousands of militiamen gathered to stop any attempt to open the courts. Just days after the Powder Alarm, over forty-five hundred militiamen came together to make up perhaps the largest assemblage of people in Worcester County ever up to that time. While militiamen in the thousands met on the Common, many local men shut themselves up in the courthouse a half mile away to prevent any judge or other official from entering. The royal officials–three judges, eighteen justices of the peace, three attorneys, and the sheriff–unable to get in the courthouse, gathered in a tavern while representatives of the committees of correspondence from various towns convened in a house across from the courthouse to plan just what the thirty-seven militia companies were going to do. In the end, the patriots forced the royal officials to sign a document promising they would not hold judicial proceedings under the "unconstitutional act of the British parliament, respecting the administration of justice in this province."[29] Then the militiamen lined both sides of the road between the courthouse and the tavern. The twenty-five officials emerged from the tavern and walked the road, their hats off, each reading out loud the document they had just signed. They walked the quarter mile to the court and back, reading the statement over and over again, some as many as thirty times. The militiamen found the process so satisfying that they rounded up a few other Tories and forced them to walk the gantlet hatless and to read statements.

Other communities took note of events in Worcester. Over the coming weeks, in Concord, Plymouth, and elsewhere outside Boston, patriots would slam the courts shut.

Thus, outside Boston, the governor's authority had vanished. So who was in charge? As yet no independent, revolutionary provincial government had come into existence. In this power vacuum, the towns, functioning in virtual independence, sent delegates to county conventions. In Boston's Suffolk County, town meetings defied Gage and chose delegates–sixty in all–to a "county congress" in Stoughton at Colonel Doty's tavern on August 16.[30] Boston's representatives included Joseph Warren and Benjamin Church. Other meetings followed, and on

September 9, at the home and tavern of Daniel and Rachel Smith Vose in Milton, Warren read what became known as the Suffolk Resolves.

They began with a long preamble bristling with vivid, hair-raising, breathless imagery–"the Dagger to our Bosoms," "curses of Slavery," "military Executioners," and "murderous Law"–and were followed by nineteen resolves. After "chearfully" acknowledging George III as "our rightful sovereign," these resolutions charged that recent acts of Parliament–"blocking up the Harbour of Boston, . . . altering the established Form of Government in this Colony, . . . screening the most flagitious Violators of the Laws of the Province from a legal Trial"–were "the Attempts of a wicked Administration to enslave America."[31]

Saying the people of Massachusetts owed no duty to obey such acts, further resolutions called for civil disobedience: sheriffs, constables, jurors, and others should ignore court orders; creditors and debtors should arbitrate their differences out of court; tax collectors should, for now, hold on to the taxes they collected. Another resolution called on the people to seize "every Servant of the present tyrannical and unconstitutional Government" should authorities attempt to arrest prominent patriots.[32]

The resolves further called for a trade boycott with Great Britain, Ireland, and the West Indies, and pledged to abstain from consuming British goods, excepting only those allowed by the Continental Congress meeting in Philadelphia.

One resolve established a committee to look into how best to promote local manufacturing, another called for Massachusetts towns to choose representatives to a provincial congress, and another, considering the possibility of widespread lawlessness in this period of uncertainty, urged people "not to engage in any Routs, Riots, or licentious Attacks upon the Properties of any Person whatsoever, as being subversive of all Order and Government; but by a steady, manly, uniform and persevering Opposition, to convince our enemies, that in a Contest so important, in a Cause so solemn, our Conduct shall be such as to merit the Approbation of the Wise, and the admiration of the brave and free of every Age and of every Country."[33]

The men meeting in Milton approved these resolves on September 9 and sent Paul Revere off to Philadelphia with a copy.

In early September, in the wake of the Powder Alarm, Gage took measures that, while arguably sensible, further raised hackles: he ordered fortifications at the Neck be repaired and strengthened. Townspeople were alarmed to see the only land route in or out of Boston being turned into a heavily armed bastion defended by a dozen or more cannons and field pieces. Wrote John Andrews to his brother-in-law in Philadelphia:

> Many of the inhabitants are serious about leaving the town, as they are in general apprehensive that when the Governor has sufficiently fortified it, *military Law* will be declar'd, and no one suffer'd to go out by his permission, notwithstanding what he may have said to the contrary. There is no knowing, Bill, what may take place with us. For my own part, I endeavor to make myself as easy as I can; but if they should come to disarming the inhabitants, the matter is settled with the town at once; for *blood* and *carnage* must inevitably ensue–which God forbid! Should ever take place.[34]

Gage looked at the numbers. He had about three thousand regulars in Boston as of late October. That compared to perhaps thirty thousand Americans who had picked up arms during the Powder Alarm. No wonder he became more defensive and cautious. He ordered the people of Boston to turn in their weapons.

Meanwhile, his letters to London bled with despair. From one: "Civil Government is near it's End, the Courts of Justice expiring one after another. . . . Nothing that is said at present can palliate, Concilating, Moderation, Reasoning is over, Nothing can be done by forceable Means."[35] From another: "[N]othing less than the conquest of almost all of New England Provinces will procure Obedience to the late Acts of Parliament."[36]

From Gage's view, months before Lexington and Concord, the revolution had already happened. The task for him was to undo it, to win back Massachusetts and the rest of New England. He had no illusions: "If you think ten thousand men sufficient, send twenty; if one million is thought enough, give two; you save both blood and treasure in the end."[37]

He then retreated on the very policies he had proposed. He urged London to suspend the Coercive Acts, at least until he had more troops. When that idea reached the king, George III dismissed it as "absurd."[38] Gage also asked for twenty thousand reinforcements, which was similarly discarded in London as ridiculous. A battalion of four hundred was dispatched.

In Philadelphia, the Congress was under way. Fifty-six men came together representing all but one colony (distant Georgia, looking for help from London to deal with restive Indians on the frontier, declined the invitation). The core question for delegates was how best to respond, if at all, to the closing of Boston's port and other measures affecting mainly Massachusetts. As for the topic of independence, that was too provocative to talk about–at least openly. As John Adams wrote, "Absolute Indepen[den]cy &c. are Ideas which Startle People here."[39] Still, independence was on the minds of many. A few, such as Sam Adams and perhaps Virginia's George Washington, had already, at least secretly, made up their minds in favor of independence. Others, such as John Adams, still wavered but were finding themselves pulled in that direction. Meanwhile, a moderate faction remained, mainly from the middle colonies, still determined to remain loyal and desperate for a way to patch up relations with the mother country.

As the delegates got to know each other and factions coalesced, political battle lines formed with Sam Adams, the Massachusetts radical, on one side and Joseph Galloway, the Pennsylvania moderate, on the other. Galloway famously sized up his foe; Adams, he wrote, "eats little, drinks little, sleeps little, thinks much, and is most decisive and indefatigable in the pursuit of his objects."[40]

Sam Adams understood quickly the difficulty of getting moderates around to his point of view. He worried about excessive patriotic fever back in Massachusetts and the possibility of attacks against British regulars. Such attacks could fracture the Congress, with horrified moderates abandoning Massachusetts. He wrote James Warren to "implore every Friend in Boston by every thing dear and sacred to Men of Sense and Virtue to avoid Blood and Tumult. They will have time enough to dye." The other provinces, he said, needed time "to think and resolve."[41]

Early on, Adams demonstrated his political savvy. Fellow Massachusetts delegate Cushing had suggested that each session begin with a prayer. Other delegates were agreeable. But that raised a sticky question: What minister should deliver this prayer? After all, among the delegates were Quakers, Anglicans, and Presbyterians, as well as Congregationalists. Deflecting the well-known assumption that people from Massachusetts were intolerant Congregationalist fanatics, Adams immediately gave ground: "I am not a religious bigot; I can hear a prayer from a gentleman of piety and virtue, who is at the same time a friend to his country."[42] Adams made the motion for the Congress to ask a local Anglican clergyman to offer the prayer. Adams well knew this would please the key delegation from Virginia, where the Church of England was strong, while also chipping away lingering assumptions about New England bigotry. It was a pattern that Adams would continue to follow: graciously retreating on small issues, nurturing friendship with the Virginians, quietly cultivating an image of moderation.

The delegates found the prayers of Jacob Duché suitable. No one knew at the time that eventually he would choose the Tory side.

Sessions ran from 9:00 a.m. to 3:00 p.m. Then, as John Adams explained in a letter to Abigail, "we adjourn and go to dine with some of the nobles of Pennsylvania at four o'clock, and feast upon ten thousand delicacies, and sit drinking Madeira, claret, and burgundy till six or seven, and then go home fatigued to death with business, company and care."[43]

After dining at the home of a Quaker, John Adams lovingly catalogued the delights: "ducks, hams, chickens, beef, pig tarts, creams custards, jellies . . . beer, porter, punch, wine"; elsewhere "sinful feasts" of "everything which could delight the eye or allure the taste; curds and creams, jellies, sweetmeats of various sorts, twenty sorts of tarts, fools, trifles, floating islands, whipped syllabubs . . . Parmesan cheese, punch, wine porter, beer, etc."[44]

As Adams ate his way around Philadelphia, he also observed the Philadelphians. Like New Yorkers, he found them wanting: "The morals of our people are much better," Adams sniffed. "Their manners are more polite and agreeable–they are purer English. Our language is better, our persons are handsomer, our spirit is greater, our laws are wiser, our religion is superior, our education is better."[45]

For both Adamses, the main work of Congress was done at these dinners and during chats between sessions. In pushing their agenda, Sam Adams and the other Massachusetts delegates applied the kind of behind-the-scenes stage-managing that had worked so well for Adams in Boston. Between sessions, the Massachusetts men buttonholed, cajoled, planned, pleaded, and bargained. Then, during the sessions, the Massachusetts delegates said little and let the Virginians take the lead. So effective was this strategy that one Maryland congressman came to believe the Massachusetts delegation was not radical at all, but moderate. Another observer decided that next to the Virginians, "the Bostonians are mere Milksops."[46]

For the Massachusetts men, the business of Congress was forgotten on Sundays. That was the day for viewing the exotic wonders of the town–such as a Catholic church, unknown in Boston. John Adams witnessed a service in a "Romish chapel" and was amazed at the "paintings, crucifixes, velvet and gold" and the "poor wretches fingering their beads."[47]

A few days into the Congress, on September 6, delegates were alarmed at the sound of church bells in the afternoon and not for a few minutes, but for many hours and from many churches. What was this all about? People soon found out. News had reached Philadelphia that the British had bombarded Boston. Confused, vague reports flew. The city destroyed? People shot in the streets? No one knew, and for a few days no one would know anything for sure–time enough for the men at the Congress to contemplate anew the gravity and urgency of their task.

On September 8, John Adams still did not know the true story of events. He wrote that day to Abigail:

> When or where this Letter will find you, I know not. In what Scenes of Distress and Terror, I cannot foresee. We have received a confused Account from Boston, of a dreadfull Catastrophy.

> The Particulars, We have not heard. We are waiting with the Utmost Anxiety and Impatience, for further Intelligence. . . . The Effect of the News We have both upon the Congress and the Inhabitants of this City, was very great–great indeed! Every Gentleman seems to consider the Bombardment of Boston, as the Bombardment of the Capital of his own Province. Our Deliberations are grave and serious indeed.[48]

Delegates soon learned that Boston was not, after all, a field of ashes. But just as delegates got the truth about Boston, they also learned about the massive Powder Alarm mobilization in the New England countryside. The people had risen up by the thousands, had taken up arms, and were willing, even eager, to take on Gage's trained redcoats.

This reality was just sinking in when, a few days later, on September 16, Revere arrived with the Suffolk Resolves. In the ensuing discussion of this bold call for civil disobedience, conservatives and moderates remained mostly silent. What else could they do? They didn't agree with the resolves. Yet to speak out against them would make them appear to be on the side of British authorities. That left the floor to the radicals, who, one after another, stood and spoke in firm support of the resolves. When it came time to vote, the Congress chose to match the spirit of resistance ignited by the Powder Alarm. It unanimously endorsed "the wisdom and fortitude" of the resolves.[49] The astonishing implication was that as long as Massachusetts was not the aggressor, Congress would support the province in a conflict. This was a conditional pledge to go to war. Massachusetts delegates were elated. John Adams wrote in his diary: "This was one of the happiest days of my life. . . . This day convinced me that America will support Massachusetts or perish with her."[50] Sam Adams wrote to an ally, "I think I may assure you that America will make a point of supporting Boston to the utmost."[51]

The vote in Philadelphia on the Suffolk Resolves gave momentum to Massachusetts and the most radical faction. They rode this momentum to an agreement on September 27 to stop imports from Great Britain and Ireland starting in December. This was less than the Massachusetts men wanted. They would have preferred to block both imports and exports. But many delegates from the Chesapeake region and farther south could not support an immediate stoppage of exports. The British market was too important for that year's tobacco and rice crops. Eventually, delegates went along with a prohibition of exports, but to begin the following autumn–September 1775–if by then American complaints were still not addressed.

The Congress seemed well on its way to giving the Massachusetts radicals most of what they wanted. Then, however, the day after the nonimportation resolution was approved, Galloway reached out to yank the Congress in a completely different direction. He laid out an enticing scheme to possibly resolve differences between Britain and its colonies and still keep America happily within the empire.

Galloway, leader of the faction opposing any boycott, framed his plan by predicting that Britain's response to any embargo would likely be war. Such a war, he emphasized, would probably end badly for the Americans, with no trained army and a poor record of cooperating with one another. Victory would be possible only with help from France or Spain, whose monarchs were far more tyrannical than George III. Thus, even if the colonies won, Americans might find themselves suffering under despotism far worse than the one they were now howling about. If the colonies lost, stinging retributions would likely follow.

Galloway raised the specter of another catastrophe–especially for the wealthy men who made up a large share of the Congress. If the colonies cut ties with Britain and war was somehow avoided, civil unrest was a distinct possibility. Without backing from Britain, the mobs inflamed by radicals might get out of control.

Stoppage of trade was thus the path to disaster. A better idea would be to remodel the relationship with the mother country. Galloway thus presented his "Plan of Union." Under this plan, each colony every three years would send delegates to a Grand Council in America. Meanwhile, the king would appoint a president-general for America. The Grand Council, the president-general, and the British Parliament would jointly handle all matters concerning two or more colonies and all matters concerning the colonies and Britain. Through this Grand Council, Americans would thus have a veto over any acts of the British Parliament.

The reaction to the plan at the Congress was mixed. Virginia's Patrick Henry was against it. He thought such a council would be just as corrupt as the British Parliament. However, South Carolina's Edward Rutledge called it "almost a perfect plan."[52]

Had this idea come up some years before, the Massachusetts men might have taken it seriously. Now, however, it was just a distraction. A motion to set the plan aside failed. The Galloway plan lived on one more day, but only one. By that time, the radicals cajoled enough waverers to narrowly but finally kill Galloway's resolution.

TWENTY-SIX

UNCLEAN BIRDS

Back in Massachusetts, the Tories regarded the Suffolk Resolves as "nothing short of a declaration of independency." They were thus shocked by the endorsement of the Suffolk document by the Continental Congress, a "blast from the trumpet of sedition."[1]

Meanwhile, Warren made good use of Sam Adams's gesture on prayer in Philadelphia. In a letter published in the *Boston Gazette*, Warren noted what Adams had done and reassured Episcopalians that they had nothing to fear from Adams and other Congregational patriots: "[T]he gentlemen of the established Church of England are men of the most just and liberal sentiments . . . and I earnestly request my countrymen to avoid every thing which our enemies make use of to prejudice our Episcopal brethren against us; by representing us as disposed to disturb them in the free exercise of their religious privileges, to which we know they have the most undoubted claim."[2]

Counties and towns continued to hold meetings in defiance of the law. While patriots had not yet formed any provincial government separate from the royally authorized one, the notion had been in the air at least since mid-August. But coming up with the idea of a provincial congress was the easy part. The hard part was bringing it off: calling for it, arranging elections, and bringing together essentially a revolutionary government under Gage's nose.

As it turned out, Gage himself made it all quite simple. In early September, he called for the scheduled fall meeting of the House of Representatives. He was desperately trying to keep the fixtures of royal government intact. Towns across the province thus duly elected their representatives and sent them off to Salem. But those representatives brought with them instructions to form a separate provincial congress. Likewise Boston told its elected representatives to dissolve the House of Representatives–the lawmaking body authorized by the governor–

and join with the representatives from other towns to form a provincial congress outside the governor's control.

Gage got wind of these instructions and soon canceled the session, blaming those instructions as well as September's "many tumults and disorders," "the extraordinary resolves" passed in many of the counties, and "the present disordered and unhappy state of the province."[3]

But representatives assembled anyway on October 5 as previously scheduled at the courthouse in Salem. With "cautious courtesy" they there awaited Gage that Wednesday. When he did not appear, they met the following two days. One resolution subsequently passed charged Gage with acting unconstitutionally and in violation of the charter by attempting to prevent the House from meeting. Thus branding Gage as the lawbreaker, the representatives resolved themselves into a provincial congress "to take into consideration the dangerous and alarming situation of public affairs in this province."[4]

The new and independent Massachusetts Provincial Congress then adjourned to meet again on Thursday, October 11, not in Salem but in Concord, first in the courthouse and then in the meetinghouse–228 members representing 212 towns. John Hancock, away in Philadelphia, was elected president. Other members included such prominent patriots as Plymouth's James Warren, Hampshire's Joseph Hawley, and Marblehead's Elbridge Gerry, as well as Boston's Sam Adams and Joseph Warren. Many would go on to have important military or political roles. Worcester's Artemas Ward would become the colonial army's first commander. William Heath and Benjamin Lincoln from Suffolk County would be Revolutionary War generals. Hancock, Adams, Gerry, and Robert Treat Paine would each sign the Declaration of Independence. Nathaniel Gorham from Middlesex would be a signer of the US Constitution. Hancock, Adams, Gerry, and York's James Sullivan would each become governor of Massachusetts. Gerry would become vice president of the United States.

From Concord, one of the first items of business of the new Provincial Congress was to send off a letter to Gage. The delegates courteously explained themselves. They weren't embarking on revolution. They were just putting matters in order:

> May it Please Your Excellency:
>
> The delegates from the several towns in the province of the Massachusetts Bay, having convened in general Congress, beg leave to address your excellency. The distressed and miserable state of the province, occasioned by the intolerable grievances and oppressions to which the people are subjected, and the danger and destruction to which they are exposed, of which your excellency must be sensible, and the want of a general assembly, have made it indispensibly necessary to collect the wisdom of

> the province by their delegates in this Congress, to concert some adequate remedy for preventing impending ruin, and providing for the public safety.[5]

Then they scolded Gage for his ongoing "hostile preparations," especially the strengthening of defensive measures on the Boston Neck, which "threatens to involve us in all the confusion and horrors of a civil war."[6] The Congress politely but firmly asked Gage to dismantle the structure at the Neck.

After sending off the message to Gage, the Congress tested its power: it directed tax collectors in the province to withhold collected revenues from the province's Loyalist treasurer. This was the first step toward starving Gage's government of money from the province.

Later in the month, the Congress–now gathering in Cambridge, where it met at times at the courthouse and others at a meetinghouse–appointed a receiver general to take in provincial taxes. With their property and lives on the line, the congressmen must have found it unsettling during one session when a man appeared in the chamber brandishing a sword. The sword, he said, had been sent by Lord North from Britain to kill them. This man appeared quite mad in both senses of the word: he was insane and angry. It turned out that he had just fled Boston after attempting to blow out the brains of two British officers. The Congress arranged to have the man delivered back to Boston and into Gage's custody.

The Provincial Congress also took more ominous steps. A Committee of Supplies was created to gather military equipment. The head of this committee was Marblehead's Gerry, "Firm, exact, perspicuous and tenacious of public and private honor."[7] The Congress also passed a measure to equip five thousand men with powder muskets and shot and recommended that one quarter of militia companies "hold themselves in readiness, on the shortest notice from the said committee of safety, to march to the place of rendezvous."[8] Thus was authorized the so-called minutemen companies.

The Congress also named a military commander. The first choice was a certain Jedidiah Preble, but he declined. The job then went to Artemis Ward, a dubious selection. A Harvard graduate in his midforties, Ward was a veteran of the French and Indian War and the selection of his fellow townsmen in Shrewsbury as representative in the Provincial Congress. However, he was not in good health, and some considered him inept in military matters. To make decisions on further military preparations, the Congress appointed a nine-member committee of safety, which included Hancock, Joseph Warren, and Church.

Behind the scenes, the Provincial Congress grappled with a larger question: What, exactly, was its goal? Should it seek the restoration of Massachusetts's old charter and bring back the old relationship with

Britain, before the troubles of the 1760s? Or should Massachusetts cut the cord and declare independence? John Adams, writing from Philadelphia, informed the Massachusetts men that the "Proposal of Some among you of re-assuming the old Charter is not approved here at all. The Proposal of Setting up a new Form of Government of our own, is less approved Still."[9]

So for now, afraid to do anything that might not sit well in Philadelphia, the Massachusetts Provincial Congress remained in limbo, neither declaring independence nor taking initiatives to restore the old charter. It would muddle along in this twilight, waiting for guidance from "the grand American Congress."[10]

Also, the Provincial Congress had to block any impulse to start shooting, while at the same time arming for war. John Adams warned that the Continental Congress opposed any kind of hostilities:

> They Dread the Thoughts of an Action because, it would make a Wound which could never be healed. It would fix and establish a Rancour, which would descend to the latest Generations: it would render all Hopes of a Reconciliation with Great Britain desperate. It would light up the Flames of War, perhaps through the whole Continent, which might rage for twenty year, and end, in the Subduction of America, as likely as in her Liberation.[11]

While juggling all of these matters, the Provincial Congress took a few minutes to discuss the contents of a letter asking it to "take into consideration the state and circumstances of the negro slaves in this province."[12] Those discussions went nowhere.

Gage, responding to the Provincial Congress, brushed off the request to dismantle the "fortress" at the Neck: "It is surely highly exasperating, as well as ungenerous, even to hint that the lives, liberties, or properties of any persons, except avowed enemies, are in danger from Britons." He also reminded the members of the Congress that "by your assembling, you are yourselves subverting the charter, and now acting in . . . violation of your own constitution."[13]

To his masters in Britain, Gage confided that the Congress was having little trouble asserting its power bit by bit: "[T]heir Edicts are implicitly obeyed throughout the Country."[14]

Meanwhile, Gage proved flexible and cooperative in working with town selectmen in dealing with crowding in a town packed with soldiers. Conflicts between soldiers and civilians were becoming more of a headache, and in November, cases of smallpox were reported among the children of a sergeant. To keep the peace, Gage and the selectmen each took steps. For example, Gage ordered soldiers to be unarmed unless on duty. Meanwhile, selectmen put in place a 9:00 p.m. curfew on servants and children. To control the smallpox, the town attended to the care of the children while Gage ordered a search among the troops for other cases. A few more cases were reported in December, but the outbreak appeared to have been contained.

Now radical lawyer Josiah Quincy was on his way to England on a desperate diplomatic mission to somehow change hearts and minds in Britain toward Boston. On September 28, he slipped out of Salem on board the *Boston Packet.* In a letter, Quincy said the trip stemmed from an "urgent solicitation of a great number of warm friends to my country and myself,"[15] though it seems remarkable that friends would ask such a sickly man to take on such a mission.

His mission was no secret to patriot leaders, but it was to almost everyone else, creating a flutter of gossip. A correspondent wrote: "Your leaving this country so privately has been a matter of general speculation. Some say you went away through fear; others that you went to make your peace; others that you were charged with important papers from the Continental Congress; many conjectured that you were gone to Holland; upon the whole it was a nine days' wonder."[16]

The Continental Congress in Philadelphia finished its business at the end of October, agreeing to meet again the next May. Much had been accomplished. For the Massachusetts radicals, the meeting was a triumph. Congress asserted that Americans would be content within the empire only if Parliament repealed the Coercive Acts, the Quebec Act, and previous controversial measures for raising revenues. In a clear reference to the massive military buildup in Boston, the Congress declared it unlawful to place a standing army in a colony without that colony's consent.

Furthermore, the Congress not only agreed to trade restrictions but set up a mechanism to enforce those restrictions. This was the Continental Association, a voluntary agreement signed by nearly every delegate. This called for enforcement in each colony of the trade restrictions and a prohibition in trading of slaves and in the use of imported tea. Anticipating hard times, it called for frugality and an end to such extravagant amusements as horse racing, cockfighting, and staging of plays, while encouraging more local industry and agriculture. Enforcement was to be carried out by the various towns and counties, each of which would set up a committee to take note of people's conduct. Violators would be ostracized and shamed by having their names published.

The Continental Congress took America to the precipice, but only that far. It never said in so many words that Parliament couldn't regulate trade. Nor did Congress criticize the king. Problems stemmed from "those designing and dangerous men, who daringly [interpose] themselves between your royal person and your faithful subjects."[17] Nor were any explicit preparations made for war except to call upon colonies to put militia "On a proper footing." Congress offered no assistance, and no move was made to establish a national military force.[18] According to John Adams, the prospect of war terrified most of the delegates: "Their opinions are fixed against hostilities and ruptures, except they should become absolutely necessary, and this necessity they do not yet see."[19]

Before finishing its work, the Congress also demonstrated breathless diplomatic double-dealing. In a message to the British people, the Americans played up anti-Catholic fears. With the laws now in place, the Congress argued, the ministry could employ the French Catholics of Canada "to reduce the ancient free Protestant colonies to the same state of slavery with themselves. . . . May not a ministry with the same armies enslave you?" Then in a letter to Canada, the Congress reached out to embrace the Catholic Canadians: "[W]e are too well acquainted with the liberality of sentiment distinguishing your nation to imagine that differences of religion will prejudice you against a hearty amity with us." The letter invited the Canadians to send delegates to the next Congress. The Canadians declined.[20]

"The once happy Boston is now become a den of thieves," Betsy Adams wrote in a letter to Sam. "[A] Cage of Every unclean Bird–Consignees, Commissioners and tools of every denomination have made this town their ark of safety–they walk upon Change everyday with great insolence."[21] She defiantly stayed put amid the Tories and troops, and there, at their home on Purchase Street, Sam joined her on his return from Philadelphia. Bells of Boston tolled to welcome Sam Adams home.

Meanwhile, the patriots lost one of their leaders. In October, "a Great Concourse of People" attended the funeral of William Molineux, the merchant who helped direct mob violence in Boston. Printer Boyle, calling Molineux an "Intrepid Assertor of the Rights of his Country," recorded that he died after "three days illness."[22] Tory Peter Oliver said Molineux–"most infamous disturber of the peace" and "a Pest to Society"[23]–killed himself.

On the other side of the Atlantic, Quincy was in London drinking tea with Franklin and immersed in a whirlwind of dinners and gossip. Though his published blast at the Boston Port Act was well circulated in London, he was not harassed or arrested. Indeed, doors were opened to him, and he was treated graciously everywhere. In good spirits and feeling vigorous, he found time for London theater. After viewing *The*

Beggar's Opera and another production, he was "satisfied in my opinion that the stage is the nursery of vice, and disseminates the seeds of it far and wide, with an amazing and baneful success."[24]

Quincy also managed a face-to-face, two-hour meeting with Lord North. The conversation between the passionate patriot and the chief enforcer of the hated policies was polite, even pleasant. According to Quincy's journal:

> We entered largely into the propriety and policy of the Boston Port Bill. In the conversation upon this subject I received much pleasure. His lordship several times smiled, and once seemed touched. We spoke considerably upon the sentiments of Americans, of the right claimed by Parliament to tax; of the destruction of the tea, and the justice of payment for it. His lordship went largely and repeatedly into an exculpation of the ministry. He said they were obliged to do what they did; that it was the most lenient measure that was proposed; that, if administration had not adopted it, they would have been called to account; that the nation were highly incensed, &c.[25]

Quincy, however, found it difficult to state his case fully because of "his lordship's propensity to converse."[26] North spoke as if Britain was locked on a course that could not be altered:

> His lordship more than thrice spoke of the power of Great Britain, of their determination to exert it to the utmost in order to effect the submission of the colonies. He said repeatedly: "We must try what we can do to support the authority we have claimed over America. If we are defective in power, we must sit down contented and make the best terms we can, and nobody then can blame us after we have done our utmost; but, till we have tried what we can do, we can never be justified in receding."[27]

North, for his part, found Quincy to be "a bad insidious man, designing to be artful without abilities to conceal his design."[28]

As for public opinion, Quincy was convinced that English people overwhelmingly sympathized with the Americans: "At present (as I am assured and as I verily believe), could the voices of this nation be collected by any fair method, twenty to one would be in favour of the Americans."[29] Quincy's sources in England again and again blamed former governors Bernard and especially Hutchinson for the ministry's stubbornness. Government ministers seemed to rely on Hutchinson, who insisted that the colonies would never unite and would certainly submit.

Quincy also fretted about what was happening in Boston. On December 7, he wrote that a ministry official was willing to bet three-to-one that Boston was already burned to the ground. By mid-December, Quincy thought war inevitable: Americans "must yet seal their faith and constancy to their liberties with blood."[30]

In Massachusetts that month, the Provincial Congress swiftly joined the Continental Association, the boycott scheme approved by the Continental Congress. Broadsides were printed up and sent out to the towns, directing them to form "Committees of Inspection" to enforce the boycott. For most towns, this task fell to the committees of correspondence. They became a kind of patriotic police force, poking into the habits of townspeople and shaming violators. Boston created its own separate seventy-four-member committee of inspection, which included Warren and ten others from the Boston Committee of Correspondence. By this time, that committee no longer played an important role. Its key members were scattered: Otis was inactive, his mind distracted; Sam Adams was busy with the Continental Congress and the Provincial Congress; Warren and Church were also spending much time with the Provincial Congress. Young and Joseph Greenleaf had left town. Molineux was dead.

Away from Boston, patriots continued to torment Tories, suspected Tories, and those who traded with Tories. Take the case of Jesse Dunbar, "an Honest Drover" who bought an ox (or cow) from a mandamus councillor and took it to Plymouth for slaughter and sale. After the beast was skinned and hung up, word spread that the animal came from a Tory. A mob assembled, produced a cart, put the carcass on the cart, and forced Dunbar into its belly. Its members then carted the man and meat four miles, forced him to pay a dollar for the service, and turned the cart over to a mob from the next town, Kingston. That mob carted Dunbar another four miles to the next town, charged him another dollar, and turned him over to a Duxborough mob. Members of that mob, after flinging the guts of the animal as well as dirt into Dunbar's face, dumped him and the carcass in front of the councillor's house.[31]

Amazingly, some people and some towns in the countryside remained stubbornly and bravely loyal. Tories in Marshfield created a "Loyal Association," agreeing to oppose the various congresses. They asked Gage for protection from patriot harassment. Gage dispatched a small force, which stayed in Marshfield until after the skirmishes at Lexington and Concord in spring 1775.

For the patriots in Massachusetts, one lesson of the September Powder Alarm was the importance of good intelligence about just what Gage and British soldiers were up to. Thus, in fall 1774, Boston's Green Dragon Tavern became the den of an information-gathering organization of patriots. The brick tavern, marked by a copper image of a dragon with a curled tail and a nasty tongue, had a common room below and a hall above, facing the street, for Masonic gatherings and other meetings. Outside was a livery stable and an expansive yard popular as a playground for neighborhood boys.

Paul Revere led these patriots, whose main task was to keep tabs on British troops. Every member was pledged to secrecy, hand on Bible, at every meeting. Information could only be passed on to key leaders: Hancock, Sam Adams, Warren, Church, and a few others. Revere also had a useful contact who mingled with Tories while secretly siding with the patriots. From that person, Revere learned that despite the pledge of secrecy from his group, Gage knew exactly what they were up to. Someone was passing on information to the British.

Gage took no action to break up the "secret" group at the Green Dragon. Possibly he figured such a move would only temporarily disrupt this spying at the likely cost of a valuable informer. So Revere and his group continued their activities, often going out in pairs to quietly observe soldiers coming and going.

Revere's observers discovered British plans to retrieve a cache of gunpowder, along with cannon and small arms, from a thinly manned fort at the entrance to the harbor at Portsmouth, New Hampshire. Revere took off on horseback–less than a week after his wife gave birth to her first child–and covered the sixty miles of frozen slush and mud to deliver the warning to allies in New Hampshire.

Patriots in Portsmouth took action to snatch the weapons before the British could scoop them up and carry them to Boston. By noon on December 14, four hundred militiamen gathered up and found suitable boats. By 3:00 p.m., during a snowstorm, they prepared to attack the fort by land and sea. Asked to surrender, the garrison bravely refused, despite the staggering odds. Shooting commenced–and thus, arguably, began the Revolutionary War, still months before Lexington and Concord. The garrison shot off three four-pounders, but militiamen soon flooded over the ramparts. After firing off some small arms, the garrison gave up, no lives lost, no one even wounded. The militia took down the king's colors. This so appalled the fort's captain, who had been allowed to keep his sword, that he drew the weapon and was wounded in the ensuing melee, becoming the first casualty of the war. The Americans confiscated the barrels of gunpowder and carried them to hiding places inland. British troops later arrived to find the fort looted.

Somehow, the skirmish at Portsmouth did not lead immediately to wider hostilities, perhaps because both sides wanted the event to be forgotten. The British military was embarrassed by yet another humiliation, and many New Englanders weren't keen about taking credit for an action in which the Americans were the aggressors.

In Massachusetts, war preparations continued. One plan from the most radical members of the Provincial Congress called for an army of eighteen thousand made up of men from throughout New England. At the same time, Massachusetts would declare its independence from Parliament while still recognizing allegiance to the king.

These proposals were too much for many in the Provincial Congress. Some envisioned a violent response from Gage. Others balked at the huge costs of an army. Suddenly, representatives one by one discovered they did not feel all that well and needed to go home. Sam Adams's miracle cure was a proposal that ill representatives be forced to resign. Representatives suddenly felt better. While remaining opposed to the creation of an army, they agreed that the countryside should be prepared to take up arms to oppose Gage's troops should they march out from Boston in a large, threatening force.

As the year closed, the Provincial Congress, aware of the flimsy status of civil government, called on the people to maintain order: "[T]he eyes, not only of North America and the whole British Empire, but all of Europe, are upon you. . . . Let us be, therefore, altogether solicitous, that no disorderly behavior, nothing unbecoming our characters as Americans, as citizens, as Christians, be justly chargeable to us."[32]

In early December, one British officer in Boston wrote blissfully to a cousin that he had fallen in love. His "American charmer," he wrote, "has a remarkably soft hand, and red pouting lips."[33] That same month in the same town, a soldier drowned off Long Wharf, two or three soldiers "dropped down dead" from "an infectious distempter,"[34] and Gage ordered an execution. Wrote Lieutenant John Barker in his diary on December 24, "A Soldier of the 10th shot for desertion; the only thing done in remembrance of Christ-Mass day."[35]

Only a few days into the new year, John Andrews reported the regulars on the verge of mutiny: "The Discontent of the Soldiers has become so general that they have doubled the guards and made one or two regiments lay under arms, as well as that they have fix'd a field piece in the Centre of town to be fir'd in case of a mutiny, whereby all those that are not concern'd in it are to appear under arms."[36]

TWENTY-SEVEN

WORLD TURNED UPSIDE DOWN

On January 1, 1775, Josiah Quincy, still in England, met up with Isaac Barré, America's favorite member of Parliament, in the spa town of Bath. Later Quincy toured Bristol, feeling excited and upbeat: "The cause of the colonies every day grows more popular; that of the ministry, more desperate. The merchants are alarmed, the manufacturers are in motion, the artificers and handicraftsmen are in amaze, and the lower ranks of the community are suffering." He was now convinced that bloodless, economic warfare could win the victory America sought if Americans could "follow the simplicity of their fathers" and deny themselves British goods.[1]

He had the slimmest reason to be hopeful. The government was indeed wavering. Ministers slipped word to Benjamin Franklin that concessions were possible. Parliament might be persuaded to give ground enough to allow Boston's port to reopen. But Franklin scorned the offer. Parliament, meanwhile, scoffed at proposals from the Continental Congress and then, in February, declared Massachusetts in a state of rebellion. The two sides were digging in their heels.

In Boston in January, thirty to forty British sailors, celebrating Twelfth Night, paraded in white shirts festooned with ribbons and garlands. They dragged "a plow" on a long rope. Accompanying them were two men, willingly tarred and feathered, representing male and female devils with bags for money. The devils stopped "every person of genteel appearance to request a remembrance of Old England, wishing 'em a merry Christmas."[2]

That same month, on a Sunday, several officers traveled out to Jamaica Pond near Roxbury where, according to a letter in the *Gazette*, they "sported themselves in Scating for several hours in open view of one of our Meeting Houses, to the Great Discomposure and Grief of the Pious and Well disposed."[3]

On another January day, in Boston, a servant tossed some ashes onto an icy place outside his master's stables to make the lane less treacherous. Some boys appeared. Fond of using the lane for sledding, they asked the servant to keep the lane icy. The servant ignored them. Soon enough, in "the true spirit of the sons of Boston,"[4] the boys chose a committee, which appeared at the master's house asking to see the master, who happened to be General Frederick Haldimand, one of Gage's top commanders. Two letters from the period tell the story. According to one:

> When the servant came to the door, he asked their business; they replied it was with the General. The servant was ordered to wait upon them into the parlour. The chairman informed the General that they were a committee from the boys, sent to make complaint of the invasion of their rights made by one of the servants that he had spoiled their sport by tossing a quantity of ashes over a spot of ground which they & their fathers before them had taken possession of for a coasting-place.[5]

The general, born in Switzerland, needed an explanation for the term "coasting." Once he understood, he called together the servants, identified the one who had thrown the ashes, and told him to fix the problem by throwing water over the ashes. The general then "treated the committee with a glass of wine." [6] Haldimand relayed the story to Gage, who, according to another letter about the incident, said "that it was impossible to beat the notion of Liberty out of the people, as it was rooted in 'em from their childhood."[7]

An American writing from Cambridge saw no peaceful way out of the thicket of distrust and anger on both the British and American sides: "I can't imagine which way matters can be compromis'd to the honour of the Crown & the security of our rights. The [Provincial] Congress have drawn a line which will never be submitted to while British blood flows in the veins of Englishmen. Our people will never be contented with less, tho' wading knee deep in maternal blood or deluging the land with our own may be the consequence."[8]

Yet amid all this, people danced. About the time that the American in Cambridge was contemplating bloody quagmires, ladies and gentlemen in Boston were dressing up for what would be the last Queen's Ball in Boston. A memoir describes women in long petticoats, ruffled gowns, and satin shoes, with curled hair powdered white and adorned with "pearl sprigs"; men in white broad cloth coats, satin waistcoats, gold or silver knee bands, hair curled and powdered, ruffled sleeves, and canes with gold heads: "The [minuet] and the Regadoon were danced with graceful air by the juveniles and the approving matron smiled sedate, and all was harmony and peace as the tiptoe step was scarcely heard so lightly did they skim along the floor."[9]

It was during this period that the *Massachusetts Gazette* and *Boston Post-Boy* published a series of pro-Loyalist essays by a writer calling himself Massachusettensis. In these seventeen essays, the first on December 12, 1774, the last on April 3, 1775, Massachusettensis pleaded for patience, restraint, and an end to the strife with Britain. He also defended Parliament and pummeled the radicals for their hypocrisy, shifting arguments, and dictatorial tactics. Many of his arguments were elegant and convincing.

At the time, and for years, many assumed Massachusettensis was lawyer Jonathan Sewall, who had moved his family to Boston in the wake of the Powder Alarm threats the year before. The author was actually another lawyer, Daniel Leonard, the mandamus councillor from Taunton and also a refugee in Boston. As Massachusettensis, Leonard ripped into the committees of correspondence, "the foulest, subtlest, and most venomous serpent that ever issued from the eggs of sedition."[10] Such committees, wrote Leonard, "once established think themselves amenable to none, they assume a dictatorial style, and have an opportunity under the apparent sanction of their several towns, of clandestinely wreaking private revenge on individuals. . . . [T]hey frequently erect themselves into a tribunal, where the same persons are at once legislators, accusers, witnesses, judges and jurors, and the mob the executioners."[11]

Leonard wrote that Americans "do in fact enjoy all the liberties and immunities of natural born subjects." An American is no different from an Englishman who moves to Ireland, where he would no longer be represented in Parliament, but would still be under the authority of Parliament.[12] Leonard furthermore questioned the patriots' sincerity in squawking about taxation without representation. If representation was such an important issue, why didn't the patriots demand it?

He also warned that war with Britain would be hopeless: "The twentieth part of the strength that Great Britain could exert, were it necessary, is more than sufficient to crush this defenceless province to atoms."[13] He furthermore scolded the patriots for interfering with the building of barracks for the soldiers and even straw to lie on, resulting in sickness and death.

Leonard said the difficulties with Great Britain stemmed mainly from the impracticality of having representation in Parliament owing to the "immutable laws of nature"–the vast distance separating America from England. Not unlike Galloway, he envisioned an American Parliament. But in Leonard's mind, that would be centuries in the future, when the American colonies overshadowed Britain in numbers, wealth, and power; when "for the good of the empire" the seat of government is moved from London to America; and when "some future George . . . may cross the Atlantic."[14]

John Adams couldn't let Massachusettensis go unanswered. He replied in twelve essays in the *Gazette* under the name Novanglus starting in late January and running to April 17, two days before the shooting began at Lexington and Concord. After indulging in a long history lesson and recounting the sins of Governors Bernard and Hutchinson and of others, Adams deflected some of Massachusettensis's arrows while hitting the mark with a few of his own.

As Novanglus, Adams defended the committees of correspondence. History, he wrote, is littered with examples of freedom being snuffed out because its champions failed to communicate: "Almost all mankind have lost their liberties through ignorance, inattention and disunion. These committees are admirably calculated to diffuse knowledge, to communicate intelligence, and promote unanimity."[15] Adams specifically defended the Boston Committee of Correspondence as legitimate and supported by the town: "Their doings have been laid before the town and approved of by it."[16]

Adams brushed aside the contention that Americans would be easily crushed in a war with Britain: "It is not so easy a thing for the most powerful State to conquer a country a thousand leagues off. How many years time, how many millions of money, did it take, with five and thirty thousand men, to conquer the poor province of Canada?"[17] Adams furthermore asserted that while Americans were united, Britain was deeply divided: "We know that millions in England and Scotland, will think it unrighteous, impolitic and ruinous, to make war upon us."[18]

Even at this late date, Adams asserted that the Whigs had no desire to make America an independent republic or a confederation of independent republics. Indeed, no charge could be "a more wicked or greater slander on the Whigs." The Whigs, he said, were the same as the Tories in acknowledging subordination to the king.[19]

Adams wrote that Parliament's authority over America had no legal basis. The only "law" Parliament can use to rule over the colonies is "the law of brickbats and cannon balls, which can be answered only by brickbats and cannon balls."[20] Parliament could regulate trade in the colonies, Adams conceded, but that authority was based on American consent.

As for representation in Parliament, that was out of the question, wrote Adams, because colonial representation would be too small for Americans to retain any meaningful control of their own affairs.

For others, there seemed to be no more to say. Sam Adams in January 1775 wrote, "We appear to be in a state of hostility."[21] Joseph Warren, writing the next month, said, "I am of the opinion, that, if once General Gage should lead his troops into the country, with design to enforce the late Acts of Parliament, Great Britain may take her leave, at least of the New-England colonies, and, if I mistake not, of all America."[22]

In early March, the *Evening Post* published an item, probably written by Warren, stating that if the British ministers failed to meet the demands of the Continental Congress, America would "publish a manifesto to the world, showing the necessity of dissolving their connection with a nation whose ministers were aiming at their ruin."[23] In such port towns as Providence, Newport, and New London, patriots were shifting gunpowder and weapons to the interior.

By this time, the second Provincial Congress had begun to meet, first in Cambridge, then Concord. Nineteen towns represented in the first Congress sent no one to the second. But other towns sent representatives for the first time. Among the rule changes for this Congress: because of the cold, and because there was no fire in their chamber, members could wear their hats while Congress was in session.

The Congress formed a committee of safety, which included Hancock, Warren, and Church, with the key duty to "alarm, muster, and cause to be assembled" militia to stop any attempt by Gage to enforce controversial acts of Parliament. On February 21, that committee voted to buy "all kinds of warlike stores" for an army of fifteen thousand.[24]

The next month, after an extended march by British troops into the countryside, the Provincial Congress resolved that, from now on, if more than five hundred troops came out of Boston "with Artillery and Baggage," a patriot army of observation would be called up. Its role would be strictly defensive.[25]

Later, the Provincial Congress took the first steps to create an army. After hearing of yet more redcoat reinforcements on their way to Boston, congressmen determined that minutemen and other militia–emergency part-time soldiers–would not be enough. A full-time military needed to be established. Authorization was given to enlist six artillery companies and to seek out officers. To pay for this and establish a firm financial footing, the Congress asked towns to hand over taxes collected but withheld from the royal government. Many towns balked. In late April, the Congress learned that its treasurer had received about one quarter of anticipated tax revenues.

The Provincial Congress never tried to order towns to pay up. Indeed, Congress in its resolutions on all legislative matters preferred the terms "advise" or "recommend." The Congress was still leaving the door open for accommodation with Great Britain. By advising and recommending rather than ordering, it still could claim that it had not seized power at all but was merely providing guidance in the absence of legitimate authority. By advising and recommending rather than ordering, the Provincial Congress was also less likely to offend the edgy Continental Congress in Philadelphia.

Gage remained cautious, alarmed about the arms colonists were accumulating but terrified of provoking a bloody clash. To learn all he could about patriot activities, he cultivated an intelligence network. Two of his wife's brothers and a cousin of hers had key roles. Also among the spies in this network was Benjamin Thompson, an ambitious, brave, brilliant, fascinating, and opportunistic young scoundrel with a taste for intrigue and a talent for winning the favors of wealthy women and powerful men. Born on Woburn farm in 1753, Thompson early on set his sights beyond his small town and the life of farming. But apprenticeships in Salem and Boston led nowhere, and training to become a physician was cut short for lack of money. Young Thompson settled for a position as a schoolteacher in tiny Concord, New Hampshire, where he seemed destined for obscurity.

Then, just three months after arriving in the New Hampshire town, nineteen-year-old Benjamin asked to marry the thirty-three-year-old daughter of the wealthy, well-connected man who helped Thompson get his teaching job. Transformed from single and poor to married and rich, Thompson quit teaching and cultivated a friendship with New Hampshire's provincial governor, who soon made Thompson–with no military background–a major in the militia.

As tensions between the colonists and British authorities heated up, Thompson remained quietly loyal. Doubts about Thompson's patriotism led to charges from the Concord (New Hampshire) Committee of Correspondence. While those charges failed to stick, the threat of tar and feathering was in the air. So Thompson left his wife and baby daughter in the care of his brother-in-law, fled to Boston, and promptly offered his services to Gage.

Gage quickly recognized Thompson's value. As a major in New Hampshire's militia, Thompson would know more than most people about the true military position of the patriots. He was also well acquainted with the area's geography. So Thompson was positioned to provide Gage with ample first-hand knowledge about the countryside.

Thompson also seems to have been helpful in gathering new information about patriot activities. In Boston, Thompson lived just around the corner from the shop and residence of Isaiah Thomas, printer of the radical *Massachusetts Spy*. Thomas later claimed that his wife, Mary Dill

Thomas, had "familiarities" with Thompson.[26] She, apparently smitten with Thompson and not ashamed of it, is supposed to have told her husband that she would "roast in Hell" rather than give up her lover,[27] who likely tapped Mary for the latest about what the patriots were up to.

Another, more important source for Thompson appears to have been a certain traitorous member of the Provincial Congress who was feeding intelligence to Gage. Thompson, freely going to and from Boston and pretending to be in sympathy with the patriots, may have been the conduit between this turncoat and Gage.

Gage's intelligence led him to contemplate a mission to Worcester forty miles to the west and the target of an earlier planned operation, now canceled. Gage knew that the town was the site of unauthorized meetings. Also, according to intelligence, that's where weapons were being manufactured and gunpowder and cannons were being gathered.

To scout the route, Gage in February ordered two officers, John Brown and Henry De Berniere, on a reconnaissance mission in the direction of Worcester to sketch rivers and roads; to note distances, fording places, locations of woods, heights of hills, the "situation" of the towns and whether they can be made "defencible"; and to scout possible locations for encampments: "The nature of the country to be particularly noticed, whether enclosed or open; if the former, what kind of inclosures, and whether the country admits of making roads for troops on the right or left of the main road, or on the sides."[28]

Pretending to be surveyors, Brown and De Berniere, with a servant, all dressed "like countrymen, in brown cloaths and reddish handkerchiefs round our necks," headed west by way of Charlestown and Cambridge. Near Watertown, they stopped at "Mr. Brewer's" tavern and ordered dinner. The black woman who served the meal was, at first, "very civil, but afterwards began to eye us very attentively." Striking up a conversation, one of the men chirped that "it was a very fine country." Her answer: "So it is, and we have got brave fellows to defend it." She recognized one of the men as an officer. She had seen him in Boston. She warned that if the threesome continued west, they should expect "very bad usage."

Their nerves rattled, the men chose not to sleep in the tavern that night and considered scampering back to Boston. But that would mean disgrace. So they pressed on. At the next tavern, the Golden Ball, innkeeper Isaac Jones made a point of offering tea as well as coffee. The officers took this as a hint that Jones was, at least secretly, a Tory: We "were not a little pleased to find, on some conversation, that he was a friend to government; he told us that he had been very ill-used by them some time before; but that since he had shewed them that he was not to be bullied, they had left him pretty quiet."

Reaching Worcester, the men stayed in a tavern where, once again the tavern keeper offered tea–"an open confession." The wary officers never admitted they were anything but surveyors. Nevertheless, the tavern keeper later sat with them, "talked politicks, and drank a bottle of wine with us–and also told us that none but a few friends to government knew we were in town."

The party then moved on to Framingham, where, in Buckminster's tavern, they watched the local militia exercising right outside their window. "[W]e did not feel very easy at seeing such a number so very near us; however, they did not know who we were, and took little or no notice of us." After the exercises, and a "learned and spirited . . . harangue" by a commander, "the whole company came into the house and drank until nine o'clock, and then returned to their respective homes full of pot-valour. We slept there that night and no-body in the house suspected us."

The British officers, undiscovered in this hive of patriots, were now feeling smug. They sent on to Boston their servant with their completed sketches, but continued with their mission in the countryside, determined to scout out a few other towns between Boston and Worcester. However, when they reached Marlborough, they became thoroughly alarmed when, in the midst of a snowstorm, "the people came out of their houses . . . to look at us." The men found shelter in the private home of Henry Barnes, a merchant recommended to them. Knowing how much risk Barnes was taking, the officers offered to seek out a tavern. Barnes said no, that his house was the only place that would be safe. But it was soon clear the house was not safe either. One of the people watching the men as they entered the town was a deserter from the British army who now was a baker in town. The man had been in Brown's company. The baker confirmed to the whole town that the "countrymen" were officers. Barnes soon learned of a possible attack on the house that very night. Brown and De Berniere, in the house only twenty minutes, had to leave immediately. Barnes "took us out of his house by the stables" and directed the men to a back road out of town: "[I]t snowed and blew as much as ever I see it in my life; however, we walked pretty fast, fearing we should be pursued."

They walked a ways, stopping to eat the little bread they carried, which they washed down with snow. Then they trudged on, wary of horsemen and watching for attack at any moment. Afraid to stop, they walked all day and into the night. Finally, after ten in the evening, and after thirty-two miles, "through a road that every step we sunk up to the ankles, and it blowing and drifting snow all the way," they arrived once again at the Golden Ball and into the care of friendly tavern keeper Jones. The men drank "mulled Madeira wine, which refreshed us very much, and went to bed and slept as sound as men could do." They arrived in Boston about noon the next day, at first unrecognized by their fellow officers or by Gage.

So a mission to Worcester was on Gage's mind. But that action, should it ever take place, would be weeks away. Meanwhile, Gage focused his attention in another direction, up the coast to Salem. Over the winter weeks, he learned that a forge in Salem was converting old ship cannons into field pieces. He also learned that eight brass guns had been imported there. In February the general decided to go after the weapons, but he took special care to ensure secrecy. So that Revere and his fellow spies would not notice, Gage ordered a unit on Castle Island to take on the task.

That force of about 240 redcoats, crammed onto a transport, slipped away from Castle Island about two hours after sunset on Saturday, February 25. They arrived at Homan's Cove, a secluded place near Marblehead, at around noon the next day. By appearances, the vessel carried only its standard crew. For the moment, the troops stayed below awaiting orders to come ashore at the quietest time of day, when New Englanders would be at their afternoon Sabbath services.

Finally, about 2:00 or 3:00 p.m., those orders came. The men formed up and started marching toward nearby Salem. There was no snow on the ground, but the day was bitterly cold. Fifes and drums played *Yankee Doodle.* The jaunty tune was a favorite for the troops. Back in 1768, the *Boston Evening-Post* reported it as the "capital piece" for the military occupying the town. It also seems to have been a venerable tune, perhaps at least a century old. People danced to it, or something like it, when it was known as *Kitty Fisher's Jig.*

By this time, the popular lyrics were those we now know– "Yankee Doodle came to town . . ."–which poked fun at an American simpleton. A story goes that a British officer, during the French and Indian War, came up with the lyrics to have a laugh at the expense of the motley American soldiers fighting alongside the regulars.

So to *Yankee Doodle,* the redcoats marched toward Salem. A local man, John Pedrick, came up on horseback from behind. He was no stranger. The commander, Colonel Alexander Leslie, knew him. A man under Leslie's command hoped to the win the heart of one of Pedrick's daughters. Leslie chose courtesy over prudence. He ordered his men to allow Pedrick to pass. Pedrick thanked Leslie and rode at an easy pace on ahead until just out of sight. Then he raced at a gallop to Salem to give the alarm. Soon bells were ringing and people were streaming out of the meetinghouses. No one doubted the British were after weapons.

To delay the soldiers, townsmen improvised. A few tore up planking from a bridge along the route. The soldiers stopped at the bridge, made repairs, and continued on their way. But the holdup gave other townsmen time to hide or carry away cannons and other war equipment.

Into town the soldiers marched, coming to a halt at the Town House Square. A local Tory spoke to the commander, and in a moment the force was heading toward the forge that was the target of the mission. But the shop could be reached only by crossing a bridge–a drawbridge–that spanned an extension of the sea called the North River. Salem men crossed the bridge ahead of the soldiers and raised the span as the troops approached. Some Salem men clambored to the top of the upraised bridge and sat "like so many hens at roost."[29]

The British were stymied. They couldn't go forward, and going back meant humiliation. Leslie ordered the bridge lowered, but no one obeyed. Barely containing his frustration and fury, he conferred with an officer. A Salem militiaman, John Felt, overheard a snippet of the conversation–something like, "You must face about this division and fire upon those people."

Felt, standing a few yards away, roared, "Fire! You had better be damned than fire! You have no right to fire without further orders! If you fire, you will all be dead men!"[30]

Felt was wrong about orders to fire, but right about the consequences. Leslie had full authority to commence shooting, but to do so would have been suicidal. The local men at the bridge were largely unarmed. A boy who watched remembered seeing only one with weapons, a pair of pistols. But had the redcoats starting shooting, all the locals would have scattered to their homes and retrieved guns. Those men would have been reinforced with hundreds of militiamen, already alerted and now streaming toward Salem. Once bullets started flying, Leslie and his men would have had to run a bloody gantlet in the dim light and cold back to their transport. Now, just like before the bloody chaos on Boston's King Street, voices could be heard taunting the soldiers, daring them to fire. "Soldiers, red jackets, lobster coats, cowards," shouted a man on the bridge. "Damnation to your government." Said another, "Fire and be damned."[31]

Leslie now realized he didn't need a bridge to get across. He ordered his men to seize several boats nearby. But his orders came moments too late. Some Salem men rushed ahead of the soldiers and commenced battering holes in the vessels. When some soldiers tried to intervene, an American bared his chest and dared soldiers to attack. A soldier obliged, though weakly. The bayonet "pricked" the Salem man, drawing a trickle of blood and giving the man something to brag about later on.[32]

Stymied again, Leslie now fumed aloud that he might very well transform a warehouse into barracks and stay in Salem until fall, if that's what it took to complete his mission. "By God, I'll not be defeated."

By now, around 5:00 p.m., night was approaching, the wind continued to bite, and no one was getting any warmer. Then a local minister stepped in and suggested a bloodless, honorable way out. Leslie, the minister, and the militia leaders made a deal. The bridge would be lowered to allow the British soldiers to cross. The soldiers would then march across and then on another few dozen yards, turn around, and march back across and back out of town.

Leslie honored the agreement. The soldiers marched across the bridge, continued a few dozen yards, and turned around. On the cold march back toward Marblehead, fifes played *The World Turned Upside Down*.[33] That tune would be heard again. According to tradition, a British band played it at the ceremonies accompanying the surrender of Cornwallis at Yorktown at the end of the American Revolution.[34]

For soldiers in Boston, the mortification of the Salem Alarm plunged morale to new depths. The mood would sink further as the bitter winter gave way to a chilly, damp, and muddy early spring. Fresh provisions in the crowded town were by now nearly exhausted. Salt rations were the order of the day for most men. Good drinking water was scarce. Some water was so wretched that men sickened from its stench.

Soldiers found alternative refreshment, some of which proved deadly. "We have lost seven by death, killed by drinking the cursed rum of this country," wrote Major John Pitcairn in February. In March he was concerned enough to alert the First Lord of the Admiralty. "The rum is so cheap that it debauches both navy and army, and kills many of them. Depend on it, my Lord, it will destroy more of us than the Yankees will."[35]

The putrid water, bad food, and cheap rum all contributed to the risk of disease. Some soldiers came down with "malignant spotted fever," perhaps typhus. Others caught "throat distemper," possibly diphtheria.[36]

The miserable soldiers, in their desperation, did desperate things and paid the price. Civilians in Boston were shocked when the military administered five hundred lashes to one soldier for selling his musket for money to buy alcohol. Whipping was not uncommon in Massachusetts, but the standard maximum number of lashes was thirty-nine.

Officers kept the men busy with drills on the Common and target practice using floats in Boston Harbor. But the boredom and wretchedness–magnified by insults shouted at every chance by Boston boys–was too much for many. Twenty-seven men disappeared from just one regiment, supposedly one of the best. Desertions became so common that Gage put more men on guard at places where soldiers might slip away. He also resumed executing would-be deserters unlucky enough to get caught. On the Common, Bostonians witnessed the shooting of a private who had failed in three attempts to get away.

For their part, Bostonians helped soldiers escape into the countryside. A Loyalist told Gage that Bostonians secretly rowed deserters across the Charles. One merchant gave a soldier money and a suit of clothes and helped him flee to Andover. Rumors generated by patriot leaders promised any deserter three hundred acres in New Hampshire.

Officers were as unhappy as the men they commanded. Gage ordered a court martial after one officer drew his sword on another. Pitcairn vented his frustration with useful suggestions to the First Lord of the Admiralty: "One active campaign, a smart action, and burning two or three of their towns, will set everything to rights."[37]

In this mood, about forty officers–bored, curious, determined to throw the rebels off balance–made an appearance at Old South Meetinghouse on the night of March 6, 1775. They were elbow-to-elbow with thousands of Bostonians to hear Joseph Warren deliver the annual address commemorating the Boston Massacre. The meetinghouse was so packed that Warren, arriving late, chose to enter by ladder through a window behind the pulpit rather than push through the crowd. Sam Adams, the event's moderator, announced to all the presence of many dozen British officers in the teeming audience and coolly invited the military men to take seats up close to the speaker. They came up to the front pews. Some sat on the very steps of the pulpit, which was draped in black.

From the great raised perch, Warren launched into his oration, with British officers a few feet away on the stairs below him and in pews in front of him. Theatrically garbed in a "Ciceronian toga," he carried forth in a "Demosthenian posture, with a handkerchief in his right hand, and his left in his breeches,"[38] describing a Massacre victim with gore oozing from his broken skull: "Take heed, ye orphan babes, lest, while your streaming eyes are fixed upon the ghastly corpse, your feet slide on the stones bespattered with your father's brains."[39]

As the speech went on, one officer seated on the pulpit stairs held out his open palm. In it for Warren to see was a handful of bullets. Warren glanced down, deftly dropped his handkerchief over the man's hand, and went on.

The speech ended without further incident. One observer thought Warren, to avoid a riot, had deliberately avoided saying the provocative term "bloody massacre." Sam Adams, speaking after Warren, did not hold back. He proposed that the town should thank Warren for his "Elegant and Spirited Oration" and that another speech should be given the next year to commemorate the "Bloody Massacre."[40]

The officers, who had sullenly sat through Warren's talk, now reacted. Some hissed. One officer shouted, "Oh! Fie! Oh! Fie!" To some ears in the crowded meetinghouse, the catcall sounded like, "Oh! Fire! Oh! Fire!" Men and women rushed to the doors. People screamed. A few clambered out the windows.[41]

As civilians rushed to the streets, a British regiment, fifes whistling and drums beating, marched past. In the confusion and noise, some people who feared a fire now were certain they were about to be attacked, not a far-fetched notion.

Miraculously, the panic dissipated. There was no fire, and the soldiers were just marching. Leaders on both sides stepped in to calm everyone. The crisis passed. A British lieutenant, in his journal, said a riot would probably have proven fatal "to Hancock, Adams, Warren, and the rest of those Villains." That would have been a pity, he wrote, "as I hope we shall have the pleasure before long" of seeing them make their exit "by the hands of the Hangman."[42]

A story later circulated that officers intended to seize Sam Adams, Hancock, and other leaders, put them in irons, and ship them to England for trial. But if British officers had wanted to arrest the patriot leaders, taking them at Old South would have made no sense. They easily could have grabbed Adams, Warren, Hancock, and others from their homes or off the streets. The leaders, even in this tense time, never hid themselves.

Gage never stopped revolutionary leaders from conducting their seditious business in Boston. Why didn't he arrest them? He had plenty of chances, and the previous August he had written that in his opinion, the arrest of leaders was essential for peace. But Gage was reluctant to do anything provocative without orders–he did not want the blame for starting a war–and specific orders to arrest leaders never came in 1774. Now, in 1775, Gage was already convinced that it was too late to arrest the leaders without provoking hostilities.

Gage's amazing tolerance may have been prudent, but it cost him the respect of his men, boiling with frustration and calling him an old woman behind his back. In March, a group of officers hacked away at the fence around John Hancock's elegant house. A few days later, according to John Andrews, "four sergeants and as many men were sent to insult John Hancock under pretense of seeing if his stables would do for barracks."[43] Hancock didn't flinch. He went to Gage and complained. Gage not only apologized, he ordered a guard placed near the Beacon Hill house to prevent any further incidents of that kind.

If these were anxious times for Gage, they were even more so for Hancock, who had more responsibilities than he could handle. He was still a town selectman and was meeting with other selectmen almost daily to handle not just routine matters and conflicts with the troops and Gage, but an outbreak of smallpox. He was also fully engaged with the Provincial Congress, meeting in defiance of Gage in Concord, and,

John Hancock, left, a mezzotint after Littleford's 1775 portrait; Dorothy "Dolly" Quincy, right, married Hancock that same year. (*Library of Congress*)

as chairman of the provincial committee of safety, frantically rounding up weapons and organizing militias. Furthermore, he was involved in the Continental Congress and planning his return to Philadelphia in April. On top of all this, he was tending his extensive and tottering business affairs.

Down on the list of Hancock's many concerns was Harvard College. As college treasurer, he was responsible for paying out of college funds the salaries of the faculty. Overwhelmed with other matters, Hancock had fumbled that responsibility. Now the president of Harvard was wondering why the college faculty had not been paid since the start of the academic year. Not especially sympathetic to Hancock's frenzied circumstances, or impressed by likelihood of war any day, Harvard president Samuel Langdon wanted answers. To be fair to Langdon, he was trying to right an unsteady ship. He had been brought in to take over for a disgraced college president who had quit and slunk out of Cambridge after his female servant was found "great with child."[44] With the college under a cloud, Langdon wanted no more scandals, and Hancock's handling of college funds was giving off the faint odor of rotten management. Hancock apologized to Langdon and promised to meet with him, eventually. Langdon continued to press Hancock, sending out a letter of reprimand to Hancock in early April, just a few weeks before the first shots were fired at Lexington.

All this was putting a strain on Hancock's personal life. At thirty-seven, he remained a bachelor. There had been a dalliance with an unsuitable servant girl when Hancock was in England. There was later a long relationship with one Sally Jackson, from a good Boston family. But that ended. Some people whispered that Hancock patronized a prostitute.[45]

Aunt Lydia was doing her utmost to engineer a match with her nephew and Dorothy "Dolly" Quincy, of the venerable Quincy family (her sister Esther was the wife of Tory attorney Jonathan Sewall). By this time, John and Dolly had been an item for about three years, and Dolly was living in the Hancock mansion. John, as early as 1770, had promised Lydia that he would ask Dolly to marry him. But Dolly, now twenty-seven, was still waiting. Aunt Lydia and Miss Dolly were too ladylike to openly bring up, as Mein did, John's "powers of manhood." But by this time the ladies may have given the subject some thought. As Hancock was fending off business creditors, dealing with the Harvard mess, and also, by the way, leading a nascent rebellion, he was also trying to keep Aunt Lydia and Miss Dolly happy, and not doing a very good job of it. But the two women, especially Dolly, were on his mind. While in Concord at the Provincial Congress, Hancock wrote a note to Dolly telling her that his work "prevents me the pleasure of seeing you so early as I expected." Drowning in responsibilities, overwhelmed with worry, he paused long enough to end the letter:

> [N]o Person on Earth can be possess'd of greater affection & regard for anyone, than I have for the Lady to whom I address this, & be fully convinc'd that no Distance of Time or place can ever Erase the Impression made & the determination I have formed being forever yours, in that Confidence & Expectation I close with the addition, of,
>
> My Dear Dolly
> Yours, for ever
> in every respect

It finished with his distinctive signature.[46]

In London, patience with Gage's cautious policy was wearing thin. In early April, Gage received from Lord Dartmouth permission to use force. Dartmouth also made clear that it was time to round up the leaders. Dartmouth told Gage that he would send along more troops, but far fewer than the twenty thousand Gage thought necessary. Dartmouth advised him to make up the difference by recruiting loyal Americans.

This was a slap in the face. Another slap was the news that three generals were being sent. Generals Henry Clinton, John Burgoyne, and William Howe would be given, in addition to the usual perquisites, £500 to hire or buy coaches for traveling in comfort and dignity in America. No such equipage had never been offered to Gage.

Now Gage had to act. Inexplicably, he ignored the specific demand to gather up the patriot leaders. By this time, most patriot leaders stayed clear of Boston, fearing arrest, but Warren remained in town, and still Gage left him alone.

Instead of rounding up leaders, Gage planned another mission to seize weapons. He had contemplated Worcester, but now he set aside that plan in favor of a mission to Concord, an easier target. Like Worcester, Concord was becoming a depot for weapons. It also was the gathering place for the illegal and independent Provincial Congress. Meanwhile, the roads to Concord were better than those to Worcester, and the distance, about twenty miles, was shorter by about half. With luck and good planning, troops could leave Boston, accomplish the mission, and return in one day.

In preparation for the Concord mission, Gage once again dispatched Brown and De Berniere, the two men who had scouted the route to Worcester. Their adventure this time was not so harrowing, but still nerve-wracking enough. They stayed at a private home in Concord, and the host felt sufficiently threatened that, when Brown and De Berniere left for Boston, he went with them.

Gage learned that the village was like a military encampment, that sentries were posted, and that the town bristled with weaponry. Also, the route to Concord via Watertown, with hills and woods, was a poor one for troops. The Lexington route was safer: more open with less risk of ambushes.

Remaining Loyalists in Concord secretly sent details to Gage about military equipment–including structure-by-structure lists of weaponry–and the mood of townspeople. Gage got word, for example, that seven tons of gunpowder had been collected in one particular building. He also learned that Hancock and Sam Adams were now in Lexington.

As April came, Gage selected the leader of the operation and defined the mission. In charge would be Lieutenant Colonel Francis Smith, an older officer known to be prudent and moderate, but also almost too fat to ride a horse. The orders were to march quickly and as secretly as possible to Concord and seize and destroy all military equipment. Gage also told Smith to take steps to prevent soldiers from stealing or destroying private property. Gage's orders were interesting for what they didn't say. Even though he had a specific demand from London to seize leaders, and good information about where leaders were, Gage gave no such order–at least not in writing. Nothing was said about finding and arresting Hancock, Sam Adams, or any other leader.

Gage was well aware of the risk of armed resistance. That's why he chose the Lexington Road over the shorter route through Watertown. With memories of the Salem fiasco fresh, he advised Smith to take control of bridges in Concord as quickly as possible after reaching the town.

Gage also understood precisely how the Americans would fight if it came to that. More than a month before the Concord mission, he wrote to London, "Should hostilities unhappily commence, the first opposition would be irregular, impetuous, and incessant from the numerous bodies that would swarm to the place of action, and all actuated by an enthusiasm wild and ungovernable."[47]

In preparation for the Concord operation, Gage ordered regiments out of Boston on short marches. He wanted the men to be in shape for marching and to be familiar with the countryside. He also wanted people outside Boston to see the men marching and to become used to their presence. Gage hoped by this tactic to make civilians at ease about redcoats in their midst when the soldiers finally marched to Concord. One of these practice marches went as far as Watertown and back, prompting jitters in the countryside.[48]

All the while these preparations were being made, the British still had to deal with the usual headaches. One was the continued smuggling by patriots of weapons out of Boston. Whole guns were tricky to take out, but parts of guns might be easily hidden. British soldiers were aware that many locks from firelocks–mechanisms for muskets–were highly valued. Some soldiers sold such locks, which were then spirited out of town. Americans also tried to take out ammunition. In March, a man was stopped trying to leave the town with thousands of "ball Cartridges"[49]–ball and powder wrapped in paper. After the military seized the cartridges, the man marched to military headquarters and demanded them back. He claimed, maybe even with a straight face, that the eighteen thousand cartridges were strictly for personal use. The request was denied.

Desertions also continued. One soldier was caught and ordered shot. But Gage, apparently sick of killing his own men and hoping the lesson had been learned, stopped the execution and later pardoned the man. The soldier had learned something, but not the lesson Gage intended to teach. He made another try at fleeing the army and this time succeeded.

Despite all efforts to keep the Concord mission secret, patriot leaders quickly figured an important mission was being planned and that it would involve Concord. One tipoff was the keen interest among British officers in the roads in the direction of Concord. The second tipoff was the sudden appearance of small boats lowered down from military vessels in the harbor. Soldiers preparing to march from Boston to Concord, unless they planned to go the long way via the Neck, would need such boats to ferry them across the Charles River.

On Saturday, April 8, Paul Revere delivered a message to Concord from Warren: Concord should expect the British the very next day.

Warren was wrong. The British soldiers did not come to Concord the next day, but the alarm caused patriots to disperse weapons to hiding places elsewhere in the countryside. The Provincial Congress adjourned. Many of the members left town.

Revere made another trip out from Boston, this time to Lexington. He carried more information about British military activities. He also worked out with others a system for getting word out when the British troops finally started moving out of town in force. For Revere and others in Boston, obtaining information about British activities was usually easy, with so many American eyes and ears. However, getting the information out of Boston was problematic. Revere knew that once an operation started, Gage would try to block riders from leaving town. Under the system Revere worked out in early April, messages would be sent out three ways: by messengers along usual routes, by messengers along secret routes, and by a system of lantern signals displayed in Boston to be seen in Charlestown, and then relayed from there.

For many civilians in Boston, the anxiety of the times was too much. On April 11, John Andrews wrote: "[W]e are all in confusion at present, the streets and Neck lin'd with waggons carrying off the effects of the inhabitants, who are either afraid, mad, crazy or infatuated . . . immagining to themselves that they shall be liable to every evil that can be enumerated, if they tarry in town."[50]

Another terrified civilian in Boston was Sarah Winslow Deming, aunt of schoolgirl Anna Green Winslow, who by this time was no longer in Sarah's care. In a letter addressed to a niece (not Anna), Sarah wrote that she wanted to leave Boston: "Many a time have I tho't that could I be out of Boston, together with my family, & friends, I could be content with the meanest fare, & slenderest accommodations. Out of Boston, out of Boston at almost any rate–away as far as possible from the infection of small pox, & the din of drums & martial Musick as its call'd, & horrors of war–but, my distress is not to be described."[51]

Her husband, however, insisted they stay, and so "we are joint sufferers, & no doubt it is Gods will it should be so."[52]

Then her anxiety soared after a visit April 15 from a friend named Barron, a British military man and probably Lieutenant Edward Barron:

> He affected a smiling countenance when he came in. I was glad to see him as ever–I pointed him to a chair, & seated myself, he rose & took the next chair by me, saying "permit me to set by you." I try'd to affect an ease I did not feel, & I tho't, & still think, that he did the same. Soon however, a gloom spread over his countenance,–after a short silence, he told me, (I have since recolected, somewhat officeously,) that . . . "the light Infantry, & . . . the Grenidier Companies were drafted from all the reg.rs & were ordered to be ready to attend whatever duty they might be called to at a minutes warning, & you know I am one." And are

you ready? Yes. After another short silence, he proceeded, unasked, to tell me many things tho' I have since tho't that he would have given direct answers to any questions I might have ask'd, so far as he was let into their secrets–but I ask'd no question of consequence. Several times I saw him catch in his handkerchief the tears that fell from his eyes. Sometimes, there was a silence of several minutes together, both before & after Mr. Deming came in. It was evident, that his soul labor'd under some heavy pressure. . . . He tarried till after dark, & then went off with a start, & in a hurrying manner. . . . Upon the whole, I judg'd & still judge that he found himself engag'd in a service, or rather business, that his soul abhor'd.[53]

TWENTY-EIGHT

BELLS A RINGING

Gage's sources told him about the dispersal of much of the weaponry stashed in Concord. They also told him the town was thoroughly alert to the possibility of a mission to find remaining weapons. So the undertaking was highly risky, while the possible reward as likely as not would be nothing. Another man might have called it off. But Gage was determined to move forward. With clear orders from London, he likely felt he had no choice. He had to do something.

By the middle of the afternoon on April 18, Revere was sure the British military was ready to move. Joseph Warren also suspected something was up but was not certain and didn't want to send out yet another false alarm. He had a trump card: a source, rarely used, who was close to Gage or the people around Gage. Warren tapped this valuable informant, who told him that soldiers intended to seize Hancock and Sam Adams in Lexington and then go on to Concord to destroy gunpowder and weapons.

Who was this source? No one knows, but circumstances and imagination have led some to point to the general's American wife. Margaret Kemble Gage had confessed how uneasy she was about the possibility of her husband's role in the deaths of Americans. Also, after the Battles of Lexington and Concord, he packed her off to Britain, an indication to some that he was unhappy with her. Some historians have also asserted that the marriage from this time was troubled and the two were estranged.[1]

However, as writer J. L. Bell points out, Gage may well have sent his wife away for her own comfort and safety: food was scarce, smallpox lingered, and an American bombardment of the town seemed likely. Also, the couple had two more children after Lexington and Concord—not a sign of a frosty bedroom. The case against Margaret Gage as the informant is flimsy.[2]

Whoever the informant was, Warren relied on his or her information. He summoned Revere, gave him a written message, and directed him first to go to Lexington to warn Hancock and Adams, and then to Concord to alert townspeople there. Warren gave a duplicate message to another rider, William Dawes, a tanner and a loyal Whig. Dawes went by way of the Neck. Some say he passed through the sentry point just before orders came to stop all outbound travel. Others say he knew one of the sentries and gave a convincing story to wheedle his way through. Revere, meanwhile, was to slip out of Boston by small boat and cross over to Charlestown. Dawes was well on his way before Revere left Boston. Revere had other business to attend to: he had to coordinate arrangements for the light signals that had been planned.

About the best place to put a light signal visible from Charlestown was in the steeple of Christ Church in the North End. That Anglican church, which later in the century acquired the nickname Old North, was inactive at the time. The congregation had cut off the salary to the rector, a passionate Loyalist. Revere knew the man who looked after the building, Robert Newman. That afternoon, Revere, Newman, and two others got together to work out how and when to display signal lanterns from the church steeple.

At about ten that evening, they met up again. Revere issued orders and went back to his home. Newman and the two others entered the church, took two lanterns from a closet, climbed the 154 steps of the church steeple, paused to light the lanterns with flint and steel, and then went up farther on a ladder to the uppermost window of the steeple. They then held out the two glowing lanterns on the north side, in the direction of Charlestown. The light of two lanterns meant the British planned to cross the Back Bay by boat to Cambridge. A single lantern would have indicated that the British intended to leave Boston by way of the only land route, the Neck. That the soldiers were on their way to Concord was assumed.

In Charlestown, patriot observers spotted the signals. They immediately sent off a rider to Cambridge and then to Lexington. They also obtained a horse for Revere and sent people out to watch for him coming over from Boston by boat. He soon appeared, rowed over silently from Boston undetected past a hulking warship. Once ashore, he was met by patriots and soon mounted a strong, fast mare. Her name, according to tradition: Brown Beauty.[3]

As it turned out, the legendary heroics of Revere, Brown Beauty, and others to alert the countryside didn't make much difference. The British military left so many clues that it virtually announced it was on the way.

Over many weeks, people outside Boston became accustomed to seeing British officers along the roads. In casual dress, they came out in ones and twos from Boston during the day and normally vanished back

"Christ Church, Boston, erected in A. D. 1723. This church contains the first Ring of Bells cast for North America." Christ Church (Old North) was chosen for the famous lantern signals because its steeple was clearly visible from Charlestown. (*Library of Congress*)

to the town by sundown. But suddenly, on April 18, officers and sergeants in small groups appeared along roadways in full uniform, their weapons bulging from under their overcoats. Also, instead of scrambling back to Boston, they lingered, walking their horses along the roads and stopping at country taverns. Furthermore, they were especially inquisitive, stopping travelers and asking many questions.

Gage had sent these men out mainly to thwart messengers like Revere. The officers and sergeants were to station themselves at places where messengers might pass and prevent Concord from receiving any warning. But these twenty officers only heightened the state of alert outside Boston. Early in the evening, well before Revere left Boston, word about the odd presence of the officers reached Adams and Hancock in Lexington. By 9:00 p.m., Lexington's Buckman Tavern was crowded with militiamen chattering about what the British might be up to. Three went out to observe the British patrols and send word to Concord. They found themselves caught by a group of nine British officers, who held them into the night.

Elsewhere, on the road to Concord, a farmer, Josiah Nelson, hearing the sound of horse hooves on the roadway, came out of his house to inquire, "Have you heard anything about when the Regulars are coming out?"[4] The farmer thought he was talking to neighbors, or at least Americans. It turned out to be a British patrol. A startled officer took a swing with his sword, giving the farmer a deep cut on his head. After the officers went on their way, Nelson got himself bandaged up and then saddled up to tell neighbors. Without any word from Boston, many in the countryside assumed British soldiers were on their way.

Revere, galloping to Lexington, ran headlong into a British patrol. He pulled up, turned Brown Beauty around, and rode off in the opposite direction. Two officers on horseback gave chase. Revere eluded them and took a roundabout way to Lexington.

Around midnight, he came to the parsonage of Reverend Jonas Clarke, a few hundred yards from Lexington Common. This had been the home of John Hancock's grandfather, the "Bishop." As many as a dozen Lexington militiamen guarded the darkened house. A sergeant, who didn't know Revere, scolded him for making so much noise. People, after all, were sleeping. Revere's famous reply: "Noise! You'll have noise enough before long! The Regulars are coming out!"[5]

Revere pounded on the door, and in a moment, windows clattered open and heads poked out. One of the heads belonged to Hancock. "Come in Revere. We're not afraid of you."[6] The house was stuffed with people–ten were Clarkes, adults and children. Others were Sam Adams, Hancock, Hancock's Aunt Lydia, and fiancée Dolly. Adams, Hancock, and Revere were soon trading information. Revere learned that Dawes had not arrived. Had British patrols snared him? Then, within a half hour, Dawes appeared. He had not been stopped. He just had a slower horse and took a longer route–seventeen miles to Revere's thirteen.

The men then displayed a surprising lack of urgency. They–Revere, Dawes, Hancock, Adams, Clarke–strolled to Buckman Tavern nearby. They had to consider the information that Dawes and Revere had brought and consult with militia leaders. Also, Dawes's horse and Brown Beauty were exhausted. They needed a break.

The men decided that some of Warren's information was likely false: the main aim of the military expedition was probably not to seize Adams and Hancock. The size of the expected force was too large for such an errand. They concluded, correctly, that the main purpose was to destroy the weapons and powder collected in Concord. A little rested and refreshed, Dawes and Revere were soon galloping off toward Concord.

About the time Dawes and Revere slipped out of Boston, the British military operation came to life. Strict orders were issued to keep troop activity as quiet as possible, as Gage clung to the fantasy that the whole matter might be accomplished as elegantly as the powder house mission months before. Gage's own second-in-command, Haldimand, knew nothing of the operation until his barber told him the morning of the battle.

In the barracks, sergeants went from bed to bed nudging soldiers awake. Orders were whispered. Soldiers slipped out back doors so as not to alert even their fellow soldiers and their own sentries. The soldiers went through the streets in small groups. A dog barked and was silenced with a bayonet. From eight hundred to nine hundred soldiers, along with a few Loyalist Americans as guides, gathered on an out-of-the-way beach fringing the Back Bay. Only the commanding officers and a handful of others knew exactly what the mission was all about. The navy provided twenty small boats to take the men over to another isolated beach, this one across the water at Lechmere Point.

As it turned out, the troops could have been drumming and fifing to their hearts' content, for every civilian with one eye open was aware that a big operation was in progress. Sarah Deming, for one, was well informed. She knew "that the soldiers were run thro the streets on tip toe," that boats had been readied, and that provisions for two days had been prepared.[7] But she was fooled on the aim of the mission: she was certain the troops were out to capture Hancock and Adams.

The boats, tied bow to stern to prevent them from scattering in the dark, inched across the water. To carry all the men across, two trips were necessary. By midnight–about the time Revere reached Lexington–the crossing was completed.

More time was spent sorting out the units and forming up. Most of these men wore red coats. The coats of officers were a distinctive scarlet. The cloth was strong, made of wool, and very dense. After the battle to come, one of these coats would be retrieved to outfit a scarecrow. More than ninety years hence, the coat would still be on patrol in a farmer's field.[8] These coats, some with tails down to about the knee, others cut at the hip, had ample decorations: lace, buttons, knots, badges. Lapels and cuffs might be blue, buff, yellow, purple, green, black, or white, depending on the regiment.

Headgear varied. The grenadiers wore the tall bearskin caps. Members of the light infantry had black leather helmets. Others wore cocked hats, most too small to fit properly, as was the fashion. This meant that tapes or other fasteners were used to attach the hat to the hair, which might be powdered white or covered with black grease, depending on the preference of the colonel in charge.

The men also wore white or buff waistcoats and breeches, and fresh white linen. Gaiters, held up by tight black garters, covered the legs from the ankle to thigh. On the men's feet were linen "marching socks," soaked in oil to make them waterproof, and square-toed shoes. The shoes were interchangeable. That is, each could be worn on either the right or left foot. Soldiers were instructed never to wear the same shoe on the same foot two days in a row, lest the shoes start "running crooked."[9]

Each soldier carried many pounds of equipment in addition to his gun. Cartridges hung from a belt over the left shoulder. A long sword was attached to a belt over the right shoulder. A belt at the waist held a bayonet and short sword. Each man had a haversack on his hip. Some had one or two canteens, the second canteen for rum. Lace adorned the clothing of men and officers. Many officers wore a crescent-shaped piece of metal suspended by a silk ribbon or silver chain so it rested just below the throat. This gorget, a vestige of medieval armor, was strictly ornamental.

By and by the men arranged themselves properly and the marching began. They learned why Lechmere Point was so isolated: it was a swamp. They waded "up to our Middles,"[10] until finally reaching a soggy road. Then more waiting. Soldiers shivered while sergeants checked to make sure every man had thirty-six rounds. More provisions, delivered by the navy, were brought up, carefully accounted for, dutifully distributed, and then promptly thrown away by half the men, who had brought their own provisions.

At about 2:00 a.m., the men started to march again. At a bridge over a small creek they stopped. Lieutenant Colonel Smith didn't want the men clomping across the wooden bridge and alerting the countryside. So he ordered the men off the road, down a bank, and into the stream. They waded across and clambered up the other side, once again soaked to the waist.

Miserable, cold, still ignorant of their mission, the troops marched on, but discipline slipped. Some men broke away to fill canteens from nearby wells. One man vanished altogether, reappearing at an isolated farmhouse. The family welcomed him, the soldier told what he knew, and soon that information was passed on.

In Cambridge, Elizabeth Rand, a widow, heard noises. Fearing thieves, she went to check on the carcass of a freshly slaughtered hog hanging outside. She stepped out in her nightdress but then quickly ducked behind her rain barrel and watched in amazement as hundreds of soldiers marched by. Still in her nightdress, she dashed to a neighbor's house. The neighbor, Samuel Tufts, had been busy with a slave pouring molten lead into molds for bullets. Tufts had heard nothing and didn't believe Rand until she took him out to the road and showed him by lantern light the distinctive square shoeprints. Tufts soon rode off to spread the news. Elsewhere along the way, at inns and farmhouses, people spotted the troops and sent out warnings.

At Menotomy (now Arlington), Smith ordered a pause. The light infantry–men trained and equipped for rapid deployment–were sent on ahead. Smith was concerned about the bridges in Concord. A humiliation like Salem had to be avoided. The bridges needed to be secured. Later, Smith heard bells and warning shots ringing out ahead and behind. He dispatched an aide to return to Boston with word that the advantage of surprise was gone; reinforcement might be needed.

Revere and Dawes, now on their way from Lexington to Concord, met up with another traveler, Doctor Samuel Prescott, who was returning to the town after an evening with his sweetheart. Prescott volunteered to work with Revere and Dawes in alerting the countryside. They took turns going up to each farmhouse along the way. About two miles along, they came upon four regulars on horseback. Prescott escaped the ambush, vanishing over a low stone wall and onto a trail leading through woods and wetlands. Dawes also escaped, but then was pitched off his horse. Shaken up, he decided he had served his country well enough for one night and hobbled back to Lexington. Revere, meanwhile, was snared by the British patrol and held with several other American travelers unlucky enough to run into the same patrol that night. One of the four captives later recalled that the bright moonlit evening was pleasant and they were treated "very civilly" by their nine captors, who soon started toward Lexington with their quarry. As they approached the town, one man offered his captors a comforting observation: "The bells a ringing, the country is alarmed, and you are all dead men."[11] The members of the patrol soon huddled and agreed that the best way to avoid becoming dead men that night was by scrambling back toward Boston as fast as possible. That meant without their prisoners. They took Brown Beauty, drove the horses of the other Americans away, freed the men, and galloped off. Revere and the others returned to Lexington on foot.

By this time, most towns nearby and in the distance had come to life as many riders, most unknown to history, went from house to house and town to town. One of these men left from Charlestown about the time Revere took off from the same place. By 2:00 a.m., this rider was twenty-five miles north of Boston, having given the news about the move on Concord to towns along the way.

The network of communications–riders supplemented by signals using lanterns, church bells, beacon fires, gunshots, and, in one town, a trumpet–worked well that night, although, mysteriously, the news completely missed some towns, such as Waltham, just two miles or so from Lexington Common.

As for Prescott, who had eluded the British between Lexington and Concord, he made his way toward Concord, spreading the news at houses along the way. He also recruited other riders on the road, including one like himself who had been out courting that spring night. Prescott reached Concord between 1:00 and 2:00 a.m. Soon the town bell was ringing, and he was off to warn the next town.

Back in Lexington about the same time, militiamen began to gather on the two-acre Common. These men were mainly dairy farmers, for Lexington had an established role as provider of milk for Boston. Most of the men were in their thirties and forties. The oldest was sixty-six. The youngest was sixteen-year-old fifer Jonathan Harrington, who appeared after his mother awakened him with the words, "Jonathan, get up! The Regulars are coming, and something must be done!"[12]

Contrary to common grade-school lessons, none of these men were, strictly speaking, minutemen, for Lexington had none. The town had ignored the suggestion of the Provincial Congress to form a special fast-response company. All of the town's militia belonged to a single company, termed training band, an expression dating from a century before. The men simply heard the alarm, grabbed their weapons, and came out.

Concord, unlike Lexington, did have minutemen, and, sure enough, only minutes after Prescott delivered his warning, designated minutemen appeared. In other towns, minutemen and fellow militiamen gathered, some at town "alarm posts," wooden pillars where notices were tacked. The alarm didn't reach some towns until after dawn and after men had started the workday. Some farmers literally left their plows in the furrows.

They had no uniforms; they wore everyday work clothes. For many, that meant large, weathered hats with low crowns and wide, floppy brims; linen shirts; vests; loose, oversize coats; breeches that fastened below the knee; thick, gray homespun stockings; and leather shoes with large buckles.

Weapons varied and included guns for shooting birds. Some men went to Concord with no weapon at all. One man was armed with a cane. Bayonets and cartridge boxes were rare. Some carried the lead bullets in handkerchiefs or under hats.

When Revere stumbled back to Lexington he went straightaway to the Clarke house. There he was stunned to discover Adams, Hancock, Miss Dolly, and Aunt Lydia still there. Hancock, who had spent hours fussing with his gun and sword, seemed determined to fight rather than flee. Adams, Clarke, and Revere teamed up to persuade Hancock to lay aside his gun. Adams and the others impressed on Hancock the importance of his work with the provincial government, and that he should leave the fighting–if there was going to be fighting–to others. With a hand on Hancock's shoulder, Adams said, "That is not our business."[13] Finally, as dawn chased away the night, Adams and Hancock climbed aboard Hancock's coach and were off, leaving behind Dolly and Aunt Lydia.

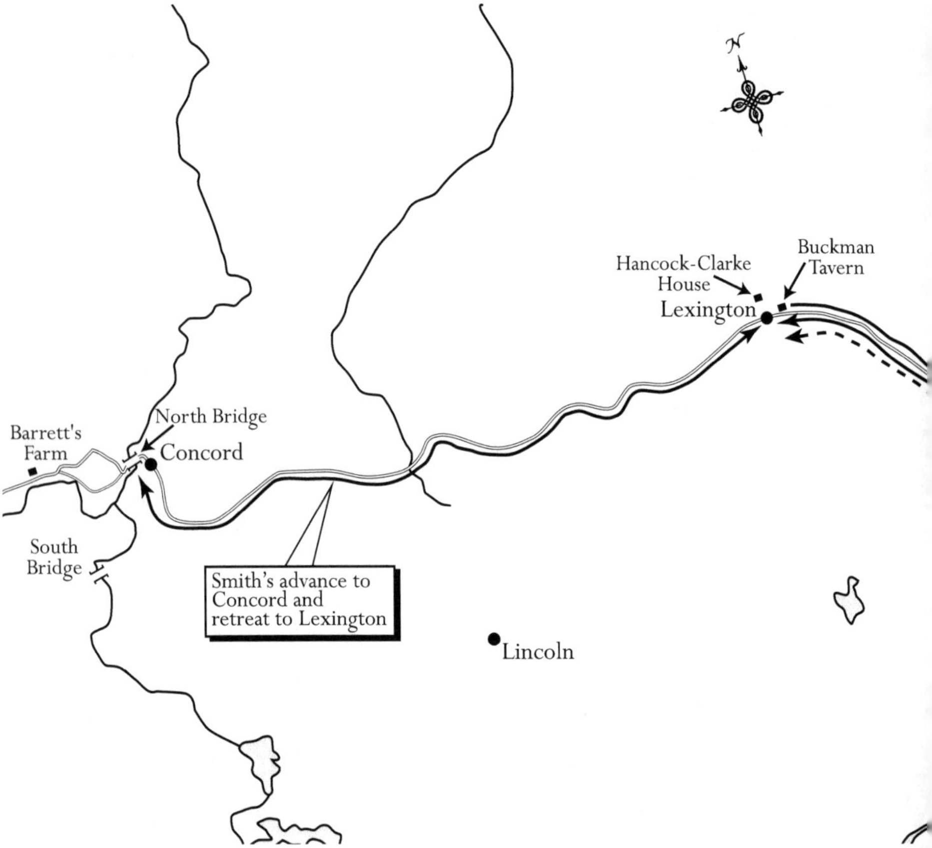

Map 5. Lexington and Concord, April 19, 1775.

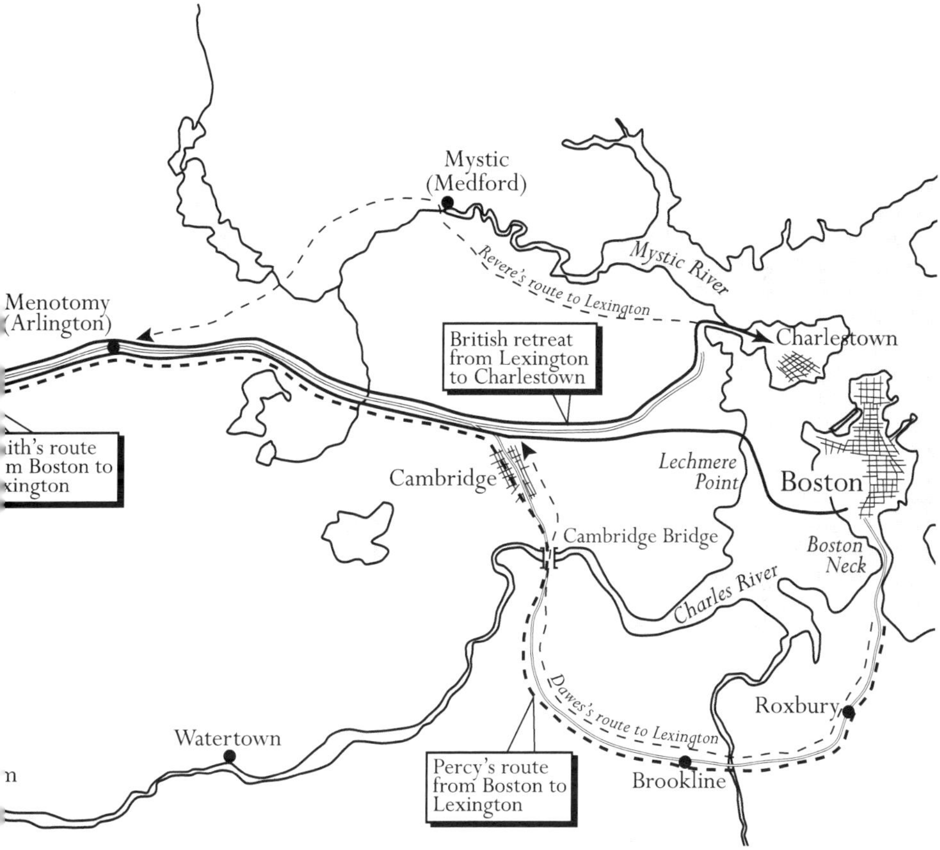
Mystic
(Medford)
Mystic River
Revere's route to Lexington
Menotomy
(Arlington)
British retreat
from Lexington
to Charlestown
Charlestown
ith's route
m Boston to
xington
Cambridge
Lechmere
Point
Boston
Cambridge Bridge
Boston
Neck
Charles River
Dawes's route to Lexington
Roxbury
Watertown
Percy's route
from Boston to
Lexington
Brookline
n

Elizabeth Clarke, then a child in the crowded Clarke house, would recall sixty-six years later the anxious scene after Hancock and Adams left: "Aunt Hancock and Miss Dolly Quincy with their cloaks and bonnets on; Aunt crying and wringing her hands and helping Mother dress the children; Dolly going round with Father to hide money, watches, and anything down in the potatoes and up garret."[14]

Back in Lexington, Revere had barely caught his breath when John Lowell, Hancock's clerk, found him and revealed another predicament. It seemed that Adams and Hancock, in getting out of town, had left behind not only Miss Dolly and Aunt Lydia, but also a trunk stuffed with important–and potentially incriminating–papers. The trunk, stashed in the Buckman Tavern facing the Common, was too heavy for one man. Two were needed to move it.

The two dashed to the tavern, where another surprise awaited Revere. Militiamen told him that the excitement was just a false alarm. The town had wisely sent out riders to confirm that the British soldiers were on their way. One rider returned saying there was no sign of the troops. The other rider had not yet reported. The militiamen who had mustered had been thus dismissed, but also were told to remain nearby just in case.

At this moment, the second rider appeared. He shouted that the regulars were indeed approaching, less than a half hour's march east. Within minutes, the air shook with blasts from alarm guns and bells. A drummer beat out the call to arms. As men poured out of the tavern and onto the Common, Revere and Lowell raced up the tavern stairs to fetch the trunk. Revere paused at a window and glimpsed the long red column on Lexington Road.

Now what? Leave the trunk and hope the British troops would not discover it? Conceal it somewhere else? But where? The two decided they would haul it into the woods nearby and hide it there. That would have to do. So they hoisted the massive chest up, wrestled it down the stairs, lugged it across the Common right through the rows of militiamen forming up, and then across a road and out of sight.

This was a time of both great excitement and paralyzing terror in the Massachusetts countryside. Women sent husbands off after hurried hugs and fearful glances. Thirty-year-old Isaac Davis was "serious and thoughtful" that morning as he prepared to leave his wife, Hannah, and four sick children, the youngest about fifteen months old. He said little, but as he went out the door to lead a group of minutemen, he turned. His only words: "Take good care of the children." Then he was gone.[15] Hannah's intuition told her those would be his last words to her, and they were.

Here and there bizarre alarms set off brief panics. A rumor spread that British soldiers had come ashore north of Boston near Ipswich and were slaughtering townspeople. This triggered a human flood along the roads heading north to New Hampshire. In Framingham, with the men gone, the women of the town locked themselves indoors with axes and pitchforks after hearing a rumor that a group of blacks were on their way to massacre them.[16]

At another town, Pepperill, the women left behind held a meeting, formed a military company, and elected a captain, Prudence Cummings Wright, mother of seven. The women took up guns and pitchforks and began patrolling the roads into the town. Their patrols snared a Tory and made him a prisoner.

The roads were filled with militia–in ones, twos, small groups, and whole companies–going in one direction passing refugees–women, children, and old men in carts and coaches packed with goods–going the opposite way. Some refugees hid in the woods. Some crowded into buildings thought to be safe: a remote building intended for smallpox victims near Charlestown, the town meetinghouse in Lexington, a minister's house in Concord.

But different men appraised the danger differently. At Menotomy, along the route of the British, one man hid himself in a hayloft while two others calmly visited the local tavern and ordered up frothing mugs of flip.

As the British soldiers in the advance column marched from Cambridge toward Lexington, they heard the warning shots and bells, glimpsed riders appearing then disappearing in the countryside, and saw beacon fires in the distance. A "very genteel man" in a sulky approached the front of the column and warned that six hundred men awaited them in Lexington.[17] Teamsters on a wagon with cordwood bound for Boston told of one thousand men waiting.

Farther on, a Lexington militiaman on his way to the Common with musket and bayonet stumbled into the column. The man quickly surrendered, whereupon the British officers took his weapons and shooed him away. The man slunk out of sight but then ran in a roundabout way to the center of town. He eventually got hold of another weapon and took his place in his company.

Still farther on, several riders approached, stopping well in front of the column. One shouted a warning not to enter the town. Another raised a weapon. Some soldiers saw flame and smoke in the dim light. Major Pitcairn, called to the front of the column, was told the column had been fired on. Pitcairn halted the column and gave new orders. Soon the men were each tearing cartridges open with their teeth and loading their muskets with gunpowder and lead balls. From the direction of Lexington came the sound of the drummer on the Common beating his call to arms.

Forward the column marched, passed a gentle bend in the road, entered the town, and headed straight toward the meetinghouse with the grassy expanse of the triangular Common beyond. Just before the meetinghouse, the road forked. The road passing to the left of the meetinghouse and skirting the left side of the Common led to Concord. The road to the right of the meetinghouse and passing in front of the Buckman Tavern led directly to the militiamen forming up in the back of the Common. The redcoats in the column would have seen the militiamen. Some may also have glimpsed two men oddly engaged in lugging a trunk across the Common.

The militiamen also saw the column. "Let the troops pass by," ordered militia Captain John Parker. A sensible choice. He had perhaps sixty to seventy men. There were 238 in this advance British column. Moments later, Parker gave further commands: "The first man who offers to run shall be shot down. Stand your ground! Don't fire unless fired upon. But if they want to have a war, let it begin here."[18]

Now the lieutenant at the head of the British column, Jesse Adair, had to make a choice. The column was approaching the fork. Should it go right or left? The direct way to Concord was to the left. But that would leave the column vulnerable to the militia. Right led toward the militia. It should have been Pitcairn's decision to make, but he was in the back of the column somewhere. Adair chose right.

As Adair led the troops to the right, Pitcairn galloped up. He led the next portion of the column to the left, along the Concord Road, and stopped the column just past the meetinghouse. Adair's men, on the other road, now swiftly deployed on the Common. Amid shouts and orders, they formed a line of battle facing the militia about sixty or seventy yards away. Three British officers galloped up and ordered the Lexington militiamen to disperse. Parker, the militia captain, now was not so eager to stand his ground. He said later that he told the men to give way. Some militiamen slowly backed off, some stayed put. No man put down his gun.

Then a shot went off. Afterward, almost everyone said it came from neither the militia nor the British infantry. Maybe it came from behind a low stone wall off the Common, or from an upper window of the Buckman Tavern, or from a pistol of one of the mounted British officers.

Some thought Pitcairn fired the first shot. But he later denied it, and other officers said Pitcairn specifically gave the order, "Soldiers. Don't fire, keep your ranks, and surround them."[19]

After the first shot or two–from wherever–the British troops began firing irregularly, and then suddenly with a volley. They quickly reloaded and continued firing. Some horses bolted. One, carrying a British lieutenant, took off straight through the militia before its rider

"A View of the Town of Concord, Plate II," a 1775 line engraving on copper, hand-colored by Amos Doolittle (1754–1832). Doolittle made a series of important contemporary illustrations of the battles of Lexington and Concord. This plate shows Maj. John Pitcairn and Lt. Col. Francis Smith, lower right, reconnoitering the surrounding countryside as their troops march into Concord. (*Albany Institute of History and Art, gift of Dr. Bela J. Ward and H. Judd Ward 1920.2.2*)

got it under control. Spectators on the fringes of the Common scattered. As a blanket of smoke shrouded the field, the British line facing the militia now moved forward, bayonets poised.

The response to all this from the militia was meager. Many fled. Some got off a shot, maybe two. One man who stood firm was Ebenezer Munroe, who had not heard Parker's orders to scatter. He fired blindly into the smoke. "The balls flew so thick, I thought there was no chance for escape, and that I might as well fire my gun as stand still and do nothing."[20]

Few of the shots from the militia found a target. A British private was shot in the thigh. Pitcairn's horse suffered two wounds.

The regulars inflicted much more carnage, mainly on militiamen attempting to disperse. One man was hit just a few yards from his home on the edge of the Common. He crawled to his own doorstep and died. Two others fell as they were running away. A Woburn man who had been taken prisoner was killed attempting to flee. Another man was killed as he emerged from the meetinghouse as the shooting started. Only two militiamen were killed along the line where they had mustered. In all, the skirmish left seven Lexington men dead and nine wounded.

The number of American casualties would certainly have been much higher if not for the orders of Lieutenant Colonel Smith, the British commander. The battle, such as it was, ended when Smith finally appeared, leading the main body of troops. Smith commanded a drummer to beat the cease-fire. The shooting stopped. The British troops slowly formed ranks again.

As the men stood in formation on the empty Common, Smith gathered his officers around him and only now revealed the point of this mission. Several astonished officers dared to suggest that the plan to go to Concord now be abandoned. With the countryside now on alert, wouldn't a quick return to Boston make more sense? Smith didn't disagree. But, he said, he had his orders.

After a victory salute–a blast from eight hundred muskets and three cheers–the march, with the advance body and main body now together, resumed toward Concord. After the troops left, the militiamen once again mustered on the Common. Now instead of sixty there were more than a hundred.

At the Clarke house, Dolly Quincy watched the mayhem on the Common from an upstairs window while Aunt Lydia peered from a doorway. A stray bullet whizzed past her head. Moments later, two wounded militiamen were carried into the Clarke home. One "insisted" he was dead, but was merely grazed. After the British troops marched on to Concord, a note came to Dolly and Lydia from Hancock asking the ladies to come by carriage to where Hancock and Adams had found refuge–a parsonage to the northwest–and, by the way, be sure to bring along the fine fresh salmon that had been a recent gift to Hancock from an admirer.[21]

TWENTY-NINE

FOR GOD'S SAKE FIRE

In Concord, minutemen and other militiamen heard from a rider who witnessed the first shots at Lexington. So the men of Concord knew the redcoats were on their way and fighting had taken place. One force of Concord minutemen marched toward Lexington with the aim of confronting the redcoats head on. But that plan evaporated when they gaped at the long red line snaking toward them to the sound of drums and fifes. The Concord men formed up on the road, pulled out their own fifes and drums, and began marching back to Concord as if leading a parade.

In Concord, militia leaders decided not to defend the town at all, but to retreat to the town's North Bridge on the far side and wait for a better opportunity. They knew time was on their side. More militiamen were joining them from the countryside. They might soon outnumber the regulars.

So the British column entered Concord without resistance. Officers permitted the men to take down and burn the town's liberty pole, a tall wooden pole erected as a symbol of freedom. As grenadiers went house to house looking for weapons, Pitcairn called on innkeeper Ephraim Jones. When Jones refused to open the door, regulars broke it down and the innkeeper soon found himself prostrate with a pistol to his head. Wishing not to have his brains blown out, Jones directed Pitcairn and his men to where three twenty-four-pounder cannon were buried. These were substantial weapons. Each gun required a team of six horses to move it and could hurl a ball more than a mile. Gage must have known about these weapons because Pitcairn plainly did. No wonder Gage ordered the Concord mission. With hostilities on the verge of breaking out, he could not allow the Americans to have such powerful guns. The troops disabled the guns, and Pitcairn asked for breakfast. Jones served it. Pitcairn paid the bill.

The British soldiers poking around Concord also discovered some wooden gun carriages, piled them up, and set them on fire. But the fire spread to the Town House, and for some minutes the townspeople and the soldiers teamed up in bucket lines to douse the blaze. Meanwhile, one light infantry company went off to take and hold the town's South Bridge while seven light infantry companies went ahead to take the North Bridge.

At the North Bridge, four companies broke off and continued marching two more miles to a house and mill suspected of being an arsenal. Indeed, it had been a collection point for weapons, but those weapons had been removed well before the troops' arrival. Hearing that the regulars were coming, men had yoked up oxen and commenced plowing, and then dropped muskets in furrows and covered them over. Musket balls were stashed in the bottoms of barrels otherwise stuffed with feathers.

The militia, augmented by men streaming in from other towns, was now swelling to a force of about five hundred. Most of those men gathered on a hilltop in view of the North Bridge, about three hundred yards away.

So as the British regulars at the bridge and the American militiamen on the hill eyed each other, one militiaman decided he wanted to chat with the men at the bridge. Leaving his gun behind, he strolled down to the bridge, had a long conversation, returned up the hill, took up his gun, and went home.[1]

The men on the hill also had a view of the town, where they could see smoke rising. A young lieutenant asked the commander, sixty-four-year-old James Barrett, "Will you let them burn the town down?"[2]

Barrett ordered the men to load their weapons but warned them not to fire first. He then directed the militiamen into a formation suited for marching, not combat. Barrett's plan, apparently, was to march over the bridge past the regulars and back into town as a kind of provocative demonstration.

So, in a long column, the militiamen marched down the hill toward the North Bridge, a fifer in the lead playing *The White Cockade*, an old Jacobite song supposed to be especially annoying to troops of Hanoverian King George.

Observing the line of militia, the British troops initially started pulling up planks from the bridge. Then they were ordered to take up "street firing" positions on the side of the bridge away from the approaching Americans. This would enable the companies to deliver continuous volleys in a compact area. However, this also involved a complex maneuver that could easily become tangled.[3]

As the line of Americans came down the hill along a curving path, the British troops appeared confused, as two of the companies crossing the bridge ran into a third. Then a shot. A regular fired without orders. Then two more shots from regulars, again without orders. Then a whole volley exploded, without a command to fire. Two militiamen fell dead, four others were wounded, and a fifth was grazed. Most shots sailed over the heads of the Americans.

The American line held steady and continued down the hill, now about fifty yards from the bridge, within killing range. Then, from American Major John Buttrick, came the command: "Fire, fellow soldiers, for God's sake fire."[4]

They did, aiming especially at the scarlet uniforms of the British officers. Shots hit four officers and killed at least three privates. With the loss of officers, the regulars seemed more confused, and soon, through the smoke, the Americans saw the regulars fleeing toward Concord. The militiamen, astonished at their own success, then fell into confusion. Some men pressed forward. Some fell back. A few simply walked away. One, saying he was sick, ran away. One American walked up to a badly wounded regular and clobbered him in the head with a hatchet.

Eventually, the militia officers restored some order. An American force of about two hundred crossed the bridge and took a position behind a low wall as the British troops assigned to hold the bridge remained in disarray and those assigned to destroy weapons were still on the far side of the bridge completing their mission.

Meanwhile, in the town center, British commander Smith heard the noise from the North Bridge and promptly led two companies of grenadiers in that direction. They soon came upon the fleeing remnants of the companies that were supposed to be holding the bridge. Smith knew that four companies were still well beyond the bridge. They needed the bridge to get safely get back to Concord.

Smith's grenadiers approached the bridge but halted two hundred yards or so from the militiamen behind the wall. In this pause in the mayhem, a Concord civilian wandered obliviously through the battlefield. This was Elias Brown, a local "crazy man" who lived by doing odd jobs. That day he was doing a brisk business selling hard cider to men on both sides.

Now the troops from beyond the bridge were returning. They hurried across the bridge. The militiamen could easily have killed many but held their fire. Some of the troops crossing the bridge came upon the regular who had been struck with the hatchet. The blow made it appear as if the man had been scalped. From this incident rumors hatched and spread that the Americans were murdering and scalping wounded soldiers.

The Battle of Concord Bridge was over. So was the mission of rooting out armaments. What had that mission accomplished? Not much. Besides finding and disabling the three twenty-four-pounder cannon, the troops discovered five hundred pounds of balls and dropped them down wells and into a pond. They also burned some carriage wheels, destroyed barrels of wooden trenchers and spoons, and broke open sixty barrels of flour presumed to be for American militia. Rebels later fished out the balls and recovered about half the flour.

Now Smith prepared for the twenty-mile retreat to Boston. Chaises were commandeered to carry wounded officers. The other wounded were supposed to march and keep up or be left behind. The British force left Concord at noon, with flankers positioned to the left and right to protect the column.

By now the countryside swarmed with militiamen who continued to stream in from towns near and far. The American force had swollen to about one thousand men. The regulars were outnumbered.

The column of British troops marched for more than a mile without incident. Then they came to the bridge at Meriam's Corner, where the British lost the protection of flankers and where the Americans were waiting. No fifes played. No drums sounded. The only sounds were the rattles of the carriages and the clomping of hooves and feet. From somewhere a shot went off. It probably came from an American. The British responded with a volley, which missed high. The Americans answered, leaving two regulars dead and an officer wounded. The column soon moved on, but not before another six or so soldiers were hit.

Protected again by flankers, the column moved along quickly through the countryside. Then after another mile, along an upward slope, the British column marched into the teeth of two strong American volleys but kept moving. Now around every bend and at every hill was an ambush, with militiamen firing from behind trees and walls. Flankers ordered to flush out the Americans became easy targets. The column pressed on. Thirty regulars fell–killed or wounded–at a stretch that became known as the Bloody Curve.

Americans were dying, too, but many fewer, and more militiamen continued to arrive. The size of the American force was approaching two thousand.

The regulars now hustled along almost at a trot. The Americans trying to keep pace in the woods and swamps along the side of the road fell behind. As the British column passed, the American militiamen swarmed onto the road in the column's wake. The disordered Americans lost ground.

But some militiamen were ahead of the column, waiting. A small militia force, hidden behind a barn close to the road, blasted the front of the column. Still the column kept moving, past the barn. There was no other choice.

After more skirmishes, the column came to the outskirts of Lexington, where the Lexington company–some men in bloody bandages–had reformed, joined by militiamen from Lincoln, and was waiting behind boulders and in ditches along the side of the road. The New England men hammered the front of the column, bringing the entire formation to a halt. A bullet found Lieutenant Colonel Smith, who fell from his horse with a wound to his thigh. Major Pitcairn galloped up and rallied the infantry to push through the ambush.

Farther on, another ambush awaited as the road led up a wooded hill, then another at the next hill. The regulars, fighting with desperate courage and astonishing discipline, swept the Americans from their hiding places, but always at a bloody cost. And still they were many miles from Boston; the column had yet to pass Lexington Common.

Now a bullet found Pitcairn, and he fell from his horse. With so many officers dead or wounded, discipline unraveled and the column began to disintegrate. Some soldiers went off to the side of the road and sat down to await American capture. An American with an empty musket came upon a sitting regular with an empty musket. "Surrender or die," said the American. The regular surrendered.[5]

On both sides, thirst now drove men to seek out water, no matter the risk. Wells close to the road became zones of fierce combat.

Still a mile from the center of Lexington, the British were running low on ammunition. Soldiers at the front, panicky and ever more desperate, moved faster, almost at a run, and started to lose touch with the flankers and the rest of the column. At the back of the column the wounded were now being left behind.

A handful of brave officers at the front somehow got ahead of the column, turned to face their men, slowed them, and brought them to order, despite the shooting all around. But those officers knew their situation was bleak. They had yet to pass through Lexington, and they could expect more fierce ambushes there and on the roadway beyond. The officers now contemplated surrender rather than being picked off in ones and twos all the way back to Boston.

Passing a bend in the road, the front of the column could see the Lexington meetinghouse in the distance. They expected to see a line of American militiamen and yet another ambush. But then the exhausted, terrified, thirst-crazed men at the front let loose cheers of joy.

What was causing such madness? There, on the heights east of the Common, was a line of men ready for battle. But they were not Americans; they were British infantrymen with artillery support. As if to welcome the broken column from Concord, a cannon, a British cannon, boomed, sending a ball in one end of the town's wooden meetinghouse and out the other.

Sure enough, regulars led by Hugh Percy had arrived in Lexington in the nick of time. From the start of the Concord operation the night before, Gage feared something would go awry. He had early on sent orders for Percy to get another ample force ready to move out. However, obsessed with secrecy, Gage sent the orders in a sealed letter to be opened only by the addressee. The letter was placed on a table and forgotten. Eventually, the orders found their way to the right people, and the rescue mission got organized–five hours late–about the time word reached Boston that something momentous was taking place, bringing the town alive with rumors and concern. At the writing school on Queen Street, just after morning prayers, schoolboys were told, "Boys, the war's begun, and you may run." Over at South Latin School, Master John Lovell dismissed his young gentlemen in a more refined style: "deponite libros"–"put down the books."[6]

The rescue force of about one thousand marched by way of Boston Neck, then through Roxbury, Brookline, and over the Charles by bridge, and into Cambridge, and on toward Lexington. Along the way, soldiers saw few people and observed that most houses were shut up. About 1:00 p.m., a wounded officer returning from Concord, alerted Percy to the trouble ahead. On entering Lexington, the rescuers formed up battle lines and were stunned to see the disorderly, panicked column rushing toward them, militiamen in pursuit.

The regulars from Concord collapsed in front of Percy's men, who now kept the Americans at bay as firing continued. To deny the Americans cover for sniping, Percy ordered three houses set on fire. For about a half hour, as the smoke from the torched buildings rose over the town, the fighting nearly stopped, with the Americans on one side of town, the British on the other. A tavern became a hospital for wounded regulars.

At that tavern, Percy huddled with his officers. A critical problem was ammunition. Not expecting so much opposition, he had not brought an ammunition wagon. That meant each man had what he carried, thirty-six cartridges. The cannons had only a few rounds. That is all the ammunition they would have to cover the fifteen miles back to Boston.

As it turned out, Gage had anticipated this problem. After Percy left with his rescue force, Gage sent out two ammunition wagons. But a handful of old New England men, too old to serve in the militia but still eager to do their bit, stopped the wagons. When the driver whipped the horses to get by, the old men simply shot the lead horses, then killed two sergeants and an officer. The remaining soldiers abandoned the wagons, threw their guns in a pond, and eventually surrendered to an old woman digging in a field.[7]

Meanwhile, a short distance from the bloody road where the destinies of a continent and empire were being worked out, Sam Adams and John Hancock, along with Dolly Quincy and Lydia Hancock, were about to become reacquainted with the gift salmon, now cooked up for dinner. Just as they were digging in, a man from Lexington rushed into the parsonage. The hysterical man had seen the flashing bayonets of the British troops returning from Concord. He was certain they would soon be coming down this road. The dinner was abandoned and the household quickly scrambled to move Hancock's great coach out of plain view and into the woods and to cover it with brush. Adams and Hancock then disappeared into a nearby swamp.

The redcoats did not pass by that road, and after a time, Hancock and Adams reappeared. By now everyone was frazzled. Quincy may also have been just a little put off that her beloved had abandoned her twice that day to the mercies of the redcoats. Furthermore, she was anxious about her father in Boston. She announced her intention to return to the town the next day to be with him.

Hancock, who for years had avoided becoming her husband, now presumed that role. "No, madam," he intoned. "You shall not return as long as there is a British bayonet left in Boston."

She pounced: "Recollect Mr. Hancock, I am not under your control yet. I shall go to my father tomorrow."[8]

In her recollections years later, she said she really was prepared to return to Boston and abandon Hancock then and there. But she did not. Aunt Lydia intervened and convinced her to stay. The parsonage, however, was now deemed too close to danger, so the foursome packed up and moved to a place farther away from Lexington. They eventually sat down again for a meal. No salmon. Their host served cold boiled salt pork, potatoes, and brown bread.

The British retreat from Lexington finally started at about 3:15 p.m. Instead of a single column, the force of eighteen hundred to nineteen hundred was divided into three columns. Percy made certain to strengthen the flanks, where parties were needed to flush out the hiding militiamen, and the rear, where he anticipated constant harassment.

On the American side, the top military commander, Artemis Ward, was absent, sick in bed in Shrewsbury. That left military command in the hands of a rotund, bald, jovial, thirty-eight-year-old farmer from Roxbury who had never experienced battle. William Heath's knowledge of military matters came mainly from books and what little he gleaned from helping out with militia training. Amazingly, he and the other American military leaders contrived a sound and straightforward strategy for wearing down the British on their march to Boston while keeping American casualties as low as possible. The New England militiamen would refrain from gathering in large groups but would surround the moving columns of regulars and move with them, finding cover and skirmishing along the way.

As Percy expected, the fighting at first was heaviest at the rear of the columns, where regulars had to march backward and companies, maneuvering in leapfrog fashion, took turns covering for each other. The redcoats, swatting at the pursuing Americans, could hear the militiamen shouting, at intervals, "King Hancock forever."[9]

Moving with the British, the Americans maintained contact with the columns and applied constant prickly harassment. Also, as the British columns moved along, other American militiamen joined the fray. Some New Englanders came on horseback and used their mobility to persistently pester the columns. They would tie the horses away from the road and crawl close enough for a shot. Then, after the columns passed, they mounted and rode around and ahead to where they could fire again.

Elsewhere along the way, seventy-eight-year-old Samuel Whittemore armed himself with a musket, two pistols, and a saber, and then waited behind a stone wall about 150 yards from the road. As the British columns drew near, he fired off five shots. A detachment was sent to flush him out. Whittemore shot three of these men. An infantryman finally got close enough to send a blast into the old man's face. Other men followed up with bayonets. Whittemore, despite at least fourteen wounds, survived and lived eighteen more years, to age ninety-six![10]

Some of the most vicious fighting was in or near Menotomy village. A British lieutenant later confided to his diary that troops had to force their way into "almost every house in the road, for the rebels had taken possession of them and galled us exceedingly, but they suffered for their temerity, for all that were found in the houses were put to death."[11]

At one house, some newly arrived militiamen joined householder Jason Russell, fifty-eight years old and lame, in attempting to defend the home against the oncoming column. Most of the Americans fled when regulars stormed the house. Russell stayed and died in his doorway.

In one house along the way, British soldiers looking for loot broke into the bedroom of Hannah Adams, where she lay with her newborn daughter and was "scarcely able to walk from my bed to the fire from being delivered in child-birth to that time." After threatening Hannah with a bayonet, the soldiers ordered her out of the house so they could burn it down. "I immediately arose, threw a blanket over me, went out, and crawled into a corn-house near the door, with my infant in my arms." They promptly set the house ablaze, even though five children remained inside. They had been hiding under a bed. The children poured home-brewed beer on the blaze, "happily" extinguished with little damage.[12] Through all this, Hannah's husband was hiding in a neighbor's barn.

While some of the regulars took time from the battle to loot houses, taverns, and churches, the columns kept moving and eventually arrived in Cambridge, where fresh American militia awaited to batter the exhausted British soldiers. Now Percy had to consider how to go the rest of the way to Boston. The preferred route was to cross the bridge over the Charles at Cambridge and march on, entering Boston via the Neck. But the Americans had effectively eliminated this choice. One of Heath's first orders as American commander had been to send out men to rip off the bridge's planking and thus thwart Percy's retreat. The American crew, raised the Yankee way to shun waste, had stacked the boards neatly nearby. Then General Gage sent out his own force to pound the planks back in place. Then the Americans returned, pulled up the planks again, this time dropping them into the Charles.

Learning that the bridge could not be used, Percy turned the columns down a narrow and little-used path leading to the road to Charlestown. He knew that once in Charlestown, his men could be protected by the warship *Somerset* and safely ferried across the water to Boston.

Percy's maneuver surprised the Americans, and the British columns suddenly escaped the circle of skirmishers who had tormented them for so many miles. The militiamen still pursued the columns, and fighting continued to be intense in the rear, but around dusk, Percy's columns approached Charlestown. The town itself was in a panic. Most of the men were gone. They had taken up arms and hours earlier left to join the militias along the road from Cambridge to Lexington. Word now reached the remaining townspeople that the British force was on its way from Cambridge. Fearing that the troops would ransack the town, many townspeople loaded up carts and tried to flee. But that was not easy. The geography of Charlestown was much like that of Boston: it occupied a peninsula–about a mile long, north to south, and about a half-mile wide at its widest point–tied to the mainland by a narrow neck, a low, narrow strip of land between the Mystic and Charles rivers. That meant one road out of town, and that was the same one the regulars would use to enter the town. The regulars, in a panic themselves, approached the town firing their weapons, killing a boy.

The civilians fleeing Charlestown turned back, and rumors spread that the soldiers were slaughtering women and children. Some terrified civilians spent the night cowering in clay pits on a hillside. But the soldiers, terrified themselves, were in no condition to do anything. After crossing Charlestown Neck to safety, many redcoats collapsed. No wonder. Some had marched forty miles over two days without sleep. Most had been under steady fire from American muskets for eight hours. The navy needed three hours to ferry the wounded across to Boston.

One officer recalled years later how, after being ferried across, he entered Boston and found his lodgings. Though his elbow was shattered, he requested not a doctor, a bed, or food–but a "dish of Tea." An acquaintance thought him "light-headed," but, he remembered, "[I]t is beyond the power of Words to express the satisfaction I felt from that Tea."[13]

In the battles and bloody retreat, the British suffered 273 casualties. That included seventy-three dead. On the American side, forty-nine were killed and forty-six were wounded or missing.

Writing the day after the battle, Lord Percy confessed surprise at the turn of events:

> Whoever looks upon [the rebels] as an irregular mob, will find himself much mistaken. They have men amongst them who know very well what they are about. . . . Nor are several of their men void of enthusiasm, as we experienced yesterday, for many of them concealed themselves in houses, & advanced within 10 yds. To fire at me & other officers, tho' they were morally certain of being put to death themselves in an instant. You may depend upon it, that as the Rebels have now had time to prepare, they are determined to go thro' with it, nor will the insurrection here turn out so despicable as it is perhaps imagined at home. For my part, I never believed, I confess, that they wd have attacked the King's troops, or have had the perseverance I found in them yesterday.[14]

THIRTY

OUR ALL AT STAKE

With the dawn, Boston awoke to a changed world. No one, though, used the word "revolution." Merchant John Rowe wrote, "[T]his unhappy affair is a Shocking Introduction to all the Miseries of a Civil War."[1] The British regulars were now effectively locked up in Boston. Until the day before, it was common enough for regulars to mosey in and out of town as they pleased. No longer. At Boston Neck, regulars on the town side and militiamen on the country side each kept close watch.

Meanwhile, alarm bordering on panic took hold of civilians, such as Sarah Deming. Terrified by news of battle and convinced that Boston would soon be charred wasteland, she had resolved the night before to leave the town "before the next setting sun, should life, & limbs be spar'd." But in the morning, her husband wakened her with the news that she "was Genl Gage's prisoner – all egress, & regress being cut off between the town & country." She was stunned: "No words can paint my distress."[2]

Then within hours came news that people could leave, but only on foot: "I then determined to try if my feet would support me thro', tho' I trembled to such a degree, that I could scarce keep my feet in my own chamber, had taken no sustenance for the day, & very sick at my stomack." She put a few things in a handkerchief, donned a cloak, and prepared to set out "upon my march" with niece Sally and slave girl Lucinda–and apparently without her husband.

Then she learned that carriages would be allowed out of town after all. However, by this time, "I was so faint that I was oblig'd to sit down." She soon summoned the strength to ask her husband to get a carriage for her and her "frighted girls." He tried, failed, and collapsed in "the easy chair, & said he had not strength to move another step. I expected to see Sally fall into hysterick fitts every minute, Lucinda holding herself up by any thing she could grasp. I bid her however git us some elixer drops, & when we had taken it in a little wine mix'd with water which happend to be boiling, I pray'd Mr. [Deming] once more to let us try to get off on foot."

With a few inquiries, they managed to obtain a carriage and by 3:00 p.m. were on their way to the Neck, where sentinels waved them through: "We had got out of ye city of destruction; such I lookt upon Boston to be, yet I could not but lift up my desires to God that he would have mercy upon, & spare the many thousands of poor creatures I had left behind. I did not however, look back after ye similitude of Lots wife. I was far from being elated with my escape."

They had no idea where to go. When her husband asked which road they should take, Sarah told him to let the horse decide. The horse veered toward Roxbury Hill, where "we met little parties, old, young, & middle aged, some with fife & drum, perhaps not an hundred in ye whole, a kind of pleasant sedateness on all their countenances. We met such parties all the way, which gave me the Idea of sheep going to the slaughter."

Sarah and the girls were left at the house of a certain Mr. Gorden. "Mr. Gorden, whom I had never seen but once . . . behaved to me as to a amiable friend of long acquaintance–spoke comfortably to me, but the ag[o-]ny of my soul, passes description–I sat down, because I could not stand."

John Deming, leaving instructions to Sarah to make her way to Providence, returned to Boston with the borrowed carriage. Sarah eventually found herself in a coach carrying twelve people–nine within ("Mrs. Gorden, Miss Mason, Mrs. Waters within two months of lying in [She is since delivered of a daughter] her three children, & fat maid, Sally & myself") and three on the outside: Lucinda, the driver, and another man. At a stop, she learned that the British in their vengeance had laid waste to Plymouth: "This to me, seemed probable, my imagination got ye mastery of my reason–I instantly concluded, that a general masecre had also taken place in Boston–O this was too much. Could I have died of terror & anguish, surely without a marvelous support from heaven, I should then have died."

Later on the journey, several men told the group that the patriots had slaughtered every soldier and Loyalist in the Tory-friendly town of Marshfield: "I said, I hopd it was a false report. You hope so madm. cryd one. Yes, indeed I do: for if it's true I do think it was very wicked; for you say they made no resistence; & I am affraid if it be as you say God will be highly offended with us, for in his account, I cannot see it to be better than murder."

Finally arriving in Providence, she noticed among the crowd "a well dress'd well looking gentleman, who look'd very particularly at me." He helped her out of the coach: "Are you Capt. Collins of Newport Sir? Are you my aunt Deming? ask'd he at the same time. It was a comfort to me to see him. I gave him my hands. O madam, sd he, I do rejoice to see you here."

Back in the care of relatives, and with the news that the reports about Plymouth and Marshfield were false, she slept well that night. She eventually moved on to find refuge in Connecticut.

A few days after Lexington and Concord, a vessel from England entered the harbor at Gloucester, Massachusetts. On board was the body of Josiah Quincy. Less than two months before, Quincy had been dining with Benjamin Franklin in London. Franklin had been confident that a firm boycott of trade was all that was needed to bring Britain around. Despite faltering health and medical advice to stay in England, Quincy was determined to personally convey to Sam Adams or Joseph Warren the views of friends of America in England, views that could not be prudently written down. He embarked on March 16, and his health quickly collapsed. As he lay dying, he dictated to a sailor his final thoughts: "I was, immediately upon my arrival, to assemble certain persons, to whom I was to communicate my trust; and, had God spared my life, it seems it would have been a great service to my country."[3] He died at thirty-one on April 26 when the ship was in sight of shore, his mission a failure. Unknown to him, thirteen days before, his only daughter had died of sickness in Boston.

For soldiers and civilians back in Boston, discomforts quickly multiplied as patriots cut off supplies of food, firewood, and other goods. One soldier wrote, "In the course of two days, from a plentiful town, we were reduced to the disagreeable necessity of living on salt provisions, and were fairly blocked up on Boston."[4] Wrote Rowe: "All Business at an end & all Communication Stop'd between the Town & Country. No Fresh Provisions of any kind brought to this market so that Boston is in a most Distressed Condition."[5]

Wives of wounded British soldiers left behind in the countryside were frantic about the fates of their husbands. Wrote one:

> [M]y husband was wounded and taken prisoner, but they use him well, and I am striving to get him . . . but it is almost impossible to get out or in, or to get any thing, for we are forced to live on salt provisions entirely, and they are building batteries round the Town, and so are we, for we are expecting them to storm us. . . . It is very troublesome times, for we are expecting the Town to be burnt down every day . . . and I hear my husband's leg is broke, and my heart is broke.[6]

Rachel Revere in Boston also fretted about her husband on the outside. She sent money with an anxious note to Paul: "I send a hundred and twenty-five pounds & beg you will take the best care of yourself & not attempt coming into this towne again & if I have an opportunity of coming or sending out anything or any of the children I shall do it. Pray keep up your spirits & trust yourself & us in the hands of a good God who will take care of us. Tis all my dependence, for vain is the help of man. Adieu my love."[7]

Paul, from Charlestown, also wrote. In late April, he advised "My Dear Girl" about packing up and leaving Boston. He was all business: "I mean that you should send Beds enough for yourself and the Children, my chest, your trunk, with Books Cloaths &c to the ferry tell the ferryman they are mine. I will provide a house here where to put them & will be here to receive them. after Beds are come over, come with the Children, except Paul."[8]

He also reminded Rachel that fresh underwear and socks would not go amiss: "I want some linnens and stockings very much."[9]

A separate note went to fifteen-year-old Paul Jr., who would be looking after his father's property: "It is now in your power to be serviceable to me, your Mother and yourself. I beg you will keep yourself at home or where your Mother sends you. Don't you come away until I send you word."[10]

Among the British soldiers in Boston, the prevailing reactions to the catastrophe were shock and fury. Fingers pointed at Smith, for moving too slowly at the beginning of the mission, and at Gage, for not anticipating the ferocity of the American resistance. Lieutenant Barker called the expedition "as ill plan'd and ill executed as it was possible to be."[11] The British soldiers were brave, he wrote, "yet were so wild and irregular, that there was no keeping 'em in any order; by their eagerness and inattention they kill'd many of our own People; and the plundering was shamefull; many hardly thought of anything else; what was worse they were encouraged by some Officers."[12]

The story of the American attacking the wounded regular at Concord was repeated and embellished. One soldier wrote that the Americans were "as bad as the Indians for scalping and cutting the dead men's ears and noses off."[13] Ann Hulton, sister of the customs commissioner, wrote that two or three British soldiers "in the Agonies of Death" had been "scalped & their Noses & ears cut off & Eyes bored out–which exasperated the Soldiers exceedingly."[14]

As for Ann's brother Henry, the customs commissioner, he insisted the operation to Lexington and Concord was a British triumph: "The affair of the 19th of April prevented the execution of a diabolical plot."[15]

British General Haldimand revealed in his notes great respect for the makeshift American army: "The Americans would be less dangerous if they had a regular army; but all the people are an army and pretend at the same time to be subject to the king."[16]

Out in the countryside, many were stunned at the turn of events. Warren wrote that despite preparations that had been made, few people expected bloodshed: "I verily believe, that the night preceding the barbarous outrages committed by the soldiery at Lexington, Concord, &c., there were not fifty people in the whole colony that ever expected any blood would be shed in the contest between us and Great Britain."[17]

Some Boston schoolboys found themselves outside the town unable to get back in. These boys, with school called off on account of the war, had simply trailed behind the relief detachment of redcoats as they marched out of town to rescue Smith's column. In Cambridge, the boys hung around the Common fully expecting to follow the British troops when they marched back. But that plan evaporated with the frenzied British retreat. Cambridge selectmen and citizens rounded up the boys, fed them, and found places for them to stay. In the days to come, some of the boys linked up with American officers and served as errand boys or in some other way. At least one boy, thirteen-year-old Benjamin Russell, happily attached himself to the army for more than three months, ignoring opportunities to go back to his home in Boston and never bothering to get word of his whereabouts to his parents. One day, as the boy was carrying provisions for the American army near Cambridge, he came upon his father and uncle in a carriage. He later recalled the touching reunion of father and son: "My father jumped from the chaise and gave me the hardest flogging I ever had."[18]

Also stranded outside Boston was Loyalist spy Benjamin Thompson, who had been visiting his mother in Woburn when fighting broke out. Making the best of his predicament, Thompson went on frequent jaunts to Watertown, where Mary Dill Thomas happened to be living while husband Isaiah was off in Worcester. Thompson also dispatched intelligence about the patriots to Boston. Well aware he was under suspicion and probably being observed, Thompson loudly complained to anyone who would listen that he was suffering from diarrhea. This gave him the excuse he needed to gather up plenty of nutgalls, swellings on oak twigs caused by certain insects. Everyone knew that a common treatment for diarrhea was tea made with nutgalls.

However, few people knew that nutgalls could also be used to make invisible ink. With this ink, Thompson wrote out intelligence on an otherwise innocuous note and sent it off to Boston. The letter should have caught the attention of the Americans inspecting correspondence going into Boston, for much of the paper appeared blank–a surprising waste of paper at a time when paper was precious. But it was passed through and found its way to military authorities, who soaked the letter in a solution of iron sulfate to expose the hidden message revealing the planned size of the patriot force and other matters.

A week after Thompson sent off this letter, watchful patriots "confined" Thompson on "suspicion of being enemical to the Liberties of this Country." But once again Thompson slipped off the hook for want of hard evidence. He stayed in the countryside and continued to spy while also making himself useful to the patriot cause by, for example, designing and supplying epaulets for uniforms.[19]

The Hastings House in Cambridge for the moment was the seat of the now revolutionary government. A committee of safety appointed by the Provincial Congress had executive authority. The first business of that committee was to find eight thousand men to lay siege to Boston. In the wake of Lexington and Concord, the great improvisational militia army evaporated, as most militiamen simply went home. Some left to get their affairs in order and intended to return. Others had no plans to join any permanent army. Few men were left to guard key posts, such as at the Boston Neck. A new force had to be assembled quickly. The committee drafted a letter for towns throughout the province. The style was distinctively Warren's:

> Gentlemen,–
> The barbarous murders committed on our innocent brethren, on Wednesday, the 19th instant, have made it absolutely necessary that we immediately raise an army to defend our wives and children from the butchering hands of the inhuman soldiery, who, incensed at the obstacles they met in their bloody progress, and enraged at being repulsed from the field of slaughter, will, without the least doubt, take the first opportunity in their power to ravage this devoted country with fire and sword. We conjure you, therefore, by all that is dear, by all that is sacred, that you give all assistance possible in forming an army. Our all is at stake. Death and devastation are the instant consequences of delay. Every moment is infinitely precious. An hour lost may deluge your country in blood, and entail perpetual slavery upon the few of your posterity who may survive the carnage.[20]

On the British side, Admiral Samuel Graves feared an American assault. Figuring the Americans would not put patriot families in danger, he ordered a ring of boats around the harbor to stop women and children from leaving the town. Graves also recognized that should the Americans obtain artillery, they might bombard Boston from Bunker Hill, on Charlestown's peninsula to the north, or from Dorchester Heights, from the south. Graves thus called for harsh measures. Looking north, he wanted Charlestown razed and Bunker Hill better fortified. Looking south, he recommended the British attack and burn Roxbury, and seize and fortify the hills of Roxbury, for control of Dorchester Heights.

But General Gage overruled Graves. Gage feared an attack on the Roxbury hills might provoke a civil uprising in Boston. Also, Gage still hoped for reconciliation, which would be snuffed out if Roxbury and Charlestown were destroyed. As for Boston, Gage would not even impose martial law or force civilians to stay. He worked with the selectmen in cobbling together an agreement: if weapons in private hands were turned over, anyone who wanted to leave the town would be free to do so. The townspeople on April 27 thus turned in hundreds of weapons, including 634 pistols, 973 bayonets, and 38 "blunderbusses," as thousands applied for passes to leave.

In early May, John Andrews reported that half the civilians had fled Boston, with another quarter waiting for permission to go: "You'll see parents that are lucky enough to procure papers, with bundles in one hand and a string of children in the other, wandering out of town . . . not knowing whither they'll go."[21] By the end of the siege, Boston's civilian population would shrivel to about thirty-five hundred from about fifteen thousand. Of those remaining thirty-five hundred, about two-thirds were Loyalists.

Refugees from Boston included sixty-three-year-old Jane Mecom, Benjamin Franklin's sister. She fled with her granddaughter and the granddaughter's father to Rhode Island. Mecom hid among her linens and clothes items related to her little business. She clarified for her brother that "this was not unlawful smuggling which you would have reproved for they were not owed for, nor any won cheated of Duties." Mecom, upon reaching Providence, got the "unspeakable Pleasure of hearing my Dear Brother was saif arrived" in America: "Blessed be God for all His mercys to me an unworthy Creature."[22]

Shoemaker George Robert Twelves Hewes sent his wife and children out of Boston to live with relatives in Wrentham. He stayed behind, apparently prevented from leaving. He was allowed to fish, however. The British permitted him to come and go from the harbor provided they could have their pick of his catch.

Meanwhile, not only did Gage fail to seize the Dorchester peninsula to the south, he did not even hold the Charlestown peninsula to the north. That was abandoned just after Lexington and Concord. Gage felt he didn't have enough men to properly hold the two key elevations north and south. This meant, then, they were free for the Americans to seize.

In the chaos after Lexington and Concord, the Americans were too confused and ill equipped to grab and fortify these important peninsulas. But they were just bold and organized enough to use the Charlestown peninsula for a provocative demonstration. On May 13,

Israel Putnam, in command of a Connecticut regiment, rounded up nearly all the soldiers stationed in Cambridge and sent them marching to Charlestown for no other purpose than to "Shoe themselves to the Regulars," according to the diary of Amos Farnsworth, a patriot soldier.[23] The line of some twenty-two hundred men, extending over a mile, crossed the Charlestown Neck, passed over Bunker Hill, went through depopulated Charlestown, skirted the shore, and gave a "War-Hoop"[24] to the *Somerset,* the British warship brooding nearby. All of Boston across the river could see the parade. British guns from the *Somerset* and Boston could easily have blasted the demonstration apart. But the British held their fire, and so did the Americans. The parade returned to Cambridge with no carnage.

However, that show rattled nerves among remaining Boston civilians, who wondered how soon patriot guns would fire upon the town and set it ablaze. Those nerves were again set on edge a few days later when a fire, starting in a barracks, destroyed or damaged twenty-seven stores, a shop, and four sheds. Gage's policies may have inhibited firefighting efforts. The military had taken possession of the fire engines and surrounded them with sentries, who wouldn't release them without the general's permission. That delayed the response by at least thirty minutes.

The British, with all their warships, should have ruled the waters. But they were not able to prevent the Americans from burning a lighthouse guarding the harbor. Nor could they stop the Americans from raiding harbor islands, a source of hay and livestock for the military. Americans set hay barns ablaze on Grape Island, Noddle's Island, and Thompson's Island. They also rounded up and carried off horses, sheep, and lambs from various islands, and sometimes skirmished with the British.

The proudest moment for the raiding Americans was the burning of a British warship in what became known as the Battle of Chelsea. In a move to trap the American raiders on Noddle's Island, the British had dispatched the schooner *Diana* to stand between the island and the mainland near Chelsea. Under fire from the *Diana* and from British marines on the island, the Americans on the island still managed to complete their rustling and burning, and flee virtually unscathed back to the mainland.

The *Diana,* however, did not escape. Knowing the danger of running aground, its captain set sail just as the tide was going out. But then the wind vanished. Quickly, with the tide ebbing and patriot guns firing all around, men in oared boats from the *Somerset* attempted to tow the *Diana* out of danger and to deeper waters. But the tide was moving too fast, and soon the vessel was stuck, listing in the mud. Boats from another warship retrieved the *Diana*'s crew, who abandoned the vessel and everything aboard. The Americans soon swarmed over it; stripped it of its sails, rigging, guns, even the clothes left behind by the sailors; and set it ablaze. The cost to the Americans of this battle was just four wounded and no deaths, even though, according to soldier Farnsworth, "Bauls Sung like Bees Round our heds."[25]

In Boston, Gage assured the selectmen that provisions would be made for the town's poor in this crisis. Also, in consideration of Tories still in the countryside, Gage arranged for a letter to be sent to Warren of the Provincial Congress indicating that anyone outside Boston wishing to move into the town would be allowed in.

For its part, the Provincial Congress set up arrangements for anyone seeking to enter Boston or Charlestown. Those people were instructed to seek passes at the "Sign of the Sun" at Charlestown Neck and at "Mr. Greaton's" house in Roxbury. The Congress also made arrangements for the five thousand or so poor people fleeing Boston to be provided for in several nearby towns.[26]

The arrangements seemed to satisfy everyone on both sides–everyone, that is, but the Tories in Boston. Like the admiral, they worried about an attack. They figured that the only reason the patriots had not already attacked and set fire to Boston was because many patriot families and much patriot property remained in the town. Now Tories watched in alarm as women and children of patriots packed up and left, taking wagonloads of goods with them. How could Gage permit this? The Tories went to the general. The two hundred or so men who had volunteered to fight with the British regulars now threatened to withdraw their service.

Gage apparently gave in, for soon people leaving town found that they could not take out certain goods, and guards started pawing through trunks and boxes. Then people found it harder to get permission to leave. The military issued passes sparingly, sometimes dividing families. For those staying in town, firewood and food were scarce and expensive. Andrews complained, "Pork and beans one day and beans and pork another, and fish when we can catch it." [27]

Meanwhile, Charlestown was becoming a ghost town. Believing rumors that the British intended to torch the town, many residents cleared out. At the same time, the Americans posted a guard at the Charlestown Neck to prevent anyone from entering the town. The situation for the few remaining poor became desperate. This got the attention of the Provincial Congress, and by and by arrangements were made to distribute these poor to other towns in the same way as had been done with the poor in Boston. By the middle of June, about two hundred people remained in Charlestown out of a population of two thousand to three thousand. By this time sentries had begun allowing civilians back into Charlestown to look after gardens or property.

Letters and messages went back and forth from Tory men in Boston and families outside. Some curious correspondence survives involving the remarkable Elizabeth Murray Campbell Smith Inman. This woman, who ran her own shop at twenty-two, who had been married and widowed twice, and who had thereby acquired considerable wealth–including no fewer than twelve houses in Boston–wed for the third time at age forty-five. As with marriage number two, Elizabeth had a prenuptial agreement. She also received from a friend curious tongue-in-cheek advice: when out for a ride, "never fail to look out at the opposite window of the Chariot, least strangers should judge you were not married." The friend also advised that to conform to the highest style, she should disagree with her husband about everything. Evidence suggests that by this measure, Elizabeth's third marriage, to retired merchant Ralph Inman, turned out to be fashionably unhappy. By the time of Lexington and Concord, Ralph and Elizabeth had been married about four years.

Identified as a Tory, Ralph found refuge in Boston, as did James Murray, Elizabeth's Tory brother. That left Elizabeth on the outside to manage the fine Inman estate, a three-story mansion with a grand porch overlooking property that included a pond and stands of pine and locust trees. In normal times, the location was exceedingly pleasant. But these were unusual times, and this was in Cambridge (the property was near the site of today's city hall). The town was an armed camp and could at any time turn into a hellish battleground.

Even so, while others fled, Elizabeth stayed on. "The women & children have all left Cambridge so we are thought wonders." She also opened her doors. In one letter she mentions others under her roof: an old man, his three-year-old grandson, and a certain "Miss Denforth." Elizabeth seemed to consider it a kind of maternal duty to stay put for the sake of the servants: "Poor Creatures, they depend on me for protection, and I do not chuse to disappint them." Less than a week after Lexington, she cheerfully wrote that all was well, patriot guards were posted about the property, and potatoes and corn were being planted.[28]

Her tone was sharper in a later letter. She felt overwhelmed with responsibilities and didn't understand why her husband continued to remain in Boston. She wrote to Ralph: "Dear Sir, . . . I hope you will make us a visit. Your advice is much wanted."[29]

But Ralph did not come out. Nor did he want her to come into town. Nor did he want her staying in Cambridge. He suggested she flee to "Limester." He probably meant Leominster. He thought it was about twenty miles from Marlborough, but he wasn't sure. He wasn't even sure it was in Massachusetts: "[I]f it should be in the other Provinces I cannot give my opinion; you must act your own judgement."[30]

Back and forth went letters between husband and wife, as well as to and from her brother, and other relatives and friends. In May, she suggested to Ralph that they abandon New England altogether. "I can move bag and baggage and meet you at any port you chuse to sail from."[31]

Mrs. James Smith (Elizabeth Murray) by John Singleton Copley. (*Reproduction © 2013, Museum of Fine Arts, Boston*)

The response to this came not from Ralph but her brother. To him, such a drastic move was "improper" and unnecessary. He fully expected the British military to soon thrash the patriots: "The greater the numbers on your side [the American side], without experienced generals, the greater will be the confusion and the more total the rout." What she needed to do was to get herself, and whatever livestock and property she could, to somewhere safe. He suggested another family farm at Brush Hill, south of Boston. "For my own part, I am as tranquil, as much at my ease as ever you knew me, from an entire Resignation to Providence and a firm persuasion that all will end for the General good."[32]

Elizabeth began packing up for the move to Brush Hill, but she wasn't happy about it. To her husband, she wrote: "Dear Sir,– to satisfy my friends I am about a most disagreeable task, that of moving from a once delightful home to wander God knows where."[33] Another letter followed, a tangle of confusion, confessing panic and revealing fear of all the dangers she faced.

Now Ralph answered with a plea for her to drop everything and come to Boston: "I will bear any hardships to have you with me. . . . Pray leave the Farm to take its Chance. Your Creatures are of no Consequence, your Hay the same. . . . [H]asten your way to Boston, where we shall be as happy as those about us; and if we cannot remain Quiet here, I will goe where ever you please. . . . I assure you I can content myself in any little Hovell that will afford me a Bare Sustinence, to have you with me."[34]

But now her innate business sense trumped her fear. She wrote back that it was more sensible for her to stay outside Boston. First of all, she reasoned, he could not afford to take care of her and of all of his servants who would come with her. Second, crops needed to be harvested. She would sleep at Brush Hill and come to Cambridge each day until the hay and other crops were in. "As we have sown it is a pitty not to reap. . . . I am sorry my letter gave you so much uneasiness."[35]

Elizabeth's connections with Tories brought her under suspicion, and when a servant muttered some accusations to patriot authorities, patriot militia for a time prevented her from leaving her Cambridge home. But over time she managed to win patriot trust. She even talked General Israel Putnam into posting guards near her property, not to keep her in but to keep riffraff out. Furthermore, in mid-May, Putnam dispatched his own son Daniel to sleep each night in the Inman mansion.

In these unsettled days, as both sides scrambled to sort themselves out, another battle ensued–the battle for public opinion in Massachusetts, in the other colonies, and in Britain. In this contest, Gage fared even worse than his soldiers did at Lexington and Concord. The patriots got their version of events out more quickly and more effectively, starting just hours after the first shots at Lexington. About the time the regulars arrived in Concord on that fateful day, the Provincial Committee of Safety had already dispatched riders with early reports about events at Lexington.

News of the battle–the patriot version–reached other colonies with amazing speed for the time. The battle occurred on April 19. New Haven got the news on the twenty-first, New York on the twenty-third, Philadelphia on the twenty-fourth, and Charleston on May 9. Americans instantly understood the importance of the battle. When news reached a hunting party in the Kentucky wilderness, the hunters named their campsite Lexington.

After the battle, the committee gathered depositions from eyewitnesses about the crucial first shots at Lexington and at Concord. Even British prisoners were asked to speak, and many did. A fast schooner out of Salem carried one hundred depositions and a letter from Warren to the "Inhabitants of Great Britain." Two weeks before Gage's official report of the battle reached the homeland, the British were reading that their soldiers were guilty of "plundering and burning of dwelling houses and other buildings, driving into the street women in child-bed [and] killing old men in their houses unarmed."[36] Some details in the depositions were horrifying. One reported the killing by British soldiers of "two aged gentlemen." The old unarmed men were "stabbed through in many places, their heads mauled, skulls broke, and their brains out on the floor and walls of the house."[37] Despite this, Warren insisted, "We profess to be [the king's] loyal and dutiful subjects" and ready "with our lives and fortunes, to defend his person, family, crown and dignity."[38] Thus at this time, reconciliation, not independence, was the aim, even among the most radical Americans in the most radical province. Probably very few patriot soldiers in their camps around Boston yet thought in terms of independence. British Lieutenant Barker, writing in his diary in May, reported, "The Rebels have erected the Standard at Cambridge; they call themselves the King's Troops and us the Parliaments. Pretty Burlesque!"[39]

In London, supporters of the government were skeptical of the patriots' "saint-like account of the skirmish at Concord"[40] but conceded defeat. This did not alter the government's opinions about its own policies. It only altered its opinion of Gage. Clearly he was not up to the task of teaching the Americans a stern lesson.

Meanwhile, Loyalist exiles in London agonized over the fate of friends and loved ones left in Boston. Elisha Hutchinson, from England, wrote helplessly, longingly, desperately to his wife in Boston with the baby he had never seen. He thanked heaven

> for making you mine for the two years that I was happy, my dear, in having you near me; for the last dear little baby; for the one I am longing to see; and for the innumerable other favors which we have experienced. Let us still trust in the same kind of providence, that he will bring us together and make us again happy in each other. However that may be, let it be our chief concern that we meet together in a world where there is no trouble, no separation.[41]

John Singleton Copley was in Italy when he heard the news of Lexington. Though a Tory and angry at the patriots, he was already certain the British would not be able to bring Americans to heel, and equally certain of the suffering to come. From Parma, he wrote to his wife in Boston:

> Whoever thinks the Americans can be easily subdued is greatly mistaken; they will keep their enthusiasm alive till they are victorious. . . . Unhappy and miserable people, once the happiest, now the most wretched! . . . [T]he day of tribulation has come, and years of sorrow will not dry the orphans' tears nor stop the widows' lamentations; the ground will be deluged with the blood of its inhabitants before peace will again assume its dominion in that country.[42]

Copley's wife, who had given birth to a boy in January, was now packing up. By fall she and three of her children would rejoin Copley in London. Left behind was the infant in the care of the Mary Pelham, the boy's grandmother (and mother of John Singleton Copley and Henry Pelham).

On May 5, the Provincial Congress passed a resolution calling Gage "an instrument in the hands of an arbitrary Ministry to enslave this people" and a man who "utterly disqualified himself to serve this Colony as a Governor." Therefore, the resolution stated, the people should not obey him.[43]

Having lost the battle, and now despised in Massachusetts and in London, Gage tried to at least rally support from other colonial governors. He sent communications to them and got some sympathy. But public opinion in the other colonies overwhelmed initiatives of those governors on Gage's behalf.

Gage also tried to get his version of events into print in Massachusetts. Loyalist printers decided the story was too hot to handle. The spineless *Boston News-Letter* informed readers: "The reports concerning this unhappy affair, and the causes that concurred to bring on the Engagement, are so various, that we are not able to collect anything consistent or regular, and cannot therefore with certainty give our readers any further account of this shocking introduction to all the miseries of a Civil War."[44]

Gage was compelled to print his own broadside. In it he charged the Americans with being the aggressors and asserted that the conduct of the American leaders "is the cause of all the misfortunes that have happened, or shall arise."[45]

Meanwhile, Whig newspapers churned out articles favorable to the patriots. The Provincial Committee of Safety had thought ahead. Even before the battle, it encouraged Isaiah Thomas, editor of the *Massachusetts Spy*, to set up a press outside Boston. Thomas smuggled his press and type out on April 16, set up shop in Worcester, obtained paper from the Provincial Congress, and began publishing a paper with the motto "Americans! Liberty or Death! Join or Die!"[46] Benjamin Edes also escaped Boston and started publishing the *Gazette* from Watertown. After the Battles of Lexington and Concord, a Salem printer published a broadside with rows of coffins representing the American dead. He added coffins in later editions as more wounded Americans succumbed.

THIRTY-ONE

NOTHING REMARKABLE

The news of Lexington and Concord was still fresh when delegates to the Second Continental Congress started for Philadelphia in May. Two of the Massachusetts delegates were John Hancock and Sam Adams, who in the days following Lexington remained harnessed together as they moved around the countryside, turning up in Worcester on April 24, poised to be off to Pennsylvania.

Hancock was in a huff because no one had arranged a proper send-off. He wanted a dignified escort for the first stage of the journey to dispel the possible impression that he and Adams were scuttling out of the province to escape danger. Hancock was also annoyed about the absence of the other three Massachusetts delegates: "Where is Mr. Cushing. Are Mr. Paine and Mr. John Adams to be with us? What are we to depend on? We travel rather as deserters, which I will not submit to."[1] John Adams, Cushing, and Paine were already on their way to the Congress.

As Hancock stewed, the Provincial Congress rounded up a suitable military escort. Then Aunt Lydia and Dolly Quincy appeared. Properly sent off, the foursome headed south on April 26. To the relief of Adams, the travelers stopped in Fairfield, Connecticut, long enough to drop off Aunt Lydia and Dolly in a mansion owned by Thaddeus Burr, a friend of Hancock's. Then Hancock and Adams went on, joining John Adams, Cushing, and Paine just north of New York City.

A triumphant welcome greeted the party in New York. Three miles out of town, musicians and eight hundred militiamen in uniform met the delegates. Church bells announced the arrival. A Connecticut delegate in the procession later wrote to his wife: "The doors, the windows, the stoops, the roofs of the piazzas, were loaded with all ranks, ages and sexes; in short, I feared every moment lest someone would be crushed to death; but no accident. A little dispute arose as we came near the town–the populace insisting on taking out our horses and drawing the carriages by hand."[2]

In Philadelphia, the men from Massachusetts got reacquainted with many of the men they met the previous fall at the First Continental Congress. These included Virginia's George Washington, now dressed in a blue and buff military uniform. The gathering also drew some who had missed the first Congress. One was the illustrious and venerable Benjamin Franklin, just returned from Britain and representing Pennsylvania. Thomas Jefferson of Virginia would also appear at this Congress. Yet another delegate was Pennsylvania's John Dickinson, the author of "Letters from a Farmer in Pennsylvania." At this Second Congress, Dickinson played a role much like Galloway's at the First Congress. Dickinson led the moderate faction still looking for reconciliation with Great Britain and an acceptable way to keep America in the empire. The setting for this Congress was the Pennsylvania State House, instead of Carpenters' Hall. Forty-eight delegates were there when the Congress opened May 10.

How vastly the world had changed since the calling of the First Continental Congress less than a year before. That meeting was conceived mainly for cool deliberation about stopping trade. This meeting began in the context of war. Would the Congress fulfill its promise to support Massachusetts? Signs were encouraging. After Peyton Randolph, president of Congress, left Philadelphia to attend Virginia's House of Burgesses, delegates chose Hancock to take Randolph's place as president. Hancock, it was said, was so startled by the selection that he hesitated to occupy the presidential chair. A Virginia delegate grabbed him, picked him up, and plopped him into the seat.

Back in Massachusetts, thousands of New Englanders responded to the Provincial Committee of Safety's call for men, and in May and June this force came together. This "grand American army," as one newspaper called it,[3] was a confusion of command and supply. Men–and boys–came from four colonies–Massachusetts supplied eleven thousand five hundred, Connecticut twenty-three hundred, New Hampshire twelve hundred, and Rhode Island one thousand. Slaves were not welcome. A resolution of the Committee of Safety insisted that "no slaves be admitted into this army upon any consideration whatsoever."[4]

But the army was not fussy about boys joining up. We know, for example, about John Greenwood, who was not quite fifteen at the time of Lexington. He grew up in Boston, but at the time of the battle was working in Falmouth, Maine, as an apprentice to a cabinetmaker. Worried about his parents, he put a few things in a handkerchief, had an early breakfast, "jumped over the back fence," and started toward Boston. He also had his fife, which he would play when he came upon men mustering. That fife enabled him to travel "free of expense" during the four and a half days it took him to get to Charlestown, where he was barred from crossing to Boston. He bided his time in a tavern, where he played his fife. Impressed patrons urged him to go to Cambridge and enlist as a fifer, which he did, for eight months at eight dollars a month.[5]

Each colony was supposed to supply its own soldiers with provisions and ammunition, but there were shortages of everything. Artemis Ward officially remained the top commander of the Massachusetts and New Hampshire men and was unofficially accepted as commander by the Rhode Island and Connecticut men. Below Ward, ranks were unclear, creating confusion, disagreement, and delay, and further adding to the difficulty of cobbling together an army from scratch.

The American soldiers were soon fighting boredom, disease, filth, and, occasionally, the British. One American soldier was Samuel Haws of Wrentham, thirty-two miles southwest of Boston. We know nothing of Haws except what he left behind in a journal, which he kept from April 19, the day he marched with other militiamen toward Lexington. He stayed on after the battle and reported biscuits "hard enough for flints," the death of a soldier after a comrade "axedentely discharged his peace," and various false alarms. Many days he had little to say. A sample of his journal:

> June the 1. Nothing remarkable hapened this day.
> the 2–8. Nothing remarkable hapened.
> the 9. We passed muster Before colonel Robinson and received one months pay.
> the 10. Their was a man Whiped for Stealing.
> the 11. Their was a soldier died at the hospittle which was the first that had died of Sickness since we incampt the same day their was two fireShips [prostitutes] drummed out of the rhodisland compy.
> the 12. Nothing Strange this day.
> the 13. Dito.[6]

Another patriot soldier, Caleb Haskell, stationed at Cambridge, recorded in June and July such events as a suicide, a desertion to the British, and punishments: thirty-nine stripes for stealing and a ride on "the wooden horse" for "abuse to . . . officers."[7] Curiously, one man was given seventy-nine stripes for "challenging his officer," while another received only twenty for striking an officer.[8] Haskell also wrote that a "very bad woman" was doused in the river and "drummed out of town." Caleb spent his time making cartridges, standing guard, and listening to at least nine sermons.[9]

Some patriot soldiers–or men pretending to be patriot soldiers–took advantage of the confusion and near lawlessness. Well-off

Loyalists in the countryside were obvious targets. One Sunday, a woman in Marlborough, her Loyalist husband stuck in Boston, had a stranger march into her house with a loaded musket and demand dinner. "I sent him the best I had upon the table. He was not contented, but insisted upon bringing in his gun and dining with me." He then demanded a horse. If she refused, he promised to "blow my brains out." He claimed to have an order from a general, but never showed it. "His language and his looks so frightful that I could not remain in the house but fled to the store and locked myself in." He followed, threatened to break in, but then scurried away when passersby intervened.[10]

Just a few miles west of the military encampment at Cambridge, the Provincial Congress met at the Congregationalist meetinghouse in Watertown. In the absence of Hancock, Warren was elected president pro tempore. Lurching along as an emergency government, this Congress was a frenzy of activity, ordering an inquiry into the shocking scalping near Concord's North Bridge, looking into establishing a network of post riders, choosing a minister to deliver a sermon to the Congress, and authorizing an invitation to "eastern tribes of indians" to join in the fight with a promise of a blanket and a ribbon for each man upon enlistment.[11] A request from "Lady Frankland" to go to Boston must have produced some tittering. Lady Frankland, as everyone knew, was the subject of just about the most romantic tale in New England. She began life as Agnes Surriage of Marblehead, and was just a poor servant girl in her bare feet scrubbing the floor of an inn when Sir Harry Frankland, well-heeled customs collector, laid eyes on her and was smitten. She moved into his fine house to be "educated" and later accompanied him to England, where his family snubbed her. By and by, they traveled to Lisbon, where they happened to be during the terrible earthquake of 1755, which killed thousands. The temblor almost killed him, too, but she plucked him out of the ruins, whereupon he decided at last to marry her, whereupon at last his family accepted her. But that was many years before. Now she was a rich widow. Lawmakers granted permission for her to go into town with "seven trunks, all the beds, and furniture to them; all the boxes and crates; a basket of chickens and a bag of corn; two barrels and a hamper; two horses and two chaises, and all the articles in the chaise, excepting arms and ammunition; one phaeton; some tongues, hams and veal; sundry small bundles."

With this permission, Lady Frankland subsequently set out for Boston, but she was stopped by armed men. Another order had to be issued for the release of the woman and her property. In the end, the Provincial Congress authorized a guard of six soldiers to escort Her Ladyship to the town.

The Congress also wrestled with the problem of raising money. In a letter to the "Inhabitants of Massachusetts," members begged: "[W]e most earnestly recommend to such of you as have cash in your hands, which you can spare from the necessary supplies of your families, that you would lend the same to the colony, by which you will put it in our power to carry in effect measures undertaken for the salvation of the country."

The Congress also appointed committees to tackle such questions as what to do with a man in Brookline with smallpox. He was ordered taken "in the most careful manner" to the "house of Ebenezer Smith in Little Cambridge," where smallpox had recently been.

Military matters, of course, occupied much of the attention of Congress. Resolutions specified the provisions the Massachusetts soldiers should receive per day:

> 1st. One pound of bread: 2d. Half a pound of beef and a half a pound of pork; and if pork cannot be had, one pound and a quarter of beef; and one day in seven they shall have one pound and one quarter of salt fish, instead of one day's allowance of meat; 3d. One pint of milk, or, if milk cannot be had, one gill of rice; 4th. One quart of good spruce or malt beer: 5th. One gill of peas or beans, or other sauce equivalent: 6th. Six ounces of good butter per week: 7th. One pound of good common soap for six men per week: 8th. Half a pint of vinegar per week per man, if it can be had.

The Congress also urged Massachusetts residents to save all the straw they could for the militiamen's use.

But the Congress recognized government shortcomings. There was no Council, which under the royal government had served as the second legislative house. There was no judicial branch. Courts had been closed since people in the countryside forced royal judges to quit or to flee to Boston. There was no governor or lieutenant governor, although the Congress's Committee of Safety took on executive functions of a governor. Civil authority was uncertain or nonexistent, a perilous situation at any time but especially with a countryside swarming with ragged and hungry men with guns.

The Provincial Congress turned to the Continental Congress. A committee, with Joseph Warren as chairman, prepared a resolution that underscored fear of both British soldiers and of the ragtag patriot army. The resolution explained the necessity in Massachusetts of raising an army "to defend us, and all America, from the further butcheries and devastations of our implacable enemies." However, this army posed a risk: "[W]e tremble at having an army, although composed of our own countrymen, established here, without a civil power to provide for and control it."

So the Massachusetts resolution asked the Continental Congress for advice on setting up a civil government. But more than that, the resolution promised to "readily submit" to the instructions of the Continental Congress. The Massachusetts Congress acknowledged the supremacy of the Congress in Philadelphia:

> We are happy in having the opportunity of laying our distressed state before the representative body of the continent, and humbly hope you will favor us with your most explicit advice, respecting the taking up and exercising the powers of civil government, which we think absolutely necessary for the salvation of our country; and we shall readily submit to such a general plan as you may direct for the colonies; or make it our great study to establish such a form of government here, as shall not only most promote our advantage, but the union and interest of all America.

Furthermore, the Massachusetts Congress offered to give over to the Continental Congress the control of the army encamped around Boston: "As the army, collecting from different colonies, is for the general defence of the rights of America, we would beg leave to suggest to your consideration, the propriety of your taking the regulation and general direction of it, that the operations may more effectually answer the purposes designed."

The Provincial Congress approved this resolution in mid-May and sent it off to Philadelphia in the care of Benjamin Church to deliver to the president of the "honorable American Congress."

As Church went off, Warren and the Provincial Congress continued to work frantically to keep the little army together and supplied. Warren dashed off a stern note to the head of the committee on supplies. Of fifteen hundred iron pots ordered, only eight hundred had been received: "You'll critically examine into this matter, and forthwith order said pots into the camp at Cambridge."[12]

In Philadelphia, delegates to the Continental Congress grappled with a most fundamental question: What, exactly, was the Congress trying to do? South Carolina's John Rutledge summed up the dilemma: "[D]o We aim at independency? Or do We only ask for a Restoration of Rights & putting of us on Our old footing?"[13]

This is why the Congress was not altogether pleased with the news in May of America's great victory at Fort Ticonderoga, which guarded the key route connecting New York's Hudson River Valley with Canada. A combined force of Connecticut men, on their own authority, and of men mainly from western Massachusetts, under the authority of the Massachusetts Committee of Safety, had marched into northern New York and seized the British fort between Lake George and Lake Champlain. The American force then took the nearby British outpost of Crown Point.

If independence were the goal, then the Continental Congress would have every reason to rejoice. But if the Congress still looked for reconciliation, those actions in the New York wilderness were calamities. This was different from Lexington and Concord. At Ticonderoga and Crown Point, the Americans were clearly the aggressors. This would only harden opinion among the British people, Parliament, and the king against making concessions to America and restoring friendship.

The Continental Congress, which hadn't authorized the expedition, dealt as best it could with the consequences, conjuring the excuse of self-defense from "indubitable evidence" that the British were plotting an invasion from Quebec. The Congress asked that an inventory be made of the cannon and other military equipment so that they could in time be returned "when the restoration of the former harmony between great Britain and these colonies so ardently wished for by the latter shall render it prudent and consistent with the overruling law of self preservation."[14]

After tackling the Ticonderoga matter, the Continental Congress took up the plea from the Massachusetts Provincial Congress for guidance about setting up a civil government and taking over the hodgepodge New England army encamped around Boston. These were critical questions. The Continental Congress, conceived as simply a meeting, was being asked to take authority, to assume the power of a national government.

At this pivotal moment, Sam Adams seemed oddly distracted by, of all things, his wardrobe. With all the turmoil and moving from place to place in Massachusetts, he had been unable to retrieve the splendid new suit he received before the First Continental Congress. Now, in Philadelphia, with little money of his own, he agonized for days before finally deciding to use the expense money given to him by the Provincial Congress to buy clothes. Meanwhile, among his fellow congressmen, his influence seemed to shrink.

Out of Sam's shadow stepped his cousin John. In speaking to the Continental Congress, he pushed hard, urging more than just support for Massachusetts. Times had vastly changed, he said. The sword had been drawn. The scabbard must be discarded. Not just Massachusetts, but every colony must now set up conventions to put in place independent governments.

The other delegates gasped. To many, independence was still a shocking idea. Adams, as he weighed in on the theme of independence, noted the expression of his audience and saw on many faces "horror, terror and detestation."[15]

Congress set aside Adams's idea of thirteen independent governments in thirteen independent colonies. But the delegates did go along with an independent government in Massachusetts "until a Governor of His Majesty's appointment will consent to govern the colony according to its charter."[16] The Continental Congress, still clinging to the idea of reconciliation, authorized an independent government only in Massachusetts, and that only temporarily.

The Continental Congress advised the Massachusetts Congress to conform as much as possible "to the spirit and substance" of its old charter before Parliament's attempt to alter it. Because the sitting royal governor and lieutenant governor were attempting to subvert the charter, they should not be obeyed, and the positions of governor and lieutenant governor should be considered vacant. The people should choose a new House of Representatives, and that House in turn should choose a Council. The House and Council then should govern the province together.

The Congress also agreed to take over the army in Massachusetts. Thus, while still seeking reconciliation with Britain, the Congress took control of a military force opposing British troops. Hand in hand with the decision to take over the army came the decision to choose a commander in chief for that army. Some were happy with Ward. He was in place and making progress in organizing the army. However, his health was uncertain.

Other names were tossed around. Perhaps Israel Putnam of Connecticut would do. Already in command of a Connecticut regiment now in Cambridge, Putnam was a war hero with plenty of military experience, gumption, and proven dedication to the patriot cause. But was Putnam, in his late fifties, too old for such a responsibility?

The name of Joseph Warren was mentioned. He was courageous, wholly dedicated, and highly respected. He had been in the thick of the shooting along the road between Lexington and Cambridge. However, his military experience was scant.

John Hancock's preference was John Hancock. At least that is what John Adams assumed. Probably Hancock would have jumped at the chance. After all, he had relished command of the Cadets in Boston. Furthermore, he had demonstrated his commitment to the cause–never mind that he had never actually seen battle or ordered men around while bullets were flying.

Another candidate was Charles Lee. Once an English officer, he became disillusioned and offered himself to the American cause. But he was an eccentric, which put some people off. Others wondered if this English transplant had the commitment required for the role of top commander.

Yet another candidate was George Washington. His military record was not stellar. He had fought under Braddock in Pennsylvania, but that expedition was a disaster. Indeed, Washington was on the losing side in every significant engagement in which he played a part. Even so, he knew what battle was like. He was tall, with a sterling character. He seemed a natural leader.

With the New England delegation unable to come together quickly on a choice, John Adams took matters in hand. This was urgent and critical. A good choice needed to be made fast. He understood that in the absence of a strong New England candidate, a southerner would be perfect as a symbol of unity among the colonies. Adams was impressed with Washington. Perhaps Adams had been moved by Washington's well-known offer earlier to raise and lead at his own expense a force of one thousand men to relieve Boston. Possibly Adams was also influenced by his colleagues back in Massachusetts. On June 4, in Watertown, Elbridge Gerry penned a letter to the Massachusetts delegation suggesting that Lee would not be suitable as general because "the pride of our people would prevent their submitting to be led by any general not an American."[17] However, Gerry liked Washington: "I should heartily rejoice to see this way the beloved colonel Washington, and do not doubt the New-England generals would acquiesce in showing to our sister colony Virginia, the respect, which she has before experienced from the continent, in making him generalissimo."[18]

Gerry said that Warren also favored Washington.

While on a walk with Sam Adams on June 14, John Adams announced his intention to nominate Washington. Sam was silent, clearly unenthused. To him, Washington's politics were suspect, leaning to moderation and a tendency to toy with reconciliation. Even so, Sam did not express dismay, and he knew of no perfect candidate, no American Cromwell blending radical passion and military genius.

At the session that day, John Adams stood and told the delegates that the man most qualified was right there among them, and that he was a man of independent wealth, "great talents," and excellent character. At this point, Hancock likely expected to hear his own name from his fellow Massachusetts delegate. Then, Adams said the candidate was from Virginia. Washington, embarrassed, slipped out of the chamber. Meanwhile, Hancock's face betrayed "mortification and resentment," according to Adams.[19] Or did Adams see what he expected to see? Hancock's later actions suggest that he fully accepted Washington's leadership and deeply admired the man. The next month, in a letter to Washington, Hancock asked for "some berth for me, in some department as you may judge most proper; for I am determined to act under you, if it be to take a firelock and join the ranks as a volunteer."[20] Later on, Hancock gave his only son the name John George Washington Hancock.

Once a motion was made to make Washington the commander, Sam Adams immediately, and significantly, seconded. Thus two

Massachusetts delegates pushed forward a Virginian to lead a New England army. Some delegates were unconvinced that Washington was the man for the job. Some pointed out that the army was now made up entirely of men from New England with a general from New England. Why put in place a new general? Paine and Cushing of Massachusetts saw no advantage of putting Washington in charge. Paine was confident that Ward could handle the responsibility. Cushing argued that New Englanders might grumble at taking orders from a "foreigner."[21]

The motion was set aside for the time being. But chatter between sessions indicated that Washington had widespread support. Those cool to the Virginian gave in, and on June 15, the nomination was sealed unanimously. Ward was made second in command and Lee third in command. Washington accepted the job, though protesting that he did not feel up to it.

Writing from Philadelphia to Gerry in Massachusetts, John Adams confessed his "great distress" about the appointments of Washington's top officers and especially with their pay: "I fear our people will think it extravagant." But Adams was altogether pleased with the appointment of Washington himself. Washington's conduct, Adams wrote, was "charming," made more appealing by his offer to serve without pay: "A gentleman of one of the first fortunes upon the Continent, leaving his delicious retirement, his family and friends, sacrificing his ease, and hazarding all in the cause of his Country! His views are noble and disinterested. He declared when he accepted the mighty trust, that he would lay before us an exact account of his expenses, and not accept a shilling for pay."[22]

Soon after appointing Washington, Congress sent Massachusetts ten companies of frontiersmen from Maryland, Pennsylvania, and Virginia. They would form with New Englanders Washington's army.

Back in Boston about this time, Gage finally declared martial law. This came in the form of a proclamation written with the help of Burgoyne, one of the three generals who had arrived in Boston by this time to give Gage a helping hand. Burgoyne wrote plays in his spare time and was thought to have some literary talent. Unintentionally, the proclamation displayed Burgoyne's skill at comic prose, especially when he sniffed at the American rebels for having "affected" to besiege the British army,[23] as if the army crammed in Boston were not really bottled up.

The proclamation announced that those armed against the regulars were "rebels and traitors." However, anyone who laid down their weapons might be forgiven–anyone, that is, except Sam Adams and John Hancock, whose crimes were of "too flagitious a nature" to justify pardons.[24]

The Provincial Congress shot back at Gage with its own generous offer of pardons to all who had fled into Boston for refuge and "to other public offenders against the rights and liberties of this country."[25] Excepted from this pardon were military men Gage and Graves, customs men Paxton and Hallowell, and Jonathan Sewall, attorney general. Sewall made the list apparently because he was assumed, incorrectly, to be the author of the Massachusettensis essays.

Elsewhere outside Boston, in the wake of the June declaration, newspapers attacked Gage with heightened virulence. The Reverend John Cleaveland of Ipswich, in an open letter to Gage in the *Essex Gazette*, didn't hold back:

> Thou profane, wicked monster of falsehood and perfidity . . . your late infamous proclamation is as full of notorious lies, as a toad or rattlesnake of deadly poison–you are an abandoned wretch. . . . Without speedy repentance, you will have an aggravated damnation in hell. . . . You are not only a robber, a murderer, and usurper but a wicked rebel: a rebel against the authority of truth, law, equity, the English constitution of government, these colony states, and humanity itself.[26]

From Salem, a writer under the pseudonym Sydney invited British soldiers and seamen to "become the glorious defenders of freedom, and join with the victorious Americans." Better that than serving Gage–"thief, robber, murderer, and common butcher of his fellow-men"–or Admiral Graves–"odious scoundrel"–who together were "the most vile and miserable wretches that ever disgraced the name of Briton."[27]

Years later, some would remember life in Boston during the siege as exciting and romantic at least some of the time. Sisters Mary and Catherine Byles, for example, would recall being serenaded by the regimental band and promenading on the Common, one on the arm of General Howe, the other on the arm of Lord Percy.

But for most, life was awful. Henry Pelham despaired over the ruin of his livelihood and hopes:

> I can't but think myself very unfortunate thus to have lost so much of the best part of my Life, to have my Bus[i]ness, upon which my happyness greatly depends, so abruptly cut short, all my bright prospects anialated, the little Property I had acquired rendered useless, myself doomed either to stay at home and starve, or leave my country my Fri[e]nds, forced to give up those flattering expectation of domestic felicity which I once fon[d]ly hoped to realize: to seek that Bread among strangers which I am thus cruelly deprived of at Home.[28]

Deaths from smallpox, dysentery, and other causes aggravated by hunger made funerals so frequent that according to Jonathan Sewall, "you meet as many dead folks as live ones on Boston streets."[29] Mourners, Sewall suggested, may have felt less sorrow than usual because every death meant a little more food for survivors.

In a letter to Thomas Hutchinson, Peter Oliver remarked, "The very rats are grown so familiar that they ask you to eat them."[30]

THIRTY-TWO

BREAST WORKS

About the time the Continental Congress decided to take over the New England army and appoint Washington, but well before word of these events reached Massachusetts, patriot leaders there toyed with the idea of grabbing the Charlestown Peninsula abandoned by the British. General Putnam, for one, wanted to seize the peninsula's 110-foot-high Bunker Hill. He was confident that if such a move drew the British out of Boston to meet the Americans in battle, the Americans would give the redcoats a good fight.[1] Certainly the American soldiers were eager for it. Though still roughly organized and poorly equipped, the men were spirited and looking for action. But Warren and Ward, among others, opposed the move to take Bunker Hill. The army was not equipped to hold such a position. The leaders finally decided to take both Bunker Hill on the Charlestown Peninsula north of Boston and Dorchester Heights on the Dorchester Peninsula south of Boston, but only when the military organization was more firmly in place and they had more gunpowder. So the Americans were content to hold tight a little bit longer to gain strength.

However, circumstances would force the Americans to move up their plan. By this time, with more British troops having arrived in Boston, Gage and his fellow generals felt confident they had the muscle to finally take and hold the high ground near Boston. They planned to start with Dorchester Heights to the south, a more important position than Bunker Hill because from Dorchester Heights the Americans could, besides firing on Boston, also lob cannonballs at ships in the harbor and thus cut off sea access to the town. But Gage and the British military still couldn't keep secrets. A "gentleman of undoubted veracity" who frequently talked with the "principal officers" in Gage's army leaked word that the British planned to move on "Dorchester and

Charlestown."[2] Word reached the Provincial Congress on June 13, five days before the operation on Dorchester Heights was to begin. The Congress decided the patriot army had to move first. On June 15, its committee of safety ordered its military leaders to seize and defend Bunker Hill now–despite the poor organization and shortage of powder. The committee chose Bunker Hill rather than Dorchester Heights probably because it seemed more of a natural extension of lines in place. A force on Dorchester Heights would have been somewhat isolated.

So soldiers mustered on Cambridge Common at about 6:00 p.m. on June 16. With them they had, according to a private, "one days provision and Blankets ready for a March somewhere, but we knew not where but we readily and cheerfully obeyed."[3] They also had tools for digging trenches, and at about 9:00 p.m., Colonel William Prescott, a forty-nine-year-old war veteran, led them on a march east to Charlestown Peninsula. Accompanying them were carriages with two cannon. Other soldiers as well as General Putnam joined the march, bringing the total number of troops to about twelve hundred.

Shaped like a triangle, the Charlestown Peninsula was about half the size of the peninsula that Boston occupied. The town of Charlestown was at the southern end, at the point closest to Boston. Besides Bunker Hill, on the northwest part of the peninsula, other elevations included Moulton's Point, a thirty-five-foot mound on the east side, and, in the center of the peninsula, a sixty-two-foot elevation with no agreed-upon name. Part of it was known as Breed's Pasture. After the battle it became known as Breed's Hill. Each of these elevations and the lands around them were grassy fields with many rail fences and a few trees.

After crossing the Charlestown Neck, the column stopped and the men were told their mission. Sixty men were sent off to deserted Charlestown to hide and watch British movements. The rest went on to Bunker Hill, where officers gathered to decide where exactly to start digging in. Bunker Hill seemed to be the prudent choice. It was close enough to the Neck to prevent the British from cutting them off from the rest of the American lines. It also offered a commanding position over vessels on the Charles and Mystic rivers. Furthermore, civilian leaders had specifically identified Bunker Hill. To dig in somewhere else was technically against orders.

But was Bunker Hill close enough to Boston to be a threat? Probably not. So if the purpose of the mission was to alarm British commanders and force them to attack, the Americans needed to dig in farther south, closer to Boston. Thus, after about thirty minutes of talk and probably at the urging of Putnam, officers decided to entrench at Breed's Hill, shorter by thirty-five feet but closer to Boston. Digging began about midnight. Working quietly so as not to alert sailors on nearby British vessels, the men fashioned trenches and walls to enable them to stand behind a barrier about chin high. The entire redoubt was about square, 130 feet on each side, with several projections to permit the Americans to shoot attacking soldiers pressed close to the walls.

Histories of the Battle of Bunker Hill typically suggest that the British were clueless about patriot activity on the Charlestown Peninsula until dawn. But a recent history by James L. Nelson asserts that the British knew something was up the night before, and that General Clinton recommended action but was ignored.[4]

And what did the Americans know of British activities in Boston? We know they were getting some intelligence from inside Boston on the very eve of battle thanks to a daring young woman. Hannah Mather, who as a girl had guided her uncle, Thomas Hutchinson, to shelter during the Stamp Act riots, was by this time twenty-three, single, and still living with her parents in Boston. Also, though a niece of the former royal governor, she had cast her lot by now with the patriot side. According to her tale told many years later, the family had applied for a pass to leave the town, but her father was not allowed to go. He was a hostage, a general admitted to Mather, adding, "and you had better stay my dear and you will be protected." She shot back: "I am a free born American and will go for free air."[5]

So that's what she did. At sunset on June 16, she and her baggage arrived at the last ferry for Charlestown. She also carried from her father "dispatches in her bossom" intended for Warren. She knew the captain in charge of inspecting outbound goods. Handing the captain the keys to her trunks, she said (if her memory is to be believed), "You may search my trunks, but don't storm my breast works." He opened one trunk, returned the keys, and responded in the only way a gallant gentleman could: "Madam your word is enough to satisfy me."[6] Mather found her way to Watertown and delivered the dispatches to Warren at about 9:00 p.m.

With the dawn of June 17, the British stirred. At early light, about 4:00 a.m., sailors aboard the warship *Lively* spotted the Americans digging away. A cannon from the *Lively* let loose a shot. Firing soon commenced from other vessels and from Copp's Hill in Boston. The entrenchments were far enough advanced that the British guns had little effect. The Americans kept working to improve, strengthen, and extend the fortifications.

In Boston, Gage, his generals, and his Council met. They decided to discard the Dorchester plan for the moment to deal with the Charlestown Peninsula, where the American position was becoming stronger with every passing minute. They immediately agreed that the Americans had to be swept off Breed's Hill. But how?

Several generals and most of the councillors wanted to land troops at Charlestown Neck and thus cut off the Americans on Breed's Hill from retreat. Gage didn't like the plan. It would put the British troops between two American forces, one larger than the British force and the other behind entrenchments. There was also a vague feeling that such an approach–to trap the Americans–was in some way dishonorable. The consensus of the British military leaders favored straightforward frontal assault on the American position. Howe would direct it; Burgoyne and Clinton would handle support from the Boston batteries. Troops would be rowed over at high tide, some seven hours away. The military leaders thus had plenty of time to send out observers or go themselves to reconnoiter the American position. But they didn't bother. Confident that the disciplined, trained redcoats would send the Americans scampering with the first smart volley, the generals planned in ignorance of the full extent of American defenses and of the many rail fences that would hinder the British advance. In their ignorance, they also failed to take full advantage of their naval supremacy. Had they taken the trouble to gather more information, they could have better positioned naval guns in the waters around the peninsula to demolish the patriot army.

As the British generals pored over maps, cannonballs rained down on Breed's Hill from five warships, several floating batteries, and Boston. Meanwhile, Prescott, amid this hail of iron, took a long look in daylight at his own position. He recognized that he was especially vulnerable to an attack from the east. With British cannonballs whistling by, men were ordered to build a new breastwork extending toward the Mystic River. The shooting was too fierce for the Americans to dig all the way to the river. However, parallel to the breastwork and a little ways north was a rail fence that could serve as a kind of flimsy barrier where patriot soldiers could be positioned. Between the breastwork and the rail fence was a two-hundred-yard gap, a weak point where attackers could pour through.

Inevitably, one of the cannonballs hit a soldier. The death of Private Asa Pollard shattered a few nerves. The courage of some erstwhile patriots evaporated, and a few slunk away. To stiffen backbones, Prescott strutted atop the works, making inspections, directing the men, but mainly demonstrating indifference to the balls flying in. The work continued, and the bombardment was mostly noise and smoke.

Across the Charles, Gage peered through field glasses and spotted Prescott. A story goes that Gage gave the glasses to a Tory councillor nearby to identify the officer. "He is my brother-in-law," said the councillor.

"Will he fight?" the general asked.

"I cannot answer for his men," the councillor said. "But Prescott will fight you to the gates of hell!"[7]

As the morning passed, the day heated up. The Americans in the trenches, joined by at least some of the men dispatched to

An engraving of the British bombardment of the American positions on and near Breed's Hill and the burning of Charlestown. (*Library of Congress*)

Charlestown, were drained. Private Peter Brown wrote, "We began to be almost beat out, being fatigued by our Labour, having no sleep the night before, very little to eat, no drink but rum, but what we hazarded our lives to get, we grew faint, Thirsty, hungry and weary." Brown also confessed that many of the common soldiers now suspected treachery and "that we were brought there all to be slain."[8]

Officers suggested to Prescott that the men should be relieved. The men, Prescott said, would stay and fight: "They had the merit of the labor, and should have the honor of the victory."[9] At nine in the morning, Prescott's officers again urged relief for the men who had been working all night. Prescott still balked, but he went along with a call for provisions and more troops.

Israel Putnam was also concerned with troop numbers. He rode off to Ward's headquarters in Cambridge to plead for more men. Ward demurred, nervous about an attack anywhere along the thin American lines. He didn't think he had men to spare. Putnam left, returned to Breed's Hill, talked with Prescott, and went back to Cambridge to again make his plea. Ward gave in a little. He gave orders for two hundred men to add to the numbers on Breed's Hill.

Prescott later sent yet another request, this time with Major John Brooks. Incredibly, however, Brooks was unable to obtain a horse. He asked for an artillery horse, held in ready to pull field pieces away. But the artillery captain turned him down. Brooks left for Cambridge on foot!

Brooks finally arrived at Cambridge at 10:00 a.m. Ward held firm but was willing to pass the question on to the Provincial Committee of Safety, which was meeting in the same house, Ward's headquarters. Finally, probably about noon, orders went out for more men to be sent to the Charlestown Peninsula.

Meanwhile, the men on Breed's Hill, waiting vainly for water, food, or relief under bright, cloudless skies, peeked nervously from time to time over at Boston, where clusters of people were gathering on rooftops and redcoats were preparing to cross the Charles.

General Putnam advised Prescott that entrenching tools should be taken away so they didn't get lost. Prescott warned that men taking away such tools would never return. Putnam insisted. Every man would come back, he said. So a call for volunteers was made. "An order was never obeyed with more readiness," recalled Ebenezer Bancroft, a captain in the patriot army. "From every part of the line volunteers ran and some picked up one, some two shovels, mattocks, &c., and hurried over the hill."[10] Some returned, but many did not.

Now the men remaining in the redoubt had no tools. In positioning cannon, men dug with their hands. "[M]any of them dug till their fingers bled," wrote Bancroft.[11]

Soon the remaining men saw boats heavily loaded with fully equipped regulars approaching a point on the peninsula, then landing and deploying. But no attack came. Not yet. Howe decided he needed more men. That would delay the attack another two hours. This would give the Americans just enough extra time for supporting troops ordered to Breed's Hill to arrive. They included Warren. The Provincial Congress had just appointed him general. But at Breed's Hill, Warren insisted on serving as a common soldier.

That morning, Warren had had a headache and was feverish after a sleepless night. He confided to Elbridge Gerry, his colleague and his roommate in Cambridge, about his intention to join the militiamen. Gerry said it would be madness for Warren to expose himself. But Warren seemed determined to be a martyr. "Dulce et decorum est pro patria mori," he said–It is sweet and becoming to die for the country.[12]

Over these hours, the British navy positioned vessels around the Charlestown Peninsula, and Gage added to guns firing from Boston. Before noon, British guns were firing from seven directions at Charlestown Neck and the trenches on Breed's Hill. The effect was terrifying, but it didn't stop determined patriot soldiers from passing over the Neck, nor did it stop soldiers from continuing to dig in. At the makeshift rail fence breastwork, the Americans added rails from other fences and stuffed gaps with hay.

After the arrival of redcoat reinforcements and a leisurely lunch, Howe finally set about arranging the attack. He had brought over cannon but couldn't find stable ground for them on the marshy soil.

Besides, most of the cannonballs sent over were too big for the weapons. So for the most part, the initial attack had no artillery support.

Howe chose to attack on two fronts–one directly at the main redoubt that the Americans had worked all night to construct and the other against the reinforced rail fence. The soldiers assigned for the assaults were well equipped, indeed too well equipped. Their gear included blankets and rations for three days. Historians have figured each soldier carried 125 pounds of equipment uphill, in the heat, in tall grass, with fences here and there to step over.[13]

Joseph Warren, after a portrait by John Singleton Copley. (*Library of Congress*)

All was finally in readiness. About twelve hours after the *Lively* alerted Boston to the Americans on Breed's Hill, the advance to sweep the Americans away began. Howe had twenty-three hundred troops. They faced maybe twenty-five hundred to thirty-five hundred Americans. With all the confusion, with many Americans deserting, and other Americans coming in to join the fight, the exact number will never be known.

As the regulars advanced, starting around 4:00 p.m., they halted from time to time to fire a volley, but to little effect. When a few isolated shots came from the American side, Prescott and other officers at the redoubt leapt up in front and kicked at the muzzles, roaring at the men to hold fire. At the rail fence, Putnam threatened to cut down any man who fired. A white stake had been driven into the ground some distance in front of the fence. Firing could begin, the men were told, only after the regulars passed that stake.

For civilians viewing from Boston rooftops, smoke rising from Charlestown about this time heightened the drama of the unfolding attack. With his men harassed by shots from Americans still hiding in the abandoned town, Howe had ordered the town burned to the ground.

The courage of the remaining men in the redoubt began to falter when they saw the redcoats marching toward them. The men looked around. Where were the reinforcements? Where were their comrades who had vanished with the tools? "It was an awful moment," Bancroft recalled. When the redcoats had reached about half the distance toward the redoubt, "our men seeing no reinforcements began by a simultaneous movement to draw off from the east side of the redoubt."

They were a heartbeat from taking off and rushing away through the opening and over the walls of the back of the earthen structure. Bancroft recalled, "This, in my opinion, was the very crisis of the day, the moment on which every thing depended." According to Bancroft, he and Prescott spoke to the men. They didn't claim that they could actually hold off the redcoats. They just asked the men not to dishonor themselves by fleeing "at the bare sight of the enemy," and that "we had no expectation of being able to hold our ground, but we wanted to give them a warm reception, and retreat."[14]

This seemed to satisfy the men. They stayed put. As the redcoats came closer, Prescott advised the men to take particular aim at the "fine coats"–the officers.[15]

At the redoubt and at the rail fence, the Americans at last opened fire and kept firing, with deadly results. Many officers crumpled to the ground. The regulars held, fired, but then pulled back.

Another assault was quickly organized. The regulars advanced, stepping over the bodies of the fallen. The Americans held their fire, waiting for the redcoats to approach even closer than before. When the American order to fire came, the results were bloodier, and again the officers were the prime targets. Those who survived cruelly prodded the men forward, striking soldiers with the hilts of their swords, or even jabbing them with the blades. The men obeyed. Some fell dead within yards of the Americans. But, as with the first attack, the regulars fell back.

Howe bravely led his men from the front, a servant close at hand to keep him well supplied with wine and other refreshments. Amazingly, the general was not killed, but he did have a wine bottle shot out of his hand. After this and the failure of the second assault, Howe soberly revised his strategy. He ordered a third assault. But this time the men could leave their knapsacks behind. Also, instead of marching into battle in rows–making each man an easy target–he ordered that the attack be made in columns focused on the redoubt by way of its weakest point, the gap between the breastwork and the rail fence. No assault would be made on the fence. Also, further reinforcements were sent over. They and other British troops would be flung at the redoubt to make, with Howe's advance, a three-sided attack. Furthermore, and against the advice of the artillery officers, Howe ordered the cannons to be moved to solid ground closer to the American lines. At last he would have artillery support.

On the American side, fresh troops arrived, passing other troops leaving the battlefield. Order was crumbling.

The British artillery proved instantly effective. Its first shots against the American position scattered militiamen in the redoubt. More men started fleeing the battlefield. With powder running out, Prescott saw

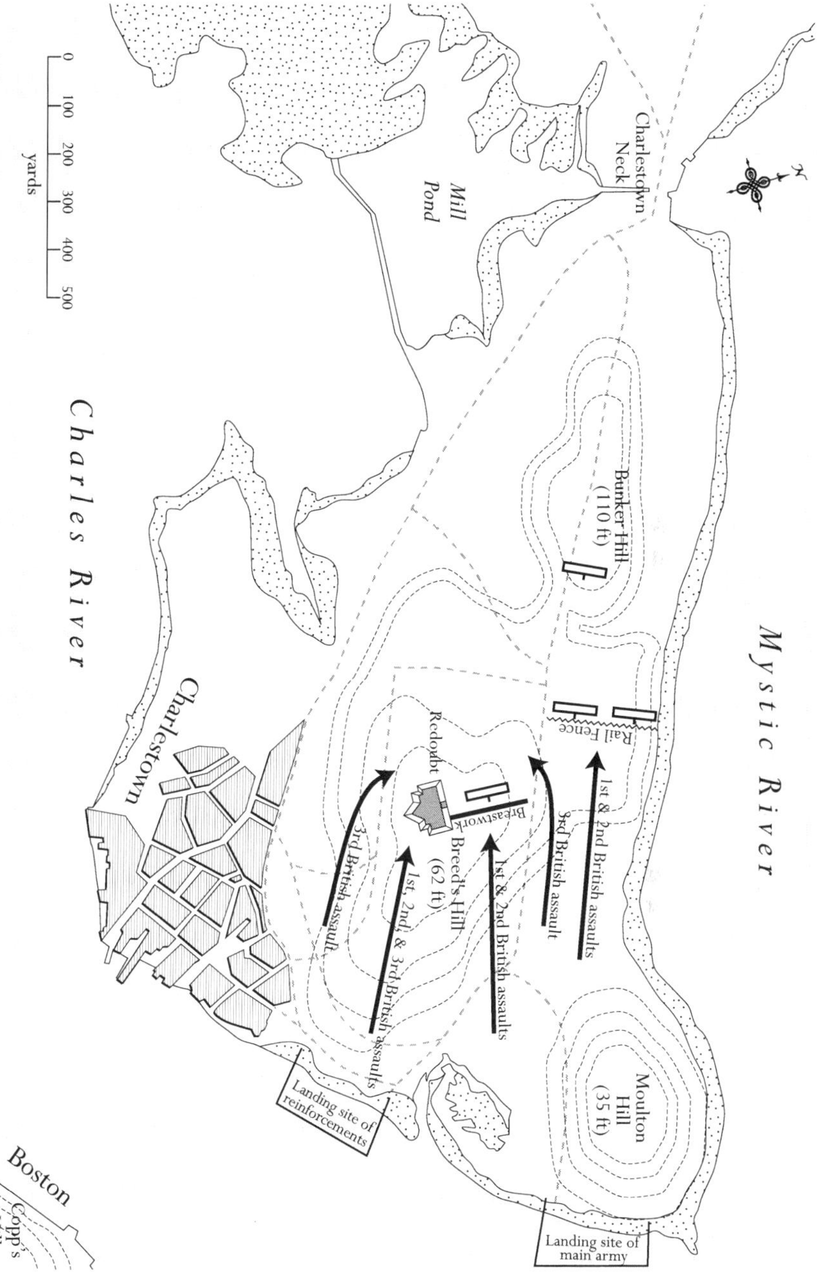

Map 6. Bunker Hill, June 17, 1775.

little hope against the advancing columns. Still, many stayed put. The remaining powder was distributed. Some men had enough for just a single shot.

The men held their fire until the head of the columns came within twenty yards. When the order to fire came, the brave, doomed regulars at the front of the columns fell. But the columns continued to advance, reaching the parapet.

With his men out of powder and the regulars about to overwhelm the redoubt, Prescott finally ordered a retreat. Some defied the order and continued to fight, even with stones. Most got away, despite the overwhelming odds. The regulars, closing in from three sides, were reluctant to fire for fear of hitting their own men. Also, the regulars, spent from the uphill climb in the heat, failed to vigorously pursue the retreating Americans, who enjoyed some protection from the men at the rail fence.

Bancroft recalled his hasty retreat. With the redoubt full of British soldiers, he held his gun "broadwise" and charged, knocking several redcoats down. After losing his gun, he then "leaped upon the heads of the throng" in the redoubt opening and was struck in the shoulder by the butt of a gun. He eventually broke away. "A shower of shot was falling all around as I ran down the hill. One struck off my hat, several marked my clothes, one struck me in the left hand, and carried off the forefinger."[16]

By 5:00 p.m., the battle was over. Among the Americans, 138 were killed, 276 wounded, and 36 missing. In the battlefield wreckage, the British found cannons that were once aboard the *Diana*. Among the dead was Warren, the lone member of Boston's radical leadership to die in battle. Among the last to leave the redoubt, he was shot in the head during the retreat. A British captain later said he "stuffed the scoundrel with another rebel into one hole, and there he and his seditious principles may remain."[17] Many months later, Paul Revere and two of Warren's brothers exhumed the body. Revere identified it by the artificial teeth he had fitted for the doctor.

On the British side, 228 were killed on the battlefield or died of wounds later. One of the dead was Pitcairn, felled by one of the last American shots. An additional 826 regulars suffered wounds but survived.

In Boston, Loyalists gathered up everything on wheels–coaches, carriages, even wheelbarrows–and brought them to the waterside to help carry the dead, dying, and wounded rowed over from the battlefield. "[L]ikewise all the physicians, surgeons, and apothecaries of Boston instantly attended the wounded officers, and gave them every assistance in their power," according to a narrative of John Clarke, a British lieutenant.[18]

Loyalist civilians took in the wounded. Captain David Johnston later credited Dorcas Griffiths and Sarah Hinson, mother and daughter prostitutes, with saving his life. "I must have died on the Street" had not Griffiths and Hinson "taken me into their house. I therefore owe my life to their humanity."[19] The women nursed other sick and wounded officers as well, as later attested by General Gage.

Decades later, shoemaker Hewes would recall watching bodies of British soldiers being "chucked" into a pit on the Common.[20] Initially, the results of the battle disheartened both sides. Customs Commissioner Hulton, writing of the battle, seethed: "[I]t grieves one, that gentlemen, brave British soldiers should fall by the hands of such despicable wretches. So compose the banditti of the country; amongst them there is not one that has the least pretention to be called a gentleman. They are a most rude, depraved, degenerate race."[21]

To the British, the battle was frightfully costly and demonstrated both the skills of the Americans and their will to fight. To the Americans, the battle was, in the end, a defeat that exposed their weaknesses: poor organization, lack of equipment, faulty communications. Especially inexcusable was the complete failure at supplying reinforcements, powder, or even water and provisions to the defenders of Breed's Hill. In the wake of the battle–the Battle of Bunker Hill, as it has always been called–the Americans were not only discouraged but also confused and panicky. After the battle, as British cannon fired balls at various American fortifications near Boston, military leaders and civilians braced for British regulars to emerge from the town any hour to smash the patriot army. On the day of the battle, Abigail Adams wrote from Braintree, "It is expected they [British regulars] will come out over the Neck tonight, and a dreadful battle must ensue."[22] For men in the Provincial Congress, it was a chaotic, fearful time. The death of Joseph Warren was hugely unsettling and a great personal loss to those who knew and admired him. We can believe Sam Adams deeply grieved, although his remarks seem stiff. Adams wrote to his wife, "The death of our truly amiable and worthy friend, Dr. Warren, is greatly afflicting."[23]

The death also created a huge void in the revolutionary leadership. As president of the Provincial Congress, Joseph Warren had been at the center of everything. The Congress quickly elected a new president, another, though unrelated, Warren. James Warren, in Watertown, scribbled a frantic letter to his wife, Mercy, in Plymouth: "It is Impossible to describe the Confusion in this place, Women and Children flying into the Country, armed Men Going to the field, and wounded Men returning from there fill the Streets." James Warren hinted to Mercy to be prepared to flee with their children: "I feel for my Dear Wife, lest her Apprehensions should hurt her health, be not concerned about me, take care of your Self. You can secure a retreat and have proper Notice in Season, and if you are safe and the Boys I shall be happy fall what will to my Interest." His thoughts leap from firearms to fruit: "I hear nothing yet but the roaring of Cannon below, but no Body regards them. I need not say that I long to see you, perhaps never more in my life. I shall try hard for it this week. I hope your Strawberries are well taken care of and that you have fine feasting on them."[24]

Amid the panic and chaos before and after Bunker Hill, the Provincial Congress juggled all the roles of government–executive, legislative, and even judicial–and matters great and small, authorizing the seizure of a vessel at Salem; ordering that a lunatic be committed; asking Paul Revere, now busy as an engraver for the Congress, to work nonstop to produce dubious currency to pay the troops; approving the disabling of coastal lighthouses; directing that a certain mother and child be taken from Watertown to Newbury and cared for at the province's expense.

Despite fears, the British did not come out to rout the confused Americans, and the standoff resumed with the British shut up in Boston and the Americans dug in at various positions around the town: just east of Cambridge, on Prospect Hill between Charlestown and Cambridge, on Winter Hill near Charlestown Neck, at Roxbury guarding the approach to Boston Neck, and elsewhere. Periodically, British guns would lob cannonballs at these fortifications, doing little damage but sending hearts aflutter. Coordination and communications among these posts were erratic and haphazard. Each position operated virtually independently. The inefficiency and disorganization was evident to all.

On cue, Washington arrived on the scene. In Watertown, the Massachusetts Congress formally received the general with a congratulatory address on July 2. Later the same day, Washington moved on to Cambridge, college town turned military headquarters. The students were gone. After dismissing students on May 1, the college handed over its buildings to the Provincial Congress. Students were told to reassemble in Concord come fall.

Apparently, Washington's arrival in Cambridge was not marked by any ceremony, no columns of troops lining the way, no committee of greeters to receive him. No one knew quite when the general was arriving. Some had expected him the day before, and so soldiers were then marched out in readiness. But on this rainy day, no preparations had been made. Someone directed Washington and his entourage to the Wadsworth House, the home of Harvard's president. The college president kept a room for himself, but the rest of the house was for Washington and the other military people.

The next day, July 3, Washington took command of a force that had no agreed-upon name. To some it was the Continental Army. To others it was the New England Army or the Army at Boston. The Continental Congress had used the term Army of the United Colonies. Washington called his men "Troops of the United Provinces of North America."[25]

What did common soldiers think of Washington's arrival? One wrote for July 2: "This day the Hon. George Washington, esq., commander-in-chief of the united forces in America, arrived in Cambridge. This afternoon had rain."[26] Another soldier scribbled the same day in his diary that "ginrale Washenton arived at Cambridge with 80 horses."[27] Private Haws wrote nothing about the momentous event. His journal for the first three days of July:

> the 1. Nothing remarkable this day.
> the 2. Dito.
> the 3. Dito.[28]

Abigail Adams soon met the commander and swooned. To John, she wrote: "You had prepared me to entertain a favorable opinion of him, but I thought the one half was not told me. Dignity with ease, and complacency, the Gentleman and Soldier look agreeably blended in him. Modesty marks every line and feature of his face."[29]

James Warren, as he saw Washington in action, was likewise in awe: "He is certainly the best man for the place he is in, important that it is, that ever lived."[30]

Among soldiers, however, Washington faced some resentment. Some sentries balked at permitting him to pass. Some officers refused to believe he was the commander in chief. Washington bought himself a ribbon to wear to set himself apart from other commanders.

Washington tried quickly to sort out leadership roles, but when he appointed Putnam as his fourth major general, another Connecticut officer quit in disgust. Taken aback and now understanding how jealousies and rivalries among commanders could doom the army, Washington determined to take more time in making such key appointments.

Meanwhile, he sought to instill some discipline and integrity among lower-ranking officers with a blizzard of demotions: a colonel and two captains for cowardice at Bunker Hill, two captains for drawing pay and provisions for men they didn't have in their companies, and a captain for being absent when the enemy appeared.

As to the rank and file, Washington soon discovered that the men were uniformly lacking in uniformity. A clergyman observed this and found it charming:

> It is very diverting to walk among the camps. They are as different in their form as the owners are in their dress; and every tent is a portraiture of the temper and taste of the persons who encamp in it. Some are made of bords, and some of sailcloth. Some partly of one and partly of another. Again others are made

> of stone and turf, brick or brush. Some are thrown up in a hurry, others curiously wrought with doors and windows, done in wreaths and withes in the manner of a basket. Some are your proper tents and marquees, looking like the regular camp of the enemy. . . . However, I think this great variety is rather a beauty than a blemish in the army.[31]

For Washington, the motley scene did not inspire confidence. He wanted uniforms for the men. Short of that, he wanted them to at least wear hunting shirts that looked more or less the same. He believed that clothes of the same kind have "a happy tendency to unite the men, and abolish those provincial distinctions, that lead to jealousy and dissatisfaction."[32] Washington also sought to bring some sort of standardization to firearms but made little progress during his months in Massachusetts.

Frustrating Washington at every step was a lack of information. How many men did he have? He expected an answer in an hour. He waited eight days. He had expected twenty thousand. He learned he had just fourteen thousand fit for duty.

Even with these disappointing numbers, Washington still had twice the force Gage had. Washington didn't know this, though. He believed Gage had about eleven thousand men. Fearing the British at any time might emerge from Boston to strike anywhere along the ten-mile arc of the American front, Washington focused on strengthening and finishing fortifications.

Along that front, sentries on both sides peered at each other but, in some places at least, genteelly held their fire when enemy soldiers within range weren't threatening. A July letter from a Rhode Island soldier described an incident involving a party of regulars cutting down trees within range of American sentries. The writer, Colonel William T. Miller, beckoned a British major for a chat: "I told him that his conduct in felling the timber so near our sentries created a jealousy, and desired him to desist from any further encroachments." The major replied: "[H]e told me he thought the trees, &c., which they were getting, were as near their lines as they were to ours, and that they had not interrupted our men in cutting hay close to the lines; and he promised me he would advance no further."[33]

Another American, a lieutenant, recorded frequent get-togethers with their British counterparts under flags of truce. These meetings were so cordial, the lieutenant "proposed to them to erect a coffee house for the convenience of such occasional conferences, upon which we held a considerable banter with good humor on both sides."[34]

But such civility was never a sure thing. After one skirmish, an American private noted in his diary, "Between sunset and dark we killed fourteen of those who came out to pick up their dead."[35]

Washington scrounged for supplies, especially gunpowder and muskets. Stocks of powder were enough for about nine rounds per man. The severity of the shortage was hidden from the men, which is partly why some amused themselves by shooting at passing geese. Orders were issued to stop such diversions. Washington was terrified that the British would learn of this shortage and overrun his army. He launched a rumor that he had eighteen hundred barrels of gunpowder, when he had only thirty-six. In about three weeks, enough additional powder was rounded up to supply each man with thirty cartridges. Washington could relax a little and think not just about defense, but also about an attack.

THIRTY-THREE

SUBURBS OF HELL

In Boston, the shortage of hay doomed the town cows. They, along with the town bull, were killed for meat, ending the supply of milk. A British officer, writing to England in August, said food shortages and deaths, as well as "insolence" of a "number of Scotch officers," had produced "inconceivable discontent" among the troops:

> With regard to diet, we are obliged to live on salt beef and salt pork, much the greater part of which is as hard as wood, as lean as carion, and as rusty as the devil. Could we have good beer, it would, in some measure, prevent their pernicious effects and alleviate the hardships we labour under; but that is impossible, our only beverage being new rum or spruce liquor, which soon throws us into the bloody flux and runs us off our legs in a few days, and has made the remains of our famished army look like so many regiments of skeletons. Could you view our hospitals and see how fast we drop off, your very heart would bleed within you. Thirty bodies are frequently thrown into a trench at a time, like those of so many dogs, no bell being suffered to toll upon the occasion. [Boston] may very justly be termed the grave of England and the slaughter house of America. Nothing is to be heard in it but execrations and clamour; nothing is to be seen but distractions and melancholy, disease and death. The soldiery, and inhabitants likewise, I am sure have done sufficient penance here for the sins of their whole lives.

The officer also confessed that the troops lived in terror of a vengeful attack by the Americans: "If we hear a gun fired upon the Neck, we are all under arms in a moment, and tremble least the Provincials should force their way into the town and put us all to the sword for the cruelty at Lexington and setting fire to the large, ancient and flourishing town of Charlestown. Certainly our conduct at both places was alike inhuman and unjustifiable; and if heaven punishes us for it, it is no more than we deserve."

Determined to resign his commission, the officer said the soldiers would all flee if they could: "'Tis well for our generals that we have no where to run to; for could the men desert, I am of the opinion that they would soon be left by themselves; but situated as we are, we must unavoidably live and die together."[1]

The Americans posted outside Boston, aware of the misery in town, encouraged British soldiers to run away. Handbills, fed into the wind to blow into the hands of British sentries, succinctly compared conditions at Prospect Hill, the American post, with those at Bunker Hill, held by the British. At Prospect Hill: "I. Seven dollars a month. II. Fresh provisions and in plenty. III. Health. IV. Freedom, ease, affluence, and a good farm." At Bunker Hill: "I. Three pence a day. II. Rotten salt pork. III. The scurvy. IV. Slavery, beggary, and want."[2]

As for civilians trapped in Boston, everyone faced disruption and disaster of one kind or another and agonizing choices. Henry Pelham was one. He desperately wanted to leave Boston but felt he could not leave his mother behind. "I am entirely at loss to know what to Do," wrote Pelham to his half-brother, John Singleton Copley. "The Total Stoppage of Business forbids me remaining here, and how to leave the place I don't know. My Hon'd Mother not inclining to undertake a Voyage and to leave her in so disagreeable a Situation would make me very uneasy."[3]

Pelham also confessed about other hopes "blasted" since the "fatal Era of the Tea's arrival." He wrote that "Miss Sally Bromfield" was "the Object of my Highest Esteem and Regard." He never confessed his love to Sally, and now he felt he never could because it would be "totally unbecoming a generous mind, under Such circumstances as mine, to disturb a Lady's repose by soliciting a Return of that Regard and attention which my Present situation forbids me to expect."[4]

Hewes, the shoemaker supporting himself by fishing, slipped out of town. After hiding his shoemaking tools in a borrowed fishing boat, he and two friends sailed off to nearby Lynn. After landing, Hewes was quickly brought before Washington, who quizzed him about conditions in Boston.

Many remaining Whigs in Boston found themselves under suspicion. Some were jailed, including schoolteachers John Leach and James Lovell and printers Peter Edes and John Gill. Edes, teenage son of Gill's partner, Benjamin Edes, was charged with concealing firearms and fed only bread and water. Other prisoners included "Soldier prisoners, and Sundry Soldier women," according to Edes's diary: "We had Some of the vilest women for our neighbours ever known, Some placed over our heads, and Some in rooms each Side of us. They acted Such Scenes as was Shocking to nature, and they used language horrible to hear, as if it came from the very Suburbs of Hell."[5]

John Leach, who taught a navigation school in Boston (he had been around the world three times before settling in Boston at age twenty-seven), was in jail several weeks before finally being charged with spying and "taking plans." Leach's wife tried to visit often but at first was turned away. Once, she smuggled a note to her husband in the toe of a stocking. Her message: Mrs. B, from out in the country, had recovered from smallpox. Eventually, jailers eased up. On one visit, she brought along seven of their children (she gave birth to seventeen!).

Other inmates included a baker confined for "speaking saucy" to an officer;[6] a certain Lucy Purham for "attempting to set the town on fire";[7] a "poor insane man" suspected of stealing;[8] a boy of about sixteen, put in a "dungeon" in irons on suspicion that he helped hide a man;[9] and an "old Dutchman" for complaining that soldiers had pilfered from his garden.[10] William Dorrington, with a son, daughter, and maid (or nurse) were in jail for "blowing up flies." Dorrington kept a smallpox hospital on Boston's west end. "Blowing up flies" was apparently a way of killing insects by setting off small explosions with gunpowder. Dorrington was probably employing the technique to cleanse some hospital rooms of bugs. British authorities, however, thought these evening explosions were meant as signals to the Americans.[11] Yet another inmate, a "most unhappy, wicked wretch,"[12] was the man who tried to kill the British officers and then brandished a sword at the Provincial Congress.

Also among the inmates were prisoners from the Battle of Bunker Hill. Many were wounded, and all were dreadfully neglected. Edes's entry for August 19:

> The poor Sick and wounded prisoners fare very hard; are many days without the comforts of life. Dr. Brown told us that they had no bread all day and the day before. He Spoke to the provost, as he had the charge of Serving the bread, who replied, let them eat the heads of the nails, and knaw the planks, and be damn'd. . . . They have no wood to burn for many days together to warm their drink, and dying men drink them cold. Some of the limbs which have been taken off it is Said, were in a State of putrifaction and not one Survived amputation.[13]

Of twenty-nine American prisoners held in the jail, eighteen were dead by September 21. Edes was released after 107 days.

More Tories toyed with leaving Boston and America altogether. One was Ralph Inman, who was thinking of sailing off to England and leaving his wife, Elizabeth, behind. Elizabeth, still living outside Boston, got wind of this in late July: "If this is the return for the many fatiguing days I have had, I leave to your better Judgement."[14] She didn't beg him to stay, nor did she beg to go with him.

By this time she was far from Cambridge. At sunset on the day of the Battle of Bunker Hill, she fled her husband's estate for a family farm south of Boston and farther away from the theater of war. Helping her and her family on her way was Daniel Putnam, under orders from his father to do just that. They left Cambridge at sunset on the day of the battle, arriving at the farm near Milton around midnight.

The Inman estate was quickly taken over by General Putnam, who made it his headquarters. The house became "barrack number one." The trees on the property soon vanished. Rickety barracks took their place.[15]

On the very day of the Battle of Bunker Hill, the Provincial Congress in Watertown got word from Philadelphia about establishing a civil government. Then, amid the military planning and all the other matters, the Watertown Congress set in motion the transition to a new government structured in the manner recommended by the Continental Congress. The Provincial Congress came together for the last time on July 19. Just over a month later, on August 23, the new Massachusetts government–gathering at the same meetinghouse in Watertown–approved its first act, declaring all the actions by the old Provincial Congress "lawful and valid."[16] James Warren, who had been president of the old Provincial Congress, was chosen speaker of the new House of Representatives. A second lawmaking house, the Council–selected by the House–met in a nearby residence. The House authorized the Council to perform the function of governor because "the late governor and deputy governor of the province have absented themselves and have refused to govern the province according to the charter."[17] The House and Council gradually put in place judicial courts. A civil government came to life, similar to the royal government of years past but with no royally appointed governor. All authority stemmed from the elected House of Representatives.

As for the Continental Congress, it adjourned on August 1 with plans to meet again September 1. As soon as Congress broke up, Hancock made a beeline to Fairfield and into the arms of Dolly. Finally, he asked her to marry him. They set a date: August 28. Hancock then dashed off to Watertown, arriving August 10. Two weeks later he was off again. Like a proper suitor, he visited Dolly's father, Edmund Quincy, who had fled Boston and found refuge in Lancaster, Massachusetts, about thirty miles west of Watertown. Quincy gave Hancock his blessing, but he was not healthy enough to make the journey to Fairfield for the wedding, so Hancock went on without him. In Fairfield, Dolly and John finally married. They were off the next day to Philadelphia in time for the next session of the Continental Congress.

John Adams, for one, was amazed. He wrote that "two of the most unlikely Things within the Compass of Possibility, have really and actually happened."[18] One was Hancock's marriage. The other had to do with Sam Adams.

About the same time Hancock and his new bride were on their way to Philadelphia, John and Sam Adams were on their way too. On the second day of the journey from Watertown, John persuaded Sam to leave his chaise and ride a "very genteel and easy little Creature." This was something of a triumph for John. Sam, living most of his life within Boston, had few opportunities to ride, didn't like it, and wasn't much good at it. John had lectured his older cousin on the importance of horsemanship. Riding was good for one's health, John said. Besides, John thought a good statesman ought to know how to look manly and capable on horseback.[19]

So for about the next three hundred miles, Sam rode and, to John's amazement, proved quite adept: "We beheld, an easy, genteel Figure upon the Horse." John had yet more to teach. Sam still didn't know how to get on and off a horse by himself. He required two servants, one to hold the bridle and stirrup, the other to give him a boost. As John wrote, "This was rather a ridiculous Circumstance still." So John gave Sam detailed instructions. "The Experiment was tried and Succeeded to Admiration."[20]

In Philadelphia, all thirteen colonies were fully represented for the first time, as Georgia, feebly represented by a single delegate from a single parish, now had a proper delegation. For the two Adamses, this was a delicate moment. They wanted a declaration of independence. After all, the war had started. What were they waiting for? But moderates still held out hope for some miraculous reconciliation, and now many moderates were in a sour mood thanks to a blunder by John Adams. The last time he was in Philadelphia, Adams, in an overly frank letter to James Warren, had complained about John Dickinson, the leading moderate. Adams called Dickinson a "piddling Genius" responsible for giving "a silly Cast to our whole Doings" and stalling aggressive but necessary measures.[21] The British intercepted the letter, and Tories published it. Now Adams felt an iciness in Philadelphia. When Adams bowed and tipped his hat to Dickinson on the street, Dickinson ignored him and stared straight ahead. In this awkward time, Adams kept his mouth shut during debates, but between sessions focused on winning over the uncommitted newcomers from Georgia.

Sam Adams, like his cousin, also managed to alienate delegates. He was willing to believe that just about anyone who contemplated reconciliation with Britain must be collecting money from the British government and possibly selling secrets as well. He was especially suspicious of New York's John Jay, an advocate of caution. By raising his concerns, Adams put more distance between himself and the hesitant majority and did nothing to undermine Jay's standing. A declaration of independence was still out of the question.

Back in Cambridge, Washington found an outlet for men itching for action. He authorized a Connecticut colonel, Benedict Arnold, to lead an expedition into Canada against the British in Quebec. A thousand men eager for adventure and a fight volunteered and soon marched off. Arnold's force would be part of a two-pronged attack. Another force would move north from Albany with the aim of taking Montreal and then joining Arnold in an assault on Quebec City.

Around that same time, Washington came into possession of a mysterious letter. Back in July, a young woman had entrusted the letter to a Newport man for delivery to an officer on a British vessel. The Newport man, suspicious and sympathetic to the patriot cause, did not deliver it, but opened it instead. It was written in code.

That man passed it on to one of Washington's generals, who delivered it directly to Washington. Washington promptly had the woman tracked down. This "subtle, shrewd jade"[22] said little at first, but then made a shocking revelation. The author of the letter was Benjamin Church, long at the very center of the patriot cause. The woman was his mistress. As James Warren described it to John Adams, Church had formed "an infamous connection with an infamous hussey."[23] Church's marital infidelity was hardly a secret; hints of it had appeared in print some six years earlier. But that Church was passing on coded letters to the enemy was stunning.

Church, who that summer had been appointed chief physician to the army, was soon arrested. Someone was sent to round up his papers. A search found nothing incriminating but signs that some letters had been removed. Meanwhile, the coded letter, dated July 22, was deciphered. It told about the strength of American forces and American military plans. It included detailed instructions for making a reply. Its ending: "Make use of every precaution or I perish."[24]

Church was brought forth to defend himself. He confessed to writing the letter but protested that he was just trying to baffle the enemy. After all, he pointed out, much of the information given was false. Church said he expected the information to reach Gage, who would then be less inclined to attack the Americans. Washington's council of war did not believe Church and found him guilty of communicating with the enemy.

For some, Church's treachery was not entirely surprising. He had raised eyebrows earlier by mingling a little too freely with Loyalists. Also, his wife was English, and Fleeming, the antipatriot partner of Mein, was related by marriage. Paul Revere, for one, had had his suspicions. Long aware that someone in the inner circle of patriots was feeding information to Gage, Revere had been amazed at how easily Church slipped into and out of Boston. Revere had been particularly taken aback when Church, on the day after Lexington and Concord, had volunteered to enter Boston to get medicine.

For most leaders, however, Church's betrayal was a huge shock. John Adams wrote to James Warren:

> I stand astonished. A Man of Genius, of Learning, of Family, of Character, a Writer of Liberty Songs and good ones too. A Speaker of Liberty orations, a Member of the Boston Committee of Correspondence, A Member of the Massachusetts Congress, an Agent for that Congress to the Continental Congress, a Member of the House, a Director General of the Hospital and Surgeon General–Good God! What shall We say of human Nature? What shall We say of American Patriots? Or rather what will the World Say?[25]

Sam Adams, also writing to Warren, said, "Our pride is sorely mortified when there are grounds to suspect that so eminent a Countryman is become a Traitor."[26]

Neither of the Adamses could quite believe Church's guilt. Sam pointed out that the information Church passed on did not seem to expose the weakness of the American army, which would be the aim of a traitor. John, after calling the incriminating letter "the oddest Thing imaginable," said, "In short I endeavor to suspend my Judgment, Don't let us abandon him for a Traitor without certain Evidence."[27]

One Boston minister urged that Church be hanged. But patriotic leaders were less severe on Church than might be expected. The Massachusetts Provincial Congress expelled him from its membership but did not charge him with any crime, perhaps because Congress had formulated no law spelling out treason against the provincial government. Treason, as it was understood at the time, was a crime against the king. Most Americans still claimed to be loyal to the king, and many clung to the hope that the king would yet reverse the course his ministers had set. Thus, it could be argued that Washington, the Adamses, Hancock, and the rest were all traitors, but Church was not.

Still, patriot leaders could not just let Church go. Eventually, the harried Provincial Congress passed the matter on to the Continental Congress, which ordered Church's transfer to a jail in Connecticut for the time being. Church would be confined, but his life spared.

As Gage gathered what intelligence he could, he became more and more convinced that an attack on the Americans from Boston would be pointless. Considering the "Strength of their Posts, and their great

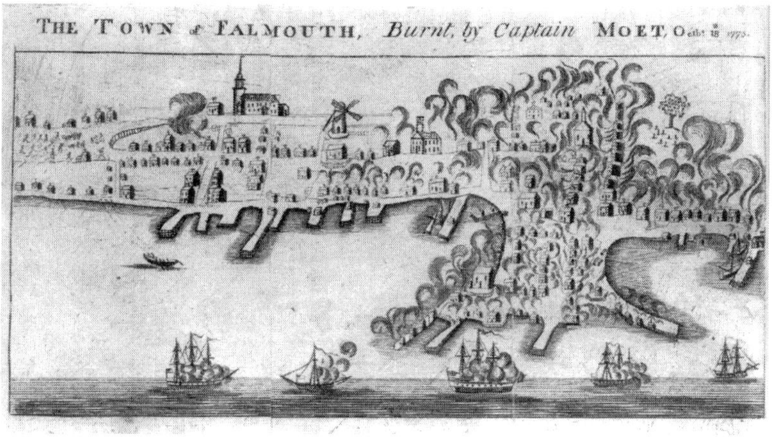

"The town of Falmouth. Burnt by Captain Moet Octbr. 18th 1775." (*Library of Congress*)

Numbers . . . considerable Loss must be expected." Besides, the British did not have enough men to maintain supplies and communications to outposts, nor the strength to reestablish the "legal Government."[28]

About this time, Gage received word that the king wished to see him in London. Clearly it would not be a social call. Gage would have some explaining to do. Frustrated and exasperated like Hutchinson and Bernard before him, Gage already knew why he failed so miserably, and it had nothing to do with shortsighted policies, vindictive measures, or boneheaded decisions on his part or on the part of the ministry or king. No, it was all a nefarious plot cooked up years before: "[T]his is no sudden Insurrection in America, but a preconcerted Scheme of rebellion, hatched years ago in Massachusetts Bay, and brought to this perfection by the help of Adherents on both Sides of the Atlantick."[29]

Almost certainly, Gage would not return as governor and general. He left for good on October 10, in the wake of yet another blunder on his watch: the burning of Falmouth, Maine, on October 4. Admiral Graves ordered the destruction after encounters with privateers (pirates authorized by the Americans to attack British shipping) along the coast and after finding the community less than welcoming to the Royal Navy. The destruction further unraveled any chance at reconciliation with America. The event horrified Americans and crystallized widespread determination to resist British authority.

Also that October, in London, thirty-seven-year-old King George III delivered to Parliament one of the most important speeches ever made by an English monarch. He told Parliament that America was in rebellion and aimed for independence. Britain would not allow it: "The object is too important, the spirit of the British nation is too high, the resources with which God hath blessed her too numerous, to give up so many colonies which she has planted with great industry, nursed with great tenderness, encouraged with many commercial advantages, and protected and defended at much expense of blood and treasure."[30]

More military force would be applied to crush this impertinence, George promised: "When the unhappy and deluded multitude, against whom this force will be directed, shall become sensible of their error, I shall be ready to receive the misled with tenderness and mercy."[31]

The speech, in the House of Lords, took about twenty minutes. Afterward the House of Commons immediately gathered in its own chamber to debate what the king said. Among the twenty or so who spoke, some were critical of the king and sympathetic with the Americans. Those included two men whom Americans long adored as their champions in England: John Wilkes and Isaac Barré. The war with the Americans was, said Wilkes, "unjust, ruinous, felonious, and murderous." He noted the bloody cost of retaking Bunker Hill. "Are we to pay as dearly for the rest of America?" Barré urged an immediate accommodation with the Americans for "if they were driven a step further in resistance" the whole continent would be lost.[32]

Among the most memorable remarks were those of Charles James Fox, a drinker, gambler, and fop who appeared occasionally in high-heeled shoes of different colors. After accusing Lord North of losing the whole continent of America, Fox said he could not "consent to the bloody consequences of so silly a contest about so silly an object, conducted in the silliest of manner that history or observation has ever furnished an instance of, and from which we are likely to derive nothing but poverty, disgrace, defeat, and ruin."[33]

But the majority in both the Lords and the Commons supported North and war. Most agreed with Alexander Wedderburn, the solicitor general, who said: "We have too long shown our forbearance and long-suffering. . . . Our thunders must go forth; America must be conquered."[34] Opponents of all-out war in America were defeated in both the Lords and the Commons by a ratio of more than 2 to 1.

In Cambridge, Washington concluded that he could never expect to win the war just by extending the siege. British sea power ensured that the British could always be supplied by sea and could presumably last forever in the bottled-up town. Meanwhile, how long could the American army hold together? He would have to attack Boston, even if it meant destroying the town.

In Philadelphia, the Continental Congress inched toward independence. When delegates from New Hampshire and then South Carolina sought advice for administering justice and policing society in this confusing time, Congress advised both colonies to form their own govern-

Map 7. The American Colonies and Canada in 1775.

ments. When Virginia asked for permission to set up a government independent of the royal governor, Congress approved that too.

Reluctantly but inexorably, the Congress was becoming more and more a national government. It was a strange sort of government, made up of one house with sixty-five representatives, more or less. The numbers fluctuated as representatives came and went. Virginia set a pattern of rotating its delegates–when one arrived, another left. Each colony had but one vote but could send as many delegates as it wished. For a while, a lone delegate represented North Carolina. New York named twelve.

This unicameral body took on legislative and executive responsibilities. Within the year, it would also take on appeals from courts and serve in a judicial capacity. It handled problems big and small, from great questions of policy to authorizing payment of $6.90 to a certain Rebecca Reynolds "for horse hire."[35] The Congress also found time to advise Americans on their habits, prodding them to wear leather waistcoats and breeches on account of the shortage of American wool.

The Congress hired clerks but normally turned over much of the day-to-day work to ad hoc and standing committees, leaving some representatives exhausted. The Congress set up a post office, began handling affairs with the Indians, provided guidance on how to treat Loyalists, dealt with matters concerning trade and roads, and settled border disputes among colonies. It even issued currency. In various ways, the individual colonies readily gave over to the Congress power they had denied Parliament.

The Congress took on all these tasks while still declaring time and time again a desire for reconciliation, not independence. In a message to the inhabitants of Ireland, for example, Congress said: "Though defamed as seditious we are ready to obey the laws. And though charged with rebellion [we] will cheerfully bleed in defence of our Sovereign in a righteous cause. What more can we say? What more can we offer?"[36]

In Boston, William Howe, the general who achieved the Pyrrhic victory at Breed's Hill, now took Gage's place as chief British commander. He was about six feet tall with dark eyes, a dark complexion, and something of a sad look about him, which was fitting because he seems to have had little enthusiasm for the war. He had once said that he would decline any offer of command in a war against the Americans. When war came, only a sense of duty compelled him to serve: "I was ordered, and could not refuse, without incurring the odious name of backwardness, to serve my country in distress."[37] He was also a man of few words. He never said anything in Parliament even though, by this time, he had been a member for more than sixteen years. He was, according to Horace Walpole, "reckoned sensible, though so silent that nobody knew whether he was or not."[38]

His family was rich and well connected. His mother was well known and highly influential. She was, some said, an illegitimate daughter of George I. Howe's brother, George Augustus, had died in America fighting in the French and Indian War. The people of Massachusetts were so moved by his valor that its lawmakers paid for a monument to his memory at Westminster Abbey. Another brother, Richard, was an admiral.

"Billy" Howe was clearly courageous. At Quebec, he had led a group of infantrymen in the daring climb up the embankment to the Plains of Abraham, preparing the way for General James Wolfe's army that followed. At Breed's Hill, he was in the thick of battle. In matching up against Washington, Howe clearly had the more impressive resume. He was forty-five, about the same age as Washington, with more experience and a more distinguished record.

But Howe had critical flaws. He lacked confidence, a drawback exacerbated by an unwillingness to find able subordinates and to take sound advice. Also, between battles he lacked diligence. Becoming preoccupied with his own pleasures, he put off military preparations or just didn't bother.

After Gage's departure, Howe kept the British on the defensive. He beefed up the fort on Bunker Hill and his lines at Charlestown. He took measures to make Boston Neck more secure. He initiated placement of batteries on the shore of the Common and on Beacon Hill. The most daring operation was a dash across the Back Bay climaxed with the capture of a few cows.

Significantly, he made no attempt to occupy Dorchester Heights. The general wasn't blind. He knew the importance of the high ground to the south. But Howe, like Gage before him, failed to seize it. He may have believed he could respond quickly enough to sweep the Americans off the heights should Washington attempt to occupy them.

Also, Howe likely felt he couldn't afford to take troops from other posts to fortify Dorchester Heights. Furthermore, had Howe stationed troops on the heights, they would have been vulnerable from patriots holding mainland positions, and then, if such an attack occurred, the British would have found it tricky to send help from Boston or Castle William by water.

In any case, Howe was thinking about leaving Boston anyway. He wanted to move operations to New York, a more important town than Boston and known to have many Loyalists. Such a move would require more ships and men, which would have to wait until spring. Thus, unwilling to risk an attack, unable to move, and unwilling to take and hold Dorchester Heights, he prepared to curl up for the winter in Boston.

In this quiet period, rules for civilians coming into town became more lax. We know of a young woman who came into town to attend a dance. Elizabeth Inman also came into town to help engineer the quiet marriage of a niece and pack off the couple to England.

Washington also prepared for winter. While gunpowder, muskets, cannon, bayonets, and flints remained in short supply, adequate quarters were found, and some food and firewood became available. Still, regional jealousies, fears, and prejudices were just below the surface and a constant source of headaches. For example, Washington found when he took over the army that the Massachusetts regiments had a surplus of officers while the Connecticut regiments had too few. The obvious solution was to put some Massachusetts officers in charge of Connecticut soldiers. But the Connecticut men would have none if it. Every platoon and company clung to its traditional right to have a say on who would command them, and they would not obey an officer from another colony.

Beyond these troubles, Washington was haunted by the fear his soldiers would simply vanish as enlistments ran out, as pay fell behind, as domestic responsibilities beckoned, and as boredom and drudgery sapped patriotic zeal.

Through these trials, Washington displayed amazing steadiness. But in letters to intimate associates, he despaired. He grumbled about the "dirty, mercenary Spirit" among the soldiers. He complained of all the compromises he had to make to keep the New England officers happy: "[I]t is beyond the powers of conception to discover the absurdities, & partiality of these People, and the trouble & vexation I have had in the New arrangement of Officers–after five, I think, different meetings of the Genl Officers I have, in a manner, been obliged to give into the humour & whimsies of the People, or get no Army."[39]

He regretted taking the job: "[C]ould I have foreseen what I have, & am like to experience, no consideration upon Earth should have induced me to accept this Command."[40]

For the American soldiers themselves, the days passed tediously. A Rhode Island soldier recorded for many days in his diary for October "nothing remarkable," "All still," "no remarks all still." He also reported the desertion of a regular to the American side; the desertion of an American to the British; a case of smallpox; the death of a soldier from "putrid fever"; and a wrestling match among men of two brigades. This soldier's main activities seem to have been standing guard and attending Sunday services. The journal also noted an attempt by an American floating battery to fire on Boston Common. A nine-pounder exploded, killing one and wounding seven.[41]

Two events lightened Washington's load of worries. One was the capture of a British brig stuffed with military supplies. The other was the arrival of Martha Washington in Cambridge on December 11. Washington welcomed his wife and her entourage in his new residence, the elegant Brattle Street home of a Tory who had fled into Boston.

While poking among the encampments and fortifications near Boston, Washington met and appraised many men. One was a hefty twenty-five-year-old who never appeared in public without a handkerchief wrapped around his left hand. This was Henry Knox, about six feet tall and 250 pounds, the same Henry Knox, bookseller, who was an eyewitness at the Boston Massacre in 1770. The handkerchief covered the stumps of two fingers blown away in a hunting accident.

Born and raised in Boston, Knox was the seventh of ten sons born to Mary Campbell and William Knox, a shipmaster. After financial setbacks, the father sold the family home on Sea Street and sailed off alone to St. Eustatius, in the West Indies, never to return. Nine-year-old Henry went to work to help out his mother. He found a job in a bookstore and, in his spare time, immersed himself in the printed word, devouring Plutarch and teaching himself to read and write French. He was also physically vigorous. Like many Boston boys, he happily took part in the annual Pope Day mayhem.

Eventually Knox opened a bookstore on Cornhill Street. At the London Book Store, Knox politely attended a clientele of "British officers and Tory ladies"[42] even as he wholeheartedly sympathized with the patriot cause.

Among the patrons was one Lucy Flucker, the plump, chatty teenage daughter of Thomas Flucker. This was the same Thomas Flucker who stood outside the locked Town House in Salem shouting Gage's proclamation for the House of Representatives to stop their business. Inevitably, amid volumes of *Tom Jones*, *Sermons to Young Men*, and *The Vicar of Wakefield*, and surrounded by inventories of German flutes, breadbaskets, and telescopes, Henry fell for Lucy. She was his "charmer." He was her "Fidelio." Thomas Flucker objected to the match, but Lucy defied her family to become Henry's wife sixteen days after the closing of Boston's port.[43]

Later identified with the patriot cause and suspected of spying, Knox was forbidden from leaving Boston. But on a June night, just before the Battle of Bunker Hill, Henry and Lucy Knox slipped out of town, bringing with them just a few belongings, including his militia sword sewn into the lining of her cloak. She never saw her parents again. Looters would ransack his Boston shop.

Henry Knox left Boston just in time to do some reconnoitering in advance of the battle. After the battle, he found a safe place for Lucy in Worcester, and then took the assignment of overseeing the building of fortifications.

It was thus at a fortification at Roxbury in July that Washington first encountered Knox. The commander was impressed with what he saw and over the subsequent weeks grew to admire the self-educated young man. Knox, fascinated with military science, had read everything he could get his hands on about gunnery and tactics. He had also been a proud member of a militia artillery company in Boston and helped found an offshoot militia group. Not surprisingly then, Washington was receptive when Knox came to him with a bold idea. By this time, the Continental Congress had decided to keep the cannon captured at Fort Ticonderoga. But those cannon remained at the fort, now abandoned by the Americans. Knox offered to lead an expedition to fetch the guns and haul them overland hundreds of miles to the outskirts of Boston. Washington knew that those Ticonderoga cannons, placed properly, were powerful enough to drive the British out of Boston. Washington gave Knox his approval, and on November 16, the bookseller and his nineteen-year-old brother set off on their mission.

Soon, winter was upon Washington's army. A Christmas Eve storm dumped a foot of snow on eastern Massachusetts. In the bitter cold, as the men scrounged for wood, Washington and his officers contemplated with dread the end of the year, when many of the enlistments would run out. If men did not reenlist, and if new recruits were not found, the army might disintegrate.

But convincing soldiers to reenlist was a hard sell. They faced dreary digging and marching; endless tedium interspersed with occasional terror and horror; high likelihood of disease; more years of cold, damp, filthy camps away from farms, businesses, wives, and children–all for infrequent payment of dubious money and a chance to fight better trained and better equipped soldiers backed by the richest empire in the world.

On December 31, a commander complained in a letter: "Many regiments have been obliged to eat their provisions raw for want of firing to cook, and notwithstanding we have burned up all the fences and cut down all the trees for a mile around the camp, our suffering has been inconceivable. . . . We have never been so weak as we shall be tomorrow."[44]

January 1 came, and indeed many thousands left, but about nine thousand remained. A new flag was unfurled: the British crosses of Saint Andrew and Saint George along with thirteen stripes. When British observers first spied the flag from Boston, they thought the Americans were surrendering.

The same day, the British sent out of Boston copies of the king's speech to Parliament, which had just arrived. Washington read it and hardened his determination "to shake off all connections with a state so unjust and unnatural."[45]

THIRTY-FOUR

AMEN

Soon after the first dawn of 1776, the Continental Congress gave Washington a polite nudge: permission to attack Boston, even if it meant destroying the town. Hancock, with his elegant mansion on Beacon Hill and more town property than anyone, roundly endorsed the resolution. His message to Washington: "May God crown your attempt with success. I most heartily wish it, though, individually, I may be the greatest sufferer."[1]

Washington intended to attack, but not yet. The commander begged for understanding and patience, noting the shortage of gunpowder and the difficulties of recruiting.

For the British troops cooped up in Boston and manning posts on the Charlestown Peninsula, the winter was a pitiless enemy. Some soldiers standing watch froze to death. Firewood was precious and almost impossible to come by as weather and privateers interfered with supplies. Boston trees, one by one, surrendered to saws and axes. The famous Liberty Tree was chopped into fourteen cords. Old barns, docks, fences, and bits of old vessels disappeared in the scramble to find fuel. Following Howe's directive, men pulled down for firewood the Congregational Old North Meetinghouse (not to be confused with today's Old North Church, the Episcopal Christ Church with the famous steeple).

The West Meetinghouse lost its steeple. Forever lost was the residence of the province's first governor, a black house more than a century old and a landmark in the center of town.

Of the buildings that survived, many suffered indignities. When officers looked about for a place to exercise their horses, they commandeered Old South and transformed its spacious sanctuary into a riding ring. Most of the pews and pulpit were stripped from the sanctuary and burned for fuel. Dirt and gravel were spread on the floor. A bar was set up for horses to jump over. A witness later saw evidence of a "grog shop" set up in the gallery. According to a diary entry, a hand-carved pew became a pigpen.

Food was scarce. In desperation, people stole. Howe cracked down. January began with the public whipping of a soldier and his wife found with filched goods.

About four thousand civilians remained in the town to suffer alongside the troops. Some–the selectmen, for example–were not allowed to leave. Most, however, were Loyalists who had chosen to stay. About half were women and children.

By this time, Ann Hulton, sister of Customs Commissioner Henry Hulton, had returned to England. But Henry and his family stayed behind. In a January letter, he thanked a friend from England for sending his "kind present of a Cheshire Cheese which was very acceptable, for every kind of provisions & fuel has been very scarce and dear."[2] The only thing cheap was rent, Hulton wrote: "Many people are glad to get a family into their houses with the furniture standing whilst they flee from fear or to join the Rebels."[3]

As to be expected, British officers enjoyed more comforts than common soldiers. Amid the privation, they had ample entertainment. One officer wrote, "We have plays, assemblies and balls, and live as if we were in a place of plenty."[4]

The town had no playhouse, so Howe made Faneuil Hall into a theater. Officers and Loyalists put on productions of, for example, *Maid of the Oaks*, a satire written by none other than General Burgoyne. Sally Flucker, Lucy's sister, played the lead.

In early January, the amateur actors staged *The Blockade*, a musical farce by Burgoyne. During the show, the audience heard the sound of guns and assumed it was part of the entertainment. As the noise continued, an actor dressed as an absurd New England farmer rushed onstage and shouted that the American army was "at it tooth and nail over in Charlestown." The line got a big laugh. But the words were not Burgoyne's. The rebels really were going at it over at Charlestown. The audience in Faneuil Hall was hearing the response from the British guns. A witness recorded events in the hall: "But soon finding their mistake a general scene of confusion ensued. They immediately hurried out of the house to their alarm posts, some skipping over the orchestra, trampling on the fiddles, and, in short, everyone making a most speedy retreat, the actors (who were all officers) calling out for water to get the paint and smut off their faces, women fainting, etc."[5]

The attack proved inconsequential. The winter continued with both sides shivering, unwilling to make a bold move.

Out of Boston came a Tory plea for the rebels to come to their senses. "An Address to the Soldiers of Massachusetts Bay Who Are Now in

Arms Against the Laws of Their Country," which appeared in January, begged the rebels not to be fooled by their leaders: "I am persuaded, my countrymen! that you are ignorant of the true rise of your disorders; the aim of your leaders hath been to keep you in ignorance; they knew that your ignorance was their protection." The address, signed "Z.Z." (really Peter Oliver), blamed corrupt and ambitious patriotic leaders, especially Sam Adams: "With his oily tongue he duped a man [Hancock] whose brains were shallow and pockets deep." Those leaders seven years earlier–before the Tea Party, before the Massacre–cooked up a plot to create "this independent empire" so they could grab the Boston estates of the Tories, said the writer. The clergy and the press went along, ramped up the patriotic frenzy, and hoodwinked the people. The rebellion was doomed, the writer warned: "[F]or God's sake, for your own sakes, for your wives and childrens sake, pause a moment and weigh the event of this unnatural civil war. You have roused the British Lion; you have incensed that power which hath crushed much greater powers than you can boast of, and hath done it without your aid too."[6]

By mid-January, Washington suspected Howe intended to abandon Boston and shift his soldiers to New York. Washington did not want to wait for that to happen. In a council of war, he argued for "making a bold attempt." The council cautioned that such a move should be made only when "practicable."[7]

While waiting for opportunities to attack the British, Washington was busy keeping his own soldiers from attacking each other. Some time that winter, a rifle corps from Virginia arrived on the Harvard campus, where Massachusetts soldiers were quartered. The Marblehead men, with their fishermen's outfits, found the backwoods gear of the Virginians curious. Ridicule was answered by snowballs, quickly degenerating into mayhem, "with biting and gouging on the one part, and knockdown on the other part, with as much fury as the most deadly enmity could create." Into this havoc rode Washington: "He leaped from his saddle, threw the reins of his bridle into the hands of a servant and rushed into the thickest of the melee, with an iron grip seized two tall, brawny savage-looking riflemen by the throat, keeping them at arm's length, alternately shaking and talking to them." The fighting stopped as men on both sides sprinted away. Thus, according to a ten-year-old messenger boy who witnessed the event, "Bloodshed, imprisonment, and hostile feelings between the different corps of the army were extinguished."[8]

On January 17, Washington received awful news about Arnold's expedition to Canada. It had sailed from Newburyport in Massachusetts, north of Boston, to the mouth of the Kennebec River in Maine. From there the men had made their way cross-country over terrain they knew little about. That overland journey was a nightmare. Just about everything went awry. The boats for the river journey leaked. Maps proved worse than useless: distances were underestimated; roads indicated on the map didn't exist. The terrain was impossibly rocky and swampy, with snarls of roots everywhere. The expedition became lost in the wilderness with no locals about to give directions. Water leaking into barrels ruined the bread inside. A huge storm washed away much of the remaining food. Dysentery and diarrhea struck. About one-third of the force turned back. The remaining soldiers, at the point of starvation, cooked up pet dogs and devoured moccasins, cartridge pouches, candlesticks, and shaving soap.

Arnold and his weary, diminished force finally arrived at Quebec City and met up with the other American force from Montreal. The Americans had expected that at Quebec, French Canadians would rise to join them in evicting the British. But the Canadians shrugged. No rising materialized. A short siege was tried. That failed. Then an attack was attempted under the cover of a snowstorm. But the storm proved more a hindrance to the American attackers than to the British defenders. The attack failed. Arnold was wounded. The other top American commander, General Richard Montgomery, was killed.

Offsetting the news about the Quebec fiasco was happier news about the Knox mission to Ticonderoga. The precious guns had been retrieved and were in Framingham, about twenty miles west of Cambridge.

About this time, John Adams prepared to once again head off to Philadelphia and another session of the Continental Congress. Before going, he stopped in Cambridge, where he dined with General and Martha Washington, a colonel and his wife, and others, including about a half dozen "Sachems and Warriors" with their squaws and children. "It was a Savage feast, carnivorous Animals devouring their Pray," wrote Adams in his diary. "Yet they were wondrous polite,"[9] bowing deeply when Washington introduced Adams as a member of the "grand Council Fire."[10]

Joining Adams on his journey the next day was Elbridge Gerry, who had taken the place of Cushing as one of the Massachusetts delegates. The two stopped at Framingham to gape at Knox's artillery and then proceeded on their journcy, taking eighteen days through rain and snow over roads alternately sticky with mud and frozen rock hard.

In Philadelphia, Adams found the mood glum. He wrote to Abigail, "There is a deep Anxiety, a kind of thoughtfull Melancholly, and some Lowness of Spirits approaching to Despondency, prevailing, through the southern Colonies, at present."[11] Delegates slumped under the weight of the crisis, anxiety over the terrifying uncertainty ahead, and complexities of the tasks at hand.

News from London crushed lingering hope of reconciliation. Parliament had passed the Prohibitory Act, which forbade trade with the thirteen American colonies, and declared that all colonial vessels and cargoes be treated like those of an enemy. Furthermore, the act authorized the British navy to seize men off American vessels and turn them into crewmen on British ships. Hancock summarized the act's significance: "[T]he making all our Vessells lawful prize don't look like a Reconcilliation."[12] Spirits were further flattened by the news of the disaster at Quebec.

Meanwhile, a spat divided the Massachusetts delegation. Delegate Robert Treat Paine was put off by remarks about him contained in a letter from James Warren to John Adams. Paine directed his anger not only at Warren but at Adams too. The Massachusetts delegation thus fractured, with Paine and Hancock on one side, and Gerry and the two Adamses on the other.

Amid this gloom and division, an electrifying pamphlet appeared anonymously that crystallized in bold, clear terms what this crisis was about and what Americans were aiming for. Some identified the author of the work as Benjamin Franklin. Others said it must be John Adams. Adams was at once amused and flattered, protesting, "I could not have written any Thing in so manly and striking a style."[13]

The author was Thomas Paine, an obscure English immigrant–in America less than fourteen months–who had embraced the American cause. The pamphlet was *Common Sense.* In everyday language that average people could understand, the pamphlet restated many old arguments while also floating ideas that had rarely been discussed openly. One was the notion of discarding the monarchy. Until *Common Sense,* Americans focused their anger on Parliament or the king's ministers. The idea of having a king had been, for the most part, sacrosanct. Paine snipped that last sentimental, centuries-old thread. He blasted the "exceedingly ridiculous" notion of a monarchy: "The state of the king shuts him from the world, yet the business of the king requires him to know it thoroughly."[14] The time for declaring independence was now. One need only to look at Boston: "that seat of wretchedness will teach us wisdom, and instruct us for ever to renounce a power in whom we can have no trust."[15] Separating from Britain "may at first seem strange and difficult, but like all other steps which we have already passed over, will in a little time become familiar and agreeable; and until an independence is declared, the continent will feel itself like a man who continues putting off some unpleasant business from day to day, yet knows it must be done, hates to set about it, wishes it over, and is continually haunted by the thoughts of its necessity."[16]

When copies of the pamphlet reached Massachusetts, people clamored for independence. Deacon Joseph Palmer of Germantown, writing to John Adams, said, "This is the time for declaring independence; we never have had such a favorable moment before, and 'tis not likely we shall have such another if we neglect this."[17]

James Warren told Adams that people in Massachusetts could not understand the "hesitancy" of the Continental Congress. "I can't describe the sighing after independence; it is universal. Nothing remains of that prudence, moderation or timidity with which we have long been plagued and embarrassed."[18]

In Cambridge, Washington's confidence grew as winter deepened. By mid-February, the general felt ready for an assault on Boston, across the frozen Back Bay. Washington himself tested the strength of the ice, venturing out onto it and jumping up and down. He had about sixteen thousand men. Tips from spies suggested only five thousand regulars were fit to fight. Washington gathered up his generals for another council of war. They did not share his enthusiasm for an attack. They argued that the British were not so weak–considering the two thousand or so Tories who would fight with the British–and the American army was not so strong–some one thousand of Washington's men had no weapons.

Washington was disheartened. But he and his generals came up with another idea: set up Knox's artillery on Dorchester Heights. That might draw the enemy out, just as at the Battle of Bunker Hill, and present an opportunity for battle more favorable to the Americans.

The plan was similar in another way to those before the Battle of Bunker Hill: fortifications would be established overnight. But the challenge of accomplishing this on the Dorchester Peninsula was more daunting. The slope was steeper, the elevation was higher, and there were enormously heavy cannon that had to be moved. Furthermore, the ground was now frozen. Soldiers would not be able to dig trenches.

Preparations were started. Men were put to work building portable makeshift fortifications made of timber, straw, and bundles of sticks. These would be moved into place with the artillery on the designated night. Barrels were also prepared. These would be filled with earth and rocks. Washington felt the barrels would project a stronger appearance. They also could be rolled downhill at an advancing enemy.

Though overwhelmed with responsibility, Washington found time in the midst of this planning to compose a gracious letter to Phillis Wheatley, the poet, who now was living in Providence and was no longer a slave. He was responding to a poem she had written in his honor. He wrote, "I thank you most sincerely for your polite notice of me, and however undeserving I may be of such encomium and pannegyrick, the style and manner exhibit striking proof of your great poetical talents."[19]

As Americans continued their preparations, the British appeared to be taking steps to evacuate Boston. Some mortars were taken off Bunker Hill. Vessels sailed out of the harbor with four hundred to five hundred men. To Washington, this was not good news. He thought he had a good opportunity now in Boston to win a clear victory that might win the war quickly. It might be many months–or years–before the Americans would have a similar chance to strike such a decisive blow.

Washington knew he couldn't stop the British from leaving. But once guns were placed on Dorchester Heights, the British, as a matter of honor, might choose to make an assault on those guns rather than slink away. It could be another Bunker Hill, but this time with the Americans better armed, organized, and prepared.

Washington knew that to attack Dorchester Heights, the British would have to take troops out of Boston. That would leave the town vulnerable. Washington thus made plans to attack the town when fighting started on Dorchester Heights. One force would attack by boat, landing at the Common. Another would land farther south. They would join and attack the rear of the British lines at Boston Neck, opening the way for another American force to enter the town by land.

Preparations ready, American cannons broke the stillness at about midnight March 2. This bombardment, far from Dorchester Heights, was meant to weaken the British while also distracting them from the Americans' true intent. The British batteries responded. The story was much the same the next night. On March 4, the American batteries bellowed with greater fury. A British captain wrote about the terrified civilians in Boston: "The inhabitants were in a horrid situation, particularly the women, who were several times drove from their houses by shot, and crying for protection."[20] An American lieutenant watching from the patriot lines said he heard the cries of women and children.

In the moonlight, the American soldiers assembled. Soon a parade of soldiers with tools and muskets made their way quietly to the Dorchester Peninsula. In the same direction went caravans of ox-drawn wagons with the timber and straw barriers, barrels of rocks and earth, and the precious guns from Ticonderoga. In the mild weather, this group of about three thousand men worked steadily, making several trips up the steep slopes, until about 3:00 a.m., when about twenty-four hundred soldiers came in to replace them and continue the work.

Meanwhile, on the Common in Cambridge, about four thousand men assembled near the college buildings, awaiting a signal from a church steeple in Roxbury to move toward boats awaiting them in the river.

At morning light, British observers looked out at Dorchester Heights and rubbed their eyes. On seeing the fortifications with twenty cannon in place, Howe was said to have remarked in amazement that the Americans had done more in one night than his army could have accomplished in three months. A London paper would later print portions of a letter by an unnamed "officer of distinction" who was in Boston: "[A]t day break we discovered two redoubts on the hills of Dorchester Point, and two smaller works on their flanks. They were raised during the night, with an expedition equal to that of the genie belonging to Aladdin's wonderful lamp. From these hills they commanded the whole town, so that we must drive them from their post, or desert the place."[21]

Howe responded immediately. For two hours, British cannons roared. But the cannonballs fell harmlessly short. The Americans were at an elevation too high for British guns to reach.

Howe huddled with his generals in Province House. He had already received a message from his admiral, Molyneux Shuldham, who had replaced Graves, that British ships were now vulnerable. British vessels, Shuldham said, could not remain in the harbor unless the rebels were swept off the heights. Howe had to attack or evacuate. There was no other course.

The prudent choice would be to slip away. Howe had intended to anyway. However, as Washington guessed, such a move now, in the face of the American challenge, seemed cowardly. Howe felt compelled to attack even under circumstances that appeared much like those of bloody Bunker Hill.

Howe set in motion a plan to move troops to Castle Island. From there, the attack would be launched against Dorchester Heights that night. The scheme horrified some officers. The soldiers were aghast. An observer watching the British soldiers waiting to embark wrote that "they looked in general pale and dejected, and said to one another it would be another Bunker Hill or worse."[22]

The Americans with telescopes from hilltops on this pleasant day could see very well that the British were making preparations not to evacuate, but to attack. This is just what Washington had hoped. To boost the spirits of his men, he reminded them of the date–the fifth of March, the anniversary of the Boston Massacre. He could anticipate the British attack at about midnight, when the British boats could ride the high tide from Castle William to the Dorchester Peninsula. Washington would wait for the British to attack, and then order the launch of boats into the Charles for the American assault on Boston.

Then, nature intervened. In the early afternoon, winds kicked up. As night fell, those winds brought hail, snow, and sleet. By midnight, when the British planned their attack, howling winds toppled fences and broke windows. The operation was put off.

By morning Howe canceled the attack and ordered an evacuation instead. Perhaps the storm gave Howe an honorable excuse. Perhaps advice from officers finally sank in. But it was almost certainly a wise decision.

With no attack by the British on Dorchester Heights, there would be no simultaneous attack by Americans on Boston. Washington decided "Providence" had stepped in "for some wise purpose." Still, the commander could "scarce forbear lamenting the disappointment."[23]

The wise purpose of Providence may have been to save Washington from disaster. At Dorchester Heights, the Americans would likely have done well, inflicting many casualties on the British. But the American assault on Boston would have been a different story. To succeed, the Americans would have had to row a mile across open water and then land in front of British cannon. Once ashore, the Americans, numbering about four thousand, still had to fight about thirty-five hundred British, all better trained, still defending the town. If the operation failed, those Americans had no way to escape. The storm may have saved both the American and the British commanders from their own blunders.

With the announcement March 6 of the evacuation, Boston became a frothy chaos. Merchant John Rowe wrote, "nothing but hurry & Confusion, every Person striving to get out of this Place."[24]

For Howe, this was mostly improvisation. He had received no orders from London since October. He had thought about evacuation, but no specific plan had been drawn up. Now he had to move quickly, and he was committed to moving not only troops and equipment but also families of soldiers and any Loyalists and their families who wanted to go.

A huge challenge would be to round up vessels and stock them with water and provisions at a time when food was scarce enough to begin with and made scarcer by storms that prevented supply ships from delivering cargoes to Boston.

Amid the bustle and confusion, the winds blew strong, making movement in the harbor treacherous. The patriot guns kept silent as work on emplacements on Dorchester Heights continued. Washington couldn't assume the activity in Boston wasn't a ruse. Howe still could attack.

Civilians in Boston agonized about the likely destruction of the town. Would Howe tear apart the town or set it on fire as the troops and Tories left? Would Washington at any moment launch a cannonade to destroy the town and the soldiers with it? Selectmen presented these concerns to Howe. He replied with a note assuring that if his soldiers were permitted to leave unmolested, he had no intention of wrecking the town.

On Friday, March 8, four of Boston's selectmen, after passing through the British lines at Boston Neck under a white flag, carried the unsigned message to American commanders, hoping for reassurance that the patriot army would not reduce the town to ashes. Uncertain of the note's authenticity, Washington made no promises. Still, the selectmen returned to Boston in a calmer frame of mind.

The next night, after spotting American soldiers moving onto a hill perilously close to the Neck, the British guns boomed for hours. A single ball killed four. But otherwise, the loud response affected nothing. Some seventy cannonballs were plucked from the hillside the next day.

The scrambling on the streets of Boston grew more frenzied. Ships became so crammed with people and equipment that despite the food crisis, hogsheads of sugar and salt, and barrels of flour were tossed into the harbor. So, too, were other goods for which there was no room: furniture, wagons, wheelbarrows, and Howe's fine coach. Surplus cannon were also plunked into the water, or else disabled.

Loyalists–both those who had found refuge in Boston from the countryside and those who had lived in Boston all their lives–had to leave almost everything they treasured behind. Their world was collapsing. "It is not easy to paint the distress and confusion of the inhabitants on the occasion," wrote the Reverend Henry Caner, rector of the Anglican King's Chapel for thirty years. "I had but six or seven hours allowed to prepare for this measure, being obliged to embark the same day."[25] His inventory of goods left behind included one thousand books, two mahogany tables, a carved mahogany desk, a harpsichord, a cow, and a calf.

The Loyalists' bitterness was immeasurable. They felt themselves as patriotic as any of the so-called patriots squawking about liberty. They had obeyed the laws, even though they, too, disagreed with many of them. For their loyalty, normally a virtue, they had suffered and now must go into exile, leaving behind the land they loved just as much as any minuteman. One Loyalist, Dr. Sylvester Gardiner, later wrote to his son-in-law:

> I found I could not stay in Boston and trust my person with a set of lawless rebels whose actions have disgraced human nature and who have treated all the King's loyal subjects that have fallen in their hands with great cruelty and for no other crime than for their loyalty to the best of Kings and a peaceable submission to the best constituted government on earth. I don't believe there ever was a people in any age or part of the world that enjoyed so much liberty as the people of America did under the mild indulgent government (God bless it) of England and never was a people under a worser state of tyranny than we are at present.[26]

Among those crowding onto the ships were many prominent Bostonians. They included Chief Justice Peter Oliver, who, after squeezing onto a vessel, had little else to do but write in his diary: "Here I took my leave of that once happy country where peace and plenty reigned uncontroulled. Until that infernal Hydra Rebellion with its hundred Heads, had devoured its happiness, spread desolation over its fertile feilds and ravaged the peacefull mansions of its inhabitants."[27]

Other prominent people on this exodus included Foster Hutchinson, brother of the former governor; John Lovell, headmaster of the Boston Latin School and Tory father of patriot James Lovell, in British custody; Benjamin Faneuil, nephew of the man who gave Boston Faneuil Hall; and Samuel Quincy, brother of Josiah Quincy. Exiles included almost one hundred Harvard graduates and eighteen clergymen.

But most of the eleven hundred Loyalists who crowded the ships were not wealthy or prominent. Heads of families included 382 farmers, mechanics, and common tradesmen. William Hill, responsible for a family of seventeen, was a baker. Among the women listed was Margaret Draper, who oversaw a family of five and had been publishing the *Massachusetts Gazette* and *Boston Newsletter* since her husband's death in 1774. Prostitutes Dorcas Griffiths and her daughter were also among the refugees.

Onboard conditions were crowded and ghastly. As he waited for departure, Benjamin Hallowell, the customs man, held his nose and crammed himself into a cabin stuffed with thirty-six others: "men, women, and children; parents, masters, mistresses, obliged to pig together on the floor, there being no berths."[28]

Howe, wishing to deprive rebels of useful materials, proclaimed on March 10 that those remaining in the town had to turn in all linen and woolen goods of possible value to the patriot army. A Loyalist with the distinctive name of Crean Brush had the assignment of enforcing the proclamation. To Brush and his men, this job was a license to loot. Rowe encountered Brush and fifteen soldiers at his warehouse: "They took from me to the Value of Twenty Two hundred & Sixty Pounds Sterling according to the best Calculations I could make, in Linens, Checks, Cloths & Woolens. This Party behaved very Insolently & with Great Rapacity & I am very well Convinced, exceeding their orders to a Great Degree."[29]

Soon other men, including drunken soldiers and sailors, joined in the plunder, smashing into houses and shops as they pleased.

By mid-March, all was ready for the departure. All that was needed was a favorable breeze. That came on March 17. Before dawn, more than eight thousand redcoats marched through Boston for the last time. By 9:00 a.m., the vessels–all 120–slipped away. But they stayed close. Near the harbor they dropped anchor. Each warship delivered a twenty-one-gun salute for the *Chatham*, Howe's flagship. The *Chatham* answered with a blast from each of its fifty guns, a reminder to those on shore that the war was only beginning.

The American soldiers watched, uncertain they were witnessing a complete evacuation. After all, British sentinels still manned the outpost at Bunker Hill. An American general galloped closer for a better look. He discovered that the "sentinels" were straw dummies clutching broken muskets.

The Americans soon realized the city was, indeed, unguarded. However, although the regulars were gone, smallpox lurked. Soldiers were sorted. Only those who had had smallpox and scars to prove it could enter the town. Washington had the scars and could have made a triumphal entrance. But he graciously gave the honor to Artemis Ward, a New Englander and the man most vigorous in pushing for the pivotal operation on Dorchester Heights.

Washington finally entered Boston on March 18, 1776, without ceremony. He found plenty of evidence of chaos and wanton destruction: provisions, rugs, and blankets strewn about; disabled cannon; abandoned military carts and wagons. A closer inspection, however, also found surprising quantities of goods left behind untouched. Structures at Hancock's Wharf held five thousand bushels of wheat. The town granary still contained one thousand bushels of beans and ten tons of hay. One lumberyard still had thirty-five thousand feet of good planks. Others made disturbing discoveries, such as the body of a child sewn up in canvas and left in a garret. The child had been dead five to six weeks, probably of smallpox.

By March 20, American commanders were confident that the risk of smallpox was slight. The main body of soldiers was permitted to enter the town. Two days later, the town was open to all.

Returning Bostonians found many houses and other buildings battered, scarred, and wrecked. Samuel Cooper, pastor of the Brattle Street Meetinghouse, entered Boston on March 26 to find "a melancholy scene. Many houses pull'd down by the British Soldiery, the Shops all shut. Marks of Rapine and Plunder ever'y where." At his own house he found "all my Beds Bedsteds, Sheets Blankets, Quilts and Coverlids, all my China Glass and Crockery Ware, &c &c, plunder'd, 2 Lookin Glasses gone 2 broke, 1 Dressing Glass gone &c."[30] The next day, Cooper got permission to snatch furniture from the abandoned houses of several departed "Enemies to our Country," including the house of Charles Paxton, customs commissioner.[31]

Others returning to Boston found less destruction than they expected. Abigail Adams reported to John that their Boston house was "very dirty, but no other damage has been done to it."[32] Two of Hancock's

Boston houses and a vessel were destroyed in the occupation. But amazingly, almost all was in order at Hancock's Beacon Hill mansion. Its former occupant, General James Grant, had once blustered that every New England town along the coast should be left in ruins. Yet Grant proved a considerate tenant. To be sure, a substantial quantity of wine had vanished from the cellar, but that was taken by Hancock's own Tory cousin, William Bowes, who had invested money with Hancock. During the occupation, Bowes felt entitled to get his money back in whatever way he could. He obtained an order from the sheriff, helped himself to Hancock's wine, and then sailed off to London.

Elsewhere, some returning residents found rent money left behind by conscientious Tory tenants. Returning Bostonians also found Tories who chose to stay. Tory Peter Oliver, who did not stay behind, later wrote about a family that was carted to the end of town, dumped into a ditch, and told not to return. According to Oliver, the crew that dumped the family also told people in the countryside not to provide the family with food or shelter.

For a few days, Howe's fleet lingered as the British retained control of Castle William, the military island in the harbor. Then, on March 20, British engineers set off an explosion on the island, destroying what they could of the fortifications. The fleet then moved farther away but remained in sight. By this time, Loyalists had been on these ships going nowhere for two weeks. One despairing man hurled himself overboard and drowned.

On March 27, most of the fleet finally vanished over the horizon. About this time, several Loyalists stood on the deck of one ship chatting. When someone remarked confidently about returning some day, merchant George Erving intoned, "Gentlemen, not one of you will ever see that place again."[33]

The fleet's destination was not New York, as Washington expected, but Halifax. Eventually, however, the British would make New York their military headquarters in America and resume the war from there.

Tributes showered down on Washington. Harvard bestowed an honorary degree. The Continental Congress struck a gold medal. Boston's selectmen and the Provincial Congress thanked him for saving the town.

In London, the news produced gnashing of teeth, especially among longtime critics of the government. At least one defender of the government responded with a shrug, saying the military had planned to abandon Boston anyway.

On April 4, Washington exited Cambridge, and most of the Continental Army soon moved off in the direction of New York. Ward remained with a holding force. Harvard would resume classes in Cambridge in June. More civilians returned to shattered Boston. Rowe, who had remained in Boston throughout the siege, was shocked to be suspected of Tory sympathies. He wrote about trying to attend ceremonies for the reburial of the remains of fellow Mason Joseph Warren: "[T]o my great mortification was very much Insulted by some Furious & hot Persons with° the least Provocation one of Brethren thought it most Prudent for me to Retire. I accordingly did so–this has caused some Uneasy Reflections in my mind as I am not conscious to myself of doing anything Prejudicial to the Cause of America either by will or deed."[34]

At the Continental Congress in Philadelphia, delegates wrestled with pesky questions: Should American ports be opened to all European vessels? Should a navy be formed? Should steps be taken to encourage privateers to attack British merchant ships?

They also agonized over independence, but they could not bring themselves to take the leap. A rumor slipped into corridors and passed from delegate to delegate: a commission sent by Britain would arrive any day to talk about patching things up. Though far-fetched, it was enough to stall the inevitable. John Adams was frustrated: "This story of commissioners is as arrant an illusion as ever was hatched in the brain of an enthusiast, a politician or a maniac."[35]

When news of the evacuation of Boston reached Philadelphia, delegates were still mesmerized by the phantom peace commission. If and when those commissioners came, should they be allowed to land? Should passports be issued? If they applied to Congress for passports, didn't that amount to recognition of American independence and the authority of the Continental Congress? Should they be sent to talk to Washington or to Congress?

When the Congress finally approached the issue of independence, delegates ran headlong into a roadblock. The Pennsylvania and New York representatives had explicit instructions to oppose any initiative to split the colonies from Britain. Maryland also hamstrung its delegates with restrictions.

The Adamses, along with Virginia's Richard Henry Lee, devised a detour. First, Lee put forward a resolution recommending to the assemblies of each of the colonies that they establish governments in places where the former government was insufficient. John Adams seconded it. This resolution seemed inoffensive. This was not really independence; it was a practical solution to a real problem. If the royal governments were not doing their job, other governments had to be established to fill the void.

It was agreed the resolution needed a preamble. John Adams, Lee, and South Carolina's John Rutledge made up the committee to draft it. On May 15, this preamble, written by Adams, stated that because the king was refusing to protect Americans, and indeed was waging war on Americans, royal authority in America should be suppressed. The term independence was not used. New York's James Duane was not fooled. He saw the maneuver for what it was–a backdoor declaration of independence. "You have no right to pass this resolution any more than Parliament has. . . . Why all this haste? Why all this urging? Why this driving?"[36]

Sam Adams clarified the issue: the king had already discarded the colonies. Not everyone saw it that way. The preamble passed, but narrowly.

Pennsylvania's James Wilson feared the consequences of this preamble once it became known. He begged for a delay in its publication, predicting "an immediate dissolution of every kind of authority; the people will instantly be in a state of nature. Why then precipitate this measure? Before we are prepared to build a new house, why should we pull down the old one?"[37]

The majority voted to publish anyway. The Maryland delegates promptly left the Congress, returning days later with new instructions. They were still ordered to remain dead set against independence. But otherwise, the measure seemed to give momentum to the drive for separation from Britain. When word of the measure reached Williamsburg, Virginia, the British flag on the capitol was yanked down. By the end of May, delegates from Rhode Island and Virginia each had specific instructions from lawmakers in their respective colonies to back independence.

Then the British government and the king delivered the crucial nudge. Word reached Philadelphia that the government was making arrangements for German mercenaries to fight Americans. About the same time, Americans learned about the king's response to a certain petition from the City of London. The petition condemned the use of mercenaries and proposed that fighting be suspended. The king brushed it aside.

This broke the hearts of the moderates at the Continental Congress. Robert Morris of Philadelphia wrote that the king's response to the petition "destroyed all hopes of reconciliation. . . . [It] breathes nothing but death and destruction, everybody sees it in the same light and it will bring us all to one way of thinking, so that you may soon expect to hear of new governments in every colony, and in conclusion a declaration of Independancy by Congress."[38]

By June 7, Congress was convinced. No one was left to argue against separating from Britain. The only question was when. Moderates representing mainly the middle colonies still wanted to be sure the people were behind them. On June 10, Congress put off the issue of independence to July 1. Meanwhile, however, the Congress laid the groundwork. Various committees were established: one to work on treaties with foreign powers; another to devise a plan of how the united colonies would work together; another to manage the war; and finally, crucially, a committee to draw up a declaration of independence.

John Adams had key roles. He chaired the committee for managing the war, making him in effect secretary of war for the collection of colonies. He also did most of the work of the committee on treaties, and was on the committee to draw up the declaration. Amid this frenzy of business, treasured letters from Abigail trickled in. In one, speaking for all women, she issued her immortal challenge to her husband as he labored to bring forth a new nation:

> I long to hear that you have declared an independency–and by the way in the new Code of Laws which I suppose it will be necessary for you to make I desire you would Remember the Ladies, and be more generous and favourable to them than your ancestors. Do not put such unlimited power into the hands of the Husbands. Remember all Men would be tyrants if they could. . . . That your Sex are Naturally Tyrannical is a Truth so thoroughly established as to admit of no dispute, but such of you as wish to be happy willingly give up the harsh title of Master for the more tender and endearing one of Friend. Why then, not put it out of the power of the vicious and the Lawless to use us with cruelty and indignity with impunity.[39]

John replied with a patronizing scoff:

> As to your extraordinary Code of Laws, I cannot but laugh. We have been told that our Struggle has loosened the bands of Government every where. That Children and Apprentices were disobedient–that schools and Colledges were grown turbulent–that Indians slighted their Guardians and Negroes grew insolent to their Masters.
>
> But your Letter was the first Intimation that another Tribe more numerous and powerfull than all the rest were grown discontented.–This is rather too coarse a Compliment but you are so saucy, I wont blot it out.
>
> Depend upon it, We know better than to repeal our Masculine systems. Altho they are in full Force, you know they are little more than Theory. We dare not exert our Power in its full Latitude. We are obliged to go fair, and softly, and in Practice you know We are the subjects.[40]

In Massachusetts, the House of Representatives sent to towns in the province a suggestion to hold meetings on the question of independence. Leaders expected a unanimous chorus in its favor and hoped to use that outcry to prod the Continental Congress. Boston went along as expected. At a town meeting in May in the Old Brick Meetinghouse, townsmen considered a motion stating "That if the Honble Continental Congress should, for the Safety of the Colonies, declare them Independent of the Kingdom of Great Britain, they, the Inhabitants, will solemnly engage, with their Lives and Fortunes to support them in the Measure." The motion passed unanimously.[41]

But many people in Massachusetts still were not sure. By June 6, most members of the House–about two-thirds according to one report–indicated that their towns backed independence. But some towns didn't respond, apparently awed by the gravity of the issue. Of those, some finally came around with formal statements in favor. While most of the hesitant towns apparently favored independence, at least one didn't. When Barnstable–the Otis family hometown–got around to voting on independence, the tally was 36 to 30 against.

During this period, the House also took time to further trash the reputation of the exiled Hutchinson. A trunk full of the former governor's letters had been found in his Milton home. A committee of the House plucked out the most damning letters and made portions available for newspapers. The letters revealed little that was not known, but extracts published out of context reinforced his perceived "perfidy, treachery, and villainy."[42]

On July 1, the Continental Congress was poised for a decision. Even though the New Jersey delegates were yet absent, the session began. John Dickinson made a last stand, speaking at length in opposition to independence. When he finished, no one stood up immediately to answer. The majority favored independence, but no one was prepared to answer Dickinson and state the case. Finally John Adams stood and summarized the arguments he knew by heart.

After Adams finished, the New Jersey delegates appeared. They had new instructions permitting them, but not requiring them, to vote for independence. They asked for a summary of the argument in favor of independence. Silence. South Carolina's Edward Rutledge poked Adams: "Nobody will speak but you upon this subject, Mr. Adams. You have all the topics so ready that you must satisfy the gentlemen from New Jersey."[43]

But his arguments, even stated twice, failed to produce unanimity. When the vote for independence was taken, four colonies still held out: South Carolina and Pennsylvania opposed; Delaware's two delegates split, one for, one against; New York's delegates abstained, saying their instructions made it impossible for them to vote in favor.

To issue a declaration of independence supported by just nine of thirteen colonies was dangerous, perhaps worse than issuing no declaration at all: it would underscore the divisions among the colonies.

Now, the pulling and tugging behind the scenes intensified. Supporters of independence maneuvered to bring the South Carolina, Pennsylvania, New York, and Delaware delegates around.

First, Delaware. One of its delegates had been missing, and that absent delegate, Caesar Rodney, was known to be strongly in favor of independence. A messenger was dispatched to urge him to make the ninety-mile journey to Philadelphia the next day.

Next, South Carolina. John Adams and Lee buttonholed Rutledge and got him, for the sake of colonial unity, to agree to independence if Delaware and Pennsylvania went along.

Next, New York. The independence faction could only hope that the rumors they had heard were true: that the New York convention directing the delegates had decided to permit the delegates to vote in favor of independence.

Finally, Pennsylvania. Three of its delegates–Franklin, John Morton, and Wilson–favored independence. The four others–Thomas Willing, Robert Morris, Dickinson, and Charles Humphreys–opposed. Morris and Dickinson agreed to a compromise. They would simply make themselves absent for the crucial vote. That would ensure that the Pennsylvania delegation would vote 3 to 2 in favor of independence.

Routine matters took up the morning session of Congress on a rainy July 2. Just after lunch, Delaware's Rodney, wet, muddy, and ill, made his appearance. A vote followed. The New York delegates abstained. The other twelve colonies voted in favor of independence. In his letter written the next day to Abigail, John Adams touched on assorted matters that she had mentioned in a letter: a petition concerning a hospital in Boston, smallpox inoculations, a letter from a cousin of Abigail's, and a journey Abigail made to Plymouth. Then, in the eighth paragraph, he remarked: "Yesterday the greatest question was decided which ever was decided in America, and a greater, perhaps, never was nor will be decided among men."[44]

The task of declaring independence was not done, however. Debate began over the declaration itself, written chiefly by Virginia's Thomas Jefferson, who had been an inconspicuous member of Congress for less than a year but was considered a graceful writer. The splendid opening sentences were untouched. Elsewhere, minor revisions were made. Then came a vote on July 4. All present voted in favor except Dickinson. The author of "Letters from a Farmer in Pennsylvania" could not bring himself to join the revolution he helped inspire.

That day the Declaration of Independence was signed–but by just one man, John Hancock, president of the Congress. This was a proud and brave moment for him, at a bittersweet time in his life. By this time Aunt Lydia was dead and Dolly was pregnant. In April, Lydia, in Fairfield, had succumbed at age sixty-two or so to a stroke. It was a blow to both John and Dolly. Aunt Lydia had been like a mother to both of them. Now helping Dolly in Philadelphia through her pregnancy was her older, unmarried sister Catherine, known as Kathy.

Later that month, the text of the Declaration reached Boston. Abigail Adams was there. Smallpox festered in the town, so she had brought herself and her brood–along with bedding, a cow, some hay, and wood–up from Braintree for variolation. They joined her sisters, other family members, a maid, and "a Negro man"–seventeen in all–crowded together in a house. The town was full of people, with thousands from the countryside, like her, flooding in to be inoculated. "Such a Spirit of inoculation never before took place," she wrote to John. "[T]he Town and every House in it, are as full as they can hold." In her letter of July 21–22 to John, she said: "Last Thursday after hearing a very Good Sermon I went with the Multitude into Kings Street to hear the proclamation for independance read and proclamed. Some Field peices with the Train were brought there, the troops appeard under Arms and all the inhabitants assembled there."[45]

When the proclamation was read from the balcony of the State House, "great attention was given to every word." When it finished, the cry from the balcony was "God Save our American States." Three cheers then "rended the air, the Bells rang, the privateers fired, the forts and Batteries, the cannon were discharged, the platoons followed and every face appeard joyfull."

Later, patriots built a bonfire on King Street and threw onto it the king's coat of arms ripped from the State House. On the street of the Massacre, the once-revered symbol of Boston's loyalty and submission to the king went up in flames and smoke. Abigail summed up: "Thus ends royall Authority in this State, and all the people shall say Amen."[46]

EPILOGUE

For Abigail Adams, the wonder of independence was a momentary distraction. She was focused on keeping her children alive. The variolation treatment proved to be a nightmare. One child, six-year-old Charles, was delirious for two days before finally recovering. Months passed before Abigail finally returned to Braintree.

Meanwhile, in Boston, like everywhere in the thirteen newly independent states, old conventions quietly vanished. After attending Anglican services on July 21, merchant John Rowe noted in his diary that the minister "omitted the petitions in the Liturgy for the King & Royal Family thinking it Prudent."[1]

Over time, references to royalty were wiped away and new heroes honored. King Street became State Street; Queen Street became Court Street. Another prominent street, which had gone by four different names–Orange, Newbury, Marlborough, and Cornhill–became Washington Street. King's Chapel, though, remained King's Chapel, and visitors to Boston will still find Hanover Street and Prince Street.

The street names changed, and so did the people. So many familiar faces were gone, never to be seen in Boston again, so many newcomers arriving. As one woman wrote in the early 1800s, "[F]rom that time to the present there has been such an inundation of strangers from every part of the [globe], that a real Bostonian is a mere rara avis, a rare bird indeed."[2]

Outside Boston, the name Hutchinson was soon erased from maps of Worcester County. The people of the town, "filled with shame to tell where we lived,"[3] set about renaming the place even before independence, first favoring the name Wilkes but then settling again on Barre. The Provincial Congress approved the new name in late 1776.

The British never returned to Boston. Until the end of the war, however, occasional rumors hinting of their return generated flutters of panic. The arrival of a French fleet in Boston Harbor in fall 1778 produced great excitement and some jitters as Bostonians lined the shore to gape at the ninety-gun flagship *Languedoc* and twenty-six other warships. The French were now allies, but they had been enemies for so many decades, and they were, to the Americans, so very foreign.

To provide fresh bread to the French military, the French set up a bakery in the town, where, for most people, wheat flour was too expensive and fresh bread but a fantasy. The smell of baking bread drew salivating throngs. People offered to buy some, but the baker would not sell. The bread was for the men on the ships, as the baker probably tried to explain, but no one in the crowd understood French. The baker knew no English. Misunderstanding led to frustrations, producing a riot. A French officer tried to intervene and was killed and then quietly buried in the vaults under King's Chapel after what might have been the first Catholic Mass ever held in Boston. The French diplomatically made no fuss. French commanders somehow blamed the death on the despicable British.

Though the war was fought elsewhere, Bostonians experienced hardships. A town meeting in 1779 set prices for goods ranging from rum, coffee, and tea, to salt, mutton, cheese, and hay. A retailer who refused to sell coffee "at the regulation Price" found himself confronted by about one hundred women who demanded keys to his store. When he refused, they put him in a cart and threatened to wheel him out of town.[4]

As the war wound down, life in Boston didn't return to the prewar normal. Newcomers took up residence in the old Tory mansions. The old economy was gone, as Britain slammed the door on New England trade with the British West Indies. Over time, though, Boston merchants cultivated new and fantastic trade routes. Boston ships skirted the remote tip of South America, glided up the Pacific coast of North America, traded for otter skins, and then set off for China for silks and other exotic goods. In Asia, "Bostonian" became a synonym for "American."

Sam Adams had hoped that Boston, once free of Tories and British authority, would emerge as a Puritan Sparta, a model of frugality, industriousness, and modesty. But other Bostonians had different ideas. They wanted a New England Paris. High living and French fashion became the rage. Old Puritan taboos were swept away. When, in 1792, the sheriff, duly enforcing the law, stopped a performance of *Richard III* and hauled the hunchback and other players off to jail, the subsequent fury started a movement to make theaters legal. A committee that included Paul Revere and John Adams's son, John Quincy Adams, went to the governor. Within a year, a proper theater opened in Boston. In 1796, one visitor from England wrote with astonishment: "The better people are all aristocrats."[5]

After independence was declared, John Adams remained hard at work at the Continental Congress, coming back to Massachusetts only for short intervals. In November 1777, Congress called on him to go to Paris to work alongside Benjamin Franklin and Arthur Lee on a possible alliance with France. Some of the French who welcomed him couldn't hide their disappointment that this was not, after all, his cousin, "le fameux Adams."[6]

He returned to America just in time to take part in the Massachusetts Constitutional Convention. In September 1779, he met with about 250 delegates in the First Church near Harvard Yard in Cambridge and was promptly named to a subcommittee to draft a state constitution. The document was almost all his work. Even the title was his own, with the choice of the word "commonwealth" rather than "state": A Constitution or Form of Government for the Commonwealth of Massachusetts.[7]

Adams's constitution reflected his distrust of a broad-based democracy. Under his original constitution, voting qualifications were more restrictive than those under the prerevolutionary charter. Adams's work has stood the test of time. It is the world's oldest functioning written constitution.

Following his work on the state constitution, Adams was off to Paris again on another diplomatic mission. Finding it difficult to work with the French or, for that matter, Franklin, he slipped away to the Netherlands for unauthorized freelance diplomacy with the Dutch. He was in Amsterdam when he heard news of the American victory at Yorktown in 1781. Adams's diplomatic groundwork now paid off. The Netherlands recognized the United States. Adams soon opened the first US embassy in the world and secured a vital loan from Dutch bankers for the infant nation. He was back in Paris in time to take part in negotiations leading to the Treaty of Paris in 1783, ending the War of Independence.

Adams continued on as a diplomat in Europe, where Abigail, with daughter Nabby, joined him. He soon had a new role: minister to the Court of St. James. He would be the US ambassador to Britain.

By the middle of 1788, the Adamses were back in Massachusetts, and in February 1789, John learned he had been elected the first vice president of the United States under the new Constitution. Like many vice presidents who came later, he was uncertain of his role and became the butt of jokes. In a debate about how to address President George Washington, senators giggled that the fitting title for portly Adams would be "His Rotundity."[8] After four years, Adams was reelected, though still he remained at a loss about what a vice president should do: "My country in its wisdom contrived for me the most insignificant office that ever the invention of man contrived or his imagination conceived."[9]

In 1797, after a close election, Adams succeeded Washington as president. The Adams presidency is regarded as an unhappy one. A blot on Adams's presidential record is the Alien and Sedition Acts, measures passed during fearful times when a war with France was expected. Under the act, a person could be fined and sent to prison just for openly criticizing the president.

Abigail Adams died in 1818, at age seventy-four. In 1820, at age eighty-five, John was chosen as a delegate to a convention in Massachusetts to revise the state constitution he had worked on years before. With Jews especially in mind, he introduced an amendment to extend religious freedom. The amendment failed.

Adams was still alive when son John Quincy Adams took the oath of office as the sixth president. John Adams, the second president, and Thomas Jefferson, the third, died on the same day, July 4, 1826, the fiftieth birthday of the United States.

John Hancock's star as a national figure faded after the Declaration of Independence. But he remained a popular and successful political figure in Massachusetts until his death.

The months after the signing of the Declaration were hard on Dolly and John Hancock. In October or perhaps November, Dolly gave birth to a girl, who was given the name Lydia, of course. Only about a month after the birth, and with Philadelphia threatened by the British, Dolly, with daughter Lydia and sister Kathy, packed up and went with John and the Continental Congress to Baltimore. When John and the Congress returned to Philadelphia in March 1777, Dolly, Lydia, and Kathy stayed behind for a time. When they did return to Philadelphia, it was only briefly. Dolly wanted to go back to Boston. After she left, John became restless, bored, and lonely. He also was stricken with grief. He received word from home that little Lydia had sickened and died. Hancock abruptly left the Congress and went home.

He lingered in Boston long enough to be with Dolly for the birth of another child, John George Washington Hancock, in May 1778. The baby's father returned to the Continental Congress that same year only to soon quit and return to Massachusetts just in time to take command as a major general of about six thousand militiamen preparing to drive the British out of Newport, Rhode Island, with the help of the French. The operation was a fiasco.

Hancock leveraged his huge popularity to become the first governor of the Commonwealth of Massachusetts in 1780, winning 90 percent of the vote. He easily won reelection in each of the next four years. Then, ill and faced with difficult economic problems in the state, he suddenly quit as governor in January 1785.

Two years later, his nine-year-old son, trying out new skates on some icy sidewalks, fell, hit his head, and died. Hancock's grief and chronically poor health did not stop him the next year from running for governor again and even promoting himself for the vice presidency of the United States. He easily won election as governor. His campaign to become vice president, however, went nowhere. He finished a distant fifth out of eleven candidates.

As governor, Hancock rarely risked his popularity by tackling issues head-on. He is remembered, however, for backing laws to help out debtors, measures that chipped away at a cause of Shays's Rebellion, unrest out of western Massachusetts that demonstrated the weakness of the young nation. Hancock also pardoned all those in the rebellion, including Shays himself.

Hancock was still governor at the time of his death in 1793. When the value of his estate was tallied, the cash came to about half of what was left to him by his uncle, and his landholdings were but a fraction of what his uncle had accumulated.

As for Harvard's snit with Hancock over college funds that Hancock, as college treasurer, appeared to mishandle, that was mostly settled in 1777. Harvard retrieved documents, notes, and related papers from Hancock and appointed another treasurer. Hancock's attorney turned over to the college almost all of the money in question. For years the college tussled with Hancock over a small amount the college felt was still owed. The problem stemmed mainly from fuzzy accounting and honest disagreement about rents and interest. The lingering issues were finally settled by Hancock's estate in 1801, eight years after Hancock's death.

As for Dolly Hancock, she remarried. Three years after John's death, she became the bride of James Scott, a widower and a ship's captain who had been a friend of Hancock's. The Scotts lived in Portsmouth, New Hampshire. After his death in 1809, she moved back to the Hancock Mansion on Beacon Hill. She sold the mansion in 1816 and moved to a smaller house in Boston. She died in 1830, at age eighty-three.

In the months before independence, Sam Adams was recognized in America and beyond as the leading revolutionary. Josiah Quincy, writing from London, said that there, Adams was thought of as "the first politician in the world." Lord North referred to rebellious Americans as "Sam Adams's crew."[10]

But as with Hancock, Adams's national influence quickly plummeted after independence was declared. He lost respect after he became associated with an attempt to dislodge Washington as commander. He also alienated many members of Congress with his penchant for intrigue.

He turned his attention to his beloved Boston and Massachusetts, where he was revered but not necessarily followed. In Boston, Adams was incensed at plans for a club that would allow dancing and card playing, and admit females over sixteen. He suggested that a mob should put an end to this club. No mob took up his recommendation.

Predictably, he stood in the way of the movement to open theaters in Boston. At a Boston town meeting, citizens claiming their "natural Theatrical rights" shouted Adams down.[11]

Adams had a role in drafting the state's constitution. According to the portion of the constitution he helped formulate, anyone who didn't go to church or who belonged to a congregation too small to support its own minister would be forced to pay a tax to support the Congregational Church in the state. This article was approved and remained the law of the state until 1833.

Adams proved fiercely unsympathetic to rebellion in independent Massachusetts. Responding to Shays's Rebellion, the man who engineered resistance to British authority declared, "The man who dares to rebel against the laws of a republic ought to suffer death."[12]

Politically, Adams seemed woefully out of touch. After the US Constitution was established, Adams ran for Congress from the district that included Boston. Voters ignored him. In 1788, he ran for lieutenant governor and lost. He finally won election to that post in 1789, but only because of strong support from Hancock, after the two had patched up old differences.

After Hancock died in 1793, Sam Adams was elected governor, but again it was through Hancock's help–this time posthumously: Adams won mainly through the support of Hancock's old followers.

Governor Adams was no longer poor, but he remained frugal and stuck in his ways. His weather-beaten house on Winter Street sorely needed paint. He continued to wear a wig, cocked hat, and knee breaches, not the style of the new generation. Like Hutchinson, he had to deal with Boston mobs, incensed by a treaty with Britain, threatening houses of the rich. Adams sympathized with the "Boys," calling the disturbances "water melon frolicks."[13] Mobs raised hell for six nights.

By this time Sam Adams and John Adams had gone their separate ways politically, so much so that Sam Adams ran as a presidential elector opposed to John Adams as president. Sam Adams lost that election and then grumbled–sounding almost like a Tory–that the opposition had flooded Boston with illegal voters.

A visitor to Boston in 1796 remarked that Governor Sam Adams was "superannuated, unpopular, and fast decaying in every respect."[14] That same year he announced that he would not seek reelection. He lived on in ill health long enough to cheer the news of Thomas Jefferson's election as president, believing that Jefferson was attuned to his revolutionary principles. Sam Adams died in 1803. His funeral procession passed the place where the Liberty Tree once stood.

After leaving public life after 1772, James Otis continued to fight madness. He could be lucid or in a frenzy. A few glasses of wine seemed to send him spinning out of control. Over the course of one two-day fury,

Otis destroyed letters and other writings, thus denying historians a clearer glimpse of this troubled and important figure.

Much of this time he spent in Barnstable, where he was regularly seen at church. He also sometimes appeared at law courts as a spectator. The last two years of his life he lodged at a farm in Andover and was stable enough to return briefly to Boston to plead a case in court.

Once he had told his sister Mercy, "I hope when God Almighty in his righteous providence shall take me out of time into eternity, that it will be by a flash of lightning." He got his wish. On a Friday afternoon in May 1783, as dark clouds gathered over Andover, Otis, cane in hand, stood near the front entryway of the house where he lived. He had just launched into a story for the family collected in the next room, when a flash of lightning exploded, striking him dead. No one else in the house was injured.[15]

In his will he left five shillings to a daughter who had married a British officer. The remainder was left to his wife and other daughter.

After his famous ride, PAUL REVERE could not return to Boston. Eventually his family joined him in Watertown, where the Provincial Congress assigned him to print money and then to establish somewhere in the province mills for making gunpowder. The mill he helped set up in Canton provided most of the powder used by Massachusetts soldiers in the first three years of the war. Revere and his family finally returned to Boston after the British evacuation. Washington sent him out to Castle Island to see what he could do to repair cannon left behind by the British. The ever-resourceful Revere made the repairs and, while he was at it, crafted a new kind of gun carriage.

Through much of the war, Revere was a commander on Castle Island, where he was plagued by desertions. He and his men were involved in the disastrous 1779 Penobscot expedition in Maine. Accusations flew about why the mission failed. Revere's reputation was so tarnished that he asked for a court-martial to clear his name. After at least six requests, he got his trial in 1782 and was acquitted.

After the war, Revere went into retailing. Working with a Boston Tory exiled in England, he was among the first to resume imports from Britain of such goods as cloth, wallpaper, playing cards, pencils, fish lines, and eyeglasses. In 1786, at age fifty-one, he wrote to a cousin: "Since my last letter I have lost one of the finest little boys that ever was born, two years and three months old, named John, for you. I have now begun to think I shall have no more children. I have had fifteen children and six grandchildren." Revere had another child the next year, the last of three sons named John.[16]

Revere continued to extend his business activity, getting into manufacturing–casting iron hardware for ships as well as stoves, anvils, and forge hammers. Then he entered the more exacting work of casting bells. According to one estimate, Revere and his son Joseph Warren Revere produced nearly four hundred bells from 1792 to 1826. Revere's largest and most famous bell still rings from Boston's King's Chapel.

Paul Revere, after the St. Memin portrait. (*Library of Congress*)

He also supplied metal parts for ships. He produced the copper bolts and spikes for the USS *Constitution*–Old Ironsides. The ship's first copper sheathing came from Britain. But when that needed to be replaced, Revere produced it. Revere copper also went onto the roof of the new State House in Boston.

When the War of 1812 broke out against Britain, and new fears arose that Boston would be attacked, Revere, close to eighty years old, was the first of some 150 or so "Mechanics of the Town of Boston" to volunteer in the town's defense. He thus joined other men, as well as boys given the day off from school, handling shovels and wheelbarrows in the construction of a fort. He received a note of thanks from the crew's leader, the first Catholic bishop of Boston. How times had changed.

Rachel Revere died in 1813 at age sixty-eight. Paul lived on without his "dear girl" until 1818, when he died at age eighty-three. His obituary said nothing about his now-famous ride.

ROBERT NEWMAN, who helped Revere with the lantern signals at Christ Church, killed himself in 1804. William Dawes, the other rider from Boston that April night, fought at Bunker Hill and later prospered from a war-related provisions business. He lived to 1799. Doctor Samuel Prescott, the rider who carried the alarm to Concord, later served as a surgeon in the Continental Army, and even later as a crewman on a privateer. He was captured by the British and died in a Halifax prison in 1777. His beloved, Lydia Mulliken, who received no word of his fate, waited for his return. She finally learned of his death in 1783. She eventually married and raised a family. According to historians, Ammi White was the Concord militiaman who clubbed to death the wounded regular at Concord Bridge. White was never tried or punished for the crime. He later married, moved to New Hampshire, and lived to age sixty-six.

Revolutionary THOMAS YOUNG, after leaving Boston before Lexington and Concord, became embroiled in the efforts to separate the region that became Vermont from New York. Young told the people of Vermont–a term Young himself coined–that they had a right to be independent of the "New York Monopolizers": "You have as good a right to choose how you will be governed and by whom as they had."[17]

New York would not go along with the secession of Vermont, and neither would the Continental Congress. Congress argued that its role was to defend the states against Great Britain, not to "recommend or countenance any thing injurious" to their "rights and jurisdictions." Congress censured a circular on the matter written by Young as "derogatory to the honour of Congress." Young never learned of this. He was already dead. Six days before, on June 24, 1777, he succumbed to a "virulent fever" while working as a surgeon at an American military hospital.[18]

Henry Knox, the stout bookseller who retrieved cannon from Fort Ticonderoga, rose to become brigadier general and then major general in the American army. After the war, he took Washington's place as army commander. In 1785, he became secretary of war under the Articles of Confederation, and in 1789 became the first secretary of war under the Constitution.

Decades into the next century, some aging participants of the revolutionary unrest in Boston were rediscovered and celebrated. One was George Robert Twelves Hewes, the poor shoemaker who had roles in the 1770 Massacre, the 1773 Tea Party, and the 1774 attack on John Malcom. In 1833, a writer found Hewes living in obscurity in New York State. The writer interviewed the old shoemaker and wrote his memoir. In this way, the people of Boston learned of his whereabouts, and in 1835, they invited him to town and made him a guest of honor on Independence Day. More interviews followed, resulting in a second memoir.

Historians, especially Alfred F. Young, used these memoirs and other information to piece together the story of this poor man's long life of struggle. By fall 1776, he and his family were in Wrentham. During the war he served at least nine months in the militia (his rank was never higher than private) and over ten months at sea as a privateer, sailing as far as the West Indies. Late in the war, he avoided the military draft by hiring a substitute.

After the war, Hewes stayed in Wrentham and then moved to Otsego County, New York, after the War of 1812. There he struggled on, apparently as a shoemaker. A comical and unflattering poem–perhaps by James Fenimore Cooper, who knew Hewes–survives:

Old Father Hewes, he makes good shoes,
And sews them well together

It has no heels but those he steals
And begs his upper leather.[19]

George Robert Twelves Hewes by Joseph Cole. (*Bostonian Society*)

Historians think Hewes and his wife, Sarah, who died in 1828, had fifteen children and some fifty or so grandchildren. Of their children, one was named Eleven, and the last was named George Robert Twelves Fifteen. Even with all the offspring, Hewes wasn't living with family, but with "a worthy gentleman," when the writer in 1833 discovered the old shoemaker.[20] The writer thought Hewes was approaching his one hundredth birthday. Actually, Hewes was closer to ninety-three, but he lived on to about ninety-eight, dying in 1840 in Richfield Springs, New York.

Where did the odd name "Twelves" come from? It was the maiden name of a grandmother.

For blacks in Massachusetts, American independence changed little. Slavery persisted and laws that discriminated against blacks remained in place. But following in the footsteps of Felix Holbrook and other prewar petitioners, blacks kept the pressure on. For example, in 1777, eight men, led by the son of a white father and mixed-race mother, asked lawmakers to free slaves twenty-one and older. In 1780, a black mariner and six others "of the African extract" used the familiar argument of no taxation without representation to demand that they be exempt from paying taxes in their town: if they were not allowed to vote in their town meetings, they should not have to pay town taxes.

These initiatives failed, but others succeeded. In 1783, a former slave won backpay for her years of unpaid labor. She received an annual pension from the rent out of the property of her former master, a Tory who fled to Britain.

Never strong in New England to begin with, slavery weakened under pressure from immigration, which lowered the cost of paid labor, thus eroding the possible economic advantage of slave labor. Finally, slavery in Massachusetts was battered to death in courtrooms. In two key cases, lawyers representing slaves latched on to a phrase in the 1780 Massachusetts Constitution: "All men are born free and equal." The state's chief justice, who had once owned a slave, ruled in 1783 that times had changed and "the idea of slavery is inconsistent with our own conduct and Constitution."[21] The state's remaining slaves were gradually freed. By the time of the first federal census in 1790, Massachusetts had no slaves.

In the months immediately after independence was declared, Bostonians briefly jailed a few Tories. Others were "exiled," not out of the country, but just out of town: four months in Medfield, or four months in Dedham, or two months in Waltham, for example. In April 1777, a mob led by "Joyce Jun'r," a figure on horseback in a red coat and white wig, brandishing a sword, carted five suspected Tories out of town, dumped them in Roxbury, and warned them never to be seen in Boston again.[22]

The congregation at the Hollis Street Meetinghouse booted Tory preacher MATHER BYLES from his pulpit. They were offended that he had stayed in town during the siege. Among their charges against Byles were that he hobnobbed with British officers and behaved during the crisis with "a grate degree of liteness and Indifference."[23] About the same time, the new government put Byles on trial, found him guilty of disloyalty, and determined that it would be "dangerous to the peace and public safety"[24] to allow him to live in Massachusetts. He was sentenced to be shipped off to the West Indies or Europe. Perhaps on account of age–he was now over seventy–or thanks to pleas from one or more local ministers, that sentence was never carried out. He was briefly confined to his house, with a sentinel standing guard. One day townspeople saw Byles, in his great wig and black clerical clothes, marching back and forth in front of his house with a musket on his shoulder. He had asked the guard to fetch some water from a nearby well. The guard kindly did the favor for the old fellow, who in exchange shouldered the musket and took over guard duties. Authorities soon agreed that Byles probably could walk around town without putting the nation's independence in peril. He was soon seen strutting "about the town in the luxuriance of his self sufficiency, looking as if he despised all mankind."[25] Byles lived on with his two unmarried daughters, the sisters who proudly strolled with British officers on the Common during the siege. How Byles and his daughters supported themselves was a mystery. After Mather Byles's death in 1788, the daughters remained as defiantly Loyalist as their father had been. Maybe more so. These descendants of rock-ribbed Puritans became Anglicans. Said a visitor: "[T]hey gloried, they triumphed, in the firm adherence of their father and his family to the royalty of England, and scorned the idea of even now being classed among the citoyennes of a republic, a republic, which as they said, they had never acknowledged and never would; regarding themselves as faithful subjects to His Majesty of Britain, whoever that majesty might be."[26]

Over fifty years after Lexington, newly crowned King William IV received a letter from one of Byles's daughters in Boston declaring the family's continued loyalty to Britain.

Bostonians generally left the Byleses alone. But as late as 1820, some locals were still put off by the sisters' defiance. That year the women received a letter from someone threatening to pull down the family's rickety old house: "The writer gives you notice that unless you alter your proud course of conduct within one month your old rotten house shall totter and your first warning will be broken glass."[27]

The sisters made certain that after their deaths, all of their possessions–portraits, letters, everything–would be shipped to Halifax and scattered among relatives in Canada so "that not a creature in the states will be any the better for what we shall leave behind us."[28]

Many Tories who left Boston hoped to return. One of the few who did was DR. JOHN JEFFRIES. He went to London, established a successful practice, and won fame as one of the first to fly by balloon across the English Channel. By 1790, he was back in Boston and accepted into the community despite his Loyalist past.

Of those Loyalists who didn't return to Boston, many ended up in New Brunswick or Nova Scotia, where they became known as United Empire Loyalists. For fifty years, they or their sons occupied many important judicial posts in Canada.

Such was the case with JONATHAN SEWALL–Loyalist attorney, friend of John Adams's, and brother-in-law of John Hancock's. The Sewalls–Jonathan, Esther, and their three children–arrived in England in late September 1775, first settling in London, where they rubbed elbows with Hutchinson and other exiles. Esther pined for New England while Jonathan stewed about "this most unnatural, causeless destructive rebellion" plotted by "the worst set of men that have ever lived from the days of Lot to this day."[29] Their lives further soured when death took their only daughter, money became tight, and expectations of a brief exile evaporated. They moved to Bristol. Jonathan changed the spelling of the family name to Sewell; it seemed more properly English. But he could not adapt to his new reality. In 1785, depressed by exile, his wife's homesickness, demands by creditors, and squabbles with the British government over money, he shut himself in his room–eating little and exercising not at all–for eighteen months. Physicians were called in. They were no help. "My malady was altogether mental," he later wrote.[30]

He finally emerged from his room determined to take Esther and his younger son to Canada, where his older son had already moved. Before leaving England, he was briefly in London, where his old friend John Adams found him. Wrote Sewell: "When Mr. Adams came in, he took my hands in both of his, and with a hearty squeeze, accosted me in these words–how do you do my dear old friend!–our conversation was just as it might be expected at the meeting of two old sincere friends after a long separation."[31]

Adams's version: "[B]oth of us, forgetting that we had ever been enemies, embraced each other as cordially as ever. I had two hours conversation with him, in a most delightful freedom, upon a multitude of subjects."[32]

In New Brunswick, Sewell's spirits rose somewhat in a place in many ways like New England. After a settlement from the British government, he even found himself well off. The couple remained unhappy, however. Her continued longing for New England made him miserable, and his declining health prevented her from visiting her old home. He died in 1796. She lived to 1810. One son became chief justice of Lower Canada and the other became Canada's attorney general.

PATRICK MCMASTER, tarred and feathered in 1770, also landed in New Brunswick. After finding refuge on Castle Island, the McMaster brothers conducted business from a makeshift warehouse on the island, returning to the town when nonimportation came to an end. After the evacuation of Boston, they first settled in Penobscot, eventually received Crown land grants, and moved to Charlotte County, New Brunswick.

Of all the Loyalists who fled Boston, none had a more fantastic life than BENJAMIN THOMPSON, the Woburn-born spy for the British military in Boston. Thompson went off to England about the time of the evacuation and quickly wormed his way into the good graces of Lord George Germaine, a key minister. From that relationship, he won several government posts, acquired a comfortable fortune, and found the resources to indulge his true passion: science. Through his experiments about, for example, the velocity of bullets, he acquired an expertise in naval gunnery and won a job as an admiral's aide. In that post, he turned his attention to an improved naval flag-based signaling system. Later, after being put in charge of clothing for British armed forces in the colonies, he studied the properties of cloth, especially silk.

He returned to America in 1781 as commander of the Loyalist King's American Dragoons. His men skirmished with patriot forces under the famous Swamp Fox, Francis Marion, in South Carolina. Later, as a commander on Long Island, New York, he enraged the community of Huntington by stripping the countryside of food, tearing down a church, chopping down dozens of apple trees, and fashioning tables and ovens out of local gravestones. Always inventive, Thompson used his spare time to design a new gun carriage that could be dismantled, carried on three horses, and then, in seventy-five seconds, reassembled.

Shortly after returning to England, Thompson set off to the Continent and landed a post in Munich as the right-hand man for the Duke of Bavaria. Put in charge of reforming the lowly regarded Bavarian military, Thompson increased military pay and ended the practice of sentencing criminals to military service. He also employed soldiers in planting gardens and in rounding up beggars, who were housed, fed, given clothes, provided medical care, and put to work producing uniforms and materiel for the military.

Later, Thompson put the military to work refashioning acres of land on the outskirts of Munich into a great public park featuring ponds and such architectural curiosities as a Chinese tower. The park endures today as the famous and beloved nine-hundred-acre English Garden.

By this time, he also had an affair and an illegitimate daughter with the ex-mistress of the Bavarian duke. This did not seem to bother the duke, who made Thompson a count of the Holy Roman Empire. (By this time Thompson had already received, from George III, a knighthood, and, from the king of Poland, the Royal Order of Stanislaus.) Thompson took the name Count Rumford–Rumford being an old name for part of Concord, New Hampshire.

Later Count Rumford decamped for Italy, where he started a new love affair with another man's wife in Florence and, in Verona, tinkered with stoves and fireplaces as part of his fascination with the nature of heat. Back in England, he acquired greater wealth as an authority on more efficient fireplaces and stoves. Tall, shallow Rumford fireplaces became hugely popular. He developed the kitchen range and came up with the first double boiler, the first convection oven, and the first pressure cooker. He conducted more groundbreaking experiments on heat, demonstrating, for example, how cold water could be brought to a boil by heat produced through friction.

Never short of chutzpah, he approached the US government with an offer to help establish a military academy. That went nowhere, but the government, eager for Rumford's expertise and willing to let bygones be bygones, did offer him an official appointment as inspector general of the artillery of the United States.

That went nowhere, too, as Rumford found other distractions in Europe. With Thomas Bernard, son of the former royal governor of Massachusetts, and others, Rumford established the Royal Institution of Great Britain, which thrives today as a charity dedicated to helping people understand science.

Rumford spent his last days in France, where he married the widow of Antoine Lavoisier, the famous chemist who discovered the role of oxygen in combustion (the wife Rumford had abandoned in New England was long since dead). Rumford's second marriage, like his first, was a disaster. He called his wife a dragon. She found him a bore. He remained devoted to science, tinkering with coffee pots and lamps, for example. He died in 1814, leaving his books to the government of the United States and money to Harvard. He also left behind a vast trove of writings on everything from the nutritional value of potatoes, to the relationship of heat to molecular motion, to the treatment of criminals, to military logistics. Most Americans never heard of him, but Franklin

Roosevelt placed Rumford alongside Benjamin Franklin and Thomas Jefferson as one of America's three greatest intellects.

Anna Green Winslow, the girl whose journal gives us a glimpse of Boston in the 1770s, did not live to see her twentieth birthday. She died in fall 1779 in Marshfield, Massachusetts, probably of tuberculosis. Her gravesite is unknown. Her Aunt Sarah Deming lived to 1788. Her slave Lucinda, whom Deming bought off a slave ship when the girl was seven, was set free after Deming's death. What became of the anxious British military man whom Sarah Deming talked to on the eve of Lexington? If that was Lieutenant Edward Barron, we know he survived Lexington because he was listed as wounded at the Battle of Bunker Hill.

The fate of Samuel Haws, the soldier from Wrentham who kept a journal, is a mystery. On February 10, 1776, he wrote in his journal, "Nothing Strange this Day,"[33] and there the journal ends. What became of him, no one knows.

Nathaniel Wheelwright, the merchant whose bankruptcy touched off a financial crisis about the time of the Stamp Act, slipped out of Boston the year of his bankruptcy, 1765, and died the next year of yellow fever in Guadeloupe. Matters concerning his bankruptcy were still being sorted out as late as 1782.

William Billings, the energetic tanner and composer, continued writing music and working the tanner's trade. Including *The New England Psalm Singer*, he produced six collections of music, and "Chester," his most famous piece, became one of the favorite tunes of the Continental Army. He also married, had six children, and was prosperous enough to buy a house. But the good times didn't last. In 1792, the *Massachusetts Magazine* noted the "distressing situation of Mr. Billings's family."[34] He died in 1800, at age fifty-four. Before he died, he saw Massachusetts finally pass, in 1783, a law protecting copyrights of authors.

Ebenezer Richardson, pardoned in 1772 after his conviction for killing the Seider boy in 1770, slipped away to Philadelphia in hopes of getting some customs job but found conditions too threatening there. He returned to Massachusetts and met up with Gage in Salem. The new governor advised him and another man to go to England. Before the two men could leave, they were confronted by a mob in Stoneham. They fled to Boston, by then a haven for Tories. By January 1775, Richardson was in London petitioning authorities for money. He received £10 and disappeared from the prying eyes of historians.

Benjamin Church, the patriot leader accused of spying for the British, was taken to a jail in Norwich, Connecticut, after his expulsion from the Massachusetts Provincial Congress. There his health declined. Responding to petitions from his doctor and his family, the Continental Congress allowed him to go to Boston in June 1776, three months after the British evacuation. Almost as soon as Church arrived in Boston, a mob attacked the house where he was staying. To prevent further disorder and to protect Church, town selectmen ordered him hauled off to jail. In July 1777, authorities planned to hand Church over to the British in exchange for American prisoners. A mob, however, rose up to block the exchange. In January 1778, Church was given permission to go into exile, provided he not return to America until the end of the war. He left for Martinique. On the way, the vessel carrying him sank with no trace.

JOSEPH WARREN left behind four children. They were initially cared for by their maternal grandmother, and local Masons provided some money for their support. Eventually, the two youngest came under the care of Mercy Scollay, with whom Warren was engaged before his death. The oldest daughter lived with her uncle's family. The oldest son was placed under the care of a minister in Chelsea. In 1777, Congress approved a motion by Sam Adams to pay for the education of the eldest son. Benedict Arnold, who had met Warren in Cambridge, took a special interest in the welfare of his children. At Arnold's instigation–before his treachery–Congress in 1780 approved more money for the support and education of Warren's three younger children.

JOSIAH QUINCY left a son, Josiah, who became president of Harvard, was elected to the US Congress, and served as Boston's mayor. His son, also Josiah, also became mayor of Boston. And his grandson, yet another Josiah, was also Boston's mayor.

At the time the redcoats left Boston, JANE FRANKLIN MECOM, sister of Benjamin Franklin, was living in Philadelphia with a niece. Learning that her Boston home had been looted, Mecom decided that for the moment, Boston was not yet safe. But Philadelphia, as it turned out, was not safe either. The war forced her to flee to Goshen, Pennsylvania, and then to Rhode Island. She spent some of 1778 making "ruffled shirts and stockings" for the American soldiers. Meanwhile, death took more of her children, and by 1779 only one remained. Mecom finally returned to Boston and lived in a house just behind Old North Church with her surviving daughter, the daughter's husband, and a daughter of one of her deceased sons. In 1786, workmen replaced the great steeple on Old North. Jane, well acquainted with her brother's inventions, was troubled: she was afraid the steeple's "Electricil wier was too small to conduct a Large Strook of Lightning." She was reassured that the thickness of the wire had been increased threefold.[35] She died in 1794, at age eighty-two.

Poet PHILLIS WHEATLEY, in 1778, married John Peters, a free black man who was a grocer and lawyer. Phillis continued to write, but with the Revolutionary War disrupting life, she could not generate interest from subscribers. In December 1784, while Peters was in debtors' prison, Phillis and two of her children died.[36]

HARBOTTLE DORR, the hardware salesman who diligently saved, indexed, and annotated newspapers, finally stopped his project at the end of 1776. In all, he collected, at "considerable Expense, and very GREAT Trouble,"[37] 3,280 newspaper pages, along with various documents of the period, and carefully, if peculiarly, crafted indexes (a story of a German man who was executed went under "H" for "hanged").[38] On the title page of one of the volumes he wrote that he hoped the collection might someday "be of some service towards Forming a political History of [this] Country, during the shameful and abandoned Administration of ye Disp[otic] Ministers of George ye 3."[39]

Soon after he stopped saving papers, Dorr, at age forty-seven, was elected town selectman, as which he evidently served to the town's satisfaction: he was reelected eleven times. He lived until 1794. His collection now is in the hands of the Massachusetts Historical Society.

The fortunes of EBENEZER MACKINTOSH, the mob leader during the Stamp Act crisis, plummeted in 1769. That year he was not only displaced as mob leader but lost his post as sealer of leather and spent some time in debtors' prison.

He possibly took part in the Boston Tea Party, as he claimed. He later vanished from Boston so quietly that Tory Peter Oliver thought he had died. But he was very much alive. By September 1774, he and his family were living in Haverhill, New Hampshire. His wife, Elizabeth, was the sister of Samuel Maverick, one of the Massacre victims. In 1777, Mackintosh enlisted in the army for two months. In Haverhill, Mackintosh served for two years as sealer of leather.

After Elizabeth's death in 1784, Mackintosh eventually married another Elizabeth–Elizabeth Chase–who already had three children. Mackintosh and his new wife had three more children. At age sixty-five, Mackintosh walked to Ohio and back to visit some of his children who had moved west. He died in 1816.

Preacher SAMUEL COOPER, who fled Boston before Lexington and Concord, returned after the British evacuation to the Brattle Street

Meetinghouse, which had been used as a barracks. Back in the pulpit, he became more outspoken about the American cause and an especially vigorous proponent of closer relations with France. Back in 1759, he had preached that the French were an "inveterate and implacable Enemy to our Religion and Liberties; inflamed with Romish Bigotry."[40] But by 1777, Cooper was calling on God to "bless the Monarch of France,"[41] now defender of Christianity and the rights of man. The French were so impressed by Cooper's aggressive touting of trade with France that the French ministry offered to pay him a stipend. Cooper accepted. Loyalists took note. A newspaper in New York commented that, in less than twenty years, Americans could expect to see Cooper "embrace the scarlet whore, and adorn the first Papal chair in America."[42] Cooper died in 1783.

Cooper's colleague, Reverend JONATHAN MAYHEW–the foe of Episcopal bishops in America–was long dead well before the start of the Revolution. But had he miraculously lived to 1852, he would certainly have died on learning that his grandson, Jonathan Mayhew Wainwright, was made Episcopal bishop of New York.

MERCY OTIS WARREN, sister of James Otis and wife of James Warren, was, like Sam Adams, dismayed by declining moral standards in Massachusetts in the years following the evacuation of Boston. She used poetry to express her grief in the pages of the *Boston Gazette* in 1778:

> Our country bleeds and bleeds at every pore
> Yet gold's the deity whom all adore,
> Except a few whose probity of soul
> No bribe could purchase nor no fears controul.[43]

She continued with her playwriting and, after the war, sent off to John Adams in London her play *The Sack of Rome* in hopes he could get it staged in London. Adams had no luck and wasn't encouraging. Getting a play produced was difficult enough, and there was no mood for anything from an American, he said.

Under a pen name, she produced a pamphlet opposing the US Constitution. She and husband James favored a union akin to that under the Articles of Confederation.

She later wrote one of the first histories of the American Revolution, which appeared in 1806. After reading her three, four-hundred-page volumes, former president John Adams sputtered to the author in ten letters, including some extending more than twenty pages. She had not mentioned the name of the great John Adams often enough: "You have carefully recorded the appointment of Mr. Jay to Madrid, in page 141, Vol. II, to have been on the 27th of September, 1779, yet have taken no notice of mine, which was on the 29th of the same month."[44] The book also restated a common complaint that Adams had become "corrupted" and "beclouded by a partiality for monarchy" during his diplomatic time in England. Adams wrote: "Corruption is a charge that I cannot and will not bear. I challenge the whole human race, and the angels and devils, too, to produce an instance of it from my cradle to this hour!" He suggested that Mrs. Warren was just getting even because Adams as president had failed to give James Warren a federal job.[45]

Mercy Otis Warren patched up her differences with John Adams before her death in 1814.

As for JAMES WARREN, he served for a time as paymaster general for the American army. Politically, he locked horns with Hancock, who managed to damage Warren's reputation so badly that Warren had trouble winning elections. Efforts to gain the office of lieutenant governor of Massachusetts and member of Congress fell short. He lived to 1808.

THOMAS HUTCHINSON, the exiled royal governor of Massachusetts, found that his stature shrank quickly soon after his arrival in England. Even before war broke out, ministers had lost interest in his insight into American affairs. Hutchinson observed that the British had no time and little love for outcast Americans: "We Americans are plenty here, and very cheap. Some of us at first coming, are apt to think ourselves of importance, but other people do not think so, and few, if any, of us are very much consulted, or enquired after."[46] By February 1776, he requested those who corresponded with him to leave off the customary "His Excellency" from addresses on letters to him: "[E]verybody laughs at such things here."[47]

When in 1775 he was blamed in the House of Commons for the troubles in America, he sat down and wrote a nineteen-page essay defending and explaining his decisions. But this attracted little attention, and no evidence exists that the king or Lord Dartmouth ever read it or even acknowledged it.

He fretted endlessly about the fate of relatives in America until they were finally reunited in London. By May 1776, some twenty-five people–including newly arrived Hutchinsons and Olivers from America–were living in his house off St. James's Street in London.

He was not completely forgotten. On the same day the Continental Congress in America approved the Declaration of Independence–July 4, 1776–Oxford University in England bestowed on Hutchinson and Peter Oliver honorary doctorates of civil laws.

Hutchinson also kept writing. He worked on the third volume of his *History of the Province of Massachusetts Bay*, which would cover his own stormy years as governor. He wrote a pamphlet that shredded assertions in the Declaration of Independence. He wondered, for example, how Americans could justify "depriving more than an hundred thousand Africans of their rights to liberty and the pursuit of happiness, and in some degree to their lives, if these rights are so absolutely unalienable."[48]

The death of his daughter Peggy in September 1777 crushed him. But he persevered with his *History*, finishing it in 1778. Though he knew he would almost certainly die in exile, he still longed to return some day, some way, to his beloved country home in Milton. Then, in July 1779, he saw his name at the top of a list from America of "conspirators against the liberties of the people" who were formally banished from Massachusetts forever. All his property there would be confiscated, including his Milton estate and even his wife's tomb. Bitter at the cruelty and ingratitude of his countrymen, and bewildered that he should be thought a traitor to the country he loved, he expressed in a letter a wish "to convince my countrymen of one truth (which I feel the force of to my own great comfort every day) that I never, in my public character, took any one step in which I did not mean to serve their true interest, and to preserve to them every liberty consistent with it, or with their connection with the kingdom."[49]

It was so unjust. Hutchinson was, as historian Bernard Bailyn observed, "More intelligent, tolerant, experienced, and perceptive–and less sanctimonious and self-righteous by far–than most who opposed him,"[50] and he was never the plotter his enemies made him out to be.

Hutchinson succumbed to a stroke on June 3, 1780. Soon after, his property at Milton was sold–to James and Mercy Otis Warren. James Warren received a congratulatory letter: "It is not always happened in like manner that the forfeited seats of the wicked have been filled with men of virtue."[51]

Schoolmaster John Lovell and schoolteacher James Lovell, father and son, were both shipped off to Halifax with the evacuation–Tory John voluntarily as an exile, patriot James involuntarily as a prisoner. John died in Halifax in 1778. James was released in late 1776 through an exchange of prisoners and returned to Boston. He was soon elected to the Continental Congress and served diligently for five years. Possibly in part because of his fluency in French, he was named chairman of the Committee on Foreign Affairs.

Customs Commissioner Henry Hulton and his family fled to Halifax from Boston in early 1776 and sailed that July to England. Hulton eventually acquired a farm in Somersetshire and resumed the life he enjoyed in Brookline–that of a gentleman farmer–while also collecting from the British government various salaries, pensions, and fees, as well as compensation for the confiscation of his Brookline property. He died in 1791, at age fifty-nine.

After THOMAS GAGE returned to London, he, like Hutchinson before him, had little influence. Gage and Hutchinson, the last two royal governors of Massachusetts, at least consoled each other. They often were together.

During a spasm of concern that the French might attack England, Gage won an assignment for about six months to help train militia.

Among other matters, he gave evidence proving that Benjamin Church indeed betrayed the patriot cause. Church's widow had asked for that evidence to bolster her request for money from the government. Gage died in London in 1787.

The *Gazette*, the voice of the patriotic cause, was reestablished in Boston and lived on for a while under BENJAMIN EDES. The paper continued long enough to oppose the adoption of the US Constitution. But it lost favor and support. By 1797, the list of subscribers had dwindled to four hundred from two thousand. The next year, Edes shut it down. In his farewell, he wrote that he had "stood on the Watch Tower and, like a faithful soldier in the cause of freedom, ever held himself ready and willing to fall or rise with the ruin or happiness of his country."[52] He also confessed that he was but a poor man "passing the gloomy valley of old age and infirmity."[53] He rejected pity: "[I]t is beneath a patriot to mourn his own misfortunes."[54]

A visitor to Edes's office in 1801 found the old man setting type. An elderly woman, perhaps a daughter, operated the press to produce shop bills. The visitor remarked on the scene's "aspect of destitution."[55] Edes died in 1803 at age eighty.

Edes's partner, JOHN GILL, stayed behind in Boston during the siege. After the evacuation, Gill ended his partnership with Edes and brought out another paper, the *Continental Journal*, which he sold in 1785. He died the same year.

Edes's son Peter, held by the British in Boston on suspicion of concealing firearms, was released from jail after 107 days. After the war, he worked as an apprentice for his father and then on his own as a printer in Rhode Island and then Maine, where he established himself as the first printer in Augusta and then Bangor. Late in life he set type for his son at a shop in Baltimore, but he returned to Bangor after that son and his wife died of cholera. Peter Edes died in Bangor in 1840.

The *Massachusetts Spy* never returned to Boston. Its publisher, ISAIAH THOMAS, had the honor in 1776 of reading the Declaration of Independence from a church balcony in Worcester, where Thomas eventually settled permanently. By 1778, Thomas resumed publishing the *Spy* in Worcester. In 1780, he was drafted as a soldier. However, deciding that dodging bullets did not fit in with his long-term plans, he sent his apprentice in his place. He later suspended publication of the *Spy* for two years partly because of a stamp tax on newspapers.

Through the *Spy* and the *Worcester Magazine*, Thomas supported the Constitution and reverentially printed everything he could about George Washington. When Washington visited Worcester in 1789, the *Spy* gave a detailed account and referred to Washington as "his Highness."[56]

Thomas also extended and expanded his businesses, becoming an important book publisher and, with partners, operating sixteen presses, five bookstores, a paper mill, and a bindery. Thomas and his partners printed more than nine hundred books. That compares to about eight hundred for Benjamin Franklin and his partners. Thomas is credited with printing the first American novel (*The Power of Sympathy*, attributed to William Hill Brown) and the first Greek New Testament in America. Later in life, he wrote *The History of Printing in America*, which for more than a century remained the best book in its field. He helped establish the American Antiquarian Society, a library for historians, and was its first president. He also contributed to the library. Thomas one day walked into a store in Boston that sold songs and bought one copy of every ballad on the shelves. This formed the core of the society's collection of secular songs.

Thomas's personal life was turbulent. He divorced Mary Dill Thomas, the apparent lover of Benjamin Thompson, in 1777. She was, he said, "destitute of that affection and regard for him which is necessary to render a State of Matrimony easy and happy." She later admitted to being unfaithful. In 1779, he married a war widow. After she died, he married a third time, but the couple later split. From his diary: "Had a meeting with Mrs. Thomas and her friends, in a friendly way. Separation thought best and agreed to. Very bad head ache and I may add, heart ache–these have attended me for the past 2 years."[57]

Thomas died in 1831. The *Spy* continued publishing until 1904.

The year of independence was a melancholy one for John Boyle, the printer who kept a diary. His young wife and their third child both died in April 1776 in Hingham. He married again and had five more children–one named George Washington and another named Dorothy Hancock–and survived to 1819.

Benjamin Russell, the thirteen-year-old refugee in Cambridge in the early days of the war, was taken directly to Worcester following the reunion with his father (and thrashing for failing to get word to his family that he was alive). In Worcester, Benjamin was apprenticed to printer Isaiah Thomas and was the apprentice who took his place in the army. During the war, he was one of the guards at the execution of Major John André for spying. Russell later established the *Massachusetts Centinel* newspaper and was elected to the Massachusetts House of Representatives and numerous other public offices. He died in 1845.

John Greenwood, the teenage fifer, stayed with the army and eventually became a dentist. He made dentures for George Washington.

John Mein's partner John Fleeming stayed behind when Mein fled to England in 1769. Fleeming opened his own printing house on King Street and married. He sold his equipment in 1773 and took his family to England. He came back to America on several occasions after 1790 as an agent for a European business. He later lived in France, where he died.

As for Mein, nothing is known of his fate. The last Sagittarius letter that we know of was published on July 23, 1774. He wrote a letter to James Murray of Boston in January 1775. That's the last trace of him.

Daniel Leonard, the Tory who wrote the Massachusettensis essays, was evacuated with his family to Halifax. He later moved to London and practiced as a barrister until appointed chief justice in Bermuda, where he lived until returning again to London, where he died in 1829.

Samuel Quincy, Loyalist brother of patriot Josiah Quincy, also joined the evacuation. His children and his wife, who disagreed with his politics, stayed behind in the care of her brother. The couple expected their separation to be only a few months, but Samuel never saw his wife again. He thought about coming back to America, but as he wrote in 1778: "[A] return to America I cannot be reconciled to until I am convinced that I am as well thought of as I know I deserve to be. I shall ever rejoice in its prosperity but am too proud to live despised where I was once respected–an object of insult instead of the child of favor."[58]

As months and then years went by, the possibility of return diminished as he was given, as he wrote, "the very flattering title of traitorous conspirator."[59] His property was confiscated. He landed a customs post in Antigua and moved there. Following the death of his wife in 1782, he remarried. In 1789, he and his second wife embarked for England. He died on the way. Thus he, brother Josiah, and, as it happened, a third brother, Edmund, all died onboard ship. Josiah died within sight of America. Samuel died in sight of England.

John Malcom, the man tarred and feathered in Boston in 1774, sailed off to England in May that same year, leaving behind his wife and five children, two born deaf. His main purpose was to ask for compensation for his suffering and to seek a job. But he also took time to put his name in for public office. In October, the year of his torment, he ran for Parliament against none other than John Wilkes. Wilkes won.

In January the following year, Malcom petitioned King George for money and a customs job, once again in Boston. He also asked for a strange sort of knighthood as a kind of revenge against his tormentors: "What I mean in the whole is if your Majesty Thinks Proper to make me a Single Knight of the Tarr, that I was so Tarred with for I like the Smell of it. this will do Me Great Honour in North America and in a Great Measure Retaliate for all my Losses and Sufferings in North America. . . . [T]he small Honour I Request of Your Majesty will forever Silence that Rebellious Mob of People at Boston that used Me so ill."[60]

Malcom did not get his knighthood or a job back in Boston. He did get an annuity and a post as an ensign in Plymouth, England. But he found it hard to get by. In 1783, writing from Plymouth, with his family still in America, he pleaded to the Commissioners on American Loyalist Claims for more support: "Pray Gentlemen consider my doleful Situation and my helpless Family now abroad that I now daily expect to arrive in Old England. O! pray then what shall I do with them, or my Self much longer for we cannot live on the Ensigns Pay."[61]

He probably never saw his family again. After he died in 1788, his widow in Boston applied to authorities in England for a pension.

Dorcas Griffiths and daughter Sarah Hinson also applied for and received a pension for a time. But that was cut off after an "Enquiry" into Griffiths's character. Someone, evidently, thought it unseemly for the government to be supporting a former prostitute. Though Griffiths had sufficient character to tend to the wounds of British men after Bunker Hill, her character was now found "to be such as by no means to justify Gov^{t} in giving her any Allowance in future." Authorities determined that Hinson did not need a pension.[62]

John Singleton Copley, with his family around him, resumed his painting career in England, creating great historical works and achieving some success, although today his fame is based largely on his earlier career as a portrait painter in America. He maintained ties with old acquaintances in Boston on both sides of the political fence. He even served as witness to the marriage in England of John Adams's daughter Nabby to William Smith in 1786.

Copley considered returning to America, but his wife was happy in England and so he never saw Boston again. Financial troubles and declining demand for his work haunted his later years. In 1811, artist

Samuel F. B. Morse (who later invented the telegraph) visited Copley and found him "very pleasant" and "agreeable." However, Morse wrote, "His Powers of mind have almost entirely left him; his late paintings are miserable."[63] He suffered a stroke in August 1815 and died less than one month later. His son John Singleton Copley, who was created Baron Lyndhurst, became the first lord chancellor of Britain born outside of Britain.

Copley's name lives on in charming Copley Square in Boston's Back Bay. Among the treasures of Boston's Museum of Fine Arts are Copley's portraits of John Adams, Sam Adams, John Hancock, Joseph Warren, James Warren, Mercy Otis Warren, and Paul Revere, as well as his *Boy with a Flying Squirrel*, with the image of his half-brother, Henry Pelham.

CLARKE COPLEY, the painter's infant son left in Boston with his grandmother, died in January 1776 at the age of about one year.

John Singleton Copley's half-brother, HENRY PELHAM, broke, heartbroken, and despairing in Boston after the Battle of Bunker Hill, left Boston in 1776 and settled in London, where he painted portraits and miniatures, worked as an engraver, and taught astronomy, geography, and perspective. He later moved to Ireland and married. His wife died after giving birth to twin sons. Pelham died in 1806, at age fifty-five or so, following a boating mishap as he was directing the construction of a tower on an island in the river Kenmare.

Did Miss Sarah Bromfield ever know she was the object of Henry's "Highest Esteem and Regard"? We suspect she suspected. Historians have found two volumes of the poetry of John Milton with the inscriptions, "For Miss Sally Bromfield with Mr H. Pelham's Sincere & Affectionate Compliments."[64] She eventually married a professor of Hebrew at Harvard and lived to 1831.

Mary Pelham, the mother of John Singleton Copley and Henry Pelham, lived on in Boston despite her sons' urging her to cross the ocean. Her death was noted in the May 4, 1789, edition of the *Boston Gazette*.

JOHN ROWE, the merchant and diarist who had remained in Boston during the siege and who was thus suspected of Tory sympathies, recovered his standing in the town and was later elected from Boston to the Massachusetts House of Representatives. He died in 1787.

RALPH INMAN, the Tory who contemplated exile to England, leaving his wife behind, stayed in Massachusetts and got back together with his wife. However, the remainder of their marriage seems to have been icy.

They continued to live in Massachusetts, despite the taint of their Tory connections. Elizabeth dared to befriend a British soldier held prisoner (a Scotsman named Campbell, he might have been related to her first husband). For her trouble, she was denounced in the press in terms that compared her to a whore.

When Elizabeth died in 1785, she left only a fraction of her wealth to Ralph and asked to be buried in the tomb of her second husband.

Christopher Monk, the Massacre victim mentioned by Hancock at the 1774 oration, lived on to 1780.

John Temple, the British customs man who got along with the Americans, reappeared in Boston in 1778. Lord North sent him to America to initiate some sort of reconciliation with the patriots. But Congress would have none of it. Temple returned to England the next year. In 1785, Britain sent Temple back to America as the first British consul to the United States. He died in New York City in 1798.

Hannah Mather, feisty patriot and niece of Thomas Hutchinson, went to Roxbury soon after slipping out of Boston and delivering her message to Joseph Warren on the eve of the Battle of Bunker Hill. She stayed with a relative there until the siege was over. In 1779, she married Joseph Crocker, a Harvard graduate, an officer in the American army, and, later, a storekeeper. A promoter of women's education and rights, Hannah was instrumental in establishing St. Ann's Lodge, a Masonic lodge for women, which fostered reading and helped set the stage for women's academies later. Apparently in connection with the lodge, Hannah drew up the "North Square Creed," an oath intended for husbands:

> I believe woman is the ostensible source of man's true happiness. I believe it was not good for man to be alone and his maker in infinite mercy provided for him a helpmeet. I believe a prudent wife is the greatest blessing man can attain in this world. . . . I firmly believe it is proper and best for every man to believe in every thing his prudent wife wishes him to believe. Therefor I do believe in every thing my good wife and other ladies of this happy circle wish me to unite in believing.[65]

Did Joseph Crocker take this oath? We don't know. But oath or no oath, the Crockers seem to have been compatible. Over sixteen years, Hannah Mather Crocker gave birth to ten children.

Students of women's rights in America know Hannah Mather Crocker for one of the first books on the subject, *Observations on the Real Rights of Women*, published in Boston in 1818.

The building known as the Town House or State House back in the 1760s and '70s survives today as the Old State House, the oldest public building in Boston. After the evacuation, it resumed its role as the seat of the Massachusetts government. In 1798, lawmakers and other state officials moved to the new State House on Beacon Hill. The town then bought the old building and leased it for shops and offices. Proposals to tear down the building emerged as early as 1826. That's when some citizens proposed "the removal of such an encumbrance" to make way for a statue of George Washington.[66]

A contemporary photograph of the Old State House. (*Library of Congress*)

The encumbrance survived and, from 1830 to 1841, served as City Hall. Related alterations were controversial: "It is like plastering and painting a matron very far in years."[67] It was during that period, in 1835, that publisher and abolitionist William Lloyd Garrison found refuge in the building to escape a mob.

After 1840, the structure entered a period of commercial use and decline. Signs and billboards blanketed the exterior, while its interior was carved up to accommodate dozens of tenants: the 1870 *Boston Directory* listed fifty. About the time a city committee recommended demolition to make room for traffic in the dense neighborhood, the city of Chicago offered to buy the building, dismantle it, and rebuild it in the Midwest boomtown. Bostonians suddenly took a new interest in the building. The city set aside money to restore it, and in 1881 it became a museum, which is its function today, owned by the city and operated by the Bostonian Society. In 1905, a subway entrance was opened under the building. In 1976, Queen Elizabeth II spoke from the famous balcony overlooking State Street.

The Old South Meetinghouse also survives, but no longer as a church. Following the British evacuation of Boston, the building was restored and served as a sanctuary for many more decades. However, in the 1860s, a committee of the church determined that the declining neighborhood was no longer suitable for the well-to-do congregation: "Our houses are far away. Business presses on all sides; and the air around this locality is corrupted by cooking and eating houses, and other establishments around us. Washington Street has become so crowded and unpleasant that it is hardly a suitable place for females to walk in the evening."[68]

In 1872, a three-day blaze swallowed up much of the neighborhood. Old South, damaged, was taken over by the city and used to house soldiers brought in to guard the blackened district. The displaced congregation, already poised to leave the neighborhood, never returned, moving to a chapel on Copley Square. Then, for a time, Old South was used as a post office.

Later, the congregation auctioned off the building and the purchaser immediately began demolition, starting with the steeple. A concerned retailer, the owner of a clothing store, was horrified and obtained a seven-day delay. As people, mainly women, worked to raise money to save the building, a further delay was granted. In the end, the building was rescued thanks mainly to one woman, Mary Hemenway, widow of one of the richest men in New England. She alone gave $100,000. Ralph Waldo Emerson, Louisa May Alcott, and Henry Wadsworth Longfellow, among others, also pitched in to help in preservation efforts. Some $400,000 was raised. The Old South Association reopened the building to the public in 1877. Over the years, the Old South Association used the building to exhibit various relics, such as a shoe that belonged to Martha Washington, to raise funds. This practice earned derision for making the building a "side show." Said the *Boston Globe*, "There is still room, however, for a fat lady."[69]

The building has since served largely as a forum for speeches. It also houses a museum and is used for such events as weddings.

Faneuil Hall, too, survives, but in a much expanded form. In 1805, architect Charles Bulfinch, builder of the new State House, took on the task of doubling Faneuil Hall's width and height while preserving its original style. He succeeded while also shifting the cupola from the center of the roof to one end. The town meetings, which made the hall such a pivotal place in the run-up to the Revolution, came to an end in 1822, when Boston adopted a city charter. That charter protected the building by including a provision prohibiting the city from selling it or from selling any part of Boston Common. The building continued to serve as a forum for important speeches by such figures as William Lloyd Garrison, Frederick Douglass, Daniel Webster, Jefferson Davis, and Susan B. Anthony. Nowadays, markets occupy the ground floor, and the meeting hall takes up most of the two floors above the ground floor. Above the hall is the museum and armory of the Ancient and Honorable Artillery Company of Massachusetts. The city owns the building and works with the US National Park Service to preserve the structure.

One of the few historic buildings in Boston that not only survives but remains in use as it was intended is Christ Church, popularly known as Old North. A North End house once occupied by Paul Revere and his family also survives as a museum.

Outside Boston, historic landmarks include Washington's headquarters in Cambridge. This house on Brattle Street was also home to Henry Wadsworth Longfellow. It is now the LONGFELLOW HOUSE–WASHINGTON HEADQUARTERS NATIONAL HISTORIC SITE, operated by the National Park Service.

Other surviving or restored historical landmarks outside Boston include the Clarke parsonage (HANCOCK-CLARKE HOUSE) and the BUCKMAN TAVERN in Lexington and the NORTH BRIDGE in Concord. Generally overlooked by tourists and ignored by guidebooks is the POWDER HOUSE, the catalyst for the Powder Alarm. The stone tower stands where it has always stood, but now as a landmark in Nathan Tufts Park in the city of Somerville.

The meetinghouse in Watertown where the Provincial Congress met is gone. But the house used as the Council chamber and executive offices for the revolutionary Massachusetts government still stands, though not in its original location. The restored EDMUND FOWLE HOUSE is a museum and headquarters of the Historical Society of Watertown.

CASTLE WILLIAM, the military post that was a refuge for customs men and their families, no longer exists. Castle Island, where the fort stood, is no longer an island. After the British blew up the fort on their way out of Boston, Washington ordered fortifications rebuilt. After the war, Massachusetts put a state prison on the island. In 1798, the US War Department reconstructed the fortifications and gave the military outpost a new name, Fort Independence. From 1834 to 1851, the fort was reconstructed again, but in granite. After the Civil War, evolving military technology made the fort obsolete.

A wooden footbridge linked the island to the mainland in 1892. An earthen causeway came along in 1925, followed by a road for automobiles in 1932. The "island" is now an extension of South Boston.

Fort Independence and Castle Island comprise a historical site and park run by the Massachusetts Department of Conservation and Recreation.

Historic structures that have vanished include the PROVINCE HOUSE, the residence of seven royal governors. It was taken over in 1776 by the independent government of Massachusetts and occupied by the government's Committee on Accounts. The Boston town treasurer rented out part of the house as a residence. Later the state treasurer lived and worked there. The state Council and other officials also later used the building. About 1806, the house was leased out. Sisters Temperance and Mercy Cook operated it as a boardinghouse starting about 1825 and, according to tradition, not only warmed beds with warming pans but also "in guileless simplicity" tucked in their boarders "in good old fashioned style."[70]

In 1835, it was a tavern known appropriately as Old Province House. During this period, Nathaniel Hawthorne visited the house and later described its state of decay and faded grandeur in detail in *Legends of the Province House.* He was told "any jar or motion was apt to shake down the dust of ages out of the ceiling of one chamber upon the floor of that beneath it."[71]

In the 1850s, the building became Ordway Hall, with black minstrel shows as the featured entertainment. That era ended on October 25, 1864, when a fire destroyed the interior, leaving only the walls standing.

The building reemerged from the 1860s to the 1920s as a lodging house and a place for tradesmen's shops. Having survived tumult and flames over almost 250 years, it couldn't stand up to the winds of commerce: wrecking balls demolished the structure in 1922 to make way for an office building and movie theater.

One surviving relic of the building is the famous Indian Archer weathervane, which, according to Hawthorne, "bedazzled the eyes of those who looked upward, like an angel of the sun." That is in the collections of the Massachusetts Historical Society.[72]

The HANCOCK MANSION, like the Province House, is also lost. John Hancock left notes indicating his wish to give the Beacon Hill landmark to the state of Massachusetts, but he died before completing arrangements. The house remained in the Hancock family, winding up in the hands of John Hancock's nephew, also named John Hancock, who died in 1859. After his death, the family immediately offered to sell the property to the state. The governor suggested that the state government buy the house and, as it was situated next to the new State House, use it as the governor's mansion. The legislature approved the purchase but then stipulated that the house never be used as a governor's mansion. Time went by, and the purchase was never completed. So in 1863, the family sold the land under the house and offered to give the house and all its contents to the city. The city dithered. The structure might have been moved across the street to the Common for about $17,000. But that would have set a precedent of putting a building in a public park. Pledges of money for the move came in, but they were not enough, and the city's enthusiasm for the project faded. The way was clear to tear down the mansion to make room for two new mansions.

Before demolition, however, architect John Hubbard Sturgis took careful measurements and made exact drawings of the building. Those enabled the state–unwilling to save the house in 1863–to build a replica of the house for the Columbian Exposition in Chicago thirty years later. Another replica was built in Ticonderoga, New York, in 1925–26 and served for a time as the headquarters of the New York State Historical Association. The structure now serves as the library and museum of the Ticonderoga Historical Society.

The HUTCHINSON MANSION in the North End, rebuilt after the Stamp Act riots, was confiscated by Massachusetts in 1779. It had several owners before finally being taken down in 1833. The company that demolished the house took away a cement capital from a pilaster and donated it to the Massachusetts Historical Society to serve as a pedestal for a bust of Washington. Later, someone at the society took offense at the Tory artifact and shunted it into a courtyard, where it was exposed to a steady flow of rusty water. It was rescued and eventually found its way to the museum of the New England Society for the Preservation of New England Antiquities, now known as Historic New England.

The HUTCHINSON HOUSE in Milton is also gone. The street where it stood has the name Adams.

NOTES

CHAPTER 1
1. "Miscellany for the Centinel," newspaper clipping pasted before the title page of a copy of Mayhew, *Sermon,* at http://archive.org/stream/godshandproviden00mayh#page/n5/mode/2up.
2. Mayhew, *Sermon,* 25.
3. Ibid., 17.
4. Brandow, "Memoirs," 82.
5. Baxter, *Hancock,* 133.
6. Fowler, *Baron,* 13.
7. Crocker, *Reminiscences,* 51.
8. Unger, *Hancock,* 12
9. Warren, *History,* 42.
10. Bernard to William Wildman Barrington, April 19, 1760, in Barrington, *Correspondence,* 12.
11. Ibid.

CHAPTER 2
1. Bell, "Boys," 204.
2. Benton, *Census,* 36.
3. Ibid., 74–75.
4. Young, *Liberty,* 106.
5. Huang, "Poor," 75.
6. Drake, *Landmarks,* 300.
7. Bridenbaugh, *Cities,* 320.
8. Herndon, *Unwelcome,* 166.
9. Gunderson, *Useful,* 130.
10. Bridenbaugh, *Cities,* 123.
11. Shurtleff, *Topographical,* 54–55.
12. Whitehill, *Boston,* 37.
13. John Adams to Benjamin Rush, August 28, 1811, in Adams, *Works* 9, 637.
14. Bridenbaugh, *Cities,* 358.
15. Field, *Tavern,* 172.
16. Salinger, *Taverns,* 57.
17. *Town Records, 1758,* 65–72.
18. Ibid.
19. Ibid., 65–79.
20. Nash, *Unknown,* 23–24.
21. Forbes, *Revere,* 31. One of the boys was Paul Revere.
22. Oliver, *Origin,* 27.
23. Hutchinson, *Massachusetts,* 290.
24. Labaree, *Massachusetts,* 114.
25. Bailyn, *Faces,* 51.
26. Bailyn, *Ordeal,* 20.
27. Bailyn, *Faces,* 62.
28. Thomas Pownall to Earl of Halifax, September 4, 1757, in Bailyn, *Ordeal,* 4–5.
29. John Adams diary 13, March 1–December 31, 1766, March 1767, *Adams Family Papers: An Electronic Archive,* Massachusetts Historical Society (MHS), http://www.masshist.org/digitaladams/aea/cfm/doc.cfm?id=D13.
30. Bailyn, *Faces,* 52–3.
31. Ibid., 53.
32. Warren, *History,* 79.
33. Bailyn, *Faces,* 44.
34. Ibid., 99.
35. Ibid., 44.
36. Ibid.
37. Hutchinson, *History,* 88.

CHAPTER 3
1. Hutchinson, *History,* 83.
2. Ibid.
3. Ibid., 84.
4. Smith, "Post," 268.
5. Kalm, *Travels,* 262–3.
6. John Adams to William Tudor, Quincy, MA, August 11, 1818, in Adams, *Works* 10, 345.
7. Jill Lepore, "Back Issues: The Day the Newspaper Died," *New Yorker,* January 26, 2009, 70–71.
8. *Boston Gazette,* March 2, 1761, in Smith, *Writs,* 172.
9. Hutchinson, *History,* 87.
10. Ibid., 88.

CHAPTER 4
1. John Adams to Judge William Tudor, March 29, 1818, in Morse, *Annals,* 223–4.
2. Putney, "Thacher," 90.
3. Beckett, *Universal,* 42.
4. Adams to Tudor, March 29, 1818, in Morse, *Annals,* 225.
5. "Adams' 'Abstract of the Argument,'" *Legal Papers of John Adams,* vol. 2, at *Founding Families,*

http://www.masshist.org/publications/apde/portia.php?id=LJA02d036.
6. Tudor, *Otis*, 68.
7. Adams to Tudor, March 29, 1818, in Morse, *Annals*, 225.
8. Ibid.
9. Hutchinson, *History*, 95.
10. Gordon, *History*, 99.
11. Bernard to unknown recipient, June 28, 1761, in Smith, *Writs*, 391.
12. Hutchinson, *History*, 102.
13. Ibid., 98.
14. Mayhew, *Discourse*, 29.
15. Ibid.
16. John Adams to E. Niles, Quincy, MA, Feb. 13, 1818, in Adams, *Works* 10, 288.
17. John Adams to Thomas Jefferson, July 18, 1818, in Cappon, *Letters*, 2:527.
18. Rossiter, "Mayhew," 541–2.
19. "Character of Dr. Mayhew," Boston, July 17, 1766, in Blackburne, *Hollis*, 2:607.
20. Bradford, *Mayhew*, 264.
21. Ibid., 258.
22. Adams to Niles, Quincy, MA, February 13, 1818, in Adams, *Works* 10, 288.
23. Thomas Hutchinson to Richard Jackson, Boston, August 3, 1763, in Waters, *Otis*, 150.

CHAPTER 5

1. Goss, *Revere*, 2:667.
2. *Boston Gazette*, September 19, 1768, in Fischer, *Revere*, 14.
3. James Gordon to William Martin, Boston, March 9, 1764, in Noble, "Letters," 390.
4. Ibid.
5. John Adams to Abigail Smith, Boston, April 13, 1764, in *Founding Families*, at http://www.masshist.org/publications/apde/portia.php?id=AFC01d025.
6. Frothingham, *Warren*, 11.
7. Ibid., 14.
8. Adams to Smith, Boston, April 13, 1764, *Founding Families: Digital Editions of the Papers of the Winthrops and the Adamses*, ed. C. James Taylor, MHS, http://www.masshist.org/publications/apde/portia.php?id=AFC01d025.
9. Ibid.
10. Louis, "Neurology," 1201.
11. Galvin, *Three*, 143.
12. John Adams to Dr. J. Morse, Quincy, MA, December 5, 1815, in Adams, *Works* 10, 190.
13. Maier, *Old*, 34.
14. Hunter, *Identity*, 159.
15. Maier, *Old*, 32.
16. John Adams Diary, June 27, 1770, in Adams, *Works* 2, 238.
17. Morgan, *Birth*, 18.
18. Tudor, *Otis*, 26–27.
19. Abigail Adams to Mary Smith Cranch, July 15, 1766, *Founding Families: Digital Editions of the Papers of the Winthrops and the Adamses*, ed. C. James Taylor, MHS, http://www.masshist.org/publications/apde/portia.php?id=AFC01d045.

CHAPTER 6

1. Cash, *Wilkes*, 2.
2. Benjamin Franklin to William Franklin, London, April 16, 1768, in Franklin, *Works* 4, 429.
3. Bell, "Bankruptcy," 16.
4. John Hancock to unknown recipient (possibly Barnards & Harrison), Boston, January 21, 1765, in Brown, *Hancock*, 61.
5. Jones, *Biography*, 92.
6. Ibid.
7. Gordon, *History*, 112.
8. John Hancock to Barnards & Harrison, October 14, 1765, in Brown, *Hancock*, 87.
9. Ibid., 88.
10. Oliver, *Origin*, 62.
11. Hutchinson to Thomas Pownall, March 8, 1766, in Morgan, *Prologue*, 124.
12. Miller, *Adams*, 53; Morgan, *Stamp*, 160. Morgan and Miller both list John Avery, Thomas Crafts, Benjamin Edes, Stephen Cleverly, Thomas Chase, George Trott, John Smith, and Henry Bass. Miller lists Joseph Field as the ninth

member, Morgan lists Henry Welles.
13. Henry Bass to Samuel Savage, Boston, December 19, 1765, in Shaw, "Savage," 688.
14. Adams, *Works* 2, 179.
15. Bass to Savage, Boston, December 19, 1765, in Shaw, "Savage," 689.
16. Morgan, *Stamp*, 120–32.
17. *Boston-Gazette and Country Journal*, March 25, 1765, in Dorr, *Annotated*, 1:45, MHS, http://www.masshist.org/dorr/volume/1/sequence/55.
18. Bernard to George Montegue-Dunk, Earl of Halifax, Aug. 15, 1765, in Morgan, *Prologue*, 106.
19. Niles, *Principles*, 451.
20. Oliver, *Origin*, 41.
21. Ibid.

CHAPTER 7

1. "Extract of a letter from Boston, in New England, August 26, 1765," in Almon, *Collection*, 10.
2. Galvin, *Three*, 97.
3. Bourne, *Cradle*, 103.
4. *Supplement to the Boston-Gazette*, Monday, August 19, 1765, in Dorr, *Annotated*, 1:166, MHS, http://www.masshist.org/dorr/volume/1/sequence/171.
5. Bernard to Halifax, August 15, 1765, in Morgan, *Prologue*, 107.
6. Hutchinson, *History*, 120.
7. Bernard to Halifax, August 15, 1765, in Morgan, *Prologue*, 108.
8. Ibid.
9. Carp, "Fire," 807.
10. Hutchinson, *History*, 122.
11. Ibid.
12. Morgan, "Hutchinson," 468; Galvin, *Three*, 72–3.
13. Hutchinson, *History*, 122.
14. *Boston Post-Boy & Advertiser*, September 2, 1765, in Dorr, *Annotated*, 1:290, MHS, http://www.masshist.org/dorr/volume/1/sequence/295.
15. Hutchinson to Richard Jackson, August 30, 1765, in Morgan, *Prologue*, 108–9.
16. Letter from Joshua Henshaw to "Couzn: David", Boston, August 28, 1765, in New England Historic Genealogical Society, *Register*, 268–9.
17. Crocker, *Reminiscences*, 91.
18. "Address of the Chief Justice," in Quincy, *Reports*, 171–3.
19. Galvin, *Three*, 107; *Town Records, 1758*, 152.
20. James Gordon to William Martin, September 10, 1765, in Noble, "Letters," 393.
21. Van Doren, *Mecom*, 78.
22. Zobel, *Massacre*, 38–39.
23. *Boston-Gazette and Country Journal*, September 2, 1765, in Dorr, *Annotated*, 1:17. MHS, http://www.masshist.org/dorr/volume/1/sequence/182.
24. Bernard Papers (Harvard College Library), iv. 62–4, in Anderson, "Mackintosh," 35–6.
25. Hutchinson, *Diary*, 1:71.
26. Ibid., 1:70–1.
27. *Boston Post-Boy & Advertiser*, September 2, 1765, in Dorr, *Annotated*, 1:182 MHS, http://www.masshist.org/dorr/volume/1/sequence/187.
28. Thomas Hutchinson to Richard Jackson, August 30, 1765, in Rantoul, "Arbitrator," 222.
29. James Gordon to William Martin, September 10, 1765, in Noble, "Letters," 394.
30. Bernard to Halifax, August 15, 1765, in Morgan, *Prologue*, 109.
31. Bernard to William Wildman Barrington, Viscount Barrington, Boston, January 28, 1768, in Barrington, *Correspondence*, 139.
32 "Pacificus" Lectures the 'Libertines' of Virginia and the 'Pumkins' of New England," in Morgan, *Prologue*, 102.
33. *Pennsylvania Journal*, March 13, 1766, in Morgan, *Prologue*, 88–92.
34. Niles, *Principles*, 457.

CHAPTER 8

1. Bernard to Board of Trade, Oct. 12, 1765, in "The King's Message, of Seventh of March, 1774," in Force, *Archives*, 1:14.

2. Boyle, "Journal," 170.
3. Ibid., 170–1.
4. Hutchinson, *History*, 136.
5. *Boston Evening-Post,* November 11, 1765, in Dorr, *Annotated,* 1;264, MHS, http://www.masshist.org/dorr/volume/1/sequence/269.
6. *Boston-Gazette and Country Journal,* November 11, 1765, in Dorr, *Annotated,* 1;268, MHS, http://www.masshist.org/dorr/volume/1/sequence/273.
7. *Boston Evening-Post,* November 11, 1765, in Dorr, *Annotated,* 1;264. MHS, http://www.masshist.org/dorr/volume/1/sequence/269.
8. *Boston Gazette,* December 2, 1765, in Morgan, *Stamp,* 243.
9. Morgan, *Stamp,* 179.
10. *Boston Gazette,* December 23, 1765, in Morgan, *Stamp,* 180.
11. Morgan, *Stamp,* 181.
12. Quincy, *Reports,* 201.
13. Ibid., 204.
14. Quincy, *Reports,* 209.
15. *Massachusetts Gazette,* March 20, 1766, in Morgan, *Stamp,* 186.
16. "'Pacificus" Lectures the 'Libertines' of Virginia and the 'Pumkins' of New England," in Morgan, *Prelude,* 101.
17. Morgan, *Stamp,* 347–8.
18. Rowe, *Letters,* 95.
19. Account from unidentified newspaper, in Brown, *Hancock,* 127.
20. Ibid., 129.
21. Ibid.
22. Mayhew, *Snare,* 13.
23. Buchanan, *Cooper,* 102.
24. "Commonplace Book of Ephraim Eliot," in Akers, *Cooper,* 182.
25. Eaton, *Byles,* 125.
26. Ibid., 144–5.
27. Oliver, *Origin,* 29.
28. Boardman, *Edes,* 96.
29. Maier, "Reason," 235.
30. Stern, "Mecom," 147.
31. Thomas Cushing to Dennis DeBerdt, Boston, December 6, 1766, in Seventy-Six Society, *Papers,* 18.
32. "Copy of an Act for granting Compensation to the Sufferers . . . " Dec. 6, 1766, in Almon, *Collection,* 135.
33. "Copy of His Majesty's Order in Council," May 13, 1767, in Almon, *Collection,* 142.
34. Zobel, *Massacre,* 49.
35. Stephens, *Unreasonable,* 40.
36. Ibid.
37. Rowe, *Letters,* 116–7.
38. Bernard to Barrington, Boston, Sept. 1, 1766, in Barrington, *Correspondence,* 113.
39. Ibid.

CHAPTER 9

1. Oliver, *Origin,* 40.
2. Miller, *Adams,* 102.
3. *Boston Gazette,* April 27, 1767, from Dorr, *Annotated,* 1:636, MHS, http://www.masshist.org/dorr/volume/1/sequence/641.
4. Bernard to William Petty, Earl of Shelburne, Sept. 21, 1767, in Frothingham, *Warren,* 30.
5. Quincy, *Memoir,* 8.
6. Ibid., 11.
7. Frothingham, *Warren,* 39.
8. *Boston Gazette,* November 9, 14, 1767, in Frothingham, *Warren,* 32.
9. *Town Records, 1758,* 221–2.
10. Stern, "Mecom," 147.
11. Ibid.
12. *Boston Gazette,* September 2, 1765, in Alden, "Scourge," 578–9.
13. *Boston Post-Boy & Advertiser* and *Boston Post-Boy &c. Extraordinary,* November 4, 1765, MHS, http://www.masshist.org/revolution/image-viewer.php?item_id=221&mode=small&img_step=3&tpc=#page3.
14. Alden, "Scourge," 581.
15. Circular Letter, Province of Massachusetts Bay, February 11, 1768, in Bradford, *Speeches,* 134–5.
16. Ibid., 135.
17. Ibid., 136.
18. Ibid., 135.
19. Ibid., 136.
20. Rowe, *Letters,* 157.

CHAPTER 10
1. Sewall, "Opinion," 501–2.
2. Commissioners of the Customs to the Lords of the Treasury, Boston, February 12, 1768, in Wolkins, "Seizure," 265.
3. Ibid.
4. Thomas Hutchinson to Richard Jackson, June 16, 1768, in Wolkins, "Seizure," 250.
5. Joseph Harrison to Marquis of Rockingham, Castle William, June 17, 1768, in Watson, "Harrison," 589–90.
6. Ibid., 590.
7. Brandow, "Memoirs," 80.
8. Harrison to Rockingham, Castle William, June 17, 1768, in Watson, "Harrison," 590.
9. Ibid.
10. Ibid.
11. Thomas Hutchinson to Richard Jackson, June 16, 1768, in Wolkins, "Seizure," 254.
12. Harrison to Rockingham, Castle William, June 17, 1768, in Watson, "Harrison," 591.
13. Ibid., 589, 592.
14. Hulton, *Letters,* 12.
15. Ibid., 17.
16. "Instructions of Boston to its Representatives in the General Court," June 17, 1768, *Papers of John Adams* 1:216–8, at *Founding Families,* http://www.masshist.org/publications/apde/portia.php?id=PJA01d105.
17. Ibid.

CHAPTER 11
1. Wolkins, "Seizure," 243.
2. Howland, *Annals,* 278.
3. Cash, *Wilkes,* 221.
4. Ibid., 225.
5. Hillsborough to Gage, June 8, 1768, in Zobel, *Massacre,* 83. It might be presumed that Hillsborough was responding to the *Liberty* riot, but that had nothing to do with this decision. Hillsborough sent the orders out on June 8, several days before the *Liberty* incident. Gage received those orders September 7, an unusually long interval even in those days of slow communications.
6. *Town Records, 1758,* 261.
7. Bernard to Hillsborough, Boston, September 16, 1768, in Seventy-Six Society, *Papers,* 103.
8. *Town Records, 1758,* 262.
9. Ibid., 263.
10. Ibid., 264.
11. "Answer of the Town of Hatfield," in Miller, "Convention," 462.
12. Frothingham, *Warren,* 96.
13. Hutchinson, *History,* 205.
14. Galvin, *Three,* 138.
15. Frothingham, *Warren,* 100.
16. *Boston Evening Post,* October 31, 1768, in Miller, "Convention," 468.
17. Ibid., 472.
18. Rowe, *Letters,* 176.
19. Quincy, *Memoir,* 18.
20. Andrew Eliot to Thomas Hollis, Boston, October 17, 1768, in Eliot, "Letters," 432.

CHAPTER 12
1. *Journal of the Times,* January 30, 1769, in Dickerson, *Boston,* 57.
2. *Journal of the Times,* April 20, 1769, in Dickerson, *Boston,* 91.
3. *Journal of the Times,* November 9, 1768, in Dickerson, *Boston,* 21.
4. *Journal of the Times,* October 19, 1768, in Dickerson, *Boston,* 8.
5. *Journal of the Times,* December 5, 1768, in Dickerson, *Boston,* 31.
6. *Journal of the Times,* April 30, 1769, in Dickerson, *Boston,* 93.
7. *Journal of the Times,* May 16, 1769, in Dickerson, *Boston,* 99.
8. *Journal of the Times,* June 14, 1769, in Dickerson, *Boston,* 108.
9. Bernard to Hillsborough, February 25, 1769, in Miller, *Adams,* 175.
10. Hood to Caldwell, April 3, 1769, in Zobel, *Massacre,* 113.
11. Ibid., 114.
12. Wroth, *Adams,* 2:295.
13. *Journal of the Times,* May 5, 1769, in Dickerson, *Boston,* 95.
14. *Boston Gazette,* May 2, 1769, in Walett, "Undoing," 219.
15. Ibid., 221.

16. Gordon, *History*, 174.
17. Ibid.
18. Ibid., 175.
19. Winsor, *Memorial*, 3:27.
20. Wroth, *Adams*, 2:331.
21. Ibid., 2:322–33.
22. Ibid., 2:322.
23. John Adams to J. Morse, Quincy, MA, January 20, 1816, in Adams, *Works* 10, 207.
24. Ibid., 208.
25. Hutchinson, *History*, 232–3.
26. Rowe, *Letters*, 188.
27. Ibid., 21.
28. Hulton, *Letters*, 19.
29. Zobel, *Massacre*, 140.
30. Ibid., 142.
31. Frothingham, *Warren*, 9.
32. *Boston Chronicle*, October 19–23, 1769, in Tyler, *Smugglers*, 132.
33. *Boston Gazette*, August 7, 1769, in Walett, "Undoing," 222.
34. Diary of John Adams, Monday, August 14, 1769, 1:341–2, at *Founding Families*, http://www.masshist.org/publications/apde/portia.php?id=DJA01d459.
35. Bowen, *Adams*, 336.
36. Dickinson, "Liberty," 55.

CHAPTER 13

1. *Boston Chronicle*, August 17-21, 1769, MHS, http://www.masshist.org/revolution/image-viewer.php?item_id=381&img_step=1&tpc=&pid=2&mode=large&tpc=&pid=2#page1.
2. Schlesinger, *Merchants*, 165.
3. Zobel, *Massacre*, 153.
4. *Boston Chronicle*, September 11, 1769; *Boston Gazette*, September 18, 1769, in Zobel, *Massacre*, 148.
5. *Town Records, 1758*, 324.
6. *Town Records, 1758*, 298.
7. Zobel, *Massacre*, 157.
8. Alden, "Scourge," 588.
9. *Pennsylvania Gazette*, September 28, 1768, in Irvin, "Tar," 201.
10. Irvin, "Tar," 205.
11. Mein to Hutchinson, October 29, 1769, in Zobel, *Massacre*, 162.
12. Zobel, *Massacre*, 162.
13. Mein to Hutchinson, undated, in Zobel, *Massacre*, 162.
14. Hutchinson, *History*, 260.
15. Hutchinson to Hillsborough, November 11, 1769, in Zobel, *Massacre*, 163.
16. Irvin, *Adams*, 85.
17. Betsy Cuming to Elizabeth Smith, November 29, 1769, and Anne Cuming to Elizabeth Smith, December 27, 1769, in Norton, *Daughters*, 157.
18. Ibid.
19. Mrs. Henry Barnes to Elizabeth Smith, November 20, 1769, in Tiffany, *Murray*, 123.
20. Duff, "Case," 390.
21. *Britannia's Intercession for the Deliverence of John Wilkes, Esq. from Persecution and Banishment*, 6th ed., Boston, 1769, 10, in Maier, *Wilkes*, 373.
22. Sons of Liberty to Wilkes, Boston, June 6, 1768, in Ford, *Wilkes*, 191.
23. William Palfrey to Wilkes, Boston, July 26, 1769, in Ford, *Wilkes*, 206.
24. Benjamin Kent to Wilkes, Boston, October 5, 1768, in Ford, *Wilkes*, 196.
25. Thomas Young to Wilkes, Boston, August 3, 1769, in Ford, *Wilkes*, 207.

CHAPTER 14

1. Fowler, *Baron*, 117.
2. *Massachusetts Gazette*, January 11, 1770, in Wroth, *Adams*, 2:397; *Boston News-Letter*, January 11, 1770, in Zobel, *Massacre*, 173.
3. Gunderson, *Useful*, 150.
4. Zobel, *Massacre*, 165.
5. Ibid., 167.
6. Ibid.
7. George Mason to unknown recipient, January 24, 1770, in Zobel, *Massacre*, 167.
8. Samuel Cooper to Thomas Pownall, January 30, 1770, in Tuckerman, "Cooper," 315.
9. Hutchinson, *History*, 267.
10. Zobel, *Massacre*, 170–1.
11. Ibid., 171.
12. Ibid.

13. Tyler, *Smugglers*, 148.
14. Bostonian, *Hewes*, 138.
15. Oliver, *Origin*, 73.
16. Zobel, *Massacre*, 172.
17. Wroth, *Adams*, 2:398.
18. John Adams to Dr. J. Morse, Quincy, MA, January 29, 1816, in Adams, *Works* 10, 210.
19. *Boston Gazette*, March 5, 1770, in Wroth, *Adams*, 2:396.
20. Wroth, *Adams*, 2:417.
21. Ibid.
22. Ibid., 2:419.
23. Ibid., 2:416–17.
24. Hutchinson to Gage, February 25, 1770, in Wroth, *Adams*, 2:398.
25. Wroth, *Adams*, 2:417.
26. Ibid., 2:418.
27. Ibid.
28. Bostonian, *Hewes*, 93–4.
29. *Boston Gazette*, March 5, 1770, in Wroth, *Adams*, 399.
30. *Boston Gazette*, February 26, 1770, in Zobel, *Massacre*, 179.
31. *Short Narrative*, Appendix, 13.

CHAPTER 15

1. Wroth, *Adams*, 3:187.
2. *Short Narrative*, Appendix, 24.
3. Wroth, *Adams*, 3:189.
4. Ibid., 3: 52; Zobel, *Massacre*, 186.
5. Wroth, *Adams*, 3:195.
6. *Short Narrative*, Appendix, 76.
7. Wroth, *Adams*, 3:198; Zobel, *Massacre*, 187.
8. Zobel, *Massacre*, 187.
9. Wroth, *Adams*, 3:182.
10. Ibid., 3:183.
11. Ibid., 3:182.
12. Ibid., 3:183.
13. Ibid.
14. Andrew Eliot to Thomas Hollis, Boston, June 28, 1770, in Eliot, *Letters*, 451.
15. *Short Narrative*, Appendix, 14.
16. Ibid., 36.
17. Ibid., 42.
18. Wroth, *Adams*, 3:76.
19. Ibid., 3:201.
20. Zobel, *Massacre*, 196.
21. Ibid., 197.
22. *Short Narrative*, Appendix, 39.
23. Wroth, *Adams*, 3:66.
24. Ibid., 3:75.
25. Zobel, *Massacre*, 200.
26. Wroth, *Adams*, 3:81.
27. *Short Narrative*, Appendix, 64–65.
28. Frothingham, *Warren*, 131.
29. Frothingham, *Warren*, 135.
30. Zobel, *Massacre*, 207.
31. Frothingham, *Warren*, 138.
32. Ibid., 139–40.
33. *Fair*, Appendix, 23.
34. Frothingham, *Warren*, 141.
35. *Fair*, Appendix, 23.
36. Adams, *Works* 10, 252.
37. *Fair*, Appendix, 25.
38. Frothingham, *Warren*, 146.
39. Ibid., 147.
40. Zobel, *Massacre*, 209.

CHAPTER 16

1. Eaton, *Byles*, 146.
2. Ibid., 146–7.
3. Puls, *Adams*, 105.
4. Wroth, *Adams*, 3:46.
5. Henry Pelham to Paul Revere, Boston, March 29, 1770, in Copley, *Letters*, 83.
6. *Short Narrative*, 8.
7. Ibid., 10.
8. Ibid., 11.
9. Ibid., 16.
10. Ibid., Appendix, 1.
11. Ibid., 10.
12. Ibid., 12.
13. *Short Narrative*, 13–4.
14. Ibid., 15–6.
15. Ibid., Appendix, 45.
16. Ibid.
17. *Fair*, Appendix, 19–20.
18. *Boston Gazette*, March 2, 1770, in Zobel, *Massacre*, 212.
19. *Boston Gazette*, March 12, 1770, in Matthews, "Preston," 6.
20. *Massachusetts Gazette Extraordinary*, June 21, 1770, in Matthews, "Preston," 6.
21. Ibid., 10.
22. Gage to Dalrymple, August 13, 1770, in Wroth, *Adams*, 3:14.
23. Thomas Hutchinson to unknown recipient, March 25, 1770, in Pownall, *Remembrancer*, 181.
24. Wroth, *Adams*, 2:402.
25. John Adams autobiography, part 1, "John Adams," through 1776,

sheet 12 of 53, *Adams Family Papers: An Electronic Archive,* MHS, http://www.masshist.org/publications/apde/portia.php?id=DJA03d285.
26. Ibid.
27. Quincy, *Memoir,* 27.
28. Zobel, *Massacre,* 221.
29. Ibid.
30. Thomas Hutchinson to unknown recipient, March 25, 1770, in Pownall, *Remembrancer,* 181.
31. *Boston Gazette,* April 9, 1770, in Zobel, *Massacre,* 223.
32. Oliver, *Origin,* 86.
33. Wroth, *Adams,* 2:412.
34. Oliver, *Origin,* 86.
35. Wroth, *Adams,* 2:427.
36. Zobel, *Massacre,* 230.
37. Ibid.
38. Rowe, *Letters,* 202.
39. Nicolson, "Scotchmen," 76.
40. Bostonian, *Hewes,* 124.
41. Nicolson, "Scotchmen," 58.
42. Hulton, "Letters," 24.
43. Ibid.
44. Ibid., 26.

CHAPTER 17
1. Maier, "Wilkes," 393.
2. Samuel Cooper to Thomas Pownall, Boston, July 2, 1770, in Tuckerman, "Cooper," 320.
3. Zobel, *Massacre,* 242.
4. William Palfrey to John Wilkes, Oct. 23–30, 1770, in Wroth, *Adams,* 3:21.
5. Zobel, *Massacre,* 245.
6. Ibid., 249–50.
7. Wroth, *Adams,* 3:57.
8. Ibid., 3:58
9. Ibid., 3:77.
10. Ibid., 3:78.
11. Ibid., 3:73.
12. Ibid., 3:71–72.
13. Zobel, *Massacre,* 260.
14. Wroth, *Adams,* 3:92–93.
15. Ibid., 3:98.
16. Ibid.
17. Preston to Gage, October 31, 1770, in Wroth, *Adams,* 3:22.
18. Wroth, *Adams,* 3:255.
19. Ibid., 3:114.
20. Ibid., 3:120.
21. Ibid., 3:130.
22. Ibid., 3:160.
23. Ibid., 3:164.
24. Zobel, *Massacre,* 282.
25. Wroth, *Adams,* 3:214.
26. Ibid.
27. Ibid., 3:233.
28. Ibid., 3:233–4.
29. Ibid., 3:230.
30. Ibid., 3:259.
31. Ibid., 3:246.
32. Ibid., 3:253.
33. Ibid., 3:266.
34. Ibid., 3:269.
35. Ibid.
36. Ibid., 3:278–9.
37. Ibid., 3:280.
38. *Boston Gazette,* December 17, 1770, in Zobel, *Massacre,* 294.
39. Samuel Quincy to Paine, December 16, 1770, in Zobel, *Massacre,* 296.
40. Zobel, *Massacre,* 299.
41. Samuel Cooper to Thomas Pownall, Boston, January 2, 1771, in Tuckerman, "Cooper," 323.
42. Hulton, *Letters,* 29.
43. Zobel, *Massacre,* 300.
44. Hulton, *Letters,* 28
45. Ibid., 29.
46. Puls, *Adams,* 110–1.
47. John Adams to James Lloyd, Quincy, MA, April 24, 1815, in Adams, *Works* 10, 162.
48. *Boston-Gazette and Country Journal,* February 10, 1772, in Dorr, *Annotated,* 4:24, MHS, http://www.masshist.org/dorr/volume/4/sequence/102.
49. Hutchinson, *History,* 287.

CHAPTER 18
1. Puls, *Adams,* 107.
2. *Town Records, 1770,* 30.
3. Puls, *Adams,* 108.
4. Ibid., 109.
5. Bernard to Hutchinson, December 5, 1769, in Lord, "Removal," 737.
6. Gordon, *History,* 202.
7. Ibid., 203.
8. Labaree, *Tea,* 80.
9. Rowe, *Letters,* 211–2.
10. Hutchinson, *History,* 332.

11. Forbes, *Revere*, 181.
12. *Town Records, 1770*, 48.
13. Lovell, "Oration," 11.
14. Gates, *Trials*, 11.
15. Ibid., 30.
16. Davis, "Billings," 169.
17. Ibid., 166.
18. Crist, "Harmony," 336.
19. Thomas Hutchinson to Hillsborough, March 27, 1770, in Bailyn, *Ordeal*, 164.
20. *Boston Gazette and Country Journal*, September 14, 1772, in Dorr, *Annotated*, 4:147, MHS, http://www.masshist.org/dorr/volume/4/sequence/225.
21. Hutchinson, *History*, 339.
22. Hutchinson to Bernard, December 3, 1771, in Hosmer, *Hutchinson*, 224.
23. John Adams diary 17, April 16–June 14, 1771, *Adams Family Papers: An Electronic Archive*, MHS, http://www.masshist.org/digitaladams/aea/cfm/doc.cfm?id=D17.
24. Miller, *Adams*, 252.
25. John Adams diary 17, April 16–June 14, 1771, *Adams Family Papers: An Electronic Archive*, MHS, http://www.masshist.org/digitaladams/aea/cfm/doc.cfm?id=D17.
26. Wells, *Adams*, 417.
27. Sainsbury, "Pro-Americans," 431.
28. Sam Adams to Arthur Lee, September 27, 1771, in Wells, *Adams*, 419.
29. Sam Adams to Arthur Lee, October 31, 1771, in Wells, *Adams*, 419.
30. Warren, *History*, 110.
31. *Boston Gazette*, October 14, 1771, in Wells, *Adams*, 425.
32. *Massachusetts Spy*, October 17 and November 22, 1771, in York, "Polemics," 92.
33. *Massachusetts Spy*, August 29, 1771, in York, "Polemics," 95.
34. Thomas, *Memoir*, 33.
35. Ibid., 34.
36. *Censor*, March 7, 1772, in York, "Polemics," 99.
37. Bailyn, *Ordeal*, 202.
38. Samuel Cooper to Thomas Pownall, Boston, November 14, 1771, in Tuckerman, "Cooper," 325–6.
39. Ibid., 326; Hutchinson, *History*, 347–8.

CHAPTER 19

1. Henry Pelham to John Singleton Copley, Boston, September 2, 1771, in Copley, *Letters*, 150–1.
2. Hutchinson, *History*, 347.
3. Frothingham, *Warren*, 173.
4. Warren, "Oration," 20.
5. Ibid., 21.
6. *Boston-Gazette and Country Journal*, May 11, 1772, in Dorr, *Annotated*, 4:77, MHS, http://www.masshist.org/dorr/volume/4/sequence/155.
7. Hutchinson to Gage, December 1, 1771, in Unger, *Hancock*, 157.
8. Lord, "Removal," 752.
9. *Massachusetts Spy*, November 11, 1771, in York, "Polemics," 92.
10. *Town Records, 1770*, 89.
11. Ibid., 90.
12. Ibid., 91.
13. Ibid., 92.
14. Ibid., 92–93.
15. Ibid., 93.
16. Miller, *Adams*, 265.
17. Ibid., 266.
18. Frothingham, *Warren*, 203.
19. *Boston Weekly News-Letter*, November 26, 1772, in Brown, *Politics*, 83–4.
20. Adams, *Writings* 2, 353; Boston, *Votes*, 4.
21. Adams, *Writings* 2, 354.
22. Ibid., 359.
23. Ibid., 361.
24. Ibid., 363.
25. Ibid., 366.
26. Ibid., 366–7.
27. Ibid., 368.
28. Ibid., 370.
29. Frothingham, *Warren*, 212.
30. Ibid.
31. Lenox, January 4, 1773, in Brown, *Politics*, 112.
32. Puls, *Adams*, 130.
33. Ibid.
34. Bradford, *Speeches*, 340.

35. Puls, *Adams*, 136.
36. Ibid.

CHAPTER 20
1. This discussion of Josiah Quincy's travels is based on Quincy, *Memoir*, 60–110.
2. Ibid., 103.
3. Ibid., 109.
4. *Town Records, 1770,* 109.
5. John Adams diary 19, December 16, 1772–December 18, 1773, *Adams Family Papers: An Electronic Archive,* MHS, http://www.masshist.org/digitaladams/aea/cfm/doc.cfm?id=D19.
6. John Adams diary 16, January 10, 1771–November 28 [i.e. , 27], 1772, *Adams Family Papers: An Electronic Archive,* MHS, http://www.masshist.org/digitaladams/aea/cfm/doc.cfm?id=D16.
7. Ibid.
8. Franklin to Thomas Cushing, London, December 2, 1772, in Franklin, *Papers*, http://www.franklinpapers.org/franklin/framedVolumes.jsp.
9. Ibid.
10. "Tract Relative to the Affair of Hutchinson's Letters," 1774, in Franklin, *Papers*, http://www.franklinpapers.org/franklin/framedVolumes.jsp.
11. Hutchinson to Thomas Whately, Boston, January 20, 1769, in Hutchinson, *Copy*, 16.
12. Hutchinson to unknown recipient, October 27, 1773, in Bailyn, *Ordeal*, 251.
13. Bailyn, *Ordeal*, 249.
14. Hutchinson to unknown recipient, July 1776, in Hutchinson, *Diary*, 2:79.
15. Bailyn, *Ordeal*, 219.
16. Hutchinson to Israel Williams, October 30, 1773, in Bailyn, *Ordeal*, 253.
17. Brown, *Politics*, 147.
18. Ibid., 11.
19. Hulton, *Letters*, 35.
20. Ibid.
21. *Town Records, 1770,* 115.
22. Rowe, *Letters*, 53.
23. Finlay, *Journal*, 29.
24. This discussion of Anna Green Winslow's journal is based on Winslow, *Diary*, 3–72.
25. This discussion of Boyle's journal is based on Boyle, *Journal*, 366–67.

CHAPTER 21
1. "Extract of a letter from Boston, dated 25th Feb., 1773," in Drake, *Tea*, 194.
2. Labaree, *Tea*, 50.
3. Ibid., 51.
4. Ibid., 71.
5. Ibid., 92.
6. Ibid., 97.
7. Puls, *Adams*, 131.
8. Ibid., 139.
9. Rowe, *Letters*, 251–2.
10. Thomas Alwyn to Col. Cushing, October 21, 1773, in Sumner, "Memoir," 110.
11. Adams, *Writings* 3, 55.
12. "Letter from Messrs. Clarke & Sons, at Boston to Mr. Abrm DuPuis," Boston, November 1773, in Drake, *Tea*, 282.
13. Copley, *Letters*, 203.
14. Ibid., 284.
15. Carp, *Defiance*, 88.
16. "Proceedings of the Inhabitants of Boston, on the 5th & 6th November, 1773," in Drake, *Tea*, 302; "Letter from Messrs. Clarke & Sons, at Boston to Mr. Abrm DuPuis," Boston, November 1773, in Drake, *Tea*, 289–90.
17. Carp, *Defiance*, 91.
18. "Petition of the Agents, & Proceedings of the Council of Boston Thereon," in Drake, *Tea*, 310.
19. "In consequence of a conference with the committees of correspondence in the vicinity of Boston, November 23, 1773. . . ," MHS, http://www.masshist.org/revolution/image-viewer.php?item_id=444&mode=transcript&img_step=1&tpc=.
20. Thomas Hutchinson to unnamed recipient (probably his eldest son), Milton, MA, November

30, 1773, in Hutchinson, *Diary*, 1:94.
21. *Boston Gazette*, November 29, 1773, in Carp, *Defiance*, 99.
22. "Proceedings of ye Body respecting the Tea," in Upton, *Proceedings*, 290–1.
23. "Dr. Williamson's Examination Before the King's Council in London," in Sparks, *Destruction*, 387.
24. "Proceedings of the Council Thereon," in Drake, *Tea*, 319–20.
25. Labaree, *Tea*, 133.
26. "Proceedings of the Town of Boston on the 29th & 30th Novembr, 1773," in Drake, *Tea*, 324.
27. Ibid., 325–6.
28. Ibid., 326.
29. "Proceedings of ye Body respecting the Tea," in Upton, *Proceedings*, 292–3.
30. "Proceedings of the Town of Boston on the 29th & 30th Novembr, 1773," in Drake, *Tea*, 326–7.
31. Ibid., 327.
32. "Proceedings of ye Body respecting the Tea," in Upton, *Proceedings*, 294.
33. Ibid., 294–5.
34. Ibid., 295.
35. Ibid.
36. Ibid., 295–6.
37. Ibid., 296.
38. Ibid.
39. "Proceedings of the Town of Boston on the 29th & 30th Novembr, 1773," in Drake, *Tea*, 330.
40. "Proceedings of ye Body respecting the Tea," in Upton, *Proceedings*, 296.
41. Hutchinson, *History*, 436–7.
42. Quincy, *Memoir*, 125.
43. Puls, *Adams*, 146.
44. Andrews, *Letters*, 326.
45. *Boston-Gazette and Country Journal*, December 20, 1773, in Dorr, *Annotated*, 4:415, MHS, http://www.masshist.org/dorr/volume/4/sequence/496.
46. Samuel Cooper to Benjamin Franklin, Boston, December 17, 1773, in Sparks, *Destruction*, 375.
47. John Adams diary 19, December 16, 1772–December 18, 1773, *Adams Family Papers: An Electronic Archive*, MHS, http://www.masshist.org/digitaladams/aea/cfm/doc.cfm?id=D19.

CHAPTER 22
1. Andrews, *Letters*, 325.
2. Labaree, *Tea*, 142.
3. Ibid., 149.
4. Forbes, *Revere*, 217.
5. *Boston-Gazette and Country Journal*, December 20, 1773, in Dorr, *Annotated*, 4:416, MHS, http://www.masshist.org/dorr/volume/4/sequence/497.
6. Labaree, *Tea*, 152.
7. Rowe, *Letters*, 258.
8. Labaree, *Tea*, 163.
9. Ibid., 174.
10. Ibid., 178.
11. Ibid., 177.
12. Morgan, *Franklin*, 199.
13. Bailyn, *Ordeal*, 255.
14. Gage to Hutchinson, London, February 2, 1774, in Hutchinson, *Diary*, 1:100.
15. Hutchinson, *Diary*, 1:100.
16. *Boston-Gazette and Country Journal*, January 10, 1774, in Dorr, *Annotated*, 4:431, MHS, http://www.masshist.org/dorr/volume/4/sequence/512.
17. *Boston Evening Post*, January 24, 1774, in Dorr, *Annotated*, 4:437, MHS, http://www.masshist.org/dorr/volume/4/sequence/518.
18. *Boston-Gazette and Country Journal*, January 3, 1774, in Dorr, *Annotated*, 4:426, MHS, http://www.masshist.org/dorr/volume/4/sequence/507.
19. *Boston Evening-Post*, January 24, 1774, in Dorr, *Annotated*, 4:437, MHS, http://www.masshist.org/dorr/volume/4/sequence/518.
20. Forbes, *Revere*, 210.
21. Hersey, "Tar," 445.
22. Ibid., 456.
23. Hutchinson to Dartmouth, Boston, January 28, 1774, in Hersey, "Tar," 449.
24. Bailyn, *Ordeal*, 269; Wroth, *Province*, 21.

25. Bailyn, *Ordeal*, 269.
26. Ibid.
27. Rowe, *Letters*, 264.
28. Hancock, *Oration*, 11–2.
29. Ibid., 16–7.
30. Ibid., 17–8.
31. This discussion of the Boston Port Bill is based on Force, *Archives*, 1:37–52.
32. "Bill for Better Regulating the Government of the Province of Massachusetts Bay," in Force, *Archives*, 1:66.
33. Ibid., 1:71–72, 83, 86.
34. "Bill for the Impartial Administration of Justice in the Province of Massachusetts Bay," in Force, *Archives*, 1:114.
35. "Bill for Better Regulating the Government of the Province of Massachusetts Bay," in Force, *Archives*, 1:88.
36. Mein, *Sagittarius*, 105.
37. Ibid., 23.
38. Ibid., 47, 65.
39. Ibid., 22, 58–9, 87, 112, 116.
40. Ibid., 103–4.
41. Ibid., 26.
42. Ibid., 57.
43. Labaree, *Tea*, 205, 209.
44. Ibid., 215.
45. Kennedy, *Statutes*, 130.
46. Andrews, *Letters*, 327.
47. Rowe, *Letters*, 269.
48. John Scollay to Arthur Lee, Boston, May 31, 1774, in Force, *Archives*, 1:369.
49. Miller, *Adams*, 300.
50. Christie, *Empire*, 199.
51. Quincy, *Memoir*, 131, 133.
52. Ibid., 327.

CHAPTER 23
1. Alden, *Gage*, 66.
2. Rowe, *Letters*, 270–1.
3. Gage to Frederick Haldimand, May 15, 1774, in Fischer, *Revere*, 41.
4. Alden, *Gage*, 14.
5. Ibid., 29.
6. Ibid., 44.
7. Rowe, *Letters*, 269.
8. Gage to Lord Barrington, September 8, 1770, in Fischer, *Revere*, 40.
9. Stark, *Loyalists*, 124.
10. Ibid., 126.
11. "An Address to Governor Hutchinson by Sundry Gentlemen of Marblehead," in Force, *Archives*, 1:358.
12. Stark, *Loyalists*, 129–30.
13. Copley to Isaac Winslow Clarke, Boston, April 26, 1774, in Copley, *Letters*, 218–9.
14. Copley, *Letters*, 218–9, 225, 237, 242.
15. Wroth, *Province*, 32.
16. *Boston Gazette*, May 30,1774, in Wroth, *Province*, 32.
17. Moore, *Notes*, 124.
18. Nash, *Unknown*, 119–20.
19. Moore, *Notes*, 112.
20. Aptheker, *History*, 6–7.
21. Ibid., 7.
22. Ibid., 8–9.
23. "Petition for freedom to Massachusetts Governor Thomas Gage, His Majesty's Council, and the House of Representatives, 25 May 1774," MHS, http://www.masshist.org/database/viewer.php?item_id=549&img_step=1&mode=transcript#page.
24. Boyle, "Journal," 375.
25. Rowe, *Letters*, 273.
26. Ibid., 274.
27. Henry Pelham to Copley, Boston, July 17, 1774, in Copley, *Letters*, 232.
28. Newell, "Diary," 353.
29. Frothingham, *Siege*, 7.
30. Breen, *Insurgents*, 113.
31. Boyle, "Journal," 377.
32. MHS, "Donations," 41.
33. Ibid., 261.
34. Ibid., 150–1.
35. Livingston, *Putnam*, 178–9.
36. MHS, "Donations," 173.
37. Andrews, "Letters," 337.
38. MHS, "Donations," 187.
39. Ibid., 270–1.
40. Christie, *Empire*, 204–5.
41. Miller, *Adams*, 305.
42. Ibid., 307.
43. Warren, *History*, 137.
44. Wroth, *Province*, 54.

CHAPTER 24

1. Frothingham, *Warren*, 330.
2. Ibid., 331.
3. Hutchinson, *Diary*, 1:313.
4. Adams, *Works*, 4, 8.
5. Percy to Duke of Northumberland, Camp at Boston, July 27, 1774, in Percy, *Letters*, 28–9.
6. Ibid., 29.
7. Andrews, "Letters," 333.
8. Ibid., 334.
9. Ibid., 335.
10. Raphael, *First*, 61.
11. Ibid., 62.
12. Ibid.
13. Smith, *Adams*, 1:161.
14. Gage to Dartmouth, August 27, 1774, in Wroth, *Province*, 49.
15. Smith, *Adams*, 1:166.
16. Ibid.
17. Bowen, *Adams*, 465.
18. Raphael, *First*, 65.
19. Joshua Loring to Thomas Gage, August 31, 1774, in Raphael, *First*, 86.
20. Declaration of Abijah Willard, August 25, 1774, in Raphael, *First*, 72.
21. Raphael, *First*, 79.
22. Ibid., 81.
23. Ibid., 85.
24. Ibid.
25. Wroth, *Province*, 47.
26. Berkin, *Sewall*, 107.
27. Force, *Archives*, 1:747–9.
28. Andrews, "Letters," 342.
29. Frothingham, *Warren*, 349.
30. Andrews, "Letters," 357.
31. Ibid.
32. Force, *Archives*, 1:802.
33. Andrews, "Letters," 371.
34. Joseph Warren to Samuel Adams, August 21, 1774, in Frothingham, *Warren*, 343–4.
35. Frothingham, *Warren*, 345, 351.

CHAPTER 25

1. Gage to Dartmouth, August 29, 31, September 2, 1774, in Wroth, *Province*, 51.
2. *Boston Evening Post*, September 5, 1774, in Dorr, *Annotated*, 4:563, MHS, http://www.masshist.org/dorr/volume/4/sequence/646.
3. Ibid.
4. Untitled paper with marginal notation "Tea Notes 1774" in Sewell Papers, Public Archives of Canada, Ottawa, in Upton, *Revolutionary*, 6.
5. *Boston Evening Post*, September 5, 1774, in Dorr, *Annotated*, 4:563, MHS, http://www.masshist.org/dorr/volume/4/sequence/646. The *Post* reported three thousand; Harbottle Dorr wrote on his copy of the *Post*, "I was told by some who belong'd to The Company's, that there were 8000 men!"
6. Sabine, *American*, 497.
7. Joseph Warren to Samuel Adams, September 4, 1774, in Raphael, *First*, 116.
8. Thomas Young to Samuel Adams, September 4, 1774, in Raphael, *First*, 117.
9. Edward Hill to John Adams, September 4, 1774, MHS, http://www.masshist.org/publications/apde/portia.php?id=PJA02d051.
10. Raphael, *First*, 118.
11. Benjamin Hallowell to Gage, September 8, 1774, in Raphael, *First*, 119.
12. Raphael, *First*, 120.
13. Sargent, *Andrews*, 39.
14. Breen, *Insurgents*, 137.
15. Sabine, *American*, 493–4.
16. Ibid., 494.
17. Ibid., 495.
18. Raphael, *First*, 125.
19. Sabine, *American*, 495.
20. Raphael, *First*, 126.
21. *Boston Gazette*, October 4–11, 1774, in Breen, *Insurgents*, 139.
22. Ibid.
23. Fischer, *Revere*, 46.
24. Stiles, *Diary*, 479–80.
25. *Connecticut Courant*, October 10, 1774, in Breen, *Insurgents*, 144.
26. *Connecticut Gazette*, September 9, 1774, in Breen, *Insurgents*, 146.
27. Paul Revere to John Lamb, September 4, 1774, in Goss, *Revere*, 1:150–3.

28. Joseph Warren to Samuel Adams, probably September 4, 1774, in Frothingham, *Warren,* 355–6.
29. Lincoln, *Journals,* 637.
30. Frothingham, *Warren,* 341.
31. *Massachusetts Gazette Supplement,* September 15, 1774, MHS, http://www.masshist.org/revolution/imageviewer.php?item_id=696&img_step=1&tpc=&pid=2&mode=transcript&tpc=&pid=2#page1.
32. Ibid.
33. Ibid.
34. Sargent, *Andrews,* 46.
35. Gage to Dartmouth, Boston, September 2, 1774, in Carter, *Gage,* 371.
36. Gage to Dartmouth, September 12, 1774, in Carter, *Gage,* 374.
37. Gage to Barrington, November 2, 1774, in Fischer, *Revere,* 51.
38. Fischer, *Revere,* 50.
39. John Adams to Joseph Palmer, Philadelphia, September 26, 1774, MHS, http://www.masshist.org/publications/apde/portia.php?id=PJA02d065.
40. Ferling, *Leap,* 114–5.
41. Sam Adams to James Warren, Philadelphia, May 21, 1774, in Adams, *Warren,* 1:26. This date is incorrect and should be some time in September, according to Maier, *Scripture,* 6.
42. Smith, *Adams,* 1:172.
43. Ibid., 1:181.
44. Ibid., 1:174–5.
45. Ibid., 1:175.
46. Ferling, *Leap,* 114.
47. Smith, *Adams,* 1:183.
48. Letter from John Adams to Abigail Adams, September 8, 1774, *Adams Family Papers: An Electronic Archive,* MHS, http://www.masshist.org/digitaladams/aea/cfm/doc.cfm?id=L17740908ja.
49. Christie, *Empire,* 209.
50. Smith, *Adams,* 1:176.
51. Frothingham, *Warren,* 367.
52. Smith, *Adams,* 1:180.

CHAPTER 26

1. Frothingham, *Warren,* 368.
2. Force, *Archives,* 1:802.
3. Lincoln, *Journals,* 4.
4. Ibid., 6.
5. Ibid., 17.
6. Ibid.
7. Warren, *History,* 164.
8. Lincoln, *Journals,* 33.
9. John Adams to William Tudor, Philadelphia, October 7, 1774, MHS, http://www.masshist.org/publications/apde/portia.php?id=PJA02d070.
10. Frothingham, *Warren,* 387.
11. John Adams to William Tudor, October 7, 1774, MHS, http://www.masshist.org/publications/apde/portia.php?id=PJA02d070.
12. Lincoln, *Journals,* 29.
13. Ibid., 20.
14. Gage to Dartmouth, November 2, 1774, in Carter, *Gage,* 383.
15. Quincy, *Memoir,* 150.
16. Nathanial Appleton to Josiah Quincy, Boston, November 15, 1774, in Quincy, *Memoir,* 174.
17. Christie, *Empire,* 212.
18. Ferling, *Leap,* 121.
19. Smith, *Adams,* 1:183.
20. Christie, *Empire,* 212–3.
21. Miller, *Adams,* 327.
22. Boyle, "Journal," 380.
23. Oliver, *Origin,* 117.
24. Quincy, *Memoir,* 198.
25. Ibid., 199.
26. Ibid.
27. Ibid., 200.
28. Hutchinson, *Diary,* 1:301.
29. Quincy, *Memoir,* 209.
30. Josiah Quincy to Joseph Reed, London, December 17, 1774, in Quincy, *Memoir,* 237.
31. Oliver, *Origin,* 155; Winsor, *Duxbury,* 140.
32. Frothingham, *Warren,* 397.
33. George Harris to Bess Dyer, December 5, 1774, in Chase, *Beginnings,* 145.
34. Andrews, "Letters," 390.
35. Barker, *British,* 14.
36. Andrews, "Letters," 393.

CHAPTER 27
1. Josiah Quincy to Mrs. Quincy, London, January 11, 1775, in Quincy, *Memoir*, 252.
2. Andrews, "Letters," 393.
3. *Boston Gazette*, January 16, 1775, in Chase, *Beginnings*, 163.
4. John Eliot to Jeremy Belknap, Boston, January 30, 1775, in Belknap, "Papers 3," 77.
5. Ibid.
6. Ibid., 78.
7. Andrews, "Letters," 398–9.
8. John Eliot to Jeremy Belknap, Cambridge, February 28, 1775, in Belknap, "Papers 3," 84.
9. Crocker, *Reminiscences*, 46.
10. Adams, *Novanglus*, 165.
11. Ibid., 165–6.
12. Ibid., 177.
13. Ibid., 182.
14. Ibid., 172–3.
15. Smith, *Adams*, 1:193.
16. Adams, *Novanglus*, 75.
17. Ibid., 29.
18. Ibid.
19. Smith, *Adams*, 1:191.
20. Ibid., 1:191–2.
21. Frothingham, *Warren*, 412.
22. Joseph Warren to Arthur Lee, February 20, 1775, in Frothingham, *Warren*, 418.
23. *Boston Evening Post*, March 6, 1775, in Frothingham, *Warren*, 428.
24. Frothingham, *Warren*, 412, 419.
25. Wroth, *Province*, 111.
26. Brown, *Thompson*, 36.
27. Ibid.
28. Gage, *Instructions*, 3. The following account of Brown and De Berniere's mission is based on Gage, *Instructions*, MHS, http://www.masshist.org/revolution/image-viewer.php?item_id=516&img_step=1&tpc=&pid=2&mode=transcript&tpc=&pid=2#page1.
29. Essex, *Proceedings*, 1:112.
30. Ibid., 1:113.
31. Ibid., 1:114.
32. Ibid., 1:115.
33. Ibid., 1:135.
34. Trevelyan, *Revolution*, 541.
35. Fischer, *Revere*, 67.
36. Ibid., 66.
37. Pitcairn to Sandwich, March 4, 1775, in Fischer, *Revere*, 69.
38. Miller, *Adams*, 330.
39. Frothingham, *Warren*, 432–3.
40. Miller, *Adams*, 330.
41. Fischer, *Revere*, 70.
42. Barker, *British*, 26.
43. Unger, *Hancock*, 188.
44. Morison, *Harvard*, 100.
45. Hersey, "Misfortunes," 22.
46. John Hancock to Dorothy Quincy, March 25, 1775, in Unger, *Hancock*, 189.
47. Fischer, *Revere*, 86.
48. Ibid.
49. Mackenzie, *Fusilier*, 42.
50. Andrews, "Letters," 402.
51. Sarah Winslow Deming Journal, 1775, MHS, http://www.masshist.org/online/siege/img-viewer.php?item_id=1898&img_step=1&tpc=&pid=21&mode=transcript&tpc=&pid=21#page1
52. Ibid.
53. Ibid.

CHAPTER 28
1. Fischer, *Revere*, 96–7.
2. Bell, *Marriage*, http://boston1775.blogspot.com/2011/04/marriage-of-thomas-and-margaret-gage.html.
3. Fischer, *Revere*, 105–6.
4. Ibid., 92.
5. Phinney, *Lexington*, 33.
6. Ibid., 17.
7. Sarah Winslow Deming Journal, 1775, MHS, http://www.masshist.org/online/siege/image-viewer.php?item_id=1898&img_step=1&tpc=&pid=21&mode=transcript&tpc=&pid=21#page1.
8. Fischer, *Revere*, 121.
9. Ibid., 122.
10. Sutherland, *Late*, 13.
11. Phinney, *Lexington*, 32.
12. Dunster, *Dunster*, 41.
13. Sumner, *Memoir*, 187.
14. Elizabeth Clarke to Lucy W. Allen, April 19, 1841, in Fowler, *Baron*, 185.
15. "Deposition of the Wife of

Captain Davis," in Adams, *Letter,* 19.
16. Fischer, *Revere,* 169.
17. Sutherland, *Late,* 15.
18. Fischer, *Revere,* 189.
19. Ibid., 194.
20. Ibid., 197.
21. Sumner, *Memoir,* 188.

CHAPTER 29
1. Amos Baker, "Affidavit of the Last Survivor," in Adams, *Letter,* 21.
2. Shattuck, *Concord,* 111.
3. Fischer, *Revere,* 212.
4. Shattuck, *Concord,* 112.
5. Fischer, *Revere,* 230.
6. Bell, "Latin," http://boston1775.blogspot.com/2007/09/south-latin-school-closes-for-war.html.
7. Fischer, *Revere,* 244.
8. Sumner, *Memoir,* 188.
9. Mackenzie, *Fusilier,* 57.
10. Fischer, *Revere,* 257.
11. Ibid.
12. Provincial, "Narrative," 20.
13. Lister, *Concord,* 34.
14. Percy to General Edward Harvey, Boston, April 20, 1775, in Percy, *Letters,* 52–3.

CHAPTER 30
1. Rowe, *Letters,* 292.
2. The following account of Sarah Deming's departure from Boston is based on Sarah Winslow Deming Journal, 1775, MHS, http://www.masshist.org/database/viewer.php?item_id=1898&img_step=1&pid=21&mode=transcript#page1.
3. Quincy, *Memoir,* 287.
4. Fischer, *Revere,* 263.
5. Rowe, *Letters,* 292–3.
6. Anonymous letter, Boston, May 2, 1775, in Force, *Archives:* 2:441.
7. Fischer, *Revere,* 267.
8. Goss, *Revere,* 1:262.
9. Ibid., 1:263.
10. Ibid.
11. Barker, *British,* 37.
12. Ibid., 39.
13. Fischer, *Revere,* 263.
14. Hulton, *Letters,* 77.
15. Brown, "Hulton," 145.
16. French, "Haldimand," 91.
17. Joseph Warren to Joseph Reed, Cambridge, May 15, 1775, in Frothingham, *Warren,* 486.
18. Buckingham, *Specimens,* 5.
19. Brown, *Thompson,* 40.
20. Frothingham, *Warren,* 466.
21. Andrews, "Letters," 406.
22. Stern, "Mecom," 147.
23. Farnsworth, "Diary," 79.
24. Nelson, *Fire,* 173.
25. Farnsworth, "Diary," 81.
26. Frothingham, *Siege,* 95.
27. Andrews, "Letters," 408.
28. Elizabeth Inman to "Friends in Boston," Cambridge, April 22, 1775, in Tiffany, *Murray,* 183–5.
29. Elizabeth Inman to Ralph Inman, April 27, 1775, in Tiffany, *Murray,* 190.
30. Ralph Inman to Elizabeth Inman, May 19, 1775, in Tiffany, *Murray,* 197–8.
31. Elizabeth Inman to Ralph Inman, Cambridge, May 20, 1775, in Tiffany, *Murray,* 201.
32. James Murray to Elizabeth Inman, Boston, May 23, 1775, in Tiffany, *Murray,* 203.
33. Elizabeth Inman to Ralph Inman, Cambridge, May 29 and 30, 1775, in Tiffany, *Murray,* 205.
34. Ralph Inman to Elizabeth Inman, June 13, 1775, in Tiffany, *Murray,* 209–10.
35. Elizabeth Inman to Ralph Inman, June 14, 1775, in Tiffany, *Murray,* 211–2.
36. Provincial, "Narrative," 4.
37. Ibid., 21.
38. MHS, *Letters,* 282.
39. Barker, *British,* 40.
40. Hinkhouse, *Preliminaries,* 188.
41. Elisha Hutchinson to Mary Watson Hutchinson, April 9, 13, June 5, 1775, in Bailyn, *Ordeal,* 333.
42. Letter from Copley to his wife, Parma, July 22, 1775, in Amory, *Copley,* 62.
43. Fischer, *Revere,* 276.
44. *Boston News-Letter,* April 20, 1775, in Fischer, *Revere,* 277.
45. Fischer, *Revere,* 277.
46. Ibid., 271.

CHAPTER 31

1. John Hancock to Committee of Safety, Worcester, April 24, 1775, in Brown, *Hancock*, 197.
2. Silas Deane to Elizabeth Saltonstall Deane, May 7, 1775, in Tourtellot, *Lexington*, 252.
3. *Essex Gazette*, June 8, 1775, according to Frothingham, *Siege*, 101.
4. Moore, *Notes*, 145.
5. Greenwood, "Memoirs," 74.
6. Haws, "Journal," 53, 54, 57.
7. Haskell, *Diary*, 6–7.
8. Ibid.
9. Ibid., 6–8.
10. Mrs. Barnes to Elizabeth Inman, April 1775, in Tiffany, *Murray*, 187–9.
11. The following account of the work of the Massachusetts Provincial Congress is based on Lincoln, *Journals*, 226–318.
12. Frothingham, *Warren*, 482–3.
13. Maier, *Scripture*, 18.
14. Ibid., 10.
15. John Adams autobiography, part 1, "John Adams" through 1776, sheet 18 of 53, *Adams Family Papers: An Electronic Archive*, in MHS, http://www.masshist.org/digitaladams/aea/cfm/doc.cfm?id=A1_18&numrecs=7&archive=autobio&hi=on&mode=&query=detestation&queryid=&rec=1&start=1&tag=text#firstmatch.
16. Smith, *Adams*, 199.
17. Gerry to the Massachusetts Delegates in Congress, at Philadelphia, Watertown, June 4, 1775, in Austin, *Gerry*, 79.
18. Ibid.
19. John Adams autobiography, part 1, "John Adams," through 1776, sheet 21 of 53, *Adams Family Papers: An Electronic Archive*, MHS, http://www.masshist.org/digitaladams/aea/cfm/doc.cfm?id=A1_21&numrecs=12&archive=autobio&hi=on&mode=&query=mortification&queryid=&rec=2&start=1&tag=text#firstmatch.
20. Hancock to Washington, July 10, 1775, in Brown, *Hancock*, 201.
21. Smith, *Adams*, 1:201.
22. John Adams to Elbridge Gerry, Philadelphia, June 18, 1775, in Force, *Archives*, 2:1020.
23. Force, *Archives*, 2:969.
24. Frothingham, *Siege*, 113.
25. Force, *Archives*, 2:1012.
26. Alden, *Gage*, 264.
27. Force, *Archives*, 2:1004.
28. Henry Pelham to Copley, May 16, 1775, in Copley, *Letters*, 325.
29. Jonathan Sewall to Thomas Robie, July, 15, 1775, in Berkin, *Sewall*, 108.
30. Hutchinson, *Diary*, 1:469.

CHAPTER 32

1. Frothingham, *Siege*, 116.
2. Force, *Archives*, 2:979.
3. Peter Brown to Sarah Brown, June 25, 1775, MHS, http://www.masshist.org/revolution/image-viewer.php?item_id=725&img_step=1&tpc=&pid=2&mode=transcript&tpc=&pid=2#page1.
4. Nelson, *Fire*, 234.
5. Crocker, *Reminiscences*, 41. In another version of this dialogue with the general, Mather wrote that she said, "No Sir, I am willing to die with my parents, but never will desert my country." Crocker, *Reminiscences*, 198.
6. Ibid., 41.
7. French, *Siege*, 260–1.
8. Peter Brown to Sarah Brown, June 25, 1775, MHS, http://www.masshist.org/revolution/image-viewer.php?item_id=725&img_step=1&tpc=&pid=2&mode=transcript&tpc=&pid=2#page1.
9. Frothingham. *Siege*, 127.
10. Hill, *Dunstable*, 59.
11. Ibid., 60.
12. Frothingham, *Warren*, 510.
13. Forbes, *Revere*, 293; French, *Siege*, 269.
14. Hill, *Dunstable*, 60–1.
15. Ibid., 61.
16. Ibid., 62.
17. Fischer, *Revere*, 285.

18. Drake, *Bunker*, 49.
19. Hersey, "Misfortunes," 18–9.
20. Young, "Hewes," 601.
21. Henry Hulton to Robert Nicholson, Boston, June 20, 1775, in Hulton, *Letters*, 99.
22. French, *Siege*, 290.
23. Frothingham, *Warren*, 521.
24. James Warren to Mercy Warren, Watertown, June 18, 1775, in Adams, *Warren*, 1:60.
25. McCullough, *1776*, 24.
26. Haskell, *Diary*, 7.
27. Nathaniel Ober Diary, MHS, http://www.masshist.org/database/viewer.php?item_id=1900&mode=transcript&img_step=9#page9.
28. Haws, "Journal," 60.
29. Abigail Adams to John Adams, July 16, 1775, *Adams Family Papers: An Electronic Archive*, in MHS, http://www.masshist.org/digitaladams/aea/cfm/doc.cfm?id=L1775 0716aa.
30. James Warren to John Adams, Watertown, November 14, 1775, in Adams, *Warren*, 1:186.
31. French, *Siege*, 308–9.
32. Ibid., 310.
33. Frothingham, *Siege*, 229.
34. Scheer, *Rebels*, 93.
35. Haskell, *Diary*, 8.

CHAPTER 33

1. Letter sent to England by an officer at Boston, Boston, August 18, 1775, in Commager, *Spirit*, 166–7.
2. French, *Siege*, 344.
3. Henry Pelham to Copley, Boston, October 10, 1775, in Copley, *Letters*, 361.
4. Ibid., 362.
5. Boardman, *Edes*, 96.
6. Ibid., 119–20.
7. Ibid., 100.
8. Peter Edes Diary, June–October 1775, MHS, http://www.masshist.org/database/viewer.php?item_id=1978&mode=transcript&img_step=20#page20.
9. Boardman, *Edes*, 104.
10. Ibid., 122.
11. Bell, "Dorringtons," http://boston1775.blogspot.ca/2009/07/dorringtons-accused-of-blowing-up-flies.html.
12. Boardman, *Edes*, 108.
13. Ibid., 102.
14. Elizabeth Inman to Ralph Inman, Brush Hill, July 30, 1775, in Tiffany, *Murray*, 215.
15. Cleary, *Murray*, 183.
16. Wroth, *Province*, 135–6.
17. Bradford, *History*, 41.
18. John Adams to James Warren, Philadelphia, September 17, 1775, in Adams, *Warren*, 1:110.
19. Ibid.
20. Ibid., 1:111.
21. John Adams to James Warren,. Philadelphia, July 24, 1775, in Adams, *Warren*, 1:88–9; Smith, Adams, 1:208.
22. James Warren to John Adams, Watertown, October 1, 1775, in Kiracofe, "Church," 447.
23. James Warren to John Adams, Watertown, October 1, 1775, in Adams, *Warren*, 1:121.
24. Bellesiles, "Church," 212–3.
25. John Adams to James Warren, Philadelphia, October 13, 1775, in Adams, *Warren*, 1:137.
26. Sam Adams to James Warren, Philadelphia, October 13, 1775, in Adams, *Warren*, 1:140.
27. John Adams to James Warren, October 18, 1775, in Adams, *Warren*, 1:142.
28. Gage to Dartmouth, August 20, 1775, in Carter, *Gage*, 413.
29. Gage to Dartmouth, Boston, September 20, 1775, in Carter, *Gage*, 416.
30. Cobbett, *Parliamentary*, 18:696.
31. Ibid., 18:696–7.
32. Ibid., 18:734, 735, 768.
33. Ibid., 18:775.
34. Force, *Archives*, 4:41.
35. Maier, *Scripture*, 15.
36. Ibid., 21.
37. McCullough, *1776*, 7.
38. Walpole, *Journal*, 460.
39. George Washington to Joseph Reed, Cambridge, November 28, 1775, in Crackel, *Washington*, 450.
40. Ibid., 449.
41. Lunt, *Diary*, 14–5.

42. McCullough, *1776*, 58.
43. Brooks, *Knox*, 24.
44. Nathanael Greene to Samuel Ward, December 31, 1775, in McCullough, *1776*, 67.
45. McCullough, *1776*, 68.

CHAPTER 34
1. John Hancock to George Washington, December 22, 1775, in Brown, *Hancock*, 205.
2. Brown, "Hulton," 149–50.
3. Ibid., 150.
4. McCullough, *1776*, 74.
5. Ibid., 75.
6. Oliver, *Origin*, 158–68.
7. McCullough, *1776*, 81.
8. Werner, *Pursuit*, 21–2.
9. John Adams diary 25, October 27, 1775–October 13, 1776. *Adams Family Papers: An Electronic Archive,* MHS, http://www.masshist.org/digitaladams/aea/cfm/doc.cfm?id=D25&numrecs=1&archive=diary&hi=on&mode=&query=carnivorous%20Animals%20&queryid=&rec=1&start=1&tag=text#firstmatch.
10. Letter from John Adams to Abigail Adams, January 24, 1776, *Adams Family Papers: An Electronic Archive,* MHS, http://www.masshist.org/digitaladams/aea/cfm/doc.cfm?id=L17760124ja.
11. Letter from John Adams to Abigail Adams, February 11, 1776, *Adams Family Papers: An Electronic Archive,* MHS, http://www.masshist.org/digitaladams/aea/cfm/doc.cfm?id=L17760211ja.
12. Hancock to Thomas Cushing, February 13, 1776, in Maier, *Scripture*, 27.
13. Letter from John Adams to Abigail Adams, March 19, 1776, *Adams Family Papers: An Electronic Archive,* MHS, http://www.masshist.org/digitaladams/aea/cfm/doc.cfm?id=L17760319ja.
14. Paine, *Common*, 255.
15. Ibid., 270–1.
16. Ibid., 291.
17. Smith, *Adams*, 1:240.
18. Ibid.
19. McCullough, *1776*, 90.
20. Ibid., 92.
21. *London Chronicle*, May 15, 1776, in McCullough, *1776*, 93–4.
22. McCullough, *1776*, 97.
23. Flexner, *Washington*, 76.
24. Rowe, *Letters*, 301.
25. McCullough, *1776*, 100.
26. Ibid., 101.
27. Forbes, *Revere*, 310.
28. Sabine, *Loyalists*, 509.
29. Rowe, *Letters*, 302.
30. Cooper, "Diary," 338.
31. Ibid.
32. Letter from Abigail Adams to John Adams, March 31–April 5, 1776, *Adams Family Papers: An Electronic Archive,* MHS, http://www.masshist.org/digitaladams/aea/cfm/doc.cfm?id=L17760331aa.
33. Tyler, *Smugglers*, 241.
34. Rowe, *Letters*, 307.
35. Smith, *Adams*, 1:249.
36. Ibid., 1:256.
37. Ibid., 1:258.
38. Morris to Silas Deane, June 5, 1776, in Rakove, *Beginnings*, 99.
39. Letter from Abigail Adams to John Adams, March 31–April 5, 1776, *Adams Family Papers: An Electronic Archive,* MHS, http://www.masshist.org/digitaladams/aea/cfm/doc.cfm?id=L17760331aa.
40. Letter from John Adams to Abigail Adams, April 14, 1776, *Adams Family Papers: An Electronic Archive,* MHS, http://www.masshist.org/digitaladams/aea/cfm/doc.cfm?id=L17760414ja.
41. *Town Records, 1770*, 235.
42. Charles Chauncy to Richard Price, July 18, 1775, in Bailyn, *Ordeal*, 336.
43. Smith, *Adams*, 1:268.
44. Ibid., 1:270.
45. Letter from Abigail Adams to John Adams, July 21–22, 1776,

Adams Family Papers: An Electronic Archive, MHS, http://www.masshist.org/digitaladams/aea/cfm/doc.cfm?id=L17760721aa.
46. Ibid.

EPILOGUE
1. Rowe, *Letters,* 314.
2. Crocker, *Reminiscences,* 94.
3. Hurd, *Worcester,* 1:344.
4. Forbes, *Revere,* 333.
5. J. S. Copley Jr. to his sisters, Boston, January 21, 1796, in Amory, *Copley,* 140.
6. McCullough, *Adams,* 189.
7. Ibid., 221.
8. Ibid., 408.
9. Ibid., 447.
10. Miller, *Adams,* 343.
11. Ibid., 367.
12. *Massachusetts Centinel,* March 31, 1787, and *Columbian Centinel,* April 2, 1794, in Miller, *Adams,* 374.
13. Miller, *Adams,* 396.
14. Amory, *Copley,* 140.
15. Tudor, *Otis,* 485.
16. Forbes, *Revere,* 376.
17. Maier, "Young," 234.
18. Ibid., 235.
19. Young, "Hewes," 613.
20. Ibid., 615.
21. Egerton, *Death,* 108.
22. Forbes, *Revere,* 327.
23. Eaton, *Byles,* 154–5.
24. Ibid., 163.
25. John Eliot to Jeremy Belknap, June 17, 1777, in Eaton, *Byles,* 158.
26. Eaton, *Byles,* 219.
27. Griffin, *Loyalists,* http://www.common-place.org/vol-07/no-04/griffin/.
28. Ibid.
29. Jonathan Sewall to Thomas Robie, March 12, 1777, in Berkin, *Sewall,* 120.
30. Berkin, *Sewall,* 140.
31. Jonathan Sewell to Judge Joseph Lee, September 21, 1787, in Berkin, *Sewall,* 142.
32. Adams, *Works* 4, 8.
33. Haws, "Journal," 90.
34. Fonder, "Billings," 8.
35. Stern, "Mecom," 147.
36. Waldstreicher, "Phillis," 110.
37. Bailyn, *Faces,* 90.
38. Ibid., 89.
39. Ibid., 90.
40. Cooper, "Sermon," 47.
41. "Sabbath after Burgoyne's surrender," in Akers, *Cooper,* 495.
42. *New York Royal Gazette,* July 1, 1778, in Akers, *Cooper,* 495.
43. *Boston Gazette,* October 5, 1778, in Hutcheson, *Warren,* 390.
44. Lepore, *Whites,* 45.
45. McCullough, *Adams,* 595.
46. Hutchinson, *Diary,* 2:40.
47. Bailyn, *Ordeal,* 345.
48. Ibid., 358.
49. Thomas Hutchinson to Edward Hutchinson, August 5, 1777, in Bailyn, *Ordeal,* 372.
50. Bailyn, *Ordeal,* 377.
51. Arthur Lee to James Warren, April 8, 1782, in Bailyn, *Ordeal,* 374.
52. Boardman, *Edes,* 11.
53. Thomas, *Memoir,* 47.
54. Boardman, *Edes,* 11.
55. Thomas, *Memoir,* 47.
56. Ibid., 64.
57. Thomas, "Diary," 113.
58. Stark, *Loyalists,* 371.
59. Ibid., 373.
60. Hersey, "Tar," 463.
61. Ibid., 469–70.
62. Hersey, "Misfortunes," 22.
63. Morse, *Letters,* 1:47.
64. Slade, "Pelham," 199.
65. Crocker, *Reminiscences,* 258.
66. Holleran, "Meetinghouse," 52.
67. *New England Palladium,* August 24, 1830, in Chase, "Architectural," 39.
68. Report by Charles Stoddard, Loring Lothrop, Avery Plumer, and the church's two pastors, April 30, 1866, in Hill, *Old South,* 2:524.
69. Holleran, "Meetinghouse," 69.
70. Watkins, "Province," 104.
71. Hawthorne, *Legends,* 14.
72. "Indian archer weathervane," MHS, http://www.masshist.org/gallery/native-americans?i=3.

BIBLIOGRAPHY

Adams, John. *John Adams: A Biography in His Own Words.* Vol. 1. Edited by James Bishop Peabody. The Founding Fathers. New York: Newsweek, 1973.

---. *The Works of John Adams.* Vol. 2. Boston: Little, Brown, 1856.

---. *The Works of John Adams.* Vol. 4. Boston: Charles C. Little and James Brown, 1851.

---. *The Works of John Adams.* Vol. 9. Boston: Little, Brown, 1854.

---. *The Works of John Adams.* Vol. 10. Boston: Little, Brown, 1856.

Adams, John, Samuel Adams, and James Warren. *Warren-Adams Letters.* Vol. 1. (Boston?): Massachusetts Historical Society, 1917.

Adams, John, and Jonathan Sewell. *Novanglus and Massachusettensis; or Political Essays.* Boston: Hews & Goss, 1819.

Adams, Josiah. *Letter to Lemuel Shattuck, of Boston, from Josiah Adams, of Framingham.* Boston: Damrell & Moore, 1850.

Adams, Samuel. *The Writings of Samuel Adams.* Vol. 2. Edited by Harry Alonzo Cushing. New York: G. P. Putnam's Sons, 1906.

---. *The Writings of Samuel Adams.* Vol. 3. Edited by Harry Alonzo Cushing. New York: G. P. Putnam's Sons, 1907.

Akers, Charles W. "'Our Modern Egyptians': Phillis Wheatley and the Whig Campaign Against Slavery in Revolutionary Boston." *Journal of Negro History* 60, no. 3 (July 1975), 397–410.

---. "Religion and the American Revolution: Samuel Cooper and the Brattle Street Church." *William and Mary Quarterly*, 3rd ser., vol. 35, no. 3 (July 1978), 477–498.

Alden, John E. "John Mein: Scourge of Patriots." *Publications of the Colonial Society of Massachusetts.* Vol. 39, *Transactions 1937–1942.* Boston: Colonial Society of Massachusetts, 1943, 571–599.

Alden, John Richard. *General Gage in America: Being Principally a History of His Role in the American Revolution.* Baton Rouge: Louisiana State University Press, 1948.

Alden, John Richard. "Why the March to Concord?" *American Historical Review* 49, no. 3 (April 1944), 446–454.

Almon, John. *A Collection of Interesting, Authentic Papers Relative to the Dispute between Great Britain and America.* London: J. Almon, 1777.

American Revolution Center. Timeline. http://timeline.americanrevolutioncenter.org/.

Amory, Martha Babcock. *The Domestic and Artistic Life of John Singleton Copley, R.A., with Notices of His Works and Reminiscences of His Son, Lord Lyndhurst, High Chancellor of Great Britain.* Boston: Houghton, Mifflin, 1882.

Anderson, George P. "Ebenezer Mackintosh: Stamp Act Rioter and Patriot." *Publications of the Colonial Society of Massachusetts.* Vol. 26, *Transactions 1924–1926.* Boston: Colonial Society of Massachusetts, 1927, 15–64, 348–361.

Andrews, Charles M. "The Boston Merchants and the Non-Importation Movement." *Publications of the Colonial Society of Massachusetts.* Vol. 19, *Transactions 1916–1917.* Boston: Colonial Society of Massachusetts, 1918, 159–259.

Andrews, John. "Letters of John Andrews, Esq., of Boston, 1772–1776." Edited by Winthrop Sargent. *Proceedings of the Massachusetts Historical Society, 1864–1865*, vol. 8. Boston: Wiggin and Lunt, 1866, 316–412.

Appleton, Nathaniel Walker. *Letters of Nathaniel Walker Appleton to his Classmate Eliphalet Pearson 1773–1784.* Edited by William Coolidge Lane. Cambridge, MA: John Wilson and Son, 1906.

Aptheker, Herbert, ed. *A Documentary History of the Negro People in the United States.* Vol. 1, *From Colonial Times through the Civil War.* New York: Citadel, 1951.

Austin, James T. *Life of Elbridge Gerry.* Boston: Wells and Lilly, 1828.

Bailyn, Bernard. *Faces of Revolution: Personalities and Themes in the Struggle for American Independence.* New York: Alfred A. Knopf, 1990.

———. *The Ideological Origins of the American Revolution.* Cambridge, MA: Harvard University Press, 1992.

———. *The Ordeal of Thomas Hutchinson.* London: Allen Lane, 1975.

Barker, John. *The British in Boston.* Cambridge, MA: Harvard University Press, 1924.

Barrington, William Wildman, and Francis Bernard. *The Barrington-Bernard Correspondence and Illustrative Matter.* Edited by Edward Channing and Archibald Cary Coolidge. New York: Da Capo, 1970.

Basch, Norma. *Framing American Divorce: From the Revolutionary Generation to the Victorians.* Berkeley: University of California Press, 1999.

Baumgarten, Linda. *What Clothes Reveal: The Language of Clothing in Colonial and Federal America.* Williamsburg, VA: Colonial Williamsburg Foundation, 2002.

Baxter, W. T. *The House of Hancock: Business in Boston, 1724–1775.* New York: Russell & Russell, 1965.

Beckett, William. *A Universal Biography.* Vol. 1. London: Mayhew, Isaac, 1834.

Belknap, Jeremy, and Ebenezer Hazard. "Belknap Papers: Part 3." *Collections of the Massachusetts Historical Society,* 6th ser., vol. 4. Boston: Massachusetts Historical Society, 1891, 1–632.

Belknap, Jeremy, and St. George Tucker. "Queries Respecting the Slavery and Emancipation of Negroes in Massachusetts, Proposed by the Hon. Judge Tucker of Virginia, and Answered by the Rev. Dr. Belknap." *Collections of the Massachusetts Historical Society,* 1st ser., vol. 4 (1835), 191–211.

Bell, J. L. "A Bankruptcy in Boston, 1765." *Massachusetts Banker,* Fourth Quarter 2008, 14–23.

———. "Captain Conner: Tea Party Thief, Scapegoat." *Boston 1775.* May 29, 2007. http://boston1775.blogspot.ca/2007/05/captain-conner-tea-party-thief.html.

———. "Colonial Boston Vocabulary: 'coasting.'" *Boston* 1775. November 15, 2006. http://boston1775.blogspot.com/2006/11/colonial-boston-vocabulary-coasting.html.

———. "Dorringtons Accused of 'Blowing Up Flies.'" *Boston 1775.* July 19, 2009. http://boston1775.blogspot.com/2009/07/dorringtons-accused-of-blowing-up-flies.html.

———. "Dr. John Jeffries: Physician, Loyalist, Aeronaut, Part 7." *Boston 1775.* August 5, 2006. http://boston1775.blogspot.com/2006/08/dr-john-jeffries-physician-loyalist_05.html.

———. "From Saucy Boys to Sons of Liberty." In James Marten, ed. *Children in Colonial America.* New York: New York University Press, 2006.

———. "George Washington's Teeth, Close Up." *Boston 1775,* April 2, 2007. http://boston1775.blogspot.com/2007/04/george-washingtons-teeth-close-up.html.

———. "John Nutting Finds Work in Boston." *Boston 1775*. September 3, 2008. http://boston1775.blogspot.com/2008/09/john-nutting-finds-work-in-boston.html.

———. "The Last Victim of the Boston Massacre?" *Boston 1775*, May 2, 2008. http://boston1775.blogspot.com/2008/05/last-victim-of-boston-massacre.html.

———. "The Marriage of Thomas and Margaret Gage." *Boston 1775*, April 13, 2011. http://boston1775.blogspot.com/2011/04/marriage-of-thomas-and-margaret-gage.html.

———. "Nailing Down Mount Whoredom." *Boston 1775*. July 27, 2009. http://boston1775.blogspot.com/search?q=whoredom.

———. "The Queen Street Writing School Closes for War." *Boston 1775*, September 21, 2007. http://boston1775.blogspot.com/2007/09/queen-street-writing-school-closes-for.html.

———. "The South Latin School Closes for War." *Boston 1775*, September 20, 2007. http://boston1775.blogspot.com/2007/09/south-latin-school-closes-for-war.html.

———. "'A Wretch of Wretches Prov'd with Child': From Scandal to Revolutionary Outrage." *New England Ancestors* 6, no. 1 (Winter 2005), 22–24, 40.

Bellesiles, Michael. "Church, Benjamin." *Encyclopedia of the American Revolution: Library of Military History*. Vol. 1. Edited by Harold Selesky. Detroit: Charles Scribner's Sons, 2006, 212–213.

———. "Temple, John." *Encyclopedia of the American Revolution: Library of Military History*. Vol. 2. Edited by Harold Selesky. Detroit: Charles Scribner's Sons, 2006.

Beneke, Chris. "Jonathan Mayhew, the British Empire, and the Idea of Resistance in Mid-Eighteenth Century Boston." *Massachusetts Historical Review* 10 (2008), 22–56.

Benton, J. H., Jr. *Early Census Making in Massachusetts*. Boston: Charles E. Goodspeed, 1905.

Benton, Josiah Henry. *Warning Out in New England*. Boston: W. B. Clarke, 1911.

Berkin, Carol. *Jonathan Sewall: Odyssey of an American Loyalist*. New York: Columbia University Press, 1974.

Bicheno, Hugh. *Rebels & Redcoats: The American Revolutionary War*. London: HarperCollins, 2003.

Blackburne, Francis. *Memoirs of Thomas Hollis*. 2 vols. London, 1780.

Block, Lawrence, ed. *Gangsters, Swindlers, Killers, and Thieves: The Lives and Crimes of Fifty American Villains*. New York: Oxford University Press, 2004.

Boardman, Samuel Lane, ed. *Peter Edes, Pioneer Printer in Maine*. Bangor, ME: The De Burians, 1901.

Boston, Town of. *Votes and Proceedings of the Freeholders and Other Inhabitants of the Town of Boston, in Town Meeting Assembled, According to Law*. Boston: Edes and Gill and T. and J. Fleet, 1772.

A Bostonian. *Traits of the Tea Party: Being a Memoir of George R. T. Hewes*. New York: Harper & Brothers, 1835.

The Bostonian Society. "History of the Old State House Building." http://www.bostonhistory.org/?s=osh&p=history.

Bourne, Russell. *Cradle of Violence: How Boston's Waterfront Mobs Ignited the American Revolution*. Hoboken, NJ: John Wiley & Sons, 2006.

Bowen, Catherine Drinker. *John Adams and the American Revolution*. Boston: Little, Brown, 1950.

Boyer, Paul S., Clifford E. Clark Jr., Joseph F. Kett, Karen Halttunen, Neal Salisbury, Harvard Sitkoff, and Nancy Woloch. *The Enduring Vision: A History of the American People.* 7th ed. Volume 1. Boston: Wadsworth, 2011.
Boyle, John. "Journal of Occurrences in Boston, 1759–1778." *New England Historical and Genealogical Register* 84 and 85 (1930, 1931), 84: 142–171, 248–272, 357–382; 85: 5–28, 118–133.
Bradford, Alden. *History of Massachusetts from July, 1775, When General Washington Took Command.* Boston: Wells & Lilly, 1825.
———. *Memoir of the Life and Writings of Rev. Jonathan Mayhew, D.D.* Boston: C. C. Little, 1838.
———, ed. *Speeches of the Governors of Massachusetts from 1765 to 1775.* Boston: Russell and Gardner, 1818.
Brandow, James C., ed. "Memoirs of a British Naval Officer at Boston, 1768–1769: Extracts from the Autobiography of William Senhouse." *Proceedings of the Massachusetts Historical Society*, 3rd ser., vol. 105 (1993), 74–93.
Brands, H. W. *The First American: The Life and Times of Benjamin Franklin.* New York: Anchor, 2002.
Breen, T. H. *American Insurgents, American Patriots.* New York: Hill & Wang, 2010.
Bridenbaugh, Carl. *Cities in Revolt: Urban Life in America, 1743–1776.* London: Oxford University Press, 1955.
Brooks, Noah. *Henry Knox: A Soldier of the Revolution.* New York: G. P. Putnam's Sons, 1900.
Brown, Abram English. *John Hancock His Book.* Boston: Lee and Shepard, 1898.
Brown, Richard D. "Massachusetts Towns Reply to the Boston Committee of Correspondence, 1773," *William and Mary Quarterly*, 3rd series, vol. 25, no. 1 (Jan. 1968), 22–39.
———. *Revolutionary Politics in Massachusetts: The Boston Committee of Correspondence and the Towns, 1772–1774.* New York: W. W. Norton, 1976.
Brown, Sanborn C. *Benjamin Thompson, Count Rumford.* Cambridge, MA: MIT Press, 1979.
Brown, Wallace, and Henry Hulton. "An Englishman Views the American Revolution: The Letters of Henry Hulton, 1769–1776." *Huntington Library Quarterly* 36, no. 1 (Nov. 1972) and no. 2 (Feb. 1973), 1: 1–26; 2: 138–151.
Buchanan, John G. "The Justice of America's Cause: Revolutionary Rhetoric in the Sermons of Samuel Cooper." *New England Quarterly* 50, no. 1 (March 1977), 101–124.
Buckingham, Joseph T. *Specimens of Newspaper Literature: With Personal Memoirs, Anecdotes, and Reminiscences.* Vol. 2. Boston: Redding, 1852.
Cappon, Lester J., ed. *The Adams-Jefferson Letters: The Complete Correspondence between Thomas Jefferson and Abigail and John Adams.* 2 vols. Chapel Hill: University of North Carolina Press, 1959.
Carp, Benjamin L. *Defiance of the Patriots: The Boston Tea Party & the Making of America.* New Haven, CT: Yale University Press, 2010.
———. "Fire of Liberty: Firefighters, Urban Voluntary Culture, and the Revolutionary Movement." *William and Mary Quarterly*, 3rd ser., vol. 58, no. 4 (Oct. 2001), 781–818.
Carter, Clarence Edwin. *The Correspondence of General Thomas Gage with the Secretaries of State, 1763–1775.* New Haven, CT: Yale University Press, 1931.
Cash, Arthur H. *John Wilkes: The Scandalous Father of Civil Liberty.* New Haven, CT: Yale University Press, 2006.

Chadwick, Bruce. *The First American Army: The Untold Story of George Washington and the Men Behind America's First Fight for Freedom.* Naperville, IL: Sourcebooks, 2007.

Chaffin, Robert J. "The Townshend Acts of 1767." William and Mary Quarterly, 3rd ser., vol. 27., no. 1 (Jan. 1970), 90–121.

Chapin, Bradley. "The American Revolution as Lese Majesty." *Pennsylvania Magazine of History and Biography* 79, no. 3 (July 1955).

Chase, Ellen. *The Beginnings of the American Revolution.* Vol. 2. New York: Baker and Taylor, 1910.

Chase, Sara B. "A Brief Survey of the Architectural History of the Old State House, Boston, Massachusetts." *Old Time New-England* 68, no. 251 (Winter/Spring 1978), 31–49.

Christie, Ian R., and Benjamin W. Labaree. *Empire or Independence.* New York: W. W. Norton, 1976.

Clark, Fiona. *Hats.* London: B. T. Batsford, 1988.

Cleary, Patricia. *Elizabeth Murray: A Woman's Pursuit of Independence.* Amherst: University of Massachusetts Press, 2000.

Cobbett, William. *The Parliamentary History of England from the Earliest Period to the Year 1803.* Vol. 18. London: T. C. Hansard, 1813.

Coburn, Frank Warren. *The Battle of April 19, 1775.* Lexington, MA: Frank Warren Coburn, 1912.

Cohen, Sheldon S. "The Turkish Tyranny." *New England Quarterly* 47, no. 4 (Dec. 1974) 564–583.

Colby, C. B. *Early American Crafts: Tools, Shops and Products.* New York: Coward-McCann, 1967.

Collins, Dr. Edward D. "Committees of Correspondence of the American Revolution." *Annual Report of the American Historical Association for the Year 1901.* Vol. 1. Washington, DC: Government Printing Office, 1902, 243–271.

Commager, Henry Steele, and Richard B. Morris, eds. *The Spirit of Seventy-Six: The Story of the American Revolution as Told by Participants.* New York: Da Capo, 1995.

Conforti, Joseph A. *Saints and Strangers: New England in British North America.* Baltimore: Johns Hopkins University Press, 2006.

Conroy, David W. *In Public Houses: Drink and the Revolution of Authority in Colonial Massachusetts.* Chapel Hill: University of North Carolina Press, 1995.

Cook, Don. *The Long Fuse: How England Lost the American Colonies, 1760–1785.* New York: Atlantic Monthly Press, 1995.

Cooper, Samuel. "Diary of Samuel Cooper, 1775–1776." *American Historical Review* 6, no. 2 (Jan. 1901), 301–341.

———. "A Sermon Preached before His Excellency Thomas Pownall, Esq." Boston: the Governor and Houses of Assembly, 1759.

Copley, John Singleton, and Henry Pelham. *Letters & Papers of John Singleton Copley and Henry Pelham, 1739–1776.* Boston: Massachusetts Historical Society, 1914.

"Correspondence in 1774 and 1775, between a Committee of the Town of Boston and Contributors of Donations for the Relief of the Sufferers by the Boston Port Bill." *Collections of the Massachusetts Historical Society.* Vol. 4 (1858), 1–279.

Cott, Nancy. "Divorce and the Changing Status of Women in Eighteenth-Century Massachusetts." *William and Mary Quarterly,* 3rd ser., vol. 33, no. 4 (Oct. 1976), 586–614.

Crackel, Theodore J., ed. *The Papers of George Washington.* Charlottesville: University of Virginia Press. http://rotunda.upress.virginia.edu/founders/default.xqy?keys=GEWN-search-1-1&expandNote=on#match.

Crawford, Mary Caroline. *Old Boston Days & Ways.* Boston: Little, Brown, 1909.

Crist, Elizabeth B. "'Ye Sons of Harmony': Politics, Masculinity, and the Music of William Billings in Revolutionary Boston." *William and Mary Quarterly,* 3rd ser., vol. 60, no. 2 (April 2003), 333–354.

Crocker, Hannah Mather. *Reminiscences and Traditions of Boston.* Eileen Hunt Botting and Sarah L. Houser, eds. Boston: New England Historic Genealogical Society, 2011.

Cummings, Abbott Lowell. "The Foster-Hutchinson House." *Old-Time New England* 54, no. 3 (Jan.–March 1964), 59–76.

Davis, Ronald L. "Francis Hopkinson and William Billings: America's First Notable Composers." In Bruce Thompson, *The Revolutionary Period: 1750–1783.* New York: Greenhaven, 2003, 158–169.

Desrochers, Robert E., Jr. "Slave-for-Sale Advertisements and Slavery in Massachusetts, 1704–1781." *William and Mary Quarterly,* 3rd ser., vol. 59, no. 3 (July 2002), 623–664.

Dickerson, Oliver Morton, ed. *Boston under Military Rule (1768–1769): As Revealed in a Journal of the Times.* Westport, CT: Greenwood, 1971.

Dickinson, John. "The Liberty Song." In Joel J. Miller and Kristen Parrish, eds. *The Portable Patriot.* Nashville, TN: Thomas Nelson, 2010.

Dornberg, John. "Count Rumford: The Most Successful Yank Abroad, Ever." *Smithsonian* 25, no. 9 (December 1994), 102–115.

Dorr, Harbottle, ed. *Harbottle Dorr Collection of Annotated Massachusetts Newspapers, 1765–1776.* Boston: Massachusetts Historical Society. http://www.masshist.org/dorr/.

Drake, Francis S. *Life and Correspondence of Henry Knox.* Boston: Samuel G. Drake, 1873.

———. *Tea Leaves: Being a Collection of Letters and Documents Relating to the Shipment of Tea to the American Colonies in the Year 1773, by the East India Tea Company.* Boston: A. O. Crane, 1884.

Drake, Samuel Adams. *Bunker Hill: The Story Told in Letters from the Battle Field by British Officers Engaged.* Boston: Nichols and Hall, 1875.

———. *Old Boston Taverns and Tavern Clubs.* Boston: W. A. Butterfield, 1917.

———. *Old Landmarks and Historic Personages of Boston.* Boston: Roberts Brothers, 1889.

———. *Our Colonial Homes.* Boston: Lee and Shepard, 1894.

Drake, Samuel G. *The History and Antiquities of Boston.* Boston: Luther Stevens, 1856.

Duff, Stella F. "The Case Against the King: The *Virginia Gazettes* Indict George III." *William and Mary Quarterly,* 3rd ser., vol. 6, no. 3 (July 1949), 383-397.

Dunster, Samuel. *Henry Dunster and His Descendants.* Central Falls, RI: E. L. Freeman, 1876.

Earle, Alice Morse. *Child Life in Colonial Days.* Williamstown, MA: Corner House, 1975.

———. *Customs and Fashions in Old New England.* New York: Charles Scribner's Sons, 1916.

———. *Home Life in Colonial Days.* Stockbridge, MA: Berkshire Traveller, 1974.

Eaton, Arthur Wentworth Hamilton. *The Famous Mather Byles.* Boston: W. A. Butterfield, 1914.

"Edmund Fowle House." Historic Watertown. http://mysite.verizon.net/vzepj3c6/id35.html.
Egerton, Douglas R. *Death or Liberty: African Americans and Revolutionary America.* New York: Oxford University Press, 2009.
Eliot, Andrew. "Letters of Andrew Eliot to Thomas Hollis." *Collections of the Massachusetts Historical Society*, vol. 4, 4th ser. Boston: Little, Brown, 1858, 398–461.
Emmons, Nathaniel. *The Cambridge Platform of Church Discipline.* Boston: Congregational Board of Publication, 1855.
Encyclopædia Britannica Online. "clergy, benefit of." http://library.eb.com/eb/article-9024344.
———. "Knox, Henry." http://library.eb.com/eb/article-9045812.
———. "Pitt, William, the Elder." http://library.eb.com/eb/article-9060225.
———. "Porteous Riots." http://library.eb.com/eb/article-9060961.
———. "Wilkes, John." http://library.eb.com/eb/article-976999.
Endicott, Charles M. *Account of Leslie's Retreat at the North Bridge in Salem, on Sunday, Feb'y, 26, 1775.* Salem: Wm. Ives and Geo. W. Pease Printers, 1856.
Essex Institute. *Proceedings of the Essex Institute.* Vol. 1. Salem, MA: Essex Institute, 1856.
A Fair Account of the Late Unhappy Disturbance at Boston in New England. London: B. White, 1770.
Farnsworth, Amos. "Amos Farnsworth's Diary." *Proceedings of the Massachusetts Historical Society.* Vol. 12, 1897–1899, 78–102.
Ferling, John. *A Leap in the Dark: The Struggle to Create the American Republic.* New York: Oxford University Press, 2003.
Field, Edward. *The Colonial Tavern: A Glimpse of New England Town Life in the Seventeenth and Eighteenth Centuries.* Providence, RI: Preston and Rounds, 1897.
Finlay, Hugh. *Journal Kept by Hugh Finlay, Surveyor of the Post Roads on the Continent of North America, during his Survey of the Post Offices between Falmouth and Casco Bay in the Province of Massachusetts, and Savannah in Georgia; begun the 13th Septr. 1773 and ended 26th June 1774.* Brooklyn: Frank H. Norton, 1867.
Fischer, David Hackett. *Paul Revere's Ride.* New York: Oxford University Press, 1994.
Fisher, Leonard Everett. *The Wigmakers.* New York: Franklin Watts, 1965.
Flexner, James Thomas. *George Washington in the American Revolution (1775–1783).* Boston: Little, Brown, 1968.
Fonder, Mark. "William Billings: A Patriot's Life?" *Bulletin of Historical Research in Music Education.* Vol. 19, no. 1 (Sept. 1970), 1–9.
Forbes, Esther. *Paul Revere and the World He Lived In.* Boston: Houghton Mifflin, 1942.
Force, Peter. *American Archives: Fourth Series. Containing a Documentary History of the English Colonies in North America, from the King's Message to Parliament of March 7, 1774, to the Declaration of Independence by the United States.* 6. vols. Washington, DC: M. St. Clair Clarke and Peter Force, 1837.
Ford, Worthington C., ed. "John Wilkes in Boston." *Proceedings of the Massachusetts Historical Society.* Vol. 47, 1913–1914, 190–215.
Founding Families: Digital Editions of the Papers of the Winthrops and the Adamses. C. James Taylor, ed. Massachusetts Historical Society. http://www.masshist.org/publications/apde/index.php.
Fowler, William M., Jr. *The Baron of Beacon Hill: A Biography of John Hancock.* Boston: Houghton Mifflin, 1980.

———. *Samuel Adams: Radical Puritan.* Reading, MA: Addison Wesley Longman, 1997.
Frankenstein, Alfred, and the editors of Time-Life Books. *The World of Copley, 1738-1815.* Alexandria, VA: Time-Life Books, 1970.
Franklin, Benjamin. *The Works of Benjamin Franklin in Twelve Volumes.* Vol. 4. New York: G. P. Putnam's Sons, 1904.
Freeman, Douglas Southall. *George Washington.* Vol. 3, *Planter and Patriot.* New York: Charles Scribner's Sons, 1951.
French, Allen. "General Haldimand in Boston 1774–1775." *Proceedings of the Massachusetts Historical Society,* 3rd ser., vol. 66 (Oct. 1936–May 1941), 80–95.
———. *The Siege of Boston.* New York: Macmillan, 1911.
Frothingham, Richard. *History of the Siege of Boston.* Boston: Charles C. Little and James Brown, 1851.
———. *Life and Times of Joseph Warren.* Boston: Little, Brown, 1865.
Gage, Thomas, and Henry De Berniere. *Gage's Instructions. New York Times* and Arno Press. http://www.gutenberg.org/files/36536/36536-h/36536-h.htm.
Galvin, John R. *Three Men of Boston: Leadership and Conflict at the Start of the American Revolution.* Washington, DC: Brassey's, 1997.
Gates, Henry Louis, Jr. *The Trials of Phillis Wheatley: America's First Black Poet and Her Encounters with the Founding Fathers.* New York: Basic Civitas Books, 2003.
Gelles, Edith B. "A Virtuous Affair: The Correspondence Between Abigail Adams and James Lovell." *American Quarterly* 39, no. 2 (Summer 1987), 252–269.
Goddard, Delano A. "Pulpit, Press, and Literature of the Revolution." In Justin Winsor, ed. *The Memorial History of Boston, including Suffolk County, Massachusetts. 1630–1880.* Vol. 3. Boston: Ticknor, 1881.
Gordon, William. *History of the Rise, Progress, and Establishment of the Independence of the United States of America.* Vol. 1. New York: Samuel Campbell, 1801.
Goss, Elbridge Henry. *The Life of Colonel Paul Revere.* 2 vols. Boston: Joseph George Cupples, 1891.
Greenwood, John. "Memoirs of the Life of the Late Mr. John Greenwood." Compiled by E. Bryan. *American Journal of Dental Science* 1, no. 4. New York, 1839, 73–77, 97–105.
———. *The Revolutionary Services of John Greenwood of Boston and New York, 1775–1783.* New York: De Vinne, 1922.
Griffin, Edward M. "Stubborn Loyalists." Common-Place. http://www.common-place.org/vol-07/no-04/griffin/.
Grolier Multimedia Encyclopedia. "Mandamus." http://gme.grolier.com.ezproxy.torontopubliclibrary.ca/article?assetid=0183500-0.
Gross, Robert A. *The Minutemen and Their World.* New York: Hill and Wang, 1976.
Gruber, Ira D. *The Howe Brothers and the American Revolution.* New York: Atheneum. 1972.
Gunderson, Joan R. *To Be Useful to the World.* New York: Twayne, 1996.
Hamilton, Alexander. *Hamilton's Itinerarium; Being a Narrative of a Journey from Annapolis.* Albert Bushnell Hart, ed. St. Louis: W. K. Bixby, 1907.
Hancock, John. *An Oration Delivered March 5, 1774, at the Request of the Inhabitants of Boston to Commemorate the Bloody Tragedy of the Fifth of March 1770.* Boston: Edes and Gill, 1774.

Harris, John. *America Rebels.* Boston: Globe Newspaper Co., 1976.
Haskell, Caleb. *Caleb Haskell's Diary: May 5, 1775–May 30, 1776.* Lothrup Withington, ed. Newburyport, MA: William H. Huse, 1881.
Haws, Samuel. "A Journal for 1775." In Abraham Tomlinson, ed. *The Military Journals of Two Private Soldiers, 1758–1775.* Poughkeepsie, NY: Abraham Tomlinson, 1855.
Hawthorne, Nathaniel. *Legends of the Province House.* Boston: James R. Osgood, 1877.
Heath, William. *Memoirs of Major General William Heath.* William Abbatt, ed. New York: William Abbatt, 1901.
Hemphill, C. Dallett. "Sibling Relations in Early American Childhoods: A Cross-Cultural Analysis." In James Marten, ed. *Children in Colonial America.* New York: New York University Press, 2006, 77–89.
Herndon, Ruth Wallis. *Unwelcome Americans: Living on the Margin in Early New England.* Philadelphia: University of Pennsylvania Press, 2001.
Hersey, Frank W. C. "The Misfortunes of Dorcas Griffiths." *Publications of the Colonial Society of Massachusetts.* Vol. 34, *Transactions 1937–1942.* Boston: Colonial Society of Massachusetts, 1943, 13–25.
———. "Tar and Feathers: The Adventures of Captain John Malcom." *Publications of the Colonial Society of Massachusetts.* Vol. 34, *Transactions 1937–1942.* Boston: Colonial Society of Massachusetts, 1943, 429–473.
Hill, Hamilton Andrews. *History of the Old South Church (Third Church).* Boston: Houghton, Mifflin, 1890.
Hill, John B. *Bi-Centennial of Old Dunstable. Address by Hon. S. T. Worcester, October 27, 1873. Also, Colonel Bancroft's Personal Narrative of the Battle of Bunker Hill.* Nashua, NH: E. H. Spalding, 1878.
Hinkhouse, Fred J. *The Preliminaries to the American Revolution as Seen in the English Press: 1763–1775.* New York: Columbia University Press, 1926.
Holleran, Michael. "The Old South: The Meetinghouse and the American Preservation Movement." *Old-Time New England* 76, no. 264 (Spring/Summer, 1998), 49–77.
Holton, Woody. *Abigail Adams.* New York: Free Press, 2009.
Hosmer, James K. *The Life of Thomas Hutchinson.* Boston: Houghton, Mifflin, 1896.
Howland, Edward. *Annals of North America.* Hartford, CT: J. B. Burr, 1877.
Huang, Nian-Sheng. "Financing Poor Relief in Colonial Boston." *Massachusetts Historical Review* 8 (2006), 73–103.
Huff, Randall. *The Revolutionary War Era.* Westport, CT: Greenwood Press, 2004.
Hulton, Ann. *Letters of a Loyalist Lady.* Cambridge, MA: Harvard University Press, 1927.
Hunter, Phyllis Whitman. *Purchasing Identity in the Atlantic World: Massachusetts Merchants, 1670–1780.* Ithaca, NY: Cornell University Press, 2001.
Hunter, Robert. *The Encyclopædic Dictionary.* Vol. 5, pt. 2. London: Cassell, Petter, Galpin, 1886.
Hurd, D. Hamilton. *History of Worcester County, Massachusetts.* Vol. 1. Philadelphia: J. W. Lewis, 1889.
Hutcheson, Maud Macdonald. "Mercy Warren, 1728–1814." *William and Mary Quarterly,* 3rd ser., vol. 10, no. 3 (July 1953), 378–402.
Hutchinson, Thomas. *The Diary and Letters of His Excellency Thomas Hutchinson, Esq.* 2 vols. Boston: Houghton, Mifflin, 1884, 1886.
———. *The History of Massachusetts from the First Settlement Thereof in 1628, until the Year 1750.* Vol. 1. Salem, MA: Thomas and Andrews, 1795.

———. *The History of the Province of Massachusetts-Bay, from the Charter of King William and Queen Mary; in 1691, until the Year 1750.* Boston: Thomas & John Fleet, 1767.
———. *The History of the Province of Massachusetts Bay, from 1749 to 1774.* London: John Murray, 1828.
Hutchinson, Thomas, and Andrew Oliver. *Copy of Letters Sent to Great-Britain, by His Excellency Thomas Hutchinson, the Hon. Andrew Oliver, and Several Other Persons Born and Educated among Us.* Boston: Edes and Gill, 1773.
Hyneman, Charles S., and Donald Lutz, eds. *American Political Writing During the Founding Era: 1760–1805.* Indianapolis: Liberty Fund, 1983.
Irvin, Benjamin H. *Samuel Adams: Son of Liberty, Father of Revolution.* New York: Oxford University Press, 2002.
———. "Tar, Feathers and the Enemies of American Liberties, 1768–1776." *New England Quarterly* 76, no. 2 (2003), 197–238.
Jensen, Merrill. *The Founding of a Nation: A History of the American Revolution, 1763–1776.* New York: Oxford University Press, 1968.
———, ed. *Tracts of the American Revolution: 1763–1776.* Indianapolis: Hackett, 2003.
Jones, A. D. *Illustrated American Biography.* Vol. 3. New York: J. Milton Emerson, 1855.
Kalm, Peter. *Travels into North America.* Vol. 1. London: Warrington, 1770.
Kaynor, Fay Campbell. "The Province House and the Preservation Movement." *Old-Time New England* 74, no. 262 (Fall 1996), 5–31.
Keighley, James. "Castle Island, Fort Independence." Brochure of the Castle Island Association. South Boston, MA.
Kennedy, W. P. M. *Statutes, Treaties and Documents of the Canadian Constitution, 1713–1929.* Toronto: Oxford University Press, 1930.
Kiracofe, James. "Dr. Benjamin Church and the Dilemma of Treason in Revolutionary Massachusetts." *New England Quarterly* 70, no. 3 (Sept. 1997), 443–462.
Knollenberg, Bernhard. "Bunker Hill Re-Viewed: A Study in the Conflict of Historical Evidence." *Proceedings of the Massachusetts Historical Society*, 3rd ser. vol. 72 (Oct. 1957–Dec. 1960), 84–100.
Labaree, Benjamin Woods. *The Boston Tea Party.* New York: Oxford University Press, 1964.
———. *Colonial Massachusetts: A History.* Millwood, NY: KTO, 1979.
Labine, Clem. "The Neo-Colonial House." *Old-House Journal* 12, no. 4 (May 1984), 73–77.
Langguth, A. J. *Patriots: The Men Who Started the American Revolution.* New York: Simon and Schuster, 1988.
Lepore, Jill. "Back Issues: The Day the Newspaper Died." *New Yorker*, Jan. 26, 2009.
———. *The Whites of Their Eyes: The Tea Party's Revolution and the Battle Over American History.* Princeton, NJ: Princeton University Press, 2010.
"Letters of John Hancock, Joseph Warren, Thomas Gage and Governor Trumbull." *Collections of the Massachusetts Historical Society.* Vol. 10 (1888), 283–312.
Lincoln, William, ed. *Journals of Each Provincial Congress of Massachusetts.* Boston: Dutton and Wentworth, 1838.
Lister, Jeremy. *Concord Fight.* Cambridge, MA: Harvard University Press, 1931.
Livingston, William Farrand. *Israel Putnam: Pioneer, Ranger, and Major-General, 1718–1790.* New York: G. P. Putnam's Sons, 1901.

Lord, Donald C., and Robert M. Calhoon. "The Removal of the Massachusetts General Court from Boston, 1769–1772. *Journal of American History* 55, no. 4 (March 1969), 735–755.

Lothrop, Samuel Kirkland. *A History of the Church in Brattle Street, Boston.* Boston: Wm. Crosby and H. P. Nichols, 1851.

Louis, Elan D. "Historical Neurology: Samuel Adams' Tremor." *Neurology* 56 (2001), 1201–1205.

Lovell, James. "Oration Delivered at Boston, April 2, 1771." In *Orations, Delivered at the Request of the Inhabitants of the Town of Boston to Commemorate the Evening of the Fifth of March, 1770.* Boston: Wm. T. Clapp, 1807.

Lunt, Paul. *Paul Lunt's Diary. May–December, 1775.* Edited by Samuel A. Green. Boston: John Wilson and Son, 1872.

Lynch, Jack. "Wilkes, Liberty, and Number 45." *Colonial Williamsburg Journal* (Summer 2003), http://www.history.org/Foundation/journal/summer03/wilkes.cfm.

Mackenzie, Frederick. *A British Fusilier in Revolutionary Boston.* Cambridge, MA: Harvard University Press, 1926.

MacNutt, W. S. "The Loyalists: A Sympathetic View." *Acadiensis* 6, no. 1 (Autumn 1976), 3–20.

Maier, Pauline. *American Scripture: Making the Declaration of Independence.* New York: Alfred A. Knopf, 1997.

———. *From Resistance to Revolution.* New York: Vintage, 1974.

———. "John Wilkes and American Disillusionment with Britain." *William and Mary Quarterly,* 3rd ser., vol. 20, no. 3 (July 1963), 373–395.

———. *The Old Revolutionaries: Political Lives in the Age of Samuel Adams.* New York: Vintage, 1982.

———. "Reason and Revolution: The Radicalism of Dr. Thomas Young." *American Quarterly* 28, no. 2 (Summer 1976), 229–249.

Martin, Alfred S. "The King's Customs: Philadelphia, 1763–1774." *William and Mary Quarterly,* 3rd ser., vol. 5, no. 2 (April 1948), 201–216.

Massachusetts Daughters of the American Revolution. *An Historic Guide to Cambridge.* Cambridge, MA: Hannah Winthrop Chapter, N.S.D.A.R., 1907.

Massachusetts Historical Society (MHS). www.masshist.org.

Matthews, Albert. "Capt. Thomas Preston and the Boston Massacre." *Publications of the Colonial Society of Massachusetts.* Vol. 7. Boston: Colonial Society of Massachusetts, 1905, 2–21.

Mayhew, Jonathan. *A Discourse Concerning Unlimited Submission and Non-Resistance to the Higher Powers.* Boston: D. Fowle, 1759.

———. *A Sermon Occasioned by the Great Fire in Boston, New-England, Thursday, May 20, 1760.* Boston: Richard Draper, 1760.

———. *The Snare Broken: A Thanksgiving Discourse Preached at the Desire of the West Church, in Boston, N.E. Friday, May 23, 1766.* London: G. Kearsley, 1766.

McCullough, David. *1776.* New York: Simon and Schuster, 2005.

———. *John Adams.* Simon and Schuster, New York, 2001.

Mein, John. *Sagittarius's Letter and Political Speculations Extracted From the Public Ledger.* Boston, 1775.

Menand, Catherine S. "The Things That Were Caesar's: Tax Collecting in Eighteenth-Century Boston." *Massachusetts Historical Review* 1 (1999), 49–77.

Metzger, Bruce M. "Three Learned Printers and their Unsung Contributions to Biblical Scholarship." *Journal of Religion* 32, no. 4 (Oct. 1952), 252–262.

Middlekauff, Robert. *The Glorious Cause: The American Revolution, 1763–1789.* New York: Oxford University Press, 1982.

Miller, John C. "The Massachusetts Convention 1768." *New England Quarterly* 7, no. 3 (Sept. 1934), 445–474.

———. *Sam Adams: Pioneer in Propaganda.* Stanford, CA: Stanford University Press, 1936.

Greenwood, George H. *Notes on the History of Slavery in Massachusetts.* New York: D. Appleton, 1866.

Morgan, Edmund S. *Benjamin Franklin.* New Haven, CT: Yale University Press, 2002.

———. *The Birth of the Republic 1763–89.* Rev. ed. Chicago: University of Chicago Press, 1977.

———, ed. *Prologue to Revolution: Sources and Documents on the Stamp Act Crisis, 1764–1766.* Chapel Hill: University of North Carolina Press, 1959.

———. "Thomas Hutchinson and the Stamp Act." *New England Quarterly* 21, no. 4 (December 1948), 459–492.

Morgan, Edmund S. and Helen M. *The Stamp Act Crisis.* New York: Collier, 1963.

Morison, John Hopkins. *An Address Delivered at the Centennial Celebration in Peterborough, N.H., Oct. 24, 1839.* Boston: Isaac R. Butts, 1839.

Morison, Samuel Eliot. *Three Centuries of Harvard: 1636–1936.* Cambridge, MA: Harvard University Press, 1986.

Morse, Edward Lind, ed. *Samuel F. B. Morse: His Letters and Journals.* Vol. 1. Boston: Houghton Mifflin, 1914.

Morse, Jedidiah. *Annals of the American Revolution.* Hartford, CT: Oliver D. Cooke & Sons, 1824.

Nash, Gary B. *The Unknown American Revolution: The Unruly Birth of Democracy and the Struggle to Create America.* London: Penguin, 2005.

National Park Service. *Boston and the American Revolution.* Washington, DC.: US Department of the Interior, 1998.

———. "Colonials and Patriots" (Old South Meeting House/Boston NHP). http://www.nps.gov/history/online_books/colonials-patriots/sitec17.htm.

———. "Faneuil Hall." (Bulletin).

———. "Longfellow House–Washington's Headquarters." http://www.nps.gov/long/index.htm.

Nelson, James L. *With Fire and Sword: The Battle of Bunker Hill and the Beginning of the American Revolution.* New York: St. Martin's, 2011.

Newell, Thomas. "Diary of Thomas Newell." *Proceedings of the Massachusetts Historical Society, 1876–1877.* Boston: Massachusetts Historical Society, 1878, 335–364.

Newell, Timothy. "A Journal Kept During the Time Y^T^ Boston was Shut Up in 1775–6." *Collections of the Massachusetts Historical Society.* Vol. 1, 4th ser. Boston: Massachusetts Historical Society, 1852, 261–276.

New-England Historical and Genealogical Register 32. Boston: New England Historic Genealogical Society, 1878.

Nicolson, Colin. *The "Infamas Govener."* Boston: Northeastern University Press, 2001.

———. "A Plan 'To Banish All the Scotchmen': Victimization and Political Mobilization in Pre-Revolutionary Boston." *Massachusetts Historical Review* 9 (2007), 55–102.

Niles, Hezekiah. *Principles and Acts of the Revolution in America.* Baltimore: William Ogden Niles, 1822.

Noble, John, ed. "Letters Communicated by Mr. Noble." *Proceedings of the Massachusetts Historical Society,* 2nd ser., vol. 13, 1899–1900, 379–424.

Norton, Mary Beth. *Liberty's Daughters: The Revolutionary Experience of American Women, 1750–1800.* Boston: Little, Brown, 1980.
Old South Association. "Old South Meeting House." http://www.oldsouthmeetinghouse.org/osmh_123456789files/mission_old_south_meeting_house_today.aspx.
Oliver, Peter. *Peter Oliver's Origin & Progress of the American Rebellion: A Tory View.* San Marino, CA: Huntington Library, 1961.
Paine, Thomas. *Rights of Man; Common Sense.* New York: Everyman's Library, 1994.
Papers of Benjamin Franklin. Yale University. http://www.yale.edu/franklinpapers/project.html.
Pemberton, W. Baring. *Lord North.* London: Longmans, Green, 1938.
Pencak, William. "The Social Structure of Revolutionary Boston: Evidence from the Great Fire of 1760." *Journal of Interdisciplinary History* 10, no. 2 (Autumn 1979), 267–278.
Percy, Hugh Earl. *Letters of Hugh Earl Percy from Boston and New York, 1774–1776.* Edited by Charles Knowles Bolton. Boston: Charles E. Goodspeed, 1902.
Phillips, James Duncan. *Salem in the Eighteenth Century.* Boston: Houghton Mifflin, 1937.
Phillips, Kevin. *1775: A Good Year for Revolution.* New York: Penguin, 2012.
Phinney, Elias. *Battle at Lexington, on the Morning of the 19th April, 1775.* Boston: Phelps and Farnham, 1825.
Plumb, J. H. *The First Four Georges.* London: Fontana/Collins, 1973.
Pownall, Thomas. *The Remembrancer, or Impartial Repository of Public Events.* London: J. Almon, 1775.
The Printer in Eighteenth-Century Williamsburg. Williamsburg Craft Series. Williamsburg, VA: Colonial Williamsburg Foundation, 2005.
Proctor, Donald J. "John Hancock: New Soundings on an Old Barrel." *Journal of American History* 64, no. 3 (Dec. 1977), 652–677.
Provincial Congress. "A Narrative of the Excursions and Ravages of the King's Troops Under the Command of General Gage." Worcester, MA: Provincial Congress, 1775.
Prown, Jules David. *John Singleton Copley: In America, 1738–1774.* Cambridge, MA: Harvard University Press, 1966.
———. *John Singleton Copley: In England, 1774–1815.* Cambridge, MA: Harvard University Press, 1966.
Puls, Mark. *Samuel Adams, Father of the American Revolution.* New York: Palgrave Macmillan, 2006.
Putney, Clifford. "Oxenbridge Thacher: Boston Lawyer, Early Patriot." *Historical Journal of Massachusetts* 32, no. 1 (Jan. 1, 2004), 90–106.
Quincy, Josiah. *The History of Harvard University.* Vol. 2. Boston: Crosby, Nichols, Lee, 1860.
———. *Memoir of the Life of Josiah Quincy, Junior, of Massachusetts Bay: 1744–1775.* Boston: Little, Brown, 1875.
Quincy, Josiah, Jr. *Reports of Cases Argued and Adjudged in the Superior Court of Judicature of the Province of Massachusetts Bay, between 1761 and 1772.* Boston: Little, Brown, 1865.
Rakove, Jack N. *The Beginnings of National Politics: An Interpretive History of the Continental Congress.* New York: Alfred A. Knopf, 1979.
Rantoul, Robert S. "Report of the Arbitrator of the Hutchinson Papers." *Proceedings of the Massachusetts Historical Society.* Vol. 13, 1873–1875. Boston: Massachusetts Historical Society, 1875, 219–232.

Raphael, Ray. *The First American Revolution: Before Lexington and Concord.* New York: New Press, 2002.
Rediker, Marcus. *Between the Devil and the Deep Blue Sea: Merchant Seamen, Pirates and the Anglo-American Maritime World, 1700–1750.* Cambridge: Cambridge University Press, 1987.
Reiff, Daniel, and the Old-House Journal editors. "Copycat Houses." *Old-House Journal* 30, no. 5 (October 2002), 76–81.
Reiss, Oscar. *Blacks in Colonial America.* Jefferson, NC: McFarland, 1997.
A Report of the Record Commissioners of the City of Boston, Containing the Boston Town Records, 1758 to 1769. Boston: Rockwell and Churchill, 1886.
A Report of the Record Commissioners of the City of Boston, Containing the Boston Town Records, 1770 through 1777. Boston: Rockwell and Churchill, 1887.
Ridpath, John Clark. *James Otis, the Pre-Revolutionist.* Project Gutenberg Etext 722, November 1996, http://www.gutenberg.org/ebooks/722.
Rossiter, Clinton. "The Life and Mind of Jonathan Mayhew." *William and Mary Quarterly,* 3rd ser., vol. 7, no. 4 (Oct. 1950), 531-558.
Rowe, John. *Letters and Diary of John Rowe.* Edited by Anne Rowe Cunningham, with extracts from a paper written for the Massachusetts Historical Society by Edward Lillie Pierce. Boston: W. B. Clarke, 1908.
Rowlinson, Hugh. "The Contribution of Count Rumford to Domestic Life in Jane Austen's Time." *Persuasions On-Line,* vol. 23, no. 1 (Winter 2002). Jane Austen Society of North America. http://www.jasna.org/persuasions/on-line/vol23no1/rowlinson.html.
Sabine, Lorenzo. *The American Loyalists.* Boston: Charles C. Little and James Brown, 1847.
———. *Biographical Sketches of Loyalists of the American Revolution.* Vol. 1. Boston: Little, Brown, 1864.
Sainsbury, John. "The Pro-Americans of London, 1769 to 1782." *William and Mary Quarterly,* 3rd ser., vol. 35, no. 3 (July 1978), 423–454.
Salinger, Sharon V. *Taverns and Drinking in Early America.* Baltimore: Johns Hopkins University Press, 2002.
Savage, Edward H. *A Chronological History of the Boston Watch and Police from 1631 to 1865.* Boston: Edward H. Savage, 1865.
Scheer, George F., and Hugh F. Rankin, eds. *Rebels & Redcoats: The American Revolution through the Eyes of Those Who Fought and Lived It.* New York: Da Capo, 1957.
Schlesinger, Arthur M. *The Birth of the Nation.* New York: Alfred A. Knopf, 1968.
———. *The Colonial Merchants and the American Revolution: 1763–1776.* New York: Atheneum, 1968.
———. "The Colonial Newspaper and the Stamp Act." *New England Quarterly* 8, no. 1 (March 1935), 63–83.
Schorow, Stephanie. *Boston on Fire.* Beverley, MA: Commonwealth Editions, 2003.
Scudder, Horace. "Life in Boston in the Revolutionary Period." In Justin Winsor, ed. *The Memorial History of Boston, including Suffolk County, Massachusetts. 1630–1880.* Vol. 3. Boston: Ticknor, 1881, 149–174.
Selesky, Harold E. "James Warren," "Mandamus Councillors," "Quebec Act," "Whigs and Tories." *Encyclopedia of the American Revolution: Library of Military History.* Vol. 2. Edited by Harold E. Selesky. Detroit: Charles Scribner's Sons, 2006.
Seventy-Six Society. *Papers Relating to Public Events in Massachusetts Preceding the American Revolution.* Philadelphia: Seventy-Six Society, 1856.

Sewall, Jonathan. "Opinion of Attorney General Jonathan Sewall in the Case of the *Lydia*, Given to the Commissioners of Customs at Boston, April 23, 1768." In Oliver M. Dickerson. "Opinion of Attorney General Jonathan Sewall of Massachusetts in the Case of the *Lydia*." *William and Mary Quarterly*, 3rd ser., vol. 4, no. 4 (Oct. 1947), 499–504.

Shammas, Carole. "How Self-Sufficient Was Early America?" *Journal of Interdisciplinary History* 13, no. 2 (Autumn 1992), 247–272.

———. "The Space Problem in Early United States Cities." *William and Mary Quarterly*, 3rd ser., vol. 57, no. 3 (July 2000), 505–542.

Shattuck, Lemuel. *A History of the Town of Concord*. Boston: Russell, Odiorne, 1835.

Shaw, Samuel S. "Savage Papers." *Proceedings of the Massachusetts Historical Society*. Vol. 44. Boston: Massachusetts Historical Society, 1911, 1–86.

Shipton, Clifford K. "The American Antiquarian Society." *William and Mary Quarterly* 2, no. 2 (April 1945), 164–172.

A Short Narrative of the Horrid Massacre in Boston. Boston: Town of Boston, 1770.

Shurkin, Joel N. *The Invisible Fire: The Story of Mankind's Triumph over the Ancient Scourge of Smallpox*. New York: G. P. Putnam's Sons, 1979.

Shurtleff, Nathaniel B. *A Topographical and Historical Description of Boston*. Boston: Boston City Council, 1871.

Slade, Denison Rogers. "Documents Drawn from the Papers of Richard Clarke, 1762–1774." *Publications of the Colonial Society of Massachusetts*. Vol. 8, *Transactions 1902–1904*. Boston: Colonial Society of Massachusetts, 1906, 78–89.

———. "Henry Pelham, Half-Brother of John Singleton Copley." *Publications of the Colonial Society of Massachusetts*. Vol. 5, *Transactions 1897, 1898*. Boston: Colonial Society of Massachusetts, 1902, 193–211.

Smith, Edgar C. "The Edes Family." *Sprague's Journal of Maine History* 9, no. 1 (1921), 32–35.

Smith, M. H. *The Writs of Assistance Case*. Berkeley: University of California Press, 1978.

Smith, Page. *John Adams*. 2 vols. Garden City, NY: Doubleday, 1962.

Smith, William. "The Colonial Post Office." American Historical Review 21, no. 2 (Jan. 1916), 258–275.

Sonneck, Oscar George Theodore. *Report on "The Star-Spangled Banner," "Hail Columbia," "Yankee Doodle."* Washington, DC: Government Printing Office, 1909.

Sparks, Jared. "Destruction of the Tea in the Harbor of Boston, December 16, 1773." *Collections of the Massachusetts Historical Society*. Vol. 4, 4th ser. Boston: Little, Brown, 1858, 373–389.

Stannard, David E. *The Puritan Way of Death: A Study in Religion, Culture, and Social Change*. New York: Oxford University Press, 1977.

Stark, James H. *The Loyalists of Massachusetts and the Other Side of the American Revolution*. Boston: W. B. Clarke, 1910.

Starkey, Marion L. *The Congregational Way: The Role of the Pilgrims and Their Heirs in Shaping America*. Garden City, NY: Doubleday, 1966.

Stephens, Otis H., and Richard A. Glenn. *Unreasonable Searches and Seizures: Rights and Liberties under the Law*. Santa Barbara, CA: ABC-CLIO, 2006.

Stern, Jeremy A. "Jane Franklin Mecom: A Boston Woman in Revolutionary Times." *Early American Studies* 4, no. 1 (Spring 2006), 147–191.

Stiles, Ezra. *The Literary Diary of Ezra Stiles, D.D., L.L.D.* Vol. 2. Edited by Franklin Bowditch Dexter. New York: Charles Scribner's Sons, 1901.

Stout, Neil R., John Temple, and Thomas Whately. "The Missing Temple-Whately Papers." *Proceedings of the Massachusetts Historical Society*, 3rd ser., vol. 104 (1992), 123–147.

Streitmatter, Rodger. *Mightier Than the Sword.* Boulder, CO: Westview Press, 2008.

Sumner, W. H. "Memoir of Governor Increase Sumner." *New England Historical and Genealogical Register* 8, no. 2 (April 1853), 105–128.

Sutherland, William, and Richard Pope. *Late News of the Excursion and Ravages of the King's Troops.* Cambridge, MA: Club of Odd Volumes, 1927.

Taussig, Charles William. *Rum, Romance and Rebellion.* New York: Minton, Balch, 1928.

Taylor, Eldad. "Evacuation of Boston, 1776, by an Eye Witness." Letter from Eldad Taylor to his wife. March 18, 1776. *New England Historical and Genealogical Register* 8, no. 3 (July 1854), 231–232.

Thomas, Benjamin Franklin. *Memoir of Isaiah Thomas.* Boston: Munsell, 1874.

Thomas, Isaiah. "Diary of Isaiah Thomas, 1805–1828, Volume II." *Transactions and Collections of the American Antiquarian Society.* Vol. 10. Worcester, MA: American Antiquarian Society, 1909.

———. *The History of Printing in America, With a Biography of Printers.* Worcester, MA: Isaiah Thomas, June 1810.

Thwing, Annie Haven. *The Crooked & Narrow Streets of the Town of Boston.* Detroit: Singing Tree Press, 1970.

Tiffany, Nina Moore, ed. *Letters of James Murray, Loyalist.* Boston, 1901.

Tourtellot, Arthur B. *Lexington and Concord: The Beginning of the War of the American Revolution.* New York: W. W. Norton, 1959.

Trevelyan, George Otto. *The American Revolution.* New York: David McKay, 1965.

Tuckerman, Frederick, ed. "Letters of Samuel Cooper to Thomas Pownall, 1769–1777." *American Historical Review* 8, no. 2 (Jan. 1903), 301–330.

Tudor, William. *The Life of James Otis of Massachusetts.* New York: Da Capo, 1970.

Tunis, Edwin. *Colonial Craftsmen and the Beginnings of American Industry.* Cleveland: World Publishing, 1965.

———. *Colonial Living.* New York: Thomas Y. Crowell, 1957.

Tyler, John W. *Smugglers & Patriots: Boston Merchants and the Advent of the American Revolution.* Boston: Northeastern University Press, 1986.

Unger, Harlow Giles. *American Tempest: How the Boston Tea Party Sparked a Revolution.* Cambridge, MA: Da Capo, 2011.

———. *John Hancock: Merchant King and American Patriot.* New York: John Wiley & Sons, 2000.

Upton, Leslie F. S., ed. *Revolutionary Versus Loyalist: The First American Civil War, 1774–1784.* Waltham, MA: Blaisdell, 1968.

———. "Proceedings of Ye Body Respecting the Tea." *William and Mary Quarterly*, 3rd ser., vol. 22, no. 2 (April 1965), 287–300.

Van Doren, Carl. *Jane Mecom: The Favorite Sister of Benjamin Franklin: Her Life Here First Fully Narrated from Their Entire Surviving Correspondence.* New York: Viking, 1950.

"A Visitor's Guide to Nathan Tufts Park." Pamphlet. Somerville, MA.

Volo, Dorothy Denneen, and James M. Volo. *Daily Life During the American Revolution.* Westport, CT: Greenwood, 2003.

Vrabel, Jim. *When in Boston: A Time Line & Almanac.* Boston: Northeastern University Press, 2004.

Waldstreicher, David. "Phillis Wheatley: The Poet Who Challenged the American Revolutionaries." In Alfred F. Young, Gary B. Nash, and Ray Raphael, eds. *Revolutionary Founders: Rebels, Radicals, and Reformers in the Making of the Nation.* New York: Alfred A. Knopf, 2011.

Walett, Francis G. "Governor Bernard's Undoing: An Earlier Hutchinson Letters Affair." *New England Quarterly* 38, no. 2 (June 1965), 217–226.

———. "The Massachusetts Council, 1766–1774: The Transformation of a Conservative Institution." *William and Mary Quarterly,* 3rd ser., vol. 6, no. 4 (Oct. 1949), 605–627.

Walpole, Horace. *Journal in the Reign of King George the Third.* Vol. 1. London: Richard Bentley, 1859.

Warden, G. B. *Boston: 1689–1776.* Boston: Little, Brown, 1970.

———. "The Caucus and Democracy in Colonial Boston," *New England Quarterly* 43, no.1 (March 1970), 19–45.

Warren, Dr. Joseph. "Oration, Delivered at Boston, March 5, 1772. In *Orations, Delivered at the Request of the Inhabitants of the Town of Boston, to Commemorate the Evening of the Fifth of March, 1770.* 2nd ed. Boston: Wm. T. Clap, 1807.

Warren, Mercy Otis. *History of the Rise, Progress and Termination of the American Revolution.* Boston: Manning and Loring, 1805.

Waters, John J., Jr. *The Otis Family in Provincial and Revolutionary Massachusetts.* New York: W. W. Norton, 1968.

Waters, John J., Jr., and John A. Schutz. "Patterns of Massachusetts Colonial Politics: The Writs of Assistance and the Rivalry between the Otis and Hutchinson Families." *William and Mary Quarterly,* 3rd ser., vol. 24, no. 4 (Oct. 1967), 543–567.

Watkins, Walter Kendall. "The Province House and Its Occupants." *Old-Time New England* 62, no. 228 (Spring 1972), 95–104.

Watson, D. H. "Joseph Harrison and the Liberty Incident." *William and Mary Quarterly,* 3rd ser., vol. 20, no. 4 (Oct. 1963), 585–595.

Webb, Alfred. *A Compendium of Irish Biography.* Dublin: M. H. Gill & Son, 1878.

Wells, William V. *Life and Public Services of Samuel Adams.* Boston: Little, Brown, 1865.

Werner, Emmy E. *In Pursuit of Liberty: Coming of Age in the American Revolution.* Westport, CT: Praeger, 2006.

Whitehill, Walter Muir, and Lawrence W. Kennedy. *Boston: A Topographical History.* Cambridge, MA: Belknap, 2000.

Whitmore, William H. *Notes Concerning Peter Pelham, the Earliest Artist Resident in New England, and His Successor Prior to the Revolution.* Cambridge, MA: John Wilson and Son, 1867.

The Wigmaker in Eighteenth-Century Williamsburg. Williamsburg Craft Series. Williamsburg, VA: Colonial Williamsburg Foundation, 2007.

Wilson, James Grant, and John Fiske, eds. *Appleton's Cycopædia of American Biography.* Vol. 2. New York: D. Appleton, 1888.

Winslow, Anna Green. *Diary of Anna Green Winslow, a Boston School Girl of 1771.* Edited by Alice Morse Earle. Boston: Houghton, Mifflin, 1894.

Winsor, Justin. *History of the Town of Duxbury, Massachusetts.* Boston: Crosby & Nichols, 1849.

———, ed. *The Memorial History of Boston.* 4 vols. Boston: James R, Osgood, 1881.

Witkowski, Terrence H. "Colonial Consumers in Revolt: Buyer Values and Behavior During the Nonimportation Movement, 1764–1776." *Journal of Consumer Research* 16, no. 2 (Sept. 1989), 216–226.

Wolf, Stephanie Grauman. *As Various as Their Land: The Everyday Lives of Eighteenth-Century Americans.* New York: HarperCollins, 1993.
Wolkins, George G. "The Seizure of John Hancock's Sloop 'Liberty.'" *Proceedings of the Massachusetts Historical Society,* 3rd ser., vol. 55 (October 1921–June 1922), 224–284.
Wood, Gordon S. *The Americanization of Benjamin Franklin.* New York: Penguin, 2004.
Woodbury, Ellen C. D. Q. *Dorothy Quincy, Wife of John Hancock with Events of Her Time.* Washington, DC: Neale, 1905.
Woodforde, John. *The Strange Story of False Hair.* New York: Drake, 1972.
Wroth, Lawrence C. *The Colonial Printer.* Charlottesville, VA: Dominion, 1964.
Wroth, L. Kinvin, ed. *Province in Rebellion: A Documentary History of the Founding of the Commonwealth of Massachusetts, 1774–1775.* Cambridge, MA: Harvard University Press, 1975.
Wroth, L. Kinvin, and Hiller B. Zobel, eds. *Legal Papers of John Adams.* 3 vols. Cambridge, MA: Belknap, 1965.
York, Neil L. "Tag-Team Polemics: The 'Centinel' and His Allies in the *Massachusetts Spy.*" *Proceedings of the Massachusetts Historical Society,* 3rd ser., vol. 107 (1995), 85–114.
Youcha, Geraldine. *Minding the Children: Child Care in America from Colonial Times to the Present.* Cambridge, MA: Da Capo, 2005.
Young, Alfred F. "Ebenezer Mackintosh: Boston's Captain General of the Liberty Tree." In Alfred F. Young, Gary B. Nash, Ray Raphael, eds. *Revolutionary Founders: Rebels, Radicals, and Reformers in the Making of the Nation.* New York: Alfred A. Knopf, 2011, 15–33.
———. "George Robert Twelves Hewes (1742–1840): A Boston Shoemaker and the Memory of the American Revolution." *William and Mary Quarterly,* 3rd series, vol. 38, no. 4 (Oct. 1981), 561–623.
———. *Liberty Tree: Ordinary People and the American Revolution.* New York: New York University Press, 2006.
Zobel, Hiller B. *The Boston Massacre.* New York: W. W. Norton, 1970.

INDEX

ACKNOWLEDGMENTS

In doing research for this book, I was fortunate to have access to some fine public libraries as well as vast online resources. Those libraries included the Boston Public Library, the Watertown Free Public Library, the Cambridge Public Library, and the Toronto Public Library. Especially useful online resources included those of the Massachusetts Historical Society, the Internet Archive, and the Boston 1775 Web log by J. L. Bell. I am grateful to the people who supported and made available these resources, without which my research would have been more difficult.

I thank my friends Judy and Ken Luginbuhl of Toronto for reading a draft of the manuscript and for their enthusiastic and helpful remarks; Robert J. Allison, Professor and Chair of the Department of History at Boston's Suffolk University, for graciously reviewing a draft and offering his comments; and John A. Nagy, Scholar-in-Residence at Saint Francis University, Loretto, Pennsylvania.

Thanks also to Paul Dangle for his work on the maps; Ron Silverman for his thorough editing; Trudi Gershenov for her jacket design; and publisher Bruce H. Franklin for his wholehearted support for this book.

Finally, I am especially grateful to my wife, Carol Damioli, for her thoughtful editing of the manuscript and for her helpful and wise advice through the years of work on this project.